COLLEGE
PRESS
NIV
COMMENTARY

ACTS

COLLEGE PRESS NIV COMMENTARY

ACTS

MARK E. MOORE, Ph.D.

COLLEGE
—P R E S S—
Joplin, Missouri

ISBN: 978-0-89900-562-1

A WORD
FROM THE PUBLISHER

Years ago a movement was begun with the dream of uniting all Christians on the basis of a common purpose (world evangelism) under a common authority (the Word of God). The College Press NIV Commentary Series is a serious effort to join the scholarship of two branches of this unity movement so as to speak with one voice concerning the Word of God. Our desire is to provide a resource for your study of the New Testament that will benefit you whether you are preparing a Bible School lesson, a sermon, a college course, or your own personal devotions. Today as we survey the wreckage of a broken world, we must turn again to the Lord and his Word, unite under his banner and communicate the life-giving message to those who are in desperate need. This is our purpose.

IN GRATEFUL
DEDICATION TO

Kenny Boles, who first introduced me
to the academic study of Acts

and

Tony Williamson, who continues to teach me
how to live Acts outrageously in our contemporary world.

PREFACE

There could hardly be a more ambitious theological task than writing a commentary on the book of Acts. The historical, sociological, textual, and theological issues at play are vast and complicated. The secondary literature is enormous and includes a plethora of opinions on virtually every issue. Moreover the contributing commentators have reputations as weighty as the tomes they have produced. So why would anyone attempt to add another volume to the overcrowded shelves of works on Acts? Put another way, what does this commentary offer aside from an update on secondary literature? Actually, there are several notable and unique features of this work:

In order to follow Luke's thoughts, one really needs a map in one hand along with the book of Acts in the other. *What* Luke says is often colored by *where* he takes you; it is *theological geography*. Previous commentaries have relied on a black and white map on a flat piece of paper. This work has opted for **geo-tags on Google Earth**. Every place mentioned in the book of Acts is listed at www.markmoore.org/actsplaces.shtml and identified by its longitude and latitude coordinates. By copying a geo-tag and pasting it into the search box of Google Earth, one can 'fly' to each site and enjoy a satellite view, topological layout, and panoramic photos.

Another feature that sets this commentary apart is the use of **ancient texts**. It is imperative that any commentary on Acts cite relevant material from Luke's social world. After all, he didn't write in a vacuum. One must know a bit about Luke's contemporaries if s/he is to grasp Luke's genius. Commentators are generally quite good about citing ancient sources. The problem is that few readers chase these references down to see what they actually say. That's understandable since most people don't have access to research libraries, nor do most have the time to dig up ancient sources even when they are available. So we have done the digging for you. [Andrew Williamson deserves special recognition for this herculean effort.] The full text of every nonbiblical reference cited in this commentary is arranged by chapter and verse at: www.markmoore.org/actsreferences.shtml. Even better, we have reproduced only the relevant passage so you will not be burdened with excessive scouring of difficult texts. Even so, there are hundreds of pages of illustrative material at your fingertips.

Finally, we have scoured the world-wide-web for **artwork** pertaining to particular events in Acts. There are hundreds available, linked by chapter and verse at www.markmoore.org/actsart.shtml. These will keep your right brain engaged as your left brain swims in the deep end of Luke's theological pool. These three sites, along with this text, offer an unprecedented opportunity to

9

grasp the genius of Luke's second volume and communicate his message with visual support.

It is, perhaps, appropriate to mention a couple of other features of this commentary that are not completely unique but may be of interest to the reader. First, I've worked hard to keep the text of the commentary accessible for the average bible student. When it was necessary to use 'big' words, I put these in a glossary for easy access (pp. 17-19). The footnotes are a different story. These are designed for students who want to go deeper and for teachers who need to engage in the thorny arguments of the text. Hence, some of the best stuff is at the bottom of the page, but admittedly, not all of it is for everyone. Second, there are hundreds of copyright-free photos from my own travels to these sites doing primary research at www.markmoore.org/actsphotos.shtml. It is my gift to you with the sincere desire that these enrich your own knowledge of this majestic book. The camera icon lets you know when to check online for the appropriate photo.

Special thanks are in order for John Hunter whose magic with interlibrary loans made a world of scholarship available in our humble library at Ozark Christian College. Vern Moore, Phil Smith, and Jeremy Bacon took on the odious responsibility of reading first drafts of each chapter long before they were passable for publication. Kenny Boles offered his expertise in checking Greek texts and transliterations. These good people (each important in my life at far deeper levels than editing) provided a kindness to the reader by reducing the errors in this manuscript. Those that remain I own as my own.

ABBREVIATIONS OF JOURNALS

ABR . . . . . . *Australian Biblical Review*
AJPT . . . . . . *Asian Journal of Pentecostal Studies*
AJSR . . . . . . *Association for Jewish Studies Review*
AJT . . . . *Asian Journal of Theology*
ATJ . . . . *Ashland Theological Journal*
ATR . . . . . . *Anglican Theological Review*
AUSS. . . . . . *Andrews University Seminary Studies*
AV. . . . . .Authorized Version—King James Version
BAG . . . . . . .A Greek-English Lexicon of the NT and Other Early Christian Literature (2nd ed.)
BAR . . . . . . *Biblical Archaeology Review*
BBR . . . . . . *Bulletin for Biblical Research*
Beginnings. . F. J. Foakes Jackson and Kirsopp Lake, *The Beginnings of Christianity*, 5 vols., 1920.
BeO . . . . *Bibbia e Oriente*
Bib. . . . . *Biblica*
BibSac . . . . . *Bibliotheca Sacra*
Bijdr . . . . . . *Bijdragen tijdschrift voor filosofie en theologie*
BJRL. . . . . . *Bulletin of the John Rylands Library*
BN. . . . . *Biblische Notizen*
BR. . . . . *Biblical Research*
BRT . . . . . . *Baptist Review of Theology*
BT. . . . . *Bible Translator*
BTF. . . . . . . *Bangalore Theological Forum*
BZ. . . . . *Biblische Zeitschrift*
CIL . . . . *Corpus Inscriptionum Latinarum* (Berlin, 1863-)
CJT . . . . *Canadian Journal of Theology*
ConJ . . . . . . *Concordia Journal*
CTM . . . . . . *Concordia Theological Monthly*
DBSJ . . . . . . *Detroit Baptist Seminary Journal*
DNTB . . . . . *Dictionary of New Testament Background* (ed. Craig Evans & Stanley Porter, IVP, 2000)
EB. . . . . *Estudios Bíblicos*
EgT . . . . *Eglise et théologie*
EJ . . . . *Evangelical Journal*
EstEcl. . . . . . *Estudios Eclesiásticos*
ETL. . . . . . . *Ephemerides theologicae Lovanienses*

ETR . . . . . . *Études théologiques et religieuses*
EvJ . . . . *Evangelical Journal*
EvQ. . . . . . . *Evangelical Quarterly*
EvT. . . . . . . *Evangelische Theologie*
ExAud. . . . . *Ex auditu*
Exp . . . . *The Expositor*
ExpTim . . . . *Expository Times*
FilNoet. . . . . *Filologia neotestamentaria*
FM . . . . *Faith and Mission*
FPh . . . . *Faith and Philosophy*
FV. . . . . *Foi et vie*
GOTR. . . . . *Greek Orthodox Theological Review*
GTJ. . . . . . . *Grace Theological Journal*
HBT . . . . . . *Horizons in Biblical Theology*
HTR . . . . . . *Harvard Theological Review*
HvTSt . . . . . *Hervormde teologiese Studies*
IDS . . . . *In die Skriflig*
IEJ. . . . . *Israel Exploration Journal*
IJFM . . . . . . *International Journal of Frontier Missions*
IJT. . . . . *The Indian Journal of Theology*
ILS . . . . *Inscriptiones Latinae Selectae* (H. Dessau, Berlin, 1892-1916)
Int. . . . . *Interpretation*
IRM . . . . . . *International Review of Missions*
ISBD . . . . . *International Standard Bible Dictionary*
JACT. . . . . . *Journal of African Christian Thought*
JASCG. . . . . *Journal of the American Society for Church Growth*
JBL . . . . *Journal of Biblical Literature*
JD . . . . *Journal of Dharma*
JEH. . . . . . . *Journal of Ecclesiastical History*
JES . . . . *Journal of Ecumenical Studies*
JETS . . . . . . *Journal of the Evangelical Theological Society*
JHS . . . . *Journal of Hellenistic Studies*
JITC . . . . . . *Journal of the Interdenominational Theological Center*
JP . . . . *Journal for Preachers*
JPT . . . . *Journal of Pentecostal Theology*
JRA . . . . *Journal of Roman Archaeology*
JRE . . . . *Journal of Religious Ethics*
JRR. . . . . . . *A Journal from the Radical Reformation*
JRS . . . . *Journal of Roman Studies*
JRT. . . . . . . *Journal of Religious Thought*
JSNT . . . . . . *Journal for the Study of the New Testament*
JSPS. . . . . . . *Journal of the Society for Pentecostal Studies*
JSS. . . . . *Journal of Semitic Studies*

JTS . . . . *Journal of Theological Studies*
LCL . . . . . . .Loeb Classical Library
LJ . . . . *Liturgisches Jahrbuch*
LTJ . . . . *Lutheran Theological Journal*
LTQ . . . . . . *Lexington Theological Quarterly*
LumVie . . . . *Lumière et vie*
LumVit . . . . *Lumen vitae*
MIR . . . . . . *Missiology: An International Review*
MissSt . . . . . *Mission Studies*
MQR. . . . . . *The Mennonite Quarterly Review*
MNeot . . . . . *Miscellanea Neotestimentica*
MR . . . . *Methodist Review*
NovT. . . . . . *Novum Testamentum*
NRTh . . . . . *La nouvelle revue théologique*
NTS. . . . . . . *New Testament Studies*
OC . . . . *Oriens Christianus*
OGIS. . . . . . *Orientis graeci inscriptiones selectae,* edited by W. Dittenberger,
            2 vols., Leipzig, 1903–1905
PEQ. . . . . . *Palestine Exploration Quarterly*
PGM . . . . . . *Papyri graecae magicae: Die griechischen Zauberpapyri.* Edited by
            K. Preisendanz. Berlin, 1928
PRS. . . . . . . *Perspectives in Religious Studies*
PSB . . . . *Princeton Seminary Bulletin*
PSTJ . . . . . . *Perkins School of Theology Journal*
RB. . . . . *Revue biblique*
RecSR . . . . . *Recherches de science religieuse*
REG . . . . . . *Revue des études grecques*
RevB . . . . . . *Revista bíblica*
RevExp . . . . *Review & Expositor*
RHPR . . . . . *Revue d'histoire et de philosophie religieuses*
RIBLA. . . . . *Revista de Interpretación Bíblica Latinoamerica*
RQ . . . . *Restoration Quarterly*
RR. . . . . *Radical Religion*
RSPT. . . . . . *Revue des sciences philsophiques et théologiques*
RSR. . . . . . . *Revue des sciences religieuses*
RTP . . . . . . *Revue de théologie et de philosophie*
RTR . . . . . . *Reformed Theological Review*
Salm . . . . . . *Salmanticensis*
SBET. . . . . . *Scottish Bulletin of Evangelical Theology*
SC. . . . . .The Second Century
ScEs. . . . . . . *Science et esprit*
ScrTh. . . . . . *Scripta theologic*
SJT . . . . *Scottish Journal of Theology*

SPhiloA . . . . *Studia Philonica Annual*
ST . . . . *Studia Theologica*
StBibTheo . . *Studia Biblica et Theologica*
Str-B . . . . . . .Strack & Billerbeck, *Kommentar Zum Neuen Testament aus Talmud und Midrasch*. 6 vols. Munich, 1922–1961
StudMiss . . . *Studia Missionalia*
SvEA . . . . . . *Svensk Exegetisk årsbok*
TDNT . . . . . *Theological Dictionary of the New Testament*. Edited by G. Kittel and G. Friedrich. Translated by G.W. Bromiley. 10 vols. Grand Rapids, 1964–1976
Them . . . . . . *Themelios*
Theof . . . . . . *Theoforum*
TJ . . . . *Trinity Journal*
TS . . . . *Theological Studies*
TynBul . . . . *Tyndale Bulletin*
TZ . . . . *Theologische Zeitschrift*
VC . . . . *Vigiliae christianae*
WLQ . . . . . . *Wisconsin Lutheran Quarterly*
WTJ . . . . . . *Westminster Theological Journal*
WW . . . . . . *Word & World*
ZAW . . . . . *Zeitschrift für die alttestamentliche Wissenschaft*
ZKG . . . . . *Zeitschrift für Kirchengeschichte*
ZMR . . . . . *Zeitschrift für Missionswissenschaft und Religionswissenschaft*
ZNW . . . . . . *Zeitschrift für die neutestamentliche Wissenschaft und die Kunde der älteren Kirche*
ZTK . . . . . . *Zeitschrift für Theologie und Kirche*

OTHER ABBREVIATIONS

Ant.. . . . . *Antiquities of the Jews* (by Josephus)

b.. . . . . *Babylonian Talmud* (followed by the name of the tractate)

c.. . . . .*circa* = "approximately" as in "about this time"

CD . . . . .Cairo (Genizah text of the) Damascus (Document) in the DSS

cf. . . . . *conferre* = "refer to" or "see"

DSS . . . . . . .Dead Sea Scrolls

e.g. . . . .*exempli gratia* = "for example"

frg. . . . . Fragment

i.e.. . . . . *id est* = "that is"

J.W. . . . . *Jewish War* (by Josephus)

LXX. . . . . . .Septuagint (Old Testament in Greek)

m. . . . . *Mishnah* (followed by the name of the tractate)

MS(S) . . . . .Manuscript(s)

MT . . . . .Massoretic Text

ns . . . . .new series (in any language)

NT . . . . .New Testament

or. . . . . *oratio,* oration

OT . . . . .Old Testament

pap. . . . . . . .papyrus

Q . . . . .Qumran (preceded by the cave number and followed by the document name or number)

T. . . . .*Testament (of)*

tg. . . . . Targum

GLOSSARY OF TECHNICAL TERMS

Agora　　　　　The 'marketplace' of the ancient city where most major social functions took place.

Amanuensis　　A personal assistant who serves as a secretary or scribe.

Anarthrous　　Lacking an article.

Angelophany　An appearance of an angel; more specifically a story form featuring the appearance of an angel that takes on commensurate literary features.

Bema　　　　　Greek word for 'Judgment Seat'—a raised platform in the *agora.*

Chiliarch　　　A Roman military leader over one thousand troops.

Cognomen　　　A Latin term for a Roman's 'last name'—the family name within the *gens.*

De facto　　　　In fact.

Diaspora　　　Literally "dispersion," used in reference to the Jewish nation that had been scattered throughout the Roman world and even beyond.

Ecclesiology　Study of the doctrines and structure of the Christian Church (Greek: *ecclesia* = church, assembly). Hence, *ecclesiastical* means "pertaining to the church."

Emic　　　　　This is a sociological term describing an "insider's" perspective or description of an event, practice, or phenomenon. It is the opposite of *etic.*

Epexegetically　This adjective describes a repetition of thought where two different expressions actually mean the same thing.

Eschatological　Pertaining to the last days. Derived from Greek word *eskatos* meaning 'last'.

Eschatology　Dealing with the death, judgment, and the final destiny of the soul. Concerning the last days.

Etic	This is a sociological term describing an 'outsider's' perspective or description of an event, practice, or phenomenon. It is the opposite of *emic*.
Glossolalia	Phenomenon of speaking in an unknown language.
Gnosticism	A group of beliefs derived from the *gnosis*, an esoteric knowledge of mysteries, mysticism, and the beginning of the world. Attaining this knowledge leads to the redemption of the person.
Hoi Polloi	A Greek term for the common masses—the proletariat; lit. 'the many'.
Inclusio	A literary device that envelops a work by using similar concepts at both the beginning and end of the work.
Incipit	Beginning words of a text or manuscript—the introduction that sets the tone for a piece.
Ipsissima vox	"Authentic voice," indicating phraseology that represents closely what was said by Jesus.
Ipso facto	Due to that very fact.
Kerugma	The original oral proclamation of the Gospel (based on the Greek word for 'preaching').
Logion	A saying, especially one attributed to Jesus.
Magnum opus	A great work of art, music, or literature. Generally the most important work by the artist or writer.
Nomen	The Latin term for "name" or more accurately, name of the *gens* or clan.
Ostracon	An ancient piece of pottery (or stone) with writing on it.
Parousia	Greek word for "coming" used in reference to Jesus' second coming
Pentateuch	The first five books of the Old Testament; synonymous with "Torah."
Physiognomy	The study of how physical attributes represent character traits (e.g., beady eyes).

Pneumatology Dealing with the study and theology of the Holy Spirit (Greek: *Pneuma* = spirit) in Christianity.

Praenomen   A Roman 'first name' or 'given name'.

Qahal   This is a Hebrew word meaning 'congregation'; it stands for the 'people of God' as a group.

Soteriology   Study of the doctrine of salvation, (Greek: *Soteria* = salvation).

Theophany   Visible manifestation of God to man.

Topos   A rhetorical term for a standard method or structure of an argument or story form.

Vorlage   The original form of a manuscript, ascertained by a hypothetical reconstruction based on extant copies.

Xenolalia   Phenomenon of speaking in a foreign language without prior ability or knowledge. This is in contradistinction from glossolalia, which is an unknown utterance or babbling.

INTRODUCTION

The book of Acts is unique. It alone recounts the early days of the Christian church, plowing through the first thirty years of her history (c. A.D. 30–62). It is also unique in that it is the only book of the Bible written by a Gentile. Fortunately, our author is thorough; his two volumes (Luke/Acts) comprise 27% of the New Testament—more actual words than we read from any other New Testament author, including Paul! Without Luke's second volume, one could argue that the story of Jesus would be incomplete. We would know about the incarnation but not the indwelling of the Spirit. We would know about the resurrection but not the ascension. We would know about the kingdom but not the church. We would know about our Jewish roots but not how our Gentile branches were grafted in. The book of Acts is simply imperative for our full understanding of the church.

Before diving headlong into the book, however, we might want to get our bearings. This book didn't just fall from heaven; it grew out of Mediterranean soil at a particular place and time. It behooves the reader to grasp some of the 'when', 'where', 'who', and 'why' questions surrounding the book before we jump into the middle of it. To that end, we will try to tackle twelve questions that, if answered, will help us read with more precision, appreciation, and clarity. Since the reader is undoubtedly eager to get to the 'good stuff', we'll make this introduction as brief as possible.[1]

(1) Why is the book entitled "Acts"?

Acts is the title offered by the New International Version. Others opt for a longer title "The Acts of the Apostles" (KJV, NASV, RSV, TEV).[2] This, however, raises the question, "Is it really the Acts of the Apostles?" After all, only two Apostles receive prominence—Peter in chapters 1–12 and Paul in chapters 13–28.[3] Furthermore, Luke hardly offers a complete portrait. For instance, Paul himself records five lashings from the Jews, three shipwrecks, and two beatings with rods that Luke never mentions (cf. 2 Cor 11:24-25). So perhaps, a more accurate, but less readable title would be "*Some* of the Acts of *Some* of the Apostles."

Of course, in the ancient world that would make no sense. There were dozens of books that began with the words "Acts of ..." that ended with the name of their hero, recounting the valiant deeds of an outstanding individual. There

---

[1] For more comprehensive introductions to the book of Acts, one is commended to Fitzmeyer 47-152; Kistemaker, 3-40; Polhill, 19-76; or Bock, 1-48.

[2] Codex vaticanus and Beza have "Acts of Apostles." However, Codex Sinaiticus has only "Acts," and this is used by the church fathers. The Muratorian canon calls it *The Acts of All the Apostles* (*Acta omnium apostolorum*).

[3] Furthermore, it appears that Luke avoids connecting Paul to the Twelve. He is mentioned as an apostle along with Barnabas in a single pericope (Acts 14:4, 6, 14).

were "The Acts of Pompey" (Josephus, *Ant.* 14.4.3 §68), "The Acts of the Divine Augustus," "The Acts of Hercules," "The Acts of Alexander," "The Acts of Hannibal," "The Acts of Paul and Thecla," etc. So perhaps we should ask, "Who is the hero of this book?" It is really not the Apostles. A more likely candidate is the Holy Spirit. If Luke's intention is to catalogue the progress of Jesus' Kingdom under the power of the Spirit, perhaps the best working title of the book would be "The Acts of the Holy Spirit."[4] Though this title does not capture the full force of the book, it is not a bad place to start. The Spirit, poured out by Jesus at Pentecost, drives the disciples further afield to spread God's global enterprise to become a universal kingdom.

(2) Who is the author?

Since the book is not signed, it takes a bit of detective work to determine its author. There are a number of clues. First, whoever wrote it was pretty smart. This person's vocabulary was extensive, his literary style smooth, and the breadth of his facts broad.[5] He knew political terms, medical words, geography, rhetoric, religion, and culture. In short, our author is one well-educated and classy reporter. Second, three stories are repeated three times: Cornelius's vision (10:1-8, 30-33; 11:13-14), Saul's conversion (9, 22, 26), and Gentile Guidelines from the Jerusalem Council (15:20, 29; 21:25; cf. 16:4). This robust emphasis on Gentile inclusion suggests our author was likely a Gentile convert himself. Thus, this emphasis is as much autobiographical as historical. Third, there are three sections in Acts when the author uses "we" (16:10-17, 20:5–21:18, and 27:1–28:16). Some have argued that this is merely a rhetorical device to make the narrative livelier—a kind of fictional literary device.[6] This is unlikely. The percentage of place names and overnight stops mentioned in the "we" sections is way out of proportion to the rest of the book. Such meticulous travel logs were hardly captivating to a reader (though *terribly* interesting to those on the boat!). In short, it looks like the author traveled with Paul during these occasions.

So there are the clues; where do they lead us? First one must scour the Epistles and Acts for a list of Paul's known companions. It is a fairly long list but it can be narrowed considerably by cross-referencing those who were potentially Paul's companions during the "we" passages in Acts. Next, one can then eliminate all those who were Jewish. Finally, we look for an individual who was educated, articulate, and possibly a physician.[7] The single name that surfaces is

---

[4] One could equally argue for "The Acts of the Church" or even "The Acts of God." Perhaps simply "Acts" leaves the book sufficiently open-ended.

[5] The quality of Greek in the book of Acts exceeds every other book of the NT except the comparable quality of Hebrews. Luke/Acts contains 732 words not found elsewhere in the NT. This vocabulary compares favorably with the famed Greek writer, Xenophon. However, when describing Jewish events our author uses Hebraisms familiar to Hellenistic Jews and follows the style of the LXX. Yet when he describes Roman events, he writes like a Roman. His chameleon style thus changes to appropriately reflect the environment of the story. This is a literary masterpiece. Cf. James Moulton, *A Grammar of New Testament Greek* (Edinburgh: T&T Clark, 1908), 2:7-8.

[6] E.g., Vernon K. Robbins, "By Land and by Sea: The We-Passages and Ancient Sea Voyages," in *Perspectives on Luke-Acts* (Edinburgh: T & T Clark, 1978), 215-242.

[7] Though Acts does implement medical vocabulary; cf. William Hobart, *The Medical Language of St. Luke* (Grand Rapids: Baker, 1954 [1882]), too much should not be made from this fact. Statistically, there is no

Luke, Paul's dear friend, the Doctor (Col 4:14).[8] This detective work is not new.[9] In fact, all the ancient sources come to the same conclusion: Muratorian Canon (170–200), Anti-marcionite prologue (160–180), Irenaeus (c. 180), Clement of Alexandria (c. 200), Tertullian (c. 200), Origen (c. 230), Eusebius (c. 325), and Jerome (c. 375). There is even a textual variant in an Armenian text of Acts 20:13 that reads, "But I, Luke, and those who were with me, went on board."

(3) What is the relationship of Luke and Acts?

From the first sentence of Acts, Luke makes his agenda clear: What Jesus began with the disciples, the Holy Spirit brings to fruition through the church. This two-volume work is deliberately linked in a number of ways. (1) Both introductions address Theophilus, and both lay out Luke's primary agenda for the book (Luke 1:1-4; Acts 1:1-5). (2) Acts begins where Luke left off. The Gospel ends with a lengthy description of the resurrection and a snippet on the ascension whereas Acts briefly mentions the resurrection and expands on the ascension. (3) The work of the Holy Spirit is a continuation of the ministry of Jesus. (4) While Luke emphasizes that the roots of Christianity are to be found in Judaism, Acts describes the international enterprise of Gentile inclusion. (5) Both volumes show intense interest in the downtrodden—Gentiles, Samaritan, Women, the poor and the sick. For Luke, the only Gentile author of the Bible, the idea that God would be available to all (not just healthy Jewish males) was *the* life-changing realization that undergirded his literary project. (6) Both show interest in supernatural beings, both angels (Luke 1:11-19, 26-38; 2:9-15, 26; 12:8-9; 15:10; 16:22; 20:36; 24:23; Acts 1:10-11; 5:19; 8:26; 10:3-7; 11:13; 12:7-15, 23; 27:23) and demons (Luke 4:33-36, 41; 6:18; 7:21; 8:2, 27-38; 9:1, 42, 49; 10:17; 11:14-24; 13:32; Acts 8, 13, 16, 19, 28).

The most prominent, link, however, is the deliberate comparsion of Peter and Paul in Acts as they reflect the ministry of Jesus from the gospels.[10] The overt linkage between the two great apostles in Acts could not be more obvious: Both healed a lame man (3:6; 14:8f), performed miracles through a personal article (Peter's shadow, 5:15 and Paul's handkerchief, 19:12), confronted a sorcerer (8:20; 13:8), raised the dead (9:36-42; 20:9-12), received and rejected worship (10:25-26; 14:11-15), were supported by a Pharisee before the Sanhedrin (5:34-35; 23:6, 7), were miraculously released from prison (5:19; 16:26), had a vision

---

greater use of medical terms in Acts than in many other works of antiquity; cf. H. J. Cadbury, *Style and Literary Method of Luke*, Part 1 (Cambridge: Harvard University Press, 1920). Nonetheless, there is a subtle clue in 28:8-10 that our author helped Paul in treating the sick on the Island of Malta (see comments there). This is augmented by Luke's vivid interest in medical descriptions of those healed as well as by the strong ancient tradition that he was a physician. His vocabulary would most certainly support that tradition; cf. A. T. Robertson, *Luke the Historian in Light of Research* (Edinburgh: T&T Clark, 1920), 90-102.

[8] According to tradition he hailed from Antioch of Syria and died in Boeatia, Greece, unmarried, at age 84. He is often portrayed in classical art as a painter. The Vatican claims to have his skull encased in silver. This fascinating artifact can be seen in the museum of St. Peter's Basilica in Rome.

[9] Cf. Rudolf Pesch, "Die Zuschreibung der Evangelien an apostolische Verfasser," *ZTK* 97 (1975): 56-71.

[10] Joel Green, "Internal Repetition in Luke-Acts: Contemporary Narratology and Lucan Historiography," in *History, Literature and Society* (ed. Ben Witherington; Cambridge: Cambridge, 1999), 283-299, views this repetition as intertextuality imitating the use and reuse of the Hebrew Bible in Jewish history and Scripture. If this is so, then Luke's method is not merely a literary device; it is a sacred apologetic.

that was recorded three times (10:9-23, 27-29; 11:4-10; 9:1-19; 22:6-12; 26:12-18), were beaten (5:40; 16:22, 23), were filled with the Holy Spirit (4:8; 9:17; 13:19), preached the Word of God with boldness (4:13, 31; 9:27, 28), and reached to both Jews and Gentiles (10:34f; 13:46f).

It is as if Luke is saying, "So goes Peter, so goes Paul." Yet this comparison needs to be taken one step backwards and one step forwards. The ministries of Peter and Paul reflect backward on that of Jesus.[11] They also project forward to the ministry of the church in expanding the fame of Jesus. Christians, even today, continue the legacy passed on from every generation, extending to the Master himself.

(4) What kind of literature is Acts?

Does it really matter whether Acts is classified as Greek history, Roman biography, or Jewish wisdom literature? One the one hand, Acts is what it is and the label we attach to it changes nothing of its contents. On the other hand, it is true that we read a romance novel differently than we would a sales contract, a news story, or a letter from our mother. *What* we read is often determined by what we *read* into it. There are three genres that bear most resemblance to Luke's work.

Acts looks a lot like *Roman biography*.[12] Luke, after all, drills down on the life of Jesus, including classic tales from his birth, puberty, and death. Acts, for its part, centers around the two primary pillars of Peter and Paul. So it is not unfair to read Luke/Acts with a biographical bent. The problem is that Roman biographical material is often notorious for injecting apocryphal tales to make the hero look larger than life. Miraculous births, messages from the gods, and heroic deeds punctuate the otherwise historical annals of an individual's life.

Other scholars have pointed out multiple features in Acts that match those of *Greek history*, such as speeches, geographical interest, political rulers, and the preface to each volume.[13] This has become somewhat of a consensus, especially among conservative scholars.[14] Since 'history' is deemed 'true', many who desire to defend the inspiration of Scripture vigilantly defend Acts as history. However, as Alexander has pointed out, history is often fraught with errors and mislead-

---

[11] David Moessner, "'The Christ Must Suffer': New Light on the Jesus—Peter, Stephen, Paul Parallels in Luke-Acts," *NovT* 28 (1986): 220-256, may well be right when he argues that this whole paradigm—call, journey, suffering—goes back to the life of Moses as the theological backdrop of Luke's two-volume project.

[12] The two most articulate proponents of this view are Charles Talbert, *Literary Patterns, Theological Themes and the Genre of Luke-Acts* (SBLMS 20; Missoula: Scholars Press, 1974) and Richard Pervo, *Profit with Delight: The Literary Genre of Acts of the Apostles* (Philadelphia: Fortress, 1987).

[13] Recent compelling arguments have shown that Luke's preface is not a key feature of 'History' but what might better be classified as 'Intellectual Biography'; cf. Loveday Alexander, "Acts and Ancient Intellectual Biography," in *The Book of Acts in Its Palestinian Setting* (ed. Richard Bauckham, vol. 1, in *The Book of Acts in Its First-Century Setting*, Grand Rapids: Eerdmans, 1995), 31–63, and "The Preface to Acts and the Historians," in *History, Literature and Society* (ed. Ben Witherington; Cambridge: Cambridge, 1999), 73–103. Others would opt for the broader term 'Apologetic'; cf. Greg Sterling, *Historiography and Self-Definitions: Josephus, Luke-Acts and Apologetic Historiography* (NovTsupp, 44; Leiden: Brill, 1992) and H.J. Cadbury, "The Purpose Expressed in Luke's Preface," *Exp* 21 (1921): 431-441.

[14] E.g., Colin Hemer, *The Book of Acts in the Setting of Hellenistic History* (Tübingen: J.C.B. Mohr, 1989); Darryl W. Palmer, "Acts and the Ancient Historical Monograph," *The Book of Acts in Its Ancient Literary Setting* (ed. Richard Bauckham, vol. 1, in *The Book of Acts in Its First Century Setting*, Grand Rapids: Eerdmans, 1993), 1-29, and Daniel Margeurat, *The First Christian Historian* (Cambridge: Cambridge University Press, 2002).

ing presuppositions while 'biography' can be both historical and true.[15] Thus, it is naïve to accept history as 'true' over against other genres.

More than any other kind of literature, Luke seems to overtly imitate *Scripture*. More specifically, much of Luke's style, vocabulary, and allusions are lifted from the pages of the LXX. He continues the scriptural tradition of the history of Israel.[16] So this is not merely history, it is God's story Luke seeks to tell. It appears that Luke would classify his own work as *Jewish History* in which God works through the lives of his Prophets and Apostles to extend the Kingdom of God.

(5) Why did Luke write his books?

This sounds like a simple question but it has generated volumes of opinions.[17] Obviously Luke is the only Evangelist to continue the story of Jesus into the first thirty years of the church (c. A.D. 30–62). He is hardly, however, a bare and unbiased historian. This is, in the best sense of the word, propaganda—it aims at convincing his readers of a particular perspective. But just what was Luke's agenda? One answer on offer is *evangelism*—he wanted to bring his friend Theophilus to faith. This answer is ultimately unsatisfying for two reasons. First, it looks rather like Theophilus is the patron of the book more than merely a recipient of it. Hence, he is likely already a believer. Second, Luke surely writes with a broader audience in mind. His two-volume work has more in common with a novel than the personal correspondence of a letter.

Others have taken Acts as an *apologetic*, showing the legal innocence of a movement that some were claiming was politically dangerous. Some go so far as to suggest it was designed for Paul's defense attorney in Rome. After all, there is a great bit of material for the courtroom. Luke proves that Roman officials were consistently friendly to Christianity. They found no fault in either Jesus or His apostles (cf. Luke 23:4 [Pilate], 14-15 [Herod]; Acts 18:14-15 [Gallio]; 23:29 [Claudius Lysias]; 24:23, 26-27 [Felix]; 25:25 [Festus]; 26:31 [Herod Agrippa II]). If, however, Luke's agenda was merely (or even primarily) judicial, he wasted a lot of space with irrelevant stories, particulary those from a Jewish environment. Even worse, he jeopardized his agenda by consistently reminding Theophilus of the multitudinous charges brought against believers. This won't really help Paul's case.

A third suggestion, most compelling for this author, is that Acts is for *catechism*. Its primary purpose is neither apologetic nor evangelistic, but educational. It teaches the church why we believe what we believe. In that sense, it is apologetic, but it is an apologetic for the already immersed not for the yet to be converted.[18] Theophilus (and many others) need to be indoctrinated concern-

[15] Loveday Alexander, "Fact, Fiction and the Genre of Acts," in *Acts in Its Ancient Literary Context* (London: T&T Clark, 2006), 133-163.

[16] Jacob Jervell, "The Future of the Past: Luke's Vision of Salvation History and Its Bearing on His Writing of History," in *History, Literature and Society* (ed. Ben Witherington; Cambridge: Cambridge, 1999), 104-126.

[17] Schuyler Brown provides a very helpful survey of the options on offer with particular reference to Luke's prologue and how that affects one's view of Luke's overall purpose; cf. "The Role of Prologues in Determining the Purpose of Luke-Acts," in *Perspectives on Luke-Acts* (Edinburgh: T & T Clark, 1978), 99-111.

[18] I. Howard Marshall has made this case with his usual perspicuity in "Luke and his 'Gospel'," in *Evangelium und die Evangelien* (Tübingen: J. C. B. Mohr, 1983), 289-308. Jacob Jervell, *Luke and the People of God: A New*

ing the story of Jesus and the foundation of the church. They need to know that their faith is reasonable, powerful, and legally defensible. This, more than any other theory, explains the totality of the work and its peculiar contours.

(6) What kinds of things were important to Luke?

A person's interests reveal a lot about their motives. By examining Luke's major themes, one gets a glimpse into what makes his heart beat. Several things stand out.[19]

1. **The Holy Spirit** punctuates the book at virtually every major juncture, by Haenchen's count, sixty-two times.[20] The Spirit shows up in the baptistery (1:5; 2:38; 10:47; 11:16; 19:1-4; cf. 8:16), fills evangelists (6:5; 11:24), commissions agents (8:29; 10:19, 44; 11:28; 13:3, 4; 16:6f; 20:23; 21:11), and assists with special tasks (4:8, 31; 7:55; 13:9, 52). The church is guided by the Spirit directly (13:2; 15:28; 16:6) or through his prophets (11:28; 20:11f), as if by Jesus himself (9:4-6, 10-16; 18:9; 23:11). In this sense, the Spirit is the hero of the book and the guiding power of God for the growth of the church.

The work of the Spirit will surface again and again in the course of the commentary but here it seems appropriate to point out an important, but not-so-obvious fact. Namely, Luke's view of the Spirit has more in common with John's pneumatology than with Paul's. That is peculiar. One would think that a traveling companion of the great Apostle would soak in the contours of his pneumatology. Nevertheless, somehow Luke arrived at John's perspective more nearly than Paul's. In essence, Paul portrayed the Spirit as the power of God working *in* the believer for *sanctification* whereas John describes him as the power of God working *through* the believer for *evangelism*.[21] These are complementary, not contradictory perspectives. Nonetheless, it is important to read the Spirit in Acts on Luke's terms rather than with a Pauline lens. Except in Acts 2:38, the work of the Spirit is more about building the kingdom than creating a Christian.

2. Luke was well aware of the Jewish roots of Christianity. Not only does he place the church in the bosom of Jerusalem for the first seven chapters, he often references the **Old Testament Scriptures** as explanation and justification of what God was doing. The following chart shows just how prolific Luke was in referencing the sacred texts of the Jews:[22]

Look at Luke-Acts (Minneapolis: Augsburg, 1972) argues convincingly that the details of Acts are precisely the kind of *internal* apologetic designed for catechism of a 'mixed' church containing both Jews and Gentiles. Loveday Alexander, "The Acts of the Apostles as an Apologetic Text," *Apologetics in* the Roman Empire (ed. Mark Edwards, et al.; Oxford: Oxford University Press, 1999), provides an excellent survey of the various approaches to Acts as an apologetic.

[19] To this brief list one might add 'geography' or perhaps more accurately stated, 'theological geography'. For Luke, a map tells a story of the movement of God. It can also describe a person's worldview. For Luke's world map in contradistinction to Chariton's and Xenophon's, see Loveday Alexander, "Narrative Maps: Refletions on the Toponomy of Acts," in *The Bible and Human Society* (ed. Daniel Carroll, D.J.A. Clines, and P.R. Davies; Sheffield: Sheffield Academic Press, 1995), 17-57.

[20] Ernst Haenchen, *Die Apostelgeschichte* (Göttingen: Bandenhoed & Ruprecht, 1956), 154. This is all the more striking given that Matthew references the spirit 11x, Mark 6x, and John 14x. For the frequency and significance of Luke's use of the Holy Spirit, cf. Joseph Fitzmyer, "The Role of the Spirit in Luke-Acts," in *The Unity of Luke-Acts* (Leuven: Leuven University Press, 1999), 165-183.

[21] Cf. Mark E. Moore, "The Comforter Has Come with Power," in *Fanning the Flame: Probing the Issues in Acts* (ed. Mark E. Moore; Joplin, MO: College Press, 2003), 192-209; Craig Keener, *The Spirit in the Gospels and Acts* (Peabody: Hendrickson, 1997); and F. F. Bruce, "The Holy Spirit in the Acts of the Apostles," *Int* 27 (1978): 166-183.

[22] These references do not include the dozens of allusions Luke makes to the OT. Nor do they include

ACTS	OT QUOTE	INTRODUCTION
1:20	Psa 69:26; Psa 109:8	David fortold (v. 16)...It is written
2:17-21	Joel 3:1-5	Spoken by Joel
2:25-28	Psa 16:8-11	David says
2:30	Psa 132:11	[Allusion]
2:31	Psa 16:10	David spoke
2:34-35	Psa 110:1	David said
3:22	Deut 18:15-16	Moses said
3:23	Deut 18:19, etc.	Moses said
3:25	Gen 22:18; 26:4	God said to Ab.
4:11	Psa 118:22	
4:25-26	Psa 2:1-2	David said by HS
7:3	Gen 12:1	God said to Ab.
7:5	Gen 48:4	[retelling]
7:6-7	Gen 15:13-14	God spoke/said
7:18	Exod 1:8	[retelling]
7:27-28	Exod 2:14	[retelling]
7:30	Exod 3:2	[retelling]
7:32	Exod 3:6	Voice of the Lord
7:33	Exod 3:5	The Lord said to him
7:34	Exod 3:7-8, 10	The Lord said to him
7:35	Exod 2:14	With the words
7:37	Deut 18:15	Moses told Israel
7:40	Exod 32:1, 23	Ancestors said to Aaron
7:42-43	Amos 5:25-27	Written in the prophet
7:49-50	Isa 66:1-2	As the prophet says
8:32-33	Isa 53:7-8	Passage of Scripture
13:22	1 Sam 13:14, etc.	God said
13:33	Psa 2:7	Second Psalm
13:34	Isa 55:3	As God said
13:35	Psa 16:10	Stated elsewhere
13:41	Hab 1:5	Prophets have said
13:47	Isa 49:6	Lord commanded us
15:16-17	Amos 9:11-12	Words of the prophets
23:5	Exod 22:27	It is written
28:26-27	Isa 6:9-10	Said through Isaiah

Several facts emerge immediately from this list. (1) Every quotation is offered in a Jewish environment. Scriptural proofs were hardly compelling to the biblically illiterate. (2) The preaching of Peter (Acts 1–4), Stephen (Acts 7), and Paul (Acts 13, 28) accounts for every citation with two exceptions: a quotation by James (15:16-17) and an editorial addition by Luke (8:32-33). (3) Virtually

the 'global' references where Peter and Paul claim support from the entire OT for the points they are making (3:18, 24; 10:43; 17:2-3; 18:28; 24:14; 26:22).

all of these quotes are from the Greek LXX (*Beginnings* 2:66-105), though most represent a fairly literal rendering of the MT.[23] This was apparently the Bible with which Luke was most familiar. (4) The interpretation of virtually all these passages is Christocenric.[24] In other words, the whole Old Testament, according to Luke,[25] pointed toward Jesus, a hermeneutic he probably inherited through the Apostles, going back to Jesus himself (cf. Luke 24:27, 44).[26]

3. **The Church**, obviously, is the content of volume two, but under the banner of "the Kingdom of God." This is the fulfillment of God's intention for the Old Testament people of God. The kingdom is larger than the church, older than the church, and will extend beyond the church, but the church is the present manifestation of God's kingdom on earth. Luke offers a strikingly honest picture of the church, portraying both the pressures without and the struggles within. In addition, he shows the expansion of the people of God throughout all corners of the Roman Empire, under persecution, yet unhindered (Acts 28:31).

4. For Luke, however, Acts is not merely the story of the church, but a particular kind of church—one that **included Gentiles**. He hints at the problem in chapter 6 with the division of the Hellenistic and Hebraic Jews. In chapter 8, Saul's rampage ravages the church and sends Philip scurrying off to Samaria. Here the gospel opened to those theologically 'icky' people of questionable stock. By the end of chapter 8, an Ethiopian 'god-fearer' emigrates into the kingdom. By chapter 10 there is a full frontal assault by God against the "dividing wall of hostility" (Eph 2:14). Chapter 15, the theological center of the book, settles the issue once and for all: Gentiles, without converting to Judasim, are full members of the kingdom of Christ. There will, henceforth, be no vacillation or reconsideration. The kingdoms of this world have become the kingdoms of the Lord and of his Christ. Abraham's seed had finally blessed all nations (Gen 26:4).

(7) To whom did Luke write Luke/Acts?

Obviously Luke addressed both books to Theophilus (whose name means "friend of God," Luke 1:3; Acts 1:1). It is tempting to see this "friend of God" as an allegory for 'any Christian'. However, the fact that he is given a specific title "most excellent" (Luke 1:3), virtually assures that he was a real person.[27] This

---

[23] James's quotation of Amos 9:11-12 (Acts 15:16-17) is the primary exception wherein the choice of the LXX over against the MT renders a markedly different interpretation.

[24] Matthew Black, "The Christological Use of the Old Testament in the New Testament," *NTS* 18 (1971): 1-14.

[25] Esp. Craig Evans and J. A. Sanders, *Luke and Scripture: The Function of Sacred Traditions in Luke-Acts* (Minneapolis: Fortress, 1993), 171-224; and Helmer Ringgren, "Luke's Use of the Old Testament," *HTR* 79 (1986): 227-235.

[26] Luke's hermeneutic, in a gross oversimplification, is basically this: what happened back in the Bible is being fulfilled among us today. Eckart Reinmuth, "Beobachtungen zur Rezeption der Genesis bei Pseudo-Philo (LAB 1–8) und Lukas (Apg 7.2-17)," *NTS* 43 (1997): 552-569, shows that Luke was not alone in his approach to Scripture.

[27] Christoph Heil, "Theophilos (Lk 1,3; Apg 1,1)," in *Licht zur Erleuchtung der Heiden und Herrlichkeit für dein Volk Israel* (ed. Christoph Müller and Josef Zmijewski, Hamburg: Philo, 2005), 7-28, provides a fairly comprehensive survey of the primary material on Theophilus including ancient and modern views on allegorizing his name as well as the inscriptional and documentary use of this common appellation. Werner Marx makes a case (though ultimately unconvincing) for his idiosyncratic view that Theophilus was none other than Agrippa II; cf. "A New Theophilus," *EvQ* 52 (1980): 17-26.

title was reserved for governors (e.g., Acts 23:26; 24:3; 26:25) and Equestrian soldiers of the Roman military. So whoever this guy was, he was on the upper rungs of the political ladder.

Both books were dedicated to Theophilus. This likely suggests he was the patron responsible for the publication of the two volumes. Such dedications were fairly common. For example, Josephus, wrote an apology for the Jews divided into two parts, dedicated to his patron:

> In the first volume of this work, my most esteemed Epaphroditus, I demonstrated the antiquity of our race. . . . I also challenged the statements of Manetho, Chaeremon, and some others. I shall now proceed to refute the rest of the authors who have attacked us. (Jospehus, *Against Apion*, 2:1)

Or again, Philo introduces the second of his two-volume work, *Every Good Man Is Free*, with the following dedication: "My former treatise, O Theodotus, was intended to prove that every wicked man was a slave. . . ." Hence, what Luke is doing is recognizable in the Greco-Roman literary world. Thus, three things can be suggested about Theophilus: (1) He was a Greek who would appreciate Luke's rhetorical flare. (2) He was the patron of the two-volume set and paid for its publication and distribution. (3) He was a Christian whose own faith would be deepened through the historical sources Luke was able to pull together in his theological treatise.

It should be obvious, however, that Luke is not merely writing to an individual. Theophilus was the patron of the book; its audience is much broader. This is a work for the entire Christian community. By telling the story of Jesus in volume 1 and the successful spread of the church in volume 2, Luke is legitimating the Christian community for converts who likely find themselves on the outskirts of society due to their allegiance to Jesus. Furthermore, one is likely on secure ground in assuming that this community was a group of Messianic Jews who had widened its circle to God-fearing Gentiles.[28]

(8) When did Luke write Acts?

The answer to this question depends on when one dates the book of Luke, which depends on when one dates Mark and Matthew. In other words, there are a number of variables. If any of these presuppositions are askew, the date could be off by decades! Hence, at the end of the day, the honest scholar has to humbly admit, "We just don't know." There are, however, two guesses that deserve special attention.

Guess #1: Luke wrote Acts in the 80s. If we can assume that Luke leaned on Mark's gospel to compose his own (a pretty good bet; cf. Luke 1:1-4), then Luke must have been composed after Mark was already distributed. Most scholars would suggest that Mark was written pretty close to A.D. 70. There are two

---

[28] This conclusion has been meticulously substantiated by Philip Esler, *Community and the Gospel in Luke-Acts* (Cambridge: Cambridges University Press, 1987).

clues. The most important clue is the prediction of the destruction of Jerusalem (Mark 13) which would be increasingly obvious during the revolutionary war of A.D. 66–70. (This, of course, presupposes that Jesus' predictive prophecy was more Mark's literary creation than Jesus' prognostication.) Secondly, it is assumed that the messianic understanding of Jesus and the political language of the gospel would be more at home in Rome in the late 60s than in Israel in the first half of the first century. Given these presuppositions (which is, in fact, the rub), Mark could be dated in the late 60s, Matthew in the 70s and Luke in the 80s. It might also be argued that Matthew and Mark were but two of a good number of accounts of Jesus' life as Luke reports: "*Many* have undertaken to draw up an account of the things that have been fulfilled among us" (Luke 1:1). One might argue that multiple gospels could not have been composed prior to the 70s, pushing Luke into the 80s.

Guess #2: Luke wrote Acts about A.D. 62. The book ends with Paul's imprisonment in Rome (about A.D. 60). (1) Since Luke doesn't mention his release or death, one might assume from the silence that Acts was composed while Paul was still in prison. This point is particularly pronounced given Luke's interest in showing the parallels between Jesus' passion and Paul's. Had Paul been killed already (as Jesus), Luke missed mentioning the greatest comparison of all between these two martyrs. Granted, this is an argument from silence. However, the silence is deafening. Luke also failed to mention the death of Jesus' brother, James (A.D. 62), the first official persecution of Christians under Nero (A.D. 64), the martyrdom of Peter and Paul (A.D. 67–68), and the destruction of Jerusalem (A.D. 70). Each of these events would have played right into Luke's theological hand. So unless he planned a third volume, it is virtually inexplicable why he failed to mention these vital details if he completed Acts in the 80s.

(2) One might also note that Acts described the state as tolerant of the church. Had Luke written in the 80s, he could hardly have described the Roman State so moderately given the rise of persecution. (3) In addition, Luke describes the church of Jerusalem in relation to the temple, Sanhedrin, sacrifice, and Sadducees, none of which had much relevance to a later Hellenized church in a diaspora setting. (4) Finally, the fact that Luke never quotes from or references the letters of Paul *may* suggest that they had not yet achieved broad circulation. This is likely a good assumption given Luke's careful use of sources when they were available (cf. Luke 1:1-4). Consequently, it appears to this author that the most likely date for the book of Acts appears to be A.D. 62.

(9) Is the Paul of Acts the same as the historical Paul of the Epistles?

Acts furnishes background material for at least ten of Paul's Epistles (1 & 2 Thess, 1 & 2 Cor, Gal, Rom, Col, Phil, Eph, and Phlm). It is only natural to compare the Paul of the Epistles and the Paul of Acts. Most Bible readers tend to trust the text. Therefore, when two authors present differing sets of data, readers intuitively harmonize them rather than stand each set in juxtaposition to one another. Perhaps that's fair. However, biblical scholars are presented with a Paul from Luke that differs substantially from Paul's self-revelation. So, did Luke 'get' Paul? Put another way, would Paul recognize himself from Luke's descriptions in Acts?[29]

In order to answer the question, one must first note the major differences: (a) In Acts, Paul is a powerful orator, but in 1 Corinthians 2:4, he denies his rhetorical prowess, and in 2 Corinthians 10:10 his opponents also disparaged Paul's speaking ability. (b) Luke only labels Paul an Apostle in one brief paragraph (Acts 14:4, 14). Paul, on the other hand, claims that title in the greeting of every letter he wrote and defended his Apostolic rights vociferously in Romans (11:13), 1 Corinthians (9:1-5; 15:9); 2 Corinthians (11:5; 12:11-12), Galatians (2:8), 1 Thessalonians (2:6-7), 1 Timothy (2:7), and 2 Timothy (1:11). His Apostolic role was paramount to Paul but minimized by Luke. (c) One of Paul's recurring themes is salvation by grace through faith or more specifically by the atoning work of Jesus' death. The epistles are riddled with this important doctrine. Luke, however, barely mentions it. In all of Acts, Paul's doctrine of salvation is clearly articulated only twice (13:38-39 and 20:28). (d) The Paul of Acts is a Law-abiding Jew, even a proud Pharisee (26:5). He circumcised Timothy (16:3), took a vow (18:18), paid for the purification rites of four Jerusalem pilgrims (21:24). In contrast, the anti-legalist Apostle of the Epistles (so it is said) would never do such things (e.g., 1 Cor 9:19-23; Gal 2:3-4; 5:3, 11-12). (e) In Acts Paul is brought directly into the church and into fellowship with the Apostles (9:10-19, 23-30), while in the epistles Paul asserts independence from them (Gal 1:15-17).

All told, these are substantial differences. However, none are necessarily contradictions or incompatible perspectives. Each of the aforementioned issues will be taken up in turn in the text. Just now, however, we should observe four important principles. First, the Epistles are Paul's emic description of himself to churches who knew him. Acts is an etic description of Paul to those who likely had never met him. It is most natural that a person's self-description differs substantially even from description of family and friends. In short, these two perspectives come from two different authors writing to different audiences, for very different purposes. One would expect different, though not contradictory, portraits. That is precisely what we have.

Second, there are several places where the Paul in Acts is clearly the Paul of the Epistles (e.g., Acts 13:38 and 20:28).[30] And it's not just his words that overlap, so do many of his life-experiences.[31] He says and does many of the same things.

---

[29] Witherington, 430-438, offers one of the better and balanced discussions of this topic.

[30] Armin D. Baum, "Paulinismen in den Missionreden des lukanischen Paulus: Zur inhaltlichen Authentizität der *oratio recta* in der Apostelgeschichte," *ETL* 82 (2006): 405-436, makes a strong case that the missionary sermons of Paul have enough verbal and ideological overlaps to assert that Luke has accurately represented his mentor; contra Philipp Vielhauer, "Zum 'Paulinismus' der Apostelgeschichte," *PSTJ* 17 (1963): 5-17.

[31] The most important passages from the Epistles pertaining to Paul in Acts are: Rom 11:1; 15:19, 22-32; 16:1; 1 Cor 1:11; 4:17; 5:9; 7:7-8; 15:32; 16:1-10, 12, 17; 2 Cor 1:8, 15-16, 19; 2:1, 9-13; 7:5-6; 9:2-4; 11:7-9, 23-27, 32-33; 12:2-4, 14, 21; 13:1-2, 10; Gal 1:13-23; 2:1-14; 4:13; Phil 3:5-6; 4:15-16; 1 Thess 2:1-2, 17-18; 3:1-3, 6. Fitzmyer offers a helpful chart to correlate the aforementioned passages with texts in Acts (134-135). Cf. F. F. Bruce, "Is the Paul of Acts the Real Paul?" *BJRL* 58 (1975–76): 282-305.

Third, Paul's theology of justification, so clear in Galatians and Romans, is not articulated in 1 Corinthians. Does that mean we have two different 'Pauls' in these books? Certainly not! No one expects Paul to be a broken record in each of his letters so why should that expectation be forced upon Luke? This is even truer since the total number of words in Paul's missionary speeches in Acts is *less than those in 2 Thessalonians.*[32] That is too little data for a fair comparison. Conclusion: Both the etic view of Paul in Acts and Paul's own emic view in the Epistles have valid claims to authenticity. The supposed contradiction between the Paul of Acts and the Epistles is to a large degree artificial, overblown, and sociologically naïve.

(10) Was Luke an accurate historian?

The rules for what counts as 'accurate history' change from place to place and from time to time. The modern penchant for chronological and geographical precision, for example, is a product of computerized measuring instruments that were simply unavailable in the ancient world. Or again, the western presupposition that spirits are separate from the physical world or that they are psychological projects of superstition, is nowhere to be found in most cultures (ancient or modern).

So perhaps the question should be rephrased: Was Luke an accurate historian according to the standards of his day? The answer is an enthusiastic "yes."[33] Though Luke has been challenged on various individual points, particularly chronology,[34] his accuracy has been established time and again. His political titles, geography,[35] sociology, and religious descriptions are as authentic and trustworthy as any historian of antiquity.[36]

The real bugaboo comes in the speeches.[37] It is often asserted that Luke

---

[32] Baum, "Paulinismen in den Missionreden," 405.

[33] W. C. van Unnik, "Luke's Second Book and the Rules of Hellenistic Historiography," in *Les Acte des Apôtres* (Leuven: Leuven University Press, 1979), 37-60, catalogues nine rules of ancient historiography and judges Luke to be exemplary at virtually every point. Cf. C. K. Barrett, "How History Should be Written," in *History, Literature and Society* (ed. Ben Witherington; Cambridge: Cambridge, 1999), 33-57. Eckhard Plümacher, "Cicero und Lukas: Bemerkungen zu Stil und Zweck der historischen Monographie," in *The Unity of Luke-Acts* (Leuven: Leuven University Press, 1999), 759-775, even compares Luke's use of history in an apologetic context favorably to that of the famed Cicero.

[34] The two most problematic Lucan passages are his claim that Quirinius was governor of Syria when Jesus was born (Luke 2:2) and that Theudas was a known rebel in the mid-thirties (Acts 5:36). Both appear to be a decade too early. Though admittedly problematic, neither is without a proposed solution.

[35] Martin Hengel has done a thorough survey of Luke's geography of Israel and shown that his descriptions of places he had not visited was expectedly less precise than his descriptions of roads he claimed to have walked with Paul. Nevertheless, Luke's descriptions are satisfactorily accurate for an ancient writer and impeccable in the "we" passages. Cf. "The Geography of Palestine in Acts," in *The Book of Acts in Its Palestinian Setting* (ed. Richard Bauckham, vol. 4 in *The Book of Acts in Its First Century Setting*; Grand Rapids: Eerdmans, 1995), 27-78.

[36] Two classics defending Luke's historicity are A. T. Robertson, *Luke the Historian in Light of Research* (Edingurgh: T&T Clark, 1920), and W. M. Ramsay, *Luke the Physician: And Other Studies in the History of Religion* (Grand Rapids: Baker, 1956).

[37] This is particularly important since Acts contains no less than 25 speeches or excerpts comprising nearly 1/3 of the entire book: Nine by Peter (1:16-22; 2:14-36; 3:12-26; 4:8-12; 5:29-32; 8:20-23; 10:34-43; 11:5-17; 15:7-11); nine by Paul (13:16-41; 14:15-17; 17:22-31; 20:18-35; 22:1-21; 24:10-21; 26:2-23; 27:21-26; 28:17-20); one each by Stephen (7:2-53) and James (15:13-21); as well as a handful of non-Christians: Gamaliel (5:35-39); Demetrius (19:25-27); the Ephesian town clerk (19:35-40), Tertullus (24:2-8), and Festus (25:24-27). Fitzmyer counts 28 speechs by adding Jesus (1:4-5, 7-8), the Twelve (6:2b-4), Gallio (18:14b-15),

made them up after the practice advocated by Thucydides (460–400 B.C.):[38]

> With reference to the speeches in this history, some were delivered be-
> fore the war began, others while it was going on; some I heard myself,
> others I got from various quarters; it was in all cases difficult to carry
> them word for word in one's memory, so my habit has been to make
> the speakers say what was in my opinion demanded of them by the vari-
> ous occasions...(*History of the Pelopennesian War*, 1.22)[39]

Often the quote stops here to give the impression that ancient historians wrote
as much fiction as fact.[40] However, reading the full paragraph gives a different
impression. Thucydides continued:

> ... of course adhering as closely as possible to the general sense of what
> they really said. And with reference to the narrative of events, far from
> permitting myself to derive it from the first source that came to hand,
> I did not even trust my own impressions, but it rests partly on what I
> saw myself, partly on what others saw for me, the accuracy of the report
> being always tried by the most severe and detailed tests possible. My
> conclusions have cost me some labour from the want of coincidence
> between accounts of the same occurrences by different eye-witnesses,
> arising sometimes from imperfect memory, sometimes from undue
> partiality for one side or the other. The absence of romance in my his-
> tory will, I fear, detract somewhat from its interest; but if it be judged
> useful by those inquirers who desire an exact knowledge of the past as
> an aid to the interpretation of the future, which in the course of hu-
> man things must resemble if it does not reflect it, I shall be content.
> In fine, I have written my work, not as an essay which is to win the ap-
> plause of the moment, but as a possession for all time.

Polybius (200–118 B.C.) would agree:

> A historical author should not try to thrill his readers by such exagger-
> ated pictures, nor should he, like a tragic poet, try to imagine the prob-
> able utterances of his characters or reckon up all the consequences
> probably incidental to the occurrences with which he deals, but simply
> record what really happened and what really was said, however com-
> monplace. For the object of tragedy is not the same as that of history
> but quite the opposite. The tragic poet should thrill and charm his au-
> dience for the moment by the verisimilitude of the words he puts into
> his characters' mouths, but it is the task of the historian to instruct and

---

and Paul's appeal to Caesar (25:8b, 10b-11) but eliminating Peter's interaction with Simon (8:20-23).

[38] Martin Dibelius has, perhaps, been the most influential representative of this view; cf. "The Speehes in Acts and Ancient Historiography," *Studies in Acts of the Apostles* (London: SCM, 1956 [1951]), 138-191.

[39] One must admit that the meaning of Thucydides' statement is far from clear. Stanley Porter points out no less than seven linguistic difficulties in understanding this (in)famous quote; cf. "Thucydides 1.22.1 and Speeches in Acts: Is there a Thucydidean View?" *NovT* 22 (1990): 121-142.

[40] It should be noted also that such 'invented' speeches can be amply illustrated. For example, Tacitus (*Ann.* 11.24) composed a speech on Claudius's conferring *ius honorum* on the citizens of Gaul which differs radically from the transcript available to us and probably to him (CIL 13.1668). Likewise, Josephus records two renditions of Herod's speech against the Arabs (*J.W.* 1.19.4 §373ff./*Ant.* 15.5.3 §127ff) which shows how free he felt to put words into Herod's mouth. Or again, *Ant.* 12.6.3 §279-284 is a rough paraphrase of 1 Macc 2:49-68.

convince for all time serious students by the truth of the facts and the speeches he narrates, since in the one case it is the probable that takes precedence, even if it be untrue, in the other it is the truth, the purpose being to confer benefit on learners. (*Hist.* 2.56. 10-12)

Quotes such as this could be multiplied by Posidonius (c. 135–51 B.C.), Cicero (106–43 B.C.), Dionysius of Halicarnassus (c. 60–7 B.C.), Livy (c. 59 B.C. –A.D. 17), Josephus (c. A.D. 37–100), Tacitus (c. A.D. 55–115), and Lucian of Samosata (c. A.D. 125–180).[41] It is simply *not* true that ancient historians played fast and loose with the facts, that they made up speeches whole cloth, created events of their liking, ignored eyewitnesses and documented sources, or prioritized propaganda to the detriment of historical facts. No historian of Luke's day could pass muster without careful attention to details, to that which actually happened. Luke wrote under these expectations and did rather well by every available means of evaluation.

(11) What can be dated in the book of Acts?

Honestly, there are very few secure dates in the book of Acts but from those few anchors we can construct a reasonable timeline of the book. The following chart shows the likely chronology of Acts with the most secure dates in bold and the guesswork italics.[42]

EVENTS IN ACTS	A.D.	OTHER HISTORICAL EVENTS
	14–37	**Tiberius Emperor of Rome**
	18–36	Joseph Caiaphas High Priest
	26–36	**Pontius Pilate, prefect of Judea** (Jos., Ant. 18 §89)
Ascension of Jesus (1:9)	30 or 33	
Pentecost (2:1-13)	30 or 33	
Conversion of Paul (9:1-19)	33–36	Three year sojourn in Arabia (Gal 1:17-18)
Paul returns to Jerusalem then flees to Tarsus (9:26-30)	36–39	Paul in Cilicia & Syria (Gal 1:18-21)
Aretas IV, King of Damasucs (2 Cor 11:32)	37–41	**Caligula Gaius Emperor of Rome**
	41–54	**Claudius Emperor of Rome**
Paul's Second Jerusalem Visit (11:30)	43	
Martyrdom of James; Death of Herod Agrippa (12:1-23; Jos. Ant. 19 § 343–352)	44	
First Missionary Journey (13:1–14:28)	45–48	

---

[41] For a full evaluation of these types of statements, cf. A. W. Mosley, "Historical Reporting in the Ancient World," *NTS* 12 (1965): 10-26.

[42] For a detailed explanation of the primary historical anchors in Acts, cf. *Beginnings* 5:445–74 and for a speculative chronology just of the life of Paul, cf. Fitzmyer, 139-141.

EVENTS IN ACTS	A.D.	OTHER HISTORICAL EVENTS
Famine under Claudius (11:28;	45 or 46	
12:25; Josephus, *Ant.* 3 §320)	45 or 46	
Council in Jerusalem (15:1-35)	49	**Jews Expelled from Rome** (18:2; Suet. Claudius 25; Tac., Ann. 13.1)
Second Missionary Journey (15:36–18:22)	49–52	*Letters to the Galatians and Thessalonians*
Paul in Corinth (18:1-18)	50–52	**Gallio proconsul of Achaia** (51–52, Dio Cassius, 60.35; 62.25)
Felix is governor of Judea (Jos., *J.W.* 2.12.8 §247; 2.13.2 §252; *Ant.* 20.7.1 §137)	52–59	
Third Missionary Journey (18:23–21:26)	53–58	**Nero Emperor of Rome (54–68)**
Paul in Ephesus	54–57	Procunsul's Celer & Helius (Tac., Ann. 13.1)
Paul in Macedonia, Illyricum & Achaia (20:1-6)	57–58	*Letters to the Corinthians*
Paul's Last Jerusalem Visit (21:17)	58	*Letter to the Romans*
Paul's Imprisonment in Caesarea (23:11–26:32)	58–59	*Luke wrote his Gospel at this time*
Festus succeeds Felix as procurator (24:27; Jos. Ant. 20.8.9-10 §182-188; 20.9.1 §197, 200; J.W. 2.14.1 §271-272)	59	Jos. Ant. 20 §160–65; Tacitus, *Ann.* 12.54
Shipwreck on Malta (27:39-44)	59 (Nov)	
Paul under house arrest in Rome (28:11)	60–62	*Letters to Phil, Col., Eph., and Phlm.*
Paul released from prison	62	Death of James, half-brother of Jesus
	64 (Jul)	**Fire of Rome and first official persecution**
Paul visits Spain, etc.	64–68	*Writing of 1 & 2 Timothy, Titus, Acts*
Paul is beheaded in Rome; Peter crucified upside down	68	**Death of Nero (June)**
	70	**Destruction of Jerusalem**

(12) Which version of Acts is authentic?

It comes as a shock to many that there are two different textual traditions of Acts: Alexandrian and Western. What that means is that some ancient manuscripts follow the so called 'Alexandrian' tradition and others follow what has been labeled the 'Western text'.[43] The Western text offers dozens of minor variations, most of which are longer additions and some of which appear to be more

---

[43] The Alexandrian text is represented by Codexes A, ℵ, B, and C while the Western text is supported by codes Beza (D), Harklean Syriac, and several papyri (29, 38, 48). For a fuller description of the Western text, cf. Frank Pack, "The 'Western' Text of Acts," *RQ4* (1960): 220-234. Barrett offers meticulous detail of the Greek manuscripts of Acts as well as ancient translations and quotations from the Church Fathers (2-20).

authentic.[44] The most important of these variations will be identified in foot-notes throughout the commentary.[45]

Most modern versions follow the Alexandrian text almost with a religious bias. That's probably justified since the science of textual criticism gives prefer-ence to the older manuscripts (in this case the Alexandrian tradition) and to shorter readings, since it is presumably more likely to add something to a bibli-cal text than to take something out. However, an analysis of the Western text shows that it also sounds Lucan.[46] This led the famed Frederick Blass, as far back as 1895, to speculate that *both* versions were Lucan; the Western version was an earlier draft and the Alexandrian version was a later 'cleaned-up' edition for Theophilus.[47] Though his theory lay dormant for decades it has recently been resurrected and revised by a number of scholars.[48] The recent burgeoning stud-ies on the Western text makes two things patently clear. First, we are far from a solution. Therefore, second, it behooves the student of Acts to pay attention to the alternative readings found in the Western text (the most important of which can be easily accessed in the footnotes of a study Bible).[49]

---

[44] For example, the detailed geography of Asia Minor and Israel are sharper in the Western text. Of eccle-siastical interest, the Western text also appears to have an anti-feminist bias; cf. Ben Witherington, "The Anti-Feminist Tendencies of the 'Western' Text in Acts," *JBL* 103 (1984): 82-84. Matthew Black has also discerned a pro-charismatic pneumatology which he believes is original; cf. "The Holy Spirit in the Western Text of Acts," in *New Testament Textual Criticism: Its Significance for Exegesis* (Oxford : Clarendon Press, 1981), 159-170.

[45] Josep Rius–Camps has provided a series of articles analyzing these major variations, what the differ-ences are, why they matter theologically, with a favorable bias toward the Western text; cf. "Las variants de la recensión occidental de los Hechos de los Apóstoles," in *Filología neotestamentaria*: Acts 1:1-3 in volume 6 (1993): 59-68; 1:4-14, 6 (1993): 219-229; 1:25-26, 7 (1994): 53-64; 2:1-13, 7 (1994) 197-207; 2:14-40, 8 (1995): 63-78; 2:41-47, 8 (1995) 199-208; 3:1-26, 9 (1996): 61-76; 4:1-22, 9 (1996): 201-216.

[46] E.g., Gijs Bouwman, "Der Anfang der Apostelgeschichte und der 'westliche' Text," in *Text and Testimony* (ed. T. Baarda, etc.; Kampen: Uitgeversmaatschappij J. H. Kok, 1988), 46-55; and Sheldon MacKenzie, "The Western Text of Acts: Some Lucanisms in Selected Sermons," *JBL* 104 (1985): 637-650. However, such proposals of Lucanisms have several flaws. (1) They often lack a sufficient methodological criterion for what counts as a Lucanism. (2) They fail to account for the minor papyri that also follow the "Western" tradition. And (3) they do not address the possibility that Luke's style was imitated by a scribal disciple just as Luke himself adopted style and vocabulary from the Septuagint.

[47] *Acta Apostolorum sive Lucae ad Theophilum liber alter: Editio philologica apparatu critico, commentario perpetuo, indices verborum illustrate* (Göttingen: Vandenhoeck & Ruprecht, 1895).

[48] The most important recent work is arguably Marie Boismard, "The Texts of Acts: A Problem of Liter-ary Criticism?" in *New Testament Criticism* (ed. E. J. Epp and Gordon Fee; Oxford: Clarendon Press, 1981): 147-157, and later expanded to a full two volumes with A. Lamouille, *Le Text Occidental des Actes des Apôtres, Reconstitution et Rehabilitation* (Paris: Editions Recherche sur les Civilisations, 1984). For a history of the important research on the Western text, cf. Joël Delobel, "The Text of Luke-Acts," in *The Unity of Luke-Acts* (ed. J. Verheyden; Leuven: Leuven University Press, 1999), 83-107 and Thomas Greer, "The Presence and Significance of Lucanisms in the 'Western' Text of Acts," *JSNT* 39 (1990): 59-76.

[49] For the eager student who would like to research the text of Acts in depth, the magisterial work of James Ropes, *The Text of Acts*, vol. 3 in *The Beginnings of Christianity* (ed. By F. J. Foakes Jackson and Kirsopp Lake; London: MacMillan, 1926) is available online as a free PDF download.

OUTLINE OF ACTS

I. **WITNESS IN JERUSALEM**—1:1–8:1a
    A. Introduction—1:1-26
        1. Continuity with Luke—1:1-5
        2. Commission to Proclaim the Kingdom—1:6-8
        3. Ascension—1:9-11
        4. Replacement of Iscariot—1:12-26
    B. Pentecost—2:1-47
        1. Miracle of Tongues—2:1-13
        2. First Gospel Message—2:14-36
        3. Response to the Message—2:37-41
        4. A Description of the Pristine Church—2:42-47
    C. Persecution—3:1-4:37
        1. Miracle of the Lame Man—3:1-10
        2. Peter Responds by Proclaiming the Name of Jesus—3:11-26
        3. The Sanhedrin Responds by Arresting Peter & John—4:1-22
        4. The Church Responds by Praying—4:23-31
    D. Community Economics and Unity—4:32-6:7
        1. Barnabas Offers a Good Example of Economic Sharing—4:32-37
        2. Ananias and Sapphira Offer a Bad Example of Economic Manipulation—5:1-11
        3. The Fearsome Power of the Apostles—5:12-16
        4. Second Arrest and First Beating of the Apostles—5:17-42
        5. Handling Benevolence for Christian Widows—6:1-7
    E. The First Christian Martyr—6:8-8:1a
        1. Stephen's Character and Arrest—6:8-15
        2. Stephen's Sermon on Jesus through Jewish History—7:1-53
        3. Stephen's Execution by Stoning—7:54-8:1a

II. **WITNESS IN SAMARIA & JUDEA**—8:1b–12:25
    A. The Gospel Extends to Samaritans—8:1b-40
        1. Philip with Simon in Samaria—8:1b-25
        2. Philip with the Eunuch en Route to Gaza—8:2—40
    B. The Conversion of the 'Apostle' to the Gentiles—9:1-31
        1. Saul with Ananias en Route to Damascus—9:1-19a
        2. Saul with Barnabas Back in Jerusalem—9:19b-31
        3. Transition: God Postures Peter with Aeneas in Lydda and Dorcas in Joppa—9:32-43

D. The Third Missionary Journey:
From Europe to Asia—18:18–20:38
  1. Interlude: Apollos the Eloquent Alexandrian—18:18-28
  2. Ephesus: Jesus is Better—19:1-41
  3. Interlude: Paul's Preparations for His Return
     to Jerusalem—20:1-12
  4. Miletus: Paul's Farewell Address to the Ephesian Elders—20:13-38

IV. WITNESS SHIFTS FROM JERUSALEM TO ROME—21:1–28:31
  A. Paul's Journey to Jerusalem—21:1-36
    1. Travel Itinerary and the Church's Reception—21:1-16
    2. Paul's Arrival and Consultation with James—21:17-26
    3. Paul's Arrest—21:27-36
  B. Paul's *Apologia*—21:37–26:32
    1. To the Jews
      a. To the Jewish People in Jerusalem and an Escape from
         Flogging—21:37–22:29
      b. To the Jewish Leaders and an Escape from an
         Assassination Plot—22:30–23:35
    2. To the Gentiles
      a. To the Gentile Governor Felix and Two-Year
         Imprisonment—24:1-27
      b. To the Gentile Governor Festus and Paul's Appeal
         to Caesar—25:1-12
    3. To King Agrippa and Paul's Proclamation of
       Innocence—25:13–26:32
  C. Journey to Rome—27:1–28:31
    1. The Storm—27:1-20
    2. The Shipwreck—27:21-44
    3. Salvation on Shore—28:1-10
    4. Arrival in Rome—the Unhindered Gospel—28:11-31

BIBLIOGRAPHY

Commentaries Cited in Parenthetical Notes

Ash, Anthony Lee. *The Acts of the Apostles*. Austin: Sweet, 1979.

Barclay, William. *The Acts of the Apostles*. Philadelphia: Westminster, 1976.

Barrett, C. K. *A Critical and Exegetical Commentary on the Acts of the Apostles*, 2 vols., International Critical Commentary. Edinburgh: T&T Clark, 1994/1998.

Bock, Darrell, *Acts*. Baker Exegetical Commentary on the New Testament. Grand Rapids: Baker, 2007.

Bruce, F. F. *Commentary on the Book of Acts*. In The New International Commentary on the New Testament, F. F. Bruce (ed.). Grand Rapids: Eerdmans, 1954.

Fernando, Ajith. *The NIV Application Commentary*. Grand Rapids: Zondervan, 1998.

Fitzmyer, Joseph. *The Acts of the Apostles*. New York: Doubleday, 1998.

Gaertner, D. *Acts*. Joplin, MO: College Press, 1993.

Haenchen, Ernst. *Die Apostelgeschichte*. Göttingen: Vandenhoeck & Ruprecht, 1965.

Harrison, Everett. *Acts: The Expanding Church*. Chicago: Moody Press, 1975.

Horton, Stanley H. *The Book of Acts*. Springfield, MO: Gospel Publishing House, 1981.

Johnson, L. Timothy, *The Acts of the Apostles*. Collegeville, MN: Liturgical Press, 1992.

Krodel, Gerhard. *Acts*. Augsburg Commentary on the New Testament. Minneapolis: Augsburg, 1986.

Larkin, William J. *Acts*. Downers Grove, IL: InterVarsity, 1995.

Longenecker, Richard N. *Acts*. In The Expositor's Bible Commentary, Frank E. Gaebelein (ed.). Grand Rapids: Zondervan, 1981.

Marshall, I. H. *The Acts of the Apostles*. Grand Rapids: Eerdmans, 1980.

McGarvey, J. W. *The Acts of the Apostles*. Cincinnati: Standard, 1892.

Parsons, Mieal C. *Acts*. In Paideia Commentaries on the New Testament. Grand Rapids: Baker, 2008.

Pesch, Rudolph. *Apostelgeschichte*. 2 vols. Evangelisch-Katholischer Kommentar zum Neuen Testament. Benzinge: Neukirchener, 1986/2003.

Polhill, J. B. *Acts*. In The New American Commentary. Nashville: Broadman, 1992.

Rackham, Richard. *Acts of the Apostles: An Exposition.* Grand Rapids: Baker, 1978.

Ramsay, William. *Cities of St. Paul: Their Influence on His Life and Thought, the Cities of Eastern Asia Minor.* Grand Rapids: Baker, 1960, c. 1907.

_____. *St. Paul the Traveller and Roman Citizen* (Grand Rapids: Baker Book House, 1962, 1897).

Reese, Gareth L. *New Testament History, Acts.* Joplin, MO: College Press, 1976.

Stott, John R. *The Spirit, the Church and the World.* Downers Grove, IL: InterVarsity, 1990.

Talbert, C. H. *Acts.* Atlanta: John Knox Press, 1971.

Willimon, William. *Acts: Interpretation, A Bible Commentary for Teaching and Preaching.* Atlanta: John Knox, 1988.

Witherington, Ben. *The Acts of the Apostles: A Socio-Rhetorical Commentary.* Grand Rapids: Eerdmans, 1998.

Bibliography of Ancient Sources

Achilles, Tatius. *The Loves of Clitophon and Leucippe.* Oxford: Printed by William Turner for John Allam, 1638.

Aelius Aristides. *The Complete Works.* Tr. Charles A. Behr. Leiden: Brill, 1981–1986.

Aeschylus. Tr. Herbert Weir Smyth. Cambridge: Harvard University Press, 1926.

Apollinaris von Laodicea. Tr. Ekkehard Mühlenberg. Göttingen: Vandenhoeck u. Ruprecht, 1969.

Apollodorus. *Apollodorus: The Library.* Tr. James George Frazer.; Cambridge: Harvard University Press, 1976.

Apollonius. *Apollonius Rhodius: The Argonautica.* Tr. R. C. Seaton. Cambridge: Harvard University Press, 2006.

Apollonius King of Tyre. Tr. Elizabeth Archibald. Rochester: Boydell & Brewer 1991.

Aratus, Solensis. *Phaenomena.* Tr. Douglas Kidd. New York: Cambridge University Press, 1997.

Aristotle. *Aristotle in 23 Volumes.* Tr. H. Rackham. Cambridge: Harvard University Press, 1952.

Artemidorus. *The Oneirocritica of Artemidorus.* Tr. Robert John White. Ann Arbor, MI: University Microfilms, 1974.

Cassius, Dio Cocceianus. *Dio's Roman History, with an English Translation.* Tr. Earnest Cary and Herbert Baldwin Foster. London: W. Heinemann, 1914.

Chariton. *Chaereas and Callirhoe.* Tr. by G.P. Goold. Cambridge: Harvard University Press, 1995.

Charles, R. H. *The Apocrypha and Pseudepigrapha of the Old Testament in English.* Oxford: Clarendon, 1976.

Chion of Heraclea: A Novel in Letters. Ed. Ingemar Düring. New York: Arno Press, 1979.

Cicero, Marcus Tullius. *Cicero.* Tr. Bailey D. R. Shackleton. Cambridge: Harvard University Press, 2002.

_____. *The Orations of Cicero.* Tr. Charles Duke Yonge. Ann Arbor, MI: University Microfilms International, 1982.

Cleomedes. *Caelestia (Meteōra).* Ed. Robert Todd. Leipzig: Teubner, 1990.

Diodorus. *Books I and II, 1-34.* Tr. Charles M. Oldfather. Cambridge: Harvard University Press, 1989.

Diogène, Laërce. *Lives of Eminent Philosophers.* Tr. Robert Drew Hicks and Herbert Long. London: W. Heinemann, 1972.

Épictète. *Epictetus.* Tr. Robert F. Dobbin. Oxford: Oxford University Press, 2007.

Epiphanius. *Epiphanius.* Tr. Karl Holl, Christian-Friedrich Collatz, et al. Berlin: W. De Gruyter, 2006.

Epstein, Isidore, and A. Cohen, eds. *Hebrew-English Edition of the Babylonian Talmud.* London: Soncino, 1974.

Euripides. *Euripides.* Tr. David Kovacs. Cambridge: Harvard University Press, 1994.

Freese, J. H., tr. *Aristotle.* Cambridge: Harvard University Press, 1926.

Guggenheimer, Heinrich W., tr. *The Jerusalem Talmud.* Berlin: De Gruyter, 2006.

Heliodorus. *An Ethiopian Romance.* Tr. Moses Hadas. Ann Arbor, MI; University of Michigan Press, 1957.

Heraclitus. *Fragments: A Text and Translation with a Commentary.* Tr. T. M. Robinson. Toronto: University of Toronto, 1991.

Herodotus. *The Histories.* Tr. A. D. Godley. Cambridge: Harvard University Press, 1920.

Homer. *The Iliad,* 2 vols. Tr. A.T. Murray. Cambridge: Harvard University Press, 1924.

_____. *The Odyssey,* 2 vols. Tr. A.T. Murray. Cambridge: Harvard University Press, 1919.

Horace. *Satire.* In *The Odes of Horace.* Tr. Jeffrey H. Kaimowitz. Baltimore: Johns Hopkins University Press, 2008.

Josephus, Flavius. *Josephus: Complete Works.* Tr. William Whiston. Grand Rapids: Kregel, 1960.

Juvenal. *Juvenal/Persius.* Tr. S. M. Braun. Cambridge: Harvard University Press, 2004.

Livy. *Livy.* Tr. B. O. Foster. Cambridge: Harvard University Press, 1951.

Lucian. *The Works of Lucian of Samosata, Complete with Exceptions Specified in the Preface.* Tr. H. W. Fowler and F. G. Fowler; Oxford: Clarendon, 1905.

Lucilius, Gaius. *Remains of Old Latin: in Four Volumes.* Ed. E. H. Warmington. Cambridge: Harvard University Press, 2006.

Maher, Michael, tr. *Targum Pseudo-Jonathan, Genesis.* Collegeville, MN: Liturgical, 1992.

McNamara, Martin, Kevin Cathcart, et al. *The Aramaic Bible: The Targums.* Edinburgh: T & T Clark, 1987.

Memar Marqah: The Teaching of Marqah. Tr. John Macdonald. Berlin: A. Töpelmann, 1963.

Neusner, Jacob, tr. *The Mishnah: A New Translation.* New Haven: Yale University, 1991.

_____. *The Tosefta.* Peabody, MA: Hendrickson, 2002.

Orosius, Paulus. *The Seven Books of History against the Pagans.* Tr. Roy J. Deferrari. Washington, DC: Washington Catholic University of America Press, 1964.

Ovid. *Metamorphoses.* Tr. Arthur Golding. London: W. Seres., 1567.

_____. *Tristia.* Tr. L.R. Lind. Athens, GA: University of Georgia Press, 1975.

Pausanias. *Pausanias: Description of Greece.* Tr. H. A. Omerod, Richard Wycherley, and W. H. S. Jones. Cambridge: Harvard University Press, 1931.

Petronius. *The Satyricon.* Tr. P.G. Walsh. Oxford: Clarendon Press, 1996.

Phaedrus. *The Fables of Phaedrus.* Tr. P.F. Widdows. Austin: University of Texas Press, 1992.

Philo, Judaeus. *The Works of Philo: Complete and Unabridged.* Tr. C. D. Yonge. Peabody: Hendrickson, 1997.

Philostratus. *Philostratus.* Tr. Ewen Bowie. Cambridge: Cambridge University Press, 2009.

Pindar. *Pindar.* Tr. William H. Race. Cambridge: Harvard University Press, 1997.

Plautus. *The Rope.* In *Roman Drama: The Plays of Plautus and Terence.* Tr. Frank O. Copley. Indianapolis: Bobbs-Merrill, 1965.

Pliny. *Pliny: Letters.* Tr. William Melmoth. Cambridge: Harvard University Press, 1961.

Pliny the Elder. *The Natural History.* Eds. John Bostock and H.T. Riley. London: Taylor and Francis, 1855.

Plutarch. *Plutarch Moralia.* Tr. Edward N. O'Neil; Cambridge: Harvard University Press, 2004.

_____. *Plutarch's Lives.* Tr. Bernadotte Perrin. London: W. Heinemann, 1914.

Polybius. *Histories.* Tr. Evelyn S. Shuckburgh. New York: Macmillan, 1889.

Pseudo-Callisthenes. *The Romans of Alexander the Great by Pseudo-Callisthenes.* Tr. Albert Wolohojian. New York: Columbia University Press, 1969.

Quintilian. *The Institutio Oratoria of Quintilian.* Tr. Harold Edgeworth Butler. London: W. Heinemann, 1921.

Quintus Curtius. *History of Alexander.* Tr. John C. Rolfe. Cambridge: Harvard University Press, 1946.

Quintus of Smyrna. *The War at Troy: What Homer Didn't Tell.* Tr. Frederick M. Comebellack. Norman: University of Oklahoma Press, 1968.

Roberts, Alexander, James Donaldson, A. Cleveland Coxe, and Allan Menzies, trs. *Ante-Nicene Fathers: The Writings of the Fathers Down to A.D. 325.* Peabody, MA: Hendrickson, 1994.

Robinson, James McConkey. *The Nag Hammadi Library in English.* San Francisco: Harper & Row, 1988.

Schaff, Philip, ed. *Nicene and Post-Nicene Fathers,* Series 1 & 2. Peabody, MA: Hendrickson, 1995, 2004.

Seneca, Lucius Annaeus. *Moral Essays.* Tr. John William Basore. Cambridge: Harvard University Press, 1928.

Silius Italicus. *Punica.* Tr. J.D. Duff. Cambridge: Harvard University Press, 1934.

Statius. *Thebaid.* In *Statius.* 2 vols. Tr. J.H. Mozley. Cambridge; Harvard University Press, 1928.

Strabo. *The Geography of Strabo.* Tr. Horace Leonard Jones and J. R. Sitlington Sterrett. Cambridge: Harvard University Press, 1982.

Suetonius. *The Lives of the Caesars.* Tr. Alexander Thomson. Whitefish: Kessinger Pub., 2000.

Tacitus. *Complete Works of Tacitus.* Tr. Alfred John Church, William Jackson Brodribb, and Sara Bryant. New York: Random House, 1942.

Thucydides. *Thucydides Translated into English; with Introduction, Marginal Analysis, Notes, and Indices.* Vol. 1. Tr. Benjamin Jowett. Oxford: Clarendon Press, 1881.

Valerius Flaccus. *Argonautica.* In *Valerius Flaccus.* Tr. J.H. Mozley. Cambridge: Harvard University Press; London: Heinemann, 1936.

Vegetius, Renatus Flavius. *Vegetius: Epitome of Military Science.* Tr. N. P. Milner. Liverpool, England: Liverpool University Press, 1996.

Vermes, Geza, tr. *The Complete Dead Sea Scrolls in English.* New York: Allen Lane/Penguin, 1997.

Virgil. *Eclogues. Georgics. Aeneid: Books 1–6.* Tr. H. R. Fairclough. Cambridge: Harvard University Press, 1934–1935.

Xenophon. *Xenophon in Seven Volumes.* Tr. Carleton L. Brownson. Cambridge: Harvard University Press, 1918.

Xenophon of Ephesus. *Ephesian Tale.* In *Three Greek Romances.* Tr. Moses Hadas. Indianapolis: Bobbs-Merrill, 1964.

Ancient Sources Abbreviations

1 En.. . . . .*1 Enoch (Ethiopic Apocalypse)*
1QM . . . .*War Scroll*
1QSb . . . .*Rule of Blessings*
2 Bar. . . . .*2 Baruch (Sryiac Apocalypse)*
2 Esd . . . .*2 Esdras*
2 Macc . . . .*2 Maccabees*
3 Macc . . . .*3 Maccabees*
4 Ezra . . . .*4 Ezra*
4QShirShabb . . . .*Songs of the Sabbath Sacrifice*
Apoc. Ab.. . . . .*Apocalypse of Abraham*
Ass. Mos.. . . . .*Assumption of Moses*
b. Sotah . . . .*Sotah*
Bar . . . . .Baruch
Barn.. . . . .*Barnabas*
Chysostom
   Hom. Act. . . . . .Homilies on the Acts of the Apostles
Josephus
   Ag. Ap . . . .*Against Apion*
   Ant. . . . .*Antiquities of the Jews*
   J.W. . . . .*Wars of the Jews*
Jub.. . . . .*Jubilees*
L.A.E.. . . . .*Life of Adam and Eve*
m. Men . . . .*Menahot*
Philo
   Flaccus . . . .*Flaccus*
   Rewards . . . .*On Rewards and Punishment*
   Moses . . . .*On the Life of Moses*
   Pss. Sol. . . . .*Psalms of Solomon*
Sir . . . . .Sirach/Ecclesiasticus/Wisdom of Jesus son of Sirach
T. Benj. . . . .*Testament of Benjamin*
T. Levi.. . . . .*Testament of Levi*
Tertullian
   Adversus Judaeos. . . . . . .An Answer to the Jews
Tg. Ps. J. . . . .*Targum Pseudo-Jonathan*
Tobit . . . . .Tobit
Wisdom . . . . .Wisdom of Solomon

ACTS 1

I. WITNESS IN JERUSALEM (1:1–8:1a)

If the book of Acts were a symphony it would have three movements roughly following the contours of Jerusalem (1–7), Judea and Samaria (8–12), and the "ends of the earth" (13–28). This first movement is dedicated to the Jewish Church in the capital city of Jerusalem ⬛, what the Jews would consider the navel of the universe. From this ethnic and geographic center, the gospel will ultimately eminate out to the farthest reaches under the centrifugal force of the Spirit.

Though Luke will describe the earliest days of Jewish Christians, his interest goes beyond historical curiosity. As the stories unfold, Luke laces clues into the narrative, showing the inevitable outward expansion of the church: the fourteen nations of Pentecost (2:9-11), the universal promise of Joel (2:17-21), the prophecy of his international rule (4:25-27), the ethnic expansion of Hellenistic widows (6:1-7), and Stephen's magisterial historical survey of God's major work *outside* of Israel (7:1-53). All this prepares the reader for the gospel to break out of its ethnocentric shell. This is not the story of a Jewish church ensconced in its traditions. It is the story of the universal kingdom, quivering on the precipice of a metamorphosis.

A. INTRODUCTION (1:1-26)

If the book of "Acts" is actually the "Acts of the Holy Spirit," then the real action begins in chapter 2. Chapter 1 is an introduction. This same phenomenon is found in Luke when the birth of Jesus is delayed until the second chapter. Both Luke and Acts set the stage through an extended introduction before the hero steps into the spotlight—Jesus in Luke and the Spirit in Acts.

Chapter 1 is a carefully crafted introduction that prepares for the debut of the Spirit. It accomplishes three things before shifting the narrative into high gear. First, it links the Gospel of Luke with the book of Acts by 'interlacing' the two works (1:1-11).[1] Like a two-part television show, the second episode begins with a flashback, reminding the viewers of where they've been. Next, it details Jesus' ascension (1:12-14), creating a gaping hole that only the Spirit can fill. Finally, it describes the restoration of the apostolic band (1:15-26). Thus, when the Spirit descends (John 14:26; 15:26; 16:7) the full retinue of Twelve Apostles can function as the official witness to Jesus' resurrection (Luke 24:48; Acts 1:8;

---

[1] These verses are carefully composed with four two-part scenes (vv. 1-3, 4-5, 6-8, 9-11), each linked with and building upon the last; cf. Rudolf Pesch, "Der Anfang der Apostelgeschichte: Apg 1,1-11: Kommentarstudie," in *Vorarbeiten: Der Anfange der Apostelgeschichte*, vol. 3 (Zürich: Neukirchener Verlag, 1971), 7-35 (esp. 7-9).

2:32; 3:15; 5:32; 10:39, 41; 13:31; 1 Cor 15:5). This brilliantly crafted introduction not only bridges the two books, it also builds the 'drum roll' to a crescendo before the Spirit makes his triumphal entrance.

1. Continuity with Luke (1:1-5)

[1]In my former book,[2] Theophilus, I wrote about all that Jesus began to do and to teach

1:1. From the very first sentence, Luke makes it clear that this is part two of his *magnum opus*. First, he mentions *Theophilus* whose name means "beloved of God."[3] The Gospel of Luke was dedicated to him.[4] Second, he mentions his "former book" which traced the ministry of Jesus—all that he *began to do and to teach*. By implication, therefore, the book of Acts will take up where the Gospel left off and carry it on through the establishment of the church in the far-reaches of the Roman Empire.[5] More specifically, Acts 1 and Luke 24 overlap substantially. Luke's Gospel ends with a lengthy description of the resurrection and a 'teaser' on the ascension (Luke 24:51). Acts, on the other hand, opens with a brief mention of the resurrection (Acts 1:3) and expands the story of the ascension (Acts 1:2, 9-11).

This kind of continuity actually runs the length of both books:

LUKE	ACTS
Introduction in **1:1-4**	Introduction in **1:1-5**
Birth of **Jesus**, chapter 2	**Outpouring** of the **Holy Spirit**, chapter 2
Kingdom of God announced to the **Jews**	**Church** of Jesus Christ opened to the to the **Gentiles**

---

[2] Luke opens volume two with a rather standard line, recognizable from about a dozen other Hellenistic documents; cf. P. W. van der Horst, "Hellenistic parallels to the Acts of the Apostles 1:1-26," *ZNW* 74 (1983): 17-18. Even though it is recognizable, it is still peculiar in that the word μέν, which would normally suggest something like "on the one hand," has no corresponding δέ —"on the other hand." This same peculiarity, however, is also found in the prologues of Xenophon's *Anabasis*, Josephus's *Antiquities,* Herodian's *History of the Empire,* etc. (and elsewhere in Luke 8:5; Acts 3:13, 21; 21:29; 27:21); cf. D. W. Palmer, "The Literary Background of Acts 1.1-14," *NTS* 33 (1987): 427.

[3] For more information on Theophilus, see the introduction under 'Recipient.' There it was argued that Theophilus was (a) a real person, not merely a metaphoric 'lover of God', contra Claire Rothschild, *Luke-Acts and the Rhetoric of History* (WUNT 11; Tübigen: Mohr Siebeck, 2004), 124-125; (b) like Luke, he was probably a Hellenistic adherent to Judaism—a Godfearer, (c) he was already a convert though he needed further instruction, and (d) he probably was the patron who funded the research and/or publication of the book.

[4] Though there are a number of books in the ancient world with similar dedications (Fitzmyer, 194-195), the one closest to Luke in both culture and time is Josephus's *Against Apion* (c. A.D. 45; 1.1.1; §1): "Through my treatise on Ancient History, most eminent [κράτιστε] Epaphroditus, I consider that, to those who will read it, I have made it sufficiently clear concerning our people, the Judeans, that it is extremely ancient and had its own original composition, and how it inhabited the land that we now possess; for I composed in the Greek language a history covering 5,000 years, on the basis of our sacred books." *Against Apion* is an apologetic tract to defend against Apian's attack of the Jews before the Emperor Caligula. This may give us a clue as to how to read Luke's two-volume work as a political apologetic for Christians in the early Roman world. Cf. G.E. Sterling, *Historiography and Self-Definition: Josephus, Luke-Acts, and Apologetic Historiography,* NovTSup 64 (Leiden: Brill, 1992).

[5] This is reminiscent of Hebrews 2:3, "This salvation, which was first announced by the Lord, was confirmed to us by those who heard him." Cf. A. Feuillet, "Commencement de l'économie chrétienne d'après He II. 3-4; Mc I. 1 et Ac I. 1-2," *NTS* 24 (1978): 163-174.

LUKE	ACTS
Acts of **Jesus**	Acts of the **Holy Spirit** through the **Apostles**
The movement pushes toward **Jerusalem** (9:51)	The movement pushes toward **Rome** (19:21)
Ends with five **trials of Jesus**	Ends with five **trials of Paul**

In a very real sense, one could say that without the book of Acts the story of Jesus would be incomplete. After all, he didn't come merely to save individuals to get them to heaven, but to create a community that would carry out God's kingdom on earth.

. . . ²until the day he was taken up to heaven, after giving instructions through the Holy Spirit to the Apostles he had chosen.⁶

1:2. The ascension (which will be discussed in detail in vv. 9-11) marks the completion of Jesus' earthly ministry. Up to that time Jesus directed[7] the Apostles. Henceforth, the Holy Spirit will instruct them (John 14:26; 16:13, 15). However, this is not a terribly drastic shift. Notice that even Jesus' teaching of the Twelve was *through the Holy Spirit.*[8] It is not as if the Spirit suddenly gets involved because Jesus left the premises. The Spirit was responsible for Jesus' conception (Luke 1:35), validated his baptism (Mark 1:10/Matt 3:16/Luke 3:22/John 1:31-34), led him into the wilderness to be tempted (Mark 1:12/Matt 4:1/Luke 4:1), empowered his ministry for preaching (John 3:34-35), miracles (Luke 4:14, 18-19), and exorcisms (Matt 12:28), and raised Jesus from the dead (Rom 1:4; 8:11; 1 Pet 3:18). This says nothing about the Spirit's role in the Old Testament in preparing for the coming Messiah. He has been intimately involved in the establishment of God's kingdom on earth and will now step onto the stage of history in his most prominent and personal role.

Though Jesus taught the Twelve a bunch of stuff, the core of his teaching, especially after the resurrection, boils down to the great commission (cf. Matt 28:18-20; Mark 16:15-18; Luke 24:47-48; John 20:21; Acts 1:8). What follows in Acts, is the story of the Holy Spirit facilitating the completion of Jesus' final directive to spread his fame to the "ends of the earth." Here, then, before Luke finishes his first breath, we have laid out the two grand themes of this book: The continued work of the *Holy Spirit* through the witness of the *Apostles.*

---

[6] The so-called "Western" text (mss D) includes an extra line at the end of this verse: "…and he ordered them to proclaim the good news"; "καὶ ἐκέλευσε κηρύσσειν τὸ εὐαγγέλιον." This addition would have three fortuitous effects. It would (a) recollect the original call of the Twelve (Luke 9:2); (b) draw a straight line between the opening of Acts and the closing commission of Luke 24:47, and (c) offer a nice inclusio since the final verse of Acts (28:31) would successfully fulfill the opening of the book. Cf. Josep Rius-Camps, "Las variantes de la recensión occidental de los Hechos de los Apóstoles (I) (Hch 1,1-3)." *FilNoet* 8 (1995): 59-78.

[7] The Greek word ἐντέλλω "giving instruction" implies a command. In other words, Jesus is not merely informing them of facts but giving them directions.

[8] Kilgallen suggests that "through the Spirit," which grammatically could describe either the teaching of Jesus or the selection of the Apostles, should be taken to mean "because of the Spirit" (διά with the genitive can be read this way, cf. Rom 8:3; 2 Cor 9:13 [*BAG* 179], though it is very rare). In other words, he suggests Jesus chose the Twelve *because* the Spirit would one day empower them for witness. Cf. John J. Kilgallen, "'The Apostles Whom He Chose Because of the Holy Spirit': A Suggestion Regarding Acts 1,2," *Bib* 81 (2000): 414-417.

Jesus designated the Apostles as his leadership task force and the primary witness to his resurrection. The word "Apostle" means "one sent with a commission," and it implies that the emissary carries the authority of the one sending him. For this group, however, the work of any individual is not nearly as important as the testimony of the group. That is to say, there were twelve of them and they represented the reconstituted Israel (cf. Luke 22:30/Matt 19:28).[9] As a corporate whole, they could proclaim the resurrection of Jesus as the signal event of God's kingdom on earth (v. 3).

Several things should be said in this regard. First, there were not just twelve Apostles named in the New Testament. There are potentially nine others.[10] With the exception of Paul, whose Apostolic claims (cf. Rom 1:1; 11:13; 1 Cor 15:1-11, etc.) will be examined as he makes his own appearance in Acts, they all appear to be delegates of a specific church, not chosen by Jesus to represent the universal church. Luke especially stresses the number and function of the Twelve (Luke 6:13; Acts 1:2, 26) even using "Twelve" as a synonym for the Apostolic band (Luke 8:1; 9:1, 12; 18:31; 22:3, 30, 47; Acts 6:2). Second, Luke uses the word "apostle" more than anyone else. In fact, Matthew, Mark, and John together only use the word four times. Luke uses it six times in his Gospel and twenty-eight more times in Acts. That is nearly half of the seventy-nine uses in the entire New Testament. Third, the Apostles are the key leaders in the Jerusalem church (cf. 1:2-5, 8, 13, 21-22, 26; 2:6, 7, 14, 37, 42-43; 4:33, 36-37; 5:2, 12, 18, 29, 40; 6:2, 6; 8:1, 14, 18; 9:27; 11:1). However, after the doors open to Gentiles in chapter 10–11, we hear almost nothing about the apostolic band. They only partner with the Elders in Jerusalem to arbitrate the dispute over circumcision (15:2, 4, 22-23). It looks, therefore, like their leadership began to yield to Elders once the church expanded ethnically. Massive tomes have been written on the Apostles. Suffice to summarize here for Luke's purposes, the Apostles are the symbolic heads of the divine state so named "the kingdom of God" and in that official capacity, they declare Jesus as the sovereign envoy of Yahweh by their testimony to his resurrection from the dead.

[3]After his suffering, he showed himself to these men and gave many convincing proofs that he was alive. He appeared to them over a period of forty days and spoke about the kingdom of God.

1:3. Verse two identifies the two primary actors of Acts—the Spirit and the Apostles. Verse three now identifies their two primary declarations—the resurrection and the kingdom of God.

Jesus offers *convincing proofs* of his bodily resurrection. The Greek word,

---

[9] For a full examination of the Twelve as representative leaders of Israel see Andrew Clark, "The Role of the Apostles," in *Witness to the Gospel: The Theology of Acts* (ed. I. H. Marshall and David Peterson; Grand Rapids: Eerdmans, 1998), 169-181 and Jacob Jervell; *Luke and the People of God: A New Look at Luke-Acts* (Minneapolis: Augsburg, 1972), 75-112.

[10] Paul and Barnabas (Acts 14:4, 14), Andronicus and Junias (Rom 16:7) [although the text may simply mean that these men were well known by the apostles], unnamed brothers (2 Cor 8:23), James, the Lord's brother (Gal. 1:19) [though this text may simply be an 'except' clause that would not have to make James an apostle], Epaphroditus, the messenger from the church (Phil 2:25), and even Jesus (Heb 3:1).

tekmērion is used only here in all the New Testament. Other Hellenistic authors use it to mean "sure evidence" (e.g., Aristotle, *Rhetoric* 1.2.16; Wis 5:11; 3 Macc 3:24; Josephus, *Ant.* 5.1.13 §38).[11] This would include his twelve appearances to more than five-hundred people in which he was seen, heard, and handled (cf. 1 John 1:1).[12] When this was not enough, Jesus even ate a piece of fish to verify he was not a ghost (Luke 24:37-43).[13]

The resurrection thus became the core of Christianity (1 Cor 15:14). It was the singular event that turned Peter from crouching in a courtyard to preaching at Pentecost. It alone explains the meteoric rise of Christianity from a band of about 120 behind locked doors to an unquenchable force under Roman persecution. It stopped Paul in his tracks on the road to Damascus, transformed Thomas from doubter to martyr, and turned James from an embittered half-brother to a pillar of the church of Jerusalem. The very sacraments of baptism and the Lord's Supper, or even a church gathering on Sunday, are predicated on the reality of the resurrection. It comes as no surprise, therefore, that the resurrection of Jesus features in virtually every sermon in the book of Acts.

During the first forty days[14] between Passover and Pentecost, Jesus appeared intermittently and talked about the *Kingdom of God*.[15] It would be difficult to make too much of the kingdom. It is not only the core of Jesus' preaching (cf. Mark 1:15; Matt 4:23; 9:35; Luke 4:43; 8:1; 9:11), it forms the bookends of Luke's second volume (1:3; 28:31).[16] It remains, however, a mystery to most contempo-

---

[11] For other nonbiblical uses see David Mealand, "The Phrase 'Many Proofs' in Acts 1,3 and Hellenistic Writers," *ZNW* 80 (1989): 134-135.

[12] (1) Mary Magdalene (Mark 16:9-11; John 20:11-18), (2) other women (Matthew 28:9-10), (3) two on the way to Emmaus (Luke 24:13-22), (4) Peter (1 Corinthians 15:5; Luke 24:36-43; John 20:19ff.), (5) ten Apostles (Mark 16:14; Luke 24:36; John 20:19ff.), (6) the Eleven (John 20:26-31), (7) the seven by the Sea of Galilee (John 21:1-23), the 500 (Great Commission?) (1 Corinthians 15:6; Matthew 28:16-20), (8) in Jerusalem (Commission Repeated?) (Mark 16:15-18), (9) James (1 Corinthians 15:7), (10) the disciples' further commission (Acts 1:3-8; Luke 24:44-49), (11) the Ascension (Acts 1:9-12; Mark 16:19-20; Luke 24:50-53).

[13] For a brief defense of the bodily resurrection of Jesus, see Mark Moore, "Did Jesus Really Rise from the Dead?" in *Humble Defense: Evidence for the Christian Faith* (ed. Mark Moore and Mark Scott; Joplin: College Press, 2004), 145-164. The most important work to date on the subject is N.T. Wright, *The Resurrection of the Son of God* (Minneapolis: Fortress, 2003). Norman Geisler, *The Battle for the Resurrection* (Nashville, Thomas Nelson, 1989) offers a classic evangelical apologetic. For a more popular but less sophisticated approach see Josh McDowell, *The Resurrection Factor* (San Bernardino, CA: Here's Life, 1989).

[14] Forty days was a highly symbolic number, particularly in Jewish literature. In general, it was used for the period of time a servant of God took to receive revelation (e.g., Exod 24:18; 34:28; Ezek 4:6; Jonah 3:4; 2 Macc 5:2; 2 Esd 14:23, 36, 45; Mark 1:13/Matt 4:2/Luke 4:2). Cf. Philippe Menoud, "'Pendant quarante jours' (Actes 1:3)," in *Noetestamentica et Patristica* (ed. Oscar Cullmann; Leiden: Brill, 1962), 148-156.

[15] Though the precise phrase "kingdom of God" (βασιλεία θεοῦ) is never found in the OT (the closest is 1 Chronicles 28:5 which uses the term "kingdom of Yahweh" (מַלְכוּת יְהוָה) the concept of God's real rule is common throughout the OT, Apocrypha, and rabbinic literature. Similar terms include Psa 103:19; 145:12 (מַלְכוּתוֹ); 145:11, 13 (מַלְכוּתְךָ); 1 Chr 17:14 (מַלְכוּתִי); 1 Chr 28:5 and 2 Chr 13:8 (יְהוָה מַמְלֶכֶת); 1 Chr 29:11 (הַמַּמְלָכָה); Obad 21 and Psa 22:29 [27] (הַמְּלוּכָה). In addition, there appears to have been a growing awareness of the kingdom of God during the second-temple period: *Jub* 1:28, "All shall know that I am the God of Israel . . . and King on Mount Zion for all eternity;" *Pss. Sol.* 17:3, "The kingdom of our God is forever over the nations in judgment"; *T. Benj.* 9:1, "The kingdom of the Lord shall not be among you, for straightway He shall take it away"; 1QM 12:7, "For Thou art [terrible], O God, in the glory of Thy kingdom"; 1QSb 4:25-26, "May you attend upon the service in the Temple of the Kingdom"; (cf. 1QM 6:6; 1QSb 5:21). To this could be added exaltation of the celestial Kingdom in the Songs of the Sabbath (4QShirShabb). For a comprehensive listing of relevant citations, see Craig A. Evans, "Daniel in the New Testament: Visions of God's Kingdom," in *The Book of Daniel: Composition and Reception* (ed. John J. Collins and Peter W. Flint; Leiden: Brill, 2001), 2:491-498.

[16] Acts is the only book outside the Gospels to thematically develop the "kingdom of God" (cf. Acts 1:3, 6; 8:12; 14:22; 19:8; 20:25; 28:23, 31); cf. Otto Merk, "Das Reich Gottes in den lukanischen Schriften," in *Jesus und Paulus* (Göttingen: Vandenhoeck & Ruprecht, 1975), 201-220.

rary Christians for whom the kingdom is either an internal, spiritual experience or a future reality (either an earthly millennial reign or synonymous with heaven). The bulk of the discussion has thus centered on whether the kingdom is a present (internal) reality or some future state yet to be inaugurated.[17] Neither of these captures Jesus' ideology of God's reign on earth—"Thy kingdom come; thy will be done on earth . . . " (Matt 6:10). As a first-century Palestinian Jew, Jesus set his sights on a renewed Israel that lived in fidelity to God's rule. The kingdom's most striking characteristic, as articulated by Jesus, is the paradoxical nature of its citizens. Rather than the economic elite or the ethnically elect, the kingdom is populated by the poor (Matt 5:3/Luke 6:20; James 2:5), the persecuted (Matt 5:10), the marginalized (Matt 11:11/Luke 7:28; Matt 8:11-12/Luke 13:29-30), "sinners" (Matt 21:31; cf. Luke 7:29), and children (Matt 18:1-4/Luke 18:16-7; Matt 19:14; Mark 10:14-15). In a sense, it is Luke's agenda to show that Christ's followers, Gentiles included, are the faithful remnant, the children of Abraham, who embody and enact the kingdom of God.

[4]On one occasion, while he was eating with them, he gave them this command: "Do not leave Jerusalem, but wait for the gift my Father promised, which you have heard me speak about. [5]For John baptized with water, but in a few days you will be baptized with[a] the Holy Spirit."

[a]5 Or *in*

1:4. Verse 3 describes Jesus' general post-resurrection discussion of the kingdom. Verses 4-5 describe a specific meal.[18] Jesus ordered them to stay in Jerusalem and wait for the power of the Holy Spirit before venturing into the hinterlands to preach the Gospel. This is virtually identical to what Jesus commanded the Apostles on the evening of his resurrection:

> This is what is written: The Christ will suffer and rise from the dead on the third day, and repentance and forgiveness of sins will be preached in his name to all nations, beginning at Jerusalem. You are witnesses of these things. I am going to send you what my Father has promised; but stay in the city until you have been clothed with power from on high. (Luke 24:46-49)

---

[17] There are three key figures in this debate. Johannes Weiss, *Die Predigt Jesu vom Reiche Gottes* (Göttingen: Vandenhoeck & Ruprecht, 1964 [1895]) opened the discussion by calling attention to Jesus' irreducibly eschatological character that necessitated a future (imminent) expectation of God's rule. C. H. Dodd, *Parables of the Kingdom* (New York: Scribner's Sons, 1936), argued that Jesus thought the kingdom was, in fact, already present in his ministry, so-called 'realized eschatology'. Norman Perrin, *The Kingdom of God in the Teaching of Jesus* (Philadelphia: Westminster, 1963), offered a mediating option of both/and, which has become the consensus today. It must be emphasized that the discussion of the kingdom has been derailed by this tangential chronological argument. The important issue is the real rule of God in and through a sociologically identifiable group of adherents.

[18] The word συναλίζω, "eating together," is used only here in the NT. There is some question, therefore, about its meaning. Etymologically it could be rendered "to salt together." Since Jesus often appeared to his disciples at a meal (Luke 24:13-22; Mark 16:14/Luke 24:36/John 20:19ff; John 21:1-23), it probably means some kind of shared meal. Though, William Hatch makes a strong lexical case for it simply meaning "to assemble" without any implication of food at the gathering ("The Meaning of Acts 1:4," *JBL* 30 [1911]: 123-128), though Daniel McConaughy shows how the old Syriac translation understood the word in terms of a sacred or solemn meal; cf. "An Old Syriac Reading of Acts 1:4 and More Light on Jesus' Last Meal before His Ascension," *OC* 72 (1988): 63-67.

Luke's strategy is obvious—he is weaving together the ending of Luke and the beginning of Acts.

It was appropriate for the Apostles to wait in Jerusalem, the capital that housed the temple (cf. Luke 24:52-53; Acts 1:12; 2:46).[19] For the Jews it was the center of the universe and the primary place of God's revelation (not to mention prophetic suffering, cf. Luke 13:33). Luke is aware of the theological significance of the city and to good effect uses Jerusalem throughout his two-volume work as geographic theology.

The *gift* for which they were to wait was the Holy Spirit (cf. Luke 24:49; Acts 2:33, 39; Gal 3:14; Eph 1:13) which Jesus promised several times (cf. Luke 11:13; 12:12; John 14:26; 15:26; etc.). The Spirit is what differentiates John's baptism from Jesus' baptism (cf. Acts 11:16; 19:1-7). This raises the question: "What is the baptism of the Holy Spirit?" Does it come with water baptism? After all, water and the Spirit are often connected (cf. John 3:3-7; Acts 2:38-39; 19:1-6; 1 Cor 6:11; Titus 3:3-7). Or is it a spiritual experience of being overwhelmed by the Spirit, perhaps manifested in the gift of tongues (e.g., Acts 2:4; 10:44-46)?[20]

1:5. The baptism of the Holy Spirit, originally prophesied by John the Baptist (Mark 1:8/Matt 3:11/Luke 3:16; John 1:33) is identified only *twice* in the book of Acts (2:1-4 and 10:44-46; 11:16) and both included tongues as a sign of God's approval. (A) At Pentecost, God was validating the Apostles as spokesmen and witnesses of the resurrection. (B) At Cornelius's house, God was validating the first Gentiles as *bona fide* prospects for conversion. In neither case was the baptism of the Holy Spirit equivalent to or necessary for salvation.[21] The Apostles were already saved, and Cornelius commenced to be baptized in water according to the normal first-century practice of Christian conversion. Thus the only two times the New Testament identifies the Baptism of the Holy Spirit, it was not for salvation but for validation.

Some scholars argue that these two episodes alone constitute the Baptism of the Holy Spirit. However, when John prophesies about this baptism (Luke 3:16), he seems to promise it to the whole crowd. Furthermore, 1 Corinthians 12:13 speaks of Spirit baptism as a universal Christian experience (cf. Eph 4:5). Thus, our initial impulse is to look for a broad fulfillment of this promise, not

---

[19] Jacob Kremer, "Die Voraussagen des Pfingstgeschehens in Apg 1, 4–5 und 8," in *Zeit Jesu: Festschrift für Heinrich Schlier* (ed. Günther Bornkamm and Karl Rahner; Freiburg: Herder, 1970), 150, proposes the *leitmotif* of waiting as a reminder of Israel's history—how often they waited for Yahweh to save them.

[20] The baptism of the Holy Spirit should be differentiated from two other Christian experiences: the *seal* of the spirit, by which an *individual* is *saved*, describes the mystic union between a believer and the Spirit. Sometimes it is referred to as the "gift" of the Holy Spirit (John 7:37-39; Acts 11:17; Rom 5:5; 1 Cor 2:12; 2 Cor 5:5); at other times it is called an "anointing" (Luke 4:18; Acts 4:27; 10:38; 2 Cor 1:21; 1 John 2:20, 27), or more specifically a "seal" (2 Cor 1:22; Eph 1:13; 4:30). Whatever it is called, it is essential for salvation (Rom 8:9; 1 Cor 6:19). The second Christian experience is the *filling* of the Spirit, by which a person is *empowered* to serve the *community* (Luke 1:15, 41, 67; 4:1; Acts 2:4; 4:8, 31; 6:3; 7:55; 9:17; 11:24; 13:9, 52).

[21] Roger Stronstad understands the Baptism of the Holy Spirit unilaterally as an experience of empowerment not of conversion or initiation; cf. *The Charismatic Theology of St. Luke* (Peabody, MA: Hendrickson, 1984) and "*The Charismatic Theology of St. Luke* Revisited," in *Defining Issues in Pentecostalism, Classical and Emergent* (Eugene, OR: Pickwick, 2008), 101-122. James Dunn, *Christ and the Spirit* (Grand Rapids: Eerdmans, 1998), argues conversely that Baptism of the Spirit was an initiation/conversion experience not merely empowerment. Both prove their points well on their chosen texts but fail to give the term "Baptism of the Spirit" the kind of flexible definition demanded by variant contexts; cf. Robby J. Kagarise, "'Baptized with the Holy Spirit': Soteriology and Empowerment in Lucan Pneumatology," *EvJ* 24 (2006): 19-33.

just two incidents. So how can the Baptism of the Holy Spirit apply to every believer if it is specifically validation of particular individuals? Perhaps the solution is simple: "Baptism of the Holy Spirit" is an umbrella term that Luke uses to describe the two 'Pentecost' experiences in Acts while Paul and John the Baptist used it more broadly for the universal experience of conversion. Readers of the Bible should give each author the latitude to use words on their own terms and in varied ways in different contexts. This is especially true when trying to describe the work of the Holy Spirit which is usually varied, mostly mystical, and often individualistic.

2. Commission to Proclaim the Kingdom (1:6-8)

This is the fifth and final great commission account which maps the movement of the remainder of the book. While there are many ways one could outline Acts, verse 8 is as good as any and better than most: Jerusalem (chs. 1–7), Judea and Samaria (chs. 8–12), and the ends of the earth (chs. 13–28). The first division reflects Pauline theology "to the Jew first" (Rom 1:16; 2:9-10) which one might assume he inherited from Jesus himself (Luke 24:47; Acts 1:4). The second division traces the strained steps toward Gentile inclusion that God forged on the anvil of physical persecution. The third division is, by far, the longest. One can nearly see Luke's broad grin at the turn of every page as he narrates the unfolding story of the ever-expanding Gospel. After this final commission, Jesus departs with such a striking display that the disciples understand they have entered a new era of salvation history.[22]

⁶So when they met together, they asked him, "Lord, are you at this time going to restore the kingdom to Israel?" ⁷He said to them: "It is not for you to know the times or dates the Father has set by his own authority. ⁸But you will receive power when the Holy Spirit comes on you; and you will be my witnesses in Jerusalem, and in all Judea and Samaria, and to the ends of the earth."

1:6-7. The Apostles still hang their hopes on a nationalistic Messianic reign.[23] While Jesus does not rebuke them for their expectation,[24] he does warn them

---

[22] Luke seems to divide time into three eras: the Jewish covenant, the life of Jesus, the mission of the church. The division between these eras is marked by the incarnation and the ascension respectively; cf. Franz Schnider, "Die Himmelfahrt Jesu—Ende oder Anfang?" in *Kontinuität und Einheit für Franz Mussner* (ed. Paul-Gerhard Müller and Werner Stenger; Freiburg: Herder, 1981), 163, 170-172.

[23] There was no agreement on what the Messiah would look like. In fact, few Jewish documents prior to Jesus discussed it at all. Nonetheless, from the references we do possess there is a general portrait with which the disciples of Jesus seem to align: This Messianic king would gather the dispersed tribes of Israel (Isa 11:11-16; *Bar* 4:36-37; 5:5-9; Philo, *Rewards* 28.164; 2 Esd 13:39-47), establish the true Jerusalem (*Pss. Sol.* 17:25, 33; *1 En.* 53:6; 90:28-29; 2 Esd 7:26; 13:36) with Yahweh as its sovereign (*Pss. Sol.* 17:1-4, 38; 1QM 19; *Shemoneh Esreh* 11), and conquer wicked enemies (*Pss. Sol.* 17:23-41; 1QM 15-19; 2 Esd 13:33-38; *1 En.* 52:4-9), especially as a judge (*1 En.* 45:3; 55:4; 61:8-10; 69:26-29; *Pss. Sol.* 17:28, 31, 48; 2 Esd 12:32-33; *2 Bar* 40:1) and warrior (Num 24:17; Psa 2; Philo, *Rewards.* 16.91-97; *2 Bar* 39:7–40:2; 70:2-6; *1 En.* 62:1-3; 2 Esd 12:32-33; 13:27-28, 35-38; *Tg. Ps.-J.* Gen 49:11; 1QM 11:5-10).

[24] Dispensational writers are quick to point out that Jesus in no way rebuked the Apostles' expectation of an earthly kingdom; e.g., Anthony Buzzard, "Acts 1:6 and the Eclipse of the Biblical Kingdom," *EvQ* 66 (1994): 197-215 (updated in *JRR* 16 [2009], 3-21). Stanley Toussaint and Jay Quine, "No, Not Yet: The Contingency of God's Promised Kingdom," *BibSac* 164 (2007): 131-147, even argue that the kingdom *cannot* come yet because certain eschatological prophecies have not been literally fulfilled (which seems dangerously close to the Apostle's error of immanent date-setting from the opposite extreme). However, if

again about trying to establish the date (cf. Mark 13:32/Matt 24:36). Such speculation is not particularly new (cf. 1 Thess 5:1-3; 2 Thess 2:1-2), but neither is it
helpful. The ascension forced a reconception of Jesus' present agenda. After all,
Jesus hardly needed to ascend vertically to reach the right hand of God. Rather,
he ascends in such a dramatic way that his closest followers would stop expecting intermittent appearances and get on with the task of universal evangelism.
Choque may well be right that Jesus' commission (v. 8) *is* the answer to their
question (v. 6).[25] Will Jesus reestablish the kingdom *now* and for *Israel?* Sort of:
Jesus' work will be through the disciples as empowered by the Holy Spirit, and
Israel will incorporate the Gentiles at the ends of the earth. This is the very program unveiled in the remainder of the book.[26]

1:8. Their initial consternation of being left as orphans (cf. John 14:18)
in the face of such a daunting commission is replaced with power through the
baptism in the Holy Spirit. This word "come upon" (*eperchomai*) is used by Luke
seven of its nine times in the New Testament. Most of the time it has a tone of
violence such as a physical assault (Luke 11:22; Acts 14:19) or judgment falling
on someone (Luke 21:26; Acts 8:24; 13:40; James 5:1). Obviously, the two times
it is used in reference to the Holy Spirit don't suggest violence but unquestioned
control over the recipient, for example, in Luke 1:35 when the Spirit comes
upon Mary's womb and creates life. Luke undoubtedly took this concept from
the LXX where the Spirit of Yahweh came upon individuals with overwhelming
power (e.g., Judg 3:10; Num 11:17; Ezek 2:2). Two references from Isaiah are
of particular importance because they relate the Spirit's work with Jesus that is
now being delegated to his Apostles: Isaiah 11:2, 4, "The Spirit of the LORD will
rest on him—the Spirit of wisdom and of understanding, the Spirit of counsel
and of power . . . but with righteousness he will judge the needy, with justice he
will give decisions for the poor of the earth." Isaiah 61:1, "The Spirit of the Sovereign LORD is on me, because the LORD has anointed me to preach good news
to the poor. . . ." The commission Jesus gives them completes what he started
through the anointing of the Holy Spirit. This commission is thus not new. It is
part two—the continuing of all Jesus began to do and to teach.

This phrase "*ends of the earth*" was not uncommon in Hellenistic literature.
In his definitive article, Unnik showed that the world, in the first century, was
conceived as a disk surrounded by oceans with its extremities being Spain/Ger-
many (west), Ethiopia (south), India (east), and Scythia (north).[27] Hence, the
"ends of the earth" is the outer ring. Though Rome is the geographical end of

---

Luke's presentation of the kingdom is correctly understood as a present reality (Acts 8:12; 14:22; 15:13-19;
19:8; 20:25; 28:23, 31) then it is not possible to bracket it off as only or even primarily a future advent.

[25] Efraín Choque, "Prioridades para la Misión en la Iglesia primitiva según Hechos 1:8: Un Modelo para
la Iglesia de hoy," in *Pensar la Iglesia hoy: Hacia una Eclesiología adventista: Estudios teológicos presentados durante
el IV Simposio bíblico-teológico Sudamericano en honor a Raoul Dederen* (ed. Raoul Dederen; Gerald A. Klingbeil;
Martin G. Klingbeil, et al.; Ríos: Editorial Universidad Adventista del Plata, 2002), 119-129.

[26] It can be seen with special clarity in Luke's summary statements about the progress of the proclamation: 2:41, 47; 4:4; 5:14; 6:7; 9:31, 42; 11:21; 12:24; 13:48; 16:5; 19:20; 28:31.

[27] W. C. Van Unnik, "Der Ausdruck 'ΕΩΣ 'ΕΣΧΑΤΟΥ ΤΗΣ ΓΗΣ (Apostelgeschichte 1:8) und sein alt-
testamentlicher Hintergrund," in *Studia biblica et semitica* (Wageningen: H. Veenman, 1966), 335-349. This
concept is seen most clearly in Demosthenes, *Epistle* 4.7 and Crates, *Epistle* 31.

Acts, it was never conceived of as the "ends of the earth" nor is it really the end of the mission given in Acts 1:8 (cf. Mark 13:10/Matt 24:14; Mark 14:9/Matt 26:13; Luke 24:47; Matt 28:19).[28] The point of Paul's discourse in Rome (Acts 28:23-28) is that the gospel would henceforth extend to Gentiles without Jewish priority. This is, of course, a point Luke has been driving at for some time. Thus, "ends of the earth," which has a clear geographic reference, ultimately becomes an ethnic reference based upon Isaiah 49:6, "It is too small a thing for you to be my servant to restore the tribes of Jacob and bring back those of Israel I have kept. I will also make you a light for the Gentiles, that you may bring my salvation to the ends of the earth." When this text is quoted in Acts 13:47 (cf. *Barn.* 14:8) the "ends of the earth" *is* the Gentiles.[29] So even though Acts 1:8 is phrased with geographic terminology, the heart is for the ethnic groups who inhabit these far-flung lands. In this simple commission, Jesus turned the diaspora on its head. Rather than being a problem to be overcome by 'ingathering', it was an opportunity to be exploited by evangelism.[30]

3. Ascension (1:9-11)

[9]**After he said this, he was taken up before their very eyes, and a cloud hid him from their sight. [10]They were looking intently up into the sky as he was going, when suddenly two men dressed in white stood beside them. [11]"Men of Galilee,"[31] they said, "why do you stand here looking into the sky? This same Jesus, who has been taken from you into heaven, will come back in the same way you have seen him go into heaven."**

1:9. There has hardly been a biblical text that has drawn more fire from skeptics.[32] Part of the problem is that Luke alone describes what happened, and he does so with mythical elements. The *cloud* represents the presence and power of God (e.g., Luke 9:34-35/Mark 9:7/Matt 17:5; Luke 21:27; Exod 16:10;

---

[28] Contra Haenchen, 115. Even less likely is Gades in Spain, contra Earle Ellis, "The End of the Earth," *BBR* 1 (1991): 123-132 and Witherington, 110-111; Ethiopia, contra T. C. G. Thornton, "To the End of the Earth in Acts 1 8," *ExpTim* 89 (1977–78): 374-375; or Palestine, contra D. R. Schwartz, "The End of the ΓΗ (Acts 1 8): Beginning or End of the Christian Vision?" *JBL* 105 (1986): 669-676.

[29] Cf. Thomas Moore, "'To the End of the Earth': The Geographical and Ethnic Universalism of Acts 1:8 in Light of Isaianic Influence on Luke," *JETS* 40 (1997): 389-399; and Bertram Melbourne, "Acts 1:8 Re-Examined: Is Acts 8 Its Fulfillment?" *JRT* 57 (2001): 1-18.

[30] The reconfiguration of the diaspora was a huge ideological shift for Christian Jews. Rather than the Messiah gathering all the scattered Jews to their homes in Jerusalem, Jesus would send envoys to the far-flung reaches of the world to claim territory for God's kingdom; cf. Karl Schmidt, "Abkehr von der Rückkehr: Aufbau und Theologie der Apostelgeschichte im Kontext des lukanischen Diasporaverständnisses," *NTS* 53 (2007): 406-424.

[31] The early Christians were known to be from Galilee. "Galileans" was even one of the synonyms for Christians in the late first century (cf. Epictetus, *Diss.* 4.7.6). That the witnesses to the ascension were from Galilee authenticates their testimony since those who witnessed Jesus' exodus were from his home territory where he debuted his ministry.

[32] Some have dismissed it as legendary, most notably G. Lohfink, *Die Himmelfahrt Jesu: Untersuchungen zu den Himmelfahrts-und Erhöhungstexten bei Lukas* (StANT 26; München: Kösel, 1971), or a reaction to the deification of the Roman Emperors; cf. Detlev Dormeyere, "Die Apotheose in Seneca 'Apocolocyntosis' und die Himmelfahrt Lk 24,50-53; Apg 1,9-11," in *Testimony and Interpretation* (New York: T&T Clark, 2004), 125-142. A more recent and startling tack comes from John Pilch, "The Ascension of Jesus: A Social Scientific Perspective," in *Kontexte der Schrift: Kultur, Politik, Religion, Sprache—Text,* Part 2 (ed. Christian Strecker; Stuttgart: Kohlhammer, 2005), 75-82, who attributes it to a "sky journey" where Jesus' spirit traveled through space in an altered state of consciousness and this was witnessed by his disciples who were in an ecstatic state.

19:9; 24:15-18; Ezek 10:3-4; Psa 18:11; Dan 7:13; 1 Thess 4:17; Rev 11:12),[33] the two men in white are clearly *angels* (cf. Luke 24:4; Mark 16:5; John 20:12),[34] and *Jesus floats* through the air like a super hero with the promise that he will return in a similar fashion.

So one might ask, "Is this a historical event or a religious metaphor?" As Dunn points out, these two are not mutually exclusive.[35] Sometimes history is described with symbolic language. Nonetheless, there are good reasons to take Luke seriously when he describes this final resurrection appearance and Jesus' ultimate disappearance from the earth. First, Luke inherits an oral tradition of Jesus' ascension that penetrates virtually every layer of New Testament sources. Though he alone describes the event (Luke 24:50-53/Acts 1:3, 9-11),[36] the debated ending of Mark shares a similar tradition (Mark 16:19). In addition, Jesus alluded to his ascension according to John 6:62, "What if you see the Son of Man ascend to where he was before!" and in John 20:17 he told Mary, "Do not hold on to me, for I have not yet returned (*anabainō*) to the Father." The ascension is, hereafter, assumed throughout the New Testament (Luke 9:51; John 3:13; Acts 2:32-33; 5:30; 7:55; Rom 8:34; 1 Cor 15:1-28; Eph 1:20-21; 4:8-10; Phil 2:9-11; Col 3:1; 1 Tim 3:16; Heb 1:3; 8:1; 10:12; 12:12; 1 Pet 3:21-22).[37] So even if Luke alone describes the event, it is predicted by Jesus and affirmed by John, Paul, Peter, and the author of Hebrews. It is simply not true that Luke stands alone in witness to the ascension.[38]

There is a second argument for the historicity of Luke's account. Namely, the ascension assumes a bodily resurrection. If Jesus resurrected merely as a spirit, there is no reason *ipso facto* to have him leave the earth. He could appear as a ghostly apparition without the limitation of space and time. Hence,

---

[33] Cf. Léopold Sabourin, "The Biblical Cloud: Terminology and Traditions," *BTB* 4 (1974): 290–311.

[34] Angels were often described as wearing white clothing: Matt 28:3; 2 Macc 11:8; *1 En* 71:1; *T. Levi* 8:2. For other developing traditions of angels, cf. Tobias Nicklas, "Angels in Early Christian Narratives on the Resurrection of Jesus: Canonical and Apocryphal Texts," in *Angels: The Concept of Celestial Beings—Origins, Development and Reception* (ed. F.V. Reiterer, T. Nicklas, and K. Schöpflin, et al.; Berlin/New York: De Gruyter, 2007), 293–311.

[35] James Dunn, "The Ascension of Jesus: A Test Case for Hermeneutics," in *The Fourth Durham-Tübingen Research Symposium: Resurrection, Transfiguration and Exaltation in Old Testament, Ancient Judaism and Early Christianity* (ed. Friedrich Avemarie and Hermann Lichtenberger; Tübingen, 1999), 301-322.

[36] The charges leveled against Luke for discrepancies in the ascension narratives between his Gospel and Acts, are, frankly, hermeneutically irresponsible. For example, in Luke he says Jesus went *toward Bethany* (πρὸς Βηθανίαν) whereas Acts locates the Ascension on the Mount of Olives (1:12). Since the Mount of Olives stands between Jerusalem and Bethany, it is perfectly acceptable to describe it as "on route" to Bethany. Or again, only in Acts 1:3 do we learn of a period of 40 days. Luke 24, makes it appear that Jesus ascended on the very day of his resurrection. But Luke never expected his readers to glean a chronology from Luke 24 without also reading Acts 1! Such literary compression, particularly where a second volume is in view, is perfectly natural. Finally, the Western text of Luke 24:51 lacks "and was taken up into heaven" [a "D" rating in UBS3 though see the arguments by A. W. Zwiep, "The Text of the Ascension Narratives" *NTS* 42 (1996): 219-244]. But even if we don't have the ascension in Luke 24 according to the Western text, it still stands in Acts 1. Hence, all one can assert about Luke 24 and Acts 1 is that the former is a condensed version of the latter. There are no real contradictions between Luke's two descriptions.

[37] For an analysis of the NT vocabulary and texts referencing the ascension, one is commended to Bruce Metzger, "The Meaning of the Ascension," in *Search the Scriptures: New Testament Studies in Honor of Raymond T. Stamm* (ed. by J. M. Myers, O. Reimherr, and H. N. Bream; Leiden: Brill, 1969), 118-128 and Joseph Fitzmyer, "The Ascension of Christ and Pentecost," *TS* 45 (1984): 409-421.

[38] Neither Luke nor the other NT authors make much of this event (theologically speaking). Hence, one must wonder what kind of motive Luke would have for making up such a tale and intruding it into his otherwise historically grounded work; cf. Fitzmyer, "Ascension of Christ," 425.

the story Luke tells assumes Jesus, at some point, stopped appearing. This assumes a body, which in turn assumes a literal resurrection, which also assumes divine intervention. Simply put, if God can raise the dead, lifting that living body through the air is hardly an insurmountable obstacle. Furthermore, one should note Luke's emphasis on eyewitnesses: "He was taken up *before their eyes*" (v. 9), "a cloud hid him from their *sight*" (v. 9), "they were *looking intently*" (v. 10, cf. Luke 4:20; 22:56; Acts 3:4, 12; 6:15; 7:55; 10:4; 11:6; 13:9; 14:9; 23:1; 2 Cor 3:7, 13), and the angels asked why they were "*looking*" into the sky (v. 11). Luke goes out of his way to emphasize a visible event witnessed by the Apostles (cf. 1:22).

Finally, one should note that Luke narrates this event with reserved sobriety. It is markedly different from the apocryphal exaggerations one encounters elsewhere in Hellenistic literature.[39] The ascension motif is sparsely found in the OT, most notably, the assumption of Elijah (2 Kgs 2:11; Sir 48:9) with due credit to Enoch (Gen 5:24).[40] While it is true that Luke sometimes compares Jesus to Elijah,[41] the stories of their departures are really quite different. One might speculate that the cloud in Jesus' narrative is a vehicle of transport like Elijah's fiery chariot[42] and that the whirlwind and angels that whisked Elijah *up* to heaven come *down* to earth in Jesus' story (cf. Acts 1:10; 2:2). But this would press the textual details to the breaking point. Besides, Elijah gives his mantle to Elisha alone. Jesus pours out his Spirit on the Twelve. These are very different commissions even if both involve the power of the Spirit.

When one turns from the Bible to stories of ascensions in the broader Greco-Roman world, Luke's sobriety and restraint are even more notable. Extrabiblical stories are generally intentionally mythological.[43] Not so with Luke. He is recording the tradition he received from eyewitnesses whose lives were radically transformed by these events.

---

[39] Josephus's story of Moses' assumption looks a great deal like Luke's version of Jesus' ascension (*Ant* 4.8.48 §326, 93 A.D.; cf. Philo, *Moses* 2.291; *Ass. of Mos.*; *b. Sotah* 13b; and Str-B 1:755), "While he was bidding farewell to Eleazaros and Iesous, and was still conversing with them, a cloud suddenly stood over him and he disappeared in a certain ravine. But he has written of himself in the sacred books that he died because he was afraid that they might dare to say that because of the abundance of the virtue surrounding him he had gone up to the Divinity." After this account, however, the stories get more exaggerated and fabulous. The stories of the assumption of Adam (*Life of Adam and Eve* 33:1–37:6, late 1st cen) and Abraham (*Apoc. Ab.* 15–29; early 2nd cen.) are notoriously fanciful. Baruch (2 Bar 46:7; 48:30, 2nd cen A.D.) and Ezra (4 Ezra 14:9, 49, c. A.D. 120) speak vaguely of an assumption, but no details are narrated.

[40] Cf. Pesch, "Der Anfang," 15-16. The ascension of Jesus also fulfills the expectations of this inaugural Psalm 110, which became the most cited OT text in the NT: Mark 12:36/Matt 22:44/Luke 20:42-43; Mark 14:62/Matt 26:64/Luke 22:69; Acts 2:33-34; Eph 1:20; Heb 1:13; 8:1; Heb. 10:12-13; cf. Acts 5:31; 7:51-52; Rom 8:34; 1 Cor. 15:25; Heb 1:3; 12:2; 1 Pet. 3:22; Rev 3:21.

[41] E.g., Luke 4:24-27; Acts 3:20-21; Str-B 4:2, 769; P. Dabeck, "Siehe, Es Erschienen Moses und Elias," *Bib* 23 (1942): 175-189.

[42] Clouds were sometimes portrayed as a chariot for the gods, cf. Craig A. Evans, "In What Sense Blasphemy? Jesus before Caiaphas in Mark 14:61-64," SBLSP 30 (1991): 215-234.

[43] E.g., the ascension of Heracles (Euripides, *Heraclidae* 910; Lucian, *Cynicus* 13; Apollodorus, *Bibliotheca* 2.7.7), Romulus (Plutarch, *Numa* 2.2-3; *Romulus* 27.6) or Augustus (Suetonius, *Augustus* 100.4); cf. Haenchen, 116, and Lohfink, *Himmelfahrt* 55-70 who cautiously point out the differences between these stories and the biblical narratives. It is important, when looking at nonbiblical parallels (*Religionsgeschichte*) to ask: (1) Is the supposed parallel real or merely surface? (2) Is the supposed parallel early enough and culturally and geographically near enough to have potentially influenced the biblical author? (3) Is there evidence that the influence flowed toward the biblical text or out from it? We must not assume that the influence was always one direction. Cf. Bruce Metzger, "Considerations of Methodology in the Study of the Mystery Religions and Early Christianity," *HTR* 48 (1955): 1–20.

Finally, the ascension functions as Jesus' final farewell in which he establishes his successors.[44] It confirms three massive theological points. (1) Jesus' work is fully finished (John 17:4, 5; 19:30; Phil 2:6, 9, 10). (2) Because of that, the epoch of the Holy Spirit can now begin (John 16:7). (3) Jesus continues as our advocate at the right hand of God (Rom 8:34; Heb 7:25) ultimately preparing for an eternity in his presence (John 14:2).

1:10-11. This is not the end of their pilgrimage with Jesus. Rather, it is the beginning of their apprenticeship under the Holy Spirit. Of course the Twelve can't see that at the moment as they stare into the sky. The two angels who *had been standing there* (Greek pluperfect, *pareist keisan*) appear for the apparent purpose of bringing these disciples back to earth.[45] Jesus will return to earth in the same way he left, to the delight of all his followers. But for now, there is much work to be done.

4. Replacement of Iscariot (1:12-26)

The Apostles were a big deal.[46] They were not the only ones to witness the resurrection; they were not the only ones at the ascension; they will not be the only ones baptized with the Holy Spirit. But they *were* the authorized foundational witness to Jesus upon which the church was built (Eph 2:19-20; cf. Matt 16:18-19; John 14:26). That there were twelve sends a clear message: The Apostles were the delegates (and judges) of the twelve tribes of Israel (Matt 19:28/Luke 22:28-30). This says something significant about Jesus' agenda for the kingdom. Nonetheless, as the church expanded and Gentiles began to outnumber Jewish Christians, this early emphasis on twelve tribes waned. Hence, this whole narrative about Matthias must reach back into the earliest annals of the Church. Luke is recording a tradition that goes back to the original eyewitnesses.[47]

[12]Then they returned to Jerusalem from the hill called the Mount of Olives, a Sabbath day's walk[a] from the city. [13]When they arrived, they went upstairs to the room where they were staying. Those present were Peter, John, James and Andrew; Philip and Thomas, Bartholomew and Matthew; James son of Alphaeus and Simon the Zealot, and Judas son of James. [14]They all joined together constantly in prayer, along with the women and Mary the mother of Jesus, and with his brothers.

[a]*12 That is, about 3/4 of a mile (about 1,100 meters)*

[44] Cf. Luke 24:50 and Sir 50:20-22. It is normal for a farewell discourse to establish a successor: Elijah/Elisha (2 Kings 2), Aaron/Eleazar (Num 20:26), Moses/Joshua (Num 27:16-19; Deut 31:14ff.; 34:9; *As. Mos.* 1:6-9); cf. Palmer, *Background*, 431.

[45] Larkin (43) is probably right to associate the two angels with the number required for legal witness in Deut 19:15.

[46] The official witness of the authorized Apostles is foundational for Luke as a source for his historical monograph. They were among the most important eyewitnesses which Luke references in his prologue (Luke 1:1-4); cf. Martin Hengel, "Der Lukasprolog und seine Augenzeugen: Die Apostel, Petrus und die Frauen," in *Memory in the Bible and Antiquity* (Tübingen: Mohr Siebeck, 2007), 195-242.

[47] "No *Sitz im Leben* for such a piece of tradition is so natural or likely as the early days of perplexity," C. H. Dodd, *According to Scriptures: The Sub-Structure of the New Testament Theology* (London: Charles Scribner's Sons, 1953), 59.

1:12. The Mount of Olives stands about two thousand cubits[48] to the east of Jerusalem and about two hundred feet higher than the city, offering a stunning panoramic view ◑. This hill is thick with biblical imagery. David escaped from Jerusalem across this mountain (2 Sam 15:30) and Yahweh's march into the city is predicted to start from there (Zech 14:4). This was the route of Jesus' triumphal entry and the slope from which he predicted the destruction of Jerusalem. It was the spot of his ascension and the presumptive place of his *parousia*. Even the ground on which they stand testifies to the importance of this event.

1:13-14. Back in the city they return to *the* upper room (the Greek text adds a definite article). This may indicate that this special room was the very place Jesus celebrated last supper ◑ (though Luke uses different vocabulary for "room") and where Jesus appeared to the Apostles (cf. Luke 24:33, 36; John 20:19, 26). It may also be the home of Mary and her son, John Mark, where the church met for prayer (Acts 12:12). Those present and accounted for are the Eleven, some women, including Jesus' mother, and his brothers. Each of these is significant. The Eleven, of course, are most significant because they set up the following narrative of Matthias's election.[49] The women are significant sociologically since Jesus was the only rabbi on record from that period to allow women to follow him as disciples (cf. Luke 8:2-3; 10:38-42; 24:22; Matt 27:55; 1 Cor 9:5). That Jesus' mother is with him is significant ecclesiastically since she became one of the key iconographical figures for Christians throughout history.[50] This will be her last appearance in Scripture. Likewise, Jesus' brothers make their final appearance. Their presence is surprising since they were antagonistic during his life (cf. John 7:2-7; cf. Mark 3:21, 31-35).[51] Apparently Jesus' resurrection appearances radically altered their allegiance (1 Cor 15:7).

The original disciples devoted themselves to prayer during the ten days between Jesus' ascension and Pentecost. This does not necessarily suggest that the disciples 'prayed down' the Holy Spirit or that this devotion to prayer was somehow exceptional. The phrase "joined . . . in prayer" has been found in inscriptions as a kind of technical term for synagogue prayer meetings (cf. Acts 2:42;

---

[48] This was the distance of a "Sabbath day's journey" (*m. Soṭah* 5.3). It was figured based on the size of the village and the call to worship within the community (Exod 16:29; Num 35:5; Josh 3:4). Since every Israelite was to gather for worship, this distance, *de facto*, must be an acceptable journey.

[49] This is the fourth time the Apostles have been listed by name (cf. Matt 10:2-4; Mark 3:16-19; Luke 6:14-16), each time with a slightly different order. However, each list can be divided into three sections which consistently begin with Peter, Philip and James (son of Alphaeus) respectively. James and John, the sons of Zebedee, were probably cousins of Jesus (cf. McGarvey, 225). Several of these men had nicknames: Simon is also called Peter; Judas appears to be Thaddaeus; Bartholomew is most likely the Nathanael of John 1; and Thomas (Aramaic) is called Didymus (Greek), both names meaning "Twin." And, of course, Iscariot, who is always last on the list, carries the unflattering appellation "the betrayer" every time he is mentioned. It is also possible that he is the only Apostle not from Galilee but from the village of Kerioth in Judea, though this point has been disputed by C. C. Torrey, "The Name 'Iscariot'," *HTR* 36 (1993): 51-62 and A. Ehrman, "Judas Iscariot and Abba Saqqara," *JBL* 97 (1978): 572-573.

[50] While this is not the right place to deal with the inappropriate excesses granted to Marian veneration, it is appropriate to remind the reader that the opposite extreme is no less flattering among those who have minimized her importance. This dear woman has provided millions with a model of humble devotion and christocentric submission. The definitive work on the history of the veneration of Mary is by Miri Rubin, *Mother of God: A History of the Virgin Mary* (New Haven: Yale University Press, 2009).

[51] The argument that these 'brothers' of Jesus were not uterine but cousins or step-brothers by Joseph is necessitated *only* by the extrabiblical belief in the perpetual virginity of Mary. There is nothing exegetically or linguistically that necessitates such a conclusion. For a fuller discussion, cf. Bruce, 44-45.

6:4).[52] In other words, these early believers were Jews who devoted themselves to standard Jewish piety while they waited for the promised Holy Spirit.

[15]**In those days Peter stood up among the believers[a] (a group numbering about a hundred and twenty) [16]and said, "Brothers, the Scripture had to be fulfilled which the Holy Spirit spoke long ago through the mouth of David concerning Judas, who served as guide for those who arrested Jesus—[17]he was one of our number and shared in this ministry." [18](With the reward he got for his wickedness, Judas bought a field; there he fell headlong, his body burst open and all his intestines spilled out. [19]Everyone in Jerusalem heard about this, so they called that field in their language Akeldama, that is, Field of Blood.)**
[a]*15 Greek brothers*

1:15. Peter takes the initiative to address the brothers[53] concerning this Apostolic vacancy. Their group numbered about one hundred and twenty. This is a significant claim since it was the number, according to some rabbinic traditions, for a Jewish group to establish its own council and become an independent community (*m. Sanh.* 1:6; cf. 1QS 6.3-4; CD 13.1-2; Marshall, 64). The language Luke uses seems to support this supposition. Literally, he says they were "named" one hundred and twenty. This indicates an appellation, a title, or a characteristic, not merely a head count. Thus, they had the characteristic of a new, independent community with organizational needs to which they must now attend.

1:16-17. Judas, formerly an apostle, abdicated his *place* (the word implies an inheritance [*klēros*]) and thus had to be replaced.[54] This introduces a difficult paradox. Judas had been one of the chosen Twelve but was 'lost' (John 17:12). Was that due to his own choice? The narrative speaks of Judas as if he got what he deserved. After all, he earned 'payment' for his wickedness. Yet it also speaks as if he was destined by God. After all, the Holy Spirit had predicted these events through the prophetic Psalms of David (v. 20) as did Jesus (John 17:12). There is no clear or convincing explanation for this paradox. We stand speechless in the midst of God's mysterious sovereignty.

1:18-19. The second paradox of this text is easier to manage. Luke reports that Judas died by falling headlong down the slope of Akeldama (the Aramaic nickname for the "Bloody Field"), a tract which he purchased with the thirty pieces of silver. This presents two apparent discrepancies.[55] First, Matthew re-

---

[52] For the uses of "προσκαρτεροῦντες . . . τῇ προσευχῇ" see T. C. G. Thornton, "'Continuing Steadfast in Prayer'—New Light on a New Testament Phrase," *ExpT* 83 (1971): 23-24.

[53] This common terminology for "Christians" (Acts 9:30; 10:23, 11:1, 29; 12:17; 14:2; 15:1, 3, 13, 22, 23, 32, 33, 36, 40; 16:2, 40; 17:6, 10, 14; 18:18, 27; 21:7, 17; 28:14, 15) was also familiar vernacular for Jewish compatriots (Acts 2:29, 37; 3:17; 7:2, 26; 10:23; 13:15, 26, 38; 22:1, 5; 23:1, 5, 6; 28:17, 21).

[54] The wording of v. 17 is likely drawn from the Targum on Gen 44:18 which reads, "Benjamin who was numbered with us among the tribes and will receive a portion and share with us in the division of the land." If this is the case, then Luke is clearly accessing an older Aramaic tradition. Cf. M. Wilcox, "The Judas Tradition in Acts i. 15-26," *NTS* 19 (1972–73): 438-452 and Ernst Nellessen, "Tradition und Schrift in der Perikope von der Erwählung des Mattias (Apg 1, 15-26)," *BZ* 19 (1975): 205-218. This text, in fact, has the appearance of a Jewish Midrash; cf. Frédéric Manns, "Un midrash chrétien: Le récit de la mort de Judas," *RSR* 54 (1980): 197-203.

[55] The differences between Matthew and Luke's account are due to varying redactional emphases. Matthew's intention is to show the culpability of Jewish leaders in the death of Jesus while Luke intends to

ports that the chief priests purchased the field after Judas returned the money. Luke says Judas purchased the field. The solution is simple: the priests purchased it *for* Judas with *his* money—it was thus Judas's purchase.[56] The second 'discrepancy' is a bit more complicated. According to Matthew, Judas died by hanging, just like the traitor Ahithophel (2 Sam 17:23). According to Luke, he died by falling and bursting open (literally "gushing out all his guts"). Is there really a contradiction here? What if the rope broke when Judas hanged himself, resulting in a nasty tumble toward the valley of Gehenna? Gordon, with a slight modification, suggests the rope broke not on Friday but Sunday after his body had bloated for a few days, thus facilitating the liberation of his intestines.[57] Though this is pure guesswork, it is not an unreasonable conjecture for harmonizing the two divergent stories.

[20]"For," said Peter, "it is written in the book of Psalms, "'May his place be deserted; let there be no one to dwell in it,'[a] and, "'May another take his place of leadership.'[b] [21]Therefore it is necessary to choose one of the men who have been with us the whole time the Lord Jesus went in and out among us, [22]beginning from John's baptism to the time when Jesus was taken up from us. For one of these must become a witness with us of his resurrection." [23]So they proposed two men: Joseph called Barsabbas (also known as Justus) and Matthias. [24]Then they prayed, "Lord, you know everyone's heart. Show us which of these two you have chosen [25]to take over this apostolic ministry, which Judas left to go where he belongs." [26]Then they cast lots, and the lot fell to Matthias; so he was added to the eleven apostles.

[a]*20* Psalm 69:25   [b]*20* Psalm 109:8

1:20. Peter cites two separate Psalms as evidence that Judas must be replaced (Psa 69:25 [LXX = 68:26; MT = 69:26] and 109:8 [LXX = 108:8]).[58] The first is a curse against the abode of David's enemies. The second is a snippet from a series of curses also against David's enemies. The problem is that both Psalms appear to be about King David, yet Peter applies them to Jesus, apparently without due consideration for the original context (so Barrett, 1:100). Is this arbitrary scriptural application? If we get inside Peter's hermeneutical head, we see four things.[59] First, the Psalms, by nature, are only loosely tied to specific

emphasize the need to replace an apostate Apostle. Cf. Luc Desautels, "La Mort de Judas (Mt 27, 3-10; Ac 1, 15-26)," *ScEs* 38 (1986): 221-239.

[56] According to Jewish regulations, the money Judas returned could not be used for temple purposes but could be used to buy a defunct piece of land for burials of the poor or pilgrims; cf. J. D. M. Derrett, "Akeldama (Acts 1:19)," *Bijdr* 56 (1995): 122-132.

[57] Cf. A. B. Gordon, "The Fate of Judas according to Acts 1:18," *EvQ* 43 (1971): 97-100. There is a third story of Judas' demise attributed to Papias by Apollinaris of Laodicea (c. 310 – c. 390; *Fragments* 18.1) in which Iscariot swelled to fantastic proportions (broader than an ox-cart) and his distended genitals produced pus, and worms came from every part of his body. This kind of apocryphal demonization of a villain, though not unfamiliar in the literature (cf. 2 Macc 9:9-10; Josephus, *Ant.* 17.6.1–8.1; §146-192; 2 Sam 20:10), is not particularly helpful in analyzing historical events.

[58] Both citations appear to be from the LXX (though close to the MT) with no meaningful alteration except the plural "their" (αὐτῶν) is changed to a singular "his" (αὐτοῦ) in Acts 1:20 to relate it exclusively to Judas; cf. Gleason Archer and C. G. Chirichigno, *Old Testament Quotations in the New Testament: A Complete Survey* (Chicago: Moody, 1983), 74-75.

[59] Peter's hermeneutical use of these two Psalms is at home in his native Judaism; cf. Tzvi Novick, "Succeeding Judas: Exegesis in Acts 1:15-26," *JBL* 129 (2010): 795-799. For further details on the NT appropriation of the Psalms and Luke in particular, cf. Jamie Grant, "Singing the Cover Versions: Psalms, Reinter-

historical events. This makes them easy to apply to contemporary and personal situations. We do the same today with the Psalms (not to mention love songs and greeting cards). Second, David stood as Israel's figurehead. Jesus as King of the Jews does the same. Thus, texts about David could be read prophetically about Jesus. Third, Psalms which deal with kingship elicited eschatological hopes.[60] For Christians, this meant explaining events in the life of Jesus by looking for appropriate parallels from the life of David. That's why the Psalms were so popular with Christians (especially Psa 2, 16, 22, 69,[61] 110, 118). It made perfect sense to Peter and his audience to see Judas as a particularly appropriate example of the enemies of King David. Finally, Peter's hermeneutic may well have been learned directly from Jesus who applied various Psalms to himself (cf. Luke 13:35; 19:38; 24:44).[62]

1:21-25. Judas's betrayal necessitated a replacement.[63] But just how does one go about replacing an Apostle? There was hardly a manual for this sort of thing. Obviously, whoever replaced Judas needed to be able to testify about Jesus' entire ministry, beginning at his baptism and running through the ascension (vv. 21-22). Peter's proclamation resulted in two candidates: Joseph (also named Barsabbas [Aramaic = Son of the Sabbath][64] and Justus [Latin, cf. Acts 18:7; Col 4:11])[65] and Matthias. The text is deliberately vague about whether they were put forward by the Apostles or by the one hundred and twenty. The important point was that the Lord[66] would make the final selection. Just as Jesus handpicked the original Twelve, now he chooses Matthias. Though an ecclesiastical 'lottery' seems strange to us, such a 'divine' selection was necessary to validate Matthias as God's man rather than man's manipulation.

---

pretation and Biblical Theology in Acts 1–4," *SBET* 25 (2007): 27-49, Richard Longeneker, *Biblical Exegesis in the Apostolic Period* (Grand Rapids: Eerdmans, 1975), 77-78, and Jacques Dupont, "La destine de Judas prophetisée par David (Actes 1:16-20)," *CBQ* 23 (1961): 41-51.

[60] Herman Gunkel was the first to deal extensively with Royal Psalms, which he limited to 2, 18, 20, 21, 45, 72, 101, 110, and 132; cf. *Einleitung in Die Psalmen* (Göttingen: Vandenhoeck & Ruprecht, 1933); Sigmund Mowinckel would add Psa 28, 44, 60, 66, 68, 80, 83, and 84; cf. *Psalmenstudien* (Amsterdam: Verlag P. Schippers, 1961). John Eaton is even more inclusive with 3, 4, 7, 9, 10, 17, 22, 23, 27, 28, 35, 40, 41, 57, 59, 61, 62, 63, 66, 69, 70, 71, 75, 89, 91, 92, 94, 108, 118, 138, 140, 143; cf. *Kingship and the Psalms* (2d ed.; Sheffield: JSOT Press, 1986), including both the Psalms cited here by Peter.

[61] Psalm 69 is referenced two other times with messianic implications: v. 9, John 2:17 and v. 21, Mark 15:36/Matt 27:48/Luke 23:36 and perhaps by Jesus himself, John 19:28-30.

[62] J. A. T. Robinson, "Did Jesus Have a Distinctive Use of Scripture?" in *Christological Perspectives* (FS H. K. McArthur; ed. R. F. Berkey and S. A. Edwards; New York: Pilgrim, 1982), 49-57; Bruce Chilton, *A Galilean Rabbi and His Bible* (Wilmington, DE: Michael Glazier, 1984); R.T. France, *Jesus and the Old Testament* (London: Tyndale Press, 1971); and Joachim Jeremias, *Neutestamentliche Theologie* (Gütersloh: G. Mohn, 1973, 1971), 13-38, claims that one can even get at Jesus' *ipsissima vox* through his unique scriptural teachings.

[63] Jauregui, in an exceptional study, traces the importance of the Twelve as a witness to the resurrection of Jesus. At Acts 1:22-26, however, he argues that Judas' replacement sets a precedent for Apostolic succession; cf. Jose Antonio Jauregui, "Function de los 'Doce': en la Iglesia de Jerusalen," *EstEcl* 63 (1988): 257-284. His arguments are hardly compelling in that they fail to demonstrate exegetically (a) how Judas's replacement is necessary for the primacy of Peter, (b) that Peter really was the leader of the Jerusalem church (cf. 11:1-2; 15:13ff), (c) why there is no mention of a replacement for James after his death (12:2), or (d) why the Apostle John was overlooked as Peter's replacement after he died.

[64] Though nothing more is heard of him in the Scriptures, according to Papias, on the authority of Philip's daughters (Acts 21:9), he was challenged by unbelievers to drink snake venom and suffered no ill effects (*Eccl. Hist.* 3.39).

[65] The irrelevant detail of the three names of the candidate not chosen virtually ensures the historicity of this account. Who but an eyewitness would care to pass on such particulars?

[66] In these first few chapters of Acts, the divine titles such as "lord" are shared by both Jesus and the Father, so it is sometimes difficult to distinguish between them (cf. 2:36; 4:24).

1:26. So they cast lots. Apparently this involved something like putting two different colored pebbles in a bowl and shaking it until one of them fell out (*m. Yoma* 3.9; 4.1).[67] This practice was not uncommon in Judaism (e.g., Josh 7:10-21; 1 Sam 14:40-42; Josephus, *J.W.* 4.3.7 §153-154).[68] It was advocated even more among the Greeks as a signal element of Democracy (Aristotle, *Ath. Resp.* 8) and among the Romans to squelch ambition or to defer to the whims of the gods.[69] For the Jews, it was recognition of Yahweh's supreme knowledge and care for his community. Proverbs 16:33, "The lot is cast into the lap, but its every decision is from the LORD."[70] For Christians, however, this will be the last lot cast. Perhaps this was because the Spirit would henceforth provide the necessary clarity for church leadership (so Fernando, 79). Nonetheless, now that Jesus is seated where he belongs and the Apostolic band is restored to its right number, the stage is set for the Spirit's grand entrance.

---

[67] Cf. Gerhard Lohfink, "Der Losvorgang in Apg 1, 26," *BZ* 19 (1975): 247-249. Some have tried to argue that the word "he was added" (συγκαταψηφίζομαι) which is used only here in the entire NT, implies a congregational vote since its root (ψῆφος) means "vote." The fact is, it means "pebble" or "amulet." Since these were used for casting votes as well as for casting lots, the root cannot help us define the connotation of the word here. The point of the passage is that Jesus, not the congregation, chose Matthias so that he had divine authorization to join the Apostolic witness. Cf. John Brug, "Acts 1:26—Lottery or Election," *WLQ* 95 (1998): 212-214.

[68] The Qumran community spoke a fair bit about lots in their "Community Rule" (1QS 1.9-11; 2.2, 4, 23; 4.25-26; 5.3; 6.13-23); cf. Francis Schmidt, "Élection et tirage au sort (1QS VI, 13-23 et Ac 1, 15-26)," *RHPR* 80 (2000): 105-117.

[69] Cf. W. A. Beardslee, "The Casting of Lots at Qumran and in the Book of Acts," *NovT* 4/4 (1960): 245-252; and Horst, *Parallels*, 25.

[70] It began with the land-allotment of the twelve tribes (Num 26:55-56; Josh 18:6) but was more common in the annual temple ritual of the release of the scapegoat (Lev 16:7-10).

ACTS 2

B. PENTECOST (2:1-47)

Pentecost is often called the birthday of the church. This is true, but still a bit of a misnomer. Indeed, the baptism of the Holy Spirit was a novel event after which Peter preached the first gospel message resulting in three thousand baptisms. However, these Jewish 'converts' would hardly think they were birthing a new religion. Rather, they believed they were fulfilling their destiny as the people of God. This early group of disciples did not become the church *as opposed to* Israel, but the church as the manifestation of God's plan *for* Israel. Pentecost neither started the church nor ended the nation. Rather, it continued the tradition, writing a new chapter in the eschatological history of God.[1]

1. Miracle of Tongues (2:1-13)

[1]When the day of Pentecost came, they were all together in one place.

2:1. Pentecost, or more accurately *Shabuoth* ("Feast of Weeks," Exod 23:16; 34:22) was one of the three great pilgrim feasts of Israel along with Passover and Tabernacles (2 Chr 8:13).[2] Though Passover had greater theological significance as the founding festival of the nation, more people actually attended Pentecost, a thanksgiving celebration of the spring harvest (Lev 23:15-21; Num 28:26-31; Deut 16:10, 16)[3] simply because of where it sat on the calendar. Those

---

[1] Especially I. H. Marshall, "The Significance of Pentecost," *SJT* 30 (1977): 347-369 and Ronald Young, "The Mission of the Church in Accord with the Mission of the Holy Spirit: Some Considerations," *Theof* 37 (2006): 287-323. Brent Laytham, "The Narrative Shape of Scriptural Authority: Plotting Pentecost," *ExAud* 19 (2003): 97-119, shows how the entire narrative shape of the Acts explicates the explosive missionary force of the Pentecost story.

[2] The Greek name "Pentecost" means *fifty*, first used of the "Feast of Weeks" in Tobit 2:1 and 2 Macc 12:31-32. Specifically it was fifty days after Passover. However, there were two ways of figuring the date (Str-B 2:598-600; E. Lohse, "πεντηκοστή" *TDNT* 6:44-53). The Pharisees (of the first century) counted fifty days after Nisan 15 so that Pentecost would fall on various days of the week (*m. Men* 10:3; *b. Men* 65a). The Sadducees, however, reckoned the fifty days from the Sabbath after Passover so that Pentecost always fell on a Sunday. Their reckoning likely held sway during Jesus' day (Bruce, 53). The old Syriac tradition (4th cen), however, conflates the ascension with Pentecost, collapsing the chronology altogether (a posture at home with John 20:17-22 and Eph 4:7-12). This emphasizes the Mosaic imagery of going up on a mountain for forty days to give the law to God's people; cf. Georg Kretschmar, "Himmelfahrt und Pfingsten," *ZKG* 66 (1955): 209-253.

[3] Prior to the first century A.D. *Jubilees* 6:17-19 and 14:20 understood Pentecost as a renewal of the Noahic and Abrahamic covenants on the very day the law was given (*Jub* 1:1). Moreover, there is evidence that the Qumran community followed this same calendar (1QS 1:8–2:25); cf. Christian Grappe, "A la jonction entre Inter et Nouveau Testament: le récit de la Pentecôte," *FV* 89 (1990): 19-27. After the third century A.D. it is clear that both Jews and Christians associated Pentecost with the giving of the law at Sinai; cf. Daniel Stökl-Ben Ezra, "Parody and Polemics on Pentecost: Talmud Yerushalmi Pesaḥim on Acts 2?" in *Jewish and Christian Liturgy and Worship* (Albert Gerhards and Clemens Lonhard, eds.; Leiden: Brill, 2007), 279-293. However, there is no clear connection between Pentecost and Sinai until A.D. 150. (*Seder Olam Rabba* 5; *b. Sabb* 88b; *b. Pesa* 68b; Str-B 2:601). Cf. Stefan Schreiber, "Aktualisierung göttlichen Handelns am Pfingsttag: Das frühjüdische Fest in Apg 2,1," *ZNW* 93 (2002): 58-77, A. J. M. Wedderburn, "Traditions and Redaction in Acts 2:1-13," *JSNT* 55 [1994]: 27-54, and Michel Gourgues, "Lecture christologique du Psaume CX

in the farthest reaches of the empire (vv. 9-11) could travel only after the winter storms had abated across the Mediterranean. This makes Pentecost the perfect time for the outpouring of the Spirit as the Jews from every nation convened in their sacred city.

While many get distracted with the miraculous 'show' of Pentecost, the point Luke is trying to drive home is the missionary foundation of the church. Though Luke is the only one to record the actual events of Pentecost, John (20:21) is well aware of the importance of the outpouring of the Spirit as the foundation of the church's universal mission.[4] The initial sermon by Peter makes it clear that this message of the Jewish Messiah is for all the dispersed tribes of Israel. The 'second Pentecost' of Cornelius will push this program beyond the ethnic bounds of Israel to those Gentiles who have faith in Jesus (10:47).[5]

Perhaps this is nitpicking detail, but when Luke says, "they were all together in one place," he is likely referring to the Twelve not the one hundred and twenty. Many simply assume the whole group spoke in tongues. Perhaps John the Baptist's universal promise of Spirit baptism makes this appropriate, particularly in light of Joel's prophecy that the Spirit was poured out on *all flesh* (Acts 2:17). However, every textual clue leads one to expect that the Twelve are emphasized.[6] (1) Acts 1:2-5 promises Spirit baptism specifically to the Twelve to empower their witness. (2) If we remove the chapter division between 1:26 and 2:1, the text reads: "The lot fell to Matthias; so he was added to the eleven *apostles*. When the day of Pentecost came, *they* were all together in one place." (3) In 2:14 Peter stands up *with the eleven* (cf. v. 7 and 36). Now, this is not to suggest that the Baptism of the Holy Spirit is only for the Apostles. It does suggest, however, that *in this context* the focus is on the testimony of the Twelve, not the empowerment of the one hundred and twenty. This is the first public proclamation of the resurrection; this responsibility falls squarely on the shoulders of the Apostolic council.

[2]Suddenly a sound like the blowing of a violent wind came from heaven and filled the whole house where they were sitting. [3]They saw what seemed to

---

et fête de la Pentecôte," *RB* 83 (1976): 5-24; contra Reinhard Neudecker, "'Das ganze Volk sah die Stimmen . . . ': Haggadische Auslegung und Pfingstbericht," *Bib* 78 (1997): 329-349 and James C. VanderKam, "Covenant and Pentecost," *CTJ* 37 (2002): 239-254. There are few textual clues that Luke has this in his mind (though cf. Fitzmyer, 234). Another common suggestion is that Pentecost is the reversal of Babel; e.g., J. Rius-Camps, "Pentecost versus Babel: Estudio critic de Hch 2," *Fil Noet* 1 (1988): 35-61; Catherine and Justo González, "Babel and Empire: Pentecost and Empire: Preaching on Genesis 11:1-9 and Acts 2:1-12," *JP* 16 (1993): 22-26. There is no exegetical evidence, however, that Luke had this in mind—there is no significant verbal correspondence between Acts 1:1-13 and Gen 11:1-9 (LXX); cf. David Smith, "What Hope after Babel? Diversity and Community in Gen 11:1-9; Exod 1:1-14; Zeph 3:1-13 and Acts 2:1-3," *HBT* 18 (1996): 169-191. Moreover, the very nature of the miracle argues against it. After all, if Babel is about the breakup of one language into multiple dialects, that was hardly reversed through the speaking of multiple foreign languages at Pentecost (Willimon, 32).

[4] Peter Brunner, "Das Pfingstereignis: eine dogmatische Beleuchtung seiner historischen Problematik," in *Volk Gottes: Zum Kirchenverständnis der katholischen, evangelischen und anglikanisch Theologie* (ed. Remigius Bäumer and Heimo Dolch; Freiburg: Herder, 1967), 230-242, demonstrates that while Luke uses his own inimitable style, nonetheless, he is not writing theological fiction but a historical event which proves to be foundational for the church.

[5] Craig S. Keener, "Why Does Luke Use Tongues as a Sign of the Spirit's Empowerment?" *JPT* 51 (2007): 177-184, and Peter T. O'Brien, "Mission, Witness, and the Coming of the Spirit," *BBR* 9 (1999): 203-214.

[6] For similar arguments see Michael Sweeney, "The Identity of 'They' in Acts 2.1," *BT* 46 (1995): 245-248.

be tongues of fire that separated and came to rest on each of them. [4]All of them were filled with the Holy Spirit and began to speak in other tongues[a] as the Spirit enabled them.

[a]*4 Or languages; also in verse 11*

2:2. The Pentecost phenomenon had a striking manifestation that was both audible and visible. The *sound* (or "blast," cf. Luke 4:37; Heb 12:19) of rushing wind (*pnoē*) filled the house.[7] The fact that it was the dry season surely made such a violent blast all the more striking. In addition, some kind of flash of light had the appearance of tongues of fire as it separated and came to rest on the Twelve.[8] We are left wanting more of a description, not only of the phenomenon, but of the house. Were they still in Mary's house?[9] If so, how did more than 3,000 hear the message? We can only assume that what started in a private home was then moved to the public space in the temple, most probably the portico of Solomon (3:11; 5:12).

2:3-4. The real interest in the text, however, is not where they were, who spoke in tongues, or even the strange appearance. The point is the gift of tongues.[10] This gift has made more of a splash than its meager biblical refer-

---

[7] Though it is tempting to see the word "wind" as a subtle allusion to the Spirit, the word here for "wind" (πνοή, only used elsewhere at 17:25) is different from that used for the spirit/wind (πνεῦμα). Nor is wind particularly associated with an appearance of God (1 Kgs 19:11, though cf. Ezek 37:9-14; contra Polhill, 97-98), though in the LXX it shows up as God's breath (2 Sam 22:16; Job 37:10 and wrath, Ezek 13:13; 2 Esd 13:10; cf. Marshall, 68).

[8] Fire is often a symbol for the presence of the Lord (Exod 3:2; 13:21-22; 19:18; 24:17; 40:38; Psa 78:14; 105:39; Isa 4:5; Dan 7:9-11; Zech 2:5) particularly in judgment (2 Sam 22:9; Job 1:16; Psa 50:3; 78:21; 97:3; Isa 10:17; 66:15; Mal 3:2). However, attempts to discern some deeper meaning for the fire here have not been particularly convincing either as a sign of judgment, cf. Blaine Charette, "'Tongues as of Fire': Judgment as a Function of Glossolalia in Luke's Thought," *JPT* 13 (2005): 173-186, or of Sinai, cf. Marquardt Friedrich-Wilhelm, "Jerusalem in Flammen des Geistes: Talmudische Weisungen hinter der Pfingsterzählung des Lukas," in *Aus zweier Zeugen Mund* (Pnina Nave Levinson, Nathan Peter Levinson, and Julius H. Schoeps eds.; Gerlingen: Bleicher Verlag, 1992), 69-80. It may, therefore, simply be that Luke is describing what was actually seen rather than some hidden theological implication. It is interesting to note that all the physical manifestations of the Spirit are described as a kind of erratic movement: Gen 1:2, "quaking" (רחפת), Mark 1:10, like a descending dove; and here, like an upside-down flame. Perhaps it is only incidental, but the combination of fire and wind was sometimes a sign of the divine presence in Hellenistic literature; cf. Pieter van der Horst, "Hellenistic Parallels to the Acts of the Apostles (2.1-47)," *JSNT* 25 (1985): 49-50. However, "tongues of fire" is a Hebraic turn of phrase describing the divine realm (cf. Isa 5:24; 30:27; *1 En* 14.8-25; 71.5-8; 1Q29; 4Q376); cf. Glen Menzies, "Pre-Lucan Occurrences of the Phrase 'Tongue(s) of Fire'," *JSPS* 22 (2000): 27-60.

[9] Though the word "house" is sometimes used for the temple (Acts 7:47; Isa 6:4), there is no contextual clue that the meeting of the original band of believers was anywhere other than the home where they had been meeting (1:13). Furthermore, that they were "sitting" probably indicates a private residence more than a public space.

[10] Some have attempted to argue that the gift is really one of hearing not speaking. This would allow the Apostles to all speak in ecstatic utterances and each individual in the audience to hear his own dialect; cf. Jenny Everts, "Tongues or Languages? Contextual Consistency in the Translation of Acts 2," *JPT* 4 (1994): 71-80. This would also explain why some in the crowd accused the Apostles of being drunk and how twelve men could speak in fifteen dialects at once (which assumes some of the fifteen localities shared a language, which is patently false; *pace* Horton, 32-34). The whole theory runs afoul, however, on the actual language of the text. Luke says they "spoke" (λαλεῖν) in tongues (Acts 2:4, 7, 11; cf. Acts 10:46; 1 Cor 12:10, etc.); cf. Klaus Haacker, "Das Pfingstwunder als exegetisches Problem," in *Verborum Veritas: Festschrift für Gustav Stählin* (Otto Böcher and Klaus Haacker, eds.; Wuppertal Theologischer Verlag Brockhaus, 1970), 125-131. For Luke, this Greek word (λαλεῖν) had particular relevance to prophetic utterances; cf. Helmut Jaschke, "λαλεῖν bei Lukas," *BZ* 15 (1971): 109-114. Furthermore, the speaking is described as a Spirit-enabled "utterance" (ἀποφθέγγομαι, v. 4) which is special vocabulary for "weighty speech" or "oracle" (used elsewhere in the NT only in Acts 2:14; 26:25; cf. LXX 1 Chr 25:1; Psa 59:7 [58:8]; Ezek 13:9, 19; Mic 5:[11] 12). Finally, it was not the crowd that was filled with the Spirit, but the Apostles.

ences might merit (1 Cor 12:27-30; 13:8-10). Aside from one dubious mention in Mark 16:17, this gift only features in Acts three times (2:4 in *Jerusalem*, 10:46 in *Caesarea*, and 19:6 in *Ephesus*) and in one disciplinary discourse in 1 Corinthians 12–14 (*Corinth*). This is, of course, a hotly debated topic.[11] Here, however, we must focus rather narrowly on a few essential points:

(1) Whatever else tongues might be in 1 Corinthians 14, here in Acts 2 it is clearly a human language (cf. vv. 9-11; 1 Cor 14:10!).[12] The normal meaning of "tongues" (*heterais glōssais*) in Greek is "foreign languages" (NRSV = "other languages"). This may explain why it was practiced (only) in four major metropolitan cities (see above). (2) Paul clearly states that not everyone can expect to receive the gift of tongues (1 Cor 12:7-11, 29-30). This is precisely the impression one gets from Luke as well. The three times we hear tongues in Acts, it was used by God to validate a specific group. In Acts 2, the Apostles were proved to be God-ordained witnesses. In Acts 10 Cornelius's Gentile home was proved acceptable for Christian conversion, and in Acts 19, Christian baptism was proved to supersede John the Baptist's immersion. Herein lies the discernable difference between tongues in Acts and 1 Corinthians—in Acts tongues serve as a sign, in 1 Corinthians the gift was for service to the body (1 Cor 14:1-8). This leads to a third point: (3) the misuse of tongues caused problems that Paul confronted head-on (1 Cor 14:6-25), and thus he imposed specific regulations for their use in the community (1 Cor 14:26-28). Nonetheless, Paul practiced tongues profusely (1 Cor 14:18), commended the gift (1 Cor 14:5), and rebuked those who hindered others from using it properly (1 Cor 14:39-40). These guidelines are as effective and sufficient today as ever.

[5]Now there were staying[13] in Jerusalem God-fearing Jews from every nation under heaven. [6]When they heard this sound, a crowd came together in bewilderment, because each one heard them speaking in his own language. [7]Utterly amazed, they asked: "Are not all these men who are speaking Galileans? [8]Then how is it that each of us hears them in his own native language?

2:5-8. This phenomenal miracle created quite a stir. Notice the various words Luke uses to describe the crowd's reaction: "bewilderment" (*suncheō*,

---

[11] For a brief survey of the field see Mark Moore, "Eyeing the Tongue: What We Can Know for Sure about Speaking in Tongues," in *Fanning the Flame: Probing the Issues in Acts* (Joplin: College Press, 2003), 210-233. Some of the more helpful monographs include Felicitas D. Goodman, *Speaking in Tongues: A Cross-Cultural Study of Glossolalia* (Chicago: University of Chicago Press, 1972); Anthony A. Hoekema, *Tongues and Spirit Baptism: A Biblical and Theological Evaluation* (Grand Rapids: Baker, 1972); John P. Kildahl, *The Psychology of Speaking in Tongues* (New York: Harper & Row, 1972); Newton Malony and Adams Lovekin, *Glossolalia: Behavioral Science Perspectives on Speaking in Tongues* (New York: Oxford, 1985); Watson Mills (ed.), *Speaking in Tongues: A Guide to Research on Glossolalia* (Grand Rapids: Eerdmans, 1986).

[12] Cf. Haacker, *Pfingstwunder*, 125-131 contra J. Behm, "γλῶσσα," TDNT, 1:719-727. It is common to assert that the tongues of 1 Cor 14 are ecstatic speech (either angelic language or gibberish depending on one's bias). But the evidence weighs in favor of human languages that could be translated. The appeal to the angelic tongues of 1 Cor 13:1 as a normative gift is highly tenuous. Paul used a series of hyperbolic and hypothetical gifts (none of which he was known to have possessed) to point out the ridiculous practice of such gifts to the exclusion of love. To paraphrase, "If you have super-duper supernatural gifts but don't love, it's useless." If an angelic tongue did actually exist, the natural reading of the text would be to assume it was a rare exception not the norm.

[13] This word (κατοικέω) is a favorite for Luke (19 of its 40 NT uses are in Acts). Normally it indicates "taking up residence" though here it apparently is used loosely for the visiting pilgrims.

only used in Acts 2:6; 9:22; 19:32; 21:27, 31), "Utterly amazed" (*existēmi* with *thaumazō*, v. 7), "Amazed and Perplexed" (*existēmi* with *diaporeō*, v. 12). Luke, stretching his extensive vocabulary, shows how the crowd was amazed, astounded, astonished, flabbergasted, stunned, perplexed, befuddled, bewildered, and generally dumbfounded. Rightly so. Not only were the Twelve speaking foreign languages, they were fluently speaking each local dialect (*dialektos*)! And all this is coming from Galilean peasants who were generally ridiculed as hillbillies (cf. John 1:46; 7:40-52; Matt 26:73; *b. Erub.* 53b).[14]

However, Luke's theological agenda is not to promote the miracle of tongues but the new age of the Holy Spirit (Luke 24:49; Acts 1:5; cf. John 7:39). It is not the phenomenon of the supernatural that so excites Luke's pen but the power of the Spirit which will launch a global mission.[15] Luke's contemporary, and probable informant, credited a similar idea to Jesus: "When the Counselor comes, whom I will send to you from the Father, the Spirit of truth who goes out from the Father, he will testify about me. And you also must testify, for you have been with me from the beginning" (John 15:26-27). To put it simply, the point is not "Spirit, miracle, WOW" but "Spirit, power, WORLD." That's why Luke highlights the fact that Jews *from every nation under heaven* had convened in Jerusalem for Pentecost. From the epicenter of Israel, the message of the Messiah would launch to the farthest reaches of the known world.

[9]"Parthians, Medes and Elamites; residents of Mesopotamia, Judea and Cappadocia, Pontus and Asia, [10]Phrygia and Pamphylia, Egypt and the parts of Libya near Cyrene; visitors from Rome [11](both Jews and converts to Judaism); Cretans and Arabs—we hear them declaring the wonders of God in our own tongues!" [12]Amazed and perplexed, they asked one another, "What does this mean?" [13]Some, however, made fun of them and said, "They have had too much wine.ᵃ"

ᵃ*13 Or sweet wine*

2:9-11. This list is fascinating. Technically, it is not a list of languages but political regions or, more specifically, eleven geographic locations sandwiched between three ethnic identities on the front side and three on the backside of the list.[16] If you play 'dot to dot' with them on a map of the Middle East, you will draw a meandering line that generally flows from North to South and then East to West. It begins with the Parthians in the Far East, and three kingdoms under their control—Medes, Elamites, and residents of Mesopotamia.[17] It ends with Rome, preceded by nine regions under their control. As it stands, however, the

---

[14] For more on the view of Galileans see Geza Vermes, *Jesus the Jew: A Historian's Reading of the Gospels* (Philadelphia: Fortress, 1973), 42-57.

[15] In addition to the global impact of Pentecost, Samuel Sahagian is probably right to see an allusion here to the life-giving Spirit against the backdrop of Genesis 1-2 and Ezekiel 37; cf. "Temps de l'Eglise—Actes 2:1-13," *ETR* 58 (1983): 359-367.

[16] The structure of the list is helpfully analyzed by Werner Stenger, "Beobachtungen zur sogenannten Völkerliste des pfingstwunders (Acts 2:7-11)," *Kairos* 21 (1979): 208-210.

[17] Martin Hengel, "'Ιουδαία in the Geographical List of Acts 2:9-11 and Syria as 'Greater Judea'," *BBR* 10 (2000): 162. In the first century B.C. Parthia captured the Roman military standards, declaring itself Rome's rival in the East. There was hardly another nation that posed more difficulties for Roman domination. Placing Parthia first in this lists established a shrill tone for Luke's original Roman audience.

list has a substantial anomaly:[18] Why does Luke place Judea between Mesopotamia and Cappadocia and not mention Syria, the actual capital of the region?
One could also ask why he mentions Judea at all, as if it would be surprising to
find Judeans in Jerusalem.[19]

One would expect a first-century list of this region to include Syria and
perhaps even skip Judea since it was under Syrian provenance.[20] This state of affairs, of course, galled the Jews. According to the them, the greater part of Syria
was promised to them by God: "On that day the LORD made a covenant with
Abram and said, 'To your descendants I give this land, from the river of Egypt
to the great river, the Euphrates'" (Gen 15:18; cf. Exod 23:31; Deut 11:24; Josh
1:4). Much of it had been, in fact, controlled by David and Solomon. Hence,
it is not surprising that some messianic expectations predicted the control of
Syria according to the ancient promise of God: "In that day people will come to
you from Assyria and the cities of Egypt, even from Egypt to the Euphrates and
from sea to sea and from mountain to mountain" (Micah 7:12; cf. Zech 9:10; Sir
44:21). Moreover, the Messiah would bring back the dispersed tribes into the
original boundaries of the Promised Land:

> In that day the Lord will reach out his hand a second time to reclaim the
> remnant that is left of his people from Assyria, from Lower Egypt, from
> Upper Egypt, from Cush, from Elam, from Babylonia, from Hamath
> and from the islands of the sea. He will raise a banner for the nations
> and gather the exiles of Israel; he will assemble the scattered people of
> Judah from the four quarters of the earth. (Isa 11:11-12)

The return of the exiles was the single most important messianic function in
the Old Testament (Isa 14:2; 43:57; 49:8-18; Jer 30:3; 31:8-25; Ezek 11:16-21; 28:24-
26; 37:1-14; Hosea 1:10-11), intertestamental literature (Tobit 13:16; 2 Esd 13:39-
47; *1 En.* 90:33; *Bar* 4:36-37; 5:5-9; Philo, *Rewards* 28.164), and rabbinic literature
(*b. Ber.* 12b; *b. Pesah* 88a; *Esth. Rab.* 1:8). Luke's claim here that all these *diaspora
Jews* were *dwelling* (*katoikeō*, see fn 13) in Jerusalem would hardly go unnoticed.

---

[18] There are two other difficulties with this list which are less important. (1) Why does Luke leave out
all the regions of Greece—Macedonia, Thessaly, and Achaia? We probably will never know, but it is clear
that Luke is well acquainted with these areas as his narrative shows in chapters 16–19. (2) Why does he list
Cretans and Arabs after Rome, basically going backwards on the map? Without these final three locations
the list has a nice round number of 12 nations. Hengel, "Geographical List," 179-180, speculates Luke
is merely listing the immediate neighbors of Judea, thus highlighting the Jewish perspective of this list
(though one wonders how Crete is seen as "neighbors in the coastal plain").

[19] This problem was noticed by the early church fathers. Tertullian, who first cites this text (c. A.D. 200)
in *Adversus Judaeos* 7.4, replaces "Judea" with "Armenia." Two centuries later, Augustine apparently follows
him (*Contra epistulam Manichaei quam vocant Fundamenti* 9). Chrysostom cites "Judea" but interprets it as
"India" (*Hom. Acts* 4). One solution (here rejected) is that Luke's list is based on the same material as a later
4th-century list by Paul of Alexandria which placed similar geographical references under the twelve zodiac
signs. Accordingly, Luke must be showing that Jesus is Lord of the universe; cf. Stefan Weinstock, "The
Geographical Catalogue in Acts 2:9-11," *JRS* 38 (1948): 43-46. Bruce Metzger pointed out two insuperable
difficulties with his theory; "Ancient Astrological Geography and Acts 2:9-11" in *Apostolic History and the
Gospel* (W. Ward Gasque and Ralph P. Martin, eds.; Great Britain: Paternoster Press, 1970), 123-133. First,
Luke's list is three centuries earlier and cannot be shown to be dependent on Paul of Alexandria. Second,
only five of the sixteen names are actually identical in the two lists. This is no greater overlap than one
would expect from any two random geographers cataloguing the Mediterranean.

[20] For copious documentation on this point see Hengel, "Geographical List," 168-170.

The Messianic age had dawned through the coming of the Spirit and the promises of God were reaching their fulfillment. Tertullian (c. A.D. 200) took it this way:

> For upon whom else have the universal nations believed, but upon the Christ who is already come? For whom have the nations believed—Parthians, Medes, Elamites, and they who inhabit Mesopotamia, Armedain, Phrygia, Cappadocia, and they who dwell in Putus and Asia and Pamphylia, tarriers in Egypt, and the inhabitants of the regions of Africa which is beyond Cyrene, Romans and proselytes, and, in Jerusalem, Jews, and all other nations. (*Adv. Jud.* 7)[21]

Taking this list as a messianic claim would explain four anomalies of this passage. (1) Verse 1: "When the day of Pentecost came" (*sumplēroō*, lit., 'was fulfilled') indicates a fullness of time, not merely a point on the calendar. (2) Verse 5: These pilgrims are described as "residing" in Jerusalem, alluding to the return from exile.[22] (3) Verse 9: Mentioning Medes and Elamites was anachronistic since these empires had been extinct for centuries. But if Luke was speaking of a messianic ideal rather than contemporary history, it would be reasonable to reach back into the annals to illustrate the Messiah's rule in important territories. And (4) verse 9: Judea is listed rather than Syria as one would expect during the reign of the Messiah over Israel. The odd element that would strike Luke's readers is that rather than *undoing* the diaspora to spread the Kingdom of God, the Messiah *used* the diaspora as the very element which effected the spread of God's Kingdom. It is not the collection of saints in a geo-political body that expands the Kingdom. It is the subversive leavening influence of believers. These 'seeds' dispersed into the farflung kingdoms of this world undermine the dominating powers of Rome, spreading Yahweh's fame among the nations of the world.

2:12-13. There are two responses from the audience. On the one hand, some in the crowd asked "What does this mean?" (v. 12). More literally, they asked, "What will become of this?" The issue is not what these tongues *mean* but what they will *bring*. This was one of those massive moments that would inevitably change everything. Some in the crowd sensed it.

On the other hand, there were mockers who accused the Apostles of being drunk on sweet wine (v. 13).[23] Normally this word (*gleukos*) means grape juice

---

[21] Gary Gilbert, "The List of Nations in Acts 2: Roman Propaganda and the Lukan Response" *JBL* 121 (2002): 497-529, rightly argues that such lists of nations were used in Roman literature and monuments as propaganda to portray the power of Rome (e.g., Virgil, *Aeneid* 1.278-279; Pliny, *Natural History* 7.2; *Res gestae divi Augusti* 26-32). Eberhard Güting, "Der geographische Horizont der sogenannten Völkerliste," *ZNW* 66 (1975): 149-169, demonstrates the relevance this has for Luke's propaganda of Gentile inclusion. Of course they should be allowed into the kingdom since God now ruled the whole world.

[22] Dietrich-Alex Koch, "Proselyten und Gottesfürchtige als Hörer der Reden von Aposelgeschichte," in *Apostelgeschichte und die hellenistische Geschichtsschreibung* (ed. Cilliers Breytenbach and Jens Schröter; Leiden: Brill, 2004), 85-87.

[23] Such an accusation, followed by a refutation, is a common feature in Luke (2:13-17; 4:18-20; 5:27-29; 6:1-2; etc.) which comes out of the Greek *progymnasmata*. It is a standard rhetorical device designed to establish one's credibility through logical refutation (cf. Quintilian, *Inst.* 5.13.53-59). Cf. Mikeal C. Parsons, "Luke and the *Progymnasmata*: A Preliminary Investigation into the Preliminary Exercises," in *Contextualizing Acts: Lukan Narrative and Greco-Roman Discourse* (ed. Todd C. Penner and Caroline Vander Stichele, SBLSymS; Atlanta: SBL, 2003): 43-64 and Julien C. H. Smith, "The Rhetorical Function of Refutation in Acts 6–7 and 10–15," in *Contemporary Studies in Acts* (ed. Thomas E. Phillips; USA: Mercer, 2009), 103-118.

(cf. Josephus, *Ant* 2.5.2 §64). But that hardly makes sense here. It is early June and the grape harvest would not be for another couple of months ◖. It simply was not possible to keep juice from fermenting for ten months.[24] Two verses might help unravel this mystery. First, the Old Testament reference to tongues, hardly a flattering portrait, compares it to drunkenness (Isa 28:7-11; cf. 1 Cor 14:21). It would not be uncommon for such mystical manifestations to be described as intoxication by opponents (cf. 1 Sam 1:14).[25] Second, Luke may be alluding to Job 32:18-19 (LXX) where Elihu claims to be filled with the Spirit like wine (the only use of *gleukos* in the LXX).[26] This is not so different from Paul's exhortation in Ephesians 5:19, "Do not get drunk on wine, which leads to debauchery. Instead, be filled with the Spirit." If this is Luke's reference point, he is using a word which aptly counters the accusation.[27]

2. First Gospel Message (2:14-36)

Naturally, Peter addresses the crowd as the spokesman for the Twelve (cf. Matt 16:19). His sermon will have three primary movements. First, he quotes Joel 2:28-32 (LXX 3:1-5) to explain the phenomenon of tongues. More than that, Joel prophesies a new era in salvation history when the Spirit of God would be poured out on all flesh (vv. 14-21). Second, Peter gives witness to the resurrection, calling on Psalm 16:8-11 as a prophetic proof-text (vv. 22-36). Together, these two world-altering events—Jesus' resurrection and the Spirit's outpouring—call for a decisive change (vv. 37-41). Since Jesus is Lord, these people from every nation are called to realign their loyalties with the Kingdom of God. Just as Jesus' address to the synagogue of Nazareth establishes the paradigm for the rest of his work in the Gospels (Luke 4:18-27), so Peter's sermon here lays out the program for Spirit's mission in Acts.[28]

[14]**Then Peter stood up with the Eleven, raised his voice and addressed the crowd: "Fellow Jews and all of you who live in Jerusalem, let me explain this to you; listen carefully to what I say.** [15]**These men are not drunk, as you suppose. It's only nine in the morning!** [16]**No, this is what was spoken by the prophet Joel."**

2:14-16. Peter deals summarily with the bogus accusation that the Apostles are drunk. Such an early drinking binge was so shameful to make it unthinkable (Cicero, *Philippic* 2.104), particularly during the hour of prayer at a sacred festival. Peter's dignified oration (*apophthengomai*, see v. 2:4), though respectful of his fellow Jews, demonstrates this phenomenon is from the Spirit, not the 'spirits'. A reference from Joel will suffice to make the point.

Before delving into Peter's sermon, a couple of preliminary remarks are in

---

[24] Cf. A. R. S. Kennedy and J. Paterson, "Wine and Strong Drink," *ISBD* 1038-1039.

[25] The same was true in Hellenistic literature; Horst, "Hellenistic Parallels," 55-56.

[26] For the full development of this theory, see Daniel R. Schwartz, "On Some New and Old Wine in Peter's Pentecost Speech (Acts 2)," *SPhiloA* 3 (1991): 256-271.

[27] If this is not Luke's reference point, these mockers are calling the Apostles lightweights who get drunk on juice. It is hardly flattering, but neither is it a very convincing argument against them.

[28] Cf. Robert Sloan, "'Signs and Wonders': A Rhetorical Clue to the Pentecost Discourse," *EvQ* 63 (1991): 225-240.

order. What we have here is a barebones summary of Peter's sermon by a historian who was not there. This raises the question, "Did Luke make up the content of Peter's sermon?" Older scholars assumed as much for several reasons. First, the sermon is couched in Greek literary and rhetorical style that is beyond the pale of a Palestinian fisherman. Second, this is Luke's vocabulary—his fingerprints are all over the sermon. Third, the Old Testament quotations are from the LXX not the Aramaic or Hebrew that Peter would have used. Fourth, parts of this sermon are reproduced in later ones through the book (most notabley vv. 25-28, 31//13:35, also vv. 34-36//7:55-56) indicating that either it was imitated by other speakers (namely Stephen and Paul) or it had a single mind behind it (i.e., Luke).

Even so, the evidence suggests that the framework of the sermon stemmed from Peter even if Luke presented it in his own style and vocabulary.[29] First, the theological ideas of this sermon match what we find in Peter's letters.[30] Second, there are a number of places where it appears Luke has translated from an Aramaic original.[31] Third, while it was common for historians to fashion a speech based upon what was probably said (Thucydides, *Hist.* 1.22; cf. Lucian, *Hist.* 58), it was always preferable to ancient historians to witness the events themselves or investigate those who were there (cf. Heraclitus, 22B frg. 101a; Dio Chrysostom, 12:71; Philo, *Confusion* 57; Seneca, *Ep. Mor.* 6.5; Papias in Eusebius, *Eccl. Hist.* 3.39.15; etc.). The point is that the church continued to keep its foundational stories alive, making it highly unlikely that Luke could have made one up to fit his own agenda.[32] Finally, it is entirely possible that Luke met Peter and personally interviewed him about this great occasion.

---

[29] Especially helpful here is William Lane, "The Speeches of the Book of Acts," in *Jerusalem and Athens: Critical Discussions of the Theology and Apologetics of Cornelius Van Til* (ed. E. R. Geehan; USA: Presbyterian and Reformed, 1971), 260-272. In addition to the arguments below, Lane suggests that the Christology presented in the speeches of Acts is early, with an emphasis on παῖς θεοῦ as well as Israel's hope.

[30] Both open with a claim to Apostolic authority (1 Pet 1:1; Acts 2:14). Both are predicated on the Jewish Diaspora who are filled/sanctified by the Spirit (1 Pet 1:2; Acts 2:9-11). The central message is the resurrection of Jesus as evidence that he is now "Lord and Christ" (1 Peter 1:3, 21; 3:21; Acts 2:24-32, 36, 38). Both speak of the "last days" as an imminent reality (1 Pet 1:5; 4:7, 17; Acts 2:17). Both emphasize prophecy (1 Pet 1:10-12; Acts 2:18, 30). Jesus suffered innocently, was raised from the dead, and then was exalted in the ascension (1 Pet 1:11; 2:22-24; 3:21-22; Acts 2:22-24, 33). The Holy Spirit is "sent from heaven" (1 Pet 1:12; Acts 2:17). Peter pleads that we "save ourselves from this corrupt generation" (1 Pet 1:13-25; 4:2-4; Acts 2:40). Jesus' destiny was chosen by God (1 Pet 1:20; Acts 2:23); though rejected by men he was vindicated by God (1 Pet 2:4; Acts 2:36). Through Jesus we have an opportunity to repent specifically through baptism (1 Pet 2:24-25, 21; Acts 2:38). In Acts 2, Peter cites Joel 2 and Psa 16 and 110. In 1 Peter he cites Lev 11:44-45 (1:16); Isa 40:6-9 (1:24); Psa 34:8 (2:3); Isa 28:16 (2:6); Psa 118:22 (2:7); Isa 8:14-15 (2:8); Exod 19:5-6 (2:9); Hos 2:23 (2:10); Psa 34:12-16 (3:10-12); Prov 11:31 (4:18); Prov 3:34 (5:5); with multiple other allusions.

[31] This would not, of course, prove it was Peter's original, but it would argue against the idea that Luke created the substance of the sermon. Fitzmyer, however, denies Luke was influenced by Aramaic transcripts: "Most of the instances cited as alleged Aramaisms are to be explained more correctly as Septuagintisms" (116). He catalogues a goodly number of words Luke has incorporated from the LXX (114-118).

[32] The presence of eyewitnesses within the early church and the deeply traditional nature of Judaism within which the gospel traditions circulated (cf. Rom 6:17; 1 Cor 11:23; 15:1-3; 1 Pet 5:1; 2 Pet 1:16; 1 John 1:1-3) make it unlikely that the traditions were created *de novo* rather than recounting events that transpired (cf. Luke 1:1-4; John 19:35; 21:24; Acts 1:21-22; 10:39, 41). A fair summary is offered by Eusebius, quoting Papias (*Eccl. Hist.* 3.39), "Whatsoever I have at any time accurately ascertained and treasured up in my memory, as I have received it from the elders, and have recorded it in order to give additional confirmation to the truth, by my testimony.... For I do not think that I derived so much benefit from books as from the living voice of those that are still surviving." For a full defense of oral tradition see Richard Bauckham, *Jesus and the Eyewitnesses: The Gospels as Eyewitness Testimony* (Grand Rapids: Eerdmans, 2006); James Dunn, *Jesus Remembered: Christianity in the Making,* vol. 1 (Grand Rapids: Eerdmans, 2003); and Kenneth E. Bailey, "Informal Controlled Oral Tradition and the Synoptic Gospels," *AJT* 5 (1991): 34-51.

[17]"**In the last days, God says, I will pour out my Spirit on all people. Your sons and daughters will prophesy, your young men will see visions, your old men will dream dreams.** [18]**Even on my servants, both men and women, I will pour out my Spirit in those days, and they will prophesy.** [19]**I will show wonders in the heaven above and signs on the earth below, blood and fire and billows of smoke.** [20]**The sun will be turned to darkness and the moon to blood before the coming of the great and glorious day of the Lord.** [21]**And everyone who calls on the name of the Lord will be saved.'**[a]

[a]*21* Joel 2:28-32

If we jump into the middle of this prophecy there are all kinds of weird and wonderful elements. For example, (1) the mention of prophecy, visions, and dreams will generate a flurry of passionate opinions. Then (2) there are those galactic catastrophes of blood and fire and billows of smoke that fuel doomsday predictions. This says nothing of the (3) "last days"[33] or the "day of the Lord."

2:17. Perhaps we would do well to read this text from the outside in rather than the inside out. In other words, let's look at the introduction and conclusion as a key to Peter's primary emphasis. The meat of his message is in the way the quote starts and ends: "I will pour out my Spirit on **all people . . . Everyone who calls on the name of the Lord will be saved**" (emphasis added). The point is simple: The outpouring of the Spirit of God inaugurates a new era in salvation history where all people have access to salvation.[34] While the miracles are intriguing and serve a valuable purpose, it is the open access to God that is earth-shattering. For Peter and his original audience, this is a message to Jews who found themselves scattered across the Empire. It was wondrous news that the Diaspora had equal access to Yahweh as those privileged to live in the sacred city. For Luke, of course, this text will push forward all the way to Cornelius's house in chapter 10.[35] There they will realize that God's ambitions were not merely for scattered Israelites, but the nations of the world (Isa 49:6).

2:18-20. With this in mind, the details make more sense. (1) Prophecy,[36] vi-

---

[33] The LXX simply reads "After this." Luke's alteration is interpretive—Pentecost inaugurates the final era in prophetic chronology.

[34] Throughout most of the OT the Spirit of God was essentially the manifestation of Yahweh's power on an earthly plane. During the later days of the OT, the concept of Spirit of God evolved into a kind of embodiment in Wisdom. This embodiment was in no way divorced from the person of God but was viewed as a personification of his power on earth. This prepared for the Christian concept of Jesus pouring out the Spirit as an individual entity distinct from the Father—a unique persona of the Godhead. John Levison traces this evolution of the concept of the Spirit through the later OT through the intertestamental period; cf. *The Spirit in First Century Judaism* (Boston: Brill, 2002) and *Filled with the Spirit* (Grand Rapids: Eerdmans, 2009).

[35] Though Sandt makes too much of Luke's supposed redaction of Joel, he is correct in pointing out that Joel 3 is not a particularly friendly message to Gentiles; Hubertus van de Sandt, "The Fate of the Gentiles in Joel and Acts 2: An Intertextual Study," *ETL* 66 (1990): 56-77. This fact alone makes it highly unlikely that this sermon is a Lucan creation, though he uses it well to promote his agenda of universal inclusion; cf. Bernd Willmes, "Lukas als Interpret von Joël 3,1-5 in Apg 2," in *"Licht zur Erleuchtung der Heiden und Herrlichkeit für dein Volk Israel": Studien zum lukanischen Doppelwerk* (ed. Christoph Müller und Josef Zmijewski; Hamburg: Philo, 2005), 227-258.

[36] Peter adds an extra line to Joel's words in v. 18, "and they will prophesy." This demonstrates an interest in prophecy that Peter exhibits elsewhere (Acts 2:30; 3:18, 21-25; 10:43; 1 Pet 1:10-12; 2 Pet 2:19-21; 3:2). Dillon attributes this interest to Lucan redaction which hardly seems necessary given Peter's demonstrable interest in prophecy in his letters (a liking he could easily have gleaned from Jesus himself); cf. Richard Dillon, "The Prophecy of Christ and His Witnesses according to the Discourses of Acts," *NTS* 32 (1986): 544-556.

sions, and dreams[37] were ways God talked to people through his Spirit. If he's talking with you, then you are on the inside of his plan. So while these communiqués have a valuable function, especially for the recipient, the more powerful message is God's availability to all people—young and old, male and female, slave and free (cf. Gal 3:28 and *Num. Rab.* 15.25, which says, "In this world a prophet was one in a thousand but in the world to come all Israel will be made prophets"). (2) This message of a universally accessible God is earth-shattering, or in Joel's description, heaven shaking. If one takes verses 19-20 literally, s/he will have to wait for some end-time event for it to be fulfilled.[38] But that is hardly necessary. This kind of language of the sun being darkened, the moon turning to blood, or stars falling from the sky, is common coin in prophetic oracles (Stott, 73; *pace* Polhill, 110). For example, we read a similar description in Isaiah 13:9-11 in reference to the fall of Babylon (cf. v. 1). Again, Egypt's demise is described as galactic turmoil in Ezekiel 32:7-11 (esp. v. 2). Such metaphors are also applied to Jerusalem in Matthew 24:29-31 (cf. vv. 1-2). These images refer to political entities as heavenly bodies. In other words, this inclusive love of God is going to shake the nations. And so it did. (3) Finally, the "last days" are not necessarily limited to a seven-year tribulation before the coming of the Lord. Though it sometimes refers to such a terminal period (2 Tim 3:1; 2 Pet 3:3; James 5:3),[39] it is perfectly natural to speak of the "last days" as the final epoch of human history from Jesus' ascension until his return (Acts 2:17; Heb 1:2; 1 Pet 1:20). During this age of the Spirit—the age of God's grace extending to all people—his gifts will be distributed without distinction of race, class, or gender. Now that *is* an Empire-rattling reality.

2:21. However, these galactic signs also inevitably conjure up images of judgment (Bock, 117). This era culminates in the coming of Christ and the ultimate judgment of those who reject him. Interestingly, verse 21 uses the term "lord" to apply specifically to Jesus while Joel has used that term to mean Yahweh. Peter conflates the two. No wonder the rejection of Jesus would have such dire consequences.

[22]"Men of Israel, listen to this: Jesus of Nazareth[40] was a man accredited by God to you by miracles, wonders and signs, which God did among you through him, as you yourselves know. [23]This man was handed over to you by God's set purpose and foreknowledge; and you, with the help of wicked men,ᵃ put him to death by nailing him to the cross. [24]But God raised him from the dead, freeing

---

[37] Because of the paucity of data, there is no way to clearly differentiate between a vision and a dream, except perhaps that one is asleep during a dream and awake during a vision.

[38] Walter Kaiser, "The Promise of God and the Outpouring of the Holy Spirit: Joel 2:28-32 and Acts 2:16-21," in *Living and Active Word* (ed. Morris Inch and Ronald Youngblood; USA: Eisenbrauns, 1983), 109-122. Or perhaps one could look backwards to the supernatural darkness at Jesus' crucifixion (Bruce, 69; Marshall, 74) but there is no solid evidence Peter saw this as fulfilled prior to the Spirit's outpouring rather than a consequence thereof.

[39] John uses the singular "last day" to refer to the Day of Judgment or resurrection (6:39, 40, 44, 54; 11:24; 12:48).

[40] It was common in ancient times to identify an individual from their town of origin. Luke certainly adopts this practice with Jesus (Luke 4:34; 18:37; 24:19; Acts 2:22; 6:14; 10:38; 22:8; 26:9). For a discussion of the derivation and meaning of the term see Bruce, 69-70, fn. 51, and G. F. Moore, "Nazarene and Nazareth," in *Beginnings* (London: MacMillan, 1920), I:426-432.

him from the agony of death,[41] because it was impossible for death to keep its hold on him."

 a 23 Or *of those not having the law* (that is, Gentiles)

2:22-23. The brutal execution of Jesus made him look like a Roman criminal and a Jewish heretic. Hence, trying to convince these Diaspora pilgrims to accept him as their Messiah is a hard sell. So Peter builds an overwhelming argument: Yahweh affirmed Jesus during his lifetime through extraordinary miracles (v. 22; cf. Luke 7:16, 22; 11:20; Acts 10:38-39; Josephus, *Ant* 18.3.3; §§63-64). This theme is echoed in Hebrews 2:3b-4: "This salvation, which was first announced by the Lord, was confirmed to us by those who heard him. God also testified to it by signs, wonders and various miracles, and gifts of the Holy Spirit distributed according to his will." Thus, it was not so much the cruelty of wicked men (i.e., the Romans) or the plots of Jewish leaders that caused Jesus' demise.[42] It was the sovereign hand of God which orchestrated his death and vindicated him through resurrection. This pattern "you killed Jesus but God raised him" is repeated a number of times throughout Acts (3:15; 4:10; 5:30; 10:39-40; 13:28-30). Here God's sovereign plan stands side by side with the free will of man without a hint of contradiction or tension.

2:24. The Apostles now testify to seeing Jesus raised from the dead. Normally this would be rejected out of hand. On this occasion, however, the Holy Spirit intervened, granting phenomenal linguistic abilities to a bunch of Galileans! Thus, their eyewitness testimony is bolstered by a miraculous manifestation.

[25]"David said about him: 'I saw the Lord always before me. Because he is at my right hand, I will not be shaken. [26]Therefore my heart is glad and my tongue rejoices; my body also will live in hope, [27]because you will not abandon me to the grave, nor will you let your Holy One see decay. [28]You have made known to me the paths of life; you will fill me with joy in your presence.'a [29]Brothers, I can tell you confidently that the patriarch[43] David died and was buried, and his tomb is here to this day. [30]But he was a prophet and knew that God had promised him on oath that he would place one of his descendants on his throne. [31]Seeing what was ahead, he spoke of the resurrection of the Christ,b that he was not abandoned to

---

[41] The "agony of death" (ὠδῖνας τοῦ θανάτου) likely comes from the "cords of death/Sheol" in Psa 18:4-5 [17:5-6]. The word for cord (חֶבֶל) and "agony" (חֵבֶל) are spelled identically except for the vowels. The LXX translators (c. 250–150 B.C.) read the Hebrew word as "agony" while the Rabbis who later pointed the MT (c. 500–900 A.D.) read the word as "cord" in Psa 18:4-5 and 116:3.

[42] Luke's narrative consistently charges the Jewish leaders with the death of Jesus (Luke 22–23; 24:20; Acts 3:13-17; 4:5, 10-11, 27; 5:30; 7:52; 10:39-40; 13:27-29). But then so does Josephus (*Ant* 18.3.3 §§63-64) and the Talmud (*b. Sanh.* 43a). Cf. Jon Weatherly, *Jewish Responsibility for the Death of Jesus*, Journal for the Study of the New Testament Supplement Series 106 (Sheffield: Sheffield Academic Press, 1994). Frank Matera, "Responsibility for the Death of Jesus according to Acts of the Apostles," *JSNT* 39 (1990): 73-93, argues persuasively that Luke is *not* anti-Semitic in his presentation, contra J. T. Sanders, *The Jews in Luke–Acts* (Minneapolis: Augsburg, 1972). Also helpful is Augusto Barbi's careful analysis of the 79 uses of *hoi Ioudaioi* in Acts; "The Use and Meaning of (*Hoi*) *Ioudaioi* in Acts," in *Luca-Atti* (ed. Gerald O'Collins and Gilberto Marconi; Assisi: Cittadella, 1991), 123-142.

[43] The term "patriarch" normally refers to Abraham, Isaac, or Jacob as founders of the twelve tribes. Here it is used of David as the founder of the royal dynasty. Sirach 47 references David as a patriarch as well, so Peter's use is certainly understandable within the literature of his day.

**the grave, nor did his body see decay. [32]God has raised this Jesus to life, and we
are all witnesses of the fact."**

[a]*28* Psalm 16:8-11   [b]*31* Or *Messiah,* "The Christ" (Greek) and "The Messiah" (Hebrew) both
mean "The Annointed One"; also in verse 36

2:25-28. As if all this validation was not enough, Jesus was also authenticated
by an ancient prophecy from Psalm 16. Peter's logic (which Paul would later
adopt, Acts 13:35-37) is fairly straightforward: David writes a Psalm that describes
a "Holy One" surviving death. Since David did not survive death (as his tomb
testified[44]), he is obviously not the subject of the Psalm. Jesus *must* be the holy
one to whom David refers since he did, in fact, survive death ◧. So far, so good.

2:29-32. However, Psalm 16 originally was not referring to postmortem
survival but rescue from a premature death. So this question looms large: Did
Peter ignore the context of the Psalm, thereby misusing it for his own theological agenda?[45] Several things should be borne in mind. First, Peter is not trying
to prove the resurrection. That was already an established fact through their
Spirit-empowered eyewitness testimony. He is merely using the Psalm to show
that there is an ancient lens through which this event might be viewed. Second,
the Jewish interpretation of the Bible was keenly aware of historical connections
between David and his promised progenitor (v. 30; cf. 2 Sam 7:12-16; 4QFlor).[46]
Thus, the idea of David's descendant living larger than he had was certainly a
fair assumption. Third, David was commonly considered a prophet in various
Jewish circles (e.g., Acts 1:16; 4:25; Heb 11:32; 11Q5 27.2-11; Josephus, *Ant* 6.8.2
§166; *Barn* 12:10; *b. Sotah* 48b).[47] The Targum, in fact, takes 2 Sam 23:1-7 to be
a prophetic, eschatological description of David's descendant. It would be natural, therefore, for David to be viewed as a prophet describing the future Messiah.
Peter says so much in verses 30-31. So, it appears that Peter used this Psalm in a
way that modern Westerners are uncomfortable with but which was perfectly at
home in the interpretive traditions of his own place and time. In essence Peter

[44]Josephus (*Ant* 13.8.4 §249/ *War* 1.2.5 §61) says Hyrcanus (135/134 B.C.) plundered the tomb of David
in Jerusalem to help pay for his campaign. Herod later plundered it again to pay for his massive building
campaigns (Josephus, *Ant* 16.7.1 §179-182). According to the legend, his men were consumed by flame
when they neared the bodies of David and Solomon. In repentance, he expanded their funerary monument. This very monument was reportedly destroyed by Hadrian's campaign (c. 133 A.D.; Dio Cassius, *Hist.*
69.14). These references substantiate the historicity of Peter's claim.

[45] Haenchen (148-149) charges that Luke gratuitously used the LXX to prove a point that cannot be
sustained by the Hebrew text. This simply is not so. These particular Hebrew words are, in fact, adequately
translated by the LXX, falling well within the range of meaning for the words in question; cf. Pierre Constant, "Forme textuelle et justesse doctrinal de l'Ancien Testament dans le Nouveau; La citation du Psaume
16 dans le discours d'Actes 2," *BRT* 2 (1992): 4-15. For a historical survey of the interpretation of this text see
Gregory V. Trull, "Views on Peter's Use of Psalm 16:8-11 in Acts 2:25-32," *BibSac* 161 (2004): 194-214.

[46] Robert F. O'Toole, "Acts 2:30 and the Davidic Covenant of Pentecost," *JBL* 102 (1983): 245-258, provides
a compelling argument for 2 Sam 7:12-16 as the literary and theological background for the use of Psalms 16
and 110. It was this conceptual promise that provided the hermeneutical engine for the use of these citations.

[47] Cf. Joseph A. Fitzmyer, "David 'Being Therefore a Prophet . . .'," *CBQ* 34 (1972): 332-339; and Damià
Roure, *Jesús y la figura de David en Mc 2:23-26: Trasfondo bíblico, intertestamentario y rabínico* (Rome: Pontificio Inst
Biblico, 1990), 53-103. Gregory V. Trull, "Peter's Interpretation of Psalm 16:8-11 in Acts 2:25-32," *BibSac* 161
(2004): 432-448, argues that David knew, in fact, that he was predicting the resurrection of Jesus. While this
may defend Peter and the text as inerrant, it forces an odd interpretation of Psa 16:3-4 which clearly does not
apply to Jesus. Moreover, it is a lot to ask of David since neither the idea of the Messiah nor of bodily resurrection had yet developed in his day (especially in view of 1 Pet 1:10-12). Furthermore, once messianic ideas *did*
emerge, there's hardly a clue that the Messiah would suffer, let alone die.

argued that the *ultimate* fulfillment of Psalm 16 was not found in David but in Jesus. If you asked Peter if he realized Psalm 16 was actually David's, request for God to spare his life, he might well say, "Well, of course, silly! But don't *you* realize how this ultimately played out? Jesus rose from the dead, hence, his status is greater than David's and thus the words spoken of David in the temporal realm are even truer of Jesus in the eternal realm." This method of Jewish interpretation is called *Pesher*—applying ancient texts to contemporary experiences (e.g., 4Q171 and 4QpHab).[48]

[33]"Exalted to the right hand of God, he has received from the Father the promised Holy Spirit and has poured out what you now see and hear. [34]For David did not ascend to heaven, and yet he said, 'The Lord said to my Lord: "Sit at my right hand [35]until I make your enemies a footstool for your feet."'a [36]"Therefore let all Israel be assured of this: God has made this Jesus, whom you crucified, both Lord and Christ."

a35 Psalm 110:1

2:33. Peter moves from the resurrection to the ascension as he affirms the Holy Spirit flowing from the Father (2:17). Verse 33 sounds and awful lot like John: "And I will ask the Father, and he will give you another Counselor to be with you forever—the Spirit of truth" (John 14:16-17a; cf. 14:26; 15:26; 16:7; 20:21-22).[49] At the same time one hears echoes of Psa 68:18 (in the form found in Eph 4:8): "When he ascended on high, he led captives in his train and gave gifts to men." Hence Peter, through Luke's record, sounds like Jesus. Furthermore, John's writings match Paul's interpretation of Psalm 68:18. Hence, lots of voices harmonize on this important point. Namely, Jesus has assumed his rightful place at God's right hand and exorcised his regal role by pouring out the long-promised Spirit.[50]

2:34-35. If Peter's verbiage does stem from Jesus himself, perhaps his interpretation of Psalm 110 does also.[51] Jesus used Psalm 110 to point out his own superiority to David, thus clarifying his messianic role (Mark 12:35-37/Matt 22:41-46/Luke 20:41-44).[52] He is no mere earthly king working for national liberation.

---

[48] For a helpful discussion of this complex hermeneutical issue, see Richard Longenecker, *Biblical Exegesis in the Apostolic Period* (Grand Rapids: Eerdmans, 1975); Wolfgang Fenske, "Aspekte Biblischer Theologie dargestellt an der Verwendung von Ps 16 in Apostelgeschichte 2 und 13," *Bib* 83 (2002): 54-70, and José Antonio Jáuregui, "Argumento Escriturístico de la Resurrección en los Hechos de los Apóstoles," *EB* 57 (1999): 389-410. They show that rabbinic documents have as many textual alterations as Christian ones. Furthermore, the LXX alterations here with Psa 16 are not necessarily more influential in developing a theology of the resurrection than the MT. Rather, the MT, LXX, and contemporary experiences informed one another as early Christians proclaimed the risen Christ; cf. Donald Juel, "Social Dimensions of Exegesis: The Use of Psalm 16 in Acts 2," *CBQ* 43 (1981): 543-556 and W. H. Bellinger, "The Psalms and Acts: Reading and Rereading," in *With Steadfast Purpose: Essays on Acts in Honor of Henry Jackson Flanders, Jr.* (Waco: Baylor University, 1990), 127-143.

[49] Cf. John Kilgallen, "A Rhetorical and Source-traditions Study of Acts 2,33," *Bib* 77 (1996): 192.

[50] Odette Mainville, "Jésus et l'Esprit dans l'Oeuvre de Luc," *ScEs* 42 (1990): 193-208, points out the massive shift this moment represents in redemptive history. The new era of Jesus' regal reign has begun when the Spirit is commissioned by the King to fill Jesus' earthly role.

[51] Given the prominence of Psalm 110 in the early church, one might ask how it gained such significance if it does not go back to the exegesis of Jesus. Psalm 110 is cited in 1 Cor 15:25; Heb 1:13; 5:6, 10; 10:13 and alluded to in Rom 8:34; Eph 1:20-22; Col 3:1; Heb 1:3; 8:1; 10:12; 12:2.

[52] The meaning of this passage is not entirely clear. Pragmatically Jesus could have posed such a perplex-

He is God's envoy, effecting redemption for humanity. Thus Jesus' rule would be linked more with Yahweh's authority than Davidic descent.

Before Jesus, Psalm 110 had not been viewed messianically, though it was read regally (*T. Job* 33:3; 1 Macc 14:41; *T. Levi* 8:3; 18:1-3, 8, 12). Yet once the assumption of Davidic authorship was accepted, Psalm 110 falls well within the ambit of messianic discourse.[53] It appears, in fact, that he is using a *haggadic* question in which two apparently contradictory scriptural views are to be reconciled:[54] On the one hand, David is the fount from which all kings spring; on the other hand, the Messiah is more than an earthly king—he is the very vice-regent of Yahweh, sitting at his own right hand.[55]

2:36. Peter uses the same logic in interpreting Psalm 110 and 16:10. Specifically, if David did not fulfill his own Psalm then he must have been prophesying about the Messiah. Since Jesus is the only one to have ascended to the right hand of God, who else could the Messiah be but Jesus? The conclusion, for Peter, is irrefutable: "*God has made this Jesus, whom you crucified, both Lord and Christ*" (cf. Luke 2:11; *Psa Sol* 17:36).

Two terms need careful definition. "Christ" is the Greek term for the Hebrew word "Messiah." It is a common misperception that there was a ready-made definition among Jesus' contemporaries that he had to correct. Supposedly, all the Jews were yammering about this coming liberator who would overthrow the Romans. In actual fact, however, there was very little discussion about the Messiah,[56] and what did exist was more of a debate than a consensus. To ask, therefore, "What is meant by Messiah?" must be followed by further questions such as "When, where, and by whom?"[57] In actuality, it was Jesus and his follow-

---

ing question in order to divert the aggression mounting against him at that moment; cf. Robert P. Gagg, "Jesus und die Davidssohnsfrage: zur Exegese von Markus 12:35-37," *TZ* 7 (1951): 18-30. However, Gagg's conclusion that the question itself is designed to deny the Davidic descent of the Messiah exceeds the textual evidence, Jesus' messianic praxis, as well as broader cultural expectations of a Davidic Messiah.

[53] The Psalm may originally have been composed *about* the king, not *by* the king (which would substantially alter its interpretation). Nonetheless, *Tg. Psa* 110 begins "Composed by David, a psalm." This shows that it was commonly assumed, in Jesus' day, to have been written by David.

[54] Bock, *Luke* (IVPNTC 3; Downers Grove, IL: InterVarsity, 1994), 1630. Hooker also urges: "We need to remember not only the Semitic idiom whereby a comparison could be expressed by using a negative (cf. Hos. 6.6 with Mark 12.33), but also that the saying is put in the form of a question, almost a conundrum," Morna Hooker, *The Gospel according to Saint Mark* (Peabody, MA: Hendrickson, 1991), 292.

[55] This logic is an extrapolation to Psa 110 of the ideology already applied to 2 Sam 7:14 and Psalm 2:7; cf. Gerhard Schneider, "Die Davidssohnfrage (Mk 12,35-37)," *Bib* 53 (1972): 89. The fact that Jesus claims prerogative of the 'right hand' virtually eliminates any interpretation of this passage that would see Jesus as removing himself from Messianic claims.

[56] The concept of Messiah was relatively rare in Judaism prior to Jesus. The term "Messiah" is not found in the apocrypha or Philo, and only twice in Josephus in two disputed references to Jesus (*Ant.* 18.63; 20.200 and *J.W.* 6.312). Furthermore, in the OT, "messiah" typically refers to Davidic kings, past or present (Pss 18:50; 89:20; 132:10-17; Hab 3:13). Surprisingly the messianic concept is relatively rare in Qumran as well. As Evans points out, there are only thirteen scrolls out of the Qumran cache of some eight hundred and seventy scrolls which contain messianic material and "only six, or at most eight, scrolls actually refer to an 'anointed' personage who is to be understood as the eschatological messiah," Craig A. Evans, "The Messiah in the Dead Sea Scrolls," in *Israel's Messiah in the Bible and the Dead Sea Scrolls* (ed. Richard S. Hess and Daniel Carroll; Grand Rapids: Baker Academic, 2003), 86. Finally, the Targumim often avoid messianic interpretation where the text would seem to beg for it (e.g., Psa 2; 110; Isa 42:1-9, 53; Ezek 34:23-24; 37:24-25).

[57] The most common conception was a *Davidic king* (Isa 11:1; Jer 23:5; *Shemoneh Esreh* 14) who would gather the dispersed tribes of Israel (Isa 11:11-16; *Bar* 4:36-37; 5:5-9; Philo, *Rewards*. 28.164; 2 Esd 13:39-47), establish the true Jerusalem (*Pss. Sol.* 17:25, 33; *1 En.* 53:6; 90:28-29; 2 Esd 7:26; 13:36) with Yahweh as its sovereign (*Pss. Sol.* 17:1-4, 38; 1QM 19; *Shemoneh Esreh* 11), and conquer wicked enemies (*Pss. Sol.* 17:23-41; 1QM 15-19; 2 Esd 13:33-38; *1 En.* 52:4-9), especially as a judge (*1 En.* 45:3; 55:4; 61:8-10; 69:26-29; *Pss. Sol.*

ers who did more to define the term "Messiah/Christ" than any group prior to or following them. To oversimplify things, Jesus' definition was like no other: The Christ is the son of God, his earthly envoy sent to serve and suffer for the redemption of humanity. This is a surprising and unprecedented description of the "Christ" that Peter has taken pains to prove.

The second term needing clarification is "Lord". This word has a range of meanings: Sir, Master, Emperor, god(s), Yahweh (LXX). So which definition does Peter intend? His explanation of Psalm 16 and 110 suggests that Jesus is certainly more than a mere mortal. He shares Yahweh's authority and nature. Both sit as judges in the heavens ready to use their enemies as a footstool! The trend to conflate divine titles with Jesus will continue in Acts, sometimes making it difficult to determine whether the subject is Yahweh or Jesus (e.g., Acts 4:24).[58] Peter is not saying that God *created* Jesus but that he made him known publicly as Lord and Christ.

3. Response to the Message (2:37-41)

[37]**When the people heard this, they were cut to the heart and said to Peter and the other apostles, "Brothers, what shall we do?"** [38]**Peter replied, "Repent and be baptized, every one of you, in the name of Jesus Christ for the forgiveness of your sins. And you will receive the gift of the Holy Spirit.** [39]**The promise is for you and your children and for all who are far off—for all whom the Lord our God will call."**

2:37. Peter's sermon struck their deepest nerve ("cut to the heart" = "pierced" or "stabbed").[59] They have just been confronted with the dark reality—their compatriots brutally murdered the long-awaited savior from God. Their minds must have been reeling. What punishment would await such a heinous crime? Is there any undoing this travesty? Is there any way to assuage the inevitable wrath of God? Their swirling thoughts are distilled into one simple question: "What should we do?"

17:28, 31, 48; 2 Esd 12:32-33; *2 Bar* 40:1) and warrior (Num 24:17; Psa 2; Philo, *Rewards.* 16.91-97; *2 Bar* 39:7-40:2; 70:2-6; *1 En.* 62:1-3; 2 Esd 12:32-33; 13:27-28, 35-38; *Tg. Ps.-J.* Gen 49:11; 1QM 11:5-10). The term "King-Messiah" may even be reflected in Luke 23:2, "λέγοντα ἑαυτὸν χριστὸν βασιλέα εἶναι" and Mark 15:32, "ὁ χριστὸς ὁ βασιλεὺς Ἰσραήλ." Helmer Ringgren, "König und Messias," *ZAW* 64 (1952): 120-147, asserts this is the only sufficient foundation for development of the messianic ideas of the first century. But there were certainly other ideas such as an "anointed" *priest* (1 Sam 2:35; Dan 9:24-26; Mal 2:4-7; 11Q13; *T. Levi* 2:11; 18:1-14; *T. Dan* 5:10), *prophet* (like Moses, Deut 18:15-18; 4Q175; John 1:19-23; 6:14; Acts 3:22; 7:37; *Sib. Or.* 5.346-350; or Elijah, Mal 3:1; 4:5; or some other prophet, Isa 61:1-3; Matt 21:11), and *perhaps* some kind of *supernatural figure* who overthrows kings (Dan 7:13-14; *1 En.* 46:1-6; 62:3-12; 69:26-29; 2 Esd 13:26, 32-38). This could be an *angelic helper* (*Sib. Or.* 2.241-244; *Apoc. Pet.* 6), the "*Son of Man*" (Psa 80:18 [17]; Dan 7:13-14; *1 En.* 46:3-4; 48:6, 10; 62:5; 69:27, 29; *Odes Sol.* 36:3), or "*Son of God*" (*1 En.* 105:2; 2 Esd 7:28-29; 13:32, 52; 14:9); though "Son of God" is most likely a royal designation based on 2 Sam 7:14; Psa 2:7-8; and 89:26-27. There was also apparently some talk of a prophetic *forerunner* to the Messiah in the form of Elijah (Mal 3:23-24; Sir 48:10-11; cf. Mark 9:11/Matt 17:10; *m. 'Ed.* 8:7; Justin, *Dial. Tryph.* 8) or Moses (Deut 18:15; 1QS 9:11-12; 4Q175 5-8; John 1:21).

[58] For a full examination of these titles see Andy Johnson, "Resurrection, Ascension and the Developing Portrait of the God of Israel in Acts," *SJT* 57 (2004): 146-162 and Polhill, 116, fn 125.

[59] This peculiar word, κατανύσσομαι, is used only once in the NT but its 18 LXX uses are, like this one, metaphorical; cf. Shawn Flynn, "The Septuagint as Interpretive Translation and the Complex Background to κατανύσσομαι in Acts 2:37," in *Studies in the Greek Bible* (ed. Francis Gignac, Jeremy Corley, and Vincent Skemp; Washington: Catholic Biblical Association of America, 2008), 229-255.

2:38-39. Peter's answer is equally simple: *Repent* and *be baptized*. This comes with two promises: *forgiveness of sins* and the gift of the *Holy Spirit*. Peter's brief response has generated an avalanche of arguments surrounding two key questions.

(1) Does God forgive our sins because we are baptized or because we repent? This, of course, is a bad way of asking the question because our sins are forgiven because of what Jesus did, not because of what we do. Nonetheless, the text itself connects these two faith-responses to our forgiveness. So what's the deal? There are two underlying issues. The first is linguistic, the second theological. *Linguistically*, the word "repent" is plural while the word "be baptized" singular. Thus, it could be translated, "All ya'll repent and each one of you be baptized." This actually makes sense since repentance (but not baptism) can be done by a group.[60] This sounds strange to western ears because we think of repentance as something an individual does for his personal peccadilloes. For Jews, however, sin, punishment, and repentance were often corporate—the action of a family, a city, or even an entire nation.

Baptism, on the other hand, was always individualistic. This observation has led some to conclude that repentance (plural) leads to forgiveness of "your" (plural) sins and that baptism (singular) is merely a parenthetical comment not connected to salvation. The simple fact, however, is that *"be baptized, every one of you,"* is also plural (*hekatos humōn*).[61] Furthermore, if baptism is a 'parenthetical comment', the *least* one could say is that baptism is the appropriate mechanism by which repentance is carried out—it is, thus, epexegetically equivalent to repentance. Bottom line: Whatever role repentance plays in leading to forgiveness, baptism is a 'twin sister' tagging along. They are unseparated in this context.

A second (and more common) linguistic argument suggests that "for" (*eis*) should be translated *"because* your sins were forgiven" not *"in order that* your sins be forgiven." Thus, one is baptized as a *result* of being saved, not as an act of conversion. To put it politely, this is a rather gratuitous definition of "for" (*eis*). This word is used 1,767 times in the New Testament. Overwhelmingly it means "into" or "unto." Hence, the natural reading of the text is that repentance and baptism leads a convert into 'the realm' of forgiveness. Because this directly links baptism with forgiveness, A. T. Robertson[62] argued that it must have an

---

[60] Etymologically "repent" means to change one's mind, but the connotation is to transfer allegiance, not merely to feel sorry for a sin (Matt 21:32; Acts 3:19). This is clearly illustrated when Josephus called a rebel named Jesus, along with his brigands to "repent and believe in me" (Josephus, *Life* 110; cf. Mark 1:15). In other words, they must forgo the rebellion and adopt an alternative program. This aptly describes the central message of John the Baptist (Matt 3:2), Jesus (Matt 4:17; Mark 1:15), and the Apostles (Mark 6:12).

[61] This grammatical rule that a pronoun must agree with its noun in person and number is called "concord." Luther B. McIntyre, "Baptism and Forgiveness in Acts 2:38," *BibSac* 153 (1996): 53-62, uses this rule to 'prove' that only repentance, and not baptism, affects forgiveness for the convert (see also N. B. Stonehouse, "Repentance, Baptism and the Gifts of the Holy Spirit," *WTJ* 13 [1950–51]: 13-15). His linguistic theory is fatally flawed at two points. First, the inclusion of ἕκατος ὑμῶν makes the baptized group plural (cf. Acts 3:26; John 7:53; Rev 20:13); cf. Ashby L. Camp, "Reexamining the Rule of Concord in Acts 2:38," *RQ* 39 (1997): 37-42. Second, Osburn produces a number of equivalent grammatical constructions in the LXX which combine the third person singular with the second person plural to the same effect as Acts 2:38 (cf. Exod 16:29; Josh 6:10; 2 Kings 10:19; Zech 7:10; 1 Macc 10:63); cf. Carroll Osburn, "The Third Person Imperative in Acts 2:38," *RQ* 26 (1983): 81-84. Simply put, those repenting and being baptized are the same plurality of persons.

[62] *Word Pictures in the New Testament.* (Nashville: Broadman, 1930), 3:35-36. His otherwise stellar grasp of the Greek language is here marred by his theological presuppositions. Cf. H. E. Dana and Julius R. Mantey,

alternate meaning (based on the peculiar translation of *eis* in Matt 12:41 and 1 Cor 2:7). Even if one granted Robertson's interpretation of these verses, which is far from certain,[63] these rare exceptions cannot be arbitrarily applied to Acts 2:38 anymore than they could be applied to Matthew 26:28, which uses the same Greek construction, "This is my blood of the covenant, which is poured out for many *for* [*eis*] *the forgiveness of sins.*" It would be ridiculous to suggest that Jesus shed his blood *because* our sins were forgiven. Thus, *eis*, as it stands, is perfectly comprehensible unless one imports a theological bias barring baptism from forgiveness.[64] Peter meant what he said, and it is clear enough as it stands: repentance and baptism effect forgiveness in the conversion of a new believer.

So why all the fuss? Well, there *is* a real danger in requiring 'works' for salvation. We are saved by grace through faith, and anything in addition to that, at least according to Paul, is a heretical imposition (e.g., Rom 4:1-25; Eph 2:8-10; Gal 5:1-5).[65] Thus, the theological objection to baptism as a requirement for salvation is rooted in the right motives. If immersion were a legalistic addition to the cross, it would, indeed, be odious. But that is *not* how the New Testament describes it. Through baptism we put on Christ (Gal 3:27) and imitate his death, burial, and resurrection (Rom 6:3-4; Col 2:12). Baptism, along with teaching, was the mechanism Jesus gave for making disciples (Matt 28:18-20).[66] Baptism is a sacrament which imparts new life (John 3:3-5).[67] In fact, if one is unwilling

---

A Manual Grammar of the Greek New Testament (New York: Macmillan, 1927), 103-105. J. C. Davis's survey of Greek lexicons, dictionaries, and grammars shows the paucity of evidence for Robertson's idiosyncratic definition of εἰς which has grown to disproportionate influence merely by the bulk of its citations; "Another Look at the Relationship between Baptism and Forgiveness of Sins in Acts 2:38," *RQ* 24 (1984): 80-88.

[63] Εἰς in Matt 12:41 and 1 Cor 2:7 can be fairly translated "because of." However, this has more to do with the idiomatic expression of each verse than an actual alternate definition of the word. The people of Jonah's day repented *into* the realm of Jonah's preaching. In other words, they changed allegiance from the ideological world of their own gods to the system of belief in Yahweh that Jonah proclaimed (Matt 12:41). Similarly, in 1 Cor 2:7, God predestined wisdom to move from a hidden place *unto* the realm of glory in which Christians exist. Put another way, God's wisdom moved from shadows to light.

[64] Bruce Compton, "Water Baptism and the Forgiveness of Sins in Acts 2:38," *DBSJ* 4 (1999): 13, argues that with the exception of Acts 22:16, forgiveness is only associated with repentance in Lucan literature (not with baptism). One must wonder why two scriptural texts are insufficient for Compton to make the connection, particularly when the precursor to Christian immersion (i.e., John's baptism) was clearly for forgiveness of sin, using the identical Greek construction found in Acts 2:38 (cf. Mark 1:4; Luke 3:3).

[65] It must be noted, however, that Jesus and the Apostles frequently attached salvation to specific 'works'. The following are imperatives connected with receiving or sustaining salvation: *Repent* (Luke 13:5; Acts 3:19; 17:30-31; Rev 2:16, 22); *Call on Christ's Name* (Acts 22:16; cf. 2:21; Rom 10:13); *Confess Christ* (Matt 10:32-33/ Mark 8:38; Rom 10:9-10; 1 John 2:23; cf. 1 Tim 6:12-13); *Be Baptized* (Acts 2:38; 22:16); *Obey Christ* (John 3:36; Heb 5:9; 2 Thess 1:8; Heb 11:8; 1 John 5:13); *Do Good Works* (Matt 7:21-23; John 15:2; Acts 26:20; Rom 4:35; James 2:20-26); *Live Holy lives* (1 Cor 6:9-11; Gal 5:13-21; Eph 5:3-12; Heb 12:14); *Forgive* (Matt 6:14-15; 18:35; James 2:13; cf. Eph 4:32); *Love* (1 John 3:10, 14; 4:7-21); *Provide Benevolence* (Matthew 25:31-46; 1 John 3:17); *Provide for Yourself and Your Dependents* (1 Tim 5:8; Eph 4:28-32; cf. 5:6); *Remain Faithful* (John 15:6; 1 Cor 10:6-13; Col 1:22-23; Heb 3:6; 10:26-31, 36-39; 12:25; 2 Pet 2:20-21; cf. Rev 2:10, 26); *Save yourself* (Acts 2:40; Phil 2:12); *Guard Your Words* (Matt 5:22-26; 12:36-37; 1 Tim 6:20-21; Jude 1:14-16; cf. James 3:6-12; Matt 7:15-20; 2 Peter 3:16); *Guard Your Doctrine* (Col 2:8, 18-19; 2 Tim 2:16-18; 2 Pet 3:16-17; 2 John 1:7-11).

[66] In the book of Acts, baptism is always a conversion event which makes one a disciple: Pentecost (Acts 2:41), Samaritans (Acts 8:12), Eunuch (Acts 8:36), Cornelius (Acts 10:47-48), Lydia (Acts 16:15), Philippian Jailer (Acts 16:33), Paul (Acts 9:18; 22:16); cf. Bernard Sauvagnat, "Se repentir, être baptisé, recevoir l'Esprit: Actes 2,37ss," *Foi et vie* 80 (1981): 77-89.

[67] This view of baptism as a saving sacrament is the majority view by professing Christians worldwide: Roman Catholics, Greek Orthodox, Eastern Orthodox, and a host of individual Protestant churches, especially those Restoration Movement churches of the Campbellite tradition. In fact, No one separated baptism from conversion until Huldrych Zwingli (c. 1529!), "On Baptism," *Zwingli and Bullinger*, in The Library of Christian Classics, vol. 24, ed. by G. W. Bromiley, 130: "In this matter of baptism — if I may be pardoned for saying it — I can only conclude that *all the doctors have been in error from the time of the apostles.*

to say "baptism saves" s/he is unable to preach the whole counsel of God (1 Pet 3:21; Mark 16:16). Obviously this has been abused by those who give mystical power to the water and magical rites to works. Baptism is a *work of God* which initiates a Spirit-led transformation in our lives; it is a gift we receive; it is an imitation of Jesus' death by which we crucify ourselves in absolute and abject devotion to our Savior. It is not our work for God but rather his work in us.

(2) Does a person receive the Holy Spirit through immersion? It probably goes without saying that the Holy Spirit is granted to those who believe: "You also were included in Christ when you heard the word of truth, the gospel of your salvation. Having believed, you were marked in him with a seal, the promised Holy Spirit" (Eph 1:13; cf. John 7:38-39; Gal. 3:2, 5). So faith is the prerequisite to receiving the Spirit. Faith is also the impetus for baptism: ". . . having been buried with him in baptism and raised with him *through your faith* in the power of God, who raised him from the dead" (Col 2:12; cf. Mark 16:16; Acts 8:12-13; 18:8; 19:4). So presumably, the person with faith in Jesus Christ would expect to receive both baptism and the Holy Spirit. It is not much of a surprise, therefore, that the Holy Spirit is connected to baptism in a number of passages: "For we were all baptized by one Spirit into one body" (1 Cor 12:13; cf. Acts 2:38-39; 19:1-6; John 3:3-7; Titus 3:3-7). This affirmation of the Spirit coming with or in baptism does not, of course, preclude his sovereignty to fill, indwell, or empower at will. The Spirit of God is hardly constrained by norms or patterns in Scripture—he can do exceedingly more than was inscribed in the Bible! The Spirit does what he wants, where he wants, when he wants without our permission.

Thus, Peter calls for two actions and promises two effects. The two actions are repentance and baptism. The two effects are forgiveness of sins and the gift of the Spirit.[68] Repentance and baptism are faith responses; forgiveness and the Spirit are gifts God gives, not rights one earns. With these two observations, Acts 2:38 can be a blessing rather than a battleground for the church.

[40]With many other words he warned them; and he pleaded with them, "Save yourselves from this corrupt generation." [41]Those who accepted his message were baptized, and about three thousand were added to their number that day.

2:40. It is a bit odd that Luke mentions Peter's "many other words" since the sermon climaxed in verse 36 with Peter's acclamation of Jesus as Lord and Christ. There is really nothing of substance that needs to be added to that confession. Luke does, however, want to inform the reader that the discussion about Jesus

---

. . . All the doctors have ascribed to the water a power which it does not have and the holy apostles did not teach" [emphasis added]. By "doctors," Zwingli meant "church fathers" who unanimously affirmed the salvific efficacy of baptism. For the primary material on the church fathers' view of baptism see Jack Cottrell, "The Biblical Consensus: Historical Backgrounds to Reformed Theology," in *Baptism and the Remission of Sins: An Historical Perspective* (ed. David Fletcher; Joplin, MO: College Press, 1990), 28-32.

[68] One should bear in mind that the Holy Spirit for Luke (as well as John), in contradistinction to Paul, is not so much the power of God working *in* you for *sanctification* as it is the power of God working *through* you for *evangelism.* Cf. Mark E. Moore, "The Comforter Has Come with Power," in *Fanning the Flame: Probing the Issues in Acts* (ed. Mark E. Moore; Joplin: College Press, 2003), 192-209; F. F. Bruce, "The Holy Spirit in the Acts of the Apostles," *Int* 27 (1978): 166-183; and Craig Keener, *The Spirit in the Gospels and Acts* (Peabody: Hendrickson, 1997).

continued for quite some time.[69] This is as one would expect. When three thousand accept Jesus as Messiah there will be much to discuss, teach, and debate.

2:41. Logistically, baptizing three thousand is quite a feat. Jews did immerse in large pools hewn into the bedrock (called *mikveh* ⬛) before entering the temple (*m. Yoma* 3.3). The question, however, is whether there would be enough of these 'baptisteries' to accommodate so many. Older critics scoffed at the idea saying it was not possible. Archaeologists, however, have put the question to rest by uncovering some forty-eight *mikvehs* adjacent to the temple mount.[70] They had stairs on either side so lines of pilgrims could walk through the baths immersing themselves for ritual cleansing. Since Christian baptism was not self-immersion, it would take considerably longer, particularly if they were teaching, exhorting, and celebrating with each convert. Even so, the sermon began at 9:00 a.m. Even if it concluded at noon, that would give the entire afternoon for baptisms (ostensibly by the entire 120). It would be a full day but certainly doable. Three thousand believed Peter's preaching, demonstrated their repentance through immersion, and were thus counted among the early believers. The 120 suddenly exploded exponentially.

4. A Description of the Pristine Church (2:42-47)

Luke now pauses his narrative to give kind of a state-of-the-church address. These little summaries punctuate his book, particularly when the church crosses a barrier—first sermon, first persecution, first internal disunity, etc. (2:42-47; 4:32-37; 5:12-16, 42; 6:7; [8:25]; 9:3; [12:24]; 28:30-31).[71] Though each summary is different, they overlap substantially surrounding two constellations of characteristics: (1) Through Apostolic witness the church grows exponentially. (2) The church clung together in unity of heart, mind, and resources.

[42]They devoted themselves to the apostles' teaching and to the fellowship, to the breaking of bread and to prayer. [43]Everyone was filled with awe, and many wonders and miraculous signs were done by the apostles. [44]All the believers were together and had everything in common. [45]Selling their possessions and goods, they gave to anyone as he had need. [46]Every day they continued to meet together in the temple courts. They broke bread in their homes and ate together with glad and sincere hearts, [47]praising God and enjoying the favor of all the people. And the Lord added to their number daily those who were being saved.

---

[69] This was apparently a common literary device to remind the reader that the speech had been abbreviated (cf. Xenophon, *Hellenica* 2.4.42; Polybius 21.14.4; 3.111.11); see van der Horst, "Hellenistic Parallels," 57. More than that, it forced the readers to use their own imaginations to fill in the gaps; cf. Kathy Maxell, "The Role of the Audience in Ancient Narrative: Acts as a Case Study," *RQ* 48 (2006): 171-180.

[70] Cf. Ronny Reich, "The Great Mikveh Debate," *BAR* 19 (1993): 52-53; Bill Grasham, "Archaeology and Christian Baptism," *RQ* 43 (2001): 113-116; and Eyal Regev, "The Ritual Baths near the Temple Mount and Extra-Purification before Entering the Temple Courts," *IEJ* 55 (2005): 194-204.

[71] Gregory E. Sterling, "'Athletes of Virtue': An Analysis of the Summaries in Acts (2:41-47; 4:32-35; 5:12-16)," *JBL* 113 (1994): 679-696, helps put these summaries on the social map of his day—how social networks formed and functioned. Cf. Andreas Lindemann, "The Beginnings of Christian Life in Jerusalem according to the Summaries in the Acts of the Apostles (Acts 2:42-47; 4:32-37; 5:12-16)," in *Common Life in the Early Church* (ed. Julian V. Hills; Philadelphia: Trinity Press International, 1998), 202-218.

2:42-43. There are four things that marked the early church. They were habitual in Apostolic teaching, mutual living,[72] Eucharistic meals,[73] and prayer. This still serves as an admirable template for 'doing church' which will win the attention and approval of unbelievers (v. 47). But this original church had a special advantage as they 'launched'. Namely (v. 43), the Apostles bore a unique and unparalleled testimony to the life, death, and resurrection of Jesus that was bolstered with miraculous signs and wonders.

2:44-45. The unity of the early disciples was not merely doctrinal, it was social and economic.[74] This utopian description of a pristine community has been attacked at three levels. (1) Luke's critics accuse him of making this stuff up in order to present the early church as an ideal community—the kind of perfect society that Plato prescribed in his *Republic* (e.g., Conzelmann, 31).[75] In other words, these summaries are literary devices to stitch together the various pieces of tradition rather than a 'news report' of what actually happened.[76] Such skepticism fails to account for the actual living conditions of the early disciples. They were practicing the same benevolence their Jewish forefathers were commanded (Deut 15:4). This was particularly important for the Galilean disciples who had left jobs and family systems to follow Jesus. It is entirely plausible that this original band of disciples, especially for a short season,[77] lived with a shared community of goods since they had just witnessed the resurrection of Jesus, his ascension, and the Baptism of the Holy Spirit at Pentecost. They were living in extraordinary times which called for extraordinary measures of social cohesion. This is not so different from the practice of the Qumran community (1QS 5.2; cf. CD 14:13; Josephus, *J.W.* 2.8.3. §§122-123; *Ant* 18.1.5 §20; Philo, *Apology* 11.10-11).[78] The early church was charismatic and eschatological, leading

---

[72] The word "fellowship" (κοινωνία) is not simply gathering together but a communal devotion to the needs of the body. It is more of a food pantry than a fellowship dinner, more of an adoption than a babysitting co-op, more of a living together than a shared family vacation. Because of the luxurious privacy afforded by Western wealth, a biblical *koinōnia* is difficult to envision let alone enact.

[73] The Greek phrase is literally "*the* breaking of bread." This seems to indicate the Lord's Supper which was originally done at 'love feasts'. It appears that these meals were originally daily, providing an opportunity for benevolence as well as spiritual remembrance of the sacrifice of Jesus; cf. William Dowd, "Breaking Bread, Acts 2:46," *CBQ* 1 (1939): 358-362.

[74] The term ἐπὶ τὸ αὐτό (v. 44; cf. Acts 1:15; 2:1, 47; 4:26) appears to be a Semitism which means something to the effect of "in unison as a body;" Justin Taylor, "The Community of Goods among the First Christians and among the Essenes," in *Historical Perspectives: From the Hasmoneans to Bar Kokhba in Light of the Dead Sea Scrolls* (ed. David Goodblatt, Avital Pinnick, and Daniel Schwartz; Boston: Brill, 2001), 148. For a helpful collection of primary references of this term see Everett Ferguson, "'When You Come Together': *Epi To Auto* in Early Christian Literature," *RQ* 16 (1973): 202-208. It likely indicates something of a "Christian synagogue" with its own social boundaries, rules, and administration (Bruce, 132).

[75] For a host of ancient authors who describe the ideal communal society see van der Horst, "Hellenistic Parallels," 59-60. The similarities are, indeed, striking; cf. Rubén R. Dupertuis, "The Summaries of Acts 2, 4, and 5 and Plato's *Republic*," in *Ancient Fiction: The Matrix of Early Christian and Jewish Narrative* (ed. Jo-Ann A. Brant, Charles W. Hedrick, and Chris Shea; Leiden: Brill, 2005), 275-295. Of course, Plato was arguing for an ideal whereas Luke was describing a reality.

[76] Esp. Heinrich Zimmermann, "Die Sammelberichte der Apostelgeschichte," *BZ* 5 (1961): 71-82.

[77] Some have speculated that the church began to practice communism but simply ran out of funds due to the overwhelming needs exacerbated by phenomenal growth, thus the need for special offerings from Christians abroad (cf. Acts 11:27-30; 24:17; Gal 2:10; Harrison, 67, 90).

[78] Justin Taylor, "The Community of Goods among the First Christians and among the Essenes," in *Historical Perspectives: From the Hasmoneans to Bar Kokhba in Light of the Dead Sea Scrolls*; Studies on the Texts of the Desert of Judah 37 (ed. David Goodblatt, Avital Pinnick and Daniel R. Schwartz; Leiden: Brill, 2001), 147-161 and Reta Halteman Finger, "The Spirituality of Eating Together," in *Vital Christianity: Spirituality,*

to a radical sacrifice, especially as they expected the imminent return of Jesus (Krodel, 118; Barrett, 1:168).

(2) Luke's critics also find certain inconsistencies with Luke's descriptions of a pristine communalism. Namely, in Acts 2:44-45 and 4:32-35 the disciples sold their property and shared everything in common. Yet Acts 5:4 states that Ananias's property was his own to do with as he chose, and 6:1-6 indicates there were, in fact, widows in need. "So," say the critics, "which story are we to believe?" Did the church live communally or did they not?

(3) A third difficulty arose when certain social theorists latched onto these texts in order to propogate their own agenda of socialism. Consequently, many exegetes have taken great pains to explain away any reflection of Communism (or more acurately 'Stalinism') so odious to the modern West. As the pendulum has radically swung both left and right, Liberation theologians offer a salutary warn against facilely dismissing the economic and social implications of these summaries.[79]

Two things should be stated in response to these aforementioned difficulties. First, these are summary statements. Their brevity makes it difficult to extract a comprehensive social program. Luke's words *do* describe a communal sharing of which the western church has been woefully negligent.[80] But it would press Luke's language beyond acceptable measures to suggest that we have here a program equivalent to Marx's *Das Capital*. Second, one of the conundrums throughout Luke's work is deciphering what is description and what is prescription. Is Luke giving us a template for all churches? Or do his summaries bear the marks of a growing, morphing, changing church? It would appear that the voluntary sale of property for the benefit of the poor was a laudable example practiced by Spirit-led believers. While this practice was always encouraged (Acts 9:36; 11:27; 12:25; 24:17; Gal 2:10; etc.), it was probably never universal (practiced by every member) or absolute (so that one sold all his/her property).[81] In

---

Justice, and Christian Practice (ed. David L. Weaver-Zercher and William H. Willimon; New York: T&T Clark, 2005), 188-200.

[79] Frank Pimentel, "La Praxis de las Comunidades Cristianas al Comenzar un Nuevo Milenio: Una Lectura comunitaria y Actualizante de Hechos 2," *RIBLA* 33 (1999): 147-163. Laude Bridel, "Espiritu Comunitario y Diaconia segun los Hechos de los Apóstoles 2, 42 y 4, 32," *Seminarios* 23 (1977): 301-308. Of course, this is also of concern to Mennonite scholars among others; cf. Reta Halteman Finger, "Cultural Attitudes in Western Christianity toward the Community of Goods in Acts 2 and 4," *MQR* 78 (2004): 235-270.

[80] Bruce (81) described this as a *haburah*—a self-ruled community with a communal meal which serves the needs of the poor among them.

[81] The two primary descriptions of communal living were "had everything in common" (εἶχον ἅπαντα κοινά [2:44]) and "they shared everything they had" (ἦν αὐτοῖς ἅπαντα κοινά [4:32]). Neither of these preclude private ownership of property even among the Hellenistic literature describing idealized communal societies; cf. Steve Walton, "Primitive Communism in Acts? Does Acts Present the Community of Goods (2:44-45; 4:32-35) as Mistaken," *EQ* 80 (2008): 103-104. The fact is, the 'friendship' tradition in Hellenistic literature is varied and sometimes discordant; cf. Alan C. Mitchell, "The Social Function of Friendship in Acts 2:44-47 and 4:32-37," *JBL* 111 (1992): 255-257. Mitchell argues cogently that Luke uses the friendship tradition to describe the real need and encourage the actual praxis in the early church of the wealthy putting some of their resources at public disposal. Clearly the church continued to meet in private homes of wealthy patrons (Krodel, 117). For example, Mary's house (Acts 12:13) had a portico out front (τὴν θύραν τοῦ πυλῶνος) indicating a large home (BAG 729 πυλών §1; Josephus, *J.W.* 5.5.3 §202). Interestingly, archaeological speculation as to the location of Mary's house may be close to the mark; cf. Jerome Murphy-O'Connor, "The Cenacle—Topographical Setting for Acts 2:44-45," in *The Book of Acts in Its Palestinian Setting* (ed. Richard Bauckham; vol. 4 in *The Book of Acts in Its First Century Setting*, Grand Rapids: Eerdmans, 1995), 303-321.

conclusion, there is no real contradiction between the summaries in Acts 2 and 4 with other information in Acts because we don't have a consistent or comprehensive social program, nor do we have a static church that was obligated to live communally. The point of this text was not a social agenda which could be unilaterally exported. The point was the love Christians had for one another which expressed itself in pragmatic care for the economically weaker members of the body. That is the universal principle to which the church must attend.

2:46-47. Their public meetings in the temple and their private meetings in homes were their most effective apologetic. So often we think of evangelism as one person sharing the gospel with another individual. This is perfectly appropriate, one could even say "imperative." Nonetheless, their corporate evangelism—the church's living example to broader society—attracted the attention of the watching world. This sort of corporate care has an irresistible magnetic pull for pre-Christians. When the church is the church the world is drawn to Jesus.

ACTS 3

C. PERSECUTION (3:1–4:31)

A powerless church is easy to ignore. A church, however, that exercises the power of the Spirit soon encounters the powers of its surrounding society. We caught a glimpse of that in chapter 2. The tongues of Pentecost were attributed to sweet wine rather than the supreme Spirit. But this dissenting opinion was soon silenced by the overwhelming miracle crowned with Peter's Spirit-empowered preaching. In the following section, the dissenting voice will be louder, longer, and more violent. The miraculous healing of the lame man will illustrate (and in some ways explain) Peter's second sermon.[1] This time, however, the authorities arrest the Apostles and warn them in no uncertain terms that their public proclamation of the crucified Jesus is social dissent that will not be tolerated.

1. Miracle of the Lame Man (3:1-10)

This story is bigger than it looks. On the surface, we have a simple healing miracle. But it is bigger than that. Luke uses this miracle as a platform for Peter's preaching. That is not to say it is an 'excuse' to get to the good stuff. Rather, the miracle and the message are interwoven so that they work together to unveil the person of Jesus. Jesus is the power behind the miracle. If he can heal our bodies, there's a good chance he can save our souls.

But this miracle is bigger than that. It really must be read in tandem with Paul's healing of the lame man in 14:8-20. Both Apostles (Peter/Paul) stared (*atenizō*) at a man crippled since birth.[2] This deliberate parallelism purposefully draws the two healings into a single focus. In both instances, the Apostles (Peter and John/Paul and Barnabas) quickly divert the praise from themselves to Jesus who himself had healed a lame man (Luke 5:18-26). Jesus' healing had led to a vituperative debate about Jesus' ability to forgive sins. If one were simply to read Luke's two-volume work attentively, she would understand that healings of lame men function as enacted parables demonstrating Jesus as the one who forgives sins.[3] What happens with a lame man's

---

[1] For Luke, miracles are generative—they drive the narrative; Matti Myllykoski, "Being There: The Function of the Supernatural in Acts 1–12," in *Wonders Never Cease: The Purpose of Narrating Miracle Stories in the New Testament and Its Religious Environment* (ed. Michael Labahn, Bert Jan Lietaert Peerbolte, and L. J. Lietaert Peerbolte; New York: T&T Clark, 2006), 146-179. Each of the miracles stem from the primary miracle of the resurrection, validate the testimony of the Apostles, and themselves are substantiated through OT prophecies.

[2] This fascinating little word ἀτενίζω means "to look intently" usually with the implication of awe or consternation. Of its fourteen NT uses, twelve are by Luke (Luke 4:20; 5:10; 22:56; Acts 1:10; 3:4, 12; 6:15; 7:55; 10:4; 11:6; 13:9; 14:9; 23:1) and two by Paul (2 Cor 3:7, 13).

[3] The deliberate echoes of Jesus' ministry in those of Peter and Paul enables the reader to view each incident, not as an isolated event but in light of the patterns previously established. Thus, it is particularly important to keep an eye on Jesus as we move through the narrative of Acts; cf. Robert C. Tannehill, "The

legs visibly and undeniably depicts what Jesus can do with our sinful souls.

But it is bigger than that. Healing the lame was one of the quintessential acts of the Messiah. Isaiah 35:6 begins, "Then will the lame leap like a deer." This was the very text Jesus referenced when John the Baptist questioned his role as Messiah (Matt 11:5/Luke 7:22). These lame men leaping were evidence that Jesus was a veteran healer and able to pass his power on to the Apostles. More than that, these liberated legs announced the inauguration of the new Messianic age. With the lame men we launch into the last days, the age of the Messiah's rule through the Spirit.

¹**One day Peter and John were going up to the temple at the time of prayer— at three in the afternoon. ²Now a man crippled⁴ from birth was being carried to the temple gate called Beautiful, where he was put every day to beg from those going into the temple courts. ³When he saw Peter and John about to enter, he asked them for money. ⁴Peter looked straight at him, as did John. Then Peter said, "Look at us!" ⁵So the man gave them his attention, expecting to get something from them. ⁶Then Peter said, "Silver or gold I do not have, but what I have I give you. In the name of Jesus Christ of Nazareth, walk."**

3:1-2. Nothing in these verses is unfamiliar for those wearing a yarmulke. It is standard Judaism. Peter and John, who tend to be running buddies (Luke 5:10; 22:8; John 13:23-25; 20:2-8; 21:20-22; Acts 3:1, 3, 11; 4:13, 19; 8:14; Gal 2:9), arrive at the Temple ⁵ around the appointed Jewish time for afternoon prayers (about 3 p.m.; cf. Acts 10:30).⁶ There at the gate Beautiful,⁷ they find a beggar who had never walked a day in his life. Since he is now over forty (4:22) he has exceeded the life expectancy of a first-century male by nearly a decade. This is, no doubt, in large part due to his friends who carried him to the entrance of the

---

Composition of Acts 3–5: Narrative Development and Echo Effect," *SBLSP* 23 (1984): 217-240. Also helpful on Luke's theme of healing in relation to salvation is Ben Witherington, "Salvation and Health in Christian Antiquity: The Soteriology of Luke-Acts in Its First Century Setting," in *Witness to the Gospel: The Theology of Acts* (ed. I. Howard Marshall and David Peterson; Grand Rapids: Eerdmans, 1998), 145-166.

⁴This word χωλός is different from "paralytic." It affects the feet, ankles, knees or hips but is not complete paralysis. For a collection of ancient medical uses of the term see Pieter W. van der Horst, "Hellenistic Parallels to Acts (Chapters 3 and 4)," *JSNT* 35 (1989): 37-38. Those with weak ankles were taken to be people of weak character (in physiognomatic literature). Luke at least ignores and perhaps subverts this common cultural perception by avoiding the ribald humor normally leveled against the lame; cf. Mikeal C. Parsons, "The Character of the Lame Man in Acts 3–4," *JBL* 124 (2005): 295-312.

⁵Herod the Great had done a spectacular job rebuilding the temple, the foundations of which can be seen to this day at the Wailing Wall . He started approximately 19 B.C. and though it would not be complete until 63 A.D., the bulk of the work was finished. Josephus describes its glorious details (*Ant* 15.11.3-4 §396-402).

⁶The times of prayer were mid-morning (roughly 9 a.m.), mid-afternoon (roughly 3 p.m.), and at sunset. The first two were also accompanied by the daily sacrifice known as the *Tamid* (Num 28:4; Josephus, *Ant* 14.4.3 §65; *m. Tamid*). It is this Jewish sacrifice to which Luke refers more than any other; cf. Dennis Hamm, "The Tamid Service in Luke-Acts: The Cultic Background behind Luke's Theology of Worship (Luke 1:5-25; 18:9-14; 24:50-53; Acts 3:1; 10:3, 30)," *CBQ* 25 (2003): 215-231.

⁷It is unfortunate that we will likely never know with certainty which gate this was. For various arguments as to the location see *Beginnings* 4:32 and 5:479-486; E. Stauffer, "Das Tor des Nikanor," *ZNW* 44 (1952–53): 44-66; Dennis Hamm, "Acts 3:1-10: The Healing of the Temple Beggar as Lucan Theology," *Bib* 67 (1986): 305-319. Perhaps the Nicanor gate is our best guess. Josephus describes this gate as two double doors, 45 feet high, covered with Corinthian bronze (*J.W.* 5.5.3 §201). In a fascinating comment, *m. Mid.* 2.3 says, "All the gates which were there were changed [and covered] with gold, except for Niqanor's gate, because a miracle was done with them," cf. *m. Yoma* 3.10.

temple to beg, thus caring for his physical needs. Though he was banned from the temple due to his disability (Lev 21:17-20),[8] he profited from the pious who went in to worship.[9] But this was his lucky day. As his friends were 'depositing' him at the gate, Peter and John bumped into him at exactly the right time.

3:3-6. As he catches their eye, he goes to work, asking for alms. Peter stares hard at him (*atenizō*) as did John, and they asked that he return their gaze (*blepō*). Perhaps he had assumed a typical posture for beggars casting his eyes to the ground. Once Peter had his full attention, he refused his request for money. This disappointment would be short-lived, of course. Peter's healing eclipses any monetary gain the lame man could have dreamed of: "In the name of Jesus Christ of Nazareth, walk (around) [*peripateō*]." Peter's charge is packed with theological innovation. First, "Jesus Christ" appears as an appellation, not as a description. In other words, "Christ" is not a descriptive title but a personal name of Jesus. Peter is the first to use "Jesus Christ" as a full name (cf. 2:38), aside from the introductions to Matthew (1:1, 18), Mark (1:1), and John (1:17) where such a fully developed Christology is expected.[10] Some would argue this is really Luke's wording, not Peter's, since "Christ" as a name would take some time to catch on. But there is no way to prove that. The resurrection validated Jesus as the Messiah, and the early believers latched onto that incredibly quickly. Peter's preaching is as valid a starting place for the use of Christ as an appellation as any.

This exalted "name" stands out all the more since it is juxtaposed to Jesus' hometown of Nazareth, a place where he had no honor ⬛. This juxtaposition of "full name" and "place of origin" is the normal way of identifying an individual, but with Jesus, it just seems odd that *the* Messiah would originate from a place of no account.

A second theological innovation of Peter's command is the "name" of Jesus. Though it has been invoked twice in the last chapter (2:21, 38), it will become a recurring theme in chapters 3–5. The "name," of course, is not some magical incantation. It represents the power and authority of the individual. Those who

---

[8] The blind and lame were classed with sinners or the impure (cf. John 9:1-2, 34; CD 15:15-20; 1 QM 7:4; 1 QSa 2:3-7; 11QT 45:14-16). Jesus, in striking contrast, considered them model kingdom citizens (cf. Luke 14:15-24; 16:19-31). It is striking that the Targumim on Zeph 3:19, Isa 35:6; and Mic 4:6-8 each replace the "lame" of the biblical text with "exiles." Craig A. Evans, "A Note on Targum 2 Samuel 5.8 and Jesus' Ministry to the 'Maimed, Halt, and Blind'," *JSP* 15 (1997): 81-82, rightly observes that this places the healing of the lame in an eschatological, Messianic context of restoration. Yet this euphemistic substitution might suggest more. Namely, the use of "exiles" effectively reinterprets the biblical texts so that the literal lame can remain marginalized. In this light, the healing of the lame and blind would be all the more poignant.

[9] Surprisingly, there is little documentation about beggars at the temple gates outside this reference, though they were found at the synagogues (Cleomedes, *De Motu circulari* 2.1, 91; Artemidorus, *Oneirocritica* 3.53). However, since alms were a particularly important part of Jewish piety, along with Torah and worship (*m. Abot* 1.2), there is little doubt about their presence.

[10] The only exception is John 17:3 where John has understandably retrojected this anachronistic title on the lips of Jesus. To John's readers at the end of the first century this would make perfect sense. Luke will use this appellation eleven times in his Gospel. In the book of Acts, thirteen uses are titular (2:31; 36; 3:18, 20; 4:26; 5:42; 8:5; 9:22; 17:3 [2x]; 18:5, 28; 26:23), five represent Jesus' appellation (9:34; 10:36; 11:17; 24:24; 28:31) and seven more are an appellation identified with the "name" of Jesus (2:38; 3:6; 4:10; 8:12; 10:48; 15:26; 16:18). Cf. Craig L. Blomberg, "Messiah in the New Testament," in *Israel's Messiah in the Bible and the Dead Sea Scrolls* (ed. Richard S. Hess and Daniel Carroll; Grand Rapids: Baker Academic, 2003), 111-141.

had been called by Jesus, who carried out his commission, were able to heal in the "name of Jesus" (3:6, 16; 4:10, 30), find courage amidst suffering because of his name (4:7, 17, 18; 5:28, 40, 41), and ultimately proclaim salvation through his name (4:12).

⁷Taking him by the right hand, he helped him up, and instantly the man's feet and ankles became strong. ⁸He jumped to his feet and began to walk. Then he went with them into the temple courts, walking and jumping,¹¹ and praising God. ⁹When all the people saw him walking and praising God, ¹⁰they recognized him as the same man who used to sit begging at the temple gate called Beautiful, and they were filled with wonder and amazement at what had happened to him.

3:7-10. Peter snatches the lame man by the hand and jerks him up.¹² Luke describes with precision what happened to the man's ankles.¹³ Predictably, the guy goes ballistic. His worship was, shall we say, aerobic! For the first time he is able to enter the temple. He had been a temple fixture at the foot of the gate Beautiful for four decades. Now he is a bundle of ADHD exuberance that the locals identify as the formerly sad, sedentary beggar. Their response was standard fare for healings: wonder (*thambos*, Luke 4:36; 5:9) and amazement (*ekstasis*, astonishment, Mark 5:42; 16:8; Luke 5:26; Acts 3:10, or a trance, Acts 10:10; 11:5; 22:17). It will come as no surprise that when Peter starts to preach, he has their undivided attention!

2. Peter Responds by Proclaiming the Name of Jesus (3:11-26)

Peter's sermons in Acts 2 and 3 have substantial similarities.¹⁴ Both begin with the phrase "Men of Israel" (2:22; 3:12). Both immediately remove the Apostles from focus (2:15-16; 3:12-13). Both present Jesus as the Jewish Messiah whom the Jews killed but God raised (2:23-24; 3:13-14, 26). Both extend an offer of repentance, forgiveness of sins, and consequent blessings for accepting Jesus (2:38; 3:19). And both bolster the Apostolic witness with prophecies presenting Jesus as the fulfillment of the great leaders of Israel: David (2:25, 35), Moses (3:22-23), and Abraham (3:25-26). These very similar sermons, however, have very different responses. In Acts 2 three thousand Jewish 'expatriates' repent and are baptized. In Acts 4 the leaders arrest and threaten the Apostles.

¹¹While the beggar held on to Peter and John, all the people were astonished and came running to them in the place called Solomon's Colonnade. ¹²When Pe-

---

¹¹ "Jumping" = ἅλλομαι = LXX Isa 35:6!

¹² This appears to be the implication of πιάζω, which is a fairly violent word. In the rest of the NT it means to capture/arrest someone (John 7:30, 32, 44; 8:20; 10:39; 11:57; Acts 12:4; 2 Cor 11:32; Rev 19:20) or to catch fish (John 21:3, 10). The recipient of the actions is hardly a volunteer!

¹³ The phrase "feet and ankles became strong" was used by ancient physicians. However, the medical vocabulary here, as elsewhere, in the book of Acts is not definitive enough to conclude from that alone that Luke was a physician; cf. *Beginnings* 4:33; contra William Hobart, *The Medical Language of St. Luke* (Grand Rapids: Baker, 1954). The strongest evidence for this still stands with Paul's direct statement, "Our dear friend Luke, the doctor" (Col 4:14).

¹⁴ For a helpful rhetorical analysis of Peter's second speech one is commended to Takaaki Haraguchi, "A Call for Repentance to the Whole Israel—Rhetorical Study of Acts 3:12-26," *AJT* 18 (2004): 267-282.

ter saw this, he said to them: "Men of Israel, why does this surprise you? Why do you stare at us as if by our own power or godliness we had made this man walk? ¹³The God of Abraham, Isaac and Jacob, the God of our fathers, has glorified his servant Jesus. You handed him over to be killed, and you disowned him before Pilate, though he had decided to let him go. ¹⁴You disowned the Holy and Righteous One and asked that a murderer be released to you. ¹⁵You killed the author of life, but God raised him from the dead. We are witnesses of this. ¹⁶By faith in the name of Jesus, this man whom you see and know was made strong. It is Jesus' name and the faith that comes through him that has given this complete healing to him, as you can all see."

3:11. This formerly lame man stopped bouncing long enough to latch onto Peter and John. The crowd gathered at the spectacle. They assembled in Solomon's Colonnade , the largest gathering place in the temple compound. It could accommodate thousands of spectators. It was a favorite meeting place for the early church (Acts 5:12; cf. 1 Kgs 7:6; John 10:23), a beautiful covered colonnade with twenty-seven foot columns supporting cedar rafters overhead. What caught their attention was not the magnificent building but the outstanding miracle. They were flabbergasted (v. 11, *ekthambos*; v. 12, *thaumazō*).

3:12. When Peter asked, "Why does this surprise you?" (v. 12) he obviously knew. Miracles were supposed to surprise people! His point was that the wonder should not be directed at him and John who had no extraordinary power or piety in and of themselves. That honor belongs to Jesus the "Holy and Righteous One" (v. 14). If a meager miracle performed on ankles merits such notoriety, how much more should the resurrection of Jesus validate him as God's Messiah?!

3:13-15. The following verses paint a pretty bleak picture. Notice the difference in God's view of Jesus (descriptions in italics) and that of Peter's audience:

VERSE	GOD:	"YOU":
13	glorified his *servant* Jesus	handed him over to Pilate to be wrongfully killed
14		disowned the *Holy and Righteous One*
15	raised him from the dead	killed the *author of life*

Jesus' brutal execution, ignoble betrayal, and extradition to the pagan Pilate make him look like a wicked thug (Luke 22:52-53; John 18:30). The wickedness, however, was not in Jesus but in his enemies. Peter's portrait is crystal clear. They stood not only as enemies of Jesus but of Yahweh himself, the God of their fathers.¹⁵ Peter was not only addressing the contemporary event of Jesus' unjust murder, he was suggesting that by rejecting Jesus, they had abandoned their national heritage. Even more, they had killed the *servant*, the *Holy and Righteous One*, the very *Author of Life*. Each of these three terms is significant.

---

¹⁵ Peter uses a kosher title for God (cf. Exod 3:6, 15, 16; 4:5; Luke 20:37; Acts 7:32) that also opened the Eighteen Benedictions, the most famous of the Jewish liturgical prayers: "Blessed art thou, O Lord our God and God of our fathers, God of Abraham, God of Isaac, and God of Jacob."

The *servant* of Yahweh in the Old Testament is normally the entire nation of Israel.[16] Nonetheless, in a number of passages the nation was embodied in a specific individual (esp. Isa 42:7; 53:11), particularly David and Moses.[17] Thus, the *servant* became a synonym for Messiah. The *Holy and Righteous One* reflects the character of Yahweh (Rev 15:4) which might be embodied in one of his prophets (Mark 6:20; 2 Kgs 4:9) or Apostles (1 Thess 2:10). The *Author of Life* is a difficult concept to translate. "Author" (*archēgos*) has the idea of "originator" or "founder" (cf. Acts 5:31; Heb 2:10; 12:2). The implication is a person who controls something because he started it. Imagine the implications of killing the very one who originated and supervises life! Jesus is thus described as the paramount person in God's eyes and Israel's history. He was abused in a most inhumane and violent way.

3:16. The risen Jesus was responsible for healing the lame man, not Peter and John. As Hamm puts it in a tidy turn of phrase, "One raising leads to another."[18] Fidelity ("faith") to his authority ("name") is what granted this healing—this complete and undeniable witness to the reality of Jesus' identity.

[17]**"Now, brothers, I know that you acted in ignorance, as did your leaders.** [18]**But this is how God fulfilled what he had foretold through all the prophets, saying that his Christ[a] would suffer.** [19]**Repent, then, and turn to God, so that your sins may be wiped out, that times of refreshing may come from the Lord,** [20]**and that he may send the Christ, who has been appointed for you—even Jesus.** [21]**He must remain in heaven until the time comes for God to restore everything, as he promised long ago through his holy prophets."**

[a]*18 Or Messiah*; also in verse 20

3:17-18. Peter's portrait in the previous verses is pretty grim. Here there is a glimmer of hope, namely, their ignorance.[19] Neither Peter's audience nor the Jerusalem hierarchy were aware of who Jesus really was (a fact also noted by Jesus [Luke 23:34] and Paul [Acts 13:27; 1 Cor 2:8]). Moreover, his suffering was foretold by the prophets. This was not merely the malice of mean men; it was the plan of the sovereign God.[20] Luke repeatedly asserts that Jesus' suffering was a divine necessity predicted in Scripture (Luke 18:31-32; 22:22; 24:26-27, 46; Acts

---

[16]Lev 25:42, 55; Deut 32:36, 43; 1 Chr 16:13; 2 Chr 6:27; Neh 1:6, 10; 2:20; Psa 105:6; Isa 41:8-9; 42:19; 43:10; 44:1-2, 21; 45:4; 48:20; 49:3, 5-7; Jer 2:14; 30:10; 46:27-28; Ezek 28:25; 37:25. Cf. J. Jeremias, "παῖς θεοῦ," *TDNT* 5:677-717 (684).

[17]*Moses*, Exod 14:31; Num 12:7, 8; Deut 34:5; Josh 1:1, 2, 7, 13, 15; 8:31, 33; 9:24; 11:12, 15; 12:6; 13:8; 14:7; 22:2, 4, 5; 1 Kgs 8:53, 56; 2 Kgs 18:12; 21:8; 1 Chr 6:49; 2 Chr 1:3; 24:6, 9; Neh 1:7-8; 9:14; 10:29; Psa 105:26; Dan 9:11; Mal 4:4; *David*, 2 Sam 3:18; 7:5 [/1 Chr 17:4], 8 [/1 Chr 17:7]; 1 Kgs 3:6; 8:24-26 [/2 Chr 6:15-17], 66; 11:13, 32, 34, 36, 38; 14:8; 2 Kgs 8:19; 20:6; 2 Chr 6:42; Psa 18:1 [0]; 36:1 [0]; 78:70; 89:5 [3], 20 [22]; 132:10; 144:10; Isa 37:35; Jer 33:22, 26; Ezek 34:23-24; 37:24.

[18]Dennis Hamm, "Acts 3:12-26: Peter's Speech and the Healing of the Man Born Lame," *PRS* 11 (1984): 202.

[19]This is not to say that ignorance is an excuse for sin, but it did make it 'forgivable' according to Jewish law (Num 15:22-31). Ignorance was commonly viewed as the cause of sin (cf. Euripides, *Hippolytus*, 1334-1335; Xenophon, *Cyropaedia* 3.1.38; Epictetus, *Disc.* 1.26.6; Plutarch, *Divine Vengeance* 6, 551E).

[20]Lubahn rightly points out the invalidity of Christian anti-Semitism due to the death of Jesus. Jesus willingly laid down his own life (John 10:15, 18) according to the preordained plan of God (Acts 3:18; 4:28). The Jewish and Roman complicity was due to divinely induced ignorance (see comments on 3:17). Cf. Erich Lubahn, "Wer ist schuld am Kreuzestode Jesu? Eine Auslegung von Apg 4,27f; 3,18," *Mission an Israel in heilsgeschichtlicher Sicht* (ed. Heinz Kremers and Erich Lubahn; Neukirchen-Vluyn: Neukirchener Verlag, 1985), 12-23.

3:18; 17:3; 26:22-23; cf. Luke 9:22; 13:33; 17:25;).[21] However, he never quoted a specific text which predicted Jesus' suffering.[22] For Luke, the prediction was not so much built on proof-texts but biographies. In verses 22-26 Jesus will be compared with Moses and Abraham, both of whom suffered in the service of God. Chapter 2 compared Jesus with David, who suffered as the Servant of the Lord. In Chapter 7 Stephen will rehearse the entire history of Israel showing Jesus as the fulfillment of a litany of national heroes, all of whom suffered for the glory of the kingdom. This particular hermeneutical move appears to have first been made by Jesus himself:

> Therefore I am sending you prophets and wise men and teachers. Some of them you will kill and crucify; others you will flog in your synagogues and pursue from town to town. And so upon you will come all the righteous blood that has been shed on earth, from the blood of righteous Abel to the blood of Zechariah son of Berekiah, whom you murdered between the temple and the altar. I tell you the truth, all this will come upon this generation. "O Jerusalem, Jerusalem, you who kill the prophets and stone those sent to you, how often I have longed to gather your children together, as a hen gathers her chicks under her wings, but you were not willing." (Matt 23:34-37).

3:19. Peter now arrives at the decisive moment of his message when he calls for decision. Those of us weaned on a church pew tend to miss the unprecedented majesty of this invitation. The original audience surely did not. After rejecting God's Messiah there was still a gracious opportunity to repent. The depth of God's kindness, forgiveness, and mercy is unfathomable.

Acts 3:19 is strikingly parallel to 2:38:

2:38	3:19
Repent	Repent
Be baptized	Turn to God
For (eis) the forgiveness of sins	So that (eis) your sins will be wiped out
You will receive the gift of the Holy Spirit	That times of refreshing may come from the Lord

[21] The theme of Jesus' scripturally mandated suffering precedes Luke and appears to go back to the historical Jesus: (1) δεῖ, Mark 8:31; Matt 26:54; Luke 13:33; 17:25; (2) κατὰ τὸ ὡρισμένον, Luke 22:22; (3) γέγραπται, Mark 9:12; 14:21; (4) ἵνα πληρωθῶσιν αἱ γραφαί, Mark 14:49; (5) πῶς οὖν πληρωθῶσιν αἱ γραφαί, Matt 26:54; and (6) τελεσθήσεται πάντα τὰ γεγραμμένα, Luke 18:31.

[22] Frankly, there are few good candidates. Though Psa 22 was used by Christian authors to describe the crucifixion, in its original context it is not clearly Messianic. The same could be said for Psa 118:22 and a handful of others (e.g., Psa 89:39-40 [38]; Jer 11:19). There are really only two OT texts which were potentially Messianic *and* included sufferings: Zech 12:10 and Isa 53. The rabbinic commentaries on each of these shows what a novel, unpalatable concept was a suffering Messiah. As Hooker says, "Thus we find, on the one hand, that those passages which speak of a 'Messiah' all avoid the concept of suffering. . . . Those references, on the other hand, which do include the concept of suffering are never found in a Messianic context," Morna D. Hooker, *Jesus and the Servant: The Influence of the Servant Concept of Deutero-Isaiah in the New Testament* (London: SPCK, 1959), 57. Zech 12:10 and Isa 53 aside, the only pre-Christian text that predicts a suffering Messiah is 2 Esd 7:29, "After those years my son the Messiah shall die, and all who draw human breath." Clearly the Messiah dies, but merely as a mortal man at the end of the present age before the new age begins.

Though the wording varies between these two invitations, the process is identical.[23] They were given the extraordinarily gracious opportunity to repent even though their rejection of Jesus was the worst sort of scandal against God. If they did repent, their sins would be forgiven[24] and they would be given a new lease on life with God. Luke translates this as "times of refreshing." This is the only time this noun "refreshment" is used in the New Testament, though the verb is found once in 2 Tim 1:16, "May the Lord show mercy to the household of Onesiphorus, because he often refreshed me and was not ashamed of my chains." Though the phrase (*kairoi anapsuxeōs*) is not found in the LXX, it is found in another Greek translation of the Old Testament (Symmachus) at a most striking place—Isaiah 32:15. Here the outpouring of the Spirit would bring a new eschatological era of fruitfulness and blessing. For Luke it likewise means "the Messianic age."[25] This is the 'season' of the Holy Spirit whose work is described as refreshment and renewal (e.g., Isa 44:1-4; John 7:38-39; Heb 4:1-13; 2 Esdras 11:46).

3:20-21. Verse 19 promised two things would result from repentance: forgiveness and refreshment. Verse 20 adds a third promise: the coming of Jesus. The question is whether Jesus' coming is a metaphor for conversion (e.g., John 14:23) or a promise of his return. It may seem odd that conversion could facilitate Christ's coming. Nonetheless, Peter's verbiage suggests that as a real possibility. Verse 20, frankly, could refer to either a spiritual relationship or the second coming. Verse 21, however, leans toward the latter: (1) Jesus "must remain in heaven" until the appointed time. That would be a strange metaphor, indeed, for the Christian life.[26] (2) This appointed time is the *renewal* of all things. That sounds more eschatological than mystical. (3) The promise through the prophets for "total" restoration surely goes beyond merely a spiritual promise to individuals.

---

[23] The Bible extends the gospel invitation with a surprising variety of verbiage: "Call on the name of the Lord" (Acts 2:21; 4:12; 9:14, 21; Rom 10:13; 1 Cor 1:2); Believe (Acts 16:30-31 [with hearing v. 32 and baptism v. 33]; Heb 10:39; cf. Luke 8:12) or have faith (Eph 2:5, 8); Believe and confess (Rom 10:9-10); "Believe and be Baptized" (Mark 16:16) or washing of rebirth and the renewal by the Holy Spirit (Tit 3:5); Respond to the message (1 Cor 1:18; 15:2; cf. 1 Thess 2:16) or love the truth (2 Thess 2:10; 1 Tim 2:4); and this odd one: "Women will be saved through childbearing" (1 Tim 2:15). None of this, of course, is viewed as 'work' to our credit, rather salvation is a work of God who chose us to be saved (Rom 5:9-10; Phil 1:28; 2 Thess 2:13; 2 Tim 1:9). That being said, Acts 2:38 and 3:19 are *not* two different invitations. The variation in wording is merely synecdoche whereby the entire process of conversion is abbreviated by one or two aspects pertinent to the present recipient(s). The absence of the word "baptism" in 3:19 no more negates it as integral than does the absence of "faith," "confession," or "calling on the name of the Lord."

[24] The word used here for "forgiven" (ἐξαλείφω) is relatively rare in the NT (elsewhere only in Col 2:14; Rev 3:5; 7:17; 21:4). It has the idea of rubbing out a written record.

[25] Luke's word for "time[s]" (καιροί) is plural, thus indicating that he has in view the interim between the ascension and the *parousia*, not the final consummation of the ages; cf. Hans F. Bayer, "Christ-Centered Eschatology in Acts 3:17-26," in *Jesus of Nazareth: Lord and Christ: Essays on the Historical Jesus and New Testament Christology* (ed. Joel B. Green and Max Turner; Grand Rapids: Eerdmans, 1994), 245; and C. K. Barrett, "Faith and Eschatology in Acts 3," in *Glaube und Eschatologie* (ed. Georg Kümmel, Erich Grässer, and Otto Merk; Tübingen: Mohr, 1985), 1-17. As Ferdinand Hahn pointed out, Luke has taken a Jewish tradition of national renewal and woven it into a new Christian eschatology; cf. "Das Problem alter christologischer Überlieferungen in der Apostelgeschichte unter besonderer Berücksichtigung von Act 3, 19-21," in *Les Actes des Apôtres: Traditions, rédaction, théologie* (ed. by J. Kremer; Leuven: Leuven University Press, 1979), 129-154.

[26] Lohfink's objection that the word "send" (ἀποστέλλω) must refer to the Christian life since it is not used for the second coming elsewhere is ill founded, for it is not elsewhere used of a spiritual indwelling either; cf. Gerhard Lohfink, "Christologie und Geschichtsbild in Apg 3, 19-21," *BZ* 13 (1969): 233-234. Moreover, when Jesus is given the title "apostle" in Heb 3:1, it is *not* a metaphor. Here the context, not lexicography, must be determinative.

A corporate and eschatological fulfillment seems to be what Peter has in mind. It is the kind of thing Jesus promised in Matthew 19:28,[27] "I tell you the truth, at the renewal of all things, when the Son of Man sits on his glorious throne, you who have followed me will also sit on twelve thrones, judging the twelve tribes of Israel." If this is Peter's intention, then the return of Jesus is, in some mysterious way, connected to conversion. That is, repentance leads not only to individuals having their sins forgiven and lives refreshed, but it may well usher in the return of Jesus. Matthew 24:14 speaks to the same issue when Jesus said, "And this gospel of the kingdom will be preached in the whole world as a testimony to all nations, and then the end will come."[28] Jesus and Peter are following a tradition well-worn by rabbis—Messiah will come when Israel lives out Torah.

22"For Moses said, 'The Lord your God will raise up for you a prophet like me from among your own people; you must listen to everything he tells you. 23Anyone who does not listen to him will be completely cut off from among his people.'ª 24Indeed, all the prophets from Samuel on, as many as have spoken, have foretold these days. 25And you are heirs of the prophets and of the covenant God made with your fathers. He said to Abraham, 'Through your offspring all peoples on earth will be blessed.'ᵇ 26When God raised up his servant, he sent him first to you to bless you by turning each of you from your wicked ways."

ª*23* Deut. 18:15, 18, 19   ᵇ*25* Gen. 22:18; 26:4

It was nothing short of revolutionary for Peter to claim that Jesus fulfilled David's prophecy (2:30). Now he is going to press the point further. Jesus is not only the 'greater David', he is the 'new Moses' *and* the blessing of Abraham. This trilogy (David, Moses, Abraham) encompassed the primary patrons of Israel (King, Law-giver, and Father).[29] There simply are no metaphors to capture the wonder and scandal of such a bodacious claim.

3:22-23. Peter cites Deuteronomy 18:15 (as will Stephen, 7:37). It is surprising how little had been made of this promise given the prominence of Moses in Jewish lore and literature.[30] Peter's comment, "You must listen to everything he

---

[27] This same expectation is expressed in different words by Paul (Rom 8:18-25), Peter (2 Pet 3:13), and John (Rev 21:1-5). This is not surprising given its OT precedent (e.g., Isa 65:17-20; 66:22).

[28] Though the promise of Matt 24:14 had immediate reference to the destruction of Jerusalem in A.D. 70, the principle it contains pushes ever outward, even to the ends of the earth, space, and time. What was true in the microcosm of Jerusalem in A.D. 70 will be true in the macrocosm of Jesus' *parousia*. Furthermore, it is not a new principle. It was founded on the exodus. The forty years wilderness wandering was a result of Israel's disobedience to God's marching orders (Num 14:33-34). Likewise, the delay of the *parousia* may be due more to the church's persistent indolence rather than God's inexhaustible patience for people to repent.

[29] A number of scholars have argued that 3:19-21 evidences the earliest Christology, namely, Jesus is the new Elijah; e.g., Haenchen, 170-172; J. A. T. Robinson, "The Most Primitive Christology of All?" *JTS* 7 n.s. (1956): 177-189; Joseph G. Kelly, "Lucan Christology and the Jewish-Christian Dialogue," *JES* 21 (1984): 688-708. Though "times of refreshing" does reflect similar ideology as Mal 4:5-6 [3:23-24], this theory has insurmountable difficulties; not least is that Luke himself records John the Baptist as Elijah (Luke 1:17; 7:27). Moreover, the stress in the first two speeches of Acts is not Jesus as Elijah, but as David, Moses, and Abraham's seed.

[30] Str-B 2:626-627; *Beginnings* 1:404-408. Aside from the overt claim Luke makes through Peter (Acts 3:22) and Stephen (7:37) and John's veiled references (John 1:19-23; 6:14), only 4Q175, Philo, *Spec. Laws* 1.64-65, and *Sib. Or.* 5.346-50 make much of this prophecy as a Messianic reference. The Samaritans, however, did have the belief that the Messiah (*Taheb*) would be a Moses figure, but their documents outlining this belief are not earlier than the fourth century (*Marqah* 4.7, 12; cf. John 1:21; 4:19, 25).

tells you," is likely a not-so-subtle reference to Deuteronomy 18:19 (borrowing words from Lev 23:29), "If anyone does not listen to my words that the prophet speaks in my name, I myself will call him to account." The people had requested a substitute for the voice of God lest the fire of Mt. Horeb consume them (Deut 18:16). God agreed and reiterated the promise for a future Moses (Deut 18:18) followed by this stern warning that the people better listen (v. 19). Peter's argument is simple. Jesus is the fulfillment of this promise for a new Moses. Since they killed him the first time, they had better listen to him now or answer to God in the near future.

3:24-26. Peter purports that from Samuel on, all the prophets unanimously predicted *this age*. Samuel is significant because he anointed David (1 Sam 16:13) inaugurating the royal dynasty through which the Messiah would come. The prophets envisioned an eschatological age characterized by forgiveness of sins, intimacy with God, and national peace and prosperity. These hopes are now fulfilled, not through materialistic or nationalistic power, but in the power of the Spirit. This is what it means, according to Peter, that Abraham's promised seed had come to bless the world. The most common understanding of the promise (Gen 22:18; cf. 12:3; 18:18; 26:4) was that the nation of Israel would bless the nations. Peter's proposal is that Jesus is the embodiment of that nation and he, himself, is the blessing (cf. Gal 3:16). How so? There is a clue in the word "raised up" (*anistēmi*). Luke uses this very word for the prophet who fulfills Moses (v. 22) as well as the fulfilled promise of Abraham's seed (v. 26). *Anistēmi* describes God raising Jesus from the dead (e.g., Luke 24:46; Acts 2:24, 32). This little play on words is a helpful reminder that Jesus' exclusive status as the eschatological David and Moses, as well as the singular seed of Abraham, was forged by God when he raised Jesus from the dead.[31]

---

[31] For substantial arguments that ἀνίστημι is, in fact, a reference to the resurrection in vv. 22 and 26 see Jacques Schlosser, "Moïse, serviteur du kérygme apostolique d'après Ac 3,22-26," *RSR* 61 (1987): 17-31; and R. F. O'Toole, "Some Observations on *Anistēmi*, 'I Raise', in Acts 3:22, 26," *ScEs* 31 (1979): 85-92.

ACTS 4

3. The Sanhedrin Responds by Arresting Peter and John (4:1-22)

Some will wonder why the Jewish leaders had the gall to persecute the Apostles after they had performed a notable miracle. How can they be so heartless as to protest the healing of a cripple?! How can they be so blind as to blatantly deny the work of God? Both of these accusations are anachronistic and misleading. First, ancients assumed that sickness was due to sin (cf. John 9:2; Job 4:7; Str-B 2:527-529). Hence, altering the lame man's fate was tantamount to tinkering with the righteous retribution of God. Second, it is a modern assumption that miracles are 'impossible' therefore undeniable evidence of the working of God. For ancients (as well as much of the non-Western world today) miracles were assumed to be probable, not merely possible. Hence, the question is not their reality but their source. If the demonstrable power comes from God, all is well. If, however, the power derives from the Devil, the community leaders have an obligation to thwart it (e.g., Mark 3:23-27/Matt 12:25-29/Luke 11:17-22).

Therefore, this Sanhedrin inquiry is ostensibly trying to ascertain whether Peter and John operate under Yahweh's authority or a more sinister jurisdiction. Of course, the sadducean party already has an opinion. They had a pretty serious prejudice against bodily resurrection (Mark 12:18/Matt 22:28/Luke 20:27; Acts 23:28; Josephus, *Ant* 18.1.3-4; §16; *J.W.* 2.8.14 §162). Since the core of apostolic preaching affirmed the resurrection, it is no great surprise that they disparage the legitimacy of these Christ followers.

¹The priests and the captain of the temple guard and the Sadducees came up to Peter and John while they were speaking to the people. ²They were greatly disturbed because the apostles were teaching the people and proclaiming in Jesus the resurrection of the dead. ³They seized Peter and John, and because it was evening, they put them in jail until the next day. ⁴But many who heard the message believed, and the number of men grew to about five thousand.

4:1. Peter and John are accosted by a group of power brokers in the temple. Luke identifies three specific groups. The *priests* officiated the temple proceedings: sacrifices, offerings, cleaning, circumcision, etc. According to Josephus there were more than 20,000 priests (*C. Ap.* 2.1.8. §108). They were arranged in twenty-four divisions, working approximately two weeks a year (in addition to special festivals). The *captain* of the temple guard kept order in the temple and distributed the payment to the priests. He was second in authority to the High Priest and likely a member of that royal family (*Beginnings* 4:40; Str-B 2:628-631). The *Sadducees* were not officials, per se, but adherents to a particular philosophy. It was the dominant 'political' party among the priests and local temple leadership. The little we know about them must be taken with a grain of salt since it is filtered through their rivals. For example, Josephus's caricature can hardly be taken at face value: "The Pharisees are friendly to one another, and are for the exercise of concord, and regard for the public; but the behavior of the Sadducees one towards another is in some degree wild, and their conversation with those that are of their own party is as barbarous as if they were strangers to them" (*J.W.* 2.8.14 §166).[1]

4:2-4. Peter's proclamation of the resurrection directly opposed the authoritative teaching of the Sadducean party. That he preached it in Solomon's Colonnade within earshot of their cloisters surely galled them. These impudent rabble-rousers must be dealt with. So they are arrested and thrown in jail until the light of day affords the legal propriety to 'investigate' their case (*m. Sanh.* 4.1). From our perspective this seems like a bogus abuse of power. It really was not. From the Jewish perspective, the Sanhedrin was obliged to interpret the written and oral law in light of contemporary experiences. And though no law had officially been broken, this extraordinary event must be evaluated by the authorities to determine if it was appropriate. From the Roman perspective (which the High Priest mediated) any disturbance of the peace that could lead to public riots was taken seriously and dealt with severely.

The verdict of the crowd, however, has already been pronounced. Five thousand men believe. This increases the Christian population to perhaps as many as fifteen thousand.[2] Thus we have Luke's third 'count' of Christians (cf. 120 in 1:15; 3000 added in 2:41).[3] What we have here is more than a church roster. In a shame/honor society, when two factions come into competition, it is ultimately the crowd that determines the victor. Thus, even before Luke narrates the 'trial', he gives the verdict by those who really matter—the people.

⁵The next day the rulers, elders and teachers of the law met in Jerusalem. ⁶Annas the high priest was there, and so were Caiaphas, John, Alexander and the other men of the high priest's family. ⁷They had Peter and John brought before them and began to question them: "By what power or what name did you do this?"

4:5-7. Verse 5 is a technical way of describing "the Sanhedrin" (cf. v. 15; Mark 8:31; 11:27; 14:43, 53-55; 15:1)[4] which was led, of course, by the High Priest

---

[1] A more virulent critique is found in *m. Sanh.* 10.1, "And these are the ones who have no portion in the world to come: He who says, the resurrection of the dead is a teaching which does not derive from the Torah. . . ." Adequate surveys of the Sadducees can be found in Steve Mason, "Chief Priests, Sadducees, Pharisees and Sanhedrin in Acts," *The Book of Acts in Its Palestinian Setting* (ed. Richard Bauckham, vol. 4 in *The Book of Acts in Its First Century Setting*; Grand Rapids: Eerdmans, 1995), 115-177 and T. W. Mason, "Sadducee and Pharisee—the Origin and Significance of the Names," *BJRL* 22 (1938): 144-159.

[2] Though ἀνδρῶν could refer to "humans"—men and women—this is not likely given the specific mention of women converts later (5:14; 8:3, 12; 9:2; 17:12; 22:4) and the fact that ἄνθρωπος would be the more appropriate term if males and females were intended.

[3] Realistic estimates for the population of Jerusalem in the first century range from 60,000-120,000; cf. Wolfgang Reinhardt, "The Population Size of Jerusalem and the Numerical Growth of the Jerusalem Church," in *The Book of Acts in Its Palestinian Setting* (ed. Richard Bauckham; vol. 4 in *The Book of Acts in Its First Century Setting*; Grand Rapids: Eerdmans, 1995), 237-265. It is theoretically possible that 5,000 males from 120,000 had converted. However, this number surely represents those Christ-followers from the surrounding villages and perhaps even those from Pentecost who lived quite apart from the city.

[4] A Sanhedrin was a local tribunal consisting of not less than twenty-three judges (*m. Sanh.* 1.1). Each

Annas and his son-in-law Caiaphas.[5] Caiaphas was the official High Priest, appointed by the Romans (A.D. 18–36) but since Jews appointed a high priest for life, it is understandable that Annas still holds sway even though his official Roman post had long since ended (A.D. 7–14). Both Annas (John 18:12b-24) and Caiaphas (Mark 14:53-65/Matt 26:57-68/Luke 22:63-65; John 18:19-24) had officiated Jesus' trial, so they had experience with the movement. They were accompanied by a couple of other movers and shakers, John[6] and Alexander, who would surely have been offended to learn that not a shred of their status was recorded by any historian other than Luke. This auspicious assembly opens the interrogation with a simple question: What is the source of your authority? Or put another way, "What gives you the right . . . ?!"

[8]Then Peter, filled with the Holy Spirit, said to them: "Rulers and elders of the people! [9]If we are being called to account today for an act of kindness shown to a cripple and are asked how he was healed, [10]then know this, you and all the people of Israel: It is by the name of Jesus Christ of Nazareth, whom you crucified but whom God raised from the dead, that this man stands before you healed. [11]He is 'the stone you builders rejected, which has become the capstone.'[a][b] [12]Salvation is found in no one else, for there is no other name under heaven given to men by which we must be saved."

[a]11 Or *cornerstone*   [b]11 Psalm 118:22

4:8. No one would blame the rugged fishermen had they cowered in fear. They stood in the center of a 'supreme court' who murdered their master and whose gaze bore down hard on them. The Sanhedrin judges sat in three concentric half-circles with the defendant(s) standing in the center (*m. Sanh.* 4.3). The oldest and most venerable would sit in the inner ring, the second ring was reserved for the less powerful, and the third ring the least. Nonetheless, all seventy-one seats were filled with men far more influential than Peter or John, mere fishermen from Galilee ◻. Yet in their reply there is not a hint of intimidation. Luke prepared the reader for this shocking turn of events by saying Peter was "filled with the Spirit." This is precisely the promise Jesus made earlier: "When you are brought before synagogues, rulers and authorities, do not worry about how you will defend yourselves or what you will say, for the Holy Spirit will teach you at that time what you should say" (Luke 12:11-12; 21:15; cf. Matt 10:17-20; Mark 13:11). Peter's empowerment was equal to the task at hand.

4:9-10. Peter's Spirit-inspired response is nothing less than brilliant. He dealt with both the sociological issue and the theological issue in one fell swoop. He identifies the healing as an "act of kindness." The word literally means "good

major city of the Jews was to have their own tribunal. The Sanhedrin of Jerusalem, of course, had special prominence because it claimed the prestige of the capital city. It was roughly three times the size of a normal Sanhedrin (71) and included the high priest (*m. Sanh.* 1.6). The Sanhedrin system first appears in Hellenistic times c. 200 B.C., though it likely had its origins in Moses' 70 elders (Num 11:16, 24-25).

[5] A box of bones was found in Jerusalem from this period with "Joseph son of Caiaphas" (Yehosef bar Qayafa') inscribed on it. It was from a wealthy burial and may, in fact, be the remains of this high priest's son. Ronny Reich, "Caiaphas Name Inscribed on Bone Box," *BAR* 18 (1992): 38-44, 76; and William Horbury, "The 'Caiaphas' Ossuaries and Joseph Caiaphas," *PEQ* 126 (1994): 32-48.

[6] This may be the Jonathan who followed Caiaphas as High Priest in A.D. 37 (Josephus, *Ant.* 18.4.3 §95).

work/service" (*euergesia*). Thus, Peter's authority is not from the devil but from God. Furthermore, this undeniably "good work" was wrought by none other than Jesus of Nazareth, killed by his countrymen, raised by God.[7] Hence, Peter used the courtroom as a pulpit to pound again the drum of resurrection. More than that, he once again makes his hearers culpable for the crucifixion.[8]

4:11. The Sanhedrin is hardly going to concede Peter's point "because he said so." So Peter enlisted a prophetic text that he heard Jesus use: Psalm 118:22 (cf. Mark 12:10-11/Matt 21:42/Luke 20:17). It was the conclusion to the parable of the vineyard which explained why Jesus was about to be rejected and killed. The problem is that this parable not only *explained* the opposition to Jesus, it *caused* it! Surely Peter did not hope for better results this time. This is not the sort of thing one is advised to say in *How to Win Friends and Influence People.* Nonetheless, the hard truth is that Jesus is the foundation stone whose rejection, far from evidence that he is a fraud, actually authenticates him as the servant God promised. Both Peter and Paul shared this view (cf. Eph 2:20; 1 Pet 2:7-8).

4:12. Moreover, Peter claimed this 'stone of offense' was the *exclusive* source of salvation. Now there is an unpopular notion. Asserting Jesus is the right way, nay, the *only* way to the Father, plays about as well in today's pluralistic world as it did amidst the Sanhedrin. Nevertheless, Peter does not stand alone. Jesus said, "I am the way and the truth and the life. No one comes to the Father except through me" (John 14:6). Paul avers, "For there is one God and one mediator between God and men, the man Christ Jesus" (1 Tim 2:5). John echoes, "No one has ever seen God, but God the One and Only, who is at the Father's side, has made him known" (John 1:18). That Jesus is the exclusive means of salvation is the opinion of the great Apostles: Peter, Paul, John, and Jesus himself. One would expect nothing short of a resurrection to authenticate such a bodacious claim.

[13]**When they saw the courage of Peter and John and realized that they were unschooled, ordinary men, they were astonished and they took note that these men had been with Jesus.** [14]**But since they could see the man who had been healed standing there with them, there was nothing they could say.** [15]**So they ordered them to withdraw from the Sanhedrin and then conferred together.** [16]**"What are we going to do with these men?" they asked. "Everybody living in Jerusalem knows they have done an outstanding miracle, and we cannot deny it.** [17]**But to stop this thing from spreading any further among the people, we must warn these men to speak no longer to anyone in this name."**

---

[7] Verse 10b is a very early standard Christian choral refrain with three elements: Jesus is the Christ, whom *you* crucified but *God* raised from the dead. It is found throughout the book of Acts (with ἀνίστημι: 2:23-24, 31-32; 13:33-34 and with ἐγείρω: 3:14-15; 4:10; 5:30; 10:39-41; 13:28-30, 37) as well as the Pauline Epistles (Rom 4:24; 8:11; 10:9; Gal 1:1; 2 Cor 4:14; Col 2:12; Eph 1:20; 1 Thess 1:10; 1 Pet 1:21; though Paul's formula lacks Luke's ever-present verdict of Jewish complicity in Jesus' death). Thus, this phrase must be read not merely as a specific statement made to a specific group of people at a specific place and time, but as a recurring theological motif; cf. Ludger Schenke, "Die Kontrastformel Apg 4,10b," *BZ* 26 (1982): 1-20.

[8] It may seem odd that Peter had accused his previous audience of killing Jesus when most of them were not even in town (Acts 2:24; 3:15). However, in a group-oriented society leaders stood for the whole group so that their sin could result in the punishment of the whole body (e.g., Exod 32:32; 1 Chr 21:8-15; Rom 9:3; CD 7:15-20; *b. Sotah* 14a); cf. Joel Kaminsky, *Corporate Responsibility in the Hebrew Bible* (JSOTSupp 196; Sheffield: Sheffield Academic Press, 1995).

4:13-14. The Sanhedrin was astounded by the courage of Peter and John. They were uneducated (*agrammatos*)[9] laymen (*idiōtēs*).[10] Yet they spoke with the composure and confidence of trained rabbis. The only other person in their experience to do this was Jesus. They had asked of him, "How did this man get such learning (*grammata*) without having studied?" (John 7:15). The Sanhedrin had no retort for Peter's defense. They were not just tongue-tied, they were hog-tied (a very unfortunate position for a Jewish judge) due to the presence of this ex-lame man standing before them.[11]

4:15-17. The defendants were ordered out of chambers. A debate ensued—they tossed options back and forth (*suneballon*) but came up with no good solution. After all, the miracle was 'outstanding'. The implication is not so much on the wonderful nature of the miracle but on its publicity. "Everyone" saw it and frankly, they loved it. So sweeping it under the carpet for damage control was simply not an option. All they could really do was threaten Peter and John to cease and desist from this kind of public propagandizing.

18Then they called them in again and commanded them not to speak or teach at all in the name of Jesus. 19But Peter and John replied, "Judge for yourselves whether it is right in God's sight to obey you rather than God. 20For we cannot help speaking about what we have seen and heard." 21After further threats they let them go. They could not decide how to punish them, because all the people were praising God for what had happened. 22For the man who was miraculously healed was over forty years old.

4:18-22. Needless to say, the Apostles were hardly intimidated by this official prohibition from preaching in Jesus' name. They promised, in fact, that they *would* practice civil disobedience. They were constrained by God's command above the law of man.[12] This undoubtedly went over about as well as pork rinds at Passover. But what could the Sanhedrin do? If they punished them, the people would make them martyrs. They knew a notable miracle when they saw one. So the Sanhedrin, with all the clout of their entire legal system, could only bark louder. Next time, however, they will bite!

4. The Church Responds by Praying (4:23-31)

The Apostles have just felt the brunt of an antagonistic legal system pushing its weight against the fledgling church. How will they respond? How can they pos-

---

[9] Peter and John, like most of the populace, had no formal rabbinic training. One must be careful not to impose modern western values on this description of the Apostles. Most people in the ancient world were functionally illiterate (probably 85–90%) with no social inferiority attached to it.

[10] Since ἀγράμματοι is an adjective and ἰδιώτης is a noun, we likely have two separate descriptions of the Apostles rather than synonymous terms in a hendiadys. For a helpful discussion of these terms see Thomas J. Kraus, "'Uneducated', 'ignorant', or even 'illiterate'?: Aspects and Background for an Understanding of ΑΓΡΑΜΜΑΤΟΙ (and ΙΔΙΩΤΑΙ) in Acts 4.13," *NTS* 45 (1999): 434-449. For combinations of similar terms see Celsus in Origen, *Contra Celsum* 1.27, and others in van der Horst, *Hellenistic Parallels*, 42.

[11] Some translations do not adequately bring out the fact that the healed man had been arrested with Peter and John and now stood with them on trial; Norman Mundhenk, "The Invisible Man (Acts 4.9-10)," *BT* 57 (2006): 203-206.

[12] It is not likely that Peter and John deliberately echoed Socrates' response at his trial, but they are strikingly similar (Plato, *Apology* 29D, "I shall obey God rather than you," "πείσομαι δὲ τῷ θεῷ μᾶλλον ἢ ὑμῖν").

sibly fight back? They have several 'weapons' in their arsenal, each with irresist-ible force.[13] First, they prayed. They took their concerns to the very throne room of God. There they leveled their complaint to the highest authority, one whom they could call *Abba*. Second, they requested the *continued* power of the Holy Spirit to validate them publicly through extraordinary signs. Finally, they would suffer—a subversive strategy, surprisingly effective. The early church understood a critical concept seemingly lost where Christianity has comfortably coexisted with or co-opted the dominant culture. They understood that Jesus called us to a cross, not a crown. Our greatest power comes not from victory but from suffer-ing. Perhaps the reason the church often lacks the power of the Spirit is because we have neglected the practice of prayer in the midst of persecution.[14]

[23]On their release, Peter and John went back to their own people and re-ported all that the chief priests and elders had said to them. [24]When they heard this, they raised their voices together in prayer to God. "Sovereign Lord," they said, "you made the heaven and the earth and the sea, and everything in them. [25]You spoke by the Holy Spirit through the mouth of your servant, our father David: 'Why do the nations rage and the peoples plot in vain?[15] [26]The kings of the earth take their stand and the rulers gather together against the Lord and against his Anointed One.'a,b"[16]

a *26* That is, Christ or Messiah   b *26* Psalm 2:1,2

4:23-24. The Apostles' report prompted a unified prayer meeting.[17] They recited and interpreted Psalm 2:1-2 for God. Then, based on this text, they asked God to keep doing the very kinds of miracles that got them in trouble in the first place!

The prayer opens with a unique address to God—"sovereign Lord" (*despota*). It is a common title for slave-masters either literally (1 Tim 6:1-2; Titus 2:9; 1 Pet 2:18) or metaphorically (2 Tim 2:21; 2 Pet 2:1). As such, it is a proper address for God in prayer (Luke 2:29; Rev 6:10).[18] What is surprising is that it can refer to Je-

---

[13] This text sets a precedent for much of the bold preaching throughout the rest of the book. It is impor-tant to understand the principles imbedded in this passage not merely for interpreting the preceding story but for all the confrontations the church will experience through the rest of the book. Cf. Beverly Gaventa, "To Speak Thy Word with All Boldness—Acts 4:23-31," *FM* 3 (1986): 76-82.

[14] For a helpful exhortation along these lines, see Chris Schofield, "Linking Prayer and Bold Procla-mation: An Exegetical Study of Acts 4:23-31 and Ephesians 6:18-20 with Implications for Contemporary Church Growth," *JASCG* 8 (1997): 63-76.

[15] This verse is a jumbled mess in Greek and hardly the kind of thing Luke would have composed. He appears to be following his source here. Wahlde makes an unlikely attempt to rehabilitate the sentence by reading it as an intricate, though confusing, chiasm; cf. Urban C. Wahlde, "The Problems of Acts 4:25a: A New Proposal," *ZNW* 86 (1995): 265-267.

[16] The term "anointed one" is the root for "Messiah." It is no surprise, therefore, that Psalm 2 was applied to Jesus by the post-Easter church.

[17] Luke presents the prayer life of the church as robust as Jesus' had been, with an obvious lineage be-tween the two. Cf. Glen Hinson, "Persistence in Prayer in Luke-Acts," *RevExp* 104 (2007): 721-736; Steve Plymale, "Luke's Theology of Prayer," *SBLsp* 29 (1990): 529-551; P. T. O'Brien, "Prayer in Luke-Acts," *TynBul* 24 (1973): 111-127. Rollin Ramsaran makes the important observation that the theme of prayer is often linked in Luke-Acts with the themes of 'Spirit' and 'Kingdom'; cf. "Rich Heroic Themes: Spirit, Kingdom and Prayer in Luke-Acts," *Leaven* 18 (2010): 179-183.

[18] The LXX uses *despota* a number of times when addressing God in prayer, not with the implication of our English word "despot" but as one with ultimate power, particularly the power to create (Fitzmyer, 308): Abraham (Gen 15:2, 8), Joshua (Josh 5:14), Jeremiah (Jer 1:6; 4:10; 15:11), Daniel (Dan 9:8, 15, 16, 17, 19), Jonah (Jonah 4:10), Judith (Jdt 9:12), Raguel (Tob 8:17), Judas Maccabeaus (2 Macc 15:22). Cf. Den-nis Hamm, "Acts 4:23-31—A Neglected Biblical Paradigm of Christian Worship (Especially for Troubled

sus as well as Yahweh: "They are godless men, who . . . deny Jesus Christ our only Sovereign (*despota*) and Lord" (Jude 1:4). Apparently Jesus, at the right hand of the Father, is, for Luke, often inseparable from Yahweh.

4:25-26. *Luke* recorded *Peter's* quotation of Psalm 2 (LXX) but attributed the poem not to *David* but ultimately to the *Holy Spirit*. Obviously there are a lot of voices talking all at once. And had Peter wanted to, he could have cited more from Psalm 2 in reference to Jesus. He expected his audience to complete the paragraph in their heads to comprehend all that was going on in the Psalm. God himself cited Psalm 2:7 (with Isa 42:1) at Jesus' baptism (Mark 1:11/Matt 3:17/Luke 3:22; cf. Heb 1:5; 5:5; *t. Levi* 18:6-8). Furthermore, the ending of the Psalm works well with the title "Despot" (the echoes of which are heard in Rev 2:27; 12:5; 19:15).

> You will rule them with an iron scepter; you will dash them to pieces like pottery. Therefore, you kings, be wise; be warned, you rulers of the earth. Serve the LORD with fear and rejoice with trembling. Kiss the Son, lest he be angry and you be destroyed in your way, for his wrath can flare up in a moment. Blessed are all who take refuge in him. (Psa 2:9-12)

[27]"Indeed Herod and Pontius Pilate met together with the Gentiles and the people[a] of Israel in this city to conspire against your holy servant[19] Jesus, whom you anointed. [28]They did what your power and will had decided beforehand should happen. [29]Now, Lord, consider their threats and enable your servants to speak your word with great boldness. [30]Stretch out your hand to heal and perform miraculous signs and wonders through the name of your holy servant Jesus." [31]After they prayed, the place where they were meeting was shaken. And they were all filled with the Holy Spirit and spoke the word of God boldly.
[a]27 The Greek is plural.

4:27-28. The key point, of course, is to relate the rulers who fought against God's anointed in Psalm 2 with those who opposed Jesus in Peter's recent experience.

PSALM 2:1-2	ACTS 4:27-28
Why do the nations rage	Gentiles (3)
and the peoples plot in vain?	People of Israel (4)
The kings of the earth take their stand	Herod and Pilate (1)
and the rulers gather together against the Lord and against his Anointed One.	[Sanhedrin, implied] (2)

This kind of interpretation was a classic apocalyptic Jewish hermeneutic called *Pesher*. In essence, it is a preaching strategy that says, "What we have just experienced was written about in Scripture." Or in short, "This is that." Once

Times)," *Worship* 77 (2003): 228. It is also found in the prayers of Josephus, *Ant* 1.18.6 §272-273; 4.3.2 §40-50; 20.4.2 §89-90.
[19] Παῖς is a word that vacillates in meaning from "son" to "servant." In view here is most likely the divine sonship of Ancient Near Eastern kings (Marshall, 105-106) and more specifically, the "servant of the Lord" in Isaiah.

again, though the parties involved are certainly culpable for the injustice per-
petrated against God's anointed, it was ultimately Yahweh that orchestrated the
events (v. 28).

4:29-30. Verse 29, "Lord consider their threats" is a page out of Hezekiah's
playbook when he laid Sennacherib's letter before the Lord in the Temple and
said, "Give ear, O LORD, and hear; open your eyes, O LORD, and see; listen to
all the words Sennacherib has sent to insult the living God" (Isa 37:17/2 Kgs
19:16). Peter is not merely asking God to hear. He is asking him to attend to the
problem. This specific kind of prayer is called 'imprecatory'. It is when you ask
God to put the hurt on your enemy so justice will be served and the righteous
vindicated. The verbiage is often brutal (e.g., Psa 58:6-11, 59:5, 13; 109:6-15;
137:8-9; 139:19-22).

This prayer, however, ends with a most surprising twist. Instead of asking
God to break teeth, smash enemies, or drop firebombs from heaven, the believers asked God to heal.[20] That, in fact, was the very activity that brought them this
trouble in the first place but it is the very thing that will bring salvation to their
countrymen. So they request the boldness to proclaim the gospel in the face of
impending persecution.[21] Their imprecation is not against their enemies but in
essence against themselves for the benefit of their enemies. There could hardly
be a more striking fulfillment of Jesus' unprecedented injunction, "Love your
enemies and pray for those who persecute you" (Matt 5:44).

4:31. God answered their prayer with an earthquake. Earthquakes were
nearly universally understood in the ancient world as an angry response from
God(s).[22] If God "stomped his foot" after "amen," these Christians would know
precisely what he was saying. It was a signal of divine judgment. As Christians
committed to love their enemies, God was assuring them that justice was still
right around the corner. It is our mandate to love our enemies; it is God's responsibility to carry out justice.

D. COMMUNITY ECONOMICS AND UNITY (4:32–6:7)

The previous section introduced the first persecution of the church. It was
bad but will get much worse in chapter 5. All the Apostles will be arrested, not just
Peter and John, and they will be beaten rather than merely threatened. Then,
in chapter 7, Stephen will be brutally stoned, laying down his life as the first
Christian martyr. In a sense, then, this current section about the unity of the early
church is an interlude into the longer section on persecution. It is not, however,
a mere tangent. Here we learn of the first two failures of the church—greed and

[20] This contrast is not merely seen in biblical prayers of imprecation but also in the prayers Josephus records: *Ant* 1.18.6 §272-273 "make him a terror to his foes"; 4.3.2 §40-50, "make manifest thy judgment in no
uncertain manner"; 20.4.2 §89-90, "come to my aid to defend me from my enemies . . . it is thy power they
have had the audacity to challenge."). Cf. Gerald Downing, "Common Ground with Paganism in Luke and
in Josephus," *NTS* 28 (1982): 546-559.
[21] Boldness (παρρησία, παρρησιάζομαι) is a key characteristic of Apostolic witness (Acts 2:29; 4:13, 29, 31;
9:27-28; 13:46; 14:3; 18:26; 19:8; 28:31). Half of the NT uses of this word in its nominal and verbal forms
are in the book of Acts.
[22] For example, Psa 114:7; Isa 29:6; Ezek 38:19; Matt 27:54; 28:2; Acts 16:26; Rev 6:12; 8:5; 11:13, 19; 16:18;
van der Horst, "Hellenistic Parallels," 44-45. Though there are some "rumblings" that emphasize the presence of God without apparent implications of judgment (cf. Exod 19:18; Psa 68:8; Isa 6:4).

prejudice—which threatened the pristine unity of the body of Christ. How does this relate to the broader context of persecution? Well, some of the trouble the church faced came from external antagonists threatening to destroy the physical body of Christians. The more nefarious threat, however, came from internal antagonists threatening the unity of the body of Christ. Both external persecution and internal corruption posed serious threats to the fledgling Christian community. But the greatest fear for the faithful was never our enemy but ourselves.

1. Barnabas Offers a Good Example of Economic Sharing (4:32-37)

It is rather unfortunate there is a chapter division between Barnabas and Ananias. The two stories are opposite sides of the same coin. Luke offers a summary of the economic unity of the church in 4:32-35, and then illustrates it with two examples. Barnabas demonstrates the right way to offer benevolence to the body (what they would have known as 'patronage'). Ananias illustrates the same impulse performed with wrong motives. One sustains life, the other brings death.

[32]All the believers were one in heart and mind. No one claimed that any of his possessions was his own, but they shared everything they had. [33]With great power the apostles continued to testify to the resurrection of the Lord Jesus, and much grace was upon them all. [34]There were no needy persons among them. For from time to time those who owned lands or houses sold them, brought the money from the sales [35]and put it at the apostles' feet, and it was distributed to anyone as he had need.

4:32-34. This is the second major summary of the church (cf. Acts 2:42-47). Like the first, it emphasizes the economic sharing among the original band of believers in Jerusalem. In the previous summary we argued that Luke was, in fact, describing a social reality not merely a literary utopia. Furthermore, this praxis reflected Jewish values, not Greek ideals (contra Conzelmann, 38 and Haenchen, 192).[23] Specifically, those early Jewish Christians seemed to have seen themselves as the rescued remnant of God (Longenecker, 310). They were living out an eschatological exodus. So the ordinance of Deuteronomy 15:4 applied directly to them: "There should be no poor among you."

If one looks closely at the key words of verse 32, there is another text reflected in this Christian community of goods: One heart, mind (or soul [*psuche*]), and possessions. These words are the backbone of the famous *Shemah* of Deuteronomy 6:4-5, "Hear, O Israel: The LORD our God, the LORD is *one*. Love the LORD your God with all your *heart* and with all your *soul* and with all your *strength*."[24] The comparison is even closer when one realizes the word "strength" was taken by some rabbis to mean one's economic wherewithal (*m. Ber.* 9.5). Thus, the

[23] For details on the social background of communal economics see Scott Bartchy, "Community of Goods in Acts: Idealization or Social Reality?" in *The Future of Early Christianity* (ed. Birger A. Pearson; Minneapolis: Fortress, 1991), 309-318; Brian Capper, "The Palestinian Cultural Context of Earliest Christian Community of Goods," in *The Book of Acts in Its Palestinian Setting* (ed. Richard Bauckham; vol. 4 in *The Book of Acts in Its First Century Setting*, Grand Rapids: Eerdmans, 1995), 323-356; and Joseph Coppens, "La koinônia dans l'Église primitive," *ETL* 46 (1970): 116-121.
[24] For this observation I am grateful to Birger Gerhardsson, "Einige Bemerkungen zu Apg 4:32," *ST* 24 (1970): 142-149.

early Christians saw their economic communion as an obligation in order to fulfill Jesus' interpretation of God's greatest two commands (Mark 12:30-31/ Matt 22:37-40; Luke 10:27; cf. 1 John 3:16-18).

Furthermore, this communal lifestyle was nothing new for the inner band of Jesus' disciples. They lived like that long before Pentecost. They had been supported in part by a group of wealthy women (Luke 8:1-3) and shared their common purse with those in need (John 6:7; 12:6; 13:29).[25] Acts 2:42-47 and 4:32-35 have their roots in the praxis of Jesus himself which was perfectly at home in the patron/client system of the first-century world.[26] It wasn't that every Christian sold what s/he had and lived in a commune. Rather, those with substantial means felt strongly the obligation to provide for the economically despondent in their fictive family. The patron provided goods and services; the client offered fidelity, thanksgiving, and praise to those who took care of him. To various degrees, all across the Empire, groups of families bound themselves to social networks for mutual support particularly provided by the economic elite. That was normal.

These Christians, however, seemed to ramp up the economic sharing beyond normal patron/client groups. They were not, however, the only ones. Among the Greeks, the Pythagoreans (4th–3rd cen. B.C.) illustrate this impulse: "At this time, then, the things belonging to each, that is, their possessions, were held in common, given to those disciples appointed for this purpose who were called 'politicians', and experienced in household management and skilled in legislation" (Iamblichus, *Vita Pythgoras* 17.72). "They would expel him from the school of the Pythagoreans. They would load him with much gold and silver (for these things were stored in common for them and were administered in common by those suitable for this purpose, who they called 'managers' because of their post). And if they ever met him by chance, they considered him someone wholly other than he who, according to them, had died" (Iamblichus, *Vita Pythagoras* 17.74).

Even closer to home were the Essenes. At Qumran 🔲 there was shared community of goods.[27] "Nor is there any one to be found among them who hath more than another; for it is a law among them, that those who come to them must let what they have be common to the whole order, insomuch that among them all there is no appearance of poverty, or excess of riches, but every one's possessions are intermingled with every other's possessions; and so there is, as it were, one patrimony among all the brethren" (Josephus *J.W.* 2.8.3 §122; cf. 1QS 5.1-3; 9.3-11; Philo, *Hypothetica* 11.4-9). One should not assume, however, that all Essenes, dispersed in perhaps as many as two hundred villages, sold everything

[25] This practice appears to have continued in the 2nd and 3rd centuries (cf. *Did.* 4.8; *Barn.* 9.8a). Though communalism has never been a universal practice of the Church, benevolence has never been abandoned as an essential praxis for believers; cf. Hans-Joachim Kraus, "Actualität des 'urchristlichen Kommunismus'," in *Freispruch und Freiheit* (ed. Walter Kreck, et al.; München: Kaiser, 1973), 306-327 and Christopher Hutson, "All Things in Common: Mutual Aid in Acts 2.42-47 and 4.32-37," *Leaven* 18 (2010): 134-189.

[26] Bartchy, "Community of Goods," 313-315. Jesus, of course, had urged his followers to sell their possessions and give to the poor (Luke 12:33-34; 18:22).

[27] For further details see S. Johnson, "The Dead Sea Manual of Discipline and the Jerusalem Church of Acts," *The Scrolls and the New Testament* (ed. K. Stendahl; rev. J. H. Chalesworth; New York: Crossroads, 1991), 129-142, 273-275.

and put it in the common pot.[28] Nonetheless, their praxis at Qumran shows that the Christians in Jerusalem were not the only ones committed to a radical lifestyle of economic sharing.

The likelihood of a radical lifestyle of economic sharing increases under four conditions: (1) An eschatological worldview where one believes God is involved in shaping current and future history. (2) A belief in the imminent return of Jesus so that our goods will soon be worthless. (3) Economic need of brothers and sisters we love. (4) A Spirit-filled church whose leaders model sacrifice and proclaim the risen Christ. While it is true that the communalism of the earliest church was neither long-lived nor broadly practiced, it is also true that the ideal has never been abandoned. Believers whose souls have been redeemed by the blood of Jesus feel most acutely the potential and imperative for social transformation at least within the church. We must model a new kind of society that models the kindness and self-sacrifice of our savior. Those living in the modern West often have the most difficult time with, as well as the deepest responsibility for, imitating the radical economic sacrifice of the early church.

[36]Joseph, a Levite from Cyprus, whom the apostles called Barnabas (which means Son of Encouragement), [37]sold a field he owned and brought the money and put it at the apostles' feet.

4:36-37. Verses 32-35 describe a radical lifestyle. It wasn't just theoretical. There were real people who sold property to provide for the needs of the poor in the church. Verses 36-37 offer a positive example in Barnabas; 5:1-11 offers a negative example in Ananias.

Barnabas's real name was Joseph, and he hailed from the tribe of Levi and the island of Cyprus.[29] This is actually a pretty normal way of introducing a person in ancient literature: Name, family, place of origin. But Luke does a couple of unique things. First, he tends to introduce with a sound bite a character who will feature more fully later in the story. In other words, we will see much more of Barnabas, but we will have to wait until chapter 9. Second, Luke gives us Joseph's Aramaic nickname, Barnabas. Luke interprets it as "Son of Encouragement."[30] He will live up to this nickname with the likes of Paul (Acts 9:27; 11:25-26), the Christians of Antioch (11:19-31), and his own relative, John Mark (Acts 15:36-41).

---

[28] Capper proves that statistically the Essenes of Palestine would have wielded significant influence and their practices would have been well-known enough to make the disciples' praxis understandable within the milieu; Brian J. Capper, "Holy Community of Life and Property amongst the Poor: A Response to Steve Walton," *EvQ* 80 (2008): 113-127.

[29] Though it was technically illegal for Levites to own land in Israel (Num 18:20; Deut 10:9), this prohibition was archaic (Jer 32:7-9; Josephus, *Life*, 76, §422). Furthermore, there is no reason to assume his land was in Palestine rather than his homeland of Cyprus. For a survey of the important role Barnabas plays in Lucan literature, cf. Jonathan Murphy, "The Role of Barnabas in the Book of Acts," *BibSac* 167 (2010): 319-341 and Robin Branch, "Barnabas: Early Church Leader and Model of Encouragment," *IDS* 41 (2007): 295-322.

[30] There is generally little reason to doubt Luke's linguistic ability. However, it has been difficult to retrace his etymological tracks. "Bar" clearly means "son." But "nabas" (נבש or נבס) has no clear connection with "encouragement." It is a lot closer to "prophet" (נְבִיא) or "Nebo" (נבו) the Babylonian god, hardly a fitting nickname for a kosher Jew (*Backgrounds*, 49). How Luke ascertained the meaning "Son of Encouragement" from "Barnabas" remains a mystery. A fuller discussion of the linguistic possibilities is provided by Sebastian Brock, "ΒΑΡΝΑΒΑΣ: ΥΙΟΣ ΠΑΡΑΚΛΗΣΕΩΣ," *JTS* 25 (1974): 93-98.

ACTS 5

2. Ananias and Sapphira Offer a Bad Example
of Economic Manipulation (5:1-11)

This is one of the more intriguing stories of the Bible. Ananias and his wife absconded with sacred funds and suffered a divine death-penalty. There are echoes here of Achan's terrifying tale (Joshua 7).[1] According to any reckoning, this is an extreme story. For some it is offensive. Of course a judgment *for* God is irrelevant (as if he needed our help) and one *against* him irreverent. Nonetheless, one might argue that the severity of the punishment fit these crimes (both Achan and Ananias), not because of the amount of money stolen, but due to the depth of its impact. Both offenses marred the pristine purity of the people of God and halted their forward progress. This 'first offense' is so devastating because it makes all subsequent sins all the easier. Perhaps that is why God took it so seriously.

[1]Now a man named Ananias, together with his wife Sapphira, also sold a piece of property.[2] [2]With his wife's full knowledge he kept back part of the money for himself, but brought the rest and put it at the apostles' feet. [3]Then Peter said, "Ananias, how is it that Satan has so filled your heart that you have lied to the Holy Spirit and have kept for yourself some of the money you received for the land? [4]Didn't it belong to you before it was sold? And after it was sold, wasn't the money at your disposal? What made you think of doing such a thing? You have not lied to men but to God."

5:1-4. This Jewish couple decided to cash in some of their property and make a sizeable donation to the Christian community. Undoubtedly they observed the honor bestowed on Barnabas after his generous gift.[3] Such honors were normal for patrons in the ancient world. Lavish thanks and copious praise were the order of the day.[4] Whatever their motives, they felt compelled to keep back part of the proceeds. As Peter made perfectly clear, there was no harm in

---

[1] There are, of course, problems in the comparison of Ananias and Achan; most notably Ananias was not violating a specific command of the Lord. Such discrepancies led Daniel Marguerat to the interesting speculation that Acts 5 is a midrash on Genesis 3, not Judges 7; "La Mort d'Ananias et Saphira (Ac 5.1-11) dans la Stratégie narrative de Luc," *NTS* 39 (1993): 222-225; and "Terreur dans l'église: Le drame d'Ananias et Saphira (Actes 5, 1-11)," *FV* 91 (1992): 77-88.

[2] The word (κτῆμα) does not, in itself, mean real-estate. It could be jewelry, livestock, cloth, coins, or other stores of wealth. But the word χωρίον in verse 8 identifies the goods sold as land.

[3] The triple repetition of the phrase "put it at the apostles' feet" (4:35, 37: 5:2) serves to connect the actions of Barnabas and Ananias. Thus, these two stories hang together as a single, cohesive narrative; cf. Soeur Anne-Etienne and Corina Combet-Galland, "Actes 4:32–5:11," *ETR* 52 (1977): 548-553.

[4] Richard S. Ascough, "Benefaction Gone Wrong: The 'Sin' of Ananias and Sapphira in Context," in *Text and Artifact in the Religions of Mediterranean Antiquity* (ed. Michel Robert Desjardins, Peter Richardson; Canada: Wilfrid Laurier University Press, 2000), 91-110, offers plentiful examples of such inscriptions of lavish praise.

111

that. The problem lay in the lie. They *said* they gave the total proceeds when, in fact, they kept a portion for themselves. The word Luke uses is peculiar; it means to pilfer or embezzle. Its only other use in the New Testament is Titus 2:10 where Paul exhorts slaves not to "steal" from their masters. Perhaps even more interesting is its use in Joshua 7:1 (LXX) describing Achan's pilfering of plunder (cf. 2 Macc 4:32). Bottom line: They stole money they had devoted to God. This chicanery was not an offense against their human brothers (merely) but against the very Spirit of God. Trying to pull a fast one on the Spirit is inescapably foolish.

There is a social setting for this story that adds color to its telling. There were a number of social groups that submitted their goods to the community. The Essenes were the closest to the Apostles in space and time.[5] It is worth noting several things about them. (1) The novices among the Essenes could listen and learn without making a full commitment to join the fellowship. Once they did decide to join, their property was sold but not yet dispersed. It was kept in waiting. In the event the novice did not prove faithful, their 'account' would be returned to them. They had to prove themselves worthy members. Only after their probationary period ended was their property actually dispersed to the community.[6] (2) There appear to be different rules about financial responsibility of members in the Dead Sea Scrolls. 1QS 5.1-3 and 9.3-11 seem to mandate selling off the property (cf. Josephus *J.W.* 2.8.3 §122; Philo, *Hypothetica* 11.4-11). However, CD 14.11b-15 indicates some level of personal property was retained by some members: "They shall place the earnings of at least two days out of every month into the hands of the Guardian and the Judges, and from it they shall give to the fatherless, and from it they shall succor the poor and the needy, the aged sick and the man who is stricken (with disease), the captive taken by a foreign people, the virgin with no near kin, and the ma[id for] whom no man cares" (cf. CD 9.10-14).[7] This suggests that there may have been different requirements for those living at Qumran from the other Essenes located in local villages. The rules may have even varied from village to village and from time to time. Variation and evolution in such communities is to be expected. (3) There were stiff penalties for lying to the leaders of the Essenes, not the death penalty, mind you, but relatively stiff: "If one of them has lied deliberately, in matters of property, he shall be excluded from the pure Meal of the Congregation for one year and shall do penance with respect to one quarter of his food" (1QS 6.25).

These facts lead to some important conclusions. First, though the story of Ananias and Sapphira has no exact parallel in Judaism of the day, the basic contours are all recognizable: voluntary communal donation, patrons seeking to get into the inner circle, and strict punishment for deception. Second, the variation in the Qumran documents suggests some flexibility in how such donations

---

[5] Henriette Havelaar, "Hellenistic Parallels to Acts 5.1-11 and the Problem of Conflicting Interpretations," *JSNT* 67 (1997): 63-82.

[6] For more details, see Brian Capper, "'In der Hand des Ananias . . .' Erwägungen zu 1 QS VI, 20 und der urchristlichen Gütergemeinschaft," *RevQ* 46 (1986): 223-236, and his "Palestinian Cultural Context," 323-356.

[7] Clearly the Qumran covenanters did not have to submit *all* private property, otherwise they could hardly be fined for infractions (cf. 1QS 7.6-8).

could be handled, hence there is no reason to think Christians had to imitate anyone else's system. Finally, and perhaps most importantly, the deception of Ananias and Sapphira was offensive because it intruded into and subverted a social network of trust and mutual support.[8] The whole patron/client system is predicated on commitment and fidelity. If that breaks down, the whole system is in jeopardy. Their sin must not, therefore, be minimized.

[5]When Ananias heard this, he fell down and died.[9] And great fear seized all who heard what had happened. [6]Then the young men came forward, wrapped up his body, and carried him out and buried him. [7]About three hours later his wife came in, not knowing what had happened. [8]Peter asked her, "Tell me, is this the price you and Ananias got for the land?" "Yes," she said, "that is the price." [9]Peter said to her, "How could you agree to test the Spirit of the Lord? Look! The feet of the men who buried your husband are at the door, and they will carry you out also." [10]At that moment she fell down at his feet and died. Then the young men came in and, finding her dead, carried her out and buried her beside her husband. [11]Great fear seized the whole church and all who heard about these events.

5:5-11. The effect of Peter's declaration was immediate and severe—Ananias dropped dead.[10] The effect of Ananias's demise was immediate and substantial—the church feared God (cf. vv. 5, 11). Naturally, the younger men in the group took care of the business of burying him. Normally a man of his means would be given an elaborate funeral with much ado. Normally his wife would be informed immediately, the family gathered, and proper mourning performed. Ananias's situation, however, is far from normal. He is given a pauper's funeral whose wrappings were nothing more than his own cloak and no one uttered a word to his wife. Likely the godly fear of divine retribution made mute the church, leaving Sapphira ignorant of the unfortunate affair.

She made her appearance after three hours. Peter interrogated her. No doubt the stunned silence of the witnesses gave her a clue that something significant had transpired but no one interceded. Peter's question was a real conundrum for her. On the one hand, if she 'outs' her husband she would have to suffer the consequences of a shamed mate, or so she thought. On the other hand, fibbing to an Apostle is not to be taken lightly. Her choice is made, the die is cast. She died for her complicity with her husband in lying to the Spirit of the Lord. She fell down at the Apostle's feet, paradoxically, where her earthly treasured had been laid (cf. 4:35, 37; 5:2). Like her husband, she breathed her

---

[8]Ascough, "Benefaction Gone Wrong," 91-110; and Bartchy, "Community of Goods," 316. The importance of the patronage system to Luke is evident by its consistent inclusion in his work (Luke 1:3; 7:1-10; 8:1-3; Acts 10:1-8; 12:12; 16:40). He even uses the word εὐεργέτης in Luke 22:25, though Jesus turns the system on its head by having the master serve his constituents (Luke 22:27).

[9]Literally, Ananias "breathed out" or "expired" (ἐκψύχω).

[10]The death of Ananias and Sapphira is but one of a string of biblical stories where God slew his own disobedient servants: Nadab and Abihu (Lev 10:2), Achan (Josh 7:25); Uzzah (2 Sam 6:7); Hananiah (Jer 28:15-17). Christians clearly saw death and sickness as a real possible result of their own sin (cf. 1 Cor 5:1-11; 11:27-32; James 5:14-16), not to mention the sin of outsiders: Herod (12:19-23); Elymas (13:11); and the seven sons of Sceva (19:16).

last. Like her husband, the young men carried her out. They laid the two next to each other in a quick and unceremonious service, the kind one expects for a criminal laid to rest without mourning or memorial. They are remembered, to this day, but only as a fearful example.

3. The Fearsome Power of the Apostles (5:12-16)

The basic contours of this summary are, by now, familiar to the reader: The Apostles' testimony is reinforced by miracles, the church gathers in unity at the temple, and their fellow Jews hold them in high esteem. There is nothing really striking here except Luke's protracted point about the extraordinary power of Peter's shadow and his cryptic statement that "no one else dared join them." Each will be taken up in turn.

[12]**The apostles performed many miraculous signs and wonders among the people. And all the believers used to meet together in Solomon's Colonnade.** [13]**No one else dared join them, even though they were highly regarded by the people.** [14]**Nevertheless, more and more men and women believed in the Lord and were added to their number.** [15]**As a result, people brought the sick into the streets and laid them on beds and mats so that at least Peter's shadow might fall on some of them as he passed by.** [16]**Crowds gathered also from the towns around Jerusalem, bringing their sick and those tormented by evil[a] spirits, and all of them were healed.**

[a]*16 Greek unclean*

5:12-14. Since these original believers were all Jewish, one is not surprised to find them assembling in Solomon's Colonnade (cf. Acts 3:19). After all, it would be more than half a century before the ultimate split between the synagogue and the church. These believers think they are *continuing* God's plan for Israel, not aborting it. And those kosher crowds in the temple were more likely to view the believers as a peculiar Jewish sect than heretical apostates.

What is confusing, however, is Luke's statement that "no one else dared join them" (v. 13) when, in fact, more men and women "believed in the Lord and were added to their number" (v. 14). This peculiar turn of phrase has led to multiple explanations. Schwartz takes this verse as evidence for a graduated membership into the church which ultimately led to the renunciation of material possessions.[11] In short, there were not many willing to attempt 'full' membership of the church given the fearful example and Ananias and Sapphira's failure. Though Schwartz can illustrate this practice with the Essenes, there is not a shred of evidence from the Bible that those who "believed in the Lord" yet had several steps before reaching the center of the Christian community. A second view suggests "them" does not mean the church in general but the Apostle's in particular. Thus, it is suggested that Christians would not hang out with the Apostles in Solomon's Colonnade (Polhill, 163). If they were doing amaz-

---

[11] Daniel R. Schwartz, "Non-Joining Sympathizers (Acts 5:13-14)," *Bib* 64 (1983): 550-555. Cf. Brian Capper, "The Interpretation of Acts 5.4," *JSNT* 19 (1983): 117-131; and "'In der Hand des Ananias . . .' 223-236.

ing miracles (including striking people dead) a close affiliation with the Twelve would not be undertaken lightly. However, the word "associate" has more to do with "affiliation" than "proximity."[12] Hence, a third option is that nonbelievers generally gave the Apostle's a wide birth. The Jewish leaders, along with the general population, held the Apostles in special esteem even if they disagreed with their doctrine vehemently. Their power and position was not to be challenged lightly. This explains why Gamaliel might be quick to defend them in the following episode.

Verse 14 mentions women believing independently of men. This is a significant moment in salvation history. In an androcentric society such as ancient Israel a woman's faith was bound up with that of her husband or father. Here we find women mentioned individually as believers. If Sapphira can be punished apart from her husband, based on her own complicity, then conversely women of faith can be judged righteous apart from their husbands' rejection of the faith. This new pattern will be reflected consistently in the remainder of the book (Acts 8:3, 12; 9:2; 16:1, 13-14; 17:4, 12, 34; 18:2; 22:4).

5:15-16. Verse 15 begins with the phrase "as a result," but as a result of what? The growth of the church? The fear of the Apostles? The death of Ananias and Sapphira? Likely what Luke has in view is verse 12, "The Apostles performed many miraculous signs and wonders . . ." The Apostles' power is the theme of this poignant little interlude. One of the most notable wonders was Peter's ability to heal with his shadow. This conjures up an image of throngs of people from nearby villages (v. 16) packing the west side of Peter's street in the morning and shifting to the east in the afternoon.

This is, indeed, a strange and wonderful miracle. As one could imagine, it has drawn fire from skeptics who easily reduce it to myth or magic imposed on the biblical text through Luke's cultural superstition. One should not be so hasty in such a judgment, however. There are several arguments in favor of the veracity of this miracle. (1) Luke eschews magic. He is eager to condemn it wherever he meets it. So why would he allow it to intrude needlessly into the story. (2) It is not necessary for the narrative. It adds virtually nothing to the previous story of Ananias and Sapphira. It is merely an addendum to the miracles already mentioned in v. 12. And it is not the direct cause of the Apostles' arrest that immediately follows. In other words, Luke included it for reasons *other* than mere rhetorical force. While it does promote Apostolic authority (a clear intention of Luke in this passage; cf. Haenchen, 201-205) it only applies to Peter. If Luke is going to make something up to beef up Apostolic authority in general, he could at least be courteous enough to include the other eleven. (3) The miraculous healing by the shadow does *not* conform to ancient myth. While many ancient texts speak of the *danger* of shadows, there is no example of shadows

---

[12] Seven of the twelve uses of the term "join" (κολλάω) are by Luke (Luke 10:11; 15:15; Acts 5:13; 8:29; 9:26; 10:28; 17:34). Each of these uses (except Acts 8:29) indicates an intimate fellowship rather than physical proximity. This aligns with the dominant use of the term in the LXX where 24 of 28 uses indicate social attachment rather than spatial connection.

curing those they touched.[13] This miracle is *counter* intuitive though similar to
Jesus (Luke 8:44) and Paul (Acts 19:12) healing with their clothing. Given the
preceding story, it would have been easier had Peter's shadow struck down some
infidels. (4) Unless Luke really is just writing fiction, it baffles the mind as to why
he would say that large crowds from surrounding villages brought their sick. If
the healing shadow was merely superstition or an occasional coincidence, one
wonders how the word spread so that wearied peasants dragged their loved ones
over considerable distances to test the rumor. If there was not something to the
shadow, it is unlikely that so many would go to such lengths to touch it. In conclusion, there is nothing in the story itself that is unbelievable except for those
who have a disinclination to accept divine intervention in the material world.

4. Second Arrest and First Beating of the Apostles (5:17-42)

The parallels between the arrest in chapter 4 and that of chapter 5 are striking. They are meant to be. What we have here is not, as is sometimes assumed, a
careless doublet of Luke.[14] Rather, these are two halves of the same persecution
that got deeper and wider as the fame of Jesus continued to spread. In chapter
4 Peter and John were threatened; in chapter 5 all Twelve were beaten. This
follows normal Jewish jurisprudence. They first clarified the offence before pun-
ishing those who committed it.

Though the persecution is intensified in this chapter, so too is the support
the Apostles receive from two unsuspected sources: an angel and a Pharisee.
God's angel intervenes to effect an escape which ultimately only releases the
prisoners to inevitable persecution.[15] And a Pharisaic sage surprisingly comes
to the defense of the Twelve reducing their potential capital offense to a misdemeanor requiring only a good beating. The tale could hardly have more delightful twists.

**[17]Then the high priest and all his associates, who were members of the party
of the Sadducees, were filled with jealousy. [18]They arrested the apostles and put
them in the public jail. [19]But during the night an angel of the Lord opened the
doors of the jail and brought them out. [20]"Go, stand in the temple courts," he
said, "and tell the people the full message of this new life."**

5:17. The Sadducees never receive a single commendation from Luke, and
frankly, they likely deserved none.[16] They were the political power behind the

---

[13] It is somewhat of an urban legend, disproved by Paschke, that shadows were believed to have healing
power; cf. Boris Paschke, "The Mystery of the Vanishing Sources: How New Testament Scholars Superfi-
cially and Uncritically Identified the Ancient Background of Luke 8:43-48, Acts 5:15, and Acts 19:12," *BN*
129 (2006): 74-80; *pace* Marshall, 115. P. W. van der Horst's citation of Pliny, *Natural History* 17.18 is hardly
apropos for the shade of trees as a botanical observation is not comparable to the shade of animals or
humans which were believed to bear the essence of the living creature; "Peter's Shadow," *NTS* 23 (1977):
204-212.
[14] First defended fully by Joachim Jeremias, "Untersuchungen zum Quellenproblem der Apostelgeschichte," *ZNW* 36 (1937): 205-221.
[15] This motif of divine deliverance was common in ancient literature; cf. Acts 12:1-19 and J. Jeremias,
TDNT 3:175-176.
[16] Labeling the Sadducees was a sociological tool designed to shift public honor from them to the church.
This was a contest that cut both ways. The Sadducees labeled the Apostles as ignorant and uneducated,

execution of Jesus (Luke 22:2-5, 52, 54) as well as the persecution of his followers. That doesn't mean they were all bad men, but in the account of the church
of Jesus there's no opportunity to highlight anything but their antagonism.

They were jealous of the Apostles. This is a sociological indication that the
Twelve were 'stealing' honor from the Sadducees by attracting the support of
the people. The ancients believed that honor was a limited resource—there was
only so much to go around.[17] If the Apostles were honored by the people, that
honor came from the invisible stock formerly held by the Sadducees.

5:18-20. Their jealousy led them to detain the Twelve overnight until the
light of day could afford a legal interrogation. However, between dusk and dawn
the angel[18] opened the jailhouse doors and ordered the Apostles to preach in
the temple courts. Obviously, this divine intervention was not for the Apostle's
release but for their affirmation. This divine display would undergird the advice
forthcoming from one of the council's senior members.

**[21]At daybreak they entered the temple courts, as they had been told, and
began to teach the people. When the high priest and his associates arrived, they
called together the Sanhedrin—the full assembly of the elders of Israel—and
sent to the jail for the apostles. [22]But on arriving at the jail, the officers did not
find them there. So they went back and reported, [23]"We found the jail securely
locked, with the guards standing at the doors; but when we opened them, we
found no one inside." [24]On hearing this report, the captain of the temple guard
and the chief priests were puzzled, wondering what would come of this. [25]Then
someone came and said, "Look! The men you put in jail are standing in the
temple courts teaching the people." [26]At that, the captain went with his officers
and brought the apostles. They did not use force, because they feared that the
people would stone them.**

5:21-26. The counsel normally convened about 10 a.m. They sent the temple guard to retrieve the prisoners but they found their cell empty. There was an
immediate investigation but everything was in order. The doors were securely
locked and the soldiers were standing at attention, but those pesky Apostles had
somehow escaped. One can imagine the consternation of the Sanhedrin.[19] The
question is not merely "Where did they go?" but "What will this lead to?"[20] They

---

[17] H. Anselm and Jerome Neyrey, "It Was Out of Envy That They Handed Jesus Over (Mk 15:10): The
Anatomy of Envy and the Gospel of Mark," *JSNT* 69 (1998): 15-56.

[18] The term "Angel of the Lord" is used eleven times in the NT, clearly derived from the fifty OT uses of
the phrase. Most of the NT uses are in the birth narratives (Matt 1:20, 24; 2:13, 19; Luke 1:11; 2:9) and the
miraculous prison breaks of Acts (5:19; 12:7, 23) with a couple of stray uses in a resurrection story (Matt
28:2) and Philip's divine guidance to the Ethiopian's chariot (Acts 8:26). Divine intervention was not an
uncommon theme in Greco-Roman literature (e.g., Euripides, *Bacchae* 443-448; Philostratus, *Apollonius*
7.38; Ovid, *Metamorphoses* 3.696-700; Artapanus, *Concerning the Jews* as reported by Eusebius, *Praep. Evang.*
9.27.23). Luke's readers would have recognized the motif.

[19] This rare word "puzzled" (διαπορέω) is only used four times in the Bible, all by Luke (Luke 9:7; Acts
2:12; 5:24; 10:17).

[20] This awkward Greek phrase "what would come of this" (περὶ αὐτῶν τί ἂν γένοιτο τοῦτο) is an optative verb which points forward to the potential consequences of this event.

and Luke retaliates by labeling them arrogant and blind. The prize of this contest is not bragging rights
but social survival via the approval of the populace. Cf. Randall Webber, "'Why Were the Heathen So Arrogant?': The Socio-Rhetorical Strategy of Acts 3–4," *BTB* 22 (1992): 19-25.

suspected foul play, not divine intervention. For the reader this is a sure sign that God is on the side of the Twelve. For the Sanhedrin, it surely indicated some sort of surreptitious plot among their own guards—some of their security detail must be secret supporters of this increasingly dangerous movement. This surely contributed to their virulent response to the Apostles. It also explains why they treat the Apostles with kid gloves. Some blasted informant bursts into the Hall of Gazith where the Sanhedrin assembled and announced that the Apostles were preaching in the Temple. The Captain of the temple guard (cf. 4:1), along with a retinue of soldiers, retrieved them. They don't dare cuff them, however, since the people love the Twelve. Their miracles made them wildly popular. Remember, this honor came from somewhere. As the Apostles get more honor, this leaves less for the Sanhedrin. Since the balance of power was shifting, they had to tread lightly lest they spark a full-scale riot.

²⁷Having brought the apostles, they made them appear before the Sanhedrin to be questioned by the high priest. ²⁸"We gave you strict orders not to teach in this name," he said. "Yet you have filled Jerusalem with your teaching and are determined to make us guilty of this man's blood." ²⁹Peter and the other apostles replied: "We must obey God rather than men! ³⁰The God of our fathers raised Jesus from the dead—whom you had killed by hanging him on a tree. ³¹God exalted him to his own right hand as Prince and Savior that he might give repentance and forgiveness of sins to Israel. ³²We are witnesses of these things, and so is the Holy Spirit, whom God has given to those who obey him."

5:27-28. The High Priest was fit to be tied. He reminded the Twelve of the explicit ban on preaching in Jesus' name (4:17-18, 21). Not only had they defied the Sanhedrin's prohibition, they had blamed their leaders for the murder of Jesus. Of course, if there is an ounce of historical truth in Matthew 27:25, this was an extraordinary protest: "All the people answered, 'Let his blood be on us and on our children!'" Annas was surely not denying involvement in the death of Jesus. Rather, he was arguing that Jesus had it coming.

5:29-30. Peter's reply could not be more direct, forceful, or offensive. They had been accused of defying the Sanhedrin's decree. To this Peter says, "Guilty as charged *because* we are obeying God whom you are opposing" (v. 29).²¹ This could not have been good for the aged priest's blood pressure. They have also been charged with implicating the Sanhedrin for Jesus' death. To this he says, "You are guilty as charged" (v. 30). Luke uses a unique Greek word, found only twice in the New Testament; it implies violence in the killing (Acts 5:31; 26:21). Peter pulled no punches.

5:31-32. As if Peter's response wasn't offensive enough, he proclaimed *again* the resurrection of Jesus. This was what got them arrested in the first place back in chapter 3! Jesus not only rose from the dead but he was seated at the

---

²¹ There are a number of times in the Bible when godly men and women practiced 'civil disobedience': Moses' parents (Exod 1:16-17), Daniel (Dan 6:10), and Shadrach, Meshach, Abednego (Dan 3:16–18). Each of these disobeyed officials only when a governmental edict prohibited what God expressly commanded or commanded what God expressly prohibited.

right hand of the Father—the place of divine royalty.[22] The man they subjected to a cursed crucifixion (cf. Acts 10:39; 13:29)[23] God raised as Prince (*archēgos*, "founder," "leader," or "originator"; cf. Acts 3:15; Heb 2:10; 12:2) and Savior (*sōtēr*). The man Annas declared deserving of death Peter proclaims as the Lord of Life. This is what one might call a difference of opinion. Peter is not trying to be belligerent. Rather, he has a message of life for all people, including the Jewish leaders. Sometimes, when one's ears are closed, all he can hear is shouting. So if Peter seems rather 'loud' here, it may just be that he is intent on offering "repentance and forgiveness of sins to Israel."

Whose opinion is right? Let the reader decide, but Peter has two witnesses on his side: The Apostles and the Holy Spirit. The Apostles stand there with a unified claim to have seen Jesus raised from the dead. The Holy Spirit stands behind them, empowering their miracles as undeniable public acclamation.[24] The crowds, much to the chagrin of the Sanhedrin, were persuaded by Peter's argument. It was time, therefore, for drastic measures.

[33]When they heard this, they were furious and wanted to put them to death. [34]But a Pharisee named Gamaliel, a teacher of the law, who was honored by all the people, stood up in the Sanhedrin and ordered that the men be put outside for a little while. [35]Then he addressed them: "Men of Israel, consider carefully what you intend to do to these men. [36]Some time ago Theudas appeared, claiming to be somebody, and about four hundred men rallied to him. He was killed, all his followers were dispersed, and it all came to nothing. [37]After him, Judas the Galilean appeared in the days of the census and led a band of people in revolt. He too was killed, and all his followers were scattered. [38]Therefore, in the present case I advise you: Leave these men alone! Let them go! For if their purpose or activity is of human origin, it will fail. [39]But if it is from God, you will not be able to stop these men; you will only find yourselves fighting against God."

5:33-34. Peter's reply was nearly lethal. The council was "furious" (*dieprionto* etymologically means "sawn through"). Had it not been for Gamaliel this would have been their last stand for the gospel.[25] This famed Pharisee[26] was well known

---

[22] Peter had used this same figure "right hand of God" in 2:33. Here it has the same implication, though with a much more aggressive audience: Jesus shares the presence and priorities of Yahweh; cf. Michel Gourgues, "Exalté à la droite de Dieu," *ScEs* 27 (1975): 303-327.

[23] Deut 21:23, "Anyone who is hung on a tree is under God's curse," cf. Gal 3:13; M. Wilcox, "Upon the Tree—Deut 21:22-23 in the New Testament," *JBL* 96 (1977): 85-99.

[24] Peter here affirms that the Holy Spirit is given to those who obey. Elsewhere the Spirit is promised to those who ask (Luke 11:13), who love Jesus (John 14:23), who believe (John 7:38-39; Gal 3:2, 5), and who repent and are baptized (Acts 2:38; 19:1-6; John 3:3-7), all of which are synecdoche.

[25] Josephus records that the Pharisees were often successful in swaying the decisions of the council (*Ant.* 18.1.4 §17).

[26] The Pharisees were one of the three major political groups of the day (Josephus, *Ant.* 18.1.2 §11). They were loosely connected by their radical devotion to the Law of God—somewhat akin to modern right-wing fundamentalists. Their name comes from the Aramaic "*perishim*," meaning "separated" and they likely evolved from the Chasidim ("godly men"), first mentioned in *Maccabees*, during the days of John Hyrcanus (134–104 B.C.). By the time of Jesus they probably numbered around 6,000. They were a constant source of tension and confrontation for Jesus (Matt 12:34-39; 15:7-8; 23:2-33; Mark 7:5-13; Luke 11:39-49; John 5:39-40; 12:48-50), mostly due to their oral traditions added to support the Scriptures. This impetus was succinctly put in *m. Abot* 1.1: "Be deliberate in giving judgment and raise up many disciples, and make a hedge about the law." In the Gospel of Luke, there are no positive statements about Pharisees. That changes in

and loved, not least because he was the grandson (or perhaps the son) of the great Hillel who died just about the time Jesus first entered the temple at age twelve. Of Gamaliel the Mishnah says, "Since Rabban Gamaliel died, the glory of the Law has ceased" (*m. Sotah* 9.15). His students, not surprisingly, were influential in establishing and codifying the oral tradition of the rabbis. His own grandson, Gamaliel II led the counsel that added to the *Eighteen Benedictions* a prayer which ultimately cemented a permanent rift between the church and synagogue: "And for slanderers let there be no hope, and let all wickedness perish as in a moment; let all Your enemies be speedily cut off, and the dominion of arrogance uproot and crush, cast down and humble speedily in our days. Blessed art thou, O Lord, who breaks the enemies and humbles the arrogant."[27] The most (in)famous of all Gamaliel's pupils was none other than Paul whose conversion, no doubt, left the Jerusalem academia stunned (Acts 22:3). Most interesting in this context is the fact that Gamaliel takes a moderate position on the Jesus movement whereas Saul, still under his tutelage, vehemently disagreed, leading a violent campaign of total eradication. One can only wonder what kind of class debate ensued over that one.

5:35-39. Gamaliel's advice is simple: If this is from God, it will survive and you will be on the wrong side. If it is from man, it will be destroyed as other human revolts have been. Whether or not Gamaliel's advice is sage or silly is rather beside the point.[28] For Luke's purpose, it was effective. The Apostles live to see another day.

Gamaliel illustrates his point with two failed revolutionaries. Judas the Galilean was a well-known rebel who stirred up a revolt during the census of Quirinius in A.D. 6 (Josephus *J.W.* 2.8.1 §118; *Ant.* 18.1.1 §4-10, 23).[29] Both Luke and Josephus would agree on the basic data. Theudas, however, presents a problem. Josephus places his rebellion during the reign of Fadus (A.D. 44-46; cf. *Ant.* 20.5.1 §97-98) about ten years later than Acts 5. So how can Gamaliel speak of events that are yet a decade in the future? And why does Luke have Gamaliel place Judas *after* Theudas (v. 37).[30] There is not yet a satisfying explanation to

---

Acts, however, where three separate incidents reflect positively on this Jewish party: Gamaliel saves the Apostles (5:34), some believe in Jesus (15:5, cf. Gal 2:4-5), and a group among the Sanhedrin defend Paul's preaching of the resurrection (23:6-10). Cf. J. D. Kingsbury, "The Pharisees in Luke-Acts," *The Four Gospels 1992* (BETL; ed. F. van Segbroeck et al.; Louvain: Leuven University/Peeters, 1992), 2.1497-1512; and J. T. Sanders, "The Pharisees in Luke-Acts," *The Living Text* (ed. D. E. Groh and R. Jewett; Lanham: University Press of America, 1985), 141-188.

[27] The twelfth prayer of the eighteen (now nineteen) Benedictions was added at Yavneh under Gamaliel II (c. A.D. 90), apparently aimed at Christians (cf. *Encyclopedia Judaica* 12:3).

[28] Those who read Gamaliel in light of the previous negative portrayal of Pharisees in Luke will likely understand his advice to be flawed. Those who concentrate on the contextual characterization of Gamaliel in Acts 5—as a hero—will take his advice to be correct. This later view is probably closer to Luke's intention since the remainder of Acts is designed to show that Gamaliel's unwitting prophecy about the church turned out to be true. Cf. William J. Lyons, "The Words of Gamaliel (Acts 5.38-39) and the Irony of Indeterminacy," *JSNT* 68 (1997): 23-49.

[29] Though Gamaliel was correct that his movement lay dormant, during the Roman campaign against Palestine in A.D. 66-70 a group of his sons and followers resurfaced under the banner of the zealots, wreaking havoc for Jews and Romans alike (*J.W.* 2.17.8 §433-434; 7.8.1 §253; *Ant.* 20.5.1 §97-102); cf. Jeffrey A. Trumbower, "The Historical Jesus and the Speech of Gamaliel (Acts 5.35-39)," *NTS* 39 (1993): 512-513. Richard Horsley, "Popular Prophetic Movements at the Time of Jesus: Their Principal Features and Social Origins," *JSNT* 26 (1986): 3-27, offers a succinct survey of the major rebel movments of the period.

[30] Some have suggested that Luke is dependent on Josephus here because Judas's sons are mentioned

this conundrum. Some have asserted that Luke simply got his facts wrong or perhaps deliberately used anachronistic examples for rhetorical effect. After all, Luke was recording a speech to which neither he nor the disciples had access. So it is asserted that he put words in Gamaliel's mouth that were true during the time Luke wrote, but not during the days of Gamaliel.[31] Given Luke's track record, however, one should be cautious about such an easy accusation against his accuracy. A second solution would be to charge Josephus with the inaccuracy. However, since he lived in Israel during the reign of Fadus, there is no reason to suspect him of error in regard to Theudas. A third solution would be to look for a second Theudas (Marshall, 122-123; Polhill, 172-173). Even though the details of Josephus and Luke are similar, there were lots of rebels during this period who could have used similar methods or even deliberately imitated one another just as Theudas himself was deliberately imitating Joshua crossing the Jordan on dry ground.[32]

[40]His speech persuaded them. They called the apostles in and had them flogged. Then they ordered them not to speak in the name of Jesus, and let them go. [41]The apostles left the Sanhedrin, rejoicing because they had been counted worthy of suffering disgrace for the Name. [42]Day after day, in the temple courts and from house to house, they never stopped teaching and proclaiming the good news that Jesus is the Christ.[a]

[a]42 Or Messiah

5:40-42. Though Gamaliel's speech spared their lives, it didn't spare their backs. The Sanhedrin could hardly afford to simply let them go. That would be tantamount to public approval. They were flogged with thirty-nine lashes,[33] verbally warned (yet again), and sent home sore and shamed. Most people would slink home to sulk in the shadows. This shameful treatment in their culture caused a humiliation deeper than the cuts from the flagellum. Yet the Apostles turned their shame into victory. Disgrace among the martyrs became bragging rights in the church. This reversal of social values was one of the most brilliant ideological maneuvers in the whole of religious history. It enabled Christians not merely to survive but to thrive under the duress of severe perse-

---

after Theudas, hence a misreading of Josephus could account for the order of Theudas and Judas in Acts 5. However, since Josephus's works were not published until c. A.D. 93 it is unlikely that Luke had access to them. Moreover, Luke mentions 400 followers of Theudas that were *not* enumerated by Josephus. The logical conclusion is that Luke is relying on a separate tradition for that bit of information and is not indebted to Josephus for any of his information.

[31] Joseph W. Swain, "Gamaliel's Speech and Caligula's Statue," *HTR* 37 (1944): 341-349, postulates a variation of this theory. Namely, Luke misplaced the material. He avers Gamaliel's speech belongs after the angelic release of Peter in Acts 12 rather than in Acts 5. While this still leaves the anachronism of Theudas, it is only off by a year rather than a decade.

[32] "Theudas" is the 34th most common name in the textual and inscriptional evidence between 330 B.C. and A.D. 200, interestingly, mentioned the same number of times as "Gamaliel"; Richard Bauckham, *Jesus and the Eyewitnesses: The Gospels as Eyewitness Testimony* (Grand Rapids: Eerdmans, 2006), 86. Hence, it was a common enough name to be confused with or reduplicated in another rebel.

[33] The Jewish law limited lashes to forty (Deut 25:3). The Jews stopped at thirty-nine lest they miscounted along the way (2 Cor 11:24; *m. Mak.* 3:10). It was better to err on the side of clemency than exceed the boundaries of the law which would make the prosecutor guilty if the victim died under the scourge (*m. Mak.* 3.14).

cution which would punctuate their chronicles. The strategy was to reinterpret persecution as a mechanism by which a person developed an affinity with Jesus (John 15:18-21; Phil 3:10-11; 2 Cor 1:5; 1 Pet 3:17-18; 4:12-16), built Christian character (Rom 5:3-5; James 1:2-4), and secured an eternal reward (Matt 5:11-12; Rom 8:17; 2 Cor 4:17-18). Paul will say, "We must go through many hardships to enter the kingdom of God" (Acts 14:22). Peter will add, "If you suffer as a Christian, do not be ashamed, but praise God that you bear that name" (1 Pet 4:16). Both reflect the teaching of Jesus, "Blessed are those who are persecuted because of righteousness, for theirs is the kingdom of heaven" (Matt 5:10).

Thus this beating did not accomplish its intended goal. On the contrary, it spurred the believers to further unity both publicly and privately. Their message was simple and incessant: Jesus is the Christ—the long-awaited Jewish Messiah (see comments on 2:36). Thus concludes the fourth summary of the church.

ACTS 6

5. Handling Benevolence for Christian Widows (6:1-7)

This story is simple enough. A group of widows felt like they were being discriminated against in the daily dole of food. Frankly, they probably had a legitimate complaint. As the church exploded, the administrative demands overloaded the Twelve. Furthermore, since the neglected party of widows spoke Greek and the primary leadership spoke Aramaic, it would be more difficult for them to keep track of these women's needs. So they delegated the ministry of benevolence to seven capable stewards who appear to be Hellenists themselves.

From this simple story a number of issues emerge. For some this text is a template for ordaining deacons in the church. Others have gleaned from this story the principle of preaching being more important than compassion. After all, feeding postpones hunger for a day; preaching rescues the soul from hell. These may or may not be valid implications drawn from this story (as will be discussed below). For Luke the agenda of the text is not the diaconate nor the relative merits of one ministry over another. Rather, his subtext (or perhaps pretext) is the expansion of the church into Gentile territory. This episode marks the first broken boundary of the narrow Jewish circle of the early church. These Hellenistic widows were Jewish by blood but lived on the fringes of Jerusalem Judaism. This confrontation pressed the issue of 'elite' Christians among the early Jewish believers. What counted as status among Jews no longer mattered for followers of the Messiah.

¹In those days when the number of disciples was increasing, the Grecian Jews among them complained against the Hebraic Jews because their widows were being overlooked in the daily distribution of food.

6:1. "In those days" is a typical Lucan marker that simply means "next I want to talk about" (cf. Luke 1:39; 2:1; 5:35; 6:12; 21:23; 23:7; 24:18; Acts 1:15; 6:1; 9:37; 11:27). There is no way to know how long this was after the start of the church. It could be months or years. The important point is the apparent neglect of the Grecian Jews. This seems all the more flagrant in the shadow of Acts 5:42, "Day after day, in the temple courts and from house to house, they never stopped teaching and proclaiming the good news that Jesus is the Christ." The Apostolic teaching went from house to house, but the church's resources apparently did not.

The Apostles were trying to do the right thing by feeding widows but got derailed by the oppressive demands of an ever-expanding congregation. The rabbis spoke of a similar system in which relief officers were sent through the community each Friday to take up alms for widows, providing them fourteen

123

meals per week (*m. Ket.* 4.12; 13.1–2; *m. Peah* 8.7; *m. Pesah.* 10.1; *b. B. Bat.* 8b). Though Jeremias asserts this practice goes back to the first century, there is no evidence that such was the case prior to the destruction of the temple in A.D. 70[1] There is no mention of this system in either of the two descriptions of famine relief (Josephus, *Ant.* 15.9.1-2 §299-316; 20.2.5 §51-53). Moreover, the frequent mention of begging in second temple Judaism may indicate that the system of benevolence later described by the rabbis had not yet fully developed. Hence, there is as much evidence that the rabbis copied the Christian example as there is that Christians copied the rabbis. Conclusion: What was happening in the church was more extreme benevolence than anything they could have seen around them with the notable exception of the Qumran community who had fled the urban area of Jerusalem (see above on 4:32-34; cf. 1 Tim 5:9-11).

There is some question about who exactly the Hellenistic widows were, but the best consensus is that they were Jewish women from the Diaspora who came to Jerusalem to die and be buried on sacred soil.[2] Archaeology bears witness to a great number of tombs and ossuaries of Hellenistic women.[3] Many of them must have accepted Jesus as their Messiah as did thousands of other Jews in Jerusalem. This massive growth of the church presented substantial cultural and administrative problems. The administrative problem is obvious. The Twelve just could not keep up with the demands to teach, heal, arbitrate disputes, communicate with Jewish leaders, distribute benevolent funds, etc. The cultural problem is more subtle. If a leader is overloaded, some of his constituents will get neglected. It is natural that those with a language and/or cultural barrier are less able to communicate their needs.[4] Hence, it is hardly surprising that they were the first to feel the pinch of the Apostles' neglect. These Greek-speaking widows ran in different circles than the Apostles. Their dress, behavior, cultural habits, and especially their food may have made them awkward or even offensive to be around. This is not to suggest they were breaking the Law of Moses. If, as we have argued, these women were devout Jews who had come to Jerusalem to be buried, they would have been zealous Jews. Their offenses were cultural, the kind that make them difficult to incorporate in social circles. Ostracized individuals are the easiest to overlook. So they grumbled.[5]

---

[1] Joachim Jeremias, *Jerusalem in the Time of Jesus* (Philadelphia: Fortress, 1969), 131-134. For the counter evidence, see Capper, "Palestinian Cultural Context," 350-351.

[2] See especially Martin Hengel, "Zwischen Jesus und Paulus: die Sieben und Stephanus (Apg 6, 1-15; 7, 54–8, 3," *ZTK* 72 (1975): 157-172; in English: "Between Jesus and Paul," pp. 6-26, in *Between Jesus and Paul: Studies in the Earliest History of Christianity* (tr. John Bowden; London: SCM, 1983). For a discussion of the various possibilities see Everett Ferguson, "The Hellenists in the Book of Acts," *RQ* 12 (1969): 159-180; also Windisch, TDNT 2:508-516. The other primary option is that they were actually Greeks whose nonkosher diet kept them separate from the other Christian widows (cf. *Beginnings* 5:59-74).

[3] Hengel, "Zwischen Jesus und Paulus," 181-185. David A. Fiensy, "The Composition of the Jerusalem Church," in *The Book of Acts in Its Palestinian Setting* (ed. Richard Bauckham; vol. 4 in *The Book of Acts in Its First Century Setting*, Grand Rapids: Eerdmans, 1995), 213-236, provides a most helpful analysis of the sociological composition of Jerusalem during the first half of the first century.

[4] Chrysostom (c. A.D. 347–407) in his commentary on Acts (*Homily* 21) wrote, "'With the Hellenists': he means those who used the Greek tongue." Clearly he understood "Hellenists" to include a language barrier not merely a cultural difference. R. Pesch, E. Gerhart, and F. Schilling point out the practical difficulties such a language barrier would cause in social differentiation between the two groups; "'Hellenisten' und 'Hebräer' zu Apg 9,19 und 6,1," *BZ* ns 23 (1979): 87-92.

[5] The Greek word (γογγυσμός) has a muted echo of the grumbling of the Israelites in the desert (Exod

COLLEGE PRESS NIV COMMENTARY

[2]So the Twelve gathered all the disciples together and said, "It would not be right for us to neglect the ministry of the word of God in order to wait on tables. [3]Brothers, choose seven men from among you who are known to be full of the Spirit and wisdom. We will turn this responsibility over to them [4]and will give our attention to prayer and the ministry of the word."

6:2. The Apostles wanted to prioritize their work of prayer and preaching. So they called a congregational meeting to delegate the distribution of food to seven Spirit-filled and wise men.[6] These three short verses raise two critical questions. First, is this passage the genesis of church deacons? Second, is the ministry of the word more important than that of benevolence? Each must be taken up in turn.

6:3. "Deacon" is a transliteration from the Greek word *diakonos*. It simply means "servant" without implying a title or office in the church.[7] While "Deacon" will eventually become an office in the church (1 Tim 3:12-13) and though the "Seven" did become the title of a recognized group (21:8)[8] it is still anachronistic and perhaps even a misnomer to call these men the first Christian Deacons. The word "deacon" is not even used in this passage though its sister word *diakonia* is used twice (vv. 1, 4) and *diakonein* once (v. 2).[9] Had Luke wanted to specify these seven as church officials, he could have used the proper title. More important, it seems, is that both Stephen and Philip transcended the boundaries of benevolence and were themselves preachers of the word in the following two chapters.[10] It could be that they merely grew in their own leadership abilities and attained higher spiritual gifts and roles. There is, however, another possi-

---

16:2-12; cf. Exod 17:3; Num 11:1; John 6:41-43, 61) though there is no indication in the text that they were unrighteous in this complaint as were their forefathers.

[6] The combination of Spirit and wisdom reminds the reader of the characteristics of the Messiah (Isa 11:2), Daniel (Dan 5:11, 14), John the Baptist (Luke 1:17), and Paul (1 Cor 2:13).

[7] Luke uses the word διακονία nine times. It refers to table service (Luke 10:40; Acts 6:1), the ministries of the Apostles (Acts 1:17, 25; 6:4; 20:24; 21:19), and benevolent offerings (Acts 11:29; 12:25). The verb (διακονέω) appears ten times, mostly in reference to table service (Luke 4:39; 10:40; 12:37; 17:8; 22:26-27 [3x]; Acts 6:2) and offerings (Luke 8:3; Acts 19:22; cf. 16:1-2, 10; 2 Tim 4:20). Bottom line: Luke uses διακονία and its cognate words primarily in reference to benevolent care surrounding the common meal. Though he uses these words with reference to the "office" of Apostle, he does not appear to use them in reference to any other office. John Collins has done the definitive study on this word surveyed over a period of eight hundred years, arguing that it should *not* be seen as humble service, but as service performed for a royal figure; *Diakonia: Re-interpreting the Ancient Sources* (Oxford: Oxford University Press, 1990). His impressive swath of data, however, fails to account for Luke's particular use of the word, likely gleaned from the *ipsissima verba* of Jesus (Mark 10:43) in which διακονία *is* an indication of humble service.

[8] Everett Ferguson tenuously argues that the verbal parallels between Acts 6:1-6 and Num 27:15-23, which the rabbis took as a sort of ordination, indicate that Jews would have seen an ordination to an office in this text; "Laying on of Hands in Acts 6:6 and 13:3," *RQ* 4 (1960): 250; also Paul Philippi, "Apostelgeschichte 6, 1-6 als Frage an die Kirche heute," in *Spiritus et institution ecclesia* (Helsinki: Societas Historiae ecclesiast, 1980), 253-265. More likely it was merely a group set aside for a particular ministry task; cf. Phillip W. Sell, "The Seven in Acts 6 as a Ministry Team," *BibSac* 167 (2010): 58-67.

[9] Luke, in fact, appears to avoid the word where it is found in his sources. Mark 9:35, "If anyone wants to be first, he must be the very last, and the servant (διάκονος) of all," whereas Luke 9:48 reads, "For he who is least among you all—he is the greatest." Again, Mark 10:43 says, "Whoever wants to become great among you must be your servant (διάκονος)," but Luke 22:26 opts for the substantive form, "The greatest among you should be like the youngest, and the one who rules like the one who serves (ὁ διακονῶν)." See further Bernhard Domagalski, "Waren die 'Sieben' (Apg 6,1-7) Diakone," *BZ* 26 (1982): 21-33. This is all the more surprising if Luke wrote from Rome, given that there were clearly deacons in that church (cf. Rom 16:1).

[10] Such is the nature of compassionate ministries. One can hardly have compassion for a person's physical condition and not their spiritual condition or vice versa; Justo L. González, "Pluralismo, justicia y mission: un studio bíblico sobre Hechos 6:1-7," *Apuntes* 10 (1990): 3-8.

bility. Perhaps the ministry of benevolence *included* the ministry of the word. It may well be that the Apostles *intended* for the seven Greek-speaking servants to deliver the meals and then sit down with the widows and instruct them in the faith. After all, the Apostles themselves were not able to communicate the word in the heart language of these dear women. This leads to our second question.

6:4. Is there a hierarchy of ministry prioritizing preaching/teaching over benevolence? That seems to be the obvious implication of the text. After all, the Apostles delegated table service *so that* they could devote their time and attention to prayer and preaching.[11] However, several other points need to be considered. First, the Apostles had a unique role as witnesses of the resurrection and were foundational for establishing orthodox Christian doctrine. The pastor at the "First Christian Church" can hardly claim to be such a cornerstone of the faith. Second, Jesus himself extolled humble service even mandating it for the highest kingdom leaders (Mark 10:42-44/Matt 20:25-27; Luke 12:35-37; John 13:1-17). This was, in fact, an essential priority for Yahweh in the Old Testament. Care for widows was one of the marks of fidelity to pure religion (cf. James 1:27).[12] Third, as was pointed out above, the ministry of the word and service at the table probably went hand in hand. Fourth, the accolades which come with preaching may impact pastors' motives more than we would like to imagine. The text says that Apostolic prayer preceded even their preaching. Thus those pastors who eschew menial service, supposedly for the proclamation of the word, betray their real agenda when they neglect to prioritize prayer which does not offer the public recognition of preaching.

[5]This proposal pleased the whole group. They chose Stephen, a man full of faith and of the Holy Spirit; also Philip, Procorus, Nicanor, Timon, Parmenas, and Nicolas from Antioch, a convert to Judaism. [6]They presented these men to the apostles, who prayed and laid their hands on them. [7]So the word of God spread. The number of disciples in Jerusalem increased rapidly, and a large number of priests became obedient to the faith.

6:5. The group selected for themselves seven men, all of whom had Greek names.[13] Though many Jews in Palestine had at least one Greek name (e.g., Philip and Andrew among the Twelve), that all seven had Greek names probably indicates they were from the Hellenistic side of this debate. This is significant. Not only were they able to speak the language and culture of the neglected widows, the unanimous selection of Hellenists sends a clear message to the church.

---

[11] A number of rabbinic statements extol the virtues of Torah study: "If he has gotten teachings of Torah, he has gotten himself life eternal" (*m. Abot* 2.7). "If the son acquired merit [by sitting and studying] before the master, the master takes precedence over the father under all circumstances" (*m. Ker.* 6.9). But study was never to exclude benevolence: "On three things does the world stand: On Torah, and on the Temple service, and on deeds of loving kindness" (*m. Abot* 1.2).

[12] F. Scott Spencer points out that if the widow texts are read in order from Luke through Acts, the reader is conditioned to expect the widows in this text to be economically oppressed as in each of the previous four widow texts (Luke 2:36-38; 7:11-17; 18:1-8; 21:1-4; cf. 20:27-40, 45-47); "Neglected Widows in Acts 6:1-7," *CBQ* 56 (1994): 715-733.

[13] In later Judaism, three men represented leadership of a synagogue whereas seven represented leadership of a city (Str–B 2:641, y. *Meg.* 3.1 [74a], 16; *m. Meg.* 3.1; *t. Meg.* 3.1; Josephus, *J.W.* 2.20.5 §570-571).

The majority group was willing to capitulate to the needs of the minority injured party. There is more at stake than who was right and who was wrong. Above any party line was the unity of the church.

Stephen will be featured in the next two chapters as the first Christian martyr. Philip will become, in a sense, the first Christian missionary, when the persecution of Saul propels him into Samaria (8:5-40; 21:8-9). The others on the list are virtual unknowns, except for Procorus and Nicolas. Procorus supposedly served as John the Evangelist's secretary and ultimately the martyred bishop of Nicodemia (Bruce, 129; *Beginnings* 4:65). Nicolas, on the other hand, does not fare so well. The early church fathers identified him as the founder of a heretical cult in Ephesus and Pergamum which Jesus rebukes in Revelation 2:6, 15 (cf. Irenaeus, *Adv. Her.*1.26.3 and Clement of Alexandria, *Stromata* 2.20.118).[14] That he was from Antioch may put him in direct relation to Luke and certainly connects him with the early missionary outreach of the church.

6:6. The Apostles forthwith confirmed the congregational selection by praying and laying their hands on the seven delegates.[15] This ceremony was not merely symbolic. Ancients believed that spiritual power was passed through physical touch. It could be a blessing (Gen 48:12-22), a curse (or at least the transfer of guilt to a sacrificial victim, Lev 1:4; 3:2; etc.), healing (Acts 9:12, 17; 28:8), commissioning a successor (Num 27:23), or a spiritual gift (Acts 6:6, 8; 8:18; 19:6; 2 Tim 1:6). Yet it was perceived as an actual transfer of spiritual power and authority.

6:7. This proved to be the right move, for the church continued to grow. In this brief 'progress report' (cf. 9:31; 12:24; 16:5; 19:20; 28:31) we find a new element: Priests were converted, not just one or two, but "crowds" of priests. Furthermore, they would have a powerful influence on their families and communities for the gospel. (There is no reason to assume these priests would have abandoned their temple duties.) The Church is nearly poised to break out of Jerusalem and spread across Judea. There is but one element missing—persecution.

E. THE FIRST CHRISTIAN MARTYR (6:8–8:1a)

The lynching of Stephen is the final phase of the Jerusalem church and the impetus for the spread of Christianity to the surrounding region. This young man represents more than a mere martyr. He is the first to preach and heal as the Apostles did. Hence, a few people from the pews are rising to the power and prominence of their leaders. Luke artistically paints the Apostles as Jesus'

---

[14] In the earliest Latin commentary on Revelation (c. A.D. 300) Victorinus of Pettau said the founders of this heresy did so "in the name of the deacon Nicolas" (cited in Bruce, 129). Though there is no way to confirm this connection of Nicolas with the Nicolaitans, neither is there any reason to doubt the testimony of the Fathers; cf. Norbert Brox, "Nicolaos und Nikolaiten," *VC* 19 (1965) 23-30; and Nikolaus Walter, "Nikolaos, Proselyt aus Antiochien, und die Nikolaiten in Ephesus und Pergamon: Ein Beitrag auch zum Thema: Paulus und Ephesus," *ZNW* 93 (2002): 200-226.

[15] The Western Text [B] of 6:3 *can* be read to suggest that it was the Apostles who not only ordained these men by laying hands on them, but were also responsible for their initial selection (as opposed to the whole congregation selecting the seven) but this is not likely the best reading; cf. *Beginnings*, 4:65 and Josep Rius-Camps, "Las Variantes del Texto Occidental de los Hechos de los Apóstoles [XI]," *FilNoet* 13 (2000): 91-92.

successors and now Stephen is commissioned by them to carry on *their* work. As Jesus' power rolls relentlessly forward through the Apostles to the people, the reader is forced to ask, "What about me? Will the work of Jesus continue through me in my own Judea?"

1. Stephen's Character and Arrest (6:8-15)

One of the seven servants, Stephen, now takes center stage. Like Barnabas he is introduced with a snippet (v. 5) before opening his full memoirs (6:8–8:1a). We're about to get an earful from Stephen; in fact, his speech is twice as long as any other in the entire book! Before hearing from Stephen himself, however, the stage must be set. His antagonists enter from the Synagogue of the Freedmen and somehow carry his case to the entire Sanhedrin. He finds himself in the very precarious position of the Apostles whose lives had hung in the balance (5:27-42). Of course, this story has no Gamaliel to alter the inevitable brutal ending. When they were unable to cast aspersions on Steven's character they cast stones.

⁸Now Stephen, a man full of God's grace and power, did great wonders and miraculous signs among the people. ⁹Opposition arose, however, from members of the Synagogue of the Freedmen (as it was called)—Jews of Cyrene and Alexandria as well as the provinces of Cilicia and Asia. These men began to argue with Stephen, ¹⁰but they could not stand up against his wisdom or the Spirit by whom he spoke.

6:8. We have a fairly full resume of Stephen. He was full of the Spirit and wisdom (v. 3, 10),[16] full of faith and the Holy Spirit (v. 5), and full of God's grace and power (v. 8). So the reader is hardly surprised that he performed miracles, even if he is the first non-Apostle to do so.[17] Nor is anyone surprised that Stephen's arguments were unassailable; that was the promise of receiving the Spirit (Luke 12:11-12; 21:12-15).

6:9-10. Stephen's rise in notoriety raised opposition. It came from the synagogue of the Freedmen,[18] whatever that was.[19] Since there are four geographic

---

[16] Aside from Stephen (6:3, 10), only Joseph (7:10) and Moses (7:22) are said to have wisdom in this passage. Clearly Joseph and Moses are Christ figures in this passage. Hence, this becomes another indication that Stephen was a particularly powerful figure, representing Jesus himself through the indwelling Spirit.

[17] The supposition that only the Apostles, or those upon whom they laid their hands, performed miracles is simply not true. Ananias (Acts 9:17) healed Saul with little chance to be 'ordained' by the Apostles in Damascus. It is true that the Apostles, as the primary witnesses to the resurrection of Jesus, receive the lion's share of attention for their healing signs. This hardly indicates, however, Luke's intention to limit miracles to the Twelve. In fact, one of the key points of the present text is the expansion of the Holy Spirit's power as the gospel penetrates ever-widening geographic and ethnic circles. It is the same literary move Luke made in the Gospel. After the Twelve were commissioned to heal and preach, there are seventy sent out with the same power and purpose. So here too we have an expansion of the Twelve in the Seven. Cf. Domagalski, "Waren die 'Sieben' (Apg 6,1-7) Diakone," 21-33.

[18] "Freedmen (as it was called)" likely represents a translation of the Latin term *libertine*. The most likely explanation of the term is prisoners of war (or their descendents) who had been emancipated. Pompey captured thousands of Jews during his Judean campaign (63 B.C.) and their descendants are likely the 'liberated' Jews spoken of here (cf. Philo, *Embassy*, 155; Tacitus, *Annals* 2.85). Cf. Hengel, "Zwischen Jesus und Paulus," 183.

[19] By synagogue we are primarily speaking about the social group rather than a particular building. There

locations listed, two from Africa (Cyrene and Alexandria) and two from Turkey (Asia and Cilicia), we cannot be sure if there were four separate synagogues, two regional synagogues, or (more likely) one synagogue for the various Hellenistic Jews who made their way back to the Holy Land from the Diaspora (see *Beginnings*, 4:66-68).[20]

The important point is that there were lots of Jews with Hellenistic roots living in Jerusalem. This clarifies several things. First, the tension in the church between the Hellenistic and Hebrew widows was likely imported prejudice from the separation already innate in the broader Jewish community. If Christian converts came from separate synagogues, it makes sense that their colloquial rivalries would not automatically disappear in the baptistery. Second, this explains Stephen's connection to Saul (Paul).[21] He too was a Hellenistic Jew (from Cilicia). If Saul held the cloaks (7:58) at Stephen's stoning, he undoubtedly participated in the previous debates *and lost* (cf. 4:14): "They could not stand up against his wisdom or the Spirit by whom he spoke" (v. 10; cf. Luke 12:12; 21:15). Third, this may explain why Paul sounds a lot like Stephen in his first recorded sermon (Acts 13). Fourth, this explains why Saul made haste to debate with this same synagogue when he returned to Jerusalem after his own conversion (9:29). Finally, Saul too was accused of threatening the temple and breeching Mosaic laws (21:28; 23:29). It looks like Saul and Stephen tussled in the same synagogue.

[11]Then they secretly persuaded some men to say, "We have heard Stephen speak words of blasphemy against Moses and against God." [12]So they stirred

---

is a dearth of archaeological evidence for synagogues as separate and dedicated buildings in Palestine; only those of Gamla, Masada ▣, and Herodium can be securely dated to the Second Temple period. This has led Fiensy and Kee, among others, to deny the existence of such buildings in Galilee during the first half of the first century A.D.; cf. David Fiensy, *The Social History of Palestine in the Herodian Period* (Lewiston, New York: Edwin Mellen, 1991), 141; and H. C. Kee, "Defining the First-Century Synagogue: Problems and Proposals," *NTS* 41 (1995): 481-500. Though Luke 7:4-5 (cf. Mark 12:39/Luke 20:46; Luke 11:43; Acts 18:7), Philo (cf. *Good Person* 81, "Sacred places which they call synagogues"; *Flaccus* 48, "sacred buildings"), and the *Theodotian Inscription* (in which one Theodotos, prior to A.D. 66, takes credit for constructing a synagogue in Jerusalem) clearly speak of physical buildings and should be taken seriously; cf. Rainer Riesner, "Synagogues in Jerusalem," in *The Book of Acts in Its Palestinian Setting* (ed. Richard Bauckham; vol. 4 in *The Book of Acts in Its First Century Setting*; Grand Rapids: Eerdmans, 1995), 179-211. It is possible, of course, that the pattern of the early church meeting in homes (Acts 2:46; 12:12; 18:7; Rom 16:5; 1 Cor 16:19; Col 4:15), later converted into dedicated buildings, was adopted from her Jewish roots (cf. *m. Ned.* 9.2, "'*Qonam* be this house if I enter it', and it was turned into a synagogue."). If this is true, then archaeologists would not necessarily be able to discern the difference between a home and a synagogue; cf. Kenneth Atkinson, "On Further Defining the First-Century A.D. Synagogue: Fact or Fiction? A Rejoinder to H. C. Kee," *NTS* 43 (1997): 491-502.

[20] The claim in *y. Meg.* 3.1 [73d] of four hundred and eighty synagogues in Jerusalem is surely a gross exaggeration. Yet it does speak to the issue at hand of multiple and potentially competing groups of Jewish worshipers. The multiplicity of synagogues likely rose from cultural differences more than geographic separation. Jerusalem is not that large of a place.

[21] Nikolaus Walter speculates that Stephen represented a Hellenistic group, *in opposition* to the Apostolic group, who took a more libertarian view of the law and temple and hence were chased out of Jerusalem (Acts 8:1b). They were responsible for the first evangelistic efforts among the Gentiles, including the conversion of Saul to 'Grace'; "Apostelgeschichte 6.1 und die Anfänge der Urgemeinde in Jerusalem," *NTS* 29 (1983): 370-393. This theory, however, runs afoul when trying to explain why Luke, the Gentile, portrayed Stephen as beholden to and in submission to the Apostles. The portrait of the primacy of the Twelve in particular and the Jerusalem church in general is consistent with Paul's offerings from the Gentiles for the Jerusalem poor (Acts 11:27-30; 20:1-6; 24:17; cf. Rom 15:25-26; 1 Cor 16:1) as well as the account of the Jerusalem council (Acts 15). The connection, however, between Stephen and Paul should not be doubted as demonstrated by Martin Hengel, "Zwischen," 201-204.

**up the people and the elders and the teachers of the law. They seized Stephen
and brought him before the Sanhedrin. ¹³They produced false witnesses, who
testified, "This fellow never stops speaking against this holy place and against
the law. ¹⁴For we have heard him say that this Jesus of Nazareth will destroy this
place and change the customs Moses handed down to us." ¹⁵All who were sitting
in the Sanhedrin looked intently at Stephen, and they saw that his face was like
the face of an angel.**

6:11-13. Stephen's enemies produced witnesses who testified that he spoke
blasphemy against Moses and God (v. 11). This got him arrested. Then, before
the Sanhedrin, they testified that he incessantly spoke against the temple and the
law (v. 13). Notice, the terms have changed, but the charge is the same: Moses/
law and God/temple. There is no way that Stephen blasphemed either Moses or
God. According to the Mishnah, blasphemy was only a misuse of the divine name
(*m. Sanh.* 7.5). In the first century, however, it was apparently any kind of slander against God, his leaders, or institutions he established (cf. Mark 14:61-64).[22]
Hence, when Stephen reinterpreted the law and the temple through Jesus, his
contemporaries took this as a personal assault against Moses and God.[23]

These "false witnesses" (v. 13) were "secretly persuaded" (v. 11). Hence,
one is right to question their motives. Nonetheless, it is doubtful that even an
unbiased court would convict them of blatant perjury. They could produce, no
doubt, specific statements from Stephen that fit the category of temple critique
as well as the abolition of the Law of Moses. What might that look like? Well,
one suspects the temple critique looked much like Hebrews 7–10 and Stephen's
evaluation of the law may have differed little from Paul's in Galatians 3–5 or
Romans 7–8. In other words, Stephen was a Christian Jew who reinterpreted the
central symbols of Israel through the lens of Jesus. For those who rejected Jesus,
this reinterpretation was heretical and blasphemous.

It is virtually certain that Stephen did, in fact, share Jesus' critique of the
temple. We are talking about a man who was arrested with the same charge as
Jesus (Mark 14:58/Matt 26:61; Mark 15:29/Matt 27:40; *Thom* 71), who prayed at
death's door for the forgiveness of his murderers (Acts 7:60; Luke 23:34), and
died with a quote of Jesus on his lips (Acts 7:59; Luke 23:46). The allusions are
unmistakable. Luke is saying, "Look at Stephen; he is just like Jesus."

6:14-15. Verse 14 says, "We have heard him say that this Jesus of Nazareth
will destroy this place." There is undoubtedly historical truth in that. After all,
Jesus quoted prophetic texts at the cleansing of the temple which threatened its
destruction (Isa 56:7; Jer 7:11). Had this been the only time Jesus indicted the

---

[22] Biblical and pseudepigraphal literature support this broader definition of blasphemy. Psa 74:18 suggests that denying God's ability is blasphemy. Isa 52:5 equates persecution of the righteous to blasphemy
(or slaying them, Tobit 1:18). Ezek 35:12 teaches that rejoicing in Israel's defeat is blasphemy, as is insulting
the temple (1 Macc 7:35–38). For more examples see Str-B 1:1016-1020; Craig A. Evans, *Mark 8:27–16:20*
(WBC 34b; Nashville: Thomas Nelson, 2001), 453-455, and Darrell Bock, "The Son of Man and the Debate
over Jesus' 'Blasphemy'," in *Jesus of Nazareth: Lord and Christ* (ed. Joel B. Green and Max Turner; Grand
Rapids: Eerdmans, 1994), 184-186.

[23] In other words, Stephen's Christology is tantamount to blasphemy; cf. Karin Finsterbusch, "Christologie
als Blasphemie: Das Hauptthema der Stephanusperikope in lukanischer Perspektive," *BN* 92 (1998): 38-54.

temple one might wonder about his intentions. On multiple occasions, however, Jesus predicted its demise. Three are recorded before the 'Cleansing of the Temple' (Luke 13:34-35; 19:42-44; John 2:19-20) and two are recorded after (Matt 23:37-39 and Mark 13:1-37/Matt 24:1-51/Luke 21:5-36). Jesus, like the prophets of old, threatened the destruction of the temple if its leaders did not repent (e.g., Isa 1:11; 28:7; Jer 6:13; 19:1-15; 26:6; Lam 4:13; Ezek 4:1-17; 22:23-31; Hos 6:6; Mic 3:9-12; Zeph 3:1-8; Zech 14:20-21; Mal 3:1).[24] Stephen reflected this same call to repent or perish (Luke 13:3-5).[25] This landed him before the high court whose glare deflected Stephen's angelic countenance (v. 15).[26]

---

[24] Jesus was hardly a solitary harbinger of the temple's destruction. *T. Levi* 10:3 predicted the tearing of the temple curtain (cf. *Liv. Pro.* 10:10-11; 12:11) and *T. Judah* 23:3 adds that the sanctuary will be consumed by fire (as does Josephus, *J.W.* 6:250; cf. *Ant.* 20.205-206). *Sib. Or.* 3:337-340 attributes the destruction to unfaithfulness, while *1 Enoch* provides an apocalyptic description of the temple's replacement (90:28-29a). This kind of critique hardly abated in later Rabbinic literature (cf. *Tg. Isa.* 5:5; *t. Menah* 13.22; *b. Yoma* 39b; *Lam. Rab.* 31.2). Cf. Craig A. Evans, "Predictions of the Destruction of the Herodian temple in the Pseudepigrapha, Qumran Scrolls, and Related Texts," *JSP* 10 (1992): 89-147. It is also significant that Jesus' major critique of the temple hierarchy revolved around economic exploitation as did that of Qumran and the later rabbis; cf. Craig A. Evans, "Early Rabbinic Sources of Jesus Research," SBLSP 20 (1981): 59-65 and "Opposition to the Temple: Jesus and the Dead Sea Scrolls," in *Jesus and the Dead Sea Scrolls* (ed. James H. Charlesworth; New York: Doubleday, 1992), 235-253. So it comes as no surprise that Stephen, one of the economic stewards of the widows, would have had something to say about their exploitation by the temple system.

[25] Thomas Söding, "Die Tempelaktion Jesu," *TTZ* 101 (1992): 63, is right that Jesus' preaching of repentance was his central call. So Stephen could hardly imitate Jesus' preaching without it.

[26] The "angelic countenance" was a rabbinic metaphor for either innocence or a divine messenger (Str-B 2:665-666). In other words, Stephen was sent by God with a message that they were rejecting.

ACTS 7

2. Stephen's Sermon on Jesus through Jewish History (7:1-53)

All the speeches Luke records are important but this one has special significance. Not only is it twice as long as any other in Acts, it stands at the gate which opens onto non-Jewish evangelism. After Stephen's death, Saul's persecution dispersed the Hellenistic Christians across Judea and Samaria. Instinctively, they told their story to their new neighbors. The result was explosive. These persecuted Christians became seedlings for new congregations unto the four winds upon which they had been dispersed.

Stephen addresses the charges leveled against him by giving reverence to Yahweh (vv. 2, 17, 32, 49-50), Moses (vv. 17-41), the Law (v. 38), and the Temple (vv. 44-50). Nonetheless, by any account his defense is subtle at best. His real purpose is to address two critical themes.[1] First is the *Universal Gospel.* Stephen's speech is less a defense of the charges leveled against him and more of a preface to coming attractions. Luke suggests that by looking backward to the Old Testament we can justify the church moving toward Gentiles in chapters 8–10. Three Jewish heroes are lined up as witnesses: Abraham (vv. 1-8), Joseph (vv. 9-19), and Moses (vv. 20-44). Though others are mentioned in passing, these make up the bulk of the speech.[2] What is most interesting about these three is that their major life work was *outside* Israel. Israel is never mentioned by name (merely alluded to by "the land," v. 45) nor is her capital city, Jerusalem. Yet we read lots of foreign geography: Mesopotamia (v. 2), Haran (vv. 2, 4), Egypt (vv. 7, 9, 10, 11, 12, 15, 17, 18, 34, 36, 39, 40), Midian (v. 29), Sinai (v. 30, 38), and Babylon (v. 43). A casual glance would give the impression that God does his greatest work in foreign lands. Hence, when Philip flees to Samaria (ch. 8), the reader is prepared to see this move is 'retro' rather than 'novel'. God has always worked in non-Jewish territory.

The theme of the *universal gospel* is also underscored with Stephen's critique of the temple. Though he hardly approaches Jesus' own severe censure of the edifice and its institutions (see comments on 6:14), he does contrast the abuse of the temple with the pristine tabernacle. The tabernacle is what got Israel into "the land." *"But"* (v. 47), the temple muddled it up. The tabernacle was the real presence of God with his sojourning people; the temple became an 'idolatrous'

---

[1] Because Stephen's defense is muted but his theological foci are amplified, a number of scholars have concluded that this sermon really is Luke's, placed on Stephen's lips (Haenchen, 240-241; Conzelmann, 43; A. F. Klijn, "Stephen's Speech—Acts vv. 2-53," *NTS* 4 [1957–1958]: 25). There is, however, no linguistic or ideological reason to believe this sermon could not have come directly from an early Hellenistic Christian like Stephen and then later redacted by Luke to fit the context of his own work; cf. Martin H. Scharlemann, "Stephen's Speech: A Lucan Creation?" *ConJ* 4 (1978): 52-57.

[2] The sermon is dominated by these three figures (86%). The introduction (a mere five words) and the conclusion together comprise only 5% of the speech with the remaining 9% devoted to a brief discussion of the temple. Clearly, therefore, the mention of Isaac, Jacob, and the Twelve Patriarchs (v. 8) as well as the surprisingly brief mention of David (vv. 45-46) and Solomon (v. 47) are little more than a literary bridge.

replacement. Lest these words seem too harsh, the reader should be aware that the phrase "made by hands" (*cheiropoētos*) is a technical term for idols in the LXX (Lev 26:2, 30; Jdt 8:18; Wis 14:8; Isa 2:18; 10:11; 16:12; 19:1; 21:9; 31:7; 46:6; Bel 1:5). So Stephen's critique of the temple, though muted, is clear enough to offend his hearers.[3]

The temple was the central symbol of Judaism, yet Yahweh's presence with his people predated this edifice by a long shot. Thus, if the temple was removed, God could still be present with his Elect. Put another way, the Gentiles in far-flung lands have as good a chance of knowing God without the temple as do the Jerusalem elite. Had Stephen heard Jesus' teachings on the temple, he too could have predicted its demise as easily as the author of Hebrews.[4] Perhaps he did; perhaps that's why feathers flew and stones were hurled.

A second critical theme of this speech is Jesus. While this may seem obvious, it is not immediately apparent from the text itself. Jesus is never directly mentioned until verse 56, *after* Stephen's defense and right before his funeral dirge. Yet Jesus pervades the entire piece. Notice that each of the three key figures—Abraham, Joseph, and Moses—are depicted as rejected prophets. Clearly there is enough material in the Old Testament on each of these men to highlight various aspects of their biographies. So it is significant that Stephen focuses on this narrow theme of rejection. Abraham had "not even a foot of ground" in the very land God promised him (v. 5), and his descendants would "be strangers in a country not their own and enslaved." Joseph was sold by his brothers (v. 9). Moses was nearly killed as a baby (v. 21). After he murdered an Egyptian in defense of an Israelite, he was chased out of Egypt because a fellow Hebrew exposed him (v. 23-28, 35)! As a final blow, the Hebrew forefathers refused to listen to him in the desert (v. 39). Luke's agenda apparently is to show that Jesus' rejection by his opponents does not put a 'black hat' on him. On the contrary, it shows that he *was*, in fact, on the right side of the fence since all God's 'good guys' were treated this way (v. 51-53).

Furthermore, Stephen's resemblance to Jesus is highlighted in how he dies. Both were falsely accused (Mark 14:56-59/Matt 26:59-63; Acts 6:11, 13). Both were charged by the Sanhedrin with threatening to destroy the temple (Mark 14:58/Matt 26:61; Acts 6:11-14). Both were misunderstood and misrepresented (Matt 26:61; Acts 6:14). Both died through unjust trials and mob action (Luke 23:34; Acts 7:59-60), with a nearly identical phrase on their lips: "Forgive them,

---

[3] Some have made too much of Stephen's temple critique; e.g., Marcel Simon, "Saint Stephen and the Jerusalem Temple," *JEH* 2 (1951): 127-142. It comprises a mere fraction of the overall speech and Luke does not use overtly negative vocabulary against the temple. Those who suspect Luke of moderating Stephen's original harsh critique also tend to date Luke after A.D. 70. So their burden of proof is to show that the Gentile Luke had some kind of motive for softening the blow of an already defunct temple from the lips of his Hellenistic hero. This seems unlikely. Cf. H. Alan Brehm, "Vindicating the Rejected One: Stephen's Speech as a Critique of the Jewish Leaders," in *Early Christian Interpretation of the Scriptures of Israel* (Sheffield: Sheffield, 1997), 265-299; Edvin Larsson, "Temple-Criticism and the Jewish Heritage: Some Reflections on Acts 6–7," *NTS* 39 (1993): 379-380; and James N. Rhodes, "Tabernacle and Temple: Rethinking the Rhetorical Function of Acts 7:44-50," in *Contemporary Studies in Acts* (ed. Thomas E. Phillips; USA: Mercer, 2009), 119-137.

[4] Cf. William Manson, "Stephen and the World—Mission of Christianity," *The Epistle to the Hebrews* (London: Hodder and Stoughton, 1966), 25-46.

for they do not know what they are doing." From beginning to end, this discourse explains God's design to validate his rejected servants and ultimately to bring this message to people beyond the pale.

¹Then the high priest asked him, "Are these charges true?" ²To this he replied: "Brothers and fathers, listen to me! The God of glory appeared to our father Abraham while he was still in Mesopotamia, before he lived in Haran. ³'Leave your country and your people,' God said, 'and go to the land I will show you.'ᵃ ⁴So he left the land of the Chaldeans and settled in Haran. After the death of his father, God sent him to this land where you are now living. ⁵He gave him no inheritance here, not even a foot of ground. But God promised him that he and his descendants after him would possess the land, even though at that time Abraham had no child."

ᵃ3 Gen. 12:1

7:1-2a. The High Priest, likely still Caiaphas (18–36 A.D.), invites Stephen to defend these charges. Given Caiaphas's previous interaction with the Jesus movement, one can be fairly certain that his mind is already made up. Stephen opens his 'defense' with what the ancient rhetoricians called an *exordium*. It was an introduction designed to 'butter-up' the hearers so they would be favorably disposed to one's case. If Luke's summary didn't excise critical information, this is as curt an *exordium* as can be found anywhere in Greek literature. With five simple Greek words—"Men, brothers, and fathers, listen!"—Stephen exhorts them, without fanfare or flattery, to pay careful attention. He is going to recount the salient points of Israel's history marching methodically through the Old Testament.[5] He is, of course, not the only writer to offer such a survey (e.g., Deut 26:4-10; Josh 24:2-15; 2 Chr 13:4-12; Neh 9:6-31; Psalms 78; 105; 106; 136; Ezekiel 20; Hebrews 11; Jdt 5:3-23; 1 Macc 2:50-68; 3 Macc 2:2-20; 2 Esd [4 Ezra] 3:3-36; Wisdom 10–18; Josephus, *Ant.* 3.5.3 §86-87; CD 1.1–2.1; 2.2–4.16). Comparing him with other authors shows just how faithful he is to Hebrew history.[6]

7:2b-3. Stephen begins with one of Israel's foundational stories—the chronicle of Abraham. The primary point is that Abraham lived faithfully to God's call even though he did not, himself, receive what was promised. He lost his father and his homeland, yet faithfully followed God's call to Canaan. He grew old with

---

[5] The following data gives the verse numbers from Acts 7 followed by the OT passages to which they refer. Verses within quotation marks indicate that Stephen cited the LXX rather than merely alluding to it: **2** (Gen 11:31; 15:7); **"3"** (Gen 12:1); **4** (Gen 11:31-32); **"5"** (Gen 12:7; 17:8); **"6-7"** (Gen 15:13-14); **8** (Exod 3:12; Gen 17:9-13; 21:4); **9** (Gen 37:11, 28; 39:2, 21-23; 45:4); **10** (Gen 39:21; 41:40-46); **11** (Gen 41:54; 42:5); **12** (Gen 42:2); **13** (Gen 45:1-16); **14** (Gen 45:9; 46:26-27; Exod 1:5; Deut 10:22); **15** (Gen 46:5; 49:33; Exod 1:6); **16** (Gen 23:16; 33:15; 50:13); **17** (Gen 47:27; Exod 1:7); **"18"** (Exod 1:8); **19** (Exod 1:10-11, 17-22); **20** (Exod 2:2; Heb 11:23); **21** (Exod 2:3); **22** (1 Kings 4:30; cf. Luke 24:19); **23-26** (Exod 2:11-13); **"27-29"** (Exod 2:14-15); **30-31** (Exod 3:2-3); **"32"** (Exod 3:6); **"33"** (Exod 3:5); **"34"** (Exod 3:7, 10); **"35"** (Exod 2:14); **36** (Exod 5:16); **"37"** (Deut 18:15 [cf. Acts 3:22]); **38** (Exod 19:17–20:26; 31:18; Deut 9:10); **39** (Num 14:3; Exod 32:1-23); **"40-41"** (Exod 32:4-6); **"42-43"** (Amos 5:25, 26); **44** (Exod 25:8-9; 26:1-37 [=36:8-38]); **45** (Joshua 3:14; 18:1; 23:9; 24:18); **46-47** (1 Kings 6:2; 8:17-21); **"48-50"** (Isaiah 66:1-2 [cf. Acts 17:24]); **51** (Exod 32:9-10; 33:3-5; 34:9; Lev 26:41); **52** (1 Kgs 19:10; 2 Chr 36:15-16; Neh 9:26; [cf. Matt 5:12; 23:31, 37]).

[6] Oda Wischmeyer, "Stephen's Speech before the Sanhedrin against the Background of the Summaries of the History of Israel (Acts 7)," in *History and Identity: How Israel's Later Authors Viewed Its Earlier History* (ed. Núria Calduch-Benages and Jan Liesen; Berlin: Walter de Gruyter, 2006), 341-358.

no heir and not a foot of ground to call home, yet never wavered in his belief in God's covenant. Finally, a single heir kept hope alive. That single heir had twins and one of them had twelve sons. Thus, God proved himself true to his word.

Stephen's rendition is unassailable in its major themes though some of the details are problematic. It is beyond the scope of this commentary to elaborate on what counted as 'accurate history' to first-century Jews or more specifically what constituted a *faithful recounting of foundational narratives*.[7] In brief, foundational narratives in the Middle East are protected by the community. Nonessential details (mostly dates and numbers), less important to the *meaning* of the story, may vary from one rendition to another (as we will see below). The core meaning of the story, however, is passionately protected by the hearers. Where Stephen's rendition of Israel's history differs in detail from the Old Testament, he is generally following a known tradition from another Jewish source.[8] He is not creating new details *de novo*. His overall flow and emphasis is a faithful retelling of Israel's story. Modern rationalists who fail to recognize how stories were told in the ancient world have been bothered by Stephen's differing details though such minutiae[9] would hardly have derailed his original audience any more than the variant details found in the Septuagint, Josephus, Philo, the Targumim,[10] or the Samaritan Pentateuch.[11] One can compare these variant

[7] The most important works on the subject, to be read in the following order, are Kenneth E. Bailey, "Informal Controlled Oral Tradition and the Synoptic Gospels," *AJT* 5 (1991): 34-51; James Dunn, "Altering the Default Setting: Re-envisioning the Early Transmission of the Jesus Tradition," *NTS* 49 (2003): 139-175; and Samuel Byrskog, "A New Perspective on the Jesus Tradition: Reflections on James D. G. Dunn's *Jesus Remembered*," *JSNT* 26 (2004): 459-471; and Richard Bauckham, *Jesus and the Eyewitnesses: The Gospels as Eyewitness Testimony* (Grand Rapids: Eerdmans, 2006).

[8] For the broad range of rabbinic traditions behind Stephen's speech, one would profit from Günter Stemberger, "Die Stephanusrede (Apg 7) und die Jüdische Tradition," in *Jesus in der Verkündigung der Kirche* (ed. Albert Fuchs; Freistadt: Plöchl, 1976), 154-174; and J. Julius Scott, "Stephen's Speech: A Possible Model for Luke's Historical Method?" *JETS* 17 (1974): 95.

[9] Liberal rationalists have anachronistically charged Stephen with error. Conservative rationalists, in response, have offered speculative, albeit plausible, 'solutions' in defense of inerrancy; cf. Rex A. Koivisto, "Stephen's Speech: A Case Study in Rhetoric and Biblical Inerrancy," *JETS* 20 (1977): 353-364. The supposed historical discrepancies in Stephen's speech include the following:

VV.	PRIMARY DISCREPANCIES	POSSIBLE SOLUTION
2-3	Where did Abraham receive his call?	Stephen compresses two calls of Abraham into one.
4	How old was Terah when he died?	Stephen follows a tradition that says 145. Another says 205.
6-7	How long was the Egyptian captivity?	Stephen follows the traditional 400 year period as opposed to specifying the 215 years of actual slavery in Egypt.
14	How many Hebrews went to Egypt?	Stephen follows the LXX, including descendants of Manasseh and Ephraim for a total of 75 rather than 70.
16	Where was Jacob buried?	Stephen, conflated the two tombs of Abraham and Joseph to press the narrative forward to Samaria.

[10] For a summary of the Targumim which align with Stephen's rendition of Hebrew history, see José Manuel Sánchez Caro, "El Trasfondo Judio del Discurso de Esteban," in *Quaere Paulum: miscelánea homenaje a Monseñor Doctor Lorenzo Turrado* (ed. Lorenzo Turrado; Salamanca: Universidad Pontifica, 1981), 63-78. He concludes that the verisimilitude of Stephen's speech with the Targumim makes it likely that this speech derived from a synagogue homily which Luke adapted to his own purpose (77-78). This author wonders why Caro credits Luke rather than Stephen directly since this debate arose out of the Synagogue of the Freedman. This seems like a more plausible scenario in support of Caro's thesis especially given the fact the Stephen's idiosyncratic interpretation of history is unique in Acts (though consistent with 1QS); cf. A. F. J. Klijn, "Stephen's Speech—Acts VII. 2-53," *NTS* 4 (1957): 25-31.

[11] At four places in Stephen's speech he is in agreement with the Samaritan version of the Pentateuch [SP] (vv. 4, 5, 32, 37). From this Abram Spiro has famously argued that Stephen was a Samaritan; "Stephen's Samaritan Background," Appendix V, in *Acts of the Apostles*, by Johannes Munck, rev. by W. F. Albright and C. S. Mann, *The Anchor Bible* (Garden City: Doubleday, 1967), 31:285-300. Charles H. Scobie has argued

renderings as driving down a four-lane highway. Certain numbers, timing of events, even locations can be conflated or altered from 'lane to lane' so long as the traffic keeps moving in the right direction and one does not take an exit ramp, diverging to an alternate route. Stephen's enemies, while objecting to his christocentric reading of Israel's history, would hardly have dallied over the kinds of variant details endemic in such retellings.

Stephen asserted that God called Abraham while he was still back in Mesopotamia. However, Genesis 11:31–12:1 makes it look like Abraham received his call in Haran years later. The solution is simple: God called Abraham twice. The first call was in Mesopotamia, more specifically, in "Ur of the Chaldeans" (cf. Gen 15:7; Neh 9:7; Philo, *Abraham* 71–72). This resulted in his family moving north to Haran en route to Canaan (Gen 11:31). After Abraham's father died, God called Abraham out of Haran *and* away from his family (Gen 12:1).[12] While Genesis concentrates on the latter call (Gen 11:31–12:1), Stephen concentrated on the former call.

7:4. Stephen testifies that Abraham stayed in Haran until the death of his father. While that is not in the Old Testament, the tradition was known to Philo (*On the Migration of Abraham*, 177). Rabbis later used this tradition to defend Abraham against criticism of abandoning his father (*Gen. Rab.* 39:7; Str-B 2:667-668). Stephen's motive may be deeper. Terah, according to rabbinic tradition, was an idolater (*Gen. Rab.* 38:13; Jub 12:1-6; cf. Josh 24:2).[13] Stephen may have in mind Abraham's complete break from idolatry now that his father was dead and he abandons his country. Regardless, it is interesting that all three heroes featured in this speech not only abandoned land, but lost parents.

7:5. When Stephen asserts that Abraham had not even a foot of ground in Palestine, he obviously excludes the cave at Machpelah which Abraham purchased as a burial plot (Gen 23:9). This hardly counts as an "inheritance" promised by God.

---

more moderately the very real connections with the SP; "The Use of Source Material in the Speeches of Acts III and VII," *NTS* 25 (1979): 399-421. Still, the evidence indicates that Stephen was primarily indebted to the LXX; cf. Earl Richard, "The Polemical Character of the Joseph Episode in Acts 7," *JBL* 98 (1979): 255-267. Where Stephen and the SP agree, it appears that both are indebted to an early Palestinian source, not that Stephen directly accessed the SP. Cf. Harold Mare, "Acts 7: Jewish or Samaritan in Character?" *WTJ* 34 (1971): 1-21; and Earl Richard, "Acts 7: An Investigation of the Samaritan Evidence," *CBQ* 39 (1977): 190-208. This conclusion is bolstered by the fact that Stephen shows reverence for David, quotes from the prophets, and is opposed to localized worship, all of which would gall Samaritan sensitivities.

[12] Abraham was seventy-five when he left Haran (Gen 12:4). Gen 11:26 says Terah was seventy years old when he became the father of Abram, Nahor, and Haran. Hence, Terah must have been one hundred and forty-five when he died. This is precisely the date given in the Samaritan Pentateuch, although both the LXX and MT of Gen 11:32 say Terah lived to 205. The most likely solution is that Stephen is following the same tradition recorded in the Samaritan Pentateuch. Although there is another solution: The chronology above assumes that Abraham was Terah's firstborn son because he is mentioned first. However, it was common for the most prominent son to be mentioned first regardless of birth order. We see this with Noah's sons (Genesis 5:32), Isaac and Ishmael (1 Chr 1:28), and Jacob's sons (1 Chr 4:1; 5:1-2). If we assume Haran was born first, then his son, Lot, could be about the same age as Abraham. Moreover, Haran's daughter married Nahor (Abraham and Haran's third brother) which *may* indicate proximity in age. This would allow Abraham to be born later, when his father was 130. Some will question the possibility of a man bearing children at 130 (e.g., Bruce, 146) though this very claim is made for Abraham at age 137 (Gen 23:1; 25:1-4; cf. Josephus, *Ant.* 1.6.5 §149-153).

[13] For this insight I am indebted to Rex A. Koivisto, "Stephen's Speech: A Theology of Errors?" *GTJ* 8 (1987): 112-113. This is certainly more compelling than Wayne Litke's bland accusation that Stephen (or Luke) just got confused; "Acts 7.3 and Samaritan Chronology," *NTS* 42 (1996): 156-160.

[6]"God spoke to him in this way: 'Your descendants will be strangers in a country not their own, and they will be enslaved and mistreated four hundred years. [7]But I will punish the nation they serve as slaves,' God said, 'and afterward they will come out of that country and worship me in this place.'ᵃ [8]Then he gave Abraham the covenant of circumcision. And Abraham became the father of Isaac and circumcised him eight days after his birth. Later Isaac became the father of Jacob, and Jacob became the father of the twelve patriarchs."

ᵃ7 Gen. 15:13,14

7:6-8. God promised Abraham a huge family and expansive lands. He died with neither. All he had was hope for God's faithfulness to his descendants through a four-hundred year[14] trek of travail. So long as they continued to mark themselves with the sign of circumcision, God would recognize their enduring faith in his promises. The greatness of Abraham was his ability to see the faithfulness of God through the slightest glimmer of hope. His single son was all the evidence he needed to remain true to Yahweh. When God provided Abraham the son he promised, Abraham followed God's prescription of circumcision. From Isaac came Jacob and from Jacob the twelve tribes of Israel. And so was born God's redemptive nation.

[9]"Because the patriarchs were jealous of Joseph, they sold him as a slave into Egypt. But God was with him [10]and rescued him from all his troubles. He gave Joseph wisdom and enabled him to gain the goodwill of Pharaoh king of Egypt; so he made him ruler over Egypt and all his palace. [11]Then a famine struck all Egypt and Canaan, bringing great suffering, and our fathers could not find food. [12]When Jacob heard that there was grain in Egypt, he sent our fathers on their first visit. [13]On their second visit, Joseph told his brothers who he was, and Pharaoh learned about Joseph's family. [14]After this, Joseph sent for his father Jacob and his whole family, seventy-five in all. [15]Then Jacob went down to Egypt, where he and our fathers died. [16]Their bodies were brought back to Shechem and placed in the tomb that Abraham had bought from the sons of Hamor at Shechem for a certain sum of money."

7:9-14. The rather muted theme of 'rejection' in the life of Abraham is now amplified in the life of Joseph. Stephen's account is brief in the extreme. He expects his hearer's to fill in the details which they obviously knew.[15] Joseph saved his entire family as well as the future of the nation because of his suffering. Out of envy (cf. 5:17; Mark 15:10) his brothers sold him into slavery. Yet God endowed him with exceptional wisdom (cf. 6:3, 10; Luke 2:40, 52)[16] which raised

---

[14] Stephen says the Egyptian captivity lasted 400 years following Gen 15:13-14. Similarly Exod 12:40 dates the entire Egyptian experience at 430 years. Josephus breaks that in half, suggesting that there were 215 years from Abraham to the bondage of Egypt and 215 in slavery (*Ant.* 2.15.2 §318). Paul follows this same chronology (Gal 3:17) which makes better sense of the genealogical lists.

[15] The same is also true for Luke's readers; cf. Kathy R. Maxwell, "The Role of the Audience in Ancient Narrative: Acts as a Case Study," *RQ* 48 (2006): 171-180.

[16] The wisdom of Joseph, though not specified in the Genesis account, was a strong theme in Jewish literature (Psa 105:22; Josephus, *Ant.* 2.5.7 §87; *Joseph and Asenath*, 4.9; *Tg. Neof.* Gen 41:43). This emphasis on the wisdom of Stephen and Joseph points to a typology of Jesus. Wisdom was such a strong metaphor for Jesus' ministry that some scholars believe it is the key to understanding his entire Messianic program (cf.

him to the second highest position in Egypt—Grand Vizier (cf. 2:33; 5:31). Only on their second visit would they recognize their brother. The same would be true of Moses (vv. 27-28). It was this 'death and resurrection' of Joseph that led to the salvation of his entire family, seventy-five in all.[17] The christological motif could not be more overt. Stephen is arguing that Jesus is God's Messiah and that his rejection only proves his affinity with the great saviors of Israel's past. The point of the story is that God was with Joseph (v. 9), not with his brothers.

7:15-16. Jacob moved the whole family to Egypt where they survived because of Joseph's God-ordained wisdom. This move sets up the following narrative with Moses whose likeness to Jesus the Savior will be most transparent. Before moving forward, however, we can't leave Jacob's or Joseph's bones entombed in Egypt. These Patriarchs merit a hero's funeral in the sacred soil of the Promised Land. So Stephen reminds his hearers that God vindicates his faithful servants by bringing them back and burying them where they belong. While it is true that Jacob and his sons were buried with Abraham in Hebron,[18] Joseph *was* buried at Shechem. It may be for brevity that Stephen conflates their burials. More likely, it serves to push the narrative forward into the non-Jewish territory of Samaria where we will find ourselves in the very next chapter. This move away from Jewish territory has deep theological import for Luke.

[17]**"As the time drew near for God to fulfill his promise to Abraham, the number of our people in Egypt greatly increased. [18]Then another king, who knew nothing about Joseph, became ruler of Egypt. [19]He dealt treacherously with our people and oppressed our forefathers by forcing them to throw out their newborn babies so that they would die. [20]At that time Moses was born, and he was no ordinary child.[a] For three months he was cared for in his father's**

Matt 12:42; 13:54; Josephus *Ant.* 18.3.3 §63; Isa 11:1-2; *Pss. Sol.* 17:27). Cf. Elisabeth Schüssler Fiorenza, *In Memory of Her: A Feminist Theological Reconstruction of Christian Origins* (New York: Crossroads, 1983); and Ben Witherington, *Jesus the Sage: The Pilgrimage of Wisdom* (Minneapolis, MN: Fortress, 1994).

[17] Stephen counts the family at seventy-five while Genesis (MT) only claims seventy (Gen 46:27; cf. Josephus, *Ant.* 2.7.4 §177-183; 6.5.6 §89; *Jub.* 44.33). The Septuagint agrees with Stephen (Gen 46:27; Exod 1:5; 4QGen-Exod[a] 17-18.2; 4QExod[b] 1.5). This is not because the Septuagint and the Hebrew Bible contradicted each other, but because Stephen, following the Septuagint, counted differently than Josephus following the MT. To be specific, the Septuagint appears to include in the count two sons of Manasseh, two of Ephraim, and one of Ephraim's grandsons (though there is some variation among ancient authors as to who might be included in these 'extra five'). Philo, aware of both 70 and 75 (*On the Migration of Abraham*, 198-202), attempts to allegorically harmonize the divergent numbers: 70 = intellect, plus 5 = the senses.

[18] The brevity of Stephen's report obscures the historical facts. When Jacob died, Joseph transported his body back from Egypt to Palestine to lay his bones to rest with Abraham at Machpelah (Gen 50:13). Later, Jacob's sons were also buried with Abraham and Jacob according to Josephus (*Ant.* 2.8.2 §199; the *Twelve Patriarchs* has even Joseph buried at Hebron). Then, after the Egyptian captivity, Joseph's bones were likewise taken out of Egypt as well, but they were buried at Shechem (Josh 24:32). Hence, Joseph is in a different tomb than his father and brothers. Yet Stephen speaks as if they are the same tomb. He even credits Abraham with the purchase of the tomb at Shechem (v. 16) when, in fact, Jacob purchased that tract of land (Gen 33:19; Joshua 24:32). Abraham purchased the cave at Machpelah near Hebron (Gen 23:16-19). Stephen conflates the two tombs into one. According to Clinton Day, "The Machpelah and Israel's Faith While in Bondage (Acts VII, 15, 16)," *MR* 81 (1899): 65-76, this is simply an error—a mental glitch under the pressure of impending death. The Western and Byzantine texts attempt to solve the problem by replacing "in Shechem" with "of Shechem" so that Abraham purchased this property from the "father of Shechem" (AV); cf. Josep Rius-Camps, "Las Variantes del Texto Occidental de los Hechos de los Apóstoles (XI)," *FilNeot* 13/25-26 (2000): 106. More likely, however, Stephen simply compressed the story given the constraints of the retelling. For Stephen and his Jewish listeners this sort of synecdoche would be understandable. It was perfectly acceptable to credit the father for a purchase of the son. This could not be truer of anyone than Jacob whose name was changed to Israel and stood for the entire nation.

house. ²¹When he was placed outside, Pharaoh's daughter took him and brought him up as her own son. ²²Moses was educated in all the wisdom of the Egyptians and was powerful in speech and action. ²³When Moses was forty years old, he decided to visit his fellow Israelites. ²⁴He saw one of them being mistreated by an Egyptian, so he went to his defense and avenged him by killing the Egyptian. ²⁵Moses thought that his own people would realize that God was using him to rescue them, but they did not. ²⁶The next day Moses came upon two Israelites who were fighting. He tried to reconcile them by saying, 'Men, you are brothers; why do you want to hurt each other?' ²⁷But the man who was mistreating the other pushed Moses aside and said, 'Who made you ruler and judge over us? ²⁸Do you want to kill me as you killed the Egyptian yesterday?'ᵇ ²⁹When Moses heard this, he fled to Midian, where he settled as a foreigner and had two sons."

ᵃ20 Or *was fair in the sight of God*   ᵇ28 Exodus 2:14

7:17-19. It was nearly time for God to fulfill his promise to Abraham. The part about "many descendants" was coming along swimmingly. The part about inheriting the land would come only through a surprising twist. A new Pharaoh rose to power (Luke labels him a "king" anachronistically for the benefit of his Greek readers). He had a different (*heteros*) character. He had no respect for Joseph, only fear for these prolific Hebrews. Though he couldn't very well keep them from reproducing, he could diminish their numbers by euthenizing their infants. This peculiar word, "dealt treacherously" (*katasophizomai*), is used only this once in the New Testament but is the very word found in Exodus 1:10 (LXX). It identified a nefarious strategy (Josephus, *Ant.* 6.11.4 §219; 8.15.5 §412). But the Hebrews had schemes of their own. Luke's abbreviation of Exodus 1:15-22 leaves out the delightful tale of the clever Shiphrah and Puah whose brave countertactics rescued untold numbers of baby boys from Pharaoh's pogrom.

7:20-22. The description of Moses as an exceptionally beautiful baby ("no ordinary child") comes straight out of Exodus 2:2 (cf. Heb 11:23; *Jub.* 47:1-9) even if one suspects his mother started the rumor. The detail of three months in hiding and his recovery by Pharaoh's daughter are biblical details (Exod 2:2-6).¹⁹ The description of Moses' education, however, is not in the Scriptures, though it was of considerable interest to several authors who tended to make him out to be some kind of a super-hero. For example, Philo describes him as a military genius (*Moses*, 1:289-291) while Josephus would add a knowledge of zoology (*Ant.* 2.10.1-2, §238-253). Eusebius credits Moses with the invention of ships, machines for laying stones, weaponry, drawing water, and philosophy as well as a military genius (*Preparation for the Gospel*, 9.26-27).²⁰ That he was well educated is probable. That he was powerful in speech seemingly contradicts Moses' self-

---

¹⁹ Luke says Pharaoh's daughter "took him" (ἀναιρέω). This word has a double entendre. It means "lifting up" as when she took him out of the water (Exod 2:10 LXX). It was also used of "adoption" in Hellenistic Greek (e.g., Plutarch, *Anton.* 36.3; Epictetus, 1.23.7), which fits the context here nicely (Polhill, 194).

²⁰ For a comprehensive list of such legends cf. Emil Schürer, *The History of the Jewish People in the Age of Jesus Christ (175 B.C.–A.D. 135)* (tr. T. A. Burkhill; rev. and ed. by Geza Vermes & Fergus Millar; Edinburgh: Clark, 1979), 2:343-344; and Ton Hilhorst, "'And Moses Was Instructed in All the Wisdom of the Egyptians' (Acts 7.22)," in *The Wisdom of Egypt: Jewish, Early Christian, and Gnostic Essays in Honour of Gerard P. Luttikhuizen* (ed. Anthony Hilhorst and George H. VanKooten; Leiden: Brill, 2005), 153-176.

assessment: "O Lord, I have never been eloquent, neither in the past nor since you have spoken to your servant. I am slow of speech and tongue" (Exod 4:10). Stephen must be talking about the *effect* of Moses speech rather than its affect. His opinion of Moses' exceptional oratorical power was shared by his contemporaries (cf. Sirach 45:3; Josephus, *Ant.* 3.1.4 §13-21; *Ant.* 2.12.3 §272). Regardless, the comment is not merely intended to describe Moses but to compare him to "Jesus of Nazareth . . . a prophet, powerful in word and deed" (Luke 24:19).

7:23-29. Stephen now recounts a well-worn tale of Moses murdering an Egyptian who beat a fellow Hebrew. Moses thought this would be understood clearly as a signal of liberation (v. 25, a detail lacking in Exod 2:11-15). He had the right pedigree to pull it off. Unfortunately, the Hebrews had no more respect for him than for Pharaoh. Now Moses, the would-be liberator, is turned fugitive. It was in this wilderness wandering that Moses bore two sons, Gershom and Eliezer. This is a seemingly irrelevant detail, unless the reader recalls that the name Gershom means, "I have become an alien in a foreign land" (Exod 2:22), and Eliezer means, "My father's God was my helper" (Exod 18:4). Here the motif of the rejected savior reaches its zenith.[21]

[30]"After forty years had passed, an angel appeared to Moses in the flames of a burning bush in the desert near Mount Sinai. [31]When he saw this, he was amazed at the sight. As he went over to look more closely, he heard the Lord's voice: [32]'I am the God of your fathers, the God of Abraham, Isaac and Jacob.'[a] Moses trembled with fear and did not dare to look. [33]Then the Lord said to him, 'Take off your sandals; the place where you are standing is holy ground. [34]I have indeed seen the oppression of my people in Egypt. I have heard their groaning and have come down to set them free. Now come, I will send you back to Egypt.'[b] [35]This is the same Moses whom they had rejected with the words, 'Who made you ruler and judge?' He was sent to be their ruler and deliverer by God himself, through the angel who appeared to him in the bush. [36]He led them out of Egypt and did wonders and miraculous signs in Egypt, at the Red Sea[c] and for forty years in the desert. [37]This is that Moses who told the Israelites, 'God will send you a prophet like me from your own people.'[d] [38]He was in the assembly[22] in the desert, with the angel who spoke to him on Mount Sinai, and with our fathers; and he received living words to pass on to us."

[a]32 Exodus 3:6   [b]34 Exodus 3:5, 7, 8, 10   [c]36 That is, *Sea of Reeds*   [d]37 Deut. 18:15

This is a classic scene; many of us still hear the voice of Charlton Heston. Flames flare around an unmolested bush, Moses walks gingerly toward it, and a booming voice from heaven bids him to remove his sandals on ground hallowed by Yahweh's presence. Who knows how close our imaginations come to reality. Yet it is inevitable that we get drawn into this scene and the unfolding narrative of

---

[21] The word in v. 25 for "rescue" is σωτηρία, more commonly rendered "salvation." The christological connections continue to mount. In v. 26, Stephen uses another christological term not found in the Exodus narrative: "reconcile." He is clearly multiplying typological references to Jesus.

[22] The word "assembly" in Greek is ἐκκλησία. This allusion to the Christian community could hardly be missed by Luke's readers. Jesus is leading God's assembly through a wilderness pilgrimage (Marshall, 143).

the Exodus. For the Jews, this was not an *important* story; it was *THE* story of Israel. This was their story and one in which they got to play a role in the continued Exodus as God perpetually rescued his nation from the bowels of slavery. Truth be told, this is our story too. Our weekly Passover meal, which we have blandly labeled 'communion', is an opportunity to remember, to confess, and to *participate* in the ongoing story of Israel, the continuous liberation of God. This Exodus theme permeates the Old Testament as the foundational metanarrative of the nation. Even in the New Testament its echoes are hardly less prominent (e.g., Mark 1:9-11/Matt 3:13-17/Luke 3:21-22; Luke 20:37; John 3:14; 6:32-33; 1 Cor 10:1-4; 2 Cor 3:13-15; 2 Tim 3:8; Heb 3:16; 11:24; 12:21; Rev 15:3). Playing off this pivotal narrative, Stephen intends to show that Jesus is the greater Moses, liberator of God's people. This will, indeed, be a hard sell with his current audience.

7:30. As Luke rehearses this well-worn tale, he introduces two novel details not found in Exodus. First, Moses was forty years old when he slew the Egyptian (v. 23). The number forty, asserted by some rabbis (Str-B 2:679-680; *Sifre* Deut 34:7 §357.14; *Exod. Rab.* 1.27, 30), is a nice round number that basically means 'full grown' (Marshall, 140; cf. Exod 2:11). After forty more years had passed, God called him through the burning bush (v. 30; cf. Exod 7:7). And in the final forty years of his life he led the Israelites through the desert (v. 36; cf. Exod 16:35; Num 14:33-34; Deut 34:7). This divides Moses' life into three distinct segments, each lasting a 'generation'. His 'first life' he spent in a palace, the second he spent in solitude herding sheep in the desert, and the third, he spent leading God's flock to the Promised Land.

The second detail that Luke emphasizes is an angel (vv. 30, 35, 38). While the angel does appear in the burning bush (Exod 3:2), there is no angel in the Old Testament giving Moses the law. This was a tradition that developed in the intertestamental period with which the New Testament concurs (cf. Deut 33:2 LXX; *Jub.* 1:27; 2:1; *T. Dan* 6.2; Gal 3:19; Heb 2:2; Josephus, *Ant.* 15.5.3 §136; Philo, *On Dreams*, 1.142-143). This tradition is a logical development of the story in Exodus 33:18-23 when Moses asked to see God's face and was refused. Well, if he could not see God's face and live, how did he speak to God face to face on Mount Sinai for forty days? Obviously, so goes the logic, it was not God himself, but his angel who acted as a mediator.

7:32-34. It was at the burning bush that Yahweh revealed his name to his servant Moses (Exod 3:15-16; cf. Acts 3:13). To know this name, or better, to have access to this name, would result in unparalleled power. The name of Yahweh had already been used one hundred and forty-three times in Genesis. Obviously the issue is not knowing *that* Yahweh was his name, but having the *right* to call on the name. We must remember that in the ancient world, name meant authority. Hence, if Moses knew the name of the one true God he could trump the lesser gods of Egypt. Given the heavy emphasis on the "name" of Jesus in Acts 3–6, this 'name-calling' should be read with special care. Notice too that when God identifies himself, he does so through his important relationships—Abraham, Isaac, and Jacob. He is a God who makes and keeps covenant. Hence, when he promises Moses his power, Moses is able to deliver. When he promises Moses a successor, you can count on a successor!

7:35-36. This is the second time Stephen quotes Exodus 2:14 (cf. v. 37), "Who made you ruler and judge over us?" (cf. *Ass. Mos.* 3.11). It is apparently a key verse, showing the utter rejection of Moses by his own people.[23] Here, however, there is an added travesty. The one they rejected as "ruler and judge" was actually "ruler and deliverer." The word "deliverer" (*lutrōtēs*) is only used here, but its cousins "redemption" (*lutrōsis*, Luke 1:68; 2:38; Heb 9:12) and "redeem" (*lutroō*, Luke 24:21; Tit 2:14; 1 Pet 1:18-19) are used exclusively of Jesus. They thought they were throwing off the shackles of an unauthorized judge when in reality they were rejecting the one who could redeem them. Though he did lead them out of Egypt with unprecedented miracles and signs, they continued to reject him in the desert. The unfortunate parallels between Jesus and Moses continue to mount.

7:37-38. Since the Israelites rejected their Savior, God promised another. Moses would return in the guise of an eschatological prophet who would finally and fully carry out the agenda first laid on Moses. Stephen's quotation of Deuteronomy 18:15-18 sounds an awful lot like Peter's (3:22). Surprisingly, this passage was seldom cited in Jewish literature and, even more shocking, never used as a clear Messianic promise before Acts![24] Furthermore, this unique combination of Abraham and Moses (cf. Acts 3:22-26) is repeated in Acts 7. Luke has recorded these sermons so as to highlight the historical contours of Abraham and Moses.[25] Jesus would fulfill the promise to Abraham that his seed would bless the whole earth and he would be the second Moses—lawgiver and savior.[26] Moses' "living words" (v. 38; cf. Deut 17:19; 32:47; Psalm 119:25, 37, 107) would become Jesus' "words of life" (John 5:24; 6:63, 68; Phil 2:16; 1 Pet 1:23; 1 John 1:1).

[39]"But our fathers refused to obey him. Instead, they rejected him and in their hearts turned back to Egypt. [40]They told Aaron, 'Make us gods who will go before us. As for this fellow Moses who led us out of Egypt—we don't know what has happened to him!'ª [41]That was the time they made an idol in the form of a calf. They brought sacrifices to it and held a celebration in honor of what

---

[23] Moses was portrayed in Jewish literature as the quintessential persecuted prophet: Josephus, *Ant.* 4.2.3. §21-22; *Pesiq. Rab.* 26.1.2; *Exod. Rab.* 30; *Eccl. Rab.* 10.1 §2. According to T. L. Donaldson, this portrait of Moses is from a Jewish, not a Gentile perspective, hence, arguing for a Palestinian origin of this material; "Moses Typology and the Sectarian Nature of Early Christian Anti-Judaism: A Study of Acts 7," *JSNT* 12 (1981): 27-52.

[24] The veiled references in 4Q175, Philo, *Spec. Laws* 1.64-65, or even *Sib. Or.* 5.346-50, hardly approach the clear claims of Peter and Stephen. Only the Samaritans come close with their prediction that the Messiah (*Taheb*) would fulfill Moses' role. But this belief cannot be substantiated prior to the 4th century (*Marqah* 4.7, 12; cf. John 1:21; 4:19, 25).

[25] Many scholars see this peculiar combination of Moses and Abraham as a Lucan idiosyncrasy; e.g., Jane E. Via, "An Interpretation of Acts 7:35-37 from the Perspective of Major Themes in Luke-Acts," *SBLSP* 14 (1978): 209-222. In other words, Luke created the speech out of whole cloth. Others argue that Stephen is responsible for these idiosyncratic ideas. However, there is no implicit reason that credit should not go originally to the Apostle Peter who undoubtedly exerted a formative influence on Stephen, an important young believer, who shared Peter's *Sitz im Leben*. Luke, in light of his own agenda, was attracted to this Judeo-Christian theme and highlighted it from his inherited records about two of his own heroes, Peter and Stephen. No other source-critical theory has greater simplicity or explanatory power.

[26] This dual emphasis of Abraham and Moses is also endemic in Paul's soteriology. In his primary passages on justification, he always places it against the backdrop of Abraham's covenant as well as the nature of Moses' law. N. T. Wright is especially helpful here in showing the metanarrative behind Paul's theology of justification in *Justification: God's Plan & Paul's Vision* (Downers Grove, IL: InterVarsity, 2009).

their hands had made. [42]But God turned away and gave them over to the worship of the heavenly bodies. This agrees with what is written in the book of the
prophets: 'Did you bring me sacrifices and offerings forty years in the desert,
O house of Israel? [43]You have lifted up the shrine of Molech and the star of
your god Rephan, the idols you made to worship. Therefore I will send you into
exile'[b] beyond Babylon.'

[a]*40* Exodus 32:1   [b]*43* Amos 5:25-27

7:39-41. The incident of the Golden Calf is the quintessential rejection of
Moses. While he was up on the mountain retrieving the Ten Commandments,
the Hebrews were at its base fashioning an idol from the gold undoubtedly tak-
en as booty from the plundered Egyptians (Exod 32:1-6). The precise description of the idol ran: "These are your gods, O Israel, who brought you up out of
Egypt." This golden calf, which Jeroboam revisited (1 Kgs 12:28), was a putative
replacement for Yahweh.[27] The form was recognizable from their sojourn in
Egypt—it looked like a familiar deity one might encounter in any of the cultic
centers of their former masters. This is a spiritual Stockholm syndrome. Stephen rightly charges, "Their hearts turned back to Egypt." The betrayal is colossal of both Moses and Yahweh.

By recalling this incident, Stephen is reversing the charges. They accused
Stephen of blasphemy against the law (6:13). He reminds them of their own
heritage in the desert. Their fathers committed gross idolatry at the very moment Moses was receiving the law. Though they would deny affinity with their
fathers, Stephen would likely remind them that they were rejecting the very
word of God embodied in Jesus the Messiah . . . if he only had the chance.

7:42-43. Because of their apostasy, God gave them over to deeper depravity
(cf. Rom 1:24-28 for a Gentile equivalent). Their idolatry reached the abys-
mal depths of worshiping heavenly bodies (e.g., Deut 17:3; 2 Kgs 17:16; 21:3;
Jer 8:2). Stephen brings in a star witness, Amos (5:25-27 LXX).[28] Things have
changed little since his time. The rejection of Yahweh through idolatry is still
pandemic. Though Molech and Rephan were distant memories, the inflamed
rejection of Yahweh burned as hot as any sacrificial pyre.[29] Stephen was aware,
no doubt, not only of the indictment of the text at hand, but of the context.
Amos blasts the Jerusalem elite who prided themselves on their sacrifices and

[27] The word "gods" (*Elohim*) is the primary term for God in the OT and is normally found in the plural. Hence, this is not an abandonment of Yahweh for foreign gods but an idolatrous representation of
the invisible God who had ostensibly abandoned them in the desert. Cf. Mark E. Moore, "Jeroboam's
Calves: Idols or Imitations," *BT* 41 (1990): 421-424. This peculiar vocabulary "made a calf" (μοσχοποιέω)
was a virulent reminder of one of Israel's darkest days of infidelity; cf. André Pelletier, "Une creation de
l'apologétique chrétienne: μοσχοποιεῖν," *RecSR* 54 (1966): 411-416.
[28] Stephen's quotation of the LXX is nearly exact except that he replaces Damascus (the departure city
of Israel) with Babylon (their final destination). Other variations are negligible. The same cannot be said
for the differences between the LXX and MT. For a detailed analysis see Gleason Archer and C. G. Chirichigno, *Old Testament Quotations in the New Testament: A Complete Survey* (Chicago: Moody, 1983), 150-153.
Fortunately, none of these changes affects the meaning of the verses.
[29] Molech (or Moloch, meaning "king") was a Phoenecian deity demanding human sacrifice. Rephan
is likely a misreading of *Kaiwan* (or *Chiun*, RSV, ESV), the Akkadian god Saturn (Amos 5:26), due to the
confusion of the *resh* (ר) for a *kaph* (כ); cf. R. Borger, "Amos 5,26, Apostelgeschichte 7,43 und Šurpa II,
180," *ZAW* 100 (1988): 70-81. It may also be read, "*pedestal* of your idols" (NIV). The point, which is still
clear enough, is that they practiced idolatry.

assemblies (Amos 5:21-23) that Yahweh had rejected. Why? Because justice was neglected (Amos 5:24). Both those who are complacent in Jerusalem and those who feel secure in Samaria (Amos 6:1) will be devastated at the coming day of the Lord. By citing this text, Stephen prepares for two things: (1) His own critique of the Jerusalem Temple (vv. 44-50), and (2) a very heated rebuke of this rebellious assembly (vv. 51-53).

⁴⁴"Our forefathers had the tabernacle of the Testimony with them in the desert. It had been made as God directed Moses, according to the pattern he had seen. ⁴⁵Having received the tabernacle, our fathers under Joshua brought it with them when they took the land from the nations God drove out before them. It remained in the land until the time of David, ⁴⁶who enjoyed God's favor and asked that he might provide a dwelling place for the God of Jacob.ᵃ ⁴⁷But it was Solomon who built the house for him. ⁴⁸However, the Most High does not live in houses made by men. As the prophet says: ⁴⁹'Heaven is my throne, and the earth is my footstool. What kind of house will you build for me?' says the Lord. 'Or where will my resting place be? ⁵⁰Has not my hand made all these things?'ᵇ"

ᵃ46 Some early manuscripts *the house of Jacob*   ᵇ50 Isaiah 66:1,2

7:44-45. The gross idolatry of Israel was even more egregious in the shadow of the Tabernacle. This tent was the center of the Hebrew camp and was officially called the "Tent of Meeting"[30] because it was the portal through which Israel encountered Yahweh (e.g., Exod 40:34-35).[31] Moses 'saw' the plans, as if he peered into the heavenly temple itself as a blueprint (Exod 26:1-37/Exod 36:8-38; Heb 8:2-5; 9:11; Rev 15:5). The care with which it was constructed, the central place it held in the community, and the visible presence of God through the pillar of cloud made the tabernacle of paramount importance. It was the center of worship and the ostensible power behind the Hebrew invasion of the Promise Land. From Joshua to David, victories were credited to the presence of Yahweh embodied in this sacred tent.[32] Both Joshua and David, heroes of Israel who loom large in the literature, are dealt with here in summary fashion. Though Stephen could use David to press further his 'rejected prophet' motif, the point has been sufficiently established with Abraham, Joseph, and Moses.[33] Now attention turns to the tabernacle/temple, the flashpoint of this agitated mob.

7:47-48. God debarred David from constructing the temple due to his bloody warfare (1 Chr 28:2-3; cf. 1 Kgs 5:3). That privilege went to his son, Solomon (1 Kgs 6:1-38).[34] While there are subtle intimations of temple critique on

---

[30] Stephen's "Tabernacle of Testimony" (σκηνὴ τοῦ μαρτυρίου) is a rough equivalent for the OT designation "Tent of Meeting" (אֹהֶל מֹעֵד).

[31] Of course, the temple also was seen as the dwelling of Yahweh (1 Kgs 8:11/2 Chr 5:14; Ezek 10:4, etc.). Rabbinic literature carries this concept as well (*Tg. Ps.-J.* Exod 39:43; *Tg. Neof.* I, 195a).

[32] The name for "Joshua" in Greek is "Jesus" (v. 45). As tempting as it is to see him as a type of Christ, the fact that Stephen only credits him with the expulsion of the nations/Gentiles (ἔθνος) mitigates any possibility that Stephen (or Luke) hail him as a messianic model.

[33] The rabbinic flourish on David is euphemistic and exaggerated in the extreme, making it all the more surprising that Stephen bypasses this opportunity to press his point further. For a helpful survey of some of the rabbinic material, see Jouette Bassler, "A Man for All Seasons: David in Rabbinic and New Testament Literature," *Int* 40 (1986): 156-169.

[34] As with Joshua and David, Solomon receives short shrift here in Luke's rendition of Stephen's speech.

Stephen's lips, they are muted. As argued above, the contrasting "but" (*de*) in verse 47 is rather weak. Moreover, while the phrase "made by hands" (v. 48) is standard criticism of idols in the LXX, it is also an appropriate description of the temple (e.g., Mark 14:58). It is unlikely that a Palestinian Jew like Stephen would seek the demolition of the Temple. None of the Apostles did, nor did the Essenes. And the fact that Stephen was a Hellenist who immigrated to Palestine might, in fact, make him *more* zealous for traditional Judaism, not less.

7:49-50. A stronger argument for Stephen's view of the temple comes from his quotation of Isaiah 66:1-2 (LXX). In short, God is claustrophobic. If the universe is the handiwork of God, then how can he be contained in a house constructed by *human* hands? This critique, of course, works equally well for both the temple and the tabernacle. It is not that Stephen disapproves of the Temple because the Tabernacle was somehow purer. His argument is that tent or temple, God transcended human construction. Solomon, even at the dedication of the temple, recognized that his *opus magnum* was hardly an adequate abode for the Almighty: "But will God really dwell on earth? The heavens, even the highest heaven, cannot contain you. How much less this temple I have built!" (1 Kgs 8:27). There is nothing new in Stephen's critique and nothing that any rabbi would not also readily confess. The temple, though grand, was not God's home, much less his protective custody. Stephen is not critiquing the temple in any derogatory way.[35] Rather, he is exalting Yahweh as a God beyond the boundaries of human engineering. If God's own creation cannot contain him, then the handiwork of one of his creatures is certainly too constricting.

[51]"You stiff-necked people, with uncircumcised hearts and ears! You are just like your fathers: You always resist the Holy Spirit! [52]Was there ever a prophet your fathers did not persecute? They even killed those who predicted the coming of the Righteous One. And now you have betrayed and murdered him— [53]you who have received the law that was put into effect through angels but have not obeyed it."

7:51. With these verses, Stephen's speech takes a drastic turn. If, as we presume, the real tension was his perceived temple critique, then it is understandable that verse 51 is the decisive turning point.[36] He hit the hot button. Surprisingly, Stephen is the one who flares up. This is Jewish smack-talk. By calling them *stiff-necked*, he compares them to a stubborn jackass who refused to be bridled. This insult was at home in the Exodus narrative (Exod 32:9; 33:3, 5; 34:9; Deut 9:6, 13; 31:27, etc.) and its implication is primarily that they would not listen to

---

This too is somewhat surprising given Luke's redactional interest in Solomon elsewhere as well as the prominence of his temple critique; cf. Peter Doble, "Something Greater than Solomon: An Approach to Stephen's Speech," in *The Old Testament in the New Testament* (ed. Steve Moyise; Sheffield: Sheffield Academic Press, 2000), 181-207.

[35] James Sweeney, "Stephen's Speech (Acts 7:2-53): Is It as 'Anti-Temple' as is Frequently Alleged?" *TrinJ* 23ns (2002): 185-210, finds the evidence lacking for a pronounced anti-temple theme.

[36] From a sociological standpoint, any threat to this central symbol of Israel, particularly given the social pressure of Hellenization and the political pressure of Roman domination, could understandably receive a lethal response. Cf. David A. deSilva, "The Stoning of Stephen: Purging and Consolidating an Endangered Institution," *StBibTheo* 17 (1989): 165-185.

God's word (2 Kgs 17:14; Neh 9:16-17, 29; Jer 7:26; 17:23; 19:15). It seems likely, therefore, that Stephen's sudden outburst, using this particular slur, was a result of the audience's obvious rejection of his message about the temple. Stephen's reaction is virulent; theirs is violent.

Stephen's second remark was even more offensive. To tell a Jew that his heart and ears were uncircumcised is to suggest that he is a Gentile in all but his genitalia (cf. Lev 26:41; Jer 4:4; 6:10; 9:26; Ezek 44:7, 9). You might as well call his mother a blue-ribbon sow. Of course, Stephen was not the first to fashion this insult. In an extended rehearsal of Hebrew history on the precipice of the Promise Land, Moses warns the Israelites against the infidelities of their forefathers in the desert: "Circumcise your hearts, therefore, and do not be stiff-necked any longer" (Deut 10:16). Paul, in a different argument, makes a similar point: "No, a man is a Jew if he is one inwardly; and circumcision is circumcision of the heart, by the Spirit, not by the written code. Such a man's praise is not from men, but from God" (Rom 2:29).[37] Their resistence was not merely to Jesus, but to the very Spirit of God. The reader of Acts has been prepared to understand the Spirit in a personal way as the embodiment of Yahweh. Stephen's original audience did not likely share this Christian perspective on the Spirit, but they would at least know that he is arguing that they were thoroughly rebellious against God as their ancestors had been.

7:52-53. Here Stephen takes up Jesus' argument from Matthew 23:29-36. Jesus, in a heated debate during his final week, exploded with a charge that his opponents were about to kill him, the pinnacle of the prophets, and thus incur the wrath of God for all his martyred envoys. In this line of logic, Stephen expects nothing but execution. The string of prophets prior to Jesus got brutalized and killed (Neh 9:26; Jer 26:20-24; Luke 6:23; 11:49; 13:34; 1 Thess 2:15; Heb 11:36-38).[38] Jesus was brutalized and killed. And so anyone following in his footsteps could hardly expect anything else. Like Peter, he pulls no punches, laying the blame for Jesus' death at their feet (Acts 3:15; 4:10; 5:30).

Stephens's enemies claim fidelity to the law (v. 53). But this law was given by Moses who was replaced by Jesus. Hence, it is disingenuous to claim to follow Moses' law and then execute his typological fulfillment (i.e., his 'spittin' image'). It is not Stephen who is guilty of blasphemy against God/temple and Moses/law, but it is, rather, his accusers. Predictably, this did not go over so well.

3. Stephen's Execution by Stoning (7:54–8:1a)

[54]**When they heard this, they were furious and gnashed their teeth at him.** [55]**But Stephen, full of the Holy Spirit, looked up to heaven and saw the glory of God, and Jesus standing at the right hand of God.** [56]**"Look," he said, "I see heaven open and the Son of Man standing at the right hand of God."**

---

[37] Other rabbis used this same metaphor as well (*b. Zebaḥ* 22b; but cf. *Gen. Rab.* 46.5.1b).

[38] The idea that the prophets of old were persecuted was common fare in Jewish literature: *1 En* 89:51-53; *Jub.* 1:12; *Sir.* 49:7; Josephus, *Ant.* 8.13.4 §330-334; 9.13.2 §265-266; *b. Sanh.* 39b; 103b; *b. Yeb.* 49b; *Cant. Rab.* 6.1.1-4; *Lam. Proem Rab.* 24.1.1b-2b.

7:54-55. It is not terribly surprising that Stephen offended the high court by turning the charges against them. The defendant became the prosecuting attorney, infuriating those with the power to punish. They were so angry that they ground their teeth together (cf. Job 16:9; Psa 35:16; 37:12; 112:10; Lam 2:16). Stephen responded by looking into heaven. Luke notes that he was full of the Holy Spirit (Acts 6:3, 5, 10). Thus, Jesus fulfilled his promise to empower his witnesses at the moment of their travail (Luke 12:11-12; 21:12-15). This explains several things. First, if his enemies were always resisting the Holy Spirit, their opposition to Stephen is inevitable. Second, this is a narrative clue as to who is in the right, not dissimilar to a white hat in a Western movie. Third, this special empowerment enables him to peer into the very throne room of God. There he saw two things: the glory of God and Jesus standing. Whether Stephen meant to or not, his claim that he saw God in heaven reinforced the very point of their conflict—the location of God's abode. It was as if Stephen said, "The temple cannot be God's home." The crowd responded with angry rejection. Stephen looks to the sky and says, "See, he's right up there!"

7:56. Even more inflammatory was his claim that Jesus was standing at God's right hand. This meant that the one they killed, God vindicated and exalted to a privileged position of power. The question is, what's he doing standing? This is the only instance in the New Testament of Jesus standing rather than sitting at the right hand of God (Matt 26:64/Luke 22:69; Mark 16:19; Acts 2:33-36; Col 3:1; Eph 1:20; Heb 1:3, 13; 8:1; 10:12-13; 12:2; Rev 3:21).[39] It is tantalizing to see him standing in honor of Stephen, the first martyr. Perhaps Jesus is standing in judgment of Stephen's enemies,[40] though judges typically sit for the verdict. More likely, Jesus was standing in solidarity with Stephen since this was the typical posture of martyrs at the point of their conviction.[41]

More inflammatory than Jesus' posture is his title—Son of Man.[42] That is

---

[39] Although in Rev 5:6 Jesus is standing in the center of the throne. Both Rev 5:6 and Acts 7:56 likely refer back to the *Merkabah* vision of Dan 7:9-14 which has given way to much mystical interpretation; cf. Phillip Munoa, "Jesus, the Merkavah, and Martyrdom in Early Christian Tradition," *JBL* 121 (2002): 303-325.

[40] Most of the "standing" texts in Acts have a judicial hint in them (Acts 2:14; 5:20; 17:22; 25:18; 27:21). Moreover, the "Son of Man" in Luke sometimes implies judgment of some sort (Luke 9:26; 12:8-9; 21:36; cf. *1 En* 49.2). Certainly one can find Yahweh standing in judgment in OT and Pseudepigraphal literature (Isa 3:13 LXX; *As. Mos.* 10.3). Cf. Franz Mußner, "Wohnung Gottes und Menschensohn nach der Stephanusperikope (Apg 6,8-8,2)," *Jesus und der Menschensohn* (ed. Rudolf Pesch und Rudolf Schnackenburg; Breiburg: Herder, 1975), 283-299; and J. Duncan Derrett, "The Son of Man Standing (Acts 7:55-56)," *BeO* 30 (1988): 71-84. The *Dialogue with Trypho* 31 (c. 135 A.D.) connected Jesus' standing with Dan 7:13 and his coming in eschatological judgment.

[41] Nicole Chibici-Revneanu, "Ein Himmlischer Stehplatz: Die Haltung Jesu in der Stephanusvision (Apg 7.55-56) und ihre Bedeutung," *NTS* 53 (2007): 459-488. Although Légasse Simon argues that the standing is nothing more than a Septuagintism for "being there"; cf. "Encore ΕΣΤΩΤΑ en Actes 7,55-56," *FilNoet* 3 (1990): 63-66. If he is correct, then commentators have made 'much ado about nothing'. Other theories are on offer. E.g., C. K. Barett takes it as a harbinger of Jesus' ready return, "Stephen and the Son of Man," in *Apophoreta: Festschrift für Ernst Haenchen* (Berlin: Töpelmann, 1964), 32-38. M. Sabbe avers it is merely a Lucan redaction of his own previous 'son of man' saying (Luke 22:69); cf. "The Son of Man Saying in Acts 7, 56," in *Les Actes des Apôtres* (ed. J. Kremer; Leuvain: Leuven University Press, 1979): 241-279.

[42] The only thing obvious about the meaning of "son of man" is the data itself. The Hebrew term אָדָם בֶּן is found in the Old Testament a hundred and seven times (אֱנָשׁ בַּר [Aramaic] is found once, Dan 7:13). Ninety four of these are found in Ezekiel; the others are in Num 23:19; Job 25:6; 35:8; Psa 8:4; 80:17; 144:3; Isa 51:12; 56:2; Jer 49:18, 33; 50:40; 51:43; Dan 8:17. Seven additional uses are found in the Apocrypha: Jdt 8:16; Wis 13:13; 14:15, 20; 15:16; 2 Esd 8:6; 16:27). "Son of Man" occurs in the Gospels eighty-two times (Matt 30x, Mark 14x, Luke 25x; John 13x) and only four times outside the Gospels (Acts 7:56; Heb 2:6; Rev

what Jesus called himself, and surprisingly, he called himself almost nothing else (save "prophet" twice by implication, Mark 6:4 and Luke 13:33).[43] Most surprising, no one other than Stephen used this title of Jesus.[44] During Jesus' earthly ministry, this term seemed to imply humility or lowly status as it did in most of its Old Testament uses (Psalm 8:4[5]; Num 23:19; Job 25:6; Isa 51:12; cf. Wis 14:20; 15:16; Jdt 8:16).[45] But Jesus also used the title to imply his future glorification. Virtually the only Old Testament passage upon which he could draw for this idea was Daniel 7:13-14:[46]

> In my vision at night I looked, and there before me was one like a son of man, coming with the clouds of heaven. He approached the Ancient of Days and was led into his presence. He was given authority, glory and sovereign power; all peoples, nations and men of every language worshiped him. His dominion is an everlasting dominion that will not pass away, and his kingdom is one that will never be destroyed.[47]

If the Sanhedrin understood this title as an assertion that Jesus was the Son of Man in Daniel 7:13-14, in combination with Psalm 110:1 at the right hand of Yahweh, they would have taken it as a blasphemous claim that Jesus was equated with God. How can we be so certain? Well, the High Priest, Caiaphas, had heard this very claim from Jesus not so long ago:

1:13; 14:14). In the Apostolic Fathers it is found only twice! "Behold again it is Jesus, not a son of man, but the Son of God, and He was revealed in the flesh in a figure" (*Barn.* 12:10). ". . . Jesus Christ, who is of the race of David according to the flesh, the son of man and Son of God" (Ignatius, *Eph.* 20:2).

[43] Maurice Casey, *The Solution to the "Son of Man" Problem* (New York: T&T Clark, 2007), has argued extensively that "Son of Man" is a generic term for humanity, not specific to an individual: "In general, therefore, (א)שׁנ(א) רב was a general term for humankind. It could be used for everyone in general, or for a more restricted group of people" (37). His conclusions have rightly been challenged by Barnabas Lindars, *Jesus, Son of Man: A Fresh Examination of the Son of Man Sayings in the Gospels* (Grand Rapids: Eerdmans, 1983), 17. The articular Greek translation is particularly striking, says Lindars, since the LXX rendering is consistently anarthrous (24). Likewise, Dunn cautions: "Casey maintains that the articular Greek could be an appropriate translation of the indefinite *bar 'enaš* as much as for the definite *bar 'enaša*. Alternatively, it may equally be possible that the definite usage *bar 'enaša* was a peculiarity of Jesus' own style, a way of particularizing the more generic/general or indefinite sense (in effect, 'that son of man')"; James Dunn, *Jesus Remembered: Christianity in the Making* (Grand Rapids: Eerdmans, 2003), 1:728.

[44] Twice Jesus is quoted using this title (Luke 24:7; John 12:34) and later this title was given to him literarily (Heb 2:6; Rev 1:13; 14:14).

[45] "The Son of Man has no place to lay his head" (Matt 8:20/Luke 9:58/Thomas 86); he was a friend of sinners (Matt 11:19/Luke 7:34); he could be blasphemed (Matt 12:32/Luke 12:10); and most importantly, the Son of Man was destined to suffer humiliating torture and death (Mark 8:31/Luke 9:22; Mark 9:31/Matt 17:22/Luke 9:44; Mark 10:33/Matt 20:18/Luke 18:31; Mark 9:12/Matt 17:12); as well as a shameful betrayal (Mark 14:21/Matt 26:24/Luke 22:22; Mark 14:41/Matt 26:45; Matt 26:2; Luke 22:48; 24:7).

[46] Dan 7:13-14 seems to be a necessary background for Jesus coming "in the glory of his Father with the holy angels" (Mark 8:38; cf. Mark 13:26/Matt 24:30/Luke 21:27; Matt 24:27/Luke 17:24; Matt 24:37/Luke 17:26; Matt 24:44/Luke 12:40; Matthew 10:23; 13:41; 16:28; 24:39; 25:31; Luke 18:8), and sitting on eschatological thrones (cf. Matt 19:28/Luke 22:30; cf. Mark 10:35-40). Furthermore, the "Son of Man" has authority on earth to forgive sins (Mark 2:10/Matt 9:6/Luke 5:24) and to judge (John 5:27); whoever confesses him before men, he will confess before Yahweh (Matt 10:32/Luke 12:8; Mark 8:38/Matt 16:27/Luke 9:26); and he is Lord of the Sabbath (Mark 2:28/Matt 12:8/Luke 6:5). These concepts derive, almost surely from Dan 7:13-14.

[47] This theology of the exalted Son of Man is echoed in Revelation 1:13-14; 14:14 as well as the first century document, *1 Enoch* 46:1: "And there I saw One who had a head of days, and His head was white like wool, and with Him was another being whose countenance had the appearance of a man, and his face was full of graciousness, like one of the holy angels" (cf. 46:3-4; 48:2; 62:5, 7, 9, 14; 63:11; 69:26, 27, 29; 71:14, 16; *Midr. Psa.* 2:9).

The high priest asked him, "Are you the Christ, the Son of the Blessed One?" "I am," said Jesus. "And you will see the Son of Man sitting at the right hand of the Mighty One and coming on the clouds of heaven." The high priest tore his clothes. "Why do we need any more witnesses?" he asked. "You have heard the blasphemy. What do you think?" They all condemned him as worthy of death. (Mark 14:61-64)

Is it, therefore, any surprise that the same basic claim resulted in a similar death sentence?

⁵⁷At this they covered their ears and, yelling at the top of their voices, they all rushed at him, ⁵⁸dragged him out of the city and began to stone him. Meanwhile, the witnesses laid their clothes at the feet of a young man named Saul. ⁵⁹While they were stoning him, Stephen prayed, "Lord Jesus, receive my spirit." ⁶⁰Then he fell on his knees and cried out, "Lord, do not hold this sin against them." When he had said this, he fell asleep. ⁸:¹And Saul was there, giving approval to his death.

7:57-58. The court erupted into mob violence.[48] They covered their ears as if to protect them from further blasphemy and shouted so as to drown out any more heresy. They rushed him,[49] threw him out (*ekballō*) of the sacred city, and executed him by stoning. This is a particularly brutal method of execution— pummeling the victim with stones until his body lies lifeless. Though there is no reason to believe that all stoning was done precisely the same way, the Mishnah (c. A.D. 200) describes it as follows:

[When] he was four cubits from the place of stoning, they remove his clothes. "In the case of a man, they cover him up in front, and in the case of a woman, they cover her up in front and behind" (the words of Rabbi Judah). And the sages say, "A man is stoned naked, but a woman is not stoned naked." The place of stoning was twice the height of a man. One of the witnesses pushes him over from the hips, so [hard] that he turns upward [in his fall]. He turns him over on his hips again [to see whether he had died]. [If] he had died thereby, that sufficed. If not, the second [witness] takes a stone and puts it on his heart. [If] he died thereby, it suffices. And if not, stoning him [the duty] of all Israelites as it is said, "The hand of the witnesses shall be first upon him

---

[48] The deadly response of the Sanhedrin would be illegal under Roman jurisprudence (cf. John 18:31). According to Josephus (*Ant.* 20.10.5 §251) Coponius (A.D. 6–9), the first prefect over Judea, was given all legal authority in the country, including *ius gladii* (*J.W.* 2.8.1 §117). The Talmud roughly aligns with this text, stating that the Jews were stripped of the right of capital punishment, excepting cases of temple violation, a generation before the destruction of the temple (*y. Sanh.* 1.1 [18a], 7.1 [24b]). Thus, Sherwin-White's assertion: "Herod and his successors jealously kept the ordinary capital jurisdiction in their hands," A. N. Sherwin-White, *Roman Society and Roman Law in the New Testament* (New York and London: Oxford University Press, 1978), 37. The only way this was a legal action was if it took place in the interim between Pilate and Marcellus (36–37 A.D.); cf. S. Dockx, "Date de la mort d'Étienne le Protomartyr," *Bib* 55 (1974): 65-73. But this was likely too late for the conversion of Saul.

[49] Interestingly, the only other "rushing" (ὁρμάω) in the New Testament was by an angry mob of idolaters in Ephesus (Acts 19:29) and a herd of pigs in Gerasa (Mark 5:13/Matt 8:32/Luke 8:33). This is not particularly complimentary company for the Jewish high court.

to put him to death, and afterward the hand of all the people" (Deut 17:7). *m. Sanh.* 6.3-4[50]

Of this Saul approved. The fact that he held the cloaks (22:20) may mean that he was in charge of the proceedings and would, if necessary, take responsibility for the execution if it came to Roman court.

7:59. As he died, Stephen looked precisely like Jesus. Jesus asked the Father to forgive his killers (Luke 23:34), and then committed his spirit to the Yahweh (Luke 23:46; cf. Psa 31:5).[51] Stephen does exactly the same, except "Jesus" replaces the "Father"! He was the one to forgive Stephen's enemies and receive his spirit. For Stephen, Jesus was God.

Stephen then falls to his knees under the battering and "falls asleep." That is an extreme euphemism describing an otherwise horrific death.[52]

8:1a. We are introduced here to the most prominent personality in the book of Acts. Saul, like Stephen, was a Hellenistic Jew who had immigrated to Jerusalem. Though we don't know their relationship, one can be fairly certain that Saul felt himself superior as a prize rabbinic student of Gamaliel. Both Stephen and Saul were far-sighted in their view of the Jewish law and its relation to the people of God. Both were zealous in the extreme over the issue of Jesus. Whatever their relationship had been, Saul now sees it as his personal responsibility to put out Stephen's fire. Saul's animosity looms like a brewing storm whose fury will not be allayed for two more chapters.

---

[50] Hegesippus describes the death of James the Just (A.D. 61) according to Mishnaic regulations. After throwing him off the pinnacle of the temple they said, "'Let us stone "James the Just".' And they began to stone him, for he was not killed by the fall; but he turned and knelt down and said, 'I entreat thee, Lord God our Father, forgive them, for they know not what they do'" (Eusebius, *Eccl. Hist.* 2.23.16).

[51] These two statements of Jesus on the cross are only found in Luke. That Luke uses them of both Jesus and Stephen indicates a deliberate comparison. Stephen, filled with the Holy Spirit *is*, in a sense, Jesus embodied. This renders Isaac Kalimi's theory highly improbable, that Luke is drawing a parallel between Stephen and the murdered Zechariah; cf. "The Murders of the Messengers: Stephen versus Zechariah and the Ethical Values of the 'New' versus 'Old' Testaments," *ABR* 56 (2008): 69-73.

[52] "Sleep" or "rest" was a common euphemism for death: Psa 7:5; 13:3; 90:5; Dan 12:2; John 11:11; Acts 13:36; 1 Cor 11:30; 15:6, 18, 20, 51; 1 Thess 4:14-15; 5:10.

ACTS 8

II. WITNESS IN SAMARIA AND JUDEA (8:1b–12:25)

We come now to the second major movement of the book according to Luke's outline in 1:8. Jerusalem fades into the background under a dark cloud of persecution. Now the curtain rises on Gentile evangelism. In the next five chapters we watch as the movement of the Spirit permeates the whole of Palestine. Three individuals and four locations will dominate this second movement in Acts, all of which portend future events.[1]

First, **Philip**, one of the original Seven, will flee to **Samaria** under the heavy hand of Saul. Through him the Holy Spirit breaks forth afresh on a people kin to Israel (8:4-25). Then, as if looking through a telescope at distant events, Philip finds himself in the baptistery with an Ethiopian 'God-fearer' who takes the gospel to the exotic land of Ethiopia (8:26-40). Both the Samaritans and the Ethiopian represent people on the outer edge of the temple. These are those who are 'almost' Jews.

Second, **Paul** is converted en route to **Damascus** (9:1-31). This marks the beginning of the ends of the earth. He, more than any other individual, is responsible for extending the Gospel to all sorts and sundry in a frenetic effort to make Jesus famous. With the help of Barnabas, and building on the foundation of some anonymous evangelists, the church of **Antioch** is birthed into a multiethnic, mission-sending society—the first group to be known as 'Christians' (11:19-30).

Third, **Peter** moves incrementally through Lydda and Joppa in order to reach **Caesarea** where he will baptize the first full-blood Gentile convert (9:32–11:18). These people were 'beyond the pale'. Two thousand years of inclusive evangelism make it nearly impossible for us to imagine how radical this move was. There are intimations throughout the Old Testament that God loved all people.[2] Yet, practically this was unimaginable. As Meyer says, "The most historically charged event of late antiquity was the entry of Mediterranean Gentiles into the Christian movement."[3] The general attitude toward Gentiles is adequately summarized by *Tg. Isa.* 10:27 "The Gentiles will be shattered before

---

[1] Each of these important steps toward global evangelism is initiated from Jerusalem, a city whose significance is recalled in the third and fourth movements of the book as well (15:1-35; 21:1-14). Thus, even though the church moves away from Jerusalem, Luke never loses sight of her roots in that sacred city. Cf. John T. Squires, "The Function of Acts 8.4–12:25," *NTS* 44 (1998): 608-617 and Jules Cambier, "Le Voyage de S. Paul à Jérusalem en Act 9:26ss et le Schéma Missionaire Théologique de S. Luc," *NTS* 8 (1962): 249-257.

[2] God promised Abraham, "All peoples on earth will be blessed through you" (Gen 12:3). The Messiah would "stand as a banner for the peoples; the nations will rally to him, and his place of rest will be glorious" (Isa 11:10) and he would be "a light for the Gentiles" (Isa 42:6; 49:6, 22). In the last days God's spirit would be poured out on all flesh (Joel 2:28) and the household of David would be restored to include all nations (Amos 9:11-12; cf. Acts 15:15-19). Cf. Deut 32:43; Psa 18:49; 67:2; 117:1; Isa 2:2; 51:4; 60:3; Jonah; Isa 49:6; *T. Levi* 14:3; *Sib. Or.* 3.195.

[3] Ben F. Meyer, *The Aims of Jesus* (London: SCM, 1979; repr., San Jose, CA: Pickwick, 2002), 247.

the Messiah." Gentiles, along with tax-collectors and thieves, render a house unclean (*m. Tehar.* 7.6). They are born accursed and are unable to repent (Wis. 12:10-11). Jesus, in contrast to the dominant cultural current, set a course that inevitably headed toward Gentile inclusion.[4] What we are about to read is not the creative propaganda of Luke for his Gentile compatriots. It is not the disciples' enlightened quest for diversity and compassion for the ostracized. It is, against all social mores and impulses, the Holy Spirit carrying out the logical and inevitable implications of Jesus' preaching and praxis.

A. THE GOSPEL EXTENDS TO SAMARITANS (8:1b-40)

The relations between Judea and Samaria were very tense going back to the civil war in Israel after the death of Solomon (c. 930 B.C.). The Samaritans considered themselves faithful to the original plan of God. The name *Samerim* means "keepers" of Torah (cf. Luke 10:33-37; 17:11-19). They had their own version of the Torah with some obvious differences from the Massoretic Text, such as Mount Gerizim replacing Jerusalem as the God-ordained place of worship (Deut 27:4; cf. John 4:20-24).[5] The Jews considered the Samaritans half-breed heretics, yet still wayward sheep of Israel's fold.[6]

After the deportation of the ten northern tribes to Assyria (c. 721 B.C.), only the poor were left in the northern kingdom (2 Kgs 17:24-41), part of which would become Samaria. Assyria's dictator, Esarhaddon (681–669 B.C.), exported people to Samaria he no longer wanted in his borders. These exiles reportedly intermarried with the Jewish remnant of the north (an accusation still unproven). The two southern tribes were later exiled to Babylon for seventy years (c. 605 B.C.). Upon their return, they rebuilt the temple (c. 538–516 B.C.). The Samaritans offered to help but were rebuffed as adversaries rather than brothers (Ezra 4:2-5). Obviously, this did not sit well with the Samaritans who successfully delayed the rebuilding of the temple until 519 B.C. by their complaints to the Persian kings under Darius (Josephus, *Ant.* 11.4.3 §84; Neh 2:10–6:14; 13:28).

[4] Though Jesus' ministry was primarily to Israel (Matt 10:5; 15:24), his principles force his followers to include Gentiles. First, Jesus used Scriptural precedent for interpreting God's rule as universal (cf. Isa 42:6; 49:6; cf. *1 En.* 48.4; Luke 2:32). Second, Jesus promised some Gentiles entrance into the kingdom: Ninevites and the Queen of Sheba (Matt 12:41-42/Luke 11:31-32); Sodom and Gomorrah (Matt 10:15/Luke 10:12; Matt 11:24); and Tyre and Sidon (Matt 11:22/Luke 10:14). All nations would stand before the throne (Matt 25:31-46). Third, some Gentiles were attracted to Jesus: the crowds of Gentiles that flocked to him (Mark 3:7-10/Matt 4:24), especially those in the temple (John 12:20-22), the several Gentiles Jesus healed (Centurion's servant [Matt 8:5-13/Luke 7:1-10], Syro-Phoenician woman [Mark 7:24-30/Matt 15:21-28], the Gerasene demoniac [Mark 5:1-20/Matt 8:21-34/Luke 8:26-39], and the leper [Luke 17:16]), not to mention John's comment that Jesus said he had sheep outside the fold of Israel (John 10:16). And Jesus deliberately engaged the Samaritan woman (John 4). Fourth, Jesus' parables indicate the radical expansion of the kingdom which well could include Gentiles (e.g., Matt 13:38, 47-48), and a Samaritan was featured in one parable as the quintessential 'saved' person (Luke 10:25-37). Fifth, Jesus "cleansed the temple" to make room, according to Isaiah 56, for the nations (Mark 11:17). Hence, the Evangelists are correct in portraying Jesus as a missionary to the Gentiles (Matt 4:15-16 [=Isa 8:23–9:1]; 12:18-21 [=Isa 42:1, 4]; Luke 2:32; 3:6 [=Isa 40:5], 38; 4:25-27; John 4:1-42; 10:16; 12:20).
[5] For a helpful survey on the primary texts on Samaritans see J. P. Meier, "The Historical Jesus and the Historical Samaritans: What Can Be Said?" *Bib* 81 (2000): 202-232.
[6] Jacob Jervell, *Luke and the People of God* (Minneapolis: Augsburg, 1972), 113-132, makes a strong case that Luke considered the Samaritans as more Jewish than Gentile. Hence, their conversion is part of the campaign "Judea and Samaria" and not yet the ends of the earth that starts proper with Cornelius.

In 409 B.C. a certain Manasseh, the son of the High Priest, was expelled from Jerusalem by Nehemiah because of an unlawful marriage. He found refuge in Samaria and through the permission of the Persian king Darius Nothus, he built a rival temple on Mount Gerizim for the Samaritans. John Hyrcanus leveled the Samaritan temple in 127 B.C. (Josephus, *Ant.* 13.9.1 §254-258) fueling immense hatred between the two groups. The Samaritans retaliated years later (c. A.D. 6–9) by scattering human bones in the temple courts to defile it (Josephus, *Ant.* 18.2.2 §29-30; cf. *m. Roš. Haš.* 2:2). The animosity of the Samaritans is shown in Jesus' ministry; they refused to house Jesus when he was headed toward Jerusalem (cf. Luke 9:52-53) though they had received him earlier (John 4:1-42).

Thereafter the Jewish literature has some rather unflattering descriptions of the Samaritans. *Ecclesiasticus* 50:25-26 lumps Samaritans together with Idumeans and Philistines as the three greatest enemies of the Jews. To say someone was demon possessed or a Samaritan was synonymous (John 8:48). Samaritans were on par with Gentiles (Matt 10:5; *m. Demai* 5.9; *m. Tehar.* 5.8) and of "doubtful status" like deaf-mutes and bastards (*m. Qidd.* 4.3). And "Samaritan women are deemed menstruants from their cradle" (*m. Nid.* 4.1).

All this shows how difficult it was to breach the Jewish boundaries into Samaritan territory. Luke has prepared his reader for this by punctuating his narrative with Samaritans at pivotal points. Just as Jesus "resolutely set out for Jerusalem" (Luke 9:51), the first place he goes is Samaria where he is rejected. We find a fictitious Samaritan in the next chapter (Luke 10:30-37) as the superior neighbor to priests and Levites. Another Samaritan emerges from a circle of lepers that Jesus heals on the liminal border of Samaria and Galilee (Luke 17:11-19). This prepared Luke's readers for this earth-altering turn of events when a Christian evangelist dares to cross the border into Samaria.

1. Philip with Simon in Samaria (8:1b-25)

¹ᵇOn that day a great persecution broke out against the church at Jerusalem, and all except the apostles were scattered throughout Judea and Samaria. ²Godly men buried Stephen and mourned deeply for him. ³But Saul began to destroy the church. Going from house to house, he dragged off men and women and put them in prison.

8:1b-3. We come now to a 'new chapter' in the book of Acts. Luke's "on that day" is used not as a chronological division but as a logical marker. Something new is happening, and in this instance, it is not good. The death of Stephen initiated a rampage against the church under Saul's supervision. The word "destroy" (*lumainō*, v. 3) is particularly vicious. It was the kind of word used to describe wild animals tearing their prey (*Beginnings*, 4:88). Saul hunted down followers of Jesus, bursting into their homes, and chasing them into exile (8:1, 4; 11:19). He extracted men and even women from their homes, threw them into prison, and ultimately to execution. He will remember with deep regret his lethal zeal: "I persecuted the followers of this Way to their death, arresting both men and women and throwing them into prison" (Acts 22:4; cf. 26:10; 1 Cor 15:9). "For you have heard of my previous way of life in Judaism, how intensely I persecuted the church of God and tried to destroy it" (Gal 1:13; cf. 1:22-23). "Even though I was once a blasphemer and a persecutor and a violent man, I was shown mercy because I acted in ignorance and unbelief. . . . Christ Jesus came into the world to save sinners—of whom I am the worst" (1 Tim 1:13, 15b).

Saul effectively scattered "all except the Apostles." This is an unfortunately nebulous statement. It may mean that the Apostles rode out the storm that swept over the whole church because of their importance as leaders in the capital city. Eusebius records Clement's memory that Jesus ordered the Apostles to stay in Jerusalem for twelve years until all the Jews could hear the gospel (*Eccl. Hist.* 5.13). How he came across this bit of oral tradition is unknown, and the fact that it is numerically allegorical may lead one to question the reliability of this tradition. Nonetheless, it does fit with the fact that the Apostles refused to leave the city. It could also be that the Sanhedrin's attempt to bully the Twelve into submission had already backfired so they left them alone. More likely, this hullabaloo arose from the Synagogue of the Freedmen and was primarily an intramural debate among the Hellenistic Jews. Since the Apostles were clearly Palestinian, they avoided the fracas.

8:2. Meanwhile, Stephen's body was buried by godly men. These kind souls were not necessarily saved. The word Luke uses to describe them indicates, by and large, Jewish piety, not faith in Jesus as Messiah (Luke 2:25; Acts 2:5; 8:2; 22:12). This begs a couple of questions: Why would they bury Stephen and wouldn't they be persecuted for doing so? The 'why' is easily answered: It was a point of piety and honor for a Jew to provide a burial for a fellow citizen. Thus, there was sufficient motive for even Sanhedrin members to bury one of their victims. One should not assume that the Sanhedrin was in total agreement on Stephen's execution anymore than they were on Jesus' execution. For example, Joseph of Arimathea, along with Nicodemus, asked for the body of Jesus and gave him a noble burial. There were dissenters who (silently?) objected to this course of action. This also answers the question about whether they would be persecuted—probably not. That is not to say these brave souls did not risk social repercussions. However, the capital punishment inflicted on Stephen was probably sufficient to deter would-be rabble-rousers and therefore probably sufficient to assuage the vengeance of the Sanhedrin. With that the Sanhedrin would probably rest. That pious Jews buried Stephen's body would not necessarily imply complicity with his doctrine. Nor would their "great mourning" (v. 2) necessarily be taken as advocacy of his pro-Jesus leanings. Mourning was an essential part of a proper burial.[7] Whether they felt Stephen's death as a personal loss is not the point. Rather, their mourning describes how nobly they acted in properly putting Stephen to rest. In short, they did it right.

---

[7] Although it should be noted that mourning for executed criminals was later prohibited (*m. Sanh.* 6.6) and thus might have serious repercussions, unless, of course, this really was a lynching rather than an official legal action.

⁴Those who had been scattered preached the word wherever they went. ⁵Philip went down to a city in Samaria and proclaimed the Christᵃ **there. ⁶When the crowds heard Philip and saw the miraculous signs he did, they all paid close attention to what he said. ⁷With shrieks, evil**ᵇ **spirits came out of many, and many paralytics and cripples were healed. ⁸So there was great joy in that city.**

ᵃ5 Or *Messiah*   ᵇ7 Greek *unclean*

8:4. The consequence of Saul's assault is predictable—the (Hellenistic) church scattered to the surrounding regions.⁸ The consequence of this dispersion is predictable—they announced the good news of faith in Jesus Christ. They were hardly a frightened group of beleaguered believers huddled in silence and solitude. They continued to boldly announce Jesus the Messiah, the long-awaited liberator of Israel.

8:5. Most would have fled to villages of Judea where they could be sheltered by family and friends. Philip, however, made a beeline to Samaria, a place not frequented by more austere legalists like Saul.⁹ Verses 5-40 will press pause on Saul. The reader should be aware, however, that this section is merely a parenthesis. Luke will later return to the dispersed Hellenists in Acts 9:1, "Meanwhile, Saul was still breathing out murderous threats against the Lord's disciples" and 11:19, "Now those who had been scattered by the persecution in connection with Stephen traveled as far as Phoenicia, Cyprus and Antioch, telling the message only to Jews." Saul the persecutor stands just offstage, ready for his next entrance. For now, Luke is going to concentrate on two fascinating transitional stories of the Samaritans and an Ethiopian noble.

8:6-8. Aside from Stephen, Philip is the only other member of the original Seven featured in Acts. His exploits will be accentuated with a delightful glimpse into his biography some two decades later when we learn that he has four virgin daughters gifted as prophetesses (Acts 21:9). This is hardly surprising given the multifaceted gifts Philip possessed. Not only was he chosen by the church to steward the meals of the widows, he apparently had considerable prowess as a preacher. As if that was not enough, he performed notable miracles and exorcisms. Philip's powers were effective on paralytics, paraplegics, and the possessed. He was doing the very thing the envoys of Jesus were empowered to do (cf. Matt 10:8; Luke 10:17-20). Consequently, the city was abuzz with joy.

⁹Now for some time a man named Simon had practiced sorcery in the city and amazed all the people of Samaria. He boasted that he was someone great, ¹⁰and all the people, both high and low, gave him their attention and exclaimed, "This man is the divine power known as the Great Power." ¹¹They followed him because he had amazed them for a long time with his magic. ¹²But when they believed Philip as he preached the good news of the kingdom of God and the

⁸ *2 Bar* 1.4 (late 1ˢᵗ cen. A.D.) says, "I will scatter this people among the Gentiles, that they may do good to the Gentiles" (cf. James 1:1; 1 Pet 1:1).
⁹ There is no way to know which city of Samaria Philip went to. Three best possibilities are Sebaste (the old "Samaria" renamed by Herod the Great which was primarily Greek and pagan), Shechem (at the foot of Mount Gerizim), or Gitta (the hometown of Simon Magus; cf. Justin, *Apol.* 1.26.56).

name of Jesus Christ, they were baptized, both men and women. [13]Simon himself believed and was baptized. And he followed Philip everywhere, astonished by the great signs and miracles he saw.

8:9-10. Philip's spiritual power was all the more notable against the backdrop of a local legend named Simon (*Beginnings* 5:151-163). According to tradition, he went on to Rome with his sidekick Helen, an ex-prostitute that he rescued and renewed as the embodiment of 'thought'. There he supposedly encountered Peter (again) and attempted to best him in the magic arts. When Peter outperformed Simon, the magician became frustrated. In one last-ditch attempt, Magus ordered his followers to bury him so he could resurrect like Jesus (Hippolytus, *Refutation* 5.2-15). And so his biography comes to an immediate and inauspicious end.

The controversy over this magician has yet to abate. Irenaeus (c. A.D. 180) considered him to be the father of Gnosticism (*Contra Haereses*, 1.23).[10] More likely, he was merely a miracle monger who cashed in on his mystical abilities. Of course, to fully exploit his 'profession', he generated a reputation to overpower the competition for people's attention, not to mention their remuneration. He projected himself as "someone great," and the general consensus agreed, even giving him semidivine status as "The Great Power," or as Justin Martyr puts it, "the highest god" (c. A.D. 165, *Apology* 1.26).[11] This, obviously, is blasphemy.

8:11-12. The crowds of Samaria had given their allegiance to Simon Magus.[12] They had for years. Now there's a new kid in town whose powers eclipse their former star. Thus they listen attentively to the message of the kingdom of God and receive joyfully the baptism of Jesus. At this point, it bears repeating that the kingdom of God was an ancient promise for national liberation. That it is now preached to Samaritans forces a reconceptualization of its contours. The return from exile of the Twelve Tribes must be more than a patriotic recapitulation of a Davidic reign. Philip's preaching sounds like the very stuff of Peter—good news of Jesus and the kingdom of God. But the fact that it was preached to non-Jews is of immense import and signals a heretofore unimagined reconfiguration of the meaning of the Messianic rule. To put it simply, Philip's message is the same as Peter's but his audience is not. This new audience alters the meaning of this old message. God's kingdom can no longer be limited to the boundaries of Palestine.

---

[10] With all due respect to the great church father, Irenaeus is most probably villainizing Simon Magus, forcing him to embody a fairly broad and variegated social movement; cf. Robert Wilson, "Simon and Gnostic Origins," in *Les Actes des Apôtres: Traditions, rédaction, théologie* (ed. by J. Kremer; Leuven: Leuven University Press, 1979), 485-491, and Karlmann Beyschlag, "Zur Simon-Magus-Frage," *ZTK* 68 (1971): 395-426. Contrariwise, Gerd Lüdemann argues in favor of Irenaeus's assessment: "The Acts of the Apostles and the Beginnings of Simonian Gnosis," *NTS* 33 (1987): 420-426.

[11] The later works of Pseudo-Clementine *Recognitions* and *Homilies* expand these legends even further, mostly for apologetic affect against Ebionites and other heretics (cf. Bruce, 178-179).

[12] The word "paid attention" (προσέχειν) is used three times in this context (vv. 6, 8, 11). That's substantial since it is only used 24x in the entire NT. It means more than "listen intently." It implies devotion, allegiance, or affiliation. More specifically, every time this word is used, it is an exhortation to either cling to orthodox doctrine or a rebuke for allegiance to heresy (e.g., Matt 7:15; 10:17; Luke 12:1; 20:46; Acts 20:28; 1 Tim 1:4; 4:1; Tit 1:14). This is not only true in the NT but also the LXX (e.g., Deut 4:23; 6:12-14; 8:11; 11:16; 12:30; 32:46) and wisdom literature (Prov 1:24-25, 30; 5:1-2; 7:24-25; Tob 4:12; Sir 11:33; 17:14; 18:27; 37:1). Cf. Axel von Dobbeler, "Mission und Konflikt: Beobactungen zu προσέχειν in Act 8,4-13," *BN* 84 (1996): 16-22.

This is the breach in the levee that will soon result in an overwhelming outpouring of God's Spirit across all tribes and tongues and lands. It is, therefore, appropriate, that Luke includes a subtle hint at the inevitable diversity in the church by mentioning that the recipients of the gospel were both men and women.

8:13. It is not so surprising that the townspeople turned their allegiance to Philip. The powerful works of the Spirit always trump lesser dilettantes who dabble in the occult (Gen 41:8-40; Exod 8:18-19; Dan 1:20; 2:27-28; 4:7-9). What is surprising, however, is that even Simon Magus converted, or at least gave every appearance of doing so. He "believed," was "baptized," and "followed" Philip wherever he went. These are the telltale signs of a bona fide disciple. Were it not for the following episode, there would be no question as to the reality of his conversion. He was as amazed as anyone else at Philip's power and preaching. Interestingly, Simon had the title "Great Power" (*dunamis megalē*, v. 10) while Philip performed great miracles (*dunameis megalas*, v. 18). Luke's play on words is undoubtedly deliberate and more than mildly entertaining.

[14]When the apostles in Jerusalem heard that Samaria had accepted the word of God, they sent Peter and John to them. [15]When they arrived, they prayed for them that they might receive the Holy Spirit, [16]because the Holy Spirit had not yet come upon any of them; they had simply been baptized into[a] the name of the Lord Jesus. [17]Then Peter and John placed their hands on them, and they received the Holy Spirit.

[a]*16 Or in*

8:14. Since this was the first non-Jewish church, it was natural for the 'mother' church in Jerusalem to send its leaders to confirm what was going on there. It would be difficult to overestimate the importance of this moment in church history. The Jesus movement could easily have splintered Christ followers into variant, ugly, and heretical groups. For those of us weaned in the modern west, such division has always been the nature of the church. But it wasn't always so, and for good reasons the Apostles worked to protect the purity of the body and promote unity between these two divergent groups.[13] That they sent Peter and John shows the importance of this issue—these guys were arguably the two primary pillars of the church (Gal 2:9). They would have the authority to declare these new believers orthodox and thereby confirm the expansion of the gospel into non-Jewish territory. That they *would* approve of the Samaritan Christians is no foregone conclusion. The last time John was in Samaritan territory, he offered Jesus a heavenly holocaust against them (Luke 9:52-56). Peter, for his part, will have to be briskly prodded to set foot in the home of Cornelius (Acts 10:9-16, 28; cf. Gal 2:11-14). Therefore, their gracious reception is not necessarily likely.

8:15-16. Verses 14 and 17 make perfect sense sociologically and historically. Theologically, verses 15-16, are a hornet's nest tucked in a thorn bush of which

[13] Dobbeler, "Mission und Konflikt" (20-22), inappropriately accuses Luke of using this story as propaganda against heterodox Christians whom he wants to label as heretics. It would be normative in the tribal culture of the Middle-East to send authoritative delegates to establish peace and order among a new group of adherents. This is particularly true for Luke for whom the Apostles are the primary witnesses.

Marshall says, "This is perhaps the most extraordinary statement in Acts" (157). Why were these believers baptized without receiving the Holy Spirit?[14] Does this mean they were not saved until Peter and John came? Is the possession of the Spirit granted by the Apostle's hands? Is this a normative conversion experience or an exception? Was the manifestation of Holy Spirit merely miraculous gifts or his indwelling of believers? These are not only complicated questions but probably ultimately unprovable. In order to help clarify this enigma, we will group the potential answers into two broad categories with two subcategories each (borrowing from Stott, 151-159).

First, the Samaritan experience could be seen as a **two-stage conversion**. Two very different groups argue for this option. *Catholics*, of course, baptize infants and later confirm them when they accept the tenets of the church as budding adults. Thus, Catholics see salvation naturally as a two-step process conforming to the Samaritan experience. Philip's baptism did save them, but there would be a later event of confirmation by the imposition of Apostolic hands for full admission into the church and reception of the Holy Spirit (cf. Fitzmyer, 400-401).[15] Likewise, *Pentecostals* commonly argue that a person is saved (with or without water baptism) and then later is baptized in the Holy Spirit (with or without the laying on of hands) which is evidenced by speaking in tongues.[16]

Second, the Samaritan experience could be seen as a **one-stage conversion**. Again, there are two options here. Some will argue that what happened here was *not normal*. After all, this is the advent of a new stage in salvation history where the plan of God is opened for the first time to non-Jews. In order to retain unity of the body, God withheld the Holy Spirit from these baptized believers.[17] Only when the Apostles laid their hands on them did they receive the Holy Spirit, thus completing their conversion. Others argue that the Samaritan experience was, in fact, *normal*, but in some way *incomplete*. It may simply be that their baptism was insincere and therefore ineffective.[18] Or it may be that their baptism was sincere,

---

[14] Obviously, the Holy Spirit is involved with the baptism of the Holy Spirit (Mt 3:11; Acts 1:5; 2:1-4; 10:44-46; 11:16). But the Spirit is also clearly connected with water baptism (Eph 4:5; 1 Cor. 12:13; Titus 3:5; John 3:5). This is natural enough since a number of texts describe the Holy Spirit in terms of working through or like water both in the OT (Psa 46:4-5; Isa 32:15; 44:3; 55:1; 58:11; Ezek 39:29; Joel 2:28) and in the NT (John 7:38-39). Even more specifically, several 'New Birth' texts mention both the water and Spirit as effective forces in the conversion process (John 3:3-7; 1 Cor 6:11; Titus 3:3-7). But is this 'water' merely a metaphor, or does it signify immersion? There is no question that the Holy Spirit is connected to immersion in Acts 2:38-39; 19:1-6 and 1 Cor 12:13. It seems fair, therefore, to interpret the other 'water' passages as baptism. The bottom line is that the Holy Spirit is clearly connected with water baptism in the process of conversion. For this same argument from a Lutheran perspective, cf. A. Andrew Das, "Acts 8: Water, Baptism, and the Spirit," *ConJ* 19 (1993): 108-134.

[15] Bock (331-332) rightly questions whether the Holy Spirit is bestowed normatively through the laying on of hands. None of the three examples of laying on of hands at conversion seem to describe what should take place with every believer (Acts 8:17; 9:17; 19:6). Most of those who receive the Spirit in Acts do so at conversion without the mention of laying on of hands (e.g., Acts 2:38; 8:26-40; 10:44-48).

[16] Max Turner, "Interpreting the Samaritans of Acts 8: The Waterloo of Pentecostal Soteriology and Pneumatology?" *Pneuma* 23 (2001): 265-286; and Gordon D. Fee, "Baptism in the Holy Spirit: The Issue of Separability and Subsequence," *Pneuma* 7 (1985): 87-99.

[17] Marshall, 157-158; Stott, 150-151; Ash, 128-129; Michael Green, *I Believe in the Holy Spirit* (Grand Rapids: Eerdmans, 1975), 161-168.

[18] E.g., James Dunn, *Baptism in the Holy Spirit* (Westminster: John Knox, 1970), 55-68; and Rudolf Bultmann, *Theology of the New Testament* (New York: Scribner, 1955 [1951]), 1:139. Although both their "faith" (cf. 16:34; 18:8) and their "one accord" (cf. 1:14; 2:46; 4:24; 5:12; 15:25) are used elsewhere to describe bona fide Christian experiences. This makes Dunn's theory unlikely.

effective, and complete. What they lacked was not the salvation or the indwelling Spirit, but the miraculous manifestations which accompanied the church for its effective establishment in these early days (Bruce, 181-183; Polhill, 218; Barrett, 413). While this may, at first, seem to be an artificial distinction, the language of verse 16 "come upon" is reserved for miraculous power rather than indwelling and the word "saw" (v. 18) indicates a visible work of the Spirit rather than an invisible "seal" (2 Cor 1:22; Eph 1:13; cf. Reese, 323). Furthermore, there is nowhere else that laying on of hands is for salvation. It is always for empowerment for ministry (e.g., Acts 6:6; 19:6-7; 1 Tim 4:14; 2 Tim 1:6). And if the Baptism of the Holy Spirit at Pentecost was to validate the Apostles (not to save them), and if this event is in any way comparable to a Samaritan Pentecost (Rackham, *Acts*, 117-118), then the Spirit's role would naturally be for empowerment, not salvation.[19] This aligns generally with Luke's pneumatology. This is a helpful oversimplification: For Paul the Holy Spirit works *in* the believer for salvation and sanctification; for Luke and John the Holy Spirit works *through* the believer for evangelism and edification.[20]

Though the Samaritan experience is an important issue for soteriology, the issue for Luke is ecclesiology. In other words, we want to argue about how and when one is saved. Luke wants to prove that the church is a place for all people. He, of course, has an existential stake in this issue. Let's not lose sight of Luke's purpose. He is pressing relentlessly forward to Gentile inclusion and so should we.

[18]When Simon saw that the Spirit was given at the laying on of the apostles' hands, he offered them money [19]and said, "Give me also this ability so that everyone on whom I lay my hands may receive the Holy Spirit." [20]Peter answered: "May your money perish with you, because you thought you could buy the gift of God with money! [21]You have no part or share in this ministry, because your heart is not right before God. [22]Repent of this wickedness and pray to the Lord. Perhaps he will forgive you for having such a thought in your heart. [23]For I see that you are full of bitterness and captive to sin." [24]Then Simon answered, "Pray to the Lord for me so that nothing you have said may happen to me." [25]When they had testified and proclaimed the word of the Lord, Peter and John returned to Jerusalem, preaching the gospel in many Samaritan villages.

8:18-19. Simon had been bested by Philip whose mentor now arrives and makes even Philip's miracles look pedestrian. Peter and John have the ability not only to perform miracles but to pass on that spiritual power at will. Simon, who made a pretty decent living through his own magic arts, sees an opportu-

---

[19] This 'Samaritan Pentecost' would match the miraculous manifestations of the Jewish (2) and Gentile (10) reception of the Spirit; cf. Michel Gourgues, "Esprit des commencements et esprit des prolongements dans les Actes: note sur la 'Pentecôtes des Samaritains'," *RB* 93 (1986): 376-385.

[20] Cf. Mark E. Moore, "The Comforter Has Come with Power," in *Fanning the Flame: Probing the Issues in Acts* (ed. Mark E. Moore; Joplin: College Press, 2003), 192-209; F. F. Bruce, "The Holy Spirit in the Acts of the Apostles," *Int* 27 (1978): 166-183. Robert Menzies, *Empowered for Witness: The Spirit in Luke-Acts* (London: T&T Clark, 2004), following E. Schweizer, "Pneuma," *TDNT* 6:389-455, offers a comprehensive analysis of Lucan pneumatology, highlighting the particular focus of Spirit empowerment as prophetic inspiration. Matthias Wenk, *Community-Forming Power: The Socio-Ethical Role of the Spirit in Luke-Acts* (London: T&T Clark, 2000), takes Menzies a step further arguing that prophetic inspiration is not merely in the word spoken but the social renewal effected by that word. Hence, pneumatology has necessary ethical implications for the renewed community of Israel.

nity here and attempts to seize it with hard cold cash. One could justify verse 19 as a benevolent impulse to empower the church. The problem, however, is Simon's offer in verse 18 to purchase this power. Derrett is undoubtedly correct that what Simon has in mind is the purchase of an authoritative office in the church not merely the spiritual ability itself.[21] The High Priesthood had, in fact, been for sale (cf. 2 Macc 4:7-10). However, one of the distinguishing marks between pagan idolatry and Yahweh is that the one true God gives his Spirit and power without cost.[22] Lest there be any doubt how seriously God takes simony one only need remember the last couple who tried to use their money for pride of place in the body of Christ (Acts 5:1-11).

8:20-21. Peter's response is violent. He curses Simon. The word "may" is optative, meaning, "I wish this upon you." Granted Peter's authoritative power it is a pretty good bet that this 'wish' would come true. And what he wishes is for Simon's money (lit., "silver") to go to destruction (*apōleia*). To put it bluntly: "May you and your money go to hell." Why is Peter in such a snit? For starters, Simon's offer emerges from the world of idolatry and black magic. These kinds of financial transactions were common among Roman cults, pagan religions, and even Judaism in her dark days of rebellious exile. Moreover, Peter says, "you thought you could *buy* the gift." This word "buy" (*ktaomai*) implies seizing control. It is not merely that Simon wanted an authoritative role in the body of Christ, he wanted to be the head. Peter saw this sin and exposed Simon's true heart (v. 21). He had no jurisdiction ("part," *meris*, cf. Acts 16:12; 2 Cor 6:15; Col 1:12) or inheritance ("share," *klēros*) among the people of God.

8:22-24. Peter calls Simon to repent in hopes that somehow God could forgive him (v. 22). Though Simon had been described as a Christian in verse 13, in verse 23, he clearly is not. He is "full of bitterness and captive to sin" (cf. Deut 29:18). While Christians can, unfortunately, have bitterness (Eph 4:31; Heb 12:15), it is a characteristic of the damned to be "full of" it (Rom 3:14). Furthermore, the Christian is in "bondage" (*sundesmos*) to the body of Christ (Eph 4:3; Col 2:19; 3:14) not "captive" to sin. Simon was destined to perdition if something didn't change. Whether Simon is sarcastic or serious in verse 24 remains a mystery. The point, for Luke, is not to describe Magus' destiny, but to warn his readers not to follow him.

8:25. Now that the Lord had validated Samaritans as *bona fide* believers, Peter and John took the opportunity to spread the fame of Jesus throughout a number of Samaritan villages on their way back to Jerusalem.[23] Perhaps we should not idealize this brief verse as a lovely little excursion with no objections, racial slurs, or threats. After all, the last time Peter and John were in Samaria

---

[21] J. Duncan M. Derrett, "Simon Magus (Acts 8:9-24)," *ZNW* 73 (1982): 61-62. It is from this Simon Magus that we coined the term "simony" in English, meaning "the buying or selling of ecclesiastical offices or positions."

[22] C. K. Barrett, "Light on the Holy Spirit from Simon Magus (Acts 8, 4-25)," in *Les Actes des Apôtres: Traditions, redaction, théologie* (ed. by J. Kremer; Leuven: Leuven University Press, 1979), 281-295.

[23] Interestingly, there is tentative evidence for Samaritan Christianity as late as the 4th–6th cen. A.D.; cf. R. Plummer, "New Evidence for Samaritan Christianity?" *CBQ* 4 (1979): 98-117.

they were refused lodging (Luke 9:51-56). It is unlikely that these Samaritan villages magically turned pro-Jewish or pro-Christian.

2. Philip with the Eunuch en Route to Gaza (8:26-40)

Few stories rival this one for intrigue, mystery, theology, and the beauty of ethnic diversity. It's just masterful. Philip, at the pinnacle of his ministry, gets the nod from the Holy Spirit for a search and rescue mission on a desolate road. There is a lone soul who desperately loved Yahweh even though his ethnic heritage and physical condition kept him at the margins. Philip announces the good news of Jesus by whom the Eunuch gained full access to the church. By the end of the day he is baptized in a lonely desert pool, and Philip is miraculously transported to another village leaving the submerged African dripping with joy as he returned home.

This story is even more fascinating when read alongside Luke 24:23-35—the two en route to Emmaus. Consider the uncanny similarities:[24] (1) An evangelist joins puzzled travelers. (2) The conversation begins with a pointed question about Jesus' death and resurrection. (3) Each ends with a sacrament, the Lord's Supper[25] (Luke 24) and Baptism (Acts 8). (4) The evangelist disappears suddenly and mysteriously only to resurface somewhere else. (5) The travelers are transformed by the event. This parallelism helps us understand better Philip's preaching to the Eunuch (see below on vv. 32-35). Perhaps more importantly, it helps us understand Philip himself. He is a 'Christ-figure' as Stephen had been. He is the mysterious sojourner who appears suddenly, opens the Scripture, supervises a sacrament, and then vanishes only to be found at another place. Part of Luke's strategy is to show how Jesus continues to be incarnate through Spirit-filled people.[26]

The danger in reading this story is getting swept up in the movement and losing the moral. This exciting little vignette plays a critical role in the transition from a Jewish church (Acts 1–7) to Gentile expansion (Acts 13–28). The Samaritan experience represents broadening boundaries with 'half-Jews'. The Ethiopian Eunuch represents those God-fearers who for geographic, ethnic, and physiological reasons would never reach the epicenter of Israel. Taken together, the Samaritans and the Ethiopian break every taboo leading up to Gen-

[24] Many have noticed the similarities between these two stories, among the better pieces are Jacques Dupont, "Le Repas d'Emmaüs," *LumVit* 31 (1957): 77-92, Joseph A. Grassi, "Emmaus Revisited (Luke 24, 13-35 and Acts 8,26-40)," *CBQ* 26 (1964): 463-467, and Coert Lindijer, "Two Creative Encounters in the Work of Luke (Lk 24:13-35 and Acts 8:26-40)," *MNeot* 2 (1978): 77-85.
[25] This is not, of course, to suggest that the two travelers *intended* to partake of the Lord's Supper at their table in Emmaus; contra Hans Dieter Betz, "The Origin and Nature of Christian Faith according to the Emmaus Legend (Luke 24:13-32)," *Int* 23 (1969): 32-46. They most certainly would *not* have remembered Jesus by eating his body and drinking his blood while they still believed his corpse was rotting. It is, rather, to suggest that this meal would be recognizable by later Christians as the very thing they were doing, meeting the risen Christ; cf. B. P. Robinson, "The Place of the Emmaus Story in Luke-Acts," *NTS* 30 (1984): 481-497.
[26] Philip's journey primarily conjures up images of Jesus. Nonetheless, particularly his running and being snatched away may be multivalent metaphors that also conjure up shades of Elijah (1 Kgs 18:12, 46; 2 Kgs 2:11, 16; Josephus, *Ant.* 8.13.6 §346). Rick Strelan, "The Running Prophet (Acts 8:30)," *NovT* 43 (2001): 31-38, further develops this theme perhaps to an extreme.

tile inclusion.[27] Thus, this episode is the final step before tackling the ultimate barrier represented by Cornelius (Acts 10–11).

[26]Now an angel of the Lord said to Philip, "Go south to the road—the desert road—that goes down from Jerusalem to Gaza." [27]So he started out, and on his way he met an Ethiopian[a] eunuch, an important official in charge of all the treasury of Candace, queen of the Ethiopians. This man had gone to Jerusalem to worship, [28]and on his way home was sitting in his chariot reading the book of Isaiah the prophet. [29]The Spirit told Philip, "Go to that chariot and stay near it." [30]Then Philip ran up to the chariot and heard the man reading Isaiah the prophet. "Do you understand what you are reading?" Philip asked. [31]"How can I," he said, "unless someone explains it to me?" So he invited Philip to come up and sit with him.

[a]27 That is, from the upper Nile region

8:26-27. The angel of the Lord, a figure closely connected with the Spirit in Jewish literature (e.g., Exod 3:2, 4, 7) charged Philip to head south from Jerusalem. This may indicate that Philip followed Peter and John back to Jerusalem (v. 25). Nonetheless, he is to follow the old trade route that led to Gaza,[28] the southernmost border of ancient Israel.[29] The timing of the Spirit is impeccable. Philip encounters the chariot at precisely the right point when the Eunuch is reading precisely the right text. Philip runs up alongside the chariot where the Ethiopian sat reading while his entourage carried him back to Africa.

Though the Ethiopian remains an enigma, Luke provides several clues as to his identity. He was an **Ethiopian**. As a nation, the Ethiopians (i.e., Nubians—modern Sudanese) were revered for their wealth (Job 28:19; Isa 45:14), wisdom (Diodorus, 3.2-8; Josephus, *Ant.* 8.6.6 §165), and military prowess (2 Chr 14:9-15; Isa 18:1-2; 20:5; Jer 46:9; Nah 3:9 ; Josephus, *Ant.* 8.10.3 §254, 8.12.1 §292-293; 10.1.4 §17; Diodorus, 1.37.5).[30] They were also considered by some not only

---

[27] Cf. G. Schneider, "Stephanus, die Hellenisten und Samaria," in *Les Actes des Apôtres: Traditions, redaction, théologie* (ed. by J. Kremer; Leuven: Leuven University Press, 1979), 222-223. Eusebius mistakenly took the Eunuch to be a Gentile (*Eccl. Hist.* 2.1.13). So did Erich Dinkler, "Philippus und der ANHP AIΘIOΨ (Apg 8,26-40)," in *Jesus und Paulus* (Göttingen: Vandenhoeck & Ruprecht, 1978), 85-95, who asserts that Luke mistakenly included the Samaritan and Ethiopian conversions since they conflict with the true Gentile conversion of Cornelius. This inhospitable skepticism borders on nonsense. Luke was well aware of what he was doing in creating a progression that climaxed in Cornelius. In fact, literarily, even the placement of the story shows the luminal Jewish character of the Eunuch. He is on the outside of the temple yet with a 'Bible' in his hand. He goes up to Jerusalem to worship yet is found on a lonely road heading away from the sacred city. He is from the 'ends of the earth' yet is a god-fearer. Thus, he is not a Gentile convert but he *is* an appropriate transitional character leading up to that pivotal moment in salvation history. Cf. Scott Shauf, "Locating the Eunuch: Characterization and Narrative Context in Acts 8:26-40," *CBQ* 71 (2009): 762-775.

[28] It is grammatically possible, though less likely, that "desert[ed]" describes to the (old) city of Gaza (destroyed 93 B.C.) rather than the road itself. Luke's good Greek offers a clever word play with "Gaza" (Γάζαν, v. 26) and "treasury" (γάζης, v. 27).

[29] The word "south" (μεσημβρία) also can be translated "noon" since the sun stood directly to the south at that hour of the day; cf. Melchor Sánchez de Toca, "Πορεύου κατὰ Μεσημβρίαν (Hch 8,26)," *EB* 55 (1977): 107-115. In fact, in its only other use in the NT it does mean 'noon' in the narrative of Saul going to Damascus (22:6). Since Gaza was the southernmost boundary of ancient Israel and Damascus was her northernmost border, the peculiar use of this odd word may be deliberate to signal to the reader that all of Judea and Samaria had now been covered. Though it would have been more obvious had Luke used the word in Saul's conversion account of chapter 9 rather than 22.

[30] Cf. Abraham Smith, "'Do You Understand What You are Reading?' A Literary Critical Reading of the Ethiopian (Kushite) Episode (Acts 8:26-40)," *JITC* 22 (1994): 64-68.

exotic, but remote—at the ends of the earth (Homer, *Odyssey*, 1.23; cf. Esther 1:1; 8:9; Isa 60:3-14; Ezek 29:10; Zech 3:10; 14:16-19; Eusebius, *Eccl. Hist.* 2.1.13). The term "Ethiopian" means "one with burnt skin."[31] Their dark skin was not an object of ridicule. What would have been an object of ridicule, however, was the fact that he was a **Eunuch** (Herodotus 8.104-106; Josephus, *Ant.* 4.8.39 §290-291; Philo, *Spec. Laws* 1.324-325; Lucian of Samosota, *The Eunuch,* 6-11).[32] The term indicates a male who had been castrated—a common experience for those serving in the high court (e.g., Esther 2:3, 14; 4:4-5).[33] After all, you don't want those around a harem or a queen mother to provide illegitimate offspring! In fact, it was so common that the title Eunuch could be applied to officials without necessarily referring to castration. For example, Potiphar, who was married, is called a Eunuch (LXX Gen 39:1, cf. Gen 40:2, 7; 2 Kgs 25:19). In this context, however, it is probable that the Ethiopian was, in fact, castrated since "Eunuch" (rather than Ethiopian or Treasurer) becomes his 'title' from here on out (vv. 32, 34, 36, 38, 39). The third thing we learn about this man is that he was the **Treasurer** for **Candace**, the queen. Candace is not a name, but a title (like 'Pharaoh' or 'Caesar').[34] She had considerable wealth! The Nubians were known for their gold. That puts the Ethiopian in the upper echelons of leadership and commerce in the entire Mediterranean. Though we cannot trace Christianity in Ethiopia back past the fourth century, it is difficult to imagine the Eunuch having little impact after his conversion.[35]

He had gone up to Jerusalem to worship. In other words, he was a godfearer. Very likely he would have loved to become a full convert but that could never happen for a eunuch. One can only imagine a man so passionate about Yahweh that he would travel hundreds of miles to worship in the sacred temple

[31] Ethiopians were famed for their dark skin; cf. Clarice Martin, "A Chamberlain's Journey and the Challenge of Interpretation for Liberation," *Semeia* 47 (1989): 105-135. For example, when examining the skin for leprosy, the Mishnah instructs: "Let a German be examined in accord with his skin for a lenient decision; and an Ethiopian [be judged] leniently by the intermediate color" (*m. Neg.* 2.1). A light-skinned German should not be judged to have leprosy due to a pale skin around a 'spot' and an Ethiopian should not be judged to have leprosy due to a dark discoloration of the 'spot'. Cf. Jer. 13:23, "Can the Ethiopian change his skin or the leopard its spots?"

[32] Though eunuchs could be prosperous under the Romans, they were still objects of scorn, particularly as illicit lovers of the elite. Titus, the general who destroyed Jerusalem, had a famous affair with a eunuch that became an object of ridicule, so much so that Emperor Domitian banned castration throughout the empire (even though he kept a favorite eunuch for his own sexual gratification). Later Hadrian intensified the ban on castration with the threat of the death penalty; cf. J. P. Balsdon, *Romans and Aliens* (Chapel Hill: University of North Carolina Press, 1979), 227-230.

[33] It was customary, according to Plutarch (*Demetrius* 25.5), for the treasuries of eastern kingdoms to be entrusted to eunuchs.

[34] One Candace (pronounced *kandākā*) met Alexander the Great (*Pseudo-Callisthenes* 226-227, cf. 228-245), others were imprisoned by Petronius (Strabo, *Geo.* 17.1.54). And Pliny records the title of these 'queens' when Nero sent an expedition to explore Ethiopia (*Nat. Hist.* 6.35). An inscription from 13 B.C. in Nubia refers to Candace as "the lady queen," cf. A. Deissmann, *Light from the Ancient East* (New York: Harper & Brothers, 1927), 352. It has not been uncommon for Candace to be confused for the Queen of Sheba in Jewish, Muslim, Persian, and Ethiopic literature; Cf. Edward Ullendorff, "Candace (Acts VIII. 27) and the Queen of Sheba," *NTS* 2 (1955): 53-56. But they are two different women. Though both are from the south, the Queen of Sheba hails from Southern Arabia on the eastern side of the Red Sea and Candace is from the African Continent on the western side.

[35] Irenaeus (*Against Heresies* 3.12.8; cf. *Beginnings* 4.98) says that the Eunuch was a missionary to Nubia, but this cannot be verified; cf. Bruce Metzger, "The Christianization of Nubia and the Old Nubian Version of the New Testament," in *Historical and Literary Studies: Pagan, Jewish, and Christian* (Leiden: Brill, 1968): 111-122.

of Jerusalem,[36] knowing that he would not actually be allowed into the Temple: "No one who has been emasculated by crushing or cutting may enter the assembly of the LORD" (Deut 23:1). He could go to the gate, he could present an offering, he could read the Torah, but he would never be allowed to participate in the Temple services. Yet he was there. There is something powerful going on in the soul of this man—some longing for God that is about to come to fulfillment on a lonely desert road.

8:28-31. The Spirit charged Philip to run up to the chariot, which is more likely some sort of an ox-cart or covered wagon. The word "stay near it" (*kollaō*) means to "stick to it" or "cling to it." It must have been a strange sight for the Ethiopian to have this Jew run alongside his chariot and just kind of 'hang out' while he rode along. Philip hears him reading from Isaiah 53 and asks, "Do you understand what you are reading?"[37] The Ethiopian does not understand and asks for help. This is hardly surprising given the perplexing nature of Isaiah 53.[38] The rabbis wrestled with this 'Servant Song' which portrayed Yahweh's envoy as suffering and rejected.[39] Some thought the suffering servant was the whole of Israel, spoken of metaphorically as an individual.[40] That can hardly be, however, since the one suffering takes on the sins of the nation (Isa 53:8b; cf. Isa 42:7). Others believed that Isaiah himself was the suffering servant (Isa 20:31). In fact, that is one of the options pondered by the Eunuch (v. 34).[41] What no one seems to have guessed is that it would refer to God's Messiah.

A suffering Messiah ran counter to virtually every known prediction. Consequently, the rabbis actually altered the text of Isaiah 53 in the Targum. Isaiah 53:3, "He was despised and forsaken of men, a man of torments and acquainted with infirmity, and like one from whom one hides his face, he was despised and we esteemed him not." Targum: "Then the glory of all the kingdoms will be for contempt and cease; they will be faint and mournful, behold, as a man of

---

[36] Since ancient Ethiopia bordered the upper Nile, he would have traveled by ship down the Nile (north, well over 1,000 miles) to the Mediterranean and sailed along the coast to Gaza where he would have continued his journey by land another 50 miles.

[37] The 'urban legend' that suggests readers in the ancient world always read aloud is based on a misinterpretation of Augustine, *Conf.* 6.3. Multiple examples of silent reading (when alone) and vocalized reading (in groups) are presented by Carsten Burfeind, "Wen hörte Philippus? Leises Lesen und lautes Vorlesen in der Antike," *ZNW* 93 (2002): 138-145.

[38] Here we have another similarity between Acts 8 and Luke 24:45 when Jesus opened the Scriptures for the two en route to Emmaus. It is comprehensible that a Christian is necessary for correct understanding of Messianic prophecy. This, however, should not be extrapolated to suggest that the Bible is somehow locked to all but professional interpreters or clergy.

[39] There is no question that Isaiah 53 had a profound influence on Pauline theology and, hence, the developing Christian Church. Isaiah 53 is cited in Rom 10:16 (53:1); 15:21 (52:15); Acts 8:32-33 (53:7-8). Echoes of Isaiah 53 include: 1 Pet 2:22-25 (53:4-7, 9); Rom 4:25 (53:4-5); 5:19 (53:11); 1 Cor 15:3 (53:4-9); Gal 1:4 (53:4-5); 2:20 (53:8-9; cf. 1 Tim 2:6 and Titus 2:14); Phil 2:7-8 (53:10-12); 2:9 (53:13); Heb 9:28 (53:12).

[40] For a survey of the exegetical suggestions see H. H. Rowley, *The Servant of the Lord and Other Essays on the OT* (London: Lutterworth Press, 1952); and C. R. North, *The Suffering Servant in Deutero-Isaiah* (London: Oxford University Press, 1948).

[41] Even earlier than the Eunuch we find another individualistic interpretation of Isaiah 53 in *T. Benj.* 3.8 when Isa 53:8 was applied to an unknown descendant of Joseph: "A blameless one shall be delivered up for lawless men, and a sinless one shall die for ungodly men." J. Jeremias and W. Zimmerli, *The Servant of the Lord* (London: SCM Press, 1957), 53, observe that "for Palestinian Judaism of the first millennium A.D. the collective application of the servant of Isa. 53 to Israel is completely unknown (it appears first in Rashi, died 1105)." Hence, the individualistic interpretations of Isaiah 53 by the Ethiopian and Philip seems to have been more likely; cf. Edward Young, "Of Whom Speaketh the Prophet This?" *WTJ* 11 (1948): 133-155.

sorrows and appointed for sicknesses; and as when the face of the Shekhinah was taken up from us, they are despised and not esteemed." Isaiah 53:4, "Surely he has borne our infirmities and carried our torments, but we considered him smitten with disease, stricken by God, and afflicted." Targum: "Then he will beseech concerning our sins and our iniquities for his sake will be forgiven; yet we were esteemed wounded, smitten before the LORD it was a pleasure to forgive the sins of us all for his sake." Isaiah 53:5, "And he was wounded by our transgressions, he was crushed by our iniquities; the chastisement of our peace was upon him, and with his stripes we were healed." Targum: "And he will build the sanctuary which was profaned for our sins, handed over for our iniquities; and by his teaching his peace will increase upon us, and in that we attach ourselves to his words our sins will be forgiven us." Hengel is correct: "In the light of all our present knowledge, the suffering and dying Messiah was not yet a familiar traditional figure in Judaism of the first century AD."[42]

³²The eunuch was reading this passage of Scripture: "He was led like a sheep to the slaughter, and as a lamb before the shearer is silent, so he did not open his mouth. ³³In his humiliation he was deprived of justice. Who can speak of his descendants? For his life was taken from the earth."ᵃ ³⁴The eunuch asked Philip, "Tell me, please, who is the prophet talking about, himself or someone else?" ³⁵Then Philip began with that very passage of Scripture and told him the good news about Jesus.

ᵃ*33* Isaiah 53:7,8

8:32-33. The particular passage Luke recorded is Isaiah 53:7 8a. Since this is the only time Luke cites an Old Testament passage—as a narrator and not on the lips of a speaker—one can assume it has particular importance to him. However, he does *not* cite either verse 6 or 8b which have clear reference to substitutionary atonement: "Each of us has turned to his own way; and the LORD has laid on him the iniquity of us all" and "for the transgression of my people he was stricken." This has led some to suggest that Luke is not aware of or not interested in the doctrine of Jesus dying for the sins of his people.[43] It is true that Luke does not emphasize this point as much as Paul or even Matthew and Mark. However, the only time Jesus 'proof-texted' a passion prediction was in

---

[42] Martin Hengel, *The Atonement: The Origins of the Doctrine in the New Testament* (trans. J. Bowden; London: SCM Press, 1981), 40. In fact, the only other passage to directly speak of the Messiah's suffering is Zech 12:10, "And I will pour out on the house of David and the inhabitants of Jerusalem a spirit of grace and supplication. They will look on me, the one they have pierced, and they will mourn for him as one mourns for an only child, and grieve bitterly for him as one grieves for a firstborn son." To this might be added 2 Esdras 7:29, "After those years my son the Messiah shall die, and all who draw human breath." Clearly the Messiah dies, but merely as a mortal man at the end of the age so that primordial time can be renewed. Psalm 89:39 [38], likewise records David's complaint against God for allowing him to suffer (even calling the king God's "servant" v. 40 [39]): "But now you have spurned and rejected him; you are full of wrath against your anointed." Neither of these last two texts, however, portrays Israel's leader suffering *on behalf* of the people.
[43] Morna D. Hooker, *Jesus and the Servant: The Influence of the Servant Concept of Deutero-Isaiah in the New Testament* (London: SPCK, 1959), 113-114, is, technically, correct that Luke missed a grand opportunity to directly connect the text of Isaiah 53 to the preaching of Jesus' substitionary death. One wonders, however, if Luke would retort: "Do I have to spell out *everything*?!" Biblical readers should keep in mind that whenever an OT text is quoted, the context must be considered. This is especially true since Luke tells us "Philip began with that very passage of Scripture and told him the good news about Jesus" (v. 35).

Luke 22:37 when he said: "'And he was numbered with the transgressors' [Isa 53:12]; and I tell you that this must be fulfilled in me. Yes, what is written about me is reaching its fulfillment."[44] Furthermore, it is clear that Luke understands that Jesus' blood purchased us: "Be shepherds of the church of God, which he bought with his own blood" (Acts 20:28). It is, of course, *highly* unlikely that Philip would have missed the meaning of Jesus' death as he moved on from this passage to preach Jesus (v. 35).[45]

Even so, Luke has good reasons for concentrating on the humiliation theme of Isaiah 53:7-8a rather than the atonement theme of Isaiah 53:6 and 8b. Humiliation and rejection spoke to the Eunuch's biography. One is inclined to agree with Parsons: "Luke may have wished to avoid these references, but not because he was reticent to contemplate or uninterested in the suffering vocation of the Servant; rather, Luke avoids citing those parts of the passage because it would have detracted from the relevance of the passage for drawing the eunuch to identify with the Servant."[46] In this text, perhaps more than any other, the Eunuch could relate to the Suffering Servant. Perhaps this was why he paused here during the reading of the scroll. Philip's message boils down to this: The Messiah himself was rejected by the Jews, so he appreciates rejected eunuchs. Interestingly, if we read this incident in the shadow of the two going to Emmaus (Luke 24:13-35), we also read of Jesus' rejection, "Did not the Christ have to suffer these things and then enter his glory?" (Luke 24:26).

Philip is invited into the chariot to discuss this important text. Starting from there, he plows through the scroll unpacking the relevance of this providential passage for the Eunuch. There is much that would be of interest to the Eunuch in the following context.[47] Philip could easily have emphasized the substitutionary importance of Jesus' death in Isaiah 53:12c, "For he bore the sin of many, and made intercession for the transgressors." And though 54:1a is addressed to women, the Eunuch would undoubtedly also feel the pain of having no progeny: "Sing, O barren woman, you who never bore a child. . . ." Verse 4b would become his song: "Do not be afraid; you will not suffer shame. Do not fear disgrace; you will not be humiliated. You will forget the shame of your youth." Perhaps Isaiah 55:1 caught his eye as it merged the themes of water and money: "Come, all you who are thirsty, come to the waters; and you who have no money, come, buy and eat! Come, buy wine and milk without money and without cost." He had already embodied Isaiah 55:5, "Surely you will summon nations you know not, and nations that do not know you will hasten to you, because of the Lord your God, the Holy One of Israel." Finally, it is not difficult to imagine the Eunuch's heart pounding like a kettle drum when he heard the words of Isaiah 56:3-5:

---

[44] André Feuillet, "Le logion sur la rançon," *RSPT* 51 (1967): 365-402.

[45] David Moessner, "The 'script' of the Scriptures in Acts: Suffering as God's 'plan' (βουλή) for the World for the 'release of sins'," in *History, Literature and Society* (ed. Ben Witherington; Cambridge: Cambridge, 1999), 218-250, catalogues a substantial list of passages that indicate Luke's awareness of and interest in atonement.

[46] Michael C. Parsons, "Isaiah 53 in Acts 8: A Reply to Professor Morna Hooker," in *Jesus and the Suffering Servant* (ed. William H. Bellinger and William R. Farmer; Harrisburg: Trinity Press, 1998), 115.

[47] Cf. Warren A. Gage and John R. Beck, "The Gospel, Zion's Barren Woman, and the Ethiopian Eunuch," *Crux* 30 (1994): 35-43.

Let no foreigner who has bound himself to the LORD say, "The LORD will
surely exclude me from his people." And let not any eunuch complain,
"I am only a dry tree." For this is what the LORD says: "To the eunuchs
who keep my Sabbaths, who choose what pleases me and hold fast to
my covenant—to them I will give within my temple and its walls a memorial and a name better than sons and daughters; I will give them an
everlasting name that will not be cut off."

This single Bible study transformed Eunuch. Here was a man who loved
God but never imagined he could share in the glorious riches of the Elect Israel.
Now in one afternoon Philip points to passage after passage that reveal Yah-
weh's heart for the nations and particularly for the marginalized like this black
Eunuch from Nubian Sudan. Though he could never enter the temple of God
in Jerusalem, he could *become* the temple of God by joining with God's church.

**[36]As they traveled along the road, they came to some water and the eunuch
said, "Look, here is water. Why shouldn't I be baptized?"[a] [38]And he gave orders
to stop the chariot. Then both Philip and the eunuch went down into the water
and Philip baptized him. [39]When they came up out of the water, the Spirit of the
Lord suddenly took Philip away, and the eunuch did not see him again, but went
on his way rejoicing. [40]Philip, however, appeared at Azotus and traveled about,
preaching the gospel in all the towns until he reached Caesarea.**

[a]*36 Some late manuscripts baptized? [37] Philip said, "If you believe with all your heart, you may." The eunuch
answered, "I believe that Jesus Christ is the Son of God."*

8:36. At the sight of a pool the Ethiopian leapt at the chance to be immersed.[48] How Philip brought up the topic of baptism from the book of Isaiah
is anyone's guess.[49] Nevertheless, it was natural enough for Philip to preach baptism as he had done already in Samaria and as his 'mentor', the Apostle Peter,
had done on the day of Pentecost.[50] One need look no further than the death
and resurrection of Jesus, the core of the gospel, to find an adequate platform
for a call to immersion in which the passion of Jesus is imitated (Rom 6:3-4).

His question is most interesting: "*Why shouldn't I be baptized?*" or more literally, "What *hinders* me from being baptized?"[51] There were plenty of hindrances

[48] There were two primary roads from Jerusalem to Gaza. One went south to Beersheva and then west to
the coast; the other was a more direct route, west-southwest down to Gaza. The most common identification of this pool has been Ein ed Dirweh on the longer route through Beersheva. It is attested in the 4th
cen. by Eusebius (*Onomasticon*, 104.31) and Jerome in the 5th cen. (*Epistle*, 103), and the Madaba Map in
the 6th century. There are, however, some good reasons to prefer *Ein Yael* as the site for the Eunuch's
baptism. It lay on the more direct route, it would have sufficient water, it had a Byzantine Christian community from the 4th–7th centuries, and the road was paved for easier travel with a chariot. Cf. Yehudah
Rapuano, "Did Philip Baptize the Eunuch at Ein Yael?" *BAR* 16 (1990): 44-49.
[49] R. J. Porter, "What Did Philip Say to the Eunuch?" *ExpT* 100 (1988): 54-55, speculates that Philip started
with Isaiah 53:7-8a and pushed forward through the scroll. When he came to Noah in Isaiah 54:9-10, he
used that text in the same way that Peter did in 1 Peter 3:21 as a metaphor for baptism.
[50] R. F. O'Toole has a convincing argument that structurally baptism is the epicenter of this text which
Luke shapes as a chiasm; cf. "Philip and the Ethiopian Eunuch (Acts VIII 25-40)," *JSNT* 17 (1983): 25-34.
This is hardly surprising since baptism and the Holy Spirit are central to each of the four major conversion
stories in Acts 8–9: Samaritans, the Eunuch, Paul, and Cornelius.
[51] This word (κωλύω) is used particularly in contexts of baptism by Luke (Acts 8:36; 10:47; 11:17; cf. Luke
11:52; 18:16). Cf. Oscar Cullmann, *Baptism in the New Testament* (London: SCM, 1950), 71-80.

for his full inclusion in the Temple but none in the church. Philip's preaching persuaded him that he could be included among the people of God. That he was a Eunuch was no barrier; that he was a foreigner was no barrier. He gets it. The God of Israel is finally and fully the God of the nations.

Before Philip could answer, the Eunuch ordered his men to stop at the pool.[52] Both entered the water. This is one of the few texts that illustrate the method of baptism by immersion (which would naturally be assumed by the definition of the word).[53] As they came up out of the water, Philip was snatched away. How? Who knows. Where? Azotus, approximately twenty miles up the coast. He would continue up the coast another sixty miles until he reached Caesarea. There he would live until we meet him again with his four virgin daughters (Acts 21:8-9). But that will have to wait another twenty years.[54]

8:38-40. Both Philip and the Ethiopian must have been terribly confused as they came up out of the water. Philip is whisked away to Azotus (OT Ashdod).[55] The Eunuch, on the other hand, is left standing in a pool of water searching for the evangelist who mysteriously joined his chariot and miraculously vanished after his immersion. The longer ending of the Western text reads, "And when they came up out of the water, the Holy Spirit fell upon the eunuch, but the angel of the Lord caught up Philip." Though the manuscript evidence for this reading is weaker, it improves on the present text by (a) returning to the angel of the Lord who initiated this whole encounter, (b) including the Holy Spirit who is responsible for the 'joy' the Ethiopian experienced, (c) balancing the exit of the Eunuch as well as Philip, and most importantly, (d) incorporating the Holy Spirit into the conversion experience.

---

[52] According to the Western text, v. 37, Philip *did* respond to the Eunuch: "If you believe with all your heart, you may." To this the Eunuch replies, "I believe that Jesus Christ is the Son of God." This sounds suspiciously like a later baptismal liturgy leading most scholars to view v. 37 as an orthodox, albeit anachronistic, addition. Jenny Heimerdinger, however, argues that it is as ancient and as authentic as the Alexandrian reading but that both were written to different audiences and both are Lucan; cf. "La foi de l'eunuquee éthiopien: le problem textual d'Actes 8:37," *ETR* 63 (1988): 521-528.

[53] Marshall (165) is technically correct that one could wade into the water and then sprinkle, but the picture this creates is rather odd and only proposed because of an ecclesiastical predisposition to sprinkling which would have been rare in the first several centuries of the Church.

[54] Eusebius repeats the tradition from three different Fathers (Papias, Polycrates, Proclus, *Eccl. Hist.* 3.31.3-5; 3.39.9; 5.24.2 respectively) that Philip died in Hieropolis in Phrygia.

[55] This miracle is narrated with such brevity that it leaves the interpreter wanting for detail. Perhaps the miracle itself is less important than the comparison(s) it makes. Here Philip is in the same role as Jesus who disappeared from the two in Emmaus only to be found later in a different location (Luke 24:31-35) and who eventually was snatched away from the earth to return to the Father (Luke 24:51; Acts 1:9-11).

ACTS 9

B. THE CONVERSION OF THE 'APOSTLE' TO THE GENTILES (9:1-31)

It would be difficult to exaggerate the impact that Paul had on Christianity. His attacks on the church prompted the first missionary activities. His conversion and subsequent preaching transformed the Jewish messianic movement into a universal religion. His intellectual genius was embedded in his thirteen New Testament letters which became a cornerstone for church doctrine and polity. Next to Jesus, he stands as the greatest founder of Christianity.

Background: Saul was born in Tarsus (Acts 22:3) probably shortly after Jesus was born in Bethlehem ⬛. His family apparently moved to the capital city of Jerusalem during his formative years of puberty, where he became a prize pupil of the great rabbi, Gamaliel (Acts 22:3; cf. Gal 1:14). His parents raised him to be deeply orthodox. He was of the tribe of Benjamin and circumcised on the eighth day (Phil 3:5). He followed in his father's footsteps, becoming a Hebrew-speaking Pharisee (Acts 23:6; Phil 3:5) and a tentmaker by trade (Acts 18:3). He was also born a Roman citizen (Acts 21:39; 22:3, 28; cf. 9:11, 30; 11:25) and was fluent in Greek language and culture (e.g., Acts 17:28; Titus 1:12), both of which he used to his advantage on his missionary ventures.

As we have seen, Saul approved of Stephen's stoning (Acts 7:58) and subsequently became the chief persecutor of the early church. With vicious rage, he invaded homes and synagogues, imprisoning and scourging both men and women (Acts 8:1-3; 22:4; 26:9-11; Gal 1:13). His reputation even preceded him in Damascus as he approached the city with letters of extradition against Christians (Acts 9:2; 22:5; cf. 26:12). The Lord pulled him up short, however, before he could carry out his murderous plot. To this event we will now attend.

1. Saul with Ananias en Route to Damascus (9:1-19a)

Saul's conversion is not merely a pivot point for his own life; it is a major event in the history of Christianity. Luke knew that. Perhaps that's why he recorded it three times (9:1-19; 22:3-16; 26:12-18).[1] The first time Luke recounts the event in third person. The second time, Paul tells his own story in the face of a hostile Jewish crowd. The third time, Paul unpacks his personal journey before King Herod and Governor Festus, two prominent Gentile rulers. Luke uses this brilliant literary strategy of 'repetition' to good effect. With each passing account, the reader is drawn deeper into the details of Saul's conversion. In 'round one' (9:1-19) Saul is a *persecutor*, transformed into a Gentile missionary by

---

[1] There are only two other events that Luke records three times: The vision of Cornelius (Acts 10:1-8, 30-33; 11:13-17) and the decision of the Jerusalem Council (Acts 15:20, 28-29; 21:25). All three events highlight sharply the spread of the gospel to Gentiles.

the intervention of Ananias. In 'round two' (22:3-16) Saul defends his *kosher heritage* before an angry Jewish mob, thus validating the continuity between Israel and the church. In 'round three' (26:12-18), Paul defends the *legality of his Gentile mission* within a Hellenistic context. Through these three narratives, the Apostle moves from passive recipient to active leadership. *In a sense, the three versions transform Saul the sinner into Paul the preacher through an intertextual conversion.*[2]

This triple report of Saul's conversion has a wonderful effect in the book of Acts. But it has also caused a bit of difficulty for historians. Obviously, the use of repetition requires the author to vary each account, adding details or altering emphases. In the process, however, Luke has created two apparent contradictions.[3] (1) 9:7 says that Paul's companions heard the sound but 22:9 says they did not hear the sound. (2) In Acts 9, Paul received his commission to preach to Gentiles through Ananias whereas in chapter 26 it comes directly from Jesus. These apparent discrepancies are really only a problem for those who ignore the function of narrative repetition. Or put more simply, some read the three passages *against* one another instead of *in conjunction with* each other. Generally speaking, Luke's accounts of Saul's conversion stand in striking alignment with Paul's autobiographical descriptions (Gal 1:13-15; 2 Cor 11:32-33; Phil 3:4-6; 1 Tim 1:12-16).[4]

(1) *Did Paul's companions hear the voice (9:7 vs. 22:9)?* A common solution is grammatical. Some have suggested that the verb "they heard" (*akouontes*) followed by genitive "voice" (*phōnēs*) means mere *hearing* (9:7) but followed by an accusative "sound" (*phōnēn*) implies *comprehension* (22:9).[5] Thus the NIV translates these nearly identical phrases very differently:[6] "They *heard* the sound" (9:7) vs. "They did not *understand* the voice" (22:9). It could be that Jesus spoke to Saul in Hebrew and his companions did not understand the sacred language (though this is unsubstantiated conjecture). Ultimately this is a failed solution for two reasons. First, there is no demonstrable grammatical difference between the genitive and accusative "voice/sound" either in the New Testament or in

---

[2] See esp. Beverly Roberts Gaventa, "The Overthrown Enemy: Luke's Portrait of Paul," *SBLsp* 24 (1985): 439-449. For a full account of Saul's increasing stature in the three narratives and the diminishing involvement of both Ananias and Saul's traveling companions, see Ronald D. Witherupp, "Functional Redundancy in the Acts of the Apostles: A Case Study," *JSNT* 48 (1992): 67-86.

[3] These two minor variations are easily reconciled compared to the radical alterations of this account in the noncanonical *Acts of Paul* wherein he hears the voice of the Father rather than that of Jesus, is converted by Judas, Jesus' brother, after which he is sent to Jericho rather than Arabia. This comparative analysis speaks favorably for the sobriety and veracity of Luke's writing; cf. Willy Rordorf, "Paul's Conversion in the Canonical Acts and in the *Acts of Paul*," *Semeia* 80 (1997): 137-144. One might also note that Luke's descriptions of Paul's conversion align so substantially with Paul's own testimonies (Rom 1:1-5; 1 Cor 15:8-11; 2 Cor 4:6; Gal 1:15-23, etc.) that Anna Maria Schwemer, "Erinnerung und Legende: die Berufung des Paulus und ihre Darstellung in der Apostelgeschichte," in *Memory in the Bible and Antiquity* (ed. Stephen Barton, Loren Stuckenbruck, and Benjamin Wold; Tubingen: Mohr Siebeck, 2007), 277-298, argues that they come from Luke's living memory of Paul's own reports.

[4] Manfred Diefenbach, "Das 'Sehen des Herrn' vor Damaskus: Semantischer Zugang zu Apg 9, 22 und 26," *NTS* 52 (2006): 409-418, contra Stephen E. Fowl, "Who's Characterizing Whom and the Difference This Makes: Locating and Centering Paul," *SBLsp* 32 (1993): 537-553.

[5] This was espoused by J. H. Moulton, *A Grammar of New Testament Greek* (Edinburgh: T&T Clark, 1906), I: 66, and later picked up by the formidable Greek scholar A. T. Robertson, *A Grammar of the Greek New Testament in the Light of Historical Research* (New York: Hodder & Stoughton, 1914), 448-449. From Robertson this view has been uncritically adopted by many commentaries even though linguistically it does not stand up under close scrutiny; cf. Robert G. Bratcher, "ἀκούω in Acts ix. 7 and xxii. 9," *ExpTim* 71 (1960): 243-245.

[6] 9:7: ἀκούοντες μὲν τῆς φωνῆς vs. 22:9: τὴν δὲ φωνὴν οὐκ ἤκουσαν.

the LXX. This 'urban legend' has been appropriately debunked.[7] Second, Luke switches from the accusative (9:4, *phōnēn*) to the genitive (9:7, *phōnēs*) and then from the genitive (22:7, *phōnēs*) to the accusative (22:9, *phōnēn*) with no discernable difference in meaning (cf. Rev 14:2, 13). So even if other authors differentiated between the accusative and the genitive, Luke does not in either context.

The fact is, *grammatically* speaking, there appears to be a discrepancy between the two accounts. *Thematically*, however, this variation makes perfect sense. It is part of Luke's narrative strategy to move Saul from a converted sinner to a powerful preacher. Thus, in each progressive account Saul's role gets more overt and focused and the role of the witnesses (Ananias and Saul's traveling companions) fades more and more into the background. Thus, the point of them "not hearing" is that they did not take an active role in the conversion.[8] Audition is not the real issue; the issue is involvement. They can "hear the voice" in chapter 9 but the later account clarifies that they were not crucial to the call of Saul—they did not participate in the event in any substantial way.[9]

(2) *Who gave Saul his commission to preach to the Gentiles?* According to chapter 9 it was Ananias. According to chapter 26 it was Jesus directly, which matches better Paul's own account of his conversion: "But when God, who set me apart from birth and called me by his grace, was pleased to reveal his Son in me so that I might preach him among the Gentiles, I did not consult any man, nor did I go up to Jerusalem to see those who were apostles before I was, but I went immediately into Arabia and later returned to Damascus" (Gal 1:15-17). So did Paul receive his commission to preach from Ananias or directly from Jesus? What Ananias said to Saul was simply that he had come to heal and baptize him (9:17). Ananias's declaration that God chose Saul to preach Jesus "to all men" was a simple summary of what Jesus had already revealed to Ananias and to Saul separately. Jesus told Ananias in his vision, "This man is my chosen instrument to carry my name before the Gentiles and their kings and before the people of Israel" (9:15). Jesus had said basically the same thing to Saul, "I will rescue you from your own people and from the Gentiles. I am sending you to them" (26:17). This commission was given by Ananias in the first account (ch. 9) where Saul is

---

[7] Horst R. Moehring, "The Verb *AKOYEIN* in Acts IX 7 and XXII 9," *NovT* 3 (1959): 80-99.

[8] Cf. Witherup, "Functional Redundancy," 84-85; and Gert Steuernagel, "ΑΚΟΥΟΝΤΕΣ ΜΕΝ ΤΗΣ ΦΩΝΗΣ (Apg 9.7) Ein Genitiv in der Apostelgeschichte," *NTS* 35 (1989): 619-624. Similar forms involving hearing/seeing are found in Deut 4:12, "Then the Lord spoke to you out of the fire. You heard the sound of words but saw no form; there was only a voice," and Wisdom 18:1, "But for your holy ones there was very great light. Their enemies heard their voices but did not see their forms, and counted them happy for not having suffered."

[9] The vocabulary and syntax of these three conversion accounts show clear signs of Lucan redaction; cf. Mark Harding, "On the Historicity of Acts: Comparing Acts 9.23-25 with 2 Corinthians 11.32-33," *NTS* 39 (1993): 518-538. (Although the core of the accounts, 9:4-9; 22:7-9; 26:14-15, has more Paulinisms and less Lucanisms; cf. Schwemer, "Erinnerung und Legende," 290-292). Thus, all three are Luke's renditions rather than independent sources awkwardly woven together. That is, the variations in each are Luke's deliberate editorial features. The later detail about "hearing/not hearing" is not a blunder but a rhetorical variation deliberately used to push the narrative forward. Cf. Daniel Marguerat, "Saul's Conversion (Acts 9, 22, 26): and the Multiplication of Narrative in Acts," in *Luke's Literary Achievement*, JSNTSs 116 (ed. C. M. Tuckett; Sheffield: Sheffield Academic Press, 1995), 127-155. More specifically, "hearing" and "seeing" are common elements in theophanies which indicate an individual was part of the action. To say these traveling companions of Paul did not hear the voice simply means they were not involved substantively in the theophany; cf. Marvin W. Meyer, "The Light and Voice on the Damascus Road," *Forum* 2 (1986): 27-35.

portrayed as passive and it was given by Jesus in the third account (ch. 26) when Saul the persecutor is turned to Paul the preacher. That makes perfect sense in light of Luke's narrative strategy. If we read the three conversion accounts in tandem rather than in tension, Luke's literary method is clear enough.

¹Meanwhile, Saul was still breathing out murderous threats against the Lord's disciples. He went to the high priest ²and asked him for letters to the synagogues in Damascus, so that if he found any there who belonged to the Way,¹⁰ whether men or women, he might take them as prisoners to Jerusalem. ³As he neared Damascus on his journey, suddenly a light from heaven flashed around him. ⁴He fell to the ground and heard a voice say to him, "Saul, Saul, why do you persecute me?"¹¹ ⁵"Who are you, Lord?" Saul asked. "I am Jesus, whom you are persecuting," he replied. ⁶"Now get up and go into the city, and you will be told what you must do."

9:1-2. In 8:3, Saul was ravaging the church like a wild animal tearing at its prey. Nothing has changed while Philip was off on his adventures in Samaria and Gaza. Saul is still spewing lethal threats against the church.¹² In fact, now he is no mere renegade leading a mob. He is an authorized vigilante with letters of extradition to the synagogues of Damascus. It was natural enough for Jewish Christians to flee to their relatives in Damascus. There was apparently a large population of Jews there. Josephus (with typical exaggeration) asserts that 10,500 Jews were killed in Damascus after the war of A.D. 70 (*J.W.* 2.20.2 §561), and if one added women and children the total rises to a staggering 18,000 (*J.W.* 7.8.7 §337).

There is no way to know if Saul's persecution would have been approved by the Roman regime reigning in Caesarea. However, the Jews had been given the right of extradition in at least one other instance in 138 B.C. (cf. 1 Macc 15:15-21). There is no reason to doubt the Sanhedrin's ability to defend their action in a Roman court if they were pressed to do so. Jesus was accused before Pontius Pilate of being a divisive rabble-rouser, and they successfully obtained a death-sentence against him (Luke 23:5). Undoubtedly Jesus' case could be used as a precedent to prove Saul was attempting to keep his disciples in check. This, of course, would save the local peace-keeping forces the trouble of a full-scale rebellion for which Saul could expect full cooperation.

9:3-4. In the third account of Saul's conversion, he describes himself as ob-

---

¹⁰ This is the first of six times the church is labeled "the Way" in the book of Acts and always in a Pauline context (Acts 9:2; 19:9, 23; 22:4; 24:14, 22; cf. 18:25-26). It was also a term used by Qumran to describe their doctrine (1QS 9:17; cf. 10:21; 11:13). It should be noted, however, that in Qumran "the Way" indicated a belief system whereas in Acts it emphasizes those who adhered to the belief system.

¹¹ From 26:14 Luke has added, "It is hard for you to kick against the goads," which some would also insert here. A goad was a sharp stick (sometimes with a metal tip on the end) which a farmer attached to his plow to prod an ox that happened to need an extra 'exhortation'. One good jab in the tender flesh of the buttocks was usually sufficiently persuasive. A particularly pugnacious beast, however, might kick back, only to find the unyielding object an uncomfortable reminder of his own stupidity. This humorous jab of Jesus is not altogether complementary to the chief persecutor of the church.

¹² Luke's terminology "breathing out lethal threats" (ἐμπνέων ἀπειλῆς καὶ φόνου) is a common Hellenistic concept which connects the lungs or breath with the seat of emotion, will, and/or psyche. My choice of "spew" connotes the same idea that Paul was full of lethal intentions that issued forth from his soul like breath expelled from the lungs. P. W. Van der Horst, "Drohung und Mord schnaubend (Acta IX I)," *NovT* 12 (1970): 257-269, offers ample primary references to illustrate this concept in Greek literature.

sessed (*emmainomai*) or perhaps better, "enraged" with the destruction of the church, going to multiple foreign cities to extradite Christians to Jerusalem for trial: "I put many of the saints in prison, and when they were put to death, I cast my vote against them. Many a time I went from one synagogue to another to have them punished, and I tried to force them to blaspheme. In my obsession against them, I even went to foreign cities to persecute them" (Acts 26:10-11). It looks like Luke hasn't told the half of Saul's pogrom. Undoubtedly Saul believes he is defending the faith. There was certainly enough authorized genocide in the Old Testament to bolster his belief in a justified 'jihad'. Second Maccabees 6:13 is surely close to his heart: "It is a sign of great kindness not to let the impious alone for long, but to punish them immediately."

Three things happened just outside the city. First, around noon (22:6; 26:13) an extraordinarily bright light flashed around them (*periastraptō*, 9:3, 22:6). Paul extrapolates: "I saw a light from heaven, brighter than the sun, blazing around me and my companions" (26:13). That it overwhelmed the bright noon sun is striking. Such a powerful light has symbolic import beyond its physical reality (cf. 2 Cor 4:4-6; Luke 2:9; 9:29). Second, the flash knocked Saul and his companions to the ground (26:14). His companions apparently scrambled to their feet while Saul was in dialogue with Jesus (9:7). Third, Saul heard Jesus ask in Aramaic, or perhaps Hebrew (*Hebrais*, 26:14), *"Saul, Saul, why do you persecute me?"*[13]

9:5-6. This must have been one of those slow-motion moments in Saul's life where his mind worked at warp speed to figure out who this voice belonged to. Could he really be on the wrong side of divine justice? Could his nemesis, Stephen, really be right? Could the rumor of Jesus' resurrection be real? These and a dozen other questions explode in his brain. He asks, "Who are you, Lord?" The word "Lord" has a range of meaning which could include something as simple as "sir," or something weightier such as "master," "King," or "sovereign." It could even connote a title for deity. Saul waits with bated breath. The answer falls from heaven with a thunderous crash: *"I am Jesus, whom you are persecuting."* This moment would stop Saul in his tracks, turn his mission on its head, and radically transform his worldview.[14]

[7]The men traveling with Saul stood there speechless; they heard the sound but did not see anyone. [8]Saul got up from the ground, but when he opened his eyes he could see nothing. So they led him by the hand into Damascus. [9]For three days he was blind, and did not eat or drink anything.

9:7-9. His companions led the blind persecutor by the hand into the city (cf. Tobit 11:16-17). There he must await further instructions. The next three days he will sit in a blind stupor wondering what his fate will be. Though these are dark days, Saul knows he won't be destroyed. Jesus promised him, "I have ap-

---

[13] The Greek, "Σαούλ" is, in fact, a transliteration of the Aramaic and Hebrew form *Sha'ul* rather than the Hellenized spelling "Σαῦλε" more common in Acts (Bruce, 200, fn. 33).

[14] Scott Bartchy, "The Domestication of a Radical Jew: Paul of Tarsus," in *Maven in Blue Jeans: A Festschrift in Honor of Zev Garber* (ed. Steven Leonard Jacobs; West Lafayette: Purdue University Press, 2009), 7-16, offers a salient warning against subverting the social sting of Saul in his Jewish context. Many of his most radical statements from his letters have been domesticated through 'Christianized' readings.

peared to you to appoint you as a servant and as a witness of what you have seen of me and what I will show you. I will rescue you from your own people and from the Gentiles. I am sending you to them . . ." (Acts 26:16b-17). Saul understands that his life will be turned upside down, but at least he will not be cast away from God for his misguided zeal. He surely also understands that Jesus, in the most concrete sense, loves his enemies.[15]

Technically, Saul was not converted on the road to Damascus but three days later after the arrival of Ananias.[16] The narrative clues are clear. While Saul fasts he is still in a state of mourning. This mourning will be lifted after his conversion. The Christian preacher, Ananias, arrives, promising Saul two things: Sight and the Holy Spirit (9:17). His sight is restored when the scales fall off his eyes (9:18). His forgiveness is embodied in baptism when Ananias exhorts him, "What are you waiting for? Get up, be baptized and wash you sins away calling on his name" (22:16). Both his healing and his baptism indicate that he is now in a new, forgiven, enlightened state. It is at this point that he will receive food, breaking his fast as a symbol of conversion.[17]

[10]In Damascus there was a disciple named Ananias. The Lord called to him in a vision, "Ananias!" "Yes, Lord,"[18] he answered. [11]The Lord told him, "Go to the house of Judas on Straight Street and ask for a man from Tarsus named Saul, for he is praying. [12]In a vision he has seen a man named Ananias come and place his hands on him to restore his sight." [13]"Lord," Ananias answered, "I have heard many reports about this man and all the harm he has done to your saints in Jerusalem. [14]And he has come here with authority from the chief priests to arrest all who

---

[15] The conversion of Saul is a psychological anomaly. If Jesus did not actually appear to him, if the bright light was not a divine revelation, and if the voice from heaven was not real sound as opposed to voices in his head, then coming up with an adequate explanation of Saul's life-transformation will be exceedingly difficult. The following psychological explanations show just how impoverished is this line of argument. J. Klausner, *From Jesus to Paul* (tr. William Stinespring; New York: MacMillan, 1943), 326-330, suggested that Saul's experience was an epileptic seizure. J. W. Bowker, "'Merkabah' Visions and the Visions of Paul," *JSS* 16 (1971): 157-173, speculates that Saul was meditating and had an epiphany akin to other 'Merkabah' visions. John J. Pilch, "Paul's Ecstatic Trance Experience near Damascus in Acts of the Apostles," *HvTSt* 58 (2002): 690-707, describes it as an ASC (altered state of consciousness) and offers a crosscultural analysis of such experience. John B. Davidson, "Religious Experience and the Conversion of the Apostle Paul: Psychological Reflections," in *With Steadfast Purpose: Essays on Acts in Honor of Henry Jackson Flanders* (ed. Naymond H. Keathley; Waco: Baylor University, 1990), 327-345, simply asserts that Saul was psychotic. Each of these theories fails at two levels. First, they ignore or discount Saul's traveling companions who also heard the voice and were knocked to the ground by the light. Second, while these theories might adequately describe what Paul experienced on the road, they do not adequately explain why Saul's experience had the effect of instantaneously turning him from persecutor to preacher. Cf. J. L. Lilly, "The Conversion of St. Paul," *CBQ* 6 (1944): 180-204; and Xavier Léon-Dufour, "L'apparition du Ressuscité à Paul," in *Resurrexit* (Vatican City: Libreria Editrice Vaticana, 1974), 266-294.

[16] Krister Stendahl, *Paul among Jews and Gentiles—and Other Essays* (Philadelphia: Fortress, 1976), 7-23, argues that Paul, technically, was not 'converted' since he did not change religions. Though it is helpful to bear in mind the continuity between Judaism and Christianity, the fact is Luke portrays Saul as a convert. He moves from darkness to light, from fasting to nourishment, and he was baptized to receive the Holy Spirit in order to carry out his commission. Cf. Philip H. Kern, "Paul's Conversion and Luke's Portrayal of Character in Acts 8–10," *TynBul* 54 (2003): 63-80.

[17] The early church would later adopt the practice of fasting before baptism (Didache 7.4; Justin, *1 Apol.* 61).

[18] The Greek text literally reads "Behold, I, Lord" (ἰδοὺ ἐγώ κύριε) and reflects the Hebrew phrase, "Here am I" (הִנֵּנִי) which was the common response when Yahweh called a person in the OT (Gen 22:1; 1 Sam 3:4; Isa 6:8, etc.). Moreover, this dual vision (a literary device Luke repeats with Peter and Cornelius), is not uncommon in Jewish literature. Likewise, these 'call visions' in chapter 10 and 11 are familiar to those acquainted with the OT; cf. Gerhard Lohfink, "Eine alttestamentliche Darstellungsform für Gotteserscheinungen in den Damaskusberichten (Apg 9; 22; 26)," *BZ* 9 (1965): 246-257.

call on your name." ¹⁵But the Lord said to Ananias, "Go! This man is my chosen instrument to carry my name before the Gentiles and their kings and before the people of Israel. ¹⁶I will show him how much he must suffer for my name."

9:10-12. Ananias is a minor character in the book of Acts but apparently a prominent figure in the early church at Damascus. We know that he was a Messianic Jew who lived a devout life according to the Law of Moses (22:12). As such, he would have been deeply involved with the local synagogue. Given the large population of Jews in the city, there were likely dozens of synagogues. Since Paul describes Ananias as "highly respected by all the Jews" of Damascus, it is reasonable to assume he was a leader in his own synagogue and known by reputation to many of the other synagogues. Furthermore, Jesus tells Ananias that Saul could be located in Judas's house on Straight Street, the major thoroughfare running east and west through town. This avenue also housed the city theater and the governor's palace. Hence, one can assume that Judas was a wealthy and prominent Jew, known personally to Ananias. If Saul is staying with Judas, most likely he was the Damascus contact who helped Saul orchestrate the persecution against Christians. Though they are working under the jurisdiction of the Sanhedrin, it is unlikely they have Roman authority to carry out this plot. Hence, Judas appears to be a zealot like Saul who likely has already parted ways with Ananias. The upshot is that Ananias is being sent into the lion's den. It was not merely Saul he had to fear, but Judas, a fellow synagogue ruler who put his money where his mouth was in supporting the persecution of local Jewish Christians. Ananias and Judas stood on opposite sides of this ugly rift in the Jewish community.

9:13-16. Ananias is well aware of Saul from Tarsus. His informants—likely recent Christian refugees from Jerusalem—have warned him about Saul's intentions as well as the letters of extradition. Understandably, he objects when Jesus asks him to go lay hands on Saul to heal him. In fact, he tries to inform Jesus of Saul's lethal intentions of which the Lord must be unaware! Obviously, Jesus is all too aware of Saul's plots. But Jesus has a plan of his own of which Ananias is unaware—Saul was predestined to preach. This is the implication of the word "chosen" (cf. Rom 9:11; 11:5, 7, 28; 1 Thess 1:4; 2 Pet 1:10). This matches Paul's own impression of his calling: "When God, who *set me apart from birth* and called me by his grace, was pleased to reveal his Son in me so that I might preach him among the Gentiles . . ." (Gal 1:15-16).

Verse fifteen reminds us that Paul preached not only to Gentiles (cf. Rom 11:13; 15:15-16; Gal 1:16; 2:7-8) but also to kings (Acts 25:22-23; 26:1) and to his own nation of Israel (9:20-22; 13:16-47; 22:1ff; 28:17ff). In the course of his new vocation, he would suffer. That, in fact, tends to be the implication of "bearing the name" of Jesus.[19] His own countrymen beat him out of jealousy, and the Gentiles beat him when he interfered with their financial gain. Second Corinthians 11:23-25 says, among other things, that he was imprisoned (cf. Acts 16:23; 21:11; 24:27; 28:30), flogged five times, beaten with rods three times (Acts 16:22-23), stoned once (Acts 14:19), shipwrecked three times. This was written c. A.D.

---
[19] Gerhard Lohfink, "Meinen Namen zu tragen (Apg 9:15)," *BZ* 10 (1966): 108-115.

55 when Paul was still in Ephesus on the third missionary journey. Thus, this list does not include being attacked in Jerusalem (Acts 21:30-31), being strung up to be flogged (Acts 22:25), or being shipwrecked for a fourth time (Acts 27). Furthermore, the material in Acts fails to mention any of the five floggings, two of the three times he was beaten with rods, or any of the first three shipwrecks. It is possible that much of this took place during the three years in Arabia and the five years in Cilicia about which Acts is silent. Needless to say, a great deal of Paul's biography and probably some of his letters have been lost. What we have, however, is sufficient to elicit our wonder, admiration, and deep gratitude for God's servant, Saul of Tarsus.

Paul's suffering would be one of his broadest platforms for preaching. Lest this seem like cruel retribution, the reader should know that Paul took a very different view of his sufferings: "I want to know Christ and the power of his resurrection and the fellowship of sharing in his sufferings, becoming like him in his death, and so, somehow, to attain to the resurrection from the dead" (Phil 3:10-11). Or again: "Now if we are children, then we are heirs—heirs of God and co-heirs with Christ, if indeed we share in his sufferings in order that we may also share in his glory. I consider that our present sufferings are not worth comparing with the glory that will be revealed in us" (Rom 8:17-18).

¹⁷Then Ananias went to the house and entered it. Placing his hands on Saul, he said, "Brother Saul, the Lord—Jesus, who appeared to you on the road as you were coming here—has sent me so that you may see again and be filled with the Holy Spirit." ¹⁸Immediately, something like scales fell from Saul's eyes, and he could see again. He got up and was baptized, ¹⁹and after taking some food, he regained his strength.

9:17-19a. It is here in Judas's house that Saul is truly converted. This should be obvious since no one is converted to Jesus by dreams, visions, angels, or voices from heaven. In the New Testament conversion is always through the faithful proclamation of Jesus by a Christian. Thus, Ananias's presence is essential. Saul's conversion is authenticated by four elements, two of which are physical and two of which are spiritual. It is typical of Lucan narratives that healing symbolizes or authenticates salvation (Luke 5:17-26; 6:6-11; 8:40-56; 11:14-28; 13:10-16). Ananias healed Saul's blindness and Jesus granted him the Holy Spirit to enlighten him. Ananias baptized him and Saul broke his fast and regained his strength. The *healing* and *eating* are physical symbols which coincide with the spiritual realities of the *Holy Spirit* and *baptism.* Together they transfer Saul from darkness to light, from weakness to strength, from persecutor to preacher.

2. Saul with Barnabas Back in Jerusalem (9:19b-31)

¹⁹ᵇSaul spent several days with the disciples in Damascus. ²⁰At once he began to preach in the synagogues that Jesus is the Son of God. ²¹All those who heard him were astonished and asked, "Isn't he the man who raised havoc in Jerusa-

lem among those who call on this name? And hasn't he come here to take them as prisoners to the chief priests?" [22]Yet Saul grew more and more powerful and baffled the Jews living in Damascus by proving that Jesus is the Christ.[a]
[a]22 Or *Messiah*

9:19b-22. Saul must have been a formidable opponent in a debate. His natural energetic zeal was supported by his rabbinic training under Gamaliel and is now bolstered by his extraordinary personal testimony. If the debate turned to Scriptural exegesis Saul was the better. If it turned to national patriotism or religious zeal, his credentials were impeccable. If it turned to personal motives, purity of heart, or raw zeal, who could question Saul's biography? Is it any wonder that he baffled[20] his opponents in the synagogues of Damascus? The people marveled that Saul, who tried to annihilate[21] the church, was now promoting it. It was a dramatic and instantaneous reversal of his life.

Saul preached Jesus as the "son of God" (v. 20) and proved that he was the "Christ" (v. 22). Both titles mean essentially the same thing. "Son of God," mentioned only here in all of Acts (cf. 13:33), was a term commonly applied to Roman emperors while "Christ" was a reference primarily to a future Jewish king (see comments on 1:6, fn. 23). Paul combines these terms synonymously a number of times (Rom 1:4; 1 Cor 1:9; 2 Cor 1:19; Gal 2:20; Eph 4:13; cf. Heb 3:6; 5:5). The incipit of Mark 1:1 introduces the whole work with this same combination of terms: "The beginning of the gospel about Jesus *Christ, the Son of God.*" Similarly, John summarizes his whole work with these synonymous terms, "These are written that you may believe that Jesus is the *Christ, the Son of God,* and that by believing you may have life in his name" (John 20:31; cf. 1 John 1:3; 2:22; 3:23; 5:20; 2 John 2:3, 9). Peter combined these terms in his great confession: "You are the *Christ, the son of the living God*" (Matt 16:16) as did Martha, "I believe that you are the *Christ, the Son of God,* who was to come into the world" (John 11:27). According to Luke even the demons understand Jesus by these combined titles, "Demons came out of many people, shouting, 'You are the *Son of God!*' But he rebuked them and would not allow them to speak, because they knew he was the *Christ*" (Luke 4:41). It was apparently no secret that Jesus' followers were making overt claims that Jesus was the Christ, the son of God. Hence, Caiaphas questioned Jesus at his trial with these very two terms, "I charge you under oath by the living God: Tell us if you are the *Christ, the Son of God*" (Matt 26:63; Mark 16:61). This politically charged claim explains why Saul's preaching in Damascus had such a dramatic impact. He was not merely making a religious claim. He was promoting Jesus as the king of the Jews and the future world ruler. This was as inflammatory in a Diaspora setting as was Stephen's temple critique in Jerusalem. Feathers will fly.

[20] This word "baffled" is used five times, only by Luke, always in reference to a crowd (2:6; 9:22; 19:32; 21:27, 31) which is always Jewish (save 19:32) and always unruly (save 2:6).
[21] This word "annihilate" (πορθέω) or "raised havoc" (NIV) is only used three times in the NT. Elsewhere it is the word Paul used to describe this same event: "For you have heard of my previous way of life in Judaism, how *intensely I persecuted* the church of God and tried to destroy it" (Gal 1:13) and "They only heard the report: 'The man who formerly persecuted us is now preaching the faith he once tried to destroy'," (Gal 1:23). Cf. Philippe Menoud, "Le sens du verbe ΠΟΡΘΕΙΝ," in *Apophoreta* (Berlin: A Töpelmann, 1964), 178-186.

²³After many days had gone by, the Jews conspired to kill him, ²⁴but Saul learned of their plan. Day and night they kept close watch on the city gates in order to kill him. ²⁵But his followers took him by night and lowered him in a basket through an opening in the wall.

9:23-25. The assassination attempt against Saul is confirmed by his own writing, "In Damascus the governor under King Aretas had the city of the Damascenes guarded in order to arrest me" (2 Cor 11:32). Though Acts claims it was the Jews who were out to get him, it is understandable that Aretas (9 B.C.–A.D. 40) would have used the locals to locate and capture this Jewish rogue.[22] Indigenous bandits and rebels even today are seldom apprehended in the Middle East without the help of native informants. Besides, there are those like Judas who are still stinging from the shame of Saul's conversion. Since the gates were heavily guarded he had to find an alternative escape route. One of Saul's accomplices lived in an upper apartment built into the city wall. In the dead of the night, Saul's disciples lowered him out the window in a large basket. His trek to Jerusalem began and ended with two poignant memories.[23] Just outside the city of Damascus, he would have recalled a bright light that changed his life. Just outside of Jerusalem, he would have recalled holding his fellow's cloaks and ending Stephen's life.

Verse 23 begins, "After many days . . ." In Galatians 1:17-18 Paul says, "I went immediately into Arabia and later returned to Damascus. Then after three years, I went up to Jerusalem to get acquainted with Peter and stayed with him fifteen days." From this information we can infer that there was a three year gap between verses 23 and 24. How much of that time was spent in Arabia is impossible to say though it is tempting to draw a parallel between Paul's three years of training under the resurrected Jesus and the Twelve being trained with Jesus during his earthly ministry. In all likelihood, Saul was neither quiet nor dormant during those three years. Given his immediate vociferous debates in Damascus after this conversion, we have every reason to believe that he preached in Arabia during his stint there. Furthermore, given his track record later in the book of Acts, it is likely that he divided synagogues and stirred up communities in Arabia (the Nabataean kingdom) which bordered the region of Damascus to the southeast. This would explain why he was chased back to Damascus by Aretas and why the locals there were eager to help the king of Arabia extradite this problematic preacher.

²⁶When he came to Jerusalem, he tried to join the disciples, but they were all afraid of him, not believing that he really was a disciple. ²⁷But Barnabas took him and brought him to the apostles. He told them how Saul on his journey had seen the Lord and that the Lord had spoken to him, and how in Damascus he

---

[22] Such differences in Luke's presentation and Paul's led Charles Masson, "A propos de Act 9:19b–25," *TZ* 18 (1962): 161-166, to correctly conclude that Luke did not utilize Paul's Epistles in constructing these accounts.

[23] This is the first of Paul's six visits to Jerusalem in Acts (9:26-30; 11:27-30; 12:25; 15:1-35; 18:22; 21:15-23). Aligning this data with the visits recorded in Galatians (1:18-20; 2:1-10) has been a vexing problem which will be taken up more fully in chapter 15. A helpful summary of the issues can be found in Ramón Trevijano Echeverría, "El Contrapunto Lucano (Hch 9, 26-30; 11, 27-30; 12, 25 y 15, 1-35) A Gal 1, 18-20 y 2, 1-10," *Salm* 44 (1998): 295-339.

had preached fearlessly in the name of Jesus. **²⁸So Saul stayed with them and moved about freely in Jerusalem, speaking boldly in the name of the Lord. ²⁹He talked and debated with the Grecian Jews, but they tried to kill him. ³⁰When the brothers learned of this, they took him down to Caesarea and sent him off to Tarsus. ³¹Then the church throughout Judea, Galilee and Samaria enjoyed a time of peace. It was strengthened; and encouraged by the Holy Spirit, it grew in numbers, living in the fear of the Lord.**

9:26-27. When Paul returns to Jerusalem, the disciples will have nothing to do with him. Though it has been three years, this is hardly a long time for the memories of widows and orphans after the decimation of their families. Those who infiltrate terrorist's organizations understand all too well that an effective spy requires years to earn the trust of an underground movement. Though the active persecution waned with Saul's conversion, the community of Christians has been conditioned to speak furtively, to look over their shoulders, and to react cautiously, particularly with a former persecutor. Were it not for the acceptance of Barnabas, much to his own potential peril, Saul would have been ostracized from the Jerusalem church. The consequent division between Jewish and Gentile Christians would likely have been immediate and detrimental to the body of Christ. Because of Barnabas, such a bitter and tragic divide in the body of Christ would now be postponed until A.D. 1054 when Catholic and Orthodox believers parted ways. Another devastating division resulted from the Protestant Reformation (c. 1517) which ultimately resulted in hundreds of splinter groups, each claiming primacy in Christian doctrine. May God raise Barnabas a thousand times over to model in our churches this self-sacrificial and dangerous practice to achieve practical Christian unity.

There is no way to know how Barnabas heard about Paul's conversion and his preaching in Damascus. Barnabas probably hosted Paul, listened to his story, and took him at his word. If this is true, then Barnabas initially took quite a risk. He could have been killed for this. He could have been cut off from the rest of the community for this dangerous maneuver. Yet his risk bore more fruit than he could possibly have imagined. Even today, we who have inherited the example and letters of Paul are deeply indebted to the 'Son of Encouragement'. One can only wonder how many Pauls have been lost through the lack of a Barnabas.

9:28-30. There are several bits of information that can be added to the narrative at this point. First, though Luke says Barnabas introduced him to the Apostles, Paul claims that on this first visit he only met Peter and James—Jesus' half-brother—and that his stay in Jerusalem was only fifteen days (Gal 1:18-19). Of course, Paul calls both Peter and James Apostles, appropriately so. Peter was clearly the spokesman for the Apostolic band and James is the key leader of the Jerusalem church (cf. 12:17; 15:13ff; 21:18). It is certainly fair for Luke, therefore, to say Paul met the Apostles (plural). It would appear, however, that most of the Apostles have already begun to disperse on preaching tours as Peter will do in the following verses.

Second, after Saul was accepted by the church of Judea, he went back to his old synagogue. There, he refuted the Grecian Jews (v. 29), paradoxically, taking over where Stephen left off. One might wonder what Saul was thinking. These men who murdered Stephen would not take well the transformation of their former assassin. Typical of Saul, he overestimated his ability to persuade and pacify his opponents. He was actually convinced that he could win them over, so much so that he argued with Jesus about it! The story is told by Paul himself in 22:17-21:

> When I returned to Jerusalem and was praying at the temple, I fell into a trance and saw the Lord speaking. "Quick!" he said to me. "Leave Jerusalem immediately, because they will not accept your testimony about me." "Lord," I replied, "these men know that I went from one synagogue to another to imprison and beat those who believe in you. And when the blood of your martyr Stephen was shed, I stood there giving my approval and guarding the clothes of those who were killing him." Then the Lord said to me, "Go; I will send you far away to the Gentiles."

This required immediate action on the part of the brothers in Jerusalem. They whisked him away to the nearest major port, Caesarea, and put him on a boat to Tarsus. There he was far enough away that his enemies would not chase him and close enough to his family that they might take care of him. For the next five or six years Saul will be silent (c. A.D. 35–40). This does not mean, of course, that he did not preach, only that Luke did not record the result of his preaching. When Barnabas goes to find him, Luke will use a word that means "to hunt him down" (11:25). Why was he so hard to find? Likely because his bold preaching offended even his kin and countrymen from whom he had to flee.

Meanwhile, the news of Saul's conversion and acceptance by the church of Jerusalem spilled over into the congregations throughout Judea. In Paul's own words, "Later I went to Syria and Cilicia. I was personally unknown to the churches of Judea that are in Christ. They only heard the report: 'The man who formerly persecuted us is now preaching the faith he once tried to destroy.' And they praised God because of me" (Gal 1:21-24).

9:31. In a typical summary statement, Luke adds that it was not merely the church of Judea that was encouraged but even Samaria and further north into Galilee. This is an interesting statement at two levels. First, it is Luke's only mention of the church in Galilee. Elsewhere the term is used to identify the home of the Apostles (1:11) and the genesis of the Jesus movement (10:37; 13:31). But only here do we learn of the church expanding into Galilee. Second, Luke describes the church in multiple areas as *the* (singular) church. Some have taken this to indicate the beginning of the concept of the 'catholic' church. That may well be. However, Giles offers a more tenable suggestion that it was still the church of a single city (i.e., Jerusalem) that had been scattered to multiple places.[24]

Of course, Luke is not primarily reporting the news of Saul but recalling the command of Jesus (1:8). This concludes part two of the book of Acts. The

---

[24] This aligns with Luke's general use of the term ἐκκλησία, indicating the believers of a specific city. K. N. Giles, "Luke's Use of the Term 'ΕΚΚΛΗΣΙΑ' with Special Reference to Acts 20.28 and 9.31," *NTS* 31 (1985): 135-142.

church enjoyed the calm after Saul's storm. They were characterized by three pillars of Christianity: The Holy Spirit, numeric growth, and a fear of the Lord.

3. Transition: God Postures Peter with Aeneas in Lydda and Dorcas in Joppa (9:32-43)

Luke is *almost* ready for the pinnacle of his book—the conversion of a Gentile when the God of Israel becomes the God of the nations. First, however, he must move all the players into position. Peter must move from Jerusalem to Caesarea. Of course, this is a huge leap; he won't make it without two intervening steps. The first step is geographical. The narrative will move Peter out of Jerusalem and toward the coast through a couple of healing miracles. Though the raising of a lame man and a dead woman are interesting in and of themselves, the point is not really Peter's power, but his location on the map. He is going to Joppa ◙! This city has obvious allusions to the story of Jonah. Here the reluctant prophet fled from God's call to preach to the Ninevites. Here, in this same city, Peter will rewrite the story line.[25]

The second step is sociological. Peter has been at the epicenter of the movement, surrounded by all things kosher. In order to change his perspective God will have to change Peter's venue. So, he draws him to the port city of Joppa and plunks him down in the home of a tanner named Simon. Simon's occupation makes him unclean. Hence, it makes Simon Peter uncomfortable. This too is a necessary preparation for Gentile inclusion. Before God thrusts Peter into the taboo of a Gentile home, he takes him to the margins of Jewish piety in the home of a tanner.

[32]As Peter traveled about the country, he went to visit the saints in Lydda. [33]There he found a man named Aeneas, a paralytic who had been bedridden for eight years. [34]"Aeneas," Peter said to him, "Jesus Christ heals you. Get up and take care of your mat." Immediately Aeneas got up. [35]All those who lived in Lydda and Sharon saw him and turned to the Lord.

9:32. After the mini-tour through Samaria with John (8:25), Peter apparently has itchy feet. He begins an itinerant ministry through Judea. More specifically, he *renewed* his itinerant ministry that he had practiced under Jesus' leadership for three full years. Such preaching tours are certainly nothing new to Peter.[26] From Jerusalem he heads northwest for twenty-five miles and lands in Lydda.[27]

---

[25] The story of Peter and Jonah have substantial overlap: Joppa, hesitancy of the evangelist, God's intervention, "arise and go" (ἀνάστηθι πορεύθητι, Jonah 3:2 LXX; and ἀναστὰς...πορεύου, Acts 10:20), Gentiles believed (Jonah 3:5; Acts 10:43-48), Jewish objection (Jonah 4:1; Acts 11:2). What is fascinating is that these two stories are not paralleled by catchwords but by pivotal incidents which follow the same track in both narratives. In other words, these stories are the same at the structural level but not at the linguistic level. Cf. Robert W. Wall, "Peter, 'Son' of Jonah: The Conversion of Cornelius in the Context of Canon," *JSNT* 29 (1987): 79-90.

[26] F. W. Beare, "The Sequence of Events in Acts 9–15 and the Career of Peter," *JBL* 62 (1943): 295-306, would like to rearrange Luke's order of events to have this preaching tour after Peter's release from prison in Acts 12:17. Though his chronology works, it runs rough shod over Luke's order based on the faulty assumption that Peter would not have made multiple itinerant tours after Jesus' resurrection as he had done before.

[27] Lydda is OT Lod (1 Chr 8:12). Its famous export was purple dye, and it would be destined become one of the noted centers of rabbinic training (*Beginnings* 4:108).

9:33. Here Peter found a bedridden paralytic, Aeneas, named after the famed hero of Homer's Illiad (13.541). The fact that he was lying on a pallet (*krabbatos*, cf. Mark 2:9-12; 6:55; John 5:8-11; Acts 5:15) rather than a proper bed probably indicates that he was from a poor family. He had been afflicted for at least eight years. The Greek text is nebulous at this point. It could mean that he had been paralyzed for eight years or since eight years old. Either way, the guy is in sad shape. He used to walk but now cannot. Therefore, he cannot work. In a poor family that is a serious handicap. He is a drain on the family resources with no ability to contribute to their well-being economically.

9:34-35. In the name of "Jesus Christ"[28] Peter orders the paralytic to get up off his pallet and straighten it up. A number of versions say "make your bed" (KJV, NLT, ESV, NASB, and ASV); the NIV is probably more accurate with, "take care of your mat." The idea is that his pallet can be straightened since he is not going to need it. The "ordering" of the "bed sheets" metaphorically mirrors the ordering of his physical health and social role in the family. In short, Peter puts him back in his proper place. The news spread up the coastal plain of Sharon to a distance of fifty miles. More specifically, the man himself traveled up and down the coast, and those who saw him gave their lives to Jesus because of his dramatic healing. As wonderful as this is, of course, Aeneas is not the complete story. He must be read in tandem with Tabitha. Both accounts call Christians "saints" (vv. 34, 41; cf. 9:13; 26:10), a rather rare occurrence in Acts; both are commanded to rise (*anastēthi*, vv. 34, 40); and both took place in the coastal plain of Sharon (Polhill, 246).

With these two we have a physical illustration of how the gospel message raises the spiritually dead and causes them to run free. Both stories play off Jesus' healing of a paralytic (Luke 5:17-26) as well as his raising the dead (Luke 7:11-16; 8:49-56). The latter, of course, conjures up memories of Elijah (1 Kgs 17:17-24) and Elisha (2 Kgs 4:32-37).

[36]In Joppa there was a disciple named Tabitha (which, when translated, is Dorcas[a]), who was always doing good and helping the poor. [37]About that time she became sick and died, and her body was washed and placed in an upstairs room. [38]Lydda was near Joppa; so when the disciples heard that Peter was in Lydda, they sent two men to him and urged him, "Please come at once!" [39]Peter went with them, and when he arrived he was taken upstairs to the room. All the widows stood around him, crying and showing him the robes and other clothing that Dorcas had made while she was still with them.

[a]*36 Both Tabitha (Aramaic) and Dorcas (Greek) mean gazelle*

---

[28] It is striking how early "Christ" became an appellation for the risen one rather than a title for the 'coming one'. In the book of Acts, thirteen uses of "Christ" are titular (2:31, 36; 3:18, 20; 4:26; 5:42; 8:5; 9:22; 17:3 [2x]; 18:5, 28; 26:23) and twelve are his name, "Jesus Christ," (9:34; 10:36; 11:17; 24:24; 28:31) sometimes even identifying "Jesus Christ" as his 'name' (2:38; 3:6; 4:10; 8:12; 10:48; 15:26; 16:18). Only after "Christ" was firmly established as Jesus' role could it be effectively used as his name. "There is no unambiguous evidence to demonstrate that 'Christ' in any of its 531 New Testament uses ever 'degenerated' into a mere second name for Jesus"; Craig L. Blomberg, "Messiah in the New Testament," in *Israel's Messiah in the Bible and the Dead Sea Scrolls* (ed. Richard S. Hess and Daniel Carroll; Grand Rapids: Baker Academic, 2003), 111-141.

9:36. About twelve miles northwest of Lydda was the major port city of Judea, called Joppa (modern Jaffa). There lived (and died) a woman named Tabitha (in Aramaic) or Dorcas (in Greek); her name meant "gazelle." She is portrayed with classic Jewish piety, showing mercy (*eleēmosunē*, v. 36) to the poor.[29] Specifically, she was famous among the widows for making clothes (v. 39).

9:37. As is all too common in third-world countries, her body was ravaged by some sickness and she died. As was the custom in the Middle East, she was immediately prepared for burial. Her body was washed (v. 37) and anointed (*m. Šabb.* 23.5), which took place the very day of death.

9:38-39. There is no time to waste! A couple of couriers were immediately dispatched to retrieve Peter who was a mere ten miles away. These spry messengers ran forthwith to Lydda and quickly found the famous Apostle. The return trip would have taken longer—Peter was not known for his foot-speed (cf. John 20:3-4). When they finally arrived, Peter climbed the stairs, undoubtedly winded, and listened to the widows' 'show and tell' of the cherished clothes from the deceased seamstress.

⁴⁰Peter sent them all out of the room; then he got down on his knees and prayed. Turning toward the dead woman, he said, "Tabitha, get up." She opened her eyes, and seeing Peter she sat up. ⁴¹He took her by the hand and helped her to her feet. Then he called the believers and the widows and presented her to them alive. ⁴²This became known all over Joppa, and many people believed in the Lord. ⁴³Peter stayed in Joppa for some time with a tanner named Simon.

9:40-43. Though Jesus had given the Apostles power to raise the dead, even on their first solo flight (Matt 10:4), this is the first recorded instance of anyone other than Jesus actually doing it. It is not surprising, therefore, that Peter follows Jesus' methodology pretty closely. When Jesus raised Jairus's daughter, he put everyone out of the room and spoke to the girl in Aramaic, "*Talitha koum,*" meaning "little girl, get up" (Mark 5:41). Peter also asks the widows to clear the room and says "*Tabitha koum,*" meaning "Gazelle, get up." There is but one letter difference in the two phrases. Dorcas responded as did Jairus's daughter: she opened her eyes, looked at Peter, and sat up in bed.

---

[29] Friederike Erichsen-Wendt, "Tabitha—Leben an der Grenze: Ein Beitrag zum Verständnis von Apg 9,36–43," *BN* 127 (2005): 67-90, rightly observes the Jewish background of this pious portrait but espouses an unlikely hypothesis that Dorcas had been a prostitute since women with this name in Rabbinic literature were often slaves and in Greco-Roman literature "Dorcas" was a common name for prostitutes. The evidence for this speculation is too thin to be convincing.

ACTS 10

C. THE GOSPEL EXTENDS TO THE GENTILES (10:1–11:18)

Acts 10:1–11:18 is the longest running narrative in the entire book and for good reason.[1] With Cornelius, the gospel finally reaches a Gentile. In a sense, this is Luke's story, symbolically autobiographical. It is, indeed, the story of the vast majority of Christians ever to accept Jesus as Messiah. Moreover, Gentile inclusion was *the* major issue facing the church in the middle of the first century. Paul tackles it in Romans 9–11 and Ephesians 2–4. The Jerusalem council addressed it in Acts 15 where the debate centered on circumcision rather than food. It may seem like circumcision and table fellowship are two separate issues, but they are not. From a Jewish perspective, if an individual converts to the Mosaic Law through circumcision his social stigma is removed. He is, for all practical purposes, a Jew. This connection is clearly seen in the criticism leveled against Peter for eating with Cornelius: "You went into the house of uncircumcised men and ate with them" (11:3). It would be difficult to overestimate the implications of Jews and Gentiles eating together. One can comprehend this ancient tension better by observing contemporary attempts at dialogue between Jewish and Arab Christians in the Middle East.

What surfaces here in chapters 10–11 is not the general issue of racism but the specific issue of table-fellowship. Some have regarded these as two separate issues (e.g., *Beginnings* 4:112). However, those in pastoral leadership know all too well the strategy of masking social problems with theological issues. The debate about eating with uncircumcised Gentiles is, in fact, a 'cover' for the real problem of Gentile inclusion in the church.[2] What is at issue is whether God loves 'them' as much as he loves 'us'. If we can dehumanize 'the other' by removing them from the 'table', then we can justify our own isolation under the guise of religious

---

[1] This complex narrative is presented in seven scenes: (1) Cornelius's vision (10:1-8), (2) Peter's vision (10:9-16), (3) messengers sent to Joppa to retrieve Peter (10:17-23a), (4) Peter & Co. return to Caesarea (10:23b-33), (5) Peter's sermon to Cornelius (10:34-43), (6) Cornelius's household is baptized with the Holy Spirit and water (10:44-48), (7) Summary and defense in Jerusalem of Cornelius's conversion (11:1-18); cf. Roland Barthes, "L'Analyse structural du Récit," *RecSR* 58 (1970): 17-37. Interestingly, it has the same basic plot as Virgil's *Aeneid* 8. According to Shea, imitating plots of previous classic works was common in antiquity. It was not viewed as plagiarism or unoriginal, rather, it was a way of establishing your text as a *polis* founding narrative. Cf. Chris Shea, "Imitating Imitation: Vergil, Homer, and Acts 10:1–11:18," in *Ancient Fiction and the Matrix of Early Christian and Jewish Narrative* (Atlanta: Society of Biblical Literature, 2005), 37-59.

[2] Mark Plunkett, "Ethnocentricity and Salvation History in the Cornelius Episode (Acts 10:1–11:18," *SBLsp* 24 (1985): 465-479; and Chris A. Miller, "Did Peter's Vision in Acts 10 Pertain to Men or the Menu?" *BibSac* 159 (2002): 302-317, show exegetically the point of the story is primarily about Cornelius not *Kashrut* (dietary laws). Karl Löhning, "Die Korneliustradition," *BZ* 18 (1974): 1-9, also demonstrates the irreducible unity of the two halves of the story. It is precisely this connection that makes Klaus Haacker's source-critical speculation unconvincing. He, following Dibelius, argues that Luke stitched together Peter's vision with Cornelius's though the two were originally independent traditions; cf. "Dibelius und Cornelius: Ein Beispiel formgeschichtlicher Überlieferungskritik," *BZ* 24 (1980): 234-251.

purity or devotion to God. Whether we do that through dress codes, alcohol prohibitions, tattoo taboos, or language filters, the strategy is the same: We label as 'unclean' the one who does not fit our parameters of a righteous life. If these rules are removed, so too is our ability to insulate ourselves and isolate the 'other'.[3]

When we talk about Gentile inclusion in the church, we must be absolutely clear. The immersion of Cornelius does not mean the subversion of Judaism or its eradication but rather its fruition.[4] God chose Abraham and destined his seed to bless the entire world. This does not mean merely that Abraham's seed—Christ (singular)—would be Israel's gift to outsiders. Rather, being incorporated in Christ allows Gentiles to be adopted into the seed (plural) of Abraham. Wilson rightly states, "Luke's aim is to demonstrate how the church's Gentile mission is both a legitimate continuation of Israel, and hence rooted in ancient traditions, and the basis of the church's institutional identity and purpose."[5] Paul put it this way: "You are all sons of God through faith in Christ Jesus, for all of you who were baptized into Christ have clothed yourselves with Christ. There is neither Jew nor Greek, slave nor free, male nor female, for you are all one in Christ Jesus. If you belong to Christ, then you are Abraham's seed, and heirs according to the promise" (Gal 3:26-29).

To that end Peter will use his keys once again to open the gospel to the Gentiles. He unlocked the front door to the church for the Jews with his Pentecost address in chapter 2. In chapter 8 he unlocked the side door so the Samaritans could come in. He is going to unlock the back door in chapter 10 to all sorts and sundry. Now the church stands wide open for any and all who respond to God's gracious invitation to become part of the elect people, expanding the bulging borders of his kingdom.

1. Scene 1: Cornelius's Vision (10:1-8)

[1]At Caesarea there was a man named Cornelius, a centurion in what was known as the Italian Regiment. [2]He and all his family were devout and God-fearing; he gave generously to those in need and prayed to God regularly.

10:1. Our story opens with a place and a name. The *place* is Caesarea, a port city constructed under Herod the Great in honor of his benefactor, *Caesar* Augustus, to whom was devoted the city's major temple (22–9 B.C.).[6] It was a mod-

---

[3] In this instance, if the *Kashrut* laws are removed, so also is the primary barrier to fellowship with Gentiles. Using the Jewish logic 'from lesser to greater', so goes the menu, so goes the guests. Cf. J. Julius Scott, "The Cornelius Incident in the Light of Its Jewish Setting," *JETS* 34 (1991): 475-484.

[4] Cornelius is presented as converting to Judaism; he is being grafted into the covenant of Abraham; cf. Mikeal Parsons, *Luke: Storyteller, Interpreter, Evangelist* (Peabody: Hendriksen, 2007), 149-190.

[5] Walter Wilson, "Urban Legends: Acts 10:1–11:18 and the Strategies of Greco-Roman Foundational Narratives," *JBL* 120 (2001): 78. Wilson goes on to argue that Luke's rhetorical strategy is similar to Greco-Roman tales of the founding of a city. Though he is careful to say he is *not* arguing that Acts is a *polis*-founding document, such an extrapolation surely does not miss the mark by much. Through Cornelius-type stories, Luke portrays the church of Jesus Christ as a distinct social entity, governed by unique principles derived from ancient Israel but whose fulfillment extends beyond all ethnic, social, gender, economic, and cultural boundaries.

[6] The literature on this city is vast, but a sufficient general coverage can be found in Avner Raban, *The Harbour of Sebastos (Caesarea Maritima) in Its Roman Mediterranean Context*, (Oxford: Archaeopress, 2009); Kenneth Holum, "Building Power: The Politics of Architecture," *BAR* 30 (2004): 36-45, 57; and Clayton Lehmann and Kenneth Holum, *The Greek and Latin Inscriptions of Caesarea Maritima* (Boston: ASOR, 2000).

ern marvel in its time, complete with theater, amphitheater, and hippodrome . It even had a man-made harbor which can be seen to this day under water, built by a fairly new invention we call "concrete."

The theater still stands nearly as majestic as in Cornelius's day against the backdrop of the Mediterranean. The defunct aqueduct is a bit more bedraggled . Nevertheless, it requires little imagination to reconstruct its full size and significance. This city was simply a magnificent architectural achievement by any reckoning. Even more important to our narrative is the fact that it was the seat of government for Judea since A.D. 6. It was here that Pilate resided, probably known personally by this centurion. Not only is the Spirit drawing Peter out of Judea and pushing him into a Gentile home, he is placing him in the seat of Roman government of the entire region. This is no small event and in no mean city.

The *name* is Cornelius, which is neither here nor there.[7] What matters is his title—centurion. These commanders of '100' were the backbone of the Roman army.[8] Since this was generally the highest office a non-noble could achieve, these natural leaders rose through the ranks, hitting this glass ceiling (cf. *Beginnings* 5:428). As leaders, they typically understood the hierarchy above them, but because of their own lineage they also could relate to the men who served under them. As a general rule they were disciplined, faithful to Rome, and diplomatic with their troops. Polybius (*Hist.* 6.24) says, "Centurions are required not to be bold and adventurous so much as good leaders, of steady and prudent mind, not prone to take the offensive or start fighting wantonly, but able when overwhelmed and hard-pressed to stand fast and die at their post." That is, in fact, the portrait of centurions in the New Testament. Each one we meet is put in a positive light. The first centurion served in Capernaum and had built the local synagogue (Matt 8:5-13/Luke 7:1-10).[9] The second centurion declared Jesus was [the] son of [a] god (Mark 15:39/Matt 27:54/Luke 23:47). The next centurion acts with legal propriety in not flogging Paul (Acts 22:25-26). The final centurion protects Paul en route to Rome, apparently even befriending him along the way (Acts 27:1, 6, 11, 31, 43).

It is no surprise, therefore, that this fellow is a noble Roman soldier. What we might not expect, however, is just how well-connected he is. Luke records that he is from the *Italian* regiment. While there is some question about just exactly what that was, it likely means that he was somehow connected to the Emperor and possibly part of his personal body-guard (*Beginnings* 5:427-445).[10]

---

[7] The name was quite common because Publius Cornelius Sulla had liberated 10,000 slaves in 82 B.C. many of whom consequently bore his name (Bruce, 214).

[8] Everett Ferguson, *Backgrounds of Early Christianity* (Grand Rapids: Eerdmans, 1987), 47-48.

[9] Luke's editing of this story makes him look even more like Cornelius. Both sent delegations to Jesus/Peter, both show reverence to the evangelist, and both recognized the problem of a Jew entering a Gentile's home; cf. Christoph Niemand, "Du centurion de Capharnaüm au centurion de Césarée; Luc 7,1-10 et sa function proleptique par rapport à Actes 10,1-11,18," in *Forschungen zum Neuen Testament und seiner Umwelt* (Frankfurt: Peter Lang, 2002), 259-270.

[10] A regiment or "company" contained approximately 600 men. Luke will also identify the name of Julius's regiment (Acts 27:1) as the "Imperial Regiment" (Σεβαστῆς). Unfortunately, we don't have sufficient historical information to differentiate between or identify these two companies. There is, however, an inscription from c. A.D. 69 recording the presence of the *Cohors II Italica ciuium Romanorum* or "second Italian cohort of roman citizens," cf. H. Dessau, *Inscriptiones Latinae Selectae* (Berlin, 1892–1916), No. 9168.

10:2. Another surprise is how *Jewish* this guy was.[11] That does not mean he was a convert, but he was a 'god-fearer'. These were Gentiles who somehow came to honor Yahweh but couldn't bring themselves to submit to circumcision (cf. 10:22, 35; 13:26).[12] There were plenty of them around! For Cornelius this meant adopting Jewish practices of *prayer* and *benevolence* for Jewish people. Luke's statement that Cornelius "prayed regularly" (*dia pantos*) most likely means that he was observing the regular Jewish times of prayer.[13] Though the NIV simply says Cornelius "gave generously to those in need," the Greek word *laos* implies Jewish people as opposed non-Jews (*ethnē*). These two acts of devotion (often found in tandem, e.g., Tob 12:8; 1 Pet 4:7-9, *Did* 15.4; *2 Clem* 16.4), along with fasting, were the most important practices for Jewish piety (cf. Matt 6:1-18).

[3]One day at about three in the afternoon he had a vision. He distinctly saw an angel of God, who came to him and said, "Cornelius!" [4]Cornelius stared at him in fear. "What is it, Lord?" he asked. The angel answered, "Your prayers and gifts to the poor have come up as a memorial offering before God. [5]Now send men to Joppa to bring back a man named Simon who is called Peter. [6]He is staying with Simon the tanner, whose house is by the sea." [7]When the angel who spoke to him had gone, Cornelius called two of his servants and a devout soldier who was one of his attendants. [8]He told them everything that had happened and sent them to Joppa.

10:3-4a. Cornelius was practicing standard Jewish piety by praying at three in the afternoon (cf. 3:1; Psa 55:17; Dan 6:10). Suddenly, he was interrupted by a vision[14] in which an angel called his name.[15] His response is typical, at least for a vision in Acts: He was terrified, asked for clarification, and addressed the heavenly voice as "Lord?" (cf. 9:5, 10f; 22:8, 10, 19; 26:15).

10:4b-6. The angel's response could not have been more encouraging. Cornelius's piety attracted God's attention. Literally, they became a "memorial" (*mnēmosunon*, cf. Mark 14:9/Matt 26:13) before God.[16] Now, that does not mean

[11] Moreover, Peter is portrayed as somewhat Hellenistic—he bears a Greek nickname, *Simon*, and is living with a tanner in Joppa. Both Peter and Cornelius overlap into each other's worlds. Thus, literarily, their paths were bound to cross; cf. Priscille Djomhoue, "Une histoire de rapprochement: Actes 10-11, 18," *FV* 104 (2005): 71-82.

[12] This is, of course, an oversimplification of the data on God-fearers. Nonetheless, it stands as a fairly reasonable supposition of Cornelius. For a more critical assessment of God-fearers, see Dietrich-Alex Koch, "The God-fearers Between Facts and Fiction," *ST* 60 (2006): 62–90 and "Proselyten und Gottesfürchtige als Hörer der Reden von Apostelgeschichte," in *Apostelgeschichte und die hellenistische Geschichtsschreibung* (ed. Cilliers Breytenbach and Jens Schröter; Leiden: Brill, 2004), 85-87.

[13] Dennis Hamm, "Praying 'Regularly' (not 'Constantly'): A Note on the Cultic Background of *dia pantos* at Luke 24:53, Acts 10:2 and Hebrews 9:6, 13:15," *ExpT* 116 (2004): 50-52, offers a helpful analysis of this phrase, showing its meaning as regular Jewish observance of prayer, especially in the LXX.

[14] Eleven of the twelve uses of this word "vision" (ὅραμα) in the NT are in Acts (Matt 17:9; Acts 7:31; 9:10, 12; 10:3, 17, 19; 11:5; 12:9; 16:9-10; 18:9) and nearly half of those are in reference to this single event.

[15] Angelophanies often follow this set formula: vision, angel, and call of a personal name (e.g., Gen 16:7-8; 22:11; 31:11; Exod 3:2-3; Luke 1:13, 30; 10:3; 27:23-24). The angel is God's envoy and virtually indistinguishable from God himself.

[16] This word in the LXX referred to the burned portion of the meat-offering (e.g., Lev. 2:2, 9, 16). Prayers and alms were sometimes compared to such holocaust offerings (Psa 141:2; Phil 4:18; Heb 13:15-16; Cf. *Beginnings* 4:113). Angels were assigned to deliver these prayers to God: "So now when you and Sarah prayed, it was I who brought and read the record (μνημόσυνον) of your prayer before the glory of the Lord. . . . I am Raphael, one of the seven angels who stand ready and enter before the glory of the Lord" (Tob 12:12, 15).

Cornelius was saved. It does mean, however, that God would respond to his piety by sending him a messenger to tell him how to be saved. God gave Cornelius the right name, the right city, and even the right address to find Simon Peter. He must make sure to get the right Simon (not the tanner). God commissioned Cornelius to summon Simon from Joppa with this promise: "He will bring you a message through which you and all your household will be saved" (11:14). What is interesting is that God already had stationed Philip in Caesarea (8:40). Why go to all the trouble to retrieve Peter rather than using a guy who was already in the neighborhood? After all, Philip was a noted evangelist in his own right. The answer lies in the fact that Cornelius was the first Gentile convert. The church was taking a bold new step, and Peter was given the authority by Jesus to 'open' the church on such occasions. The issue was not convenience but commission.

10:7-8. Without delay, Cornelius carried out his orders. He related the vision in full detail[17] to two servants and a personal body guard and immediately sent them on their way. Assuming that his vision ended by 4 p.m. and the three envoys could pack by 5 p.m., they traveled thirty miles overnight, arriving in Joppa around noon the following day (10:9). This calculates to just over 1.5 miles per hour which is not bad for traveling in the dark without sleep. Once they picked up Peter, their return trip would take more than twice as long, actually arriving in Caesarea after two days of travel (10:23b-24, 30).

2. Scene 2: Peter's Vision (10:9-16)

⁹**About noon the following day as they were on their journey and approaching the city, Peter went up on the roof to pray. ¹⁰He became hungry and wanted something to eat, and while the meal was being prepared, he fell into a trance. ¹¹He saw heaven opened and something like a large sheet being let down to earth by its four corners. ¹²It contained all kinds of four-footed animals, as well as reptiles of the earth and birds of the air. ¹³Then a voice told him, "Get up, Peter. Kill and eat." ¹⁴"Surely not, Lord!" Peter replied. "I have never eaten anything impure or unclean." ¹⁵The voice spoke to him a second time, "Do not call anything impure that God has made clean." ¹⁶This happened three times, and immediately the sheet was taken back to heaven.**

10:9. Normally Jews ate two meals a day. The first was mid-morning and the second was late afternoon. It is no wonder Peter was famished when brunch was two hours late! As he waited for the meal he decided to pray on the roof. Houses in the Middle East were designed with flat roofs which served as kind of a balcony (Deut 22:8) and sometimes even a guest room (2 Kgs 4:10; Prov 21:9; 25:24). It offered Peter a quiet place to pray where he could enjoy the coastal breeze (cf. 1 Sam 9:25-26; 2 Sam 11:2; Mark 13:15/Matt 24:17/Luke 17:31). More importantly, he busied himself with prayer. After all, it was noon, one of the three appointed times of prayer for Jews (cf. Psa 55:17; Dan 6:10). Those

[17] ἐξηγέομαι is a word that describes what a reporter or historian might do in relating the details of a story. It is only found six times in the NT, almost always by Luke (Luke 24:35; John 1:18; Acts 10:8; 15:12, 14; 21:19).

familiar with Luke's writings are not terribly surprised that Peter has a vision at this point since Luke often associates prayer with a revelation from God (cf. Luke 1:13; 3:21; 9:29; Acts 1:24; 4:31; 10:2-3, 9-10; 13:2; 22:17).

10:10-12. During his prayer he fell into a trance. This word *ekstasis*, from which we get "ecstasy," often means merely "amazement" (Mark 5:42; 16:8; Luke 5:26; Acts 3:10). In the context of prayer, however, Luke uses it to describe a vision (cf. Acts 11:5; 22:17) or what modern psychologists might label an *altered state of consciousness* (ASC).

Peter saw in his vision something like a large sheet being lowered to the earth by its four corners. It contained a bunch of different animals under three categories: land mammals, reptiles (creepy-crawlies[18]), and birds. It looked like Noah's ark had belched. That is, in fact, the point. These three categories come from Genesis 6:20: "Two of every kind of bird, of every kind of animal [livestock] and of every kind of creature that moves along the ground will come to you to be kept alive" (cf. Rom 1:23). God assembled the animals for Noah as a sign of imminent judgment. Little does Peter know that this assembly will be the undoing of judgment against Gentiles.

10:13-16. The Lord bade Peter to kill something and eat it. He objected. He had kept kosher law all his life. The Old Testament dietary regulations were clear (Lev 11 and Deut 14). You could only eat land animals with divided hoofs and which chew the cud. Water creatures were clean only if they had both fins and scales. Insects had to have six legs with a hinged back leg for jumping and birds must be vegetarians. Now, these rules sound rather bizarre to the modern ear, but they were set in stone for Jews. Dietary laws, along with Sabbath and circumcision, were the key marks of Judaism in a pluralistic world. If you remove these regulations, Peter's identity as a Jew is in jeopardy.

Undoubtedly Peter thinks this is a test. He is going to prove himself faithful to the divine ordinance of the Mosaic Law. What he was about to discover is how the law has been fulfilled in Jesus so that these rules of separation were obsolete. The reader must keep in mind this vision is a metaphor for humanity. These animals represent real people. The Levitical code itself makes this perfectly clear: "I am the LORD your God, who has set you apart from the nations. You must therefore make a distinction between clean and unclean animals and between unclean and clean birds. Do not defile yourselves by any animal or bird or anything that moves along the ground—those which I have set apart as unclean for you" (Lev 20:24b-25).

Peter uses two synonyms to describe these animals: "impure" and "unclean" (a hendiadys according to Haenchen, 300). "Impure" (*koinos*) is literally "common." "Unclean" (*akathartos*) carries the implication of "defiled" or even "evil." Together they describe the elaborate system of purity among the Jews.[19] All of

---

[18] This is, in fact, the implication of the Greek word ἑρπετόν as well as its Hebrew counterpart רֶמֶשׂ.

[19] Colin House, "Defilement by Association: Some Insights from the Usage of KOINOS/KOINOῩ in Acts 10 and 11," *AUSS* 21 (1983): 143-153 and Clinton Wahlen, "Peter's Vision and Conflicting Definitions of Purity," *NTS* 51 (2005): 505-518, offer an interesting, though ultimately unconvincing suggestion that κοινόν should not be understood as a synonym for ἀκάθαρτον. Rather, it is a third category for things rendered unkosher by contact with something defiled. They suggest that Peter saw a mixture of animals and

life had its proper order—who you could eat with, what you could wear, when to work and rest, how to marry and have children. There were biblical laws and unwritten social transcripts that guided everything.[20] Behind it all was the need for order, divinely sanctioned, telling one how to live life. Here Peter's table is about to be overturned and with it the whole of his world.

Three times Peter is told to eat. Three times he refuses, boasting that he had always avoided the "impure and unclean." The heavenly voice rebuked Peter with Peter's own words, "Stop *defiling* [*koinoō*] what God has *cleansed* [*katharizō*]." Two grammatical observations are in order here. First, the Greek construction, "do not" with the present imperative, implies "Stop doing what you are in the process of doing." This is not theoretical; it is occurring at the present time. Second, the NIV has Peter "calling" them unclean whereas in Greek he was "making them unclean." In actuality, labeling the other as unclean *does* makes them unclean within one's social network. So the translation is accurate to that extent (cf. Hauk, *TDNT* 3:809). Peter's labels have real consequences. In other words, it is simply not true that, "Sticks and stones may break your bones but *names can never harm you.*"

This is a massive revelation to Peter with world-altering consequences. But it is not new. One day the Pharisees chided Jesus for allowing his disciples to eat with unclean hands (Mark 7:1-23/Matt 15:1-20). It was a rather lengthy story, betraying its importance, concluding with these words of Jesus, "Don't you see that nothing that enters a man from the outside can make him 'unclean'? For it doesn't go into his heart but into his stomach, and then out of his body" (Mark 7:18-19a). Mark, in a parenthetical explanation said, "In saying this, Jesus declared all foods 'clean'" (Mark 7:19b). This is not to suggest that Jesus' statement was understood by his disciples on the spot as abrogation of Mosaic dietary laws. It is to suggest that the principles Jesus taught, applied and extrapolated by the Holy Spirit in the early church, resulted in the eradication of the food barrier between Jews and Gentiles. If Mark, as Peter's amanuensis, heard first-hand about his experience with Cornelius, it would explain why he added this parenthetical explanation to Mark 7 which, in reality, is the genesis of Acts 10.[21] This is hardly an astounding assertion. Paul came to the same conclusion: "I am fully convinced that no food is unclean in itself" (Rom 14:14). "But food does not bring us near to God; we are no worse if we do not eat, and no better if we do" (1 Cor 8:8). "Eat anything sold in the meat market without raising questions of conscience" (1 Cor 10:25).

All this runs counter to the normal Jewish ethic, summarized adequately by *Jubilees* 22:16, "Separate thyself from the nations, and eat not with them; and

those normally clean had been defiled by contact with the unclean. This does align with the use of the term in 1 Macc 1:47, 62, but it fails to explain why the animals were rendered unclean by contact with other animals or why Luke does not clarify that the sheet contained both clean and unclean things.

[20] Cf. *DNTB*, 874-882, and Carlos R. Sosa, "Pureza y Impureza en la narrativa de Pedro, Cornelio y el Espíritu Santo en Hechos 10," *Kairos* 41 (2006): 56-78.

[21] It is also interesting that right after Jesus' debate over clean and unclean we find him ministering to a Gentile woman (Mark 7:24-30/Matt 15:21-28). Hence, the discussion of clean and unclean food in both Mark 7 and Acts 10 is immediately applied to 'unclean' Gentiles.

do not according to their works, and become not their associate; for their works are unclean, and all their ways are a pollution and an abomination and uncleanness." The Mishnah declares even the Gentile's house unclean, "Dwelling places of gentiles [in the land of Israel] are unclean" (*m. Ohal* 18.7). Tobit 1:10-11 recognizes the reality of some Diaspora Jews associating with Gentiles, but the ideal is still abstinence: "After I was carried away captive to Assyria and came as a captive to Nineveh, everyone of my kindred and my people ate the food of the Gentiles, but I kept myself from eating the food of the Gentiles." Gentiles, of course, recognized how Jews shunned them. Tacitus, in describing the Jewish religion (from an antagonist's perspective) said:

> They regard the rest of mankind with all the hatred of enemies. They sit apart at meals, they sleep apart, and though, as a nation, they are singularly prone to lust, they abstain from intercourse with foreign women; among themselves nothing is unlawful. Circumcision was adopted by them as a mark of difference from other men. Those who come over to their religion adopt the practice, and have this lesson first instilled into them, to despise all gods, to disown their country, and set at naught parents, children, and brethren. (Tacitus, *Hist.* 5.5)

[17]While Peter was wondering about the meaning of the vision, the men sent by Cornelius found out where Simon's house was and stopped at the gate. [18]They called out, asking if Simon who was known as Peter was staying there. [19]While Peter was still thinking about the vision, the Spirit said to him, "Simon, three[a] men are looking for you. [20]So get up and go downstairs. Do not hesitate to go with them, for I have sent them." [21]Peter went down and said to the men, "I'm the one you're looking for. Why have you come?" [22]The men replied, "We have come from Cornelius the centurion. He is a righteous and God-fearing man, who is respected by all the Jewish people. A holy angel told him to have you come to his house so that he could hear what you have to say." [23a]Then Peter invited the men into the house to be his guests.

[a]*19* One early manuscript *two*; other manuscripts do not have the number.

10:17-18. The Spirit timed this perfectly. While Peter pondered this vexing vision,[22] the messengers arrived at the gate of the little villa by the sea.[23] They shouted from the gate, inquiring whether the said Simon was being hosted in this home. Meanwhile, the Spirit on the roof ordered Peter to go down and go with these men without *question* (*diakrinō*) which literally means "without judging them." He has just been told in the vision to *stop* calling animals unclean and now he is instructed to apply that principle to three yet unknown messengers at the gate.

---

[22] The word for "wonder" (διαπορέω) is used only four times and all by Luke. The other three times the "perplexed" persons were vexed (Luke 9:7; Acts 2:12; 5:24). In other words, this vision is not just confusing, it is disturbing.

[23] Pardon the poetic license, but the fact that Simon's house had a gate suggests the standard architecture of a Roman villa with a central courtyard surrounded by living quarters and workrooms. It is likely, therefore, that the tanner has a business substantial enough to support his family and a small staff.

10:19-22. When Peter obeyed, he found at the gate a Roman soldier and a couple of Gentile servants. He had an inquiry of his own: "What's your business?" These three began the 'hard-sell' on Cornelius, knowing the latent animosity Jews felt toward Roman soldiers. They tried to make Cornelius look as kosher as possible—he was "righteous," "God-fearing," "respected by all the Jews,"[24] and called by a "holy angel." Little do they know the deal had already been sealed by the Spirit up on the roof.

10:23a. Peter now, in a surprising twist, invited them in as his guests! That's a bit awkward. He himself was a guest and invites unwelcomed Gentiles into his host's home. We are about to see what a furor this whole Cornelius incident caused all the way up in Jerusalem because Peter entered a Gentile's home (11:1). Is it any less defiling to have 'them' come into a Jewish home? This is not to suggest that Peter acted inappropriately, outside his Apostolic authority, or without the consent of the tanner. It is simply to point out the social tension behind the text. It is also to point out the whole system of hospitality that is riddled through this passage.[25] The technical term for "guest" was used of Peter (9:43; 10:6, 18, 23, 32) and now of the messengers (10:23). Since hospitality was an expression of solidarity beyond mere benevolence, we understand that the movement of the Spirit toward Gentile inclusion has already begun.

4. Scene 4: Peter & Co. Return to Caesarea (10:23b-33)

[23b]**The next day Peter started out with them, and some of the brothers from Joppa went along. [24]The following day he arrived in Caesarea. Cornelius was expecting them and had called together his relatives and close friends. [25]As Peter entered the house, Cornelius met him and fell at his feet in reverence. [26]But Peter made him get up. "Stand up," he said, "I am only a man myself." [27]Talking with him, Peter went inside and found a large gathering of people. [28]He said to them: "You are well aware that it is against our law for a Jew to associate with a Gentile or visit him. But God has shown me that I should not call any man impure or unclean. [29]So when I was sent for, I came without raising any objection. May I ask why you sent for me?"**

10:23b-24. The very next day (*epaurion*)[26] the group set out for Caesarea. Caesarea was not only the home of the centurion; it was the center of the Roman rule in Palestine. That made it the geographical antithesis of Jerusalem. They were not merely crossing a geographic boundary but a social boundary, and the church would never be the same after this move.[27]

---

[24] Though they try to speak in Jewish terms, the messengers failed with this description. They said Cornelius was respected (lit., well spoken of, μαρτυρέω) by all the Jewish people (ὅλου τοῦ ἔθνους). But the Jews described themselves as "people" (λαός) and everyone else as "ethnic groups" (ἔθνους).

[25] Arterbury has constructed a fairly thorough model of ancient hospitality, showing how this present text accurately reflects standard social practices; cf. Andrew E. Arterbury, "The Ancient Custom of Hospitality, the Greek Novels, and Acts 10:1–11:18," PRS 29 (2002): 53-72.

[26] Luke uses this word to press the narrative forward in a quick succession of events (v. 9, 23, 24). Just as the days were compressed in quick succession of narrative time, so were the cities compressed in a narrow succession of narrative space—from Jerusalem to Lydda to Joppa to Caesarea.

[27] Ute E. Eisen, "Boundary Transgression and the Extreme Point in Acts 10:1–11:18," in *On the Cutting Edge: The Study of Women in Biblical Worlds* (ed. Jane Schaberg, Alice Bach, and Esther Fuchs; New York: Con-

Peter brings with him six brothers (11:12). This delegation of Seven seems to represent an official delegation of leaders (cf. 6:5).[28] And the three from Cornelius met the criterion from the Mosaic Law of a valid legal witness on behalf of the centurion (Deut 17:6). The ten set out for Caesarea and reached their goal in two days. There they found Cornelius waiting eagerly (*prosdokaō*). He had assembled his Gentile family (*sungenēs*) and intimate circle of friends. In other words, aside from Peter and his six companions, everyone else was Gentile. They had the same heritage as Cornelius, the same diet, dress, and social customs.

10:25-26. Cornelius greeted Peter as he would a commanding officer, by bowing before him in reverent submission. The word (*proskuneō*) is specifically used for worship. Talk about a cultural *faux-pas!* For a Jew, such reverence shown to a man was blasphemous. For example, Paul will go ballistic when the Lystrans attempt to make a sacrifice to Barnabas and him (Acts 14:11-15). Even the angel of Revelation 22:8-9 rebuked John for falling down before him (cf. *Ascen. Isa.* 7:21). So it is not surprising that Peter raised Cornelius to his feet and set the record straight: he was only a human messenger.

10:27-29. In verse 27, Peter talked with Cornelius and entered his house. Both actions were 'forbidden' according to Jewish custom (v. 28). There was, of course, no Mosaic injunction prohibiting interaction between Jews and Gentiles except intermarriage. The word Peter used (*athemitos*) does not mean "illegal" but "contrary to custom"—it was taboo. We are talking here about an oral tradition not Scripture. The rabbis followed Hillel's advice: "Be deliberate in giving judgment, and raise up many disciples, and *make a hedge about the law*" (*m. Abot* 1.1). In other words, the oral law augmented and clarified the written Law of Moses so as to protect any unwitting violation of the biblical commands. In this case, if one didn't even talk with a Gentile or enter his house, he could hardly be seduced into intermarriage or violated by unclean foods or idols. Those who were raised in a Protestant tradition have difficulty sensing the weight of oral law or its binding importance on the community. Peter was crossing a fixed boundary and would have to answer for his actions (11:1-4).

The social boundaries between Jews and Gentiles were being removed, and Peter sensed that. Through his vision of unclean animals, through the Spirit-guided messengers of Cornelius, through his reflection on Jesus' teaching about clean and unclean as well as his treatment of outsiders, Peter was finally getting it. God's heart is for the nations and Peter had better stop labeling outsiders as unclean. Now that Peter's ears are opened, he asks Cornelius why he was summoned (v. 29).

[30]Cornelius answered: "Four days ago I was in my house praying at this hour, at three in the afternoon. Suddenly a man in shining clothes stood before me

---

tinuum, 2003), 154-170, shows how the geographic boundaries of this text represent social and ideological boundaries. The movement from one physical place to another represents the movement of philosophical worldviews not just physical bodies.

[28] As suggested at 6:5 they may represent leaders of the entire city as opposed to a single synagogue (cf. Str-B 2:641, y. *Meg.* 3, 74a, 16; *bab Meg.* 3.1; *t. Meg.* 3.1; Josephus, *J.W.* 2.20.5 §570-571). This would be particularly appropriate since Caesarea was the Gentile counterpart for Jerusalem. These delegates could speak to the validity of the new city as a center of Christianity.

COLLEGE PRESS NIV COMMENTARY

³¹and said, 'Cornelius, God has heard your prayer and remembered your gifts to the poor. ³²Send to Joppa for Simon who is called Peter. He is a guest in the home of Simon the tanner, who lives by the sea.' ³³So I sent for you immediately, and it was good of you to come. Now we are all here in the presence of God to listen to everything the Lord has commanded you to tell us."

10:30-33. Cornelius repeats in first-person what Luke already reported in third-person (10:3-6). The only substantive difference is that the angel (v. 3) is described as "a man in shining clothes" (v. 30). Everything else is virtually identical: three in the afternoon, God responding to Cornelius's prayers and offerings, call of Simon Peter, and the house of Simon Tanner by the sea. This repetition, however, is not mere redundancy. It not only underscores the importance of the narrative, it draws the reader into the story by hearing afresh the details of the vision from Cornelius's own perspective.[29] Peter asked why he was summoned by Cornelius. The answer is, "You were summoned by God in answer to my prayers." Jesus already gave Peter a pattern to follow when a centurion responded in faith and supported the Jewish nation through benevolence (Matt 8:5-13/Luke 7:1-10).

5. Scene 5: Peter's Sermon to Cornelius (10:34-43)

Peter's sermon to Cornelius & Co. differs from the previous two sermons (Acts 2 and 3) in two substantial ways. First, Jesus is portrayed as "Lord of All" (v. 36) and "Judge" (v. 42) rather than as Messiah. This makes sense since these Gentiles are more accustomed to imperialistic imagery than Jewish motifs. Second, there is not a single Old Testament quote. Rather, it reads more like a CNN report on contemporary events in Israel. Peter mentions Galilee, Judea, Nazareth, and Jerusalem as well as John the Baptist and Jesus, both of whom were executed under Roman rulers.

In spite of these differences, however, Peter still sounds like Peter. His Aramaic verbiage isn't obscured, even through the Greek translation of his speech (Bruce, 226). It is pointless to speculate whether this Greek version is Peter's actual attempt to talk to Cornelius in the trade language of the day, whether it is some court reporter's rendition, or whether it is Luke's later edition. We just can't know. What we do know is that this speech, like the others in Acts, drives at the resurrection—the core of the gospel. This is the foundational message not only for the Jews but also for the Greeks. Jesus' died for our sins, and God raised him to life, vindicating him as both Lord and Christ. More specifically, the point of Peter's Pentecost sermons (Acts 2 and 10) is identical. Acts 2:21, via Joel 2:32, reads, "And everyone who calls on the name of the Lord will be saved." Peter had no idea how true that was until this third sermon when he applied this principle of God's wide welcome to the Gentiles.

³⁴Then Peter began to speak: "I now realize how true it is that God does not show favoritism ³⁵but accepts men from every nation who fear him and do what is right."

[29] William Kurz, "Effects of Variant Narrators in Acts 10–11," *NTS* 43 (1997): 570-586.

10:34-35. This is now the third time this crucial point has been made: God accepts Gentiles into his community. The first affirmation came from the heavenly voice, ostensibly Jesus: "Do not call anything impure that God has made clean" (v. 15).[30] Peter reiterates this idea in verse 28: "God has shown me that I should not call any man impure or unclean." Now for a third time the point is made that God does not show *favoritism* (vv. 34 and 43!). This Greek word (*prosōpolēmtēs*) etymologically means God does not *lift the face* (e.g., Esth 4:11; 5:2). The idea is that God does not pay attention to *who* is standing before him but judges impartially based upon *what* was done (cf. Gen 4:7; John 5:29; Rom 2:6; 2 Cor 5:10; Rev 20:12). The judges of the Old Testament were not to be 'face-takers' but were to judge impartially, without consideration of a person's status, wealth, or filial relationship (Exod 23:3; Lev 19:15). This rule was well-known. What is novel in this context is that it is being applied to Gentiles on behalf of Yahweh. Both Paul and James pick up on this idea in their letters, affirming the impartiality (*prosōpolēmpsia*) of God (Rom 2:11; Eph 6:9) which we are to imitate (Col 3:25; James 2:1, 9).

Thus the covenant of Yahweh is now opened to all nations. God's 'elect' are now those who respond to his invitation, not merely those who were born to a chosen bloodline (cf. Matt 3:9/Luke 3:8; Matt 8:11; 22:14). These elect are those who "do what is right." This is not, of course, antithetical to God's grace. Rather, it is a Jewish reflection of covenant loyalty. "Doing what is right" is not what merits inclusion in the covenant but what is manifested *by* inclusion in the covenant.

³⁶You know the message³¹ God sent to the people of Israel, telling the good news of peace through Jesus Christ, who is Lord of all. ³⁷You know what has happened throughout Judea, beginning in Galilee after the baptism that John preached— ³⁸how God anointed Jesus of Nazareth with the Holy Spirit and

---

[30] The NIV interpretively records these words in red ink.

[31] The Greek of verses 36-37 is a confusing mess even if the general meaning is clear enough (esp. against the backdrop of Psa 107:20; 147:18; Isa 52:7). There are no less than *four difficulties.* (1) "The word" (τὸν λόγον) of verse 36 begins the sentence but it is an accusative, not a nominative (as in English). The subject of the sentence is actually "God" from verse 34, assumed to be the subject of the verb "he sent" (ἀπέστειλεν). (2) The relative pronoun "which" (ὅν) that modifies "the word" is absent in some of the major manuscripts, so it is difficult to tell whether it belongs. Without it, the meaning is substantially different as we will see below. (3) Some translations treat τὸν λόγον as if it is an apposition to ῥῆμα in verse 37 even though the best understanding of ῥῆμα with γενόμενον is not "message" (KJV, RSV, ASV, VUL) but "events" (NIV, NASB, ESV). That is, "events" took place not a mere "message", (e.g., Luke 2:15, 17; *Jos. Asen.* 17:1-3); cf. Christoph Burchard, "A Note on 'PHMA in Josas 17:1 f.; Luke 2:15, 17; Acts 10:37," *NovT* 27 (1985): 281-295. (4) In verse 37, the word ἀρξάμενος appears to modify ῥῆμα, but it is masculine, not neuter. Hence it doesn't match anything in the sentence. The nearest masculine word it could match is "the message" (εὐαγγελιζόμενος) back in v. 36 but that connection creates more dissonance than merely accepting a flawed gender ending on the backside of ἀρξάμενος. So what are the *interpretive possibilities?* (A) Retain the "ὅν" (v. 36) so that the "events" (γενόμενον ῥῆμα) of v. 37 are connected to the "message" (τὸν λόγον) of v. 36. This makes vv. 36-37 a single sentence describing the ministry of Jesus (RSV, ASV, KJV). (B) Drop the "ὅν" (v. 36) and separate vv. 36 and 37 into two sentences (NIV, NEB) or combine the sentences but describe the "message" of v. 36 separately from the "events" of v. 37 (NASB, ESV). (C) Retain the "ὅν" (v. 36), but instead of connecting "the word" with what follows, connect it to the preceding revelation (vv. 34-35)—that God does not show favoritism. Thus, vv. 34-36 become one sentence rather than vv. 36-37. This makes good sense of the passage in that the dominant theme of Peter's sermon becomes the focus of attention. Cf. Harald Riesenfeld, "The Text of Acts 10:36," in *Text and Interpretation* (eds. E. Best and R. McL. Wilson; Cambridge: Cambridge, 1979), 191-194. For a history of this interpretation preceding Riesenfeld, cf. Frans Neirynck, "Acts 10,36a τὸν λόγον ὅν," *ETL* 60 (1984): 118-123.

power, and how he went around doing good and healing all who were under the power of the devil, because God was with him.

10:36-38. Peter summarizes the life of Jesus under three banners: John the Baptist, God's anointing Jesus with the Spirit, and Jesus' ministry of healing. There are several interesting traits of Peter's summary. First, it is geographically laden (which Luke would like). He mentions Judea, Galilee, Nazareth, and Jerusalem (v. 39). That these places are irrelevant to the narrative of Acts as well as to Cornelius's conversion suggests they are authentic memoirs of an eye-witness.[32] Who else would think to include them but one whose calloused feet remembered the journey? In fact, this summary account of Jesus' ministry follows precisely the outline of the book of Mark, most likely because both Mark and Luke are dependent on the presentation of Peter for the ministry of Jesus.[33] Second, going back to The Baptist is not particularly important to testifying about Jesus, but it is necessary as part of Peter's Apostolic witness, as Luke pointed out in 1:22. Third, Peter connects the baptism of John with Jesus' anointing by the Holy Spirit. This recalls the baptism of Jesus where Yahweh cites the Royal Psalm 2 and sends the Spirit in the form of a dove (Mark 1:10-11/Matt 3:16-17/ Luke 3:22/John 1:31-33). This anointing also recalls Jesus' inaugural address in his hometown synagogue where he claimed to personally fulfill Isaiah 61:1-2a (cf. Luke 4:16-30). This is most significant since it was in this sermon that Jesus claimed his ministry would extend beyond the boundaries of ethnic Israel. Finally, Jesus' healings (inclusive of exorcisms) were a rescue mission of those souls oppressed by the devil. In other words, the Kingdom of God was invading the territory won by Satan.

According to Peter, Cornelius was aware of these events. This is undoubtedly the case. One could hardly have lived through the last decade in Israel (even in the administrative capital of Caesarea) and be unaware of the Jesus movement that proliferated throughout the country. Paul made a similar assertion to Herod Agrippa II in Acts 26:26 (cf. 2:22). John the Baptist had somewhat of a cult following, and Jesus exceeded him in both popularity and power. The question is, therefore, not *what* happened. Everyone knew that. The question is what *to do* with it. Jesus had been crucified under Pontius Pilate. That puts him on the wrong side of justice, especially for a centurion in the Roman military machine. How could he possibly assent that this 'cursed' Jew was now a global Judge?

Peter makes four claims about Jesus that Luke picks up on for anti-imperialistic propaganda. First, Jesus is identified as "**Lord of all**" (*houtos estin pantōn kurios*). The English translation reduces the impact by rendering the title as a relative clause: "who is Lord of all." However, given the fact that this was a common epitaph for the Emperor[34] and given the strength of *houtos* ("this one"), it might be better to render it as a title: "This one is Lord of All." It is not the

---

[32] Frans Neirynck, "Le livre des Actes, 6: Ac 10:36-43 et l'Évangile," *ETL* 60 (1984): 109-117, makes a persuasive case that this pericope is pre-Lucan material.
[33] Papias famously attributed Mark's material to Peter's preaching in Rome (Eusebius, *Eccl. Hist.* 3.39).
[34] For a collection of primary inscriptions and references see Kavin Rowe, "Luke–Acts and the Imperial Cult: A Way through the Conundrum?" *JSNT* 27 (2005): 291-293.

Emperor who is really running the world, it is Jesus. Peter made the same point with more Jewish verbiage (equally shocking) in his Pentecost address: "God has made this Jesus, whom you crucified, both Lord and Christ" (2:36).

Second, Jesus brings **peace** to the Jewish people. The centurion thought this was *his* role to enforce the *pax romana* of the Emperor.[35] Peter's counterclaim was that true peace only comes through Jesus Christ.[36] Peace is not enforced from above but offered from below. Through the Messiah of Israel, all nations could share in the election of God's people. Paul will put it this way, "For he himself is our peace, who has made the two one and has destroyed the barrier, the dividing wall of hostility, by abolishing in his flesh the law with its commandments and regulations. His purpose was to create in himself one new man out of the two, thus making peace" (Eph 2:14-15).

Third, Jesus went about **doing good** (*euergeteō*). This Greek word in its noun form is "patron." The centurion thought of himself in those terms. Both he (Acts 10:2) and the centurion of Capernaum (Luke 7:4-5) used their resources to bless the Jewish people where they were stationed. Apparently this was not uncommon for centurions in the Mediterranean world.[37] This is particularly interesting in light of Jesus' earlier statement concerning Roman authorities: "The kings of the Gentiles lord it over them; and those who exercise authority over them call themselves Benefactors [*euergetai*]" (Luke 22:25). If Luke 22 can be drawn alongside Acts 10, the Emperor (i.e., king) and his underlings (e.g., centurion) are but parodies of the real rule of Yahweh which can alone bring peace on earth.

Finally, Jesus is **judge** (v. 42). While this might be read as a statement against the emperor, most cases were tried a little closer to home, under the jurisdiction of the local authority of the centurion (e.g., Cicero, *Phil.* 1.8.20; Juvenal, *Sat.* 16.7-34).[38] The upshot is that Jesus has replaced the Emperor and his envoys as the sole ruler of import. Such anti-imperialistic propaganda, though appropriately subtle, could still smack of treason if it landed in the wrong hands. Moreover, if Gentile evangelism began with anti-imperialistic implications, such preaching may have become programmatic for those who followed in Peter's wake.

For Cornelius, Peter's preaching of Jesus, will require a major alteration of his identity as a Roman official. And for Peter, the recognition of Cornelius as an acceptable candidate for conversion will require a transformation of his identity

[35] Though centurions in the NT have sterling reputations, this was not particularly the case in the Roman world. They were generally considered oppressive and greedy, particularly since they often worked in conjunction with tax collectors to make sure Caesar got his due. Furthermore, pertinent to the present context, they enforced the Imperial Cult so odious to Christians and Jews. Since Caesarea was noted for the practice of the Imperial Cult with its central temple to Roma and Augustus (Josephus, *Ant.* 15.339; *J.W.* 1.414), the portrait of this centurion is antithetical to what one might expect. He was generous rather than greedy, and he was devoted to Yahweh, not Zeus or the Divine Emperor. This is so striking that Justin Howell labels this story as rhetorical irony; "The Imperial Authority and Benefaction of Centurions and Acts 10.34-43: A Response to C. Kavin Rowe," *JSNT* 31 (2008): 25-51.

[36] Marshall (191) is right to spiritualize this peace as synonymous with salvation (cf. Luke 1:79; 2:14; Rom 5:1; Eph 2:17; 6:15) so long as we don't bracket off the pragmatic, present, and corporate sociological manifestations of the peace on earth that Jesus intended to bring through the Kingdom of God (cf. Luke 1:68-71; 2:14; Rom 14:19; 2 Cor 13:11; Gal 6:16; Eph 2:14; Col 1:20). It was, after all, a message of peace to the "people of Israel," not to individuals.

[37] Cf. Howell "Imperial Authority and Benefaction," 31-32, for extrabiblical references.

[38] Cf. Ibid., 36-37.

as a Jewish Christian leader.[39] Both men will have their worlds irrevocably transformed by this event. Jesus simply will not leave well-enough alone.

**[39]"We are witnesses of everything he did in the country of the Jews and in
Jerusalem. They killed him by hanging him on a tree, [40]but God raised him from
the dead on the third day and caused him to be seen. [41]He was not seen by all
the people, but by witnesses whom God had already chosen—by us who ate and
drank with him after he rose from the dead. [42]He commanded us to preach to
the people and to testify that he is the one whom God appointed as judge of
the living and the dead. [43]All the prophets testify about him that everyone who
believes in him receives forgiveness of sins through his name."**

10:39-41. Jesus' ministry was authenticated by his powerful miracles. His
death was vindicated by his resurrection, and the resurrection was verified by his
Apostolic witnesses.[40] That is the point of this pericope—Cornelius can believe
in Jesus because Peter is a *bona fide*, God-ordained, eyewitness to the events. Yes,
Jesus was killed in a most shameful way. He was hung on a tree which is a Jewish
description of crucifixion (cf. Deut 21:23; Acts 5:30; 10:39; 13:29; Gal 3:13; 1 Pet
2:24).[41] Normally, that would mean that he was a villain. In this case, however, it
indicates the sinfulness of those responsible for putting him to death. The proof
is in the resurrection. If God raised him to life, this unprecedented fact would
vindicate an otherwise notorious death.

Why should Cornelius believe Peter that Jesus was raised? Aside from the
obvious, that God identified Peter in a vision as an authentic witness, there are
three primary evidences Peter provides his would-be convert. First, Peter (& Co.)
are valid witnesses. Jesus was not seen by the *hoi polloi* (i.e., the masses, v. 41). God
made him appear (v. 40)[42] before the chosen band of Apostles (v. 41). Now, we
would normally think "the more the merrier" when it comes to the number of
witnesses. But here we are to weigh the *quality* of the witnesses rather than count
their *quantity*. This is no rumor foisted upon the masses, it is God's revelation to
those 'in the know'. Second, because a resurrection is hard to swallow, Jesus ate
and drank with the Apostles to prove his corporeal resurrection reality (cf. Luke
24:30, 41-43; Acts 1:4; 1 John 1:1). Thus, he was no mere apparition or ghost. He
was physically raised. Third, this was not a novel or new theological creation by
the early church but it was prophesied by the sages of old (v. 43)—it was planned
by God. In short, the resurrection of Jesus was not a rumor, it was not a fantasy or
a phantom, and it was not a half-cocked novelty concocted by some innovative
quacks. It was nothing less than God's hand intervening in human affairs.

10:42-43. Peter stood with the other Apostles, announcing the reality of Je-

---

[39] Cf. Susan Bond, "Acts 10:34-43," *Int* 56 (2002): 80-83.

[40] Notice that Peter says "we" (v. 39). While that could refer to him and the six brothers from Joppa, it
more likely refers to the group of Apostles who alone were given the right and responsibility to serve as
authoritative witnesses to the resurrection.

[41] Cf. M. Wilcox, "'Upon the Tree'—Deut. 21:22-23 in the New Testament," *JBL* 96 (1977): 85-99.

[42] Ο θεὸς ... ἔδωκεν αὐτὸν ἐμφανῆ γενέσθαι implies God's hand in generating the resurrection appearances. This is similar to the divine passive in Luke 24:31 in which God 'revealed' Jesus to the disciples,
"Then their eyes were opened and they recognized him."

sus' resurrection. As if that is not enough, behind the Apostles stand the prophets, announcing forgiveness of sins through Jesus. It is hard to know what texts Peter might have in mind. They are frustratingly few. There is, of course, Isaiah 53:4-5, 12b:

> Surely he took up our infirmities and carried our sorrows, yet we considered him stricken by God, smitten by him, and afflicted. But he was pierced for our transgressions, he was crushed for our iniquities; the punishment that brought us peace was upon him, and by his wounds we are healed. . . . For he bore the sin of many, and made intercession for the transgressors.

The problem, of course, is that the New Testament writers never press this text into service for substitutionary atonement. And after that, the proof-texts get pretty thin. If we are looking for a single statement that predicts the Messiah dying for the sins of individuals we come up short.[43] This is especially awkward since Peter says, "All the prophets testify about him," as if the Messianic savior is discussed liberally through the pages of the Old Testament. If, however, we look at the whole story line of the Old Testament, we see the metanarrative of a wayward nation in desperate need of a savior. This is a nation, in metaphoric terms, divorced from her God, or to use the terminology of N.T. Wright, "in exile."[44] Israel is still experiencing the drastic consequence of her rebellion, and only a savior can rescue her from exile. One might retort, "But he is speaking to a Gentile. What would Cornelius care about Jewish exile metaphors?" Ah, but is Cornelius not a God-fearer? Is his conversion not an issue of becoming part of the family of Abraham (Gal 3:28-29)? Does not Peter clarify that this is a message to the "people of Israel" (v. 36)? Is it not imperative that this first Gentile convert understand clearly that salvation is through the Jewish people? To use Paul's analogy, Peter is not planting a new olive tree, but grafting in a new branch to the native root (Rom 11:11-24).

Because of the resurrection, Jesus is substantiated not only as the Messiah of Israel but as Judge of all the living and the dead. This is exactly what Peter affirmed about pagans in his letter: "They will have to give account to him who is ready to judge the living and the dead" (1 Pet 4:5). Paul, likewise, gave his assent: ". . . Christ Jesus, who will judge the living and the dead . . ." (2 Tim 4:1; cf. Rom 2:16; 14:9; 2 Cor 5:10). This idea goes back to Jesus who saw himself as the eschatological arbiter of Yahweh's divine justice (cf. Matt 19:28; John 5:22-30; 9:39).

6. Scene 6: Cornelius's Household Is Baptized with the Holy Spirit and Water (10:44-48)

[44]While Peter was still speaking these words, the Holy Spirit came on all who heard the message. [45]The circumcised believers who had come with Peter

---

[43] Marshall (193) delimits the prophecy to Jesus forgiving sins, not suffering vicariously. If that is the case, there are several relevant texts (Isa 33:24; 53:4-6, 11; Jer 31:34; Dan 9:24) but hardly a prophetic consensus.

[44] N.T. Wright, *Jesus and the Victory of God* (Grand Rapids: Eerdmans, 1996); also David W. Pao, *Acts and the Isaianic New Exodus* (Grand Rapids: Baker Academic, 2003).

were astonished that the gift of the Holy Spirit had been poured out even on the Gentiles. [46]For they heard them speaking in tongues[a] and praising God. Then Peter said, [47]"Can anyone keep these people from being baptized with water? They have received the Holy Spirit just as we have." [48]So he ordered that they be baptized in the name of Jesus Christ. Then they asked Peter to stay with them for a few days.

[a]*46 Or* other languages

10:44-46. At the climax of Peter's sermon, the Holy Spirit interrupted: "Everyone who believes in him receives forgiveness of sins through his name." That, in a nutshell, is the message. That, in a nutshell, is the gospel.

The Holy Spirit burst into the room or perhaps more accurately, "spilled out" from heaven (v. 45) and "fell" upon the Gentiles (v. 44). The picture of the Holy Spirit being "poured out" like water is precisely the imagery of Pentecost (2:17, 18, 33; via Joel 2:28-32; cf. Isa 44:3; John 3:3-5). And that is precisely the point. The supernatural experience of tongues at Pentecost in Jerusalem was reproduced in Caesarea! They too praised God in miraculous utterances (v. 46, cf. 2:11).[45] Hence, there was no differentiation between the Jews in their capital city and the Gentiles in their seat of power. Peter's circumcised comrades were flabbergasted. If God no longer recognized the boundaries between Jew and Gentile, then the lines of the Kingdom of God had to be redrawn based upon different criteria. It was no longer adherence to the Temple or fidelity to the Mosaic Law but rather faith in Jesus Christ that determined Abrahamic lineage.

10:47-48. Peter called for Cornelius's house to be baptized. Well, actually, he asked a rhetorical question of his fellow Jews but the effect was the same.[46] Luke interprets Peter's question of verse 47 as a command in verse 48. In fact, the word for "command" (*prostassō*) is quite strong. In its other six uses in the New Testament, only Jesus (Matt 8:4/Mark 1:44; Luke 5:14) or God (Matt 1:24; Acts 10:33; 17:26) gives a command. It is as if Peter is representing divine justice. If the Holy Spirit authenticated this Gentile household, they should be fully incorporated into the Christian community through Christian baptism. Once these Gentile converts had the approval of the heavenly Spirit and the recognition of the earthly body of Christ, they were as fully Christian as anyone else—without circumcision!

Cornelius & Co. asked Peter to stay for a few days as part of the normal

---

[45] Elser's rationalistic skepticism drives his conclusion that these tongues were glossolalia rather than xenolalia based on Paul's critique in 1 Cor 14 rather than Luke's previous presentation in 2:1-13. Nevertheless, his argument, based on modern sociological analysis of tongues, is sound. Namely, if 'outsiders' or 'unbelievers' speak in tongues, the 'in-group' is obligated to baptize them as a sign of acceptance. Philip F Esler, "Glossolalia and the Admission of Gentiles into the Early Christian Community," *BTB* 22 (1992): 136-142. Polhill (263, fn. 109) points out that "speaking in tongues" (λαλούντων γλώσσαις, v. 46) is more similar to the verbiage of 1 Cor 12-14 and may, on that basis, be a different kind of tongues than chapter 2:1-13 (though the Western text inserts ἑτέραις, conforming to Luke's earlier report). This is unlikely since the content of the tongues was clearly interpreted (v. 46). If one simply reads Luke on his own terms, without the imposition of Paul's harangue in 1 Cor 14, s/he would naturally assume Acts 2 and 10 are the same phenomenon.

[46] Verse 47 is reminiscent of the Ethiopian's questions, "Why shouldn't I be baptized?" In fact, both Peter and the Ethiopian use the word "hinder" (κωλύω): "What hindrance is there to baptism?" Perhaps this is Luke's subtle reminder that the two stories are to be read in tandem.

hospitality code (replete throughout this passage). His acceptance would emphasize the fact that they were brothers in Christ, and it would afford the opportunity for a more thorough indoctrination into the primary tenets of the faith. Thus a boundary had been breached so that the distant borders could be reached. Let the flood of evangelism roll on.

ACTS 11

7. Scene 7: Summary and Defense in Jerusalem
of Cornelius's Conversion (11:1-18)

This is the final scene in the Cornelius episode and it is critical. It allows yet another view of the visions of Peter and Cornelius, this time from a Jewish/Christian perspective in Jerusalem. As word gets out, feathers fly. As Peter reports, the church rejoices. At last, the dividing wall crumbles. The reader should take a moment to consider the import of this text in light of contemporary events in Israel. Peace in the Middle East is possible only through Israel's Messiah. But it will require the same vitality of preaching, the same willingness to suffer, the same humility in accepting 'the other', and the same intervention of the Holy Spirit of God.

¹The apostles and the brothers throughout Judea heard that the Gentiles also had received the word of God. ²So when Peter went up to Jerusalem, the circumcised believers criticized him ³and said, "You went into the house of uncircumcised men and ate with them."

11:1-2. Rumor got back to the boys down south. "Judea" is not merely a geographic designation. It is the seat of Jewish power, kind of like saying "Wall Street" or "The White House." It is not the place on a map that is important, but the power that place represents. These 'guardians of orthodoxy' heard tell of this uncircumcised household in the seat of Roman power staking claim to the Jewish Messiah. Such a bold move needs some sort of explanation. It is not that they were resistant to the Spirit or racist against the Gentiles. They were, however, concerned that Peter had gone rogue, that he had personally pushed the church in a novel direction without approval of the Apostles and Elders.

Specifically, they were concerned that these Gentiles received access to the "Word of God" without submitting to the Law of Moses. In Luke, the "Word of God" is not the Torah but rather the preached message of the gospel (cf. Luke 5:1; 8:21; 11:28; Acts 4:31; 8:14; 13:5, 7, 46; 18:11).[1] What takes place here is virtually identical to the aftermath of the Samaritans' conversion earlier: "When the apostles in Jerusalem heard that Samaria had accepted the word of God, they sent Peter and John to them" (Acts 8:14). This time, however, Peter is on the defensive and instead of going *to* Samaria to check it out, he returns *to* Jerusalem to be checked out.[2]

---

[1] Luke's use of the term differs from Mark and Matthew for whom "Word of God" seems to imply Scripture in their single use of the phrase (Mark 7:13/Matt 15:6). Perhaps Luke was influenced by Paul or John who also imply "the preached gospel" by this term (2 Cor 2:17; 4:2; Col 1:25; Rev 1:2, 9; 6:9; 20:4; cf. Heb 13:7).
[2] The Western text is a bit longer, adding several points to the text; cf. *Beginnings* 4:124 and Édouard Delebecque, "La montée de Pierre de Césarée à Jérusalem selon le Codex Bezae au chapitre 11 des Actes

11:3. Notice, however, that the objection is not to Peter's preaching but to his eating. Preaching to pagans was obviously a good thing (particularly if it implied judgment, *a la* Jonah). One can't very well justify an objection against announcing the righteousness of God. One can, however, justify objecting to a breach of purity.[3] Peter has crossed a line. In doing so, his behavior implied that Jewish codes of ethics, which differentiated them from pagans, were no longer necessary. Or perhaps more accurately, the Mosaic Law didn't give Jews special status before Yahweh. Hence, these Gentiles were not an addendum to the Church, they were a radical transformation of it. Their inclusion suggested that the circumcised believers no longer had a 'corner on the market' so to speak; they no longer occupied 'chief seats'. In religious circles, the beauty of compassion tends to end abruptly at the point where it implies that the 'chosen' are not superior to the 'unclean initiates'.

[4]Peter began and explained everything to them precisely as it had happened: [5]"I was in the city of Joppa praying, and in a trance I saw a vision. I saw something like a large sheet being let down from heaven by its four corners, and it came down to where I was. [6]I looked into it and saw four-footed animals of the earth, wild beasts, reptiles, and birds of the air. [7]Then I heard a voice telling me, 'Get up, Peter. Kill and eat.' [8]I replied, 'Surely not, Lord! Nothing impure or unclean has ever entered my mouth.' [9]The voice spoke from heaven a second time, 'Do not call anything impure that God has made clean.' [10]This happened three times, and then it was all pulled up to heaven again."

11:4-10 = 10:9-16. Indeed, Peter did recount the tale "precisely as it had happened."[4] Verses 5-10 are virtually identically to Act 10:9-16 with few minor variations: (1) Most obviously, Acts 10:9-16 is Luke's third-person account of Peter's vision. Acts 11:5-10 is Peter's more robust firsthand account. The reader is thus drawn more deeply and personally into Peter's experience in the second telling.[5]

(2) The introduction to the first account is more detailed. There, Luke set the scene by describing the time of day (noon, 10:9), the place (roof, 10:9), and Peter's hunger while the meal was belatedly prepared (10:10). This second account avoids any laborious repetition of these details but does remind the reader that Peter was in the city of Joppa when he fell into a trance during the midday prayers. Here, however, we get an additional detail that this "trance" was a "vision" (*horama*). Luke uses this word to describe *Moses* and the burning bush (Acts 7:31), *Peter's* vision of the sheet (Acts 10:17; 11:5; cf. 12:9); and *Paul's* apparition of the Macedonian man (Acts 16:9-10). Thus, for Luke, visions were

---

des Apôtres," *ETL* 58 (1982): 106-110. (1) Peter spent a long time in the area traveling about strengthening the churches. (2) He *desired* to go to Jerusalem and did so on his own initiative. (3) Like Paul in Acts 15, he reported Gentile evangelism to the leaders of Jerusalem and met with their approval. It was the circumcision advocates who caused the trouble.

[3] The issue was not inclusion of pagans but Peter's breach of *Kashrut*; cf. Emmanuelle Steffek, "Quand juifs et païens se mettent à table (Ac 10)," *ETR* 80 (2005): 103-111.

[4] The word (καθεξῆς) implies "in sequential order" and is used only five times in the NT, all by Luke (Luke 1:3; 8:1; Acts 3:24; 11:4; 18:23).

[5] Luke has already used this narrative device to good effect with the double rendition of Cornelius's vision in 10:3-6 and 10:30-33. Cf. Kurz, "Variant Narrators," 570-586.

destiny altering events that moved major players across boundaries which they, themselves, would never have been inclined to cross.

(3) Peter added a fourth category of animals, "wild beasts," to Luke's earlier triad of four-footed animals, creeping things, and birds, which is still perfectly Jewish (e.g., Psa 148:10). (4) Finally, Peter's conclusion provided a more vivid eyewitness account (Bruce, 234-235), replacing the word "taken back [*analambanō*] to heaven" with the rare word "pulled up [*anaspaō*] to heaven." All in all, the information is identical. What changes is the readers' depth of appreciation for Peter and for the importance of this event.

¹¹"**Right then three men who had been sent to me from Caesarea stopped at the house where I was staying. ¹²The Spirit told me to have no hesitation about going with them. These six brothers also went with me, and we entered the man's house. ¹³He told us how he had seen an angel appear in his house and say, 'Send to Joppa for Simon who is called Peter. ¹⁴He will bring you a message through which you and all your household will be saved.' ¹⁵"As I began to speak, the Holy Spirit came on them as he had come on us at the beginning.**

11:11-15 = 10:17-48. We again have two parallel accounts of Peter's encounter with Cornelius. This time, however, it is only a brief synopsis. The 628 words of the first account have been reduced to 101 words here in chapter 11. The parallels are evenly distributed so as to give an accurate summary of all the events.[6] The only really *new* information is that Peter's circumcised companions were six in number (v. 12b) and an added line from Cornelius's angelic vision: "He [Peter] will bring you a message through which you and all your household will be saved" (v. 14). One other difference is, perhaps, worth mentioning. Though chapter 10 gives a summary of Peter's sermon, 11:15 gives the impression that Peter was just getting started. In Aramaic, the expression "I began" is often not a chronological marker, but like the English word "then" simply transitions into the next topic of discussion. Those familiar with this particular Aramaic expression will not trouble themselves with a supposed discrepancy between the two accounts.

¹⁶"**Then I remembered what the Lord had said: 'John baptized with[a] water, but you will be baptized with the Holy Spirit.' ¹⁷So if God gave them the same gift as he gave us, who believed in the Lord Jesus Christ, who was I to think that I could oppose God?" ¹⁸When they heard this, they had no further objections and praised God, saying, "So then, God has granted even the Gentiles repentance unto life."**
[a]*16 Or in*

11:16-18. Peter's reply stands squarely on his Apostolic authority. Not only did he hold the keys of the kingdom, and not only had he been center stage at the beginning of the church, but he had personally followed Jesus in his most intimate circle. Peter had received a private promise[7] from the resurrected Jesus concerning

---

[6]Acts 11:11 = 10:17; 11:12a = 10:20; 11:12b = 10:23b; 11:12c = 10:25a; 11:13a = 10:30; 11:13b = 10:32a; 11:15a = 10:44; 11:15b = 10:47b.

[7]Interestingly, the only other use of this term "word of the Lord" (τοῦ ῥήματος τοῦ κυρίου, v. 16) is Luke 22:61 where Jesus made another private promise to Peter that he would betray him.

the Pentecostal baptism of the Holy Spirit: "On one occasion, while he was eating with them, he gave them this command: 'Do not leave Jerusalem, but wait for the gift my Father promised, which you have heard me speak about. For John baptized with water, but in a few days you will be baptized with the Holy Spirit'" (Acts 1:4-5). In a striking fulfillment, the Holy Spirit fell on the Apostolic witnesses, resulting in 3,000 conversions. Now, for the second time in the book, this "Baptism of the Holy Spirit" is clearly identified. The Jewish Pentecost (Acts 2) is identical (*isos*, v. 17) to the Gentile Pentecost (Acts 10).[8] This validation of the Holy Spirit, according to Peter, trumps circumcision as a mark of inclusion in the Kingdom of God. It trumps dietary laws, dress codes, ethnicity, geography, gender, or economics. Hence, the Spirit-baptized believer can bypass the 'community rules' laid out under the old covenant. Peter notes how unhealthy, ungodly, and unwise it would be to continue to recognize barriers of fellowship around the table. A rejection of God's 'chosen' is opposition to Yahweh himself. As if this argument is not powerful enough, Peter, for the very first time, invokes the full title: The Lord Jesus Christ (v. 17).[9]

Happily, these godly protagonists capitulate to Peter's report. In fact, not only did they cease and desist in their objections against the Apostle, they praised God who graciously granted the nations the same opportunity of election as Israel through faith in Jesus the Messiah.

D. THE ECLIPSE OF THE JEWISH CHURCH
IN JERUSALEM (11:19–12:25)

This section is perplexing, not in its content but in its arrangement. It focuses on Antioch (11:19-30 & 13:1-4) but with a major interlude in Jerusalem (12:1-25). Luke has forged ahead from Caesarea to Antioch, tracing the major forays into Gentile territory but then backtracks to Jerusalem for an additional episode in the sacred city. Thus one might ask, "Is chapter 12 an awkward insertion that interrupts the otherwise seamless flow between 11:29 and 12:25?" Though a number of theories are on offer,[10] the most attractive comes from Longenecker

---

[8] That these two events were identical argues against the baptism of the Holy Spirit being primarily soteriological. In Acts 2, it validated the Apostles' testimony and in Acts 10 it validated the Gentiles as potential converts. It may conjoin with faith and baptism in Acts 10 as a part of the conversion experience, but that is not its primary role contra Robby Kagarise, "'Baptized with the Holy Spirit': Soteriological and Empowerment in Lucan Pneumatology," *EJ* 24 (2006): 19-33. In a related argument, Lim Yeu Chuen attempts to revive an older Pentecostal argument that tongues should be normative for every Christian; "Acts 10: A Gentile Model for Pentecostal Experience," *AJPS* 1 (1998): 62-72. His argument fails to persuade at two points. First, the baptism of the Holy Spirit is not a conversion experience in Acts 2. Hence, it is a misnomer to identify it as an experience predicated on conversion. Second, both Acts 2 and 10 are church-founding experiences. The baptism of the Spirit provided essential validation for the 'birth' of the Jewish and Gentile churches respectively. It is tenuous to suggest that what happened in the founding of the church should be normative for each individual Christian who subsequently joins the body of Christ.

[9] Luke reserves this title for the weightiest of occasions. He only uses it two more times—when James penned a letter authenticating the Gospel of Grace preached by Paul and Barnabas (15:26) and when he concluded his second volume with a crescendo of Paul's preaching (28:31).

[10] E.g., Martin Hengel and Anna Maria Schwemer, *Paul between Damascus and Antioch* (London: SCM, 1997), 256-257, see Acts 12 as a flashback, out of chronological sequence. The purpose, they assert, was to explain why the offering was given to the Elders and not the Apostles (11:30) who had been run out of town by the persecution of Agrippa. Haenchen (331) builds an argument on the loose chronological marker "about this time" (12:1) that Barnabas and Saul endured the persecution of Agrippa alongside James and Peter, thus linking the two churches of Antioch and Jerusalem in benevolence *and* suffering.

who identifies this entire chapter as a literary 'linkage' between the ministries of Peter and Paul: "The surprising interruption of the story of Barnabas and Paul in 11.27-30/12.25 by a story about Peter in 12:1-24 is . . . the result of Luke's concern to establish a strong literary transition from Petrine to the Pauline cycle of his narrative."[11] If Longenecker is correct, chapter 12 is neither awkward nor unrelated but is an important and artistic piece that links the two major players of the book. Here we watch as Peter steps offstage, giving way to the work of the now converted Apostle to the Gentiles.

1. The First 'Christian' Church in Antioch (11:19-30)

[19]**Now those who had been scattered by the persecution in connection with Stephen traveled as far as Phoenicia, Cyprus and Antioch, telling the message only to Jews. [20]Some of them, however, men from Cyprus and Cyrene, went to Antioch and began to speak to Greeks[12] also, telling them the good news about the Lord Jesus. [21]The Lord's hand was with them, and a great number of people believed and turned to the Lord.**

11:19. Luke takes us back to the persecution of Saul. In fact, the word "scattered" (*diaspeirō*) is only used three times in the whole New Testament, once here and twice in chapter 8 (vv. 1, 4). Luke thus links the two texts. In essence, before we can move beyond Peter's recent adventures, we must recall the tale of terror concerning Saul.[13] The consequence of his pre-Christian persecution continues. He sent Christians fleeing for their lives to the Island of Cyprus, to Cyrene on the northern shore of Africa,[14] Phoenicia (modern Lebanon), and to Antioch far beyond the pale of Jerusalem jurisdiction.

Antioch was a city strategically designed by Seleucus Nicaonor in 300 B.C. (Josephus, *Apion* 2.4 §39). It was located fifteen miles up the Orontes River as a protected port off the Mediterranean coast.[15] He laid it out with a grid of streets

---

[11] Bruce W. Longenecker, "Lukan Aversion to Humps and Hollows: The Case of Acts 11.27–12.25," *NTS* 50 (2004): 197. Not only does he identify this 'AbaB' linking device as common and valued by Lucian and Quintilian (185-187), he also shows how Luke uses it in each of the major transitions of the book: 1:1–8:3; 8:4–12:25; 13:1–19:41; 20:1–28:31 (201-204).

[12] The word Ἑλληνιστάς likely implies not merely ethnic Greeks (NIV, RSV, NASB, ASV, Vulgate) but also 'pagans'—what Jews might call "goyim" or "Gentiles" (ESV, NKJV, NLT "Hellenists", KJV "Grecians"). Cf. Pierson Parker, "Three Variant Readings in Luke-Acts," *JBL* 83 (1964): 167-168. The same would be true regardless of whether one follows the textual variant Ἕλληνας in P⁷⁴, ℵᶜ, A, D*, 1518. In this context, the implication of "Greeks" is not a specific ethnic group but a synecdoche for all non-Jews (cf. Gal 3:28; Col 3:11).

[13] Luke uses this word "persecution" (θλῖψις) sparingly (5 of its 43 NT uses). In fact, he never uses it in his Gospel even where he parallels Synoptics material (Mark 4:17/Matt 13:21/Luke 8:13; Mark 13:19/Matt 24:21; Mark 13:24/Matt 24:29). Furthermore, elsewhere in Acts he only has it once on the lips of Stephen (7:10-11) and twice Paul (14:22; 20:23), who uses it himself 22x in his letters.

[14] Clearly, the Jewish population of Cyrene had a strong connection with her roots in the land of Israel. Simon from Cyrene carried the cross of Jesus (Mark 15:21/Matt 27:32/Luke 23:26), pilgrims from Cyrene were present at Pentecost (Acts 2:10), the Synagogue of the Freedmen had members from Cyrene (Acts 6:9) and Lucius, one of the leaders of the church of Antioch, hailed from Cyrene (13:1).

[15] Syrian Antioch was the most important of more than two dozen ancient cities that bore the same name. Today Syrian Antioch sits on the very southern tip of Turkey. For more thorough information on the ancient city see Glanville Downey, *Ancient Antioch* (Princeton: University Press, 1963); Wayne Meeks and R. Wilcken, *Jews and Christians in Antioch* (Missoula: Scholars, 1978); and R. E. Brown and J. P. Meier, *Antioch and Rome* (New York: Paulist, 1982).

which could maximize the exposure to cool afternoon breezes from the sea. This valuable commercial center boasted a population of 500,000 or more, the third largest city of the Empire behind Rome and Alexandria (Josephus, *J.W.* 3.2.4 §29). But it was not just an architecturally designed city; it was socially engineered to promote Hellenism. This led to a multicultural city with four ethnic districts, each separated by walls within the city. Needless to say, they did not exactly 'celebrate diversity' in the same way moderns might in the western world. Moreover, it was a moral cesspool due to the cult of Apollo in Daphne, just five miles away.[16] Juvenal remarked sarcastically that "the sewage of the Syrian Orontes has for long been discharged into the Tiber" (cf. *Sat.* 3.62).[17] The large Jewish population there made it ripe for the spread of the gospel (Josephus, *J.W.* 7.3.3 §43; cf. Acts 6:5).[18]

11:20-21. Initially these beleaguered believers shared the good news of Jesus only with fellow Jews. But a group of these refugees somehow rubbed shoulders with Greeks who took an interest in their *Messiah*. Of course, that terminology made no sense to the Greeks, so the word "*Lord*" (a title commonly attributed to the Emperor) served as an acceptable substitute.[19] There is no evidence that they heard about Peter's recent expedition to Caesarea and used it as justification for their own actions. Nor is there mention of the prompting of the Holy Spirit or the inspiration from the ancient prophets to propel them into these uncharted waters. Rather, it appears to be the natural result of living as a Christian community in the midst of a diverse population. Their Greek neighbors were drawn to this liberating and universal message of Jesus, and God approved their evangelistic efforts by adding his "hand" to the mix.[20] This increased the boldness of the Jewish evangelists as well as the numbers who turned to the Lord in faith and repentance.

The reader should note this seemingly mundane statement (v. 20). These unnamed evangelists, surprisingly, are the only group in the entire book to have deliberately crossed ethnic and geographic lines for the sake of the gospel. Certainly Paul and Barnabas will be featured in powerful missionary travels. However, their efforts were either in their native lands or prompted by a vision of God, a natural impediment, or raw persecution that propelled them onward and out-

---

[16] The fame of this cult was such that Tacitus (*Annals* 2.83) identified Antioch with the term "at Daphne" (ἡ ἐπί Δάφνη).

[17] Bruce, 238, ponders whether this "sewage" for Juvenal included the Christians who arose on the banks of the Orontes.

[18] Cf. Natalio Fernández Marcos, "El Protoluciánico: Revisión griega de los Judíos de Antioquía?" *Biblica* 64 (1983): 423-427, and S. E. Johnson, "Antioch, the Base of Operations," *LTQ* 18 (1983): 64-73.

[19] The word "Lord" (κύριος) is used 3x in these two verses with no distinction between Jesus and Yahweh. This indicates the view these evangelists had of Jesus. If it is correct that this represents a final stage of an evolutionary development of the proclamation of Jesus (*e.g., Beginnings* 4:129), it tells how quickly such a Christology came to full fruition.

[20] The "hand" of the Lord is generally a metaphor for his power, particularly militarily might exercised against Israel's enemies (Exod 9:3; Josh 4:24; Judg 2:15; 1 Sam 5:6, 9; 6:9; 7:13; Psa 75:8; Jer 25:17; 51:7; Acts 13:11) or punishment against his people (Exod 16:3; Deut 2:15; Josh 22:31; Ruth 1:13; Job 19:21; Isa 40:2; 51:17), but it can also signify God's miraculous revelation or guidance through prophets (2 Kgs 3:15; 2 Chr 28:19; Ezra 7:6, 28; Prov 21:1; Ezek 1:3; 3:14, 22; 33:22; 37:1; 40:1; Luke 1:66) as well as the general blessings or rewards in this life (2 Chr 30:12; Job 12:9; Eccl 2:24; Isa 25:10; 41:20; 49:4; 62:3; 66:14; Acts 4:30).

ward. For the participant in the modern missionary movement, these Cypriots and Cyrenians serve as a compelling model seldom matched between then and the explosion of the lay-missionary movement late in the twentieth century.[21]

²²News of this reached the ears of the church at Jerusalem, and they sent Barnabas to Antioch. ²³When he arrived and saw the evidence of the grace of God, he was glad and encouraged them all to remain true to the Lord with all their hearts. ²⁴He was a good man, full of the Holy Spirit and faith, and a great number of people were brought to the Lord. ²⁵Then Barnabas went to Tarsus to look for Saul, ²⁶and when he found him, he brought him to Antioch. So for a whole year Barnabas and Saul met with the church and taught great numbers of people. The disciples were called Christians first at Antioch.

11:22. When Philip opened the gospel in Samaria, the Apostles in Jerusalem sent Peter and John as delegates to check it out (8:14). The same thing is happening here. The Church of Jerusalem caught wind of this multiethnic church and wanted to authenticate it by sending an authoritative delegate. Since Peter had just defended Gentile evangelism, why do they need to validate it? Well, first of all, they are not validating Gentile evangelism but a new church movement. This is not merely a Gentile household receiving Jesus but a whole multiethnic church. They had never seen one of those before. They needed to make sure it was orthodox. Second, they were not merely authenticating it but validating it. This was not merely a stamp of approval, it was about blessing. If the church of Jerusalem recognized and authenticated the work in Antioch, the church remained a single entity.

11:23-24. It was appropriate that Barnabas was the one chosen for this assignment. (1) Antioch was planted by Hellenists from Cyprus and Cyrene. Since Barnabas was from Cyprus, he likely knew these Christian Jews, so his encouragement and/or rebuke would carry more weight. (2) Barnabas was personally known to the Apostles from the early days of the church and (3) they had nicknamed him "Son of Encouragement." Rightly so, for he consistently fought for the underdog, giving money to the poor (4:36-37), introducing Paul to the Apostles (9:27), and defending John Mark (15:36-39). (4) His own ethnic and geographic background enabled him to understand the multicultural setting of Antioch. (5) He apparently had such personal gravitas that he was mentioned first among the leaders of the church at Antioch (13:1), he was the dominant leader of the first missionary journey (13:2, 7), and the people of Lystra mistook him for none other than Zeus (14:12). He is, in colloquial terms, the big man on campus. (6) Aside from all this, he is described as a "good man, full of the Holy Spirit and faith" (11:24). These are descriptions Luke reserved elsewhere for Joseph of Arimathea ("good man," Luke 23:50) and Stephen ("Full of the Holy Spirit and faith," Acts 6:5). As a result of Barnabas's leadership, the church at Antioch exploded.

---

[21] John H. Orme has drawn from this passage a number of helpful missionary principles; cf. "Antioquía: Paradigma para la Iglesia y la misión," *Kairós* 25 (1999): 29-36.

11:25-26. We may never know Barnabas's motives in bringing Saul to Antioch. Perhaps the church needed Saul's gifts, perhaps Saul needed an opportunity for ministry, or perhaps Barnabas needed a hand. We do know at least two things. First, Barnabas went to great lengths to locate Saul. The word "look" (*anazēteō*, v. 25) implies a difficult search (cf. Luke 2:44-45). Why was Saul hard to find? It is not likely that he was silent during these 'silent' years. If he preached in Arabia during his stint there, earning for himself enemies, it is probable he was doing the same thing at Tarsus. If Saul's preaching in Tarsus led to similar persecution, he might be on the run. In addition, this might explain some of the sufferings he lists in 2 Corinthians 12:23-26 for which Luke does not account. Second, Barnabas's decision paid big dividends. Saul shared the teaching load, blessing the burgeoning body of believers. The church grew among the Gentiles with unprecedented success.

"*The disciples were called Christians first at Antioch.*" Though this term "Christian" is only used in two other passages in the entire New Testament (Acts 26:28; 1 Pet 4:16), it came to be the dominant designation for believers in the Messiah Jesus. But why did it start here? What, precisely did the term mean? And did it originate as a self-designation or did others label the church "Christians"?

Two terms require clarification. First, the word "**called**" (*chrēmatizō*) in Greek literature originally meant "to do business." Later it morphed into the idea of accepting the *title* of an office or a *name* one inscribes in official records, whether a family name or national citizenship.[22] In other words, *chrēmatizō* is most appropriate in a public or even a legal context. Moreover, *chrēmatizō* is *active* not *passive*. Thus, the NIV's "were called" would more accurately be rendered "took the name."[23] The Patristic fathers understood "Christians" as a *self*-designation, not a label placed upon the church derisively by unbelievers.[24] In conclusion, the church at Antioch assumed the name "Christian" but what did they have in mind?

The term "Christian" is interesting because it is a Hebrew word with a Latin ending which was transliterated into Greek. First, the Latin ending *iani* was used to designate groups that were devoted to a particular political leader.[25] Second, if a Latin ending is appended to a Hebrew title in Antioch, there is a strong possibility that it originated in a social or legal setting. All the first-century non-biblical sources that mention "Christ" or "Christian" associate them with public disorders.[26] One wonders, therefore, if there were not some turbulent results of

---

[22] Elias J. Bickerman, "The Name Christians," *HTR* 42 (1949): 110-112, establishes this with a plethora of primary sources. Elsewhere in the NT "called" (χρηματίζω) indicates a supernatural warning (Matt 2:2, 12; Heb 8:5; 11:7; 12:25; cf. LXX Jer 25:30; 26:2; 30:2; 36:2, 4) or revelation (Luke 2:26; Acts 10:22; cf. LXX Jer 29:23) seven out of its nine uses.

[23] Justin Taylor, "Why Were the Disciples First Called 'Christians' at Antioch? (Acts 11, 26)," *RB* 101 (1994): 83. Cf. Bickerman, 12-14, for the excellent discussion of this grammatical point.

[24] Though most commentators view "Christians" as a term of derision given the church by outsiders, this author suggests that the linguistic evidence points to a self-designation. Ignatius (d. c. A.D. 98–117), the bishop of Antioch, was the first to use this term broadly, and he took it as a self-designation of the church as well. Others who agree with this view include Bickerman, "The Name," 14; H. B. Mattingly, "The Origin of the Name Christiani," *JTS* 9 (1958): 26-37, and C. Spicq, "Ce que signifie le titre de Chretien," *ST* 14 (1961): 68-78.

[25] E.g., "Herodianoi," "Pompeiianoi," or "Augustianoi," cf. Taylor, "Christians," 76-78.

[26] E.g., Josephus, *Ant.* 18.3.3 §64; Tacitus, *Annals* 15.44; Pliny, *Epistles* 10.96-97; Lucian, *Alexander* 25.38.

the multiethnic evangelism in Antioch that brought the believers face to face with civic rulers who wondered what to call them.[27] As a cross-cultural group, they fit no known category. Legal documents would require some kind of appellation for the factions involved. It appears that the believers labeled themselves "*Christiani.*" Notice, they are not "Jesusiani." The point is not their love for the person of Jesus but their loyalty to the Messiah/King whose rule is extending beyond the borders of Israel.[28] It was a bold move, to be sure, but one true to the ancient hopes of Israel and appropriate for the new converts from the Greco-Roman world whose allegiance to Caesar must now give way to fidelity to the King of kings.[29] "To express this relationship between the Messiah and his elect, the disciples at Antioch, speaking to the pagan world, could not style themselves: 'slaves of Christ'. . . . The term χριστιανοί on the other hand, made it clear that they were agents, representatives of the Messiah."[30]

[27]During this time some prophets came down from Jerusalem to Antioch. [28]One of them, named Agabus, stood up and through the Spirit predicted that a severe famine would spread over the entire Roman world. (This happened during the reign of Claudius.) [29]The disciples, each according to his ability, decided to provide help for the brothers living in Judea. [30]This they did, sending their gift to the elders by Barnabas and Saul.

11:27. "During this time" is not really a chronological marker.[31] It is a loose connective that simply means "next I want to talk about." This is the fourth and last time Luke will use it in Acts. This likely indicates that the earlier material in Acts is more distant to Luke and thus more difficult to nail down on a calendar. As stated earlier, this material (11:27–12:25) is both literary and logical. Literarily it links the Cornelius episode with Paul's mission to the Gentiles. Logically, it explains the crucial transition away from Apostolic hegemony in the early church.

11:28-29. One of the prophets from Jerusalem, Agabus, will feature again in Acts 21:28, warning Paul of the impending persecution in Jerusalem. There he looks like a classic Old Testament theatrical prophet, using Paul's belt as a stage prop to make his point.[32] Here he predicts a famine which ravaged the Empire during the reign of Claudius (A.D. 41–54). There was no known Empire-wide (*oikoumenē*) famine during Claudius's reign. However, such a hyperbole is perfectly appropriate to describe the severe famine in Judea under Tiberius Alexander (A.D. 46–48) which was likely linked to the devastating floods of Egypt (A.D. 45–46). This natural disaster destroyed much of their crops, resulting in a

[27] Taylor, "Christians," 84-91, offers plausible historical reconstruction for riots in Antioch as the *Sitz im Leben* of this passage.

[28] Cf. Baruch Lifshitz, "L'origine du nom des Chretiens," *VC* 16 (1962): 65-70.

[29] *Chrtistiani* would, therefore, have essentially the same meaning as δοῦλος Χριστοῦ as well as the OT term "Servant of the Lord." This is not a "slave" *per se*, but a "minister" or an "officer" of the court.

[30] Bickerman, "The Name Christians," 123.

[31] Literally "In those days" (Ἐν ταύταις δὲ ταῖς ἡμέραις, cf. Luke 1:39; 2:1; 5:35; 6:12; 21:23; 23:7; 24:18; Acts 1:15; 6:1; 9:37; 11:27).

[32] The gift of prophecy was revered in the NT church (Acts 15:32; 21:9-10; 1 Cor 12:28; 14:29; Eph 4:11), and itinerant prophets continued with popularity in the second century (*Didache* 11:7-12).

drastic increase in food prices the following years.[33] Consequently, the church in Antioch summoned their resources and sent a collection to the suffering saints in Jerusalem. Their decision was deliberate. The word Luke chooses to describe it (*horizō*) is elsewhere used only of a decree of God (Luke 22:22; Acts 2:23; 10:42; 17:26, 31; Rom 1:4; Heb 4:7) which is almost always a declaration about Jesus (save Acts 17:26 and Heb 4:7). It would be too much to suggest that God prompted the believers in Antioch to serve their brothers in Jerusalem as if they were Jesus. It would not be too much, however, to say that this decision was prompted by God through the prophets and leaders of the church.

Perhaps even more significantly, the economic sharing in Antioch showed that this church was a *bona fide* extension of the Jerusalem believers who practiced the same kind of benevolence (cf. Acts 2:44-45; 4:32-37).[34] Perhaps it is no accident that Barnabas was a prominent leader among both groups. The Christians in Antioch sent relief to sustain those in Judea because they were "brothers" in the most real and important sense of the word! This act of compassion is not a result of Christianity changing their ethical system. Families in the Middle East always took care of each others' needs. What changed was not their ethics but the boundary lines of 'family'.

11:30. Barnabas and Saul were the natural delegates to deliver the offering to Jerusalem. What is surprising is not who took the offering but who received it—the Elders. This leadership position comes straight out of Israel. Hence, it would be natural for the early church, essentially a messianic synagogue, to structure their leaders from familiar patterns. The surprise, therefore, is not the presence of Elders but the absence of Apostles.[35] Though they will make one final appearance in Jerusalem (15:4, 6, 22-23), there is now a virtual silence of the Twelve after dominating the first half of the book. The "Apostles" are mentioned twenty-five times in chapters 1–11 and in every chapter except 3 (which concentrates on Peter and John), 7 (Stephen's historical survey), and 10 (Peter and Cornelius). Their 'disappearance' is most likely explained by their own itinerant travels as well as the transition to local leaders. As the church expands to diverse places, peoples, and cultures, Elders are needed to lead in culturally specific and appropriate ways.

---

[33] This theory is articulated by Kenneth Gapp, "The Universal Famine under Claudius," *HTR* 28 (1935): 258-265. There were other noted famines as well: Suetonius, *Claudius* 18.2; Tacitus, *Annals* 12.43; Dio Cassius, *Hist.* 60.11; Orosius, *Hist.* 7.6.17; Josephus, *Ant.* 3.15.3 §320.

[34] Just as Jerusalem was the capital of Jewish evangelism, so Antioch now becomes the center for Gentile mission. This heavy emphasis on Antioch may be explained by Luke's own biography. There was a strong tradition that Luke lived in Antioch at the time of Barnabas's and Saul's arrival (*Beginnings* 2:247-249). Here in verse 28, the Western text includes the first "we" of the book, placing Luke at the scene with this additional line: "There was great rejoicing as *we* conversed together. . . ." Cf. Eduard Delebecque, "Saul et Luc avant le premier voyage missionnaire: comparaison des deux versions des Actes 11:22-26," *RSPT* 66 (1982): 551-559. In addition, the anti-Marcionite prologue of the third Gospel (c. 170 A.D.) reads: "Luke was an Antiochian of Syria" (cf. Bruce 17, ftn. 6). Eusebius repeats this tradition (*Eccl. Hist.* 3.4.7) as does Jerome (*On Illustrius Men*, 7; *Preface to Commentary on Matthew*).

[35] Hengel and Schwemer (256-257) argue that the Apostles would naturally be the ones to receive the funds (Acts 4:37; 5:2). This does not account, however, for the election of the Seven Evangelists who took over the task of benevolence. It may be that between chapter 4 and 11 the dispersed Evangelists were replaced by Elders in overseeing the economic needs of the Jerusalem church.

EXCURSUS

EXCURSUS ON PAUL'S VISITS TO JERUSALEM

One of the most vexing problems of this book is aligning the visits of Paul in Acts with those in Galatians 1–2. *The book of Acts records five visits of Paul to Jerusalem:* (1) After his time in Damascus, 9:26-30; (2) famine relief offering, 11:27-30; 12:25; (3) Jerusalem Council, 15:1-34; (4) between the 2nd and 3rd missionary journeys, 18:22; (5) second offering and arrest, 21:15-23. *Paul's Epistles only record three visits to Jerusalem* (Gal 1:18; 2:1-10; Rom 15:26-28). That, in and of itself, is no real problem. After all, one can hardly expect either corpus to slavishly follow the details of the other. The difficulty is in attempting to align the visits of Acts and the Epistles. The first and last visits are no problem—they align perfectly (Gal 1:18 [=Acts 9:26-30]; 2:1; and Rom 15:26-28 [= Acts 21:15-23]). The difficulty is with the second visit of the Epistles (Gal 2:1-10). Is it to be equated with the second visit in Acts (11:27-30; 12:25) or with the third visit in Acts (15:1-34)? Strong arguments can be made for either option:[36]

Option #1, Galatians 2:1-10 = Acts 11:27-30; 12:25:[37] In Galatians 1, Paul makes a big deal out of the fact that he was instructed by Jesus directly rather than through men, even the Apostles. He claims that he only visited Jerusalem twice. Once for two weeks after his three-year stint in Arabia/Damascus. Then his next visit was fourteen years later when the Apostles asked him to remember the poor (Gal 2:1, 10). If Paul failed to mention a third visit (between these two), his opponents could accuse him of withholding pertinent information simply to make his argument look stronger.[38] Furthermore, there is no mention in this chapter of the Apostolic decree (Acts 15:24-29) which Paul subsequently delivered to the churches he established (Acts 15:30; 16:4; 21:25). If Galatians 2 is a response to the Jerusalem council, how could he fail to mention this vital document?[39] What we have in Galatians 2 is not the Jerusalem decree, but a private meeting in which the 'Pillars' of the church exhorted Paul and Barnabas to remember the poor, the very issue highlighted in Acts 11:27-30. (One won-

---

[36] Some have abandoned altogether a chronological explanation. Haenchen (325-230) argues that Acts 11 and 15 tell of the same visit but Luke confused them as two separate occasions. Similarly, Ramón Trevijano Echeverría, "El Contrapunto Lucano (Hch 9, 26-30; 11, 27-30; 12, 25 y 15, 1-35) A Gal 1, 18-20 y 2, 1-10," *Salm* 44 (1998): 295-339, argues that Luke conflated his sources on Paul's journeys to Jerusalem just as he did with Jesus' journeys in the Gospel of Luke, so that Acts 11:27-30 = Gal 2:1-10 *and* Acts 15:1-3 = Gal 2:1-5; similarly see Georg Strecker, "Die sogenannte zweite Jerusalemreise des Paulus," *ZNW* 53 (1962): 67-77. Robert Funk, "The Enigma of the Famine Visit," *JBL* 75 (1956): 130-136, avers that this famine visit belongs with Paul's final visit to Jerusalem where Agabus is also mentioned and where Paul offers help to the Jerusalem Christians (24:17) as instructed (Gal 2:10). This 'misplacement' allows Luke to connect Barnabas with the offering, since he was there when the Apostles gave the command to take it up, even though he and Paul had since parted ways (15:39). Though these explanations work logically, they demand that Luke radically dissected his sources to engineer them for his own literary agenda. There is little evidence that Luke treated his sources in such a cavalier fashion either here or elsewhere.

[37] Supported by Bruce (244, 298-300), Ash (167), Marshall (204-205, 243-248), Stott (206, 242-243), Witherington (375, 440-449, 817-820), Bock (496), and David Trobisch, "The Council of Jerusalem in Acts 15 and Paul's Letter to the Galatians," in *Theological Exegesis* (Grand Rapids: Eerdmans, 1999), 331-338.

[38] Although, if his point is about *Apostolic* teaching, it might be reasonable to omit a visit in which he met no Apostles. The Apostles are, in fact, conspicuously absent in Acts 11:30.

[39] A point stressed by Joe Morgado, "Paul in Jerusalem: A Comparison of His Visits in Acts and Galatians," *JETS* 37 (1994): 64.

ders, however, why they would give this exhortation when Paul was holding a bag of coins collected from their Gentile brothers).[40] This option also alleviates the severe criticism of Peter in Galatians 2:11-14. He blew it by abandoning the Gentile fellowship. If he did that *after* Acts 15 then it was not merely a personal failure but a breach of the decree by the Jerusalem Council!

Option #2, Galatians 2:1-10 = Acts 15:1-34:[41] The striking similarities between Galatians 2 and Acts 15 are hard to ignore. It is the same issue, in the same place, with the same players. Galatians is not merely similar to Acts 15 but also to Romans (not to mention 1–2 Corinthians). One would assume, therefore, these books were written close to the same time, pushing the production of Galatians after the council of Acts 15. Perhaps Paul's silence of the Jerusalem council in Galatians 2 is precisely because they *already had* the decree in a separate document. Another clue to the later date of Galatians is 4:13, "As you know, it was because of an illness that I first preached the gospel to you." If this implies a second visit to Galatia that would almost certainly postdate the counsel (although Paul's return trip through Galatia might count as a second visit, Acts 14:21). Moreover, Paul's Apostolic authority and precedence over Barnabas would seem to require a date later than Acts 11.[42] Finally, Paul claimed he returned to Jerusalem with Barnabas and Titus fourteen years after his first visit to Jerusalem. This fits the later date of Acts 15 a lot easier than that of 11.[43]

There is no question that this question is perplexing, and each solution has both strengths and weaknesses. With that caveat, it seems to this author that the solution with the least problems is to equate Galatians 2 with this present famine relief visit in Acts 11.

---

[40] Bruce, 244, notes that this meeting was prompted by a "revelation" (Gal 2:2) and wonders if that might be connected with Agabus's prophetic visit. He dates this visit at c. A.D. 46, which would postdate chapter 12.

[41] Supported by Rackham (140-141, 183, 238-240), Reese (424-425, 527-533), Polhill (275, 321-323, 327, 334-335), Johnson (6, 7, 208, 270), Gaertner (188-189, 231-236, 243), Fitzmyer (539-542).

[42] Robert Stein, "The Relationship of Galatians 2:1-10 and Acts 15:1-35: Two Neglected Arguments," *JETS* 17 (1974): 239-242.

[43] Herod Agrippa died in A.D. 44 (Acts 12:23). If this chapter is in correct chronological order, that would place the Jerusalem council c. A.D. 50. Thus Paul's conversion would be 17 years earlier c. A.D. 33. If, however, one parallels Galatians 2 with Acts 11, the fourteen years must be reckoned from Paul's conversion rather than his first Jerusalem visit and counted inclusively not to have Paul converted prior to Jesus' crucifixion. For a reasonable defense of this earlier dating see William B. Decker, "The Early Dating of Galatians," *RQ* 2 (1958): 132-138.

ACTS 12

2. The First State-Sponsored Persecution in Jerusalem (12:1-25)

As we turn the page to chapter 12, we expect Luke to lead onward into Gentile territory. He's been heading in that direction for the past four chapters. Surprisingly, he takes another look at Jerusalem in the rearview mirror. Though it may seem out of place at first, Luke deliberately recounts this tale in order to exit Peter stage left, leaving full space for Saul center stage. This is neither a flashback nor a tangent. It is a literary mechanism to link the ministries of Peter and Paul. Chapter 12 not only joins the two major players of the book, it explains the transition away from both the Apostolic founders and the city of Jerusalem as the center of the church.

[1]It was about this time[1] that King Herod arrested some who belonged to the church, intending to persecute them. [2]He had James, the brother of John, put to death with the sword. [3]When he saw that this pleased the Jews, he proceeded to seize Peter also. This happened during the Feast of Unleavened Bread. [4]After arresting him, he put him in prison, handing him over to be guarded by four squads of four soldiers each. Herod intended to bring him out for public trial after the Passover.

12:1. The chapter opens with a historical note on Herod Agrippa I, the last king of Israel.[2] Perhaps a bit of his biography will help set the stage.[3] His own father, Aristobulus, had been murdered by Herod the Great in 7 B.C. on suspicion of plotting patricide to obtain his father's throne. Agrippa was four years old at the time and carried in his veins the royal blood of his grandmother, Miriamne, daughter of the Jewish High Priest. For fear of his paranoid paternal grandfather, Agrippa was sent to Rome where he was raised as a favorite in the royal palace. There he became fast friends with Gaius (Caligula), his childhood

---

[1] Luke opens the story with another one of his notoriously vague chronological markers, "about this time," cf. Luke 1:39; 2:1; 5:35; 6:12; 21:23; 23:7; 24:18; Acts 1:15; 6:1; 9:37; 11:27. This also likely indicates that Luke is relying on secondhand sources where he does not have as specific information as when he joins the narrative later on. Paradoxically, this chapter contains the first incident we are able to date definitively since Herod Agrippa I died in A.D. 44.

[2] Luke is fond of mentioning this notorious family. He tells of Herod the Great (Luke 1:5), though he leaves it to Matthew (2:1-19) to recount the murder of the children of Bethlehem. Luke (3:1, 19-20; 9:7-9) aligns with Mark (6:14-29) and Matthew (14:1-12) in narrating the beheading of John the Baptist by Herod Antipas, the son of Herod the Great. There the parallels end. Only Luke tells of Herod Philip's reign (Luke 3:1), Antipas's attempt to arrest Jesus (Luke 13:31-35), and his interview of Jesus at his terminal trial (Luke 23:7-12). Moreover, his fascination with the family continues in the book of Acts, telling of Agrippa I (grandson of Herod the Great) executing James (Acts 12:1-24), and his son, Agrippa II interviewing Paul (Acts 25:13–26:32). In addition, he mentions both Agrippa II's sisters: Berenice, his traveling 'companion' (Acts 25:13; 26:30), and Drusilla, the wife of Governor Felix (Acts 24:24).

[3] Most of the pertinent information comes from Josephus, *Ant.* 18.5.3 §126; 18.5.4 §131-134; 18.6.1-5 §143-169; 18.6.6 §179-204; 18.6.10–18.8.8 §228-301; 19.4.1 §236-244; 19.4.5 §265; 19.5.1 §274-277; 19.5.3 §288; 19.6.1–19.9.1 §292-354.

playmate. In fact, it was his affection for Gaius that caused his temporary imprisonment when he was overheard wishing for the death of Emperor Tiberias, so
his grand-nephew, Gaius, could take the throne. Upon Tiberias's death, Gaius
did rise to power and with him went Herod (A.D. 37). He inherited the former
Tetrarchies of Philip and Lysanias (cf. Luke 3:1) as well as the title "king of the
Jews." Two years later his reign was expanded to include Galilee and Perea when
Gaius deposed Antipas, Agrippa's crooked uncle. In A.D. 41, after the assassination of Gaius, Claudius took the throne and favored Agrippa further with the
entire realm of Judea which had been under a Roman procurator since A.D. 6.

By any account, his life was paradoxically tragic and successful. Even the
Jews were comparatively fond of him. For example, during the Feast of Tabernacles in the Sabbatical year (A.D. 40), he read aloud from Deuteronomy 17:14-
20. When he came to verse 5, he wept for the words: "Be sure to appoint over
you the king the LORD your God chooses. He must be from among your own
brothers. Do not place a foreigner over you, one who is not a brother Israelite"
(cf. *m. Sotah* 7.8). He knew all too well his own Edomite heritage. The crowds,
however, remembered that his grandmother, Miramne, was a Jewish princess,
whose blood made him Jewish. They cried, "Do not be afraid, Agrippa, you are
our brother, you are our brother, you are our brother." It was with this tragic
figure that Luke opens the window onto a most fascinating scene with which he
will conclude the narrative of Peter.

Though persecution is nothing new to the church, this episode is different. In Acts 4–5, only the Apostles suffered, and they did so under the heavy
hand of the Sanhedrin. In chapter 7–8, it was the malice of Saul and his zealous comrades that scattered the Hellenists under threat of pseudo-legal lynching. Here, for the first time, an officer of Rome leverages his political position
against Christians. On the one hand, it's nice to make such an impact that you
get noticed by the power brokers. On the other hand, this is hardly the kind of
press or pressure the church desired.

EXCURSUS
PERSECUTION

Polycarp rightly said, "The blood of the martyrs is seed [*of the church*]" (Tertullian, *Apology*, 50). It is a missiological principle that the church often grows due
to persecution. People tend to be more interested in something worth dying for
than something worth living for. Moreover, the church, in a brilliant sociological
maneuver, turned the shame of persecution into the honor of being like Jesus:
"I want to know Christ and the power of his resurrection and the fellowship
of sharing in his sufferings, becoming like him in his death, and so, somehow,
to attain to the resurrection from the dead" (Phil 3:10-11; cf. Acts 4:21). Jesus
promised that his followers would receive the same abuse he did (Mark 13:9/
Luke 21:12; John 15:18-20). If we don't die from the maltreatment, it forges in
us a character and witness that is worth the suffering: "Consider it pure joy, my

brothers, whenever you face trials of many kinds, because you know that the testing of your faith develops perseverance. Perseverance must finish its work so that you may be mature and complete, not lacking anything" (James 1:2-4; cf. 1 Pet 4:12-16). If, on the other hand, we die the martyr's death, God promises a co-inheritance with Christ (Rom 8:17; 2 Cor 4:17) which Paul says will be well worth it: "I consider that our present sufferings are not worth comparing with the glory that will be revealed in us" (Rom 8:18).

This all sounds idealistically wonderful. But the glorification of martyrdom is kind of like a Hollywood rendition of *Braveheart* or *Saving Private Ryan*. We are moved. The musical score and emotional story of bravery obfuscates the raw historical reality of grueling pain, social turmoil, and lifelong losses for orphans and widows. The brutality of persecution is an evil through which the church survives, even thrives, but it should never be glorified, encouraged, or accepted.

12:2-4. James, John's brother, was the first Apostolic martyr, drinking the cup Jesus promised (Mark 10:39). Surprisingly, Luke devotes a mere seven Greek words to his memory.[4] One would expect more. Then again, that is seven more words than any other Apostolic martyr receives, including Luke's heroes, Peter and Paul. He does point out that James was executed with a sword, a Roman-style decapitation as opposed to a Jewish stoning. This is terrifying, not for the mode of execution, but for the fact that it demonstrates Roman involvement. Things could easily snowball here into a systematic annihilation of the church in other Roman arenas. Fortunately, it did not, largely due to the fact that Herod's motive was not *anti*-Christian but *pro*-Jewish. The Jerusalem leaders saw the Apostles as a threat to their power in Jerusalem. Herod, in a macabre P. R. stunt takes out one of its key leaders. The response was so favorable that Herod then went for the most notable agent of the church.

Peter was taken during the Feast of Unleavened Bread (Passover),[5] which fell unusually late that year, on May 1, A.D. 44. This prevented an immediate public trial and execution (cf. Mark 14:2/Luke 22:2). Herod's timing was shrewd. Since Passover was the national day of liberation, it was then that Jewish sensibilities against a non-Davidic king would have been heightened. Herod can't do anything about his illegitimate regal heritage. He can, however, prove his worth to the Jewish leaders by using his power to accommodate their agenda. In the meantime, Peter was guarded by sixteen soldiers who took turns watching him, four at a time.[6] One might guess that such a heavy guard was suggested by the Jewish leaders after Peter's last escape (5:19).

---

[4] Eusebius (*Eccl. Hist.* 2.9) records a fascinating story he inherited from Clement of Alexandria (*Hypotyposes* 7). So the tale is told: "The one [soldier] who led James to the Judgment-seat, when he saw him bearing his testimony, was moved, and confessed that he was himself also a Christian. They were both therefore, led away together; and on the way he begged James to forgive him. And he, after considering a little, said, 'Peace be with thee', and kissed him. And thus they were both beheaded at the same time."

[5] If one wanted to be persnickety, Luke has made it look like the "Days of Unleavened Bread" preceded Passover when, in fact, the order is the reverse. The Passover meal kicks off the seven day festival of "Unleavened Bread." There terms are, of course, often used interchangeably.

[6] This may, in fact, only be the night guards who would rotate their watches every three hours from 6-9 p.m., 9 p.m.-12 a.m., 12-3 a.m., and 3-6 a.m. (cf. Vegetius, *On Military Affairs*, 3.8).

⁵So Peter was kept in prison, but the church was earnestly praying to God for him. ⁶The night before Herod was to bring him to trial, Peter was sleeping between two soldiers, bound with two chains, and sentries stood guard at the entrance. ⁷Suddenly an angel of the Lord appeared and a light shone in the cell. He struck Peter on the side and woke him up. "Quick, get up!" he said, and the chains fell off Peter's wrists. ⁸Then the angel said to him, "Put on your clothes and sandals." And Peter did so. "Wrap your cloak around you and follow me," the angel told him. ⁹Peter followed him out of the prison, but he had no idea that what the angel was doing was really happening; he thought he was seeing a vision. ¹⁰They passed the first and second guards and came to the iron gate leading to the city. It opened for them by itself, and they went through it. When they had walked the length of one street, suddenly the angel left him. ¹¹Then Peter came to himself and said, "Now I know without a doubt that the Lord sent his angel and rescued me from Herod's clutches and from everything the Jewish people were anticipating."

12:5. The Greek structure of this verse is marvelous. It comes in two parts which contrast one another in the same way we might say in English: "On the one hand . . . but on the other hand." On the one hand, Peter was locked in prison, but on the other hand the church was *earnestly* praying. Luke uses this word "earnestly" (*ektenōs*) only one other time—when he describes Jesus' passionate prayer in Gethsemane 📷 (Luke 22:44). The reader is to understand that the fervent prayers of the church are far more potent than Herod's schemes. Their prayers were undoubtedly inflamed by the celebration of Passover which bore hopes of eschatological liberation.[7] This was the right night for God to return and make things right.

12:6-8. Luke sketches the scene in vivid detail. The hourglass grows thin; in the morning Herod would bring Peter out to a kangaroo court. The charges would likely look like Stephen's: threatening the temple, blaspheming the law, and disturbing the peace. He is chained to two soldiers with two more standing guard at the locked door.[8] What grabs ones attention is Peter's *inattention*—he is sleeping just hours before his execution!

Suddenly an "Angel of the Lord" appeared. This title is used fifty times in the Old Testament and is the backdrop for its eleven uses in the New Testament (half of which are in the birth narratives, Matt 1:20, 24; 2:13, 19; 28:2; Luke 1:11; 2:9; Acts 5:19; 8:26; 12:7, 23). This is the second story of an angel releasing someone from prison (Acts 5:19), and both would have been familiar to Jewish ears. There were other such stories floating around out there.[9]

[7] August Strobel points out the strong connections Luke makes between this event and the description of Passover. Both took place at night (Exod 12:12; Acts 12:6), both stressed speed (Exod 12:11; Acts 12:7), and both used the words ζῶσαι and ὑποδῆσαι (Exod 12:11 LXX; Acts 12:8). Hence, Luke intends the reader to see this event in light of the redemptive hopes embedded in the Passover celebration (and continued in the Christian community into the 4th and 5th century according to *Epistola Apostolorum* 15). Cf. "Passa-Symbolik und Passa-Wunder in Act. xii. 3ff.," *NTS* 4 (1958): 210-215. The allusions to the resurrection of Jesus are less apparent but still provocative; cf. Walter Radle, "Befreiung aus dem Gefängnis: Die Darstellung eines biblischen Grundthemas in Apg 12," *BZ* 27 (1983): 92-95.
[8] Paradoxically, Agrippa had, himself, been chained to a guard while in Rome (Josephus, *Ant.* 18.6.7 §196) which was standard practice (Seneca, *Epistles* 5.7).
[9] Talbert (52-53), points to several similar stories: Euripides, *Bacchae* 443-448; Philostratus, *Apollonius*

The bright light accompanying the angel failed to rouse Peter. So the angel struck him in the side to wake him up and ordered him to get dressed and follow him out of the cell. Since his fetters had fallen off miraculously, Peter was free to obey.

12:9-11. Even while Peter was following the angel out of the prison, he thought it was a dream.[10] He's still pretty dazed from his latest REM cycle.[11] Of course, waltzing past the guards undetected and through the city gate which opened by itself gave the whole experience a surrealistic touch.[12] One can hardly blame Peter for feeling as if he were dreaming. It was only after walking the full length of a city street that the angel disappeared and Peter "came to himself." Standing alone in the cold air of a Passover night, he realized he had been dramatically *rescued.* Luke uses this word elsewhere to describe God's remarkable rescue of Joseph in Egypt (7:10) and later the entire nation of Israel (7:34). The word can mean "to pluck" (cf. Matt 5:29; 18:9) as in the case of Claudius Lysias "snatching" Paul from the irate mob pummeling him to death (23:27). Thus God commissioned his angel to pluck Peter from the clutches of Herod.

[12]When this had dawned on him, he went to the house of Mary the mother of John, also called Mark, where many people had gathered and were praying. [13]Peter knocked at the outer entrance, and a servant girl named Rhoda came to answer the door. [14]When she recognized Peter's voice, she was so overjoyed she ran back without opening it and exclaimed, "Peter is at the door!" [15]"You're out of your mind," they told her. When she kept insisting that it was so, they said, "It must be his angel." [16]But Peter kept on knocking, and when they opened the door and saw him, they were astonished. [17]Peter motioned with his hand for them to be quiet and described how the Lord had brought him out of prison. "Tell James and the brothers about this," he said, and then he left for another place. [18]In the morning, there was no small commotion among the soldiers as to what had become of Peter. [19a]After Herod had a thorough search made for him and did not find him, he cross-examined the guards and ordered that they be executed.

12:12. Once Peter realized the reality of the situation, he naturally went to Mary's house. It is common to speculate that this is the very place Jesus

---

7.38; Ovid, *Metamorphoses* 3.696-700; Artapanus, *Concerning the Jews* (as reported by Eusebius, *Praep. Evang.,* 9.27.23. Cf. J. Jeremias, *TDNT* 3:175-176. Due to the nature of the story and its similarities to other legends of the day, even scholars as conservative as Bruce (249-251) and Marshall (209) have entertained the possibility that the "angel" was a human agent who rescued Peter by quite natural, albeit surreptitious, means. I dare say Luke would be shocked if he ever learned that this was not a miraculous release. His rendition of the story gives not a hint of such an interpretation.

[10] Virtually every version translates ὅραμα as "vision" rather than "dream." That is proper since the word implies something that is seen, not to mention the fact that it is accompanied by the infinitive βλέπειν. However, dreams and visions are virtually indistinguishable in Acts. Dreams (ἐνύπνιον) are mentioned only in Acts 2:17 when quoting Joel's prophecy. Elsewhere, night "visions" (i.e., "dreams"), are simply called ὅραμα (16:9-10; 18:9). The visions of Cornelius (10:3) and Peter (10:17, 19; 11:5) were during the day. The visions of Ananias (9:10) and Saul (9:12) have no chronological marker. And the visions of Peter in Jerusalem (12:9) and Paul in Troas (16:9) and Corinth (18:9) were at night.

[11] Luke's wording is quite colorful. He uses the pluperfect (ᾔδει) to say, "Peter was in the present state of not understanding the reality of what he was experiencing."

[12] A door opening automatically is a feature found elsewhere. For example, Josephus claims that the brass Eastern Gate of the Temple opened at midnight on its own accord during the Roman siege (*J.W.* 6.5.3 §293).

celebrated his last Passover and where the 120 Christian's gathered (1:13-15) though there is no way to prove it. It was a well-known gathering place where they *convened* (*sunathroizō*, cf. 19:25) a considerable group for an emergency prayer meeting.

Luke introduces Mary's son, John Mark, preparing the reader for his coming debut on the missionary team (12:25) as a junior helper of Barnabas and Saul (13:5).[13] He was a cousin of Barnabas (Col 4:10, *anepsios*). After he abandoned the first missionary journey (13:13) Paul blacklisted him. In fact, when Paul suggested a return trip to the churches they planted, a delighted Barnabas was ready to give his cousin a second chance (15:37, 39). Paul, still bitter, refused, resulting in a rather dramatic breakup of the famous missionary team. The story of John Mark ends in Acts on a rather dour note. Fortunately, the epistles redeem his portrait. John Mark ministered with Paul during his Roman imprisonment according to Colossians 4:10 (cf. Philemon 1:24). And later, Paul appealed to Timothy (John's ostensible replacement on the second missionary journey) to bring John Mark with him "because he is helpful to me in my ministry" (2 Tim 4:11). The great Apostle was not alone in his regard for John Mark; Peter (the "pillar," Gal 2:9) calls him "my son Mark" (1 Pet 5:13, if, indeed this is the same "Mark"). John Mark's story is of reconciliation. One wonders whether the Gospel of Mark would ever have been written were it not for the gracious encouragement of Barnabas and Peter, who also knew a thing or two about second chances.

12:13-15. Mary's house was apparently a well-to-do home with a gate leading into the central courtyard. The 'guard' at the gate was a teenage girl (*paidiskē*) which was typical. This servant's role was not to fight off intruders, but merely to warn the security guards if something was amiss in the middle of the night (cf. John 18:16-18). Who better than a teenage girl to stay up late at night and scream real loud?

When Peter knocked, Rhoda (meaning "rose") went to the door. At the sound of his voice, the giddy girl runs to the assembly *without opening the door!* This touch of humor was typical in Greek plays. The 'running servant' who plays the buffoon was a standard motif that won uproarious applause from delighted audiences.[14] Rhoda announces excitedly that Peter had been released. Their prayers to God quickly turn to insults of the girl. They called her a "raving lunatic" (*mainomai*) which places her in the company of Jesus (John 10:20), Paul (Acts 26:24-25), and Spirit-filled Christians (1 Cor 14:23).[15] When she persisted, they insisted, "The

---

[13] It is entirely possible that we have met this lad before. In the second Gospel, likely written by this young man under Peter's tutelage (cf. Eusebius, *Eccl. Hist.* 2.15; 3.39.14-15; 5.8.3; 6.14.6), there is a strange story about a youth among Jesus' disciples in the Garden of Gethsemane. One of the soldiers took hold of his linen tunic and the spry young man wriggled free leaving the soldier with nothing but an extra 'shirt' and a striking memory of a frightened streaker (Mark 14:51-52). If this is not an autobiographical memoir, its inclusion is befuddling.

[14] Albert Harrill, "The Dramatic Function of the Running Slave Rhoda (Acts 13.13-16): A Piece of Greco-Roman Comedy," *NTS* 46 (2000): 150-157.

[15] Paradoxically, Rhoda is the only 'sane' one. Luke has used this motif before with the women coming from Jesus tomb. They were rejected as 'crazy' but they alone knew the truth (Luke 24:11).

voice you heard must be Peter's guardian angel."[16] The implication, of course, is that Herod prematurely executed Peter and thus his angel was released from his duty. How odd—the church prays (ostensibly) for Peter's release but immediately interprets his appearance as his death. Oh *we* of little faith.

12:16-17. Meanwhile, Peter kept knocking, obviously hoping not to wake the neighbors. He was, after all, a fugitive. Finally they opened the door. Much to their amazement, there he stood, in the flesh. Their excitement, no doubt, gave way to exuberant exclamations that put Peter in jeopardy. He motions with his hand for silence and likely moved the meeting inside, behind locked doors. After recounting his miraculous release, Peter went into hiding, and to this day the location has been kept secret.[17] Some say he snuck away to Rome,[18] and others suggest Antioch (cf. Gal 2:11-14),[19] but there's no way to know.

More significantly, Peter asks the group to inform James about the incident. Apparently, James, Jesus' brother, had become the key leader of the Jerusalem church.[20] This will be even more obvious during the Jerusalem Council (Acts 15:13-21) and later when Paul returned to Jerusalem with an offering (Acts 21:18). Paul himself called James a "pillar" of the church (Gal 2:9) and recounted Jesus' personal appearance to his half-brother (1 Cor 15:7). James would be stoned to death in c. A.D. 62 when the High Priest Ananus exercised the death penalty in the thin interval between the death of Procurator Festus and the arrival of his replacement, Albinus (Josephus, *Ant.* 20.9.1 §197; cf. Eusebius, *Eccl. Hist.* 2.23). As Peter leaves, James is left as the most notable leader of the Jerusalem believers.

12:18-19. One can only imagine the uproar the following morning. The guards opened the cell to relieve their colleagues only to find Peter's chains lying limp on the floor. Herod's detectives scoured the city for Peter but to no avail. He then examined the sixteen soldiers charged with Peter's security detail. To a man, they denied complicity. Since Herod was not prepared to entertain the idea of an angelic release, he concluded there must be a nefarious conspiracy among his ranks and thus, he had all sixteen executed.[21]

---

[16] There was, apparently, a belief that the guardian angel of an individual could take the human form of the individual they were to protect (Str-B 1:781-783; cf. Tobit 5:4). While there is no definitive scriptural proof for guardian angels, there are some robust Jewish traditions based upon such passages as Psa 91:11; Dan 3:28; 6:22; Matt 18:10; and Heb 1:14. There was also a belief that the soul of the departed person hung around for several days before departing to the netherworld.

[17] The peculiar thesis of Robinson (and later Smaltz) that Peter did actually die and this whole story is an allegory of his demise should be taken no more seriously than they take the biblical text; cf. Donald Robinson, "Where and When Did Peter Die?" *JBL* 64 (1945): 255-267 and Warren M. Smalz, "Did Peter Die in Jerusalem?" 71 (1952): 211-216.

[18] E.g., John Wenham, "Did Peter Go to Rome in A.D. 42?" *TB* 23 (1972): 94-102.

[19] E.g., Robert E. Osborne, "Where Did Peter Go?" *CJT* 14 (1968): 274-277.

[20] Robert Wall, "Successor to 'the Twelve' According to Acts 12:1-17," *CBQ* 53 (1991): 628-643, and Richard Bauckham, "James and the Jerusalem Church," in *The Book of Acts in Its Palestinian Setting* (ed. Richard Bauckham, vol. 4 in *The Book of Acts in Its First Century Setting*; Grand Rapids: Eerdmans, 1995), 415-480, argue persuasively for the historicity of the transition described here.

[21] Roman law mandated guards receive the punishment of their prisoners if they allowed them to escape (cf. Acts 16:27; 27:42). Though Herod was raised in Rome and familiar with Roman law, he would not necessarily have to follow it to the letter in his own court. The fact that there was an apparent conspiracy among his soldiers is impetus enough to execute them. In all fairness, the Greek word ἀπαχθῆναι probably means "to execute," but *may merely* mean "lead off to prison" (cf. *Beginnings* 4:139; e.g., Gen 39:22; 40:3; 42:16), though Luke does use the word for the execution of Jesus (Luke 23:26).

¹⁹ᵇThen Herod went from Judea to Caesarea and stayed there a while. ²⁰He had been quarreling with the people of Tyre and Sidon; they now joined together and sought an audience with him. Having secured the support of Blastus, a trusted personal servant of the king, they asked for peace, because they depended on the king's country for their food supply. ²¹On the appointed day Herod, wearing his royal robes, sat on his throne and delivered a public address to the people. ²²They shouted, "This is the voice of a god, not of a man." ²³Immediately, because Herod did not give praise to God, an angel of the Lord struck him down, and he was eaten by worms and died. ²⁴But the word of God continued to increase and spread. ²⁵When Barnabas and Saul had finished their mission, they returned from[a] Jerusalem, taking with them John, also called Mark.

[a]25 Some manuscripts *to*

12:19b-20a. Herod returned to his luxurious seaport palace in Caesarea, some sixty-five miles northwest of Jerusalem. He has bigger problems to deal with. The major import/export cities of Tyre and Sidon were out of sorts with Caesarea.[22] Though we can't be sure, a good guess is that Tyre and Sidon raised import duties to inflate the prices of vanity items imported from around the world. In response, Herod raised the prices of food exported from his province, upon which these coastal cities were dependent (cf. 1 Kgs 5:9-11).

12:20b-23. A delegation from Tyre and Sidon secured the good graces of Blastus, a trusted steward of the King's inner court. This maneuver worked. They got their food and Herod got a bunch of devoted fans. One day they all gathered in the theater to pay homage to the King. Their acclamation, however, became Herod's death-knell. It is a fascinating tale told by both Luke and Josephus. Their accounts are strikingly similar, though Josephus's longer rendition offers more details (*Ant.* 19.8 §343; cf. Eusebius, *Eccl. Hist.* 2.10).

Our story begins "On the appointed day" (v. 21) when Herod provided "shows in honor of Caesar" (*Ant.* 19.8 §343). The most likely guess is that this was Claudius Caesar's birthday (August 1; cf. Suetonius, *Life of Claudius*, 2.1) when people would pray for the Emperor's safety.[23] According to Josephus, it was the second day of the shows when Herod arrived in a garment woven of silver. The morning sun burst against his raiment and reflected resplendently across the crowd. This moment was like an epiphany for the nobles gathered in the theater who began to shout, "Be thou merciful to us; for although we have hitherto reverenced thee only as a man, yet shall we henceforth own thee as superior to mortal nature," or in the words of Luke (v. 22), "This is the voice of a god, not of a man."

Josephus reports that Herod didn't flinch. He received their flattery, knowing it was blasphemous.[24] Basking in the glory of the moment, the king looked

---

[22] Tyre and Sidon were quintessential enemies of ancient Israel. Hence, for one steeped in LXX language and ideas, this partnership with them would harbinger ominous consequences. In that light, Mark Strom is correct to point out the ideological and structural similarities between Acts 12 and God's curse on the King of Tyre in Ezekiel 28; "An Old Testament Background to Acts 12:20-33," *NTS* 32 (1986): 289-292.

[23] Another guess would be a celebration of the founding of Caesarea. But that would put the celebration on March 5, a full eleven months after the death of James. Such an extended gap would make the connection of God's retribution of James with the death of Herod less obvious.

[24] Karl Schmidt points out the similarities between this incident and that of Nero making peace with the

up and saw an owl sitting on a rope overhead. He shuddered. For years ago, while he was in house arrest in Rome, a fellow prisoner prophesied that he would see two owls in his lifetime. The first would harbinger his release from prison, the second the end of his life (*Ant.* 18.6.7 §195). Immediately he was struck with a severe pain in his abdomen and said,

> I, whom you call a god, am commanded presently to depart this life;
> while Providence thus reproves the lying words you just now said to me;
> and I, who was by you called immortal, am immediately to be hurried
> away by death. But I am bound to accept of what Providence allots, as
> it pleases God; for we have by no means lived ill, but in a splendid and
> happy manner.

Herod was carried into his palace where he suffered for five days in violent pain before dying of what Luke diagnosed as worms. Although intestinal worms were a perennial problem in third-world conditions of the ancient Mediterranean, it was also, a literary motif to describe the ugly death of a villain (Isa 66:24; Judith 16:17).[25] Hence, Luke is saying this 'King' was cursed by God for killing the Lord's servant, and he got what he deserved. He had lived fifty-four years, reigning seven in Israel and three of those with the title King. None of that now matters. He died an ignominious death as the last King of Israel.

12:24-25. In spite of Herod's persecution, the church grew. Luke gives yet another progress report on the health of the church amidst tribulation (cf. 6:7; 9:31). As the chapter opened, James was dead, Peter was in prison, and Herod was gaining popularity. By the end of the chapter, Herod was dead, Peter was free, and the church was gaining in power.

Meanwhile, Barnabas and Saul return to Antioch[26] with a new helper—John Mark. This postures the team for their first foray onto the mission field. Obviously, the unnamed evangelists in Antioch set the precedent. And, obviously, Barnabas and Saul have already traveled extensively. But this time, they are pressed into service by the Holy Spirit rather than persecution or the deprivation of a famine. This glorious new chapter of world mission awaits in chapter 13.

Parthians through the envoy Tiridates (A.D. 66; cf. Tacitus, *Ann.* 15.29; Seutonius, *Nero* 13; Dio Cassius, *Hist.* 63.1-6); cf. "Der Friede von Cäsarea: Apg 12,20-22 und die Krönung des armenischen Königs Tiridates," *BZ* 52 (2008): 110-117. The wicked emperor forced Tiridates to lay his crown before him and *acknowledge him as a god*. In return, Nero acknowledged peace between the two countries (at a huge financial cost to the Parthians). Of course, this incident is more than twenty years after Agrippa's death. Hence, Schmidt's assertion that Luke patterned his account from Nero forces an unnecessary anachronism on the biblical text. His data does, however, enable one to propose a similar *Zeitgeist* for both accounts. In fact, the deification of Emperors in Rome had its impetus in the regal deification of Eastern empires. The veneration Herod experienced in an Eastern province in A.D. 44 was exported to Rome in A.D. 66.

[25] A number of other tragic figures shared this fate: Job (7:5); Antiochus IV (2 Macc 9:5-12); Herod the Great (Josephus, *Ant.* 17.6.5 §169-170); Alexander the impostor (Lucian, *Alexander* 59); Galerius (Eusebius, *Eccl. Hist.* 8.16.4); Judas Iscariot (Papias, quoting Apollinarius of Laodicea [c. 310 – c. 390], *Fragments* 18.1); and a certain High Priest who had a ritual breach on the day of Atonement (*b. Yoma* 19b).

[26] The Greek text actually says Barnabas and Saul "returned unto Jerusalem" (ὑπέστρεψαν εἰς Ἰερυσαλήμ). Clearly, however, they returned *from* Jerusalem. Two primary solutions have been offered. First, follow one of the minority variant readings which actually has ἐξ or ἀπό rather than εἰς. Second, attach the εἰς Ἰερυσαλήμ to the mission described in the return trip: "Barnabas and Saul returned, having completed their mission unto Jerusalem"; cf. J. Dupont, "La Mission de Paul à Jerusalem (Actes 12, 25)," *NovT* 1 (1956): 275-303. Though neither solution is entirely satisfactory, the clear sense of the verse is hardly impaired by this awkward turn of phrase.

ACTS 13

III. WITNESS IN ROMAN PROVINCES (13:1–20:37)

This central section contains Paul's three missionary journeys, some of the most entertaining adventures in the book. This description is not to minimize the historical or spiritual value of the material. It is to point out, however, as Pervo has aptly done, how Luke has used the best literary devices of his day to draw the reader into the story.[1] The travel adventures, the near escapes from death, the courtroom dramas, the tension of antagonistic opposition, etc., add familiar elements from classic novels. By any account, what we are about to read is riveting literature.

In essence, we have three major elements in this central section: (1) The first missionary journey in the East—Syria, Cyprus, Galatia (chs. 13–14). (2) The Jerusalem Council over Gentile inclusion (ch. 15). (3) The second (chs. 16–18) and third (chs. 19–20) missionary journeys in the West— Macedonia, Achaia, and Asia. Theologically, this whole central section is designed to illustrate the ever expanding gospel to the Roman world. The three missionary journeys are balanced on either side of the Jerusalem council. This council serves to justify the missionary activity by grounding it in Jerusalem through the support of the key leaders of the 'mother' church—James, Peter, Barnabas, and Paul. Jesus, the Jewish Messiah, is proclaimed abroad as Lord of the nations.

A. THE FIRST 'MISSIONARY' JOURNEY: FROM SYRIA TO CYPRUS AND GALATIA (13:1–14:28)

Much of modern missions arises from the principles established in Paul's three missionary journeys. This first journey in particular is full of essential insights for the core commission of the church. For example, here we learn about the Holy Spirit as the primary sending agent amidst a church that serves, prays, and fasts. We have a pattern of a sending church and mission teams. From this journey we derive the principle of reciprocal missions, strategic locations, and the establishment of local leaders. For those whose heart beats the great commission, the following stories will quicken the pulse. In full force and in earnest, the mission of the church reaches its stride.

1. Barnabas and Saul Commissioned by the Holy Spirit (13:1-3)

[1]In the church at Antioch there were prophets and teachers: Barnabas, Simeon called Niger, Lucius of Cyrene, Manaen (who had been brought up with

---

[1] Richard Pervo, *Profit with Delight: The Literary Genre of Acts of the Apostles* (Philadelphia: Fortress, 1987).

Herod the tetrarch) and Saul. ²While they were worshiping the Lord and fasting, the Holy Spirit said, "Set apart for me Barnabas and Saul for the work to which I have called them." ³So after they had fasted and prayed, they placed their hands on them and sent them off.

13:1. The team returns to Antioch. This is the largest city they will serve, save Rome. (For details of the city see comments under 11:19). The church of Antioch was blessed by a group of gifted prophets and teachers, bracketed by the leadership of Barnabas and Saul.[2] According to Paul, these are the most important spiritual gifts, exceeded only by the Apostles (1 Cor 12:28-29; cf. Eph 4:11) who were also primary teachers (John 14:26; Acts 2:42; 4:2, 18; 5:21, 25, 28; 2 Tim 1:11-13).[3] That's only natural. Prophets were responsible for delivering messages received directly from God.[4] Teachers were responsible for articulating correct doctrine from God's word (Rom 15:4) within the community.[5] Thus, it is primarily through prophets and teachers that a community of believers comes to know right doctrine and proper application of God's will (Col 1:28; 1 Tim 4:6; Heb 5:12-6:2).

Luke lists five important individuals from the church at Antioch:

NAME	ORIGIN	ETHNICITY
Barnabas	Cyprus	Hellenistic Jew
Simeon (Niger)	———	Black (African?)
Lucius	Cyrene	North African
Manaen	Israel	Greek/Herodian
Saul	Tarsus/Jerusalem	Hebraic Jew

---

[2] There is no way to tell whether the five men listed below each had the gift of prophecy *and* teaching or whether some in the group were prophets and others were teachers. Though τε rather than καί separates Manaen and Saul from the rest of the group, this is more likely a literary variation of Luke than a categorization (Cf. *Beginnings*, 4:141).

[3] Apostles are the only Christian teachers in the first half of the book of Acts. In the second half, after Antioch, only Paul teaches properly (Acts 17:19; 18:11; 21:21, 28; cf. 1 Cor 4:17; 11:2; 2 Thess 2:15; 3:6; 1 Tim 2:7; 2 Tim 3:10). This function is, in the Epistles, an essential role of church leaders (1 Tim 1:7; 3:2; 4:6, 11, 13; 5:17; 6:2; 2 Tim 2:2, 24; Tit 2:1-3, 15).

[4] The word *prophet* (or one of its cognates) is used 582x in the Bible (NIV). These are fairly evenly distributed between the OT (384x) and the NT (198x) given their relative size. However, at least 87 of the 198 NT uses refer back to the OT (Matt 11:9; 21:26, 46; Mark 11:32; Luke 1:76; 7:26; 20:6), Jesus (Matt 13:57; 14:5; 21:11; Mark 6:4; Luke 7:16, 39; 13:33; 24:19; John 4:19; 6:14; 7:40; 9:17; Acts 3:22; 7:37), or false prophets (Matt 7:15, 22-23; 24:11, 24; 2 Thess 2:2; 1 John 4:1; Rev 2:20; 16:13; 19:20; 20:10). This leaves the following passages to refer to Christian prophets: Matt 10:41; 23:34; Acts 2:17-18; 11:27; 13:1; 15:32; 19:6; 21:9, 10; Rom 12:6; 1 Cor 11:4-5; 12:10, 28-29; 13:2, 8-9; 14:1, 3-6, 22, 24, 29-32, 37, 39; Eph 2:20; 3:5; 4:11; 1 Thess 5:20; 1 Tim 1:18; Rev 1:13; 10:11; 11:3, 6, 10, 18; 18:20, 24; 19:10; 22:7, 9, 10, 18-19. The bulk of these are in Acts, 1 Corinthians, and Revelation. Interestingly, of the 59 prophets and prophetesses named in the Bible, only 7 are Christians: Agabus (Acts 11:28); Judas (Acts 15:32); Silas (Acts 15:32); Philip's Daughters (Acts 21:8, 9); Paul (1 Tim 4:1); Peter (2 Pet 2:1, 2); John (Rev 1:1). This, in no way, minimizes the importance of Christian prophecy but does speak to the importance of Christian teachers by comparison. For a robust argument for the contemporary value of prophecy; cf. Jack Deere, *Surprised by the Voice of God: How God Speaks Today through Prophecies, Dreams, and Visions* (Grand Rapids: Zondervan, 1996).

[5] Teachers in the church were roughly equivalent to rabbis (used 16x) or "teachers of the law" (used 54x in the Synoptics as well as John 8:3; Acts 4:5; 6:12; 23:9; 1 Tim 1:7). Their importance increases with the proliferation of *false* teachers whose pernicious doctrines endanger disciples (Acts 15:1; Rom 16:17; Eph 4:14; Col 2:22; 1 Tim 1:3, 6-7; 4:2; 6:3; 2 Tim 2:17; 4:3; Tit 1:11; Heb 13:9; 2 Pet 2:1-3; 2 John 1:10; Rev 2:14-15, 20, 24). For this reason, teachers will be judged more severely (James 3:1; cf. Rom 2:20ff.).

This is a diverse group of leaders at several levels. *Economically:* Manaen, having been raised in Herod's household,[6] was a wealthy aristocrat, and Barnabas had property he could liquidate for the benevolent support of the poor (4:36-37). Simeon, who was called "Niger" (meaning "black") may be a displaced Jew from Africa who had less economic means. *Culturally:* Barnabas and Saul were both Hellenistic Jews. Manaen was a Herodian. Lucius, as his Latin name would suggest, is likely Roman (cf. 11:19-20), and since he is from Cyrene, he is probably one of the founding members of the church (cf. 11:20).[7] *Nationally:* These five men represent Africa, Syria, Cyprus, Cilicia, and Israel.

Because of the diversity of their wallets, skin color, and cultural backgrounds, these leaders could represent all constituent groups of the church in Antioch. Moreover, they could lead evangelistic forays into virtually every corner of this multicultural city. Simeon could speak to dark-skinned immigrants, Saul could debate in synagogues, Manaen could deal with the wealthy patricians, and Lucius could serve immigrants. In addition, because of this diverse leadership, the church in Antioch would be more likely to avert the kind of racial division that scourged the nascent church of Jerusalem (Acts 6:1). In our own day, the church would be wise to raise up leaders from a variety of socio-economic strata to evangelize and represent the diversity of people we find in our communities. If we fail in this, we may consign the next generation of Christians to churches that are myopic and schismatic, albeit homogenous and comfortable.

13:2-3. Not only were these men gifted, they[8] also opened their lives to the guidance of the Spirit through the disciplines of worship, fasting, and prayer (cf. Luke 2:37; Acts 14:23). These three disciplines postured them to hear the Holy Spirit and implement his agenda for the church.

The specific word for **worship** (*leitourgeō*) is about *public service* to the church rather than *private worship* of God. In the Septuagint, *leitourgeō* primarily described priests offering sacrifices in the temple (e.g., Num 18:2; Exod 28:31, 39; 29:30; Joel 1:9).[9] That's also how it is used in Hebrews (10:11). But since the church is the Christian equivalent of the temple, the sacrifices offered amongst its people are the acts of charity needed for its sustenance: "For if the Gentiles have shared in the Jews' spiritual blessings, they owe it to the Jews *to share* (*leitourgeō*) with them their material blessings" (Rom 15:27).[10] This verse is most interesting in light of the offering Barnabas and Saul just delivered to the Jewish church in Jerusalem on behalf of the Gentile Believers in Antioch.

These leaders were also **fasting**. This is hardly a surprise; Jesus expected his

---

[6] The word σύντροφος, literally means "suckled by the same nurse." It seems to indicate that Manaen was a comrade and peer of Herod rather than a servant to him. He is also a likely source for Luke's considerable interest in the Herodian family.

[7] H. J. Cadbury, "Lucius of Cyrene," in *Beginnings* 5:489-495, rightly argues against the interesting, although unlikely, possibility that Lucius is another name for Luke, the author of Luke/Acts.

[8] "They" may, in fact, refer to the entire congregation, not merely these five men.

[9] In secular Greek it meant to serve the state at one's own expense. This may apply here as well if the church was seen as its own social organization and the leaders served as patrons. Their homes would serve as meeting places and their properties dispersed for the welfare of the poor among them.

[10] The noun form of this word (λειτουργία) has the same two implications in the NT: Priestly service (Luke 1:23; Heb 8:6; 9:21) and Christian benevolence (2 Cor 9:12; Phil 2:17, 30).

disciples to fast after he was gone (Matt 9:14-15/Mark 2:18-20/Luke 5:34-35). Fasting is often a sign of grief (Jdgs 20:26; 2 Sam 1:12; 12:16, 21, 22; 1 Kgs 21:27; Ezra 8:23; Neh 1:4; 9:1; Esther 4:3; Psa 35:13; Dan 6:18; 9:3; Joel 2:12-17; Jonah 3:5; Zech 7:5) particularly in conjunction with repentance (Acts 9:9; Joel 2:12-17; Jonah 3:5; Neh 9:1; 2 Sam 12:15-23; 1 Kgs 21:27-29). Here, however, it is more likely a natural exercise of intense prayer in seeking the will of God (cf. 2 Sam 12:16-23; 2 Chron 20:3; Ezra 8:23; Esther 4:16; Mark 9:29; Luke 2:37; Acts 14:23).

Finally, this group of leaders **prayed**. Again, this is hardly surprising. Prayer, along with teaching, is one of the two primary responsibilities to which the Apostles devoted themselves as church leaders (6:4). In other words, the kinds of things the Apostles were doing in Jerusalem, these godly leaders were imitating in Antioch. In fact, just as the seven evangelists had been set apart by the laying on of the Apostles' hands, so now, Barnabas and Saul were 'ordained' to the task of church planting among the Gentiles. This is not to say they were set apart as clergy; they were, after all, already recognized leaders of the church of Antioch.[11]

Though this is commonly called *the first missionary journey,* that label is a bit misleading. After all, they are not going to distant shores, but to Barnabas's home on Cyprus. What is at play here is not exactly global conquest. Rather it is spiritual reciprocity. They offered financial resources to the Christians of Jerusalem from whom came their spiritual bread. Then, because the church of Antioch was birthed by brave missionaries who dared to cross cultural lines (11:19-20), they sent missionaries back to the territory of Cyprus that had provided them their primary evangelists. This principle of reciprocity bore great fruit well beyond Antioch's borders.

It must have been difficult for the church at Antioch to lose two of its key leaders to the mission field. However, church leaders who are in tune with the Holy Spirit will ever be aware of these two principles: Spiritual reciprocity (Rom 15:27) and global opportunity. If the Spirit calls, the primary question is not, "What will it cost?" but "What will it take?"

2. Cyprus: Ministry in Barnabas's Native Island (13:4-12)

⁴The two of them, sent on their way by the Holy Spirit, went down to Seleucia and sailed from there to Cyprus. ⁵When they arrived at Salamis, they proclaimed the word of God in the Jewish synagogues. John was with them as their helper. ⁶They traveled through the whole island until they came to Paphos. There they met a Jewish sorcerer and false prophet named Bar-Jesus, ⁷who was an attendant of the proconsul, Sergius Paulus. The proconsul, an intelligent man, sent for Barnabas and Saul because he wanted to hear the word of God.

The easiest way for Barnabas and Saul to get to Cyprus was to hop on a boat heading downstream on the Orontes. The river snakes its way to the coast

---

[11] Contra Rackham, 191-193, who sees this as an ordination to the role of Apostles. Ernest Best, "Acts xiii:1-3," *JTS* 11 (1960): 344-348 and S. Dockx, "L'ordination de Barnabé et de Saul d'après Actes 13, 1-3," *NRTh* 98 (1976): 238-250, argue that the ordination was for the vocation of missionary (or church planters), not Apostles.

so that the water ride is considerably longer than how the crow flies, but is still easier than walking the seventeen miles overland to Seleucia, the major port of Antioch. From Seleucia they boarded a seafaring vessel that ferried them one hundred and thirty miles across to Salamis.

Salamis was apparently a substantial city with an aqueduct that could have served up to one hundred thousand inhabitants. The synagogues of Salamis provided them a natural connection and platform for preaching the Jewish Messiah (cf. 13:14; 14:1; 17:1, 10; 18:4, 19; 19:8).[12] But it is more. Paul felt a spiritual obligation to preach to Jews first before turning to Gentiles (cf. Rom 1:16). Interestingly, of the twenty three times synagogues are mentioned in the book, Saul/Paul is involved in every one of them (if we assume that Stephen and Saul shared the same home-synagogue of the Freedmen, 6:9).

Luke inserts a seemingly trivial comment that John Mark assisted the veteran evangelists. He is simply called a *servant* (*hupēretēs*). Though this word can mean "officer" or "guard" (Matt 5:25; 26:58/Mark 14:54, 65; John 7:32, 45-46; 18:3, 12, 18, 22; 19:6; Acts 5:22, 26), Luke uses it for those who handle the Scriptures either metaphorically (Luke 1:2) or literally (Luke 4:20). It is, in fact, the word Jesus used to describe Paul's role as a missionary (Acts 26:16; cf. 1 Cor 4:1). Beyond this, Luke offers no further job description for the junior evangelist.

Though their time in Salamis likely spanned several weeks since they preached in multiple synagogues, there was no mention of any opposition or results. Perhaps they moved quickly beyond Salamis because the previous missionary venture there was sufficiently successful (11:19). They pressed on to Paphos, the capital city on the far side of the island.[13] Though Cyprus is only eighty-five miles across (from Salamis to Paphos), its interior is mountainous .[14] It would have been much easier to follow the southern coastal road more than one hundred miles across idyllic scenery.[15]

Once in Paphos , they met up with Bar-Jesus, probably in the synagogue. That's a bit of a paradox since Bar-Jesus (Aramaic meaning "Son of Jesus") was a sorcerer and a false prophet. One might ask, "Why hadn't a guy like that been excommunicated from the synagogue?" Well, part of the answer lies in the popularity of sorcery in the first century (e.g., Acts 8:9-10; Herodotus, *Hist.* 1.101, 140), even among the Jews (Pliny, *Nat. Hist.* 30.2.11; Josephus, *Ant.* 8.2.5 §42-49; 20.7.2 §142; cf. *Beginnings* 5:164-188). Unfortunately, the same charge could be leveled against Christians (Acts 19:19).

This fortuitous meeting drew Barnabas and Saul out of their narrow Jewish circles and connected them to the proconsul. Sergius Paulus was the highest Ro-

---

[12] The fact that there were multiple synagogues in Salamis speaks to the strong Jewish population of the city. Apparently the Jews of Cyprus were well represented (cf. Philo, *Embassy to Gaius*, 282, and Josephus, *Ant.* 13.10.4 §284-287).

[13] After the earthquake of 15 B.C., Paphos was rebuilt by the Romans, renamed Sebaste, and made into the administrative city of the Island (Dio Cassius, *Hist.* 54.23.7). Earthquakes were common on Cyprus; Seneca said, "How often has this calamity laid Cyprus waste? How often has Paphos fallen into ruin?" (*Epistle* 91).

[14] Salamis and Paphos were the two major cities of the island and were used in the Sibylline Oracles to represent the whole of the island (4.168-169; 5.605-608). Luke likely had something similar in mind.

[15] Admittedly, this is only one of three routes available to the team; cf. Merill F. Unger, "Archaeology and Paul's Tour of Cyprus," *BibSac* 117 (1960): 231.

man ruler of the island.[16] He heard about these extraordinary visitors who spoke the very words of God. In the ancient world it was common for political officials to consult with spiritual advisors to determine the will of the gods for their domain. With that intent, Sergius Paulus summoned the missionary team.

[8]But Elymas the sorcerer (for that is what his name means) opposed them and tried to turn the proconsul from the faith. [9]Then Saul, who was also called Paul, filled with the Holy Spirit, looked straight at Elymas and said, [10]"You are a child of the devil and an enemy of everything that is right! You are full of all kinds of deceit and trickery. Will you never stop perverting the right ways of the Lord? [11]Now the hand of the Lord is against you. You are going to be blind, and for a time you will be unable to see the light of the sun." Immediately mist and darkness came over him, and he groped about, seeking someone to lead him by the hand. [12]When the proconsul saw what had happened, he believed, for he was amazed at the teaching about the Lord.

13:8. Bar-Jesus, AKA Elymas,[17] likely introduced Barnabas and Saul to Sergius Paulus or at least the proconsul heard him talking about these extraordinary evangelists and invited them for a consult. Soon, however, their rising popularity threatened Elymas's status. He, like so many other religious mystics in the Middle East, was privileged to work for the government in a semi-official capacity. His private counsel often drove the public policy of Sergius Paulus for which he was probably paid handsomely. But the proconsul's interest in Jesus jeopardized Elymas's good gig. He turned against his Jewish compatriots and attempted to subvert Sergius Paulus's conversion.

13:9-10. At this Saul, *glared* at him (*atenizo*).[18] This malevolent gaze would frighten the superstitious Elymas who dabbled in dark magic, for the eye was believed to be the portal of the soul through which destructive power could pass (Str-B 2.713-715). Not only did Paul pierce his soul, he revealed it: "you are full of deceit (*dolos*) and trickery." The word *deceit* literally describes the bait laid in a trap. It is a rather revealing description of the sorcerer. Then, in a tragic paradox, Paul played off Bar-Jesus' name. "You are not a son of Jesus," exclaimed Saul, "You are a son of Satan!" The whole scene is reminiscent of Peter's vituperative confrontation of Simon Magus (Acts 8:20-23).

In a parenthetical note, Luke noted a change from Saul's Hebrew *signum* to his Greek *cognomen* (technically Saul did not change his name but changed which

---

[16] Cyprus had been a Senatorial province since 22 B.C. This means it was ruled by a proconsul and did not have legions stationed there as would be the case under an Imperial province (*Beginnings*, 1:195-199). Luke used the precise political term to describe Sergius Paulus's position (ἀνθύπατον). For the sketchy inscriptional evidence of Sergius Paulus as proconsul; see B. van Elderen, "Some Archaeological Observations on Paul's First Missionary Journey," in *Apostolic History and the Gospel* (W. Ward Gasque and Ralph P. Martin, eds.; Great Britain: Paternoster Press, 1970), 151-166.

[17] Luke translates *Elymus* as "sorcerer." The etymology of the name is impossible to identify since we don't know whether the Greek translation *Elymus* comes from Arabic, Hebrew, or Aramaic. However, L. Yaure, "Elymas—Nehelamite—Pethor," *JBL* 79 (1960): 297-314, has identified some likely candidates. *Elymus* may derive from the Arabic word *Alimun* meaning "wise." If it comes from Hebrew, the source might be Alima (אלימא) meaning "strong." Or, as Yaure argues, it could come from the Aramaic word for "dreamer" (*haloma*).

[18] Luke uses this word twelve of its fourteen times in the NT (Luke 4:10; 22:56; Acts 1:10; 3:4, 12; 6:15; 7:55; 10:4; 11:6; 13:9; 14:9; 23:1; 2 Cor 3:7, 13). It means "to stare intently."

of his given names he went by). Apparently it was also a change of leadership. From here on out, Luke will always mention Paul *before* Barnabas with two obvious exceptions: (1) When the people of Lystra took the two for a couple of gods (Acts 14:12, 14). Since Barnabas was identified with Zeus and Paul with Hermes, the more prominent 'god' got mentioned first. (2) When the pair returns to Jerusalem, where Barnabas was still the more prominent figure, Paul took a backseat once again (Acts 15:12, 25). The question, however, is why the change of name? There are several reasonable possibilities, none of which are mutually exclusive. First, as they move into Gentile territory, it makes more sense for Paul to use his Greek *cognomen* rather than his Hebrew *signum*, "Saul."[19] Second, *Paul* means "dwarfish." This may be a way of humbling himself in the work of Christ (Augustine, *On the Spirit*, 12), though if the name was really derogatory, one might wonder why it was such a popular name. Third, Sergius Paulus was Saul's first notable Gentile convert. In honor of the supposed 'inauguration' of his Gentile mission, Paul might have used his own *cognomen* to memorialize this moment.

13:11-12. Paul's diatribe turns into a curse. On behalf of the Lord, Paul declares Elymas's punishment: absolute blindness. When you can't see the light of the sun, you are stone-cold blind. Instantly, the lights went out for Bar-Jesus and a mist came over his eyes. With the image of the room still burned in his now darkened retina, he began to grope for assistance from the courtiers (cf. Deut 28:28-29). Though the text does not say so specifically, it looks like his comrades avoided him like the plague. They are not about to let Elymas touch them in case the curse is contagious! One should not assume that Paul struck Elymas blind from a puerile rage or egotistical vendetta. Nor should one imagine that Paul got sadistic pleasure from wielding such power. This blindness for Paul was undoubtedly reminiscent of his own biography. When he, like Elymas, attempted to keep converts from the Way, Jesus met him on the road and struck him blind for three days. It was this curse that led him to life. Surely this was Paul's motive, and surely blindness speaks metaphorically to Elymas's spiritual condition (cf. John 3:19-20; 9:39).

Such a striking display attracted the attention of everyone in the room, not least of whom the Proconsul. Though some have questioned whether such a high official would have converted so quickly (e.g., *Beginnings* 4:147) such skepticism is unwarranted. There was not yet a ban on Christianity. Therefore, there is no reason to think Sergius Paulus would have encountered any negative repercussions from conversion. Moreover, there were a number of high officials who, in spite of persecution and social ostracization, were delighted to make Jesus Lord: Nicodemus (John 19:39), Dionysius (Acts 17:34), and Saul himself (Gal 1:13-16) come immediately to mind. The annals of history are full of men and women of rank who, at the peril of their positions, converted to Christianity.

---

[19] It was common for Jews to have a 'by-name' distinct from his *nomen* and *pronomen* (Str-B 2:712-713). Cf. Colin J. Hemer, "The Name of Paul," *TB* 36 (1985): 179-183, and G. A. Harrer, "Saul who also is called Paul," *HTR* 33 (1940): 19-33.

3. Pisidian Antioch: Paul's First Recorded Sermon (13:13-52)

This is a classic piece of Christian rhetoric.[20] Paul has three proofs leading up to a bifurcated conclusion. **Proof #1**: All Hebrew history points to Jesus as its fulfillment (vv. 16-23). Like Stephen (from whom he might as well have plagiarized this point), Paul marches through Egypt, the conquest, the judges, and the kings. Finally, arriving at David, he brings Jesus into full frontal view as the fulfillment of God's promise to his royal seed. **Proof #2**: The Kingdom of God is unfolding before our very eyes in the contemporary events of John the Baptist and Jesus' death, burial, and resurrection (vv. 24-31). Though the shameful death of Jesus appears to discredit him, **Proof #3**: The Scriptures (Psalms 2; 16; Isaiah 55) predicted this very thing (vv. 32-37). Notably, Psalm 16, to which Paul gives the greatest attention, is the very text Peter used at Pentecost.[21]

These proofs led to the irresistible conclusion that forgiveness of sins is found in Jesus (vv. 38-39). It is in these two verses that Luke's Paul sounds most like the Paul of the Epistles.[22] His message of justification through Jesus apart from the law rings with pure clarity. This conclusion, however, also has a dark side. If one rejects salvation in Jesus, he will be rejected by God. This final warning from Habakkuk (1:5) threatens an eschatological judgment like the exile of old. The sermon is a masterpiece of Christian rhetoric that leaves the reader breathless. In fact, it had a similar impact on its original audience which returned *en masse* the following week to determine where this revelation would take them.

[13]From Paphos, Paul and his companions sailed to Perga in Pamphylia, where John left them to return to Jerusalem. [14]From Perga they went on to Pisidian Antioch. On the Sabbath they entered the synagogue and sat down. [15]After the reading from the Law and the Prophets, the synagogue rulers sent word to them, saying, "Brothers, if you have a message of encouragement for the people, please speak."

---

[20] It is also not dissimilar to other known synagogue homilies such as 4Q174 1.1-16 or other early Christian *kerygma* such as *Ascension of Isaiah* or Ignatiuus of Antioch; cf. Richard Bauckham, "Kerygmatic Summaries in the Speeches of Acts," in *History, Literature, and Society in the Book of Acts* (ed. Ben Witherington; Cambridge: Cambridges Universtiy Press, 1996), 185-217.

[21] This, sermon attributed to Paul, is actually a composite of three earlier pieces: 13:16-23 parallels 7:2-46 (Stephen), 13:24-33 reflects 10:37-43 (Peter) [13:27 = 3:17-18], and 13:35-37 is nearly identical to 2:25-31 (Peter). The only really new material is vv. 38-41, which look very Pauline. This has led some to suggest that we are not really reading Paul's emphasis here but Luke's. But is it really more likely that Luke would create these accounts? Though Luke is inclined to use his own wording, he is not wont to invent entire pericopae. The idiosyncratic Jewish hermeneutic applied to Psalm 16 by Peter and the intricate and traditional survey of Hebrew history by Stephen would more naturally come from a Hebrew rather than a Greek. Hence, if there is copying going on in Acts 13, why would one credit it to Luke's investigations when Paul was an eyewitness? He was standing ringside when Stephen preached, and it would be unlikely that Saul missed Peter's Pentecost sermon in the Portico of Solomon. Conclusion: Paul's first recorded sermon borrows themes he found difficult to refute when he heard them from his enemies.

[22] There is, of course, great debate about whether Luke's Paul is the historic Paul we find in his undisputed letters. It may be telling that in Paul's conclusion (vv. 38-39), when he is not quoting Scripture or reproducing other's arguments, that he sounds most 'himself'. Armin D. Baum, "Paulinismen in den Missionreden des lukanischen Paulus: Zur inhaltlichen Authentizität der *oratio recta* in der Apostelgeschichte," *ETL* 82 (2006): 405-436, mounts a strong argument that there are sufficient verbal and ideological overlaps between the mission speeches of Paul and his letters to assert with a good deal of confidence that Luke has accurately represented his hero; contra Philipp Vielhauer, "Zum 'Paulinismus' der Apostelgeschichte," *PSTJ* 17 (1963): 5-17.

13:13. Our team travels north to Pamphylia. Crossing the Mediterranean, they land in modern day Turkey in the ancient town of Perga ◘. There John Mark left the team. No explanation is given. Perhaps that's for the best; the creative speculation of scholars may be far more interesting than reality. John may have objected to Paul taking the lead over his cousin Barnabas, or perhaps he was homesick. Maybe the trip took longer than he expected and this move north meant an inevitably prolonged journey. It is possible that Paul got malaria or some other nasty disease (cf. Gal 4:13-14) that required the team to move to the higher elevation of Pisidian Antioch (3,600') and John was not willing to endanger his health (Ramsay, *Traveller,* 89-97). One could even suppose that John Mark did not like the direction the mission was taking, moving into pure Gentile evangelism. *Why* he left is as much of a mystery as *where* he went. One might suppose that he returned home to his mother Mary in Jerusalem. All we really know is that this 'abandonment' embittered Paul against his young helper and for years he refused to reconcile (cf. Acts 15:36-40).

13:14-15. From Paphos the team could have crossed the Mediterranean to the coast of Pamphylia and snaked their way seven miles north up the Cestrus river, dropping them on the doorstep of Perga (cf. Strabo, *Geo.* 14.4.1-3).[23] At that point they would have walked the *via Sebaste* north near the region of Pisidia, in broader Galatia (Bruce, 267, fn. 20).[24] This trek to Pisidian Antioch was long and arduous, traversing a hundred miles of mountains, rivers, and bandits. Perhaps Paul reflected on this difficult journey when he wrote: "I have been constantly on the move. I have been in danger from rivers, in danger from bandits, in danger from my own countrymen, in danger from Gentiles; in danger in the city, in danger in the country, in danger at sea; and in danger from false brothers" (2 Cor 11:26).

When they arrived in Antioch,[25] as expected, they attended the Sabbath service. As expected, following the normal liturgical readings, the synagogue rulers called on them to preach a "word of exhortation" (cf. Heb 13:22).[26] It would be

---

[23] The observation that the Cester River was navigable to within 3-4 miles of Perga, an important crossroads of southern Turkey, explains why the team chose to sail up to its borders and then head quickly north. On the return visit they took time to preach at Perga, then on to the port of Attalia (14:25-26) which they bypassed on their way into Turkey. Cf. Douglas A. Campbell, "Paul in Pamphylia (Acts 13.13-14a; 14.24b-26): A Critical Note," *NTS* 46 (2000): 595-602.

[24] Mark Wilson, "The Route of Paul's First Journey to Pisidian Antioch," *NTS* 55 (2009): 471-483, makes a strong case for Paul taking the western route north into Pisidian Antioch and the central route south, passing to the east of Lake Limnae. Pisidian Antioch was actually in Phrygia, though it lay near Pisidia from whence it derived this designation (Strabo, *Geo.* 12.6.4). Inscriptional evidence suggests the real possibility that Sergius Paulus had relatives in Pisidian Antioch (Robert Tannehill, *Narrative Unity of Luke-Acts: A Literary Interpretation* (Philadelphia: Fortress, 1986, 1990), 2:163. This may explain why Paul and Barnabas set out to preach there.

[25] Antioch was but one of the 16 cities by that name, established by Seleucus Nikator to honor his father (c. 300 B.C.). Augustus made it a Roman colony and the major military installation of the region of Galatia. For further details on the city see Ramsay, *Cities,* 247-314.

[26] The service described here by Luke aligns precisely with other historical descriptions of synagogue liturgy: (a) Recitation of the Shema, (b) prayers by a synagogue official, (c) lectionary reading from the Law and the Prophets, (d) homily, (e) benedictions. E. Schürer, *The History of the Jewish People in the Age of Jesus Christ* (tr. S. Tylor and P. Christie; Edinburgh: T & T Clark, 1892) 2:447-454, offers further details of the synagogue service. It is a bit unusual that there would be more than one synagogue ruler. But this can be easily explained if a previous ruler retained the title in retirement (e.g., Mark 5:22). There appears to be some inscriptional evidence to that effect; cf. W. Schrage, *TNDT,* 7:844-447.

a rare treat for a congregation this deep into Gentile territory to host two guests from Jerusalem so well trained in Scripture.[27]

[16]**Standing up, Paul motioned with his hand and said: "Men of Israel and you Gentiles who worship God, listen to me!** [17] **The God of the people of Israel chose our fathers; he made the people prosper during their stay in Egypt, with mighty power he led them out of that country,** [18]**he endured their conduct[a] for about forty years in the desert,** [19]**he overthrew seven nations in Canaan and gave their land to his people as their inheritance.** [20]**All this took about 450 years. After this, God gave them judges until the time of Samuel the prophet.** [21]**Then the people asked for a king, and he gave them Saul son of Kish, of the tribe of Benjamin, who ruled forty years.** [22]**After removing Saul, he made David their king. He testified concerning him: 'I have found David son of Jesse a man after my own heart; he will do everything I want him to do.'** [23]**From this man's descendants God has brought to Israel the Savior Jesus, as he promised."**

[a]*18* Some manuscripts *and cared for them*

13:16. In a classic posture of Roman rhetoric, Paul stood and waved his hand to signal the inception of his speech (cf. 19:33; 21:40; cf. Polybius 1.78.3; Josephus, *Ant.* 4.8.48 §323; 8.11.2 §275).[28] He identified his audience as both Jews and Gentile "God-fearers."[29] The parallels here between Stephen and Paul are substantial.

STEPHEN, ACTS 7:2-46	PAUL, ACTS 13:16-23
Formal appellation followed by, "listen to me" (2)	Formal appellation followed by, "listen to me" (16)
God called "our father Abraham" (2); "Later Isaac became the father of Jacob, and Jacob became the father of the twelve patriarchs" (8)	"The God of the people of Israel chose our father" (17)
They prospered in Egypt through Joseph (9-17)	They prospered in Egypt (17)

[27] Philo, *Spec. Laws* 2.15 §62 states that any educated person attending the service can give the sermon: "Some of those who are very learned explain to them what is of great importance and use, lessons by which the whole of their lives may be improved" (cf. Luke 4:16).

[28] This is the first of Paul's three main speeches in the book (Acts 13:16b-41; 17:22b-31; 20:18b-35). Though there is ample reason to credit Paul with the theme, content, and rhetorical structure of each address, Luke's fingerprints are also all over these speeches. In other words, he took Paul's words and presented them in his own style. That much is to be expected. What is not to be missed, however, is that Luke has not only shaped each individual speech, he has shaped our view of Paul through these speeches. These three sermons help us see the great preacher in Luke's intended light; cf. Michel Quesnel, "Paul prédicateur dans les Actes des Apôtres," *NTS* 47 (2001): 469-481.

[29] There appears to be a distinction between Jews (by birth), proselytes (by conversion), and "God-fearers" who were attracted to the Jewish faith but were unwilling to submit to circumcision. The popularity of Jewish religion in the ancient world is well-documented. For instance, in the town of Aphrodisias, an inscription on a synagogue pillar (c. A.D. 4–5th cen.) lists more than 50 names of "God-fearers" (θεοσεβεῖς) separate from the Jewish donors. Cf. Dietrich-Alex Koch, "The God-fearers between Facts and Fiction," *ST* 60 (2006): 62-90, and "Proselyten und Gottesfürchtige als Hörer der Reden von Aposelgeschichte," in *Apostelgeschichte und die hellenistische Geschichtsschreibung* (ed. Cilliers Breytenbach and Jens Schröter; Leiden: Brill, 2004), 85-87, as well as Irina Levinskaya, "God-fearers: Epigraphic Evidence," in *The Book of Acts in Its Diaspora Setting* (ed. Richard Bauckham, vol. 5 in *The Book of Acts in Its First Century Setting*, Grand Rapids: Eerdmans, 1996), 51-82.

STEPHEN, ACTS 7:2-46	PAUL, ACTS 13:16-23
"God was using him [Moses] to rescue them" (18-35)	With mighty power God rescued them (17)
Israel was disobedient 40 years in the desert (36-44)	Israel was disobedient 40 years in the desert (18)
God overthrew the nations in Canaan (45a)	God overthrew the seven (cf. Deut 7:1) nations in Canaan (19)
Egyptian slavery for 400 years (6)	Egyptian slavery and Canaan conquest took 450 years [Egypt 400, Wilderness 40, Conquest 10] (20a) Judges up through Samuel (20b) Saul ruled as the first king of Israel for 40 years (21)
David provided a dwelling place for God (45b-46)	David, the forerunner of Jesus (22-23)

13:17-25. Aside from the fact that Acts 7 is much longer than Paul's sermon, these two renditions of Hebrew history follow the same course (except for a couple of elements Paul includes that Stephen omits). This is hardly surprising. There were standard details of Jewish history. While details could vary from telling to telling, the basic framework was remarkably consistent.[30] Some of the details, such as Saul's forty-year reign[31] and his tribal roots in Benjamin may have interested Paul (Saul) because of his own similar heritage (cf. Phil 3:5).

King Saul's rejection (1 Sam 13:13-14; 15:23-28) precipitated David's rule. He was "a man after God' own heart" (v. 22).[32] He became the quintessential king of Israel so that 2 Samuel 7:12-13 promised his royal seed a perpetual place on the throne: "When your days are fulfilled and you lie down with your ancestors, I will raise up your offspring after you, who shall come forth from your body, and I will establish his kingdom. He shall build a house for my name, and I will establish the throne of his kingdom forever." This promise reverberates through the Psalms and Prophets: "I will place over them one shepherd, my servant David, and he will tend them; he will tend them and be their shepherd" (Ezek 34:23; cf. Psalms 89; 132; Isa 11:1-4; 16:5; Jer 23:5; 30:9; Ezek 37:24; Micah 4:6-13; Zech 9:9; 12:7-9). It was picked up through various intertestamental writers (*Pss. Sol.* 17:4, 21-32; 4Q174 1:10-13; 4QPBless), Qumran (CD 7.15-16; 4Q174; 4Q252 fr. 1, VI) and Rabbinic texts (*b. Sanh.* 98b; *b. Meg.* 17b; *b. Hag.* 14a).

It comes as no surprise, therefore, that David looms large in the New Testa-

---

[30] For a list of the standard elements used in other ancient renditions of Hebrew history see Oda Wischmeyer, "Stephen's Speech before the Sanhedrin against the Background of the Summaries of the History of Israel (Acts 7)," in *History and Identity: How Israel's Later Authors Viewed Its Earlier History* (ed. Núria Calduch-Benages and Jan Liesen; Berlin: Walter de Gruyter, 2006), 341-358.

[31] Josephus, *Ant.* 6.14.9 §378 claims a 40 year rule for Saul which contradicts his later assertion of a 20-year rule in *Ant.* 10.8.4 §143. The longer rule may factor in the co-regency with the prophet Samuel.

[32] This quotation actually stitches together phrases from three separate OT texts: Psa 49:20 [LXX 48:21] "I have found David," 1 Sam 13:14 "A man after my own heart," Isa 44:28, "He will do everything I want him to do." Cf. 1 Clement 18:1-3, "But what must we say of David that obtained a good report? Of whom God said, I have found a man after My heart, David the son of Jesse: with eternal mercy have I anointed him."

ment. As early as Romans 1:3, Jesus was confessed as a Davidic descendant (cf. Rom 15:7-13; 2 Tim 2:8; Heb 7:14-17; Rev 5:5; 22:16). Interestingly, this confession sounds a lot like the Paul of Acts 13:23, 33-37.[33] Peter (Acts 2:30-31) and James (Acts 15:16-18) are also reported to have affirmed Jesus' Davidic lineage.

All this leads inevitably to Jesus, the Savior of Israel (v. 23). Read against the backdrop of the Exodus narrative and the lineage of the Kings, Savior (*sōtēr*) is a regal title, not merely a description. Furthermore, "saving" or "rescue" is what Jesus does for the nation, not merely what he does for pious individuals. In short, this is a national discourse. This might have been all the more poigniant to a group of Jews, painfully aware that they were *not* living in Israel under a Davidic king.

[24]"**Before the coming of Jesus, John preached repentance and baptism to all the people of Israel. [25]As John was completing his work, he said: 'Who do you think I am? I am not that one. No, but he is coming after me, whose sandals I am not worthy to untie.' [26]Brothers, children of Abraham, and you God-fearing Gentiles, it is to us that this message of salvation has been sent. [27]The people of Jerusalem and their rulers did not recognize Jesus, yet in condemning him they fulfilled the words of the prophets that are read every Sabbath. [28]Though they found no proper ground for a death sentence, they asked Pilate to have him executed. [29]When they had carried out all that was written about him, they took him down from the tree and laid him in a tomb. [30]But God raised him from the dead, [31]and for many days he was seen by those who had traveled with him from Galilee to Jerusalem. They are now his witnesses to our people.**"

13:24-26. Paul now shifts from ancient history to contemporary events. Specifically he uses King David as a bridge to Jesus with John the Baptist as the final stepping stone. John the Baptist was the harbinger of the coming King. He preached repentance and baptism[34] (two sides of the same coin).[35] This repentance was to prepare the nation who came out to John to receive their coming king, Jesus.[36] When Paul called the crowd "Children of Abraham," including believing Gentiles (Gal 3:7-8; cf. Matt 3:9-10/Luke 3:8-9), it served as a reminder that this message of salvation was national in import.

[33] This is especially so since Acts 13:33-37 combines elements of 2 Sam 7:12-16 with Psalm 2 and 89:4-5 [3-4; LXX 88:3-4], which is a pre-Pauline, Jewish messianic hermeneutic also shared by 1 Macc 2:57; *Pss. Sol.* 17; *Ben Sir.* 47; 4Qflor; and 4QBt3⁸; cf. Eduard Schweizer, "The Concept of the Davidic 'Son of God' in Acts and Its Old Testament Background," in *Studies in Luke-Acts* (ed. L. E. Keck and J. L. Martyn; Nashville: Abingdon, 1966), 186-188.

[34] John features regularly in the book of Acts. He is mentioned by Jesus (1:5), Peter (10:37; 11:16), Paul (13:24-25), and Luke, the narrator (18:25). Interestingly, every time John is mentioned, so is his baptism. That makes sense, actually; John's 'nickname' was *Baptizer.* Harmut Stegemann, *The Library of Qumran: On the Essenes, Qumran, John the Baptist, and Jesus* (Leiden: Brill Academic, 1998) 218, comments, "Until John's appearance, neither in Judaism nor in the world around had anyone baptized other persons." Thus, while immersion would have been familiar, John's interpretation of it as an entry rite performed by him on another was certainly novel.

[35] As Merklein observes, outside the book of Revelation, "repentance" in the New Testament is almost exclusively a feature of John and Jesus' preaching; cf. Helmut Merklein, "Die Umkehrpredigt bei Johannes dem Täufer und Jesus von Nazaret," *BZ* 25 (1981): 29-30.

[36] Clearly John was not calling merely for a personal spiritual experience in baptism but a social transformation of the nation with economic impact that would most affect those in power; cf. Bruce J. Malina and Richard L. Rohrbaugh, *Social-Scientific Commentary on the Synoptic Gospels* (Minneapolis: Fortress, 1992), 38.

John the Baptist, a national hero, considered Jesus so exalted that he was unworthy to touch the lowest part of his body in taking off his sandals (cf. Matt 3:11/Mark 1:7/Luke 3:16/John 1:27). In the book of Acts, only Paul recalls this famous saying of John. It is entirely possible that Paul remembered this saying from his own visit to the Baptist in the desert. As a zealous young rabbinic student in Jerusalem, surely he made the twenty mile trek to the Jordan River to hear this flamboyant prophet who was all the rage.

13:27-31. Unfortunately, John's esteem of Jesus was not universal. In fact, the power brokers in Jerusalem mistook the Messiah for a rebel and condemned him to death. (On the ignorance of the Jewish leaders in connection with fulfilling prophecy, see comments on 3:17-18; cf. Luke 23:34; 1 Cor 2:8).[37] Paul, of all people, knew what it was like to shed innocent blood, fueled by the vengeance of misguided zeal. They sentenced Jesus to death under Pontius Pilate, condemning him to crucifixion on a "tree" (see comments on 10:39). This too was from God. The prophetic words heard each Sabbath in the Synagogue predicted the suffering of God's servant (see comments on 10:43). Normally, this shame would indicate that he was *not* God's man. But God himself intervened and validated him by raising him from the dead! This glorious reality has been verified by the Apostolic witnesses who accompanied Jesus (Luke 24:48; Acts 1:8; 2:32; 3:15; 5:32; 10:39, 41; 13:31; 1 Cor 15:5).

As is apparent from the chart below, none of this is new material for Luke. Though the verbiage is reworked, both the content and sequence of 13:24-33 follows 10:37-43. Certainly there were standard ways of explaining the gospel which likely derived from Peter and the other eyewitnesses.[38] Nonetheless, one would not suspect Paul's preaching was dependent on Peter with whom he had spent scarcely more than a fortnight (Gal 1:18). Consequently, one might assume that Luke is responsible for the similarity in the two arrangements.

PAUL'S ADDRESS TO ANTIOCH, ACTS 13:24-33	PETER'S ADDRESS TO CORNELIUS, ACTS 10:37-43
24, **John preached baptism** and repentance	37, **John preached baptism**
25, One greater is coming after me	38, God anointed him to do great miracles (cf. 2:22)
26, The message is for both Jews and Gentiles	
27–29, Jewish rulers (in ignorance) **killed Jesus on a tree** (cf. 2:23)	39, Jews in Jerusalem **killed Jesus on a tree**
30, "**God raised him from the dead** on the third day" (cf. 2:24)	40, "**God raised him from the dead**"
31, He was **seen** (for many days) by select **witnesses**	40, God caused him to be **seen** by select **witnesses**

[37] Cf. Frank Matera, "Responsibility for the Death of Jesus according to Acts of the Apostles," *JSNT* 39 (1990): 73-93.

[38] Richard Bauckham, *Jesus and the Eyewitnesses: The Gospels as Eyewitness Testimony* (Grand Rapids: Eerdmans, 2006).

PAUL'S ADDRESS TO ANTIOCH, ACTS 13:24-33	PETER'S ADDRESS TO CORNELIUS, ACTS 10:37-43
32, We **preach** the promise of God	42, God commanded us to **preach** Jesus as Judge
33, The promise was fulfilled as **prophesied** (Psalm 2)	43, The **prophets** testify that all who believe in him have forgiveness of sins

[32]"We tell you the good news: What God promised our fathers [33]he has fulfilled for us, their children, by raising up Jesus. As it is written in the second Psalm: 'You are my Son; today I have become your Father.'[b] [34]The fact that God raised him from the dead, never to decay, is stated in these words: 'I will give you the holy and sure blessings promised to David.'[c] [35]So it is stated elsewhere: 'You will not let your Holy One see decay.'[d] [36]For when David had served God's purpose in his own generation, he fell asleep; he was buried with his fathers and his body decayed. [37]But the one whom God raised from the dead did not see decay. [38]Therefore, my brothers, I want you to know that through Jesus the forgiveness of sins is proclaimed to you. [39]Through him everyone who believes is justified from everything you could not be justified from by the law of Moses. [40]Take care that what the prophets have said does not happen to you: [41]'Look, you scoffers, wonder and perish, for I am going to do something in your days that you would never believe, even if someone told you.'[e]"

[a]*33 Or have begotten you*   [b]*33 Psalm 2:7*   [c]*34 Isaiah 55:3*   [d]*35 Psalm 16:10*   [e]*41 Hab. 1:5*

13:32-37. Now Paul announces the "good news" (*euangelizō*). Notice, this is not a *new* message; it is the ancient promise to the Hebrew fathers—Jesus is raised from the dead so he can offer forgiveness of sins (Luke 1:77; 5:20-24; 7:47-49; 23:34; 24:47; Acts 2:28; 5:31; 10:43; 26:18). So far, Paul has offered two proofs for Jesus the Messiah: #1, all Hebrew history prefigures and points to this *Messianic king* (vv. 16-23). #2, the *Kingdom of God* is unfolding before their very eyes through the contemporary events of John the Baptist and Jesus' death, burial, and resurrection (vv. 24-31). We now come to proof #3: The *resurrection* is substantiated by ancient prophecies. Paul, as he is wont to do in the Epistles, stacks several proof-texts together, each of which is drawn from the LXX, the translation most familiar to his Greek-speaking audience.

Quotation #1. Verse 33, "You are my Son; today I have become your Father" (Psa 2:7). Paul offers this verse as a proof-text for the resurrection of Jesus. The problem is that Psalm 2 doesn't address the resurrection. So is Paul fair to interpret the Psalm in a way the author would likely not recognize? Yes! This very verse has been used twice before by Luke to refer to Jesus, first at his baptism (Luke 3:22/Mark 1:11/Matt 3:17) and later at the transfiguration (Luke 9:35/ Mark 9:7/Matt 17:5). Both of these episodes prefigure the death, burial, and resurrection of Jesus. Furthermore, Peter used this very Psalm to explicate the execution of Jesus under Pilate and the chief priest (Acts 4:25-28, citing Psalm 2:1-2). Each of the previous Lucan uses of Psalm 2 references the passion and/ or resurrection of Jesus. According to the traditional Christian interpretation, the one true king is Jesus. Hence, Psalm two must be *his* enthronement Psalm (Str-B 3:675-677).[39] Therefore, the events surrounding his death, burial, and resurrection are naturally read back into the ancient text. To the original witnesses of the resurrection, this is not only a *fair* way to read the text, it is the *only* way it can be correctly understood (cf. 2 Pet 1:16-21; Heb 1:1-5; 5:5-10).[40]

Quotation #2. Verse 34, "I will give you the holy and sure blessings promised to David" (Isa 55:3). Just as Psalm 2 was understood as Yahweh's direct address to Jesus, so the same hermeneutical move is now made with Isaiah 55:3.[41] Again, the original text says nothing about resurrection. Logically, however, it must necessitate resurrection for the crucified Jesus. If God's promise of an eternal throne is really about Jesus, then there is no way God can leave him in the grave. In light of this, Paul cites one final, definitive text.

Quotation #3. Verse 35, "You will not let your Holy One see decay" (Psa 15[16]:10 LXX). This is the very same passage Peter cited on the day of Pentecost. Though Paul's citation and explanation are only a fourth as long as Peter's, the logic is the same.[42] Luke hardly needs to give Paul equivalent space to unpack the same argument. The basic point is as clear here as it was at Pentecost— David died and decayed. Therefore, Psalm 16 must speak of the coming Messiah rather than the ancient King. Since Jesus is the one whom God raised from the dead, that validates him as David's descendant and true heir to the throne.

13:38-39. Of the entire sermon, these two verses sound most like the Paul of the Epistles.[43]

| 38a, "…through **Jesus** the **forgiveness of sins** [*hamartia*] is proclaimed to you" | Col 1:14, "…**in whom** we have redemption, the **forgiveness of sins** [*hamartia*]." |
| | Eph 1:7, "**In him** we have redemption through his blood, the **forgiveness of sins** [*paraptōma*]…" |

[39] Given the similar vocabulary of Acts 13:33-36 with 2 Sam 7:12-15, Dale Goldsmith suggests that our present text, though citing Psalm 2, is a *pesher* on the Nathan oracle; cf. "Acts 13:33-37: A Pesher on 2 Sam 7," *JBL* 87 (1968): 321-324. Nathan predicted that Yahweh would "raise up" David's offspring. Though Qumran took that as the "house" of David (4QFlor), Christians may have extrapolated the promise to the body of Jesus.

[40] Such an eschatological reading of Psalm 2 had already been taken in 4QFlor; cf. Darrell Bock, *Proclamation from Prophecy and Pattern: Lucan Old Testament Christology.* JSNTss 12 (Sheffield: JSOT Press, 1987), 246. This strengthens the possibility that such a Christian use of Psalm 2 is Pre-Pauline; cf. Gert Jacobus Steyn, *Septuagint Quotations in the Context of the Petrine and Pauline Speeches of the Acta Apostolorum* (Netherlands: Kok Pharos, 1995), 170-174.

[41] The first half of the citation is a paraphrase; only the last five words are identical to the LXX (τὰ ὅσια Δαυὶδ τὰ πιστά).

[42] The variations between the accounts are slight: (1) different vocabulary is used, (2) Paul's brief quotation of Psalm 16:10 represents the wording of the LXX [15:10] more accurately, (3) Peter, preaching in Jerusalem, points out the local tomb of David.

[43] As Baum points out ("Paulinismen in den Missionsreden," 405), it is tricky to compare the 'Paul' of Acts with his self-disclosure in the Epistles. These documents come from different periods and were written to different audiences and for different purposes. Furthermore, Paul's combined missionary speeches in Acts are shorter than 2 Thessalonians! That being said, one should be cautious about accusing Luke of misrepresenting Paul in his speeches. Luke's etic presentation in Acts may be as historically valid as Paul's emic revelation in the Epistles; cf. Witherington, 430-438.

38c-39, "Through him everyone who believes is **justified** [*dikaioō*] from everything you could not be justified from by the **law of Moses**."	Rom 3:8, "…a man is **justified** [*dikaioō*] by faith apart from observing the **law**" (cf. 3:20-22; 4:13; 10:4)
	Gal 2:16, "…a man is not **justified** [*dikaioō*] by observing the **law**, but by faith in Jesus Christ" (cf. 3:11, 24)
	Phil 3:9, "…not having a **righteousness** [*dikaiosunē*] of my own that comes from the **law**, but that which is through faith in Christ."

Justification by faith in Jesus apart from the law is a core Christian doctrine elucidated most clearly by Paul. It is fair to say that after Paul presented the standard review of Hebrew history and the traditional witness of Jesus' death and resurrection, he concludes the sermon with his own unique emphasis. This is Paul at his finest. If you would give Paul any one sentence from the entire book of Acts with which to summarize his doctrine, this would likely be at the top of a very short list.

13:40-41. Paul's critique of the law was a known flashpoint. On his final visit to Jerusalem more than a decade after this sermon, James warned him, "You see, brother, how many thousands of Jews have believed, and all of them are zealous for the law. They have been informed that you teach all the Jews who live among the Gentiles to turn away from Moses, telling them not to circumcise their children or live according to our customs" (21:20-21). While that is an obvious misrepresentation of Paul's view, it derives from such statements as Paul just made. The Law of Moses was no longer essential to salvation; Gentiles could be a part of the people of God without adherence to the now obsolete covenant. For some, this was a message of liberation. For others it was heresy.

Apparently there were those in the crowd who objected to Paul's teaching. So he responded with the ominous words of Habakkuk 1:5 (cf. Isa 28:21-22; 29:14).[44] Originally this predicted the rise of Nebuchadnezzar.[45] He was, unquestionably, one of Israel's greatest enemies. Surprisingly, this pagan became God's instrument to discipline his people. This was extraordinarily unexpected. Presently, God is doing something else just as unprecedented. Rather than using a pagan to punish his people, God is using his people, particularly his Messiah, to bless pagans by including them in his covenant salvation.

[42]As Paul and Barnabas were leaving the synagogue, the people invited them to speak further about these things on the next Sabbath. [43]When the congregation was dismissed, many of the Jews and devout converts to Judaism followed Paul and Barnabas, who talked with them and urged them to continue in the grace of God. [44]On the next Sabbath almost the whole city gathered to hear the

[44] The LXX "Look, you scoffers!" sounds quite a bit different than the MT "Look at the nations." Interestingly, the text of Acts 13:41 is closer to 1QpHab than either the MT or the LXX; cf. Steyn, *Septuagint Quotations*, 190. It appears that both Paul and the Qumran covenanters read the "nation" with a pejorative interpretive paraphrase: "scoffers."

[45] Paul was not the first to interpret Habakkuk as a *pesher* on current events. 1QpHab 2.1 had applied Habakkuk's warnings to the Roman invasion of Israel in 63 B.C.

word of the Lord. ⁴⁵When the Jews saw the crowds, they were filled with jealousy and talked abusively against what Paul was saying. ⁴⁶Then Paul and Barnabas answered them boldly: ⁴⁶ "We had to speak the word of God to you first. Since you reject it and do not consider yourselves worthy of eternal life, we now turn to the Gentiles. ⁴⁷For this is what the Lord has commanded us: 'I have made you^a a light for the Gentiles, that you may bring salvation to the ends of the earth.'^b"
^a47 The Greek is singular.   ^b47 Isaiah 49:6

13:42-43. With this rather austere ending to the sermon, Paul and Barnabas make for the door having already made a powerful impression. The congregation pleaded (*parakaleō*)⁴⁷ with them to return the following Sabbath and continue their teaching. Many of them, both Jews and Greek proselytes, chased after the two preachers to catch any tidbits of the gospel they could. Paul and Barnabas exhorted them to cling to God's grace. This undoubtedly refers back to Paul's message of salvation in Jesus apart from the Law of Moses (vv. 40-41). That was the key issue and the dividing line between Christians and non-Messianic Jews.

13:44-45. The next week the place was packed. Luke's claim that "nearly the whole city gathered" is an obvious hyperbole. But it was apropos, for the great numbers generated a jealousy among the Jews. This was not a petty squabble for popularity. Rather, in sociological terms, it was envy over the honor the apostles gained from the crowd. Since honor was believed to be a limited resource, that huge gain in the apostle's popularity was honor wrested from the Jews of the synagogue.⁴⁸ Slander began to fly.

13:46-47. In a number of places in Acts, when the Jews rejected the gospel messages, Paul turned full-force to the Gentiles: here in Antioch (13:46), Corinth (18:6), Ephesus (19:8-10), and Rome (28:23-28).⁴⁹ This principle is voiced by Jesus himself (22:18-21; cf. Luke 13:29-30) as well as Paul in his own words (Rom 1:16; 2:9-10). It never means that the work among the Jews has ended, but that in a specific city the evangelists will leave the synagogue and concentrate on Gentile evangelism. Jesus was not merely the savior of Israel but the hope of the Gentiles (Luke 2:30-32; 3:6). To that end Jesus commissioned the Apostles (Luke 24:47; Acts 1:8) and particularly Paul (Acts 9:15; 22:15; 26:16-18). None of this is novel or new; the initial promise to Abraham was that his seed would bless the nations (Gen 12:1-3; cf. Gal 3:16). Yahweh is too large to be confined to Israel; he wants to save the whole world. Paul's citation of Isaiah 49:6

⁴⁶This word (παρρησιάζομαι) is only found nine times in the New Testament and always in reference to Paul (Acts 9:27, 28; 18:26; 26:26; Eph 6:20; 1 Thess 2:2) with Barnabas tagging along a couple of times (Acts 13:46; 14:3). In Yiddish one might call this *chutzpah*.
⁴⁷The NIV's "invited" is a bit weak for this word which Luke uses to imply a strong request (Luke 7:4; 8:31-32, 41; 15:28; Acts 9:38; 16:9, 15, 39; 19:31; 21:12; 24:4; 25:3; 28:20) or exhortation (Luke 3:18; Acts 2:40; 11:23; 14:22; 15:32; 16:40; 20:1-2; 27:33-34). Only once might it have indicated a nonurgent invite (Acts 8:31).
⁴⁸For a description of this sociological phenomenon see H. Anselm and Jerome Neyrey, "It Was Out of Envy That They Handed Jesus Over (Mk 15:10): The Anatomy of Envy and the Gospel of Mark," *JSNT* 69 (1998): 15-56.
⁴⁹Cf. Robert C. Tannehill, "Rejection by Jews and Turning to Gentiles: The Pattern of Paul's Mission in Acts," *SBLsp* 25 (1986): 130-141.

(v. 47) is worth quoting in full: "It is too small a thing for you to be my servant to restore the tribes of Jacob and bring back those of Israel I have kept. I will also make you a light for the Gentiles, that you may bring my salvation to the ends of the earth." Originally "the light for the Gentiles" was the entire nation of Israel but later, because she went wayward, it was embodied in the person of Jesus (Luke 2:30-32). Now, during the Christian dispensation, the "light for the Gentiles" is again expanded from the person of Jesus to the evangelists to whom he has commissioned the vocation of the nation.

⁴⁸When the Gentiles heard this, they were glad and honored the word of the Lord; and all who were appointed for eternal life believed. ⁴⁹The word of the Lord spread through the whole region. ⁵⁰But the Jews incited the God-fearing women of high standing and the leading men of the city. They stirred up persecution against Paul and Barnabas, and expelled them from their region. ⁵¹So they shook the dust from their feet in protest against them and went to Iconium. ⁵²And the disciples were filled with joy and with the Holy Spirit.

13:48. Though the Jews were jealous, the Gentiles were delighted. They "*honored* the *word of the Lord*." This first term, "honored" (*doxazō*), means "to bring glory" which can be done verbally through praise or behaviorally through showing deference. That seems to be the meaning here—the new converts submitted to and aligned their lives with this new message of grace. The second term "Word of the Lord" (used three times in this context (vv. 44, 48, 49) is Luke's idiosyncratic term (Acts 8:25; 15:35, 36; 16:32; 19:10, 20),[50] synonymous with the "Word of God" (cf. Luke 5:1; 8:21; 11:28; Acts 4:31; 8:14; 13:5, 7, 46; 18:11) except that it always implies the oral presentation of the gospel rather than the written Scriptures.

"All who were appointed to eternal life believed." The word "appointed" means "enrolled" or "inscribed."[51] It seems to allude to one's name being added to the book of life (Exod 32:32-33; Psa 69:28; Dan 12:1; Luke 10:20; Phil 4:3; Rev 13:8; 20:12-15; 21:27).[52] This is one of the clearest statements of God's election in all of Scripture and should not be minimized. However, this does not mean that the human response to the gospel is irrelevant. Without diminishing God's definitive role in determining one's salvation, the context of this passage clearly describes the human initiative of those who became Christians. First, in verses 40-41, Paul gave a warning about rejecting the message. This implies that their own volition played a role in their salvation. Second, verse 46 indicates that some made the wrong choice which determined their destiny: "You reject it and do not consider yourselves worthy of eternal life." Third, before they were "appointed" by God they "honored the Word of the Lord." Moreover, the Greek phrase places their belief *before* their appointment: ". . . having believed [*main verb*] they had been appointed [*perfect passive participle*]." Though this rather wooden trans-

---

[50] The only other place this term is found in the NT is 1 Peter 1:25 though it is found 222x in the OT.
[51] Cf. Dan 6:13[12] Theodotion.
[52] The Book of Life was a common metaphor in other Jewish and Christian literature (Jubilees 30:20, 22; 1 Enoch 47:3; 104:1; 108:3; *b. Ros. Has.* 16b; *Tg.* Isa. 4:3.

lation is awkward English, it points out the dominant role their faith-response played in their own salvation. Here the paradox of the sovereignty of God and the freewill of humans sits comfortably side by side.

13:49-52. The message of grace swept the area. With the rise of the gospel came the increase of antagonism. Specifically, the Jews who rejected Jesus as their Messiah, incited some of the leading Greeks of the city to leverage their power against the apostles and expel them from the city. There were God-fearing women, likely proselytes,[53] and leading men of the city, likely the husbands of those influential women. The synagogue rulers influenced their powerful proselytes who convinced their husbands to enact a city-wide ban on Paul and Barnabas.

Consequently, Paul and Barnabas shook the dust from their feet as a sign of rejection and left for the next major city, Iconium, ninety miles down the *Via Sebaste*. This sign of rejection was no mere child's play. They were cursing the city as unclean under the authority of Jesus (Luke 9:5/Mark 6:11/Matt 10:14; Luke 10:11; Acts 18:6; 22:22-23; Str-B 1:571). The Christians left behind, far from beleaguered, were filled with the joy that comes from the Holy Spirit (cf. Luke 10:21; Rom 14:17; 15:13; Gal 5:22; 1 Thess 1:6).

---

[53] Greek women were apparently particularly prone to convert to Judaism (Josephus, *J.W.* 2.20.2 §560; Juvenal, *Satire* 6.542-545).

ACTS 14

4. Iconium, Lystra, and Derbe: Persecution and Stoning (14:1-20)

It would be a gross oversimplification to label chapter 14 "More of the Same." Nonetheless, it is at least that. "More of the Same" does not mean "boring" or "irrelevant." Part of Luke's strategy is to establish patterns through which the reader can extrapolate the habitual practices and experiences of the early church. To that end, this chapter is a valuable tool for the reader to capture three critical recurring themes. First, in Iconium (vv. 1-7) Paul goes to the **Jews first**. The gospel divides them and they persecute the preachers. This will continue to be standard fare. Second, in Lystra (vv. 8-20) Paul heals a lame man following Peter's pattern in chapter 3. This leads to a **sermon to pagans** that centers on God the creator. This theme is repeated in Athens when Paul preaches to pagan philosophers (17:22-31). Finally, Paul and Barnabas revisit their new church plants to establish **local Elders** (vv. 21-28). The general theme of church leadership has been addressed with the replacement of Iscariot in 1:12-26 and the Seven Evangelists of 6:1-7. The specific topic of Elders was introduced in 11:30 at Antioch and will receive full exposition in chapter 20:17-28. These three themes not only reach back to previous narratives, they project, for the reader, what is to come.

¹At Iconium Paul and Barnabas went as usual into the Jewish synagogue. There they spoke so effectively that a great number of Jews and Gentiles believed. ²But the Jews who refused to believe stirred up the Gentiles and poisoned their minds against the brothers. ³So Paul and Barnabas spent considerable time there, speaking boldly for the Lord, who confirmed the message of his grace by enabling them to do miraculous signs and wonders. ⁴The people of the city were divided; some sided with the Jews, others with the apostles. ⁵There was a plot afoot among the Gentiles and Jews, together with their leaders, to mistreat them and stone them. ⁶But they found out about it and fled to the Lycaonian cities of Lystra and Derbe and to the surrounding country, ⁷where they continued to preach the good news.

14:1-2. Paul and Barnabas flee from Antioch. Ninety miles east they land in Iconium (Modern Konya 📷). This lovely fertile plain (3,370') is an oasis in an otherwise arid region. Fruitful orchards and prolific sheep made this a profitable commercial center on the Via Sebaste.[1]

Their pattern is, by now, recognizable: Head straight to the synagogue

---

[1] For a fuller description of the city; cf. Merrill F. Unger, "Archaeology and Paul's Visit to Iconium, Lystra, and Derbe," *BibSac* 118 (1961): 107-112. Xenophon places Iconium in Phrygia c. 401 B.C. (*Anabasis* 1.2.19), though later writers put it in Lycaonia, sharing the same region as Lystra and Derbe (Cicero, *Letters to his Friends* 15.4.2 and Pliny the Elder, *Natural History* 5.25). It was apparently on the edge of both regions and had also been under the control of several dynasties including the ancient Phrygians, Greeks and Jews (312–65 B.C.), and, in Paul's day, the Romans who dignified the city with the name of the Emperor, "Claudiconium."

and preach to Jews while interested Gentiles eavesdrop. The Jewish response is beginning to be a pattern as well. A goodly number believed in Jesus as the Messiah. Those who didn't, however, stirred up the Gentiles against the evangelists (cf. 13:50).[2] The 'why?' is obvious: Paul's preaching of grace eradicates the boundaries between Jews and Gentiles, thus threatening their traditions (not to mentions spiritual superiority). Minority groups (like the Diaspora Jews) often cling tenaciously to traditional ways of life as a matter of social survival. Paul threatened their equilibrium with a message they deemed heretical. The more difficult question is not 'why?' but 'what?' What did the Jews of Iconium say to the Gentiles to turn them against the apostles? Here we can only speculate but this much cannot miss the mark by far: (1) Jesus was crucified. Thus Rome deems him a rebel. Adopting Jesus as Messiah could endanger one's standing with the government. (2) Christianity was a new religion not the ancient tradition. The reader must jettison here the Western presumption that new is good and old is inferior. The ancients believed precisely the opposite. That which is new innovation is untried and thus untrue. (3) In the second century, Rome had a legal injunction against new religious movements. It is probable that what became 'illegal' in the second century was already a prejudice in the first.

14:3-7. Paul's reaction is *not* what one would expect.[3] *Because* of the persecution, he digs in his heels and hunkers down for an extended stay in Iconium.[4] Though oppressed by unbelievers, God's support through miraculous power provided sufficient public popularity to protect them from lethal persecution (cf. 5:12; Heb 2:1-4). Nonetheless, the divided city made their stay precarious (cf. Matt 10:34-36). They always stood a breath away from a lynching. In fact, their antagonists, both Jewish and Gentile, plotted to take them out. Just like at Antioch, the persecutors won the support of some important officials to leverage their clout against the evangelists. That the planned execution was a stoning means its primary perpetrators were Jewish.

---

[2] The word (κακόω, v. 2), translated "poisoned their minds," could be rendered, "did them harm." Though the NIV translation is good, the double-entendre of doing them harm has been lost. True, the apostles were the ones harmed, but so too were the Gentiles who thereby lost the opportunity to respond to the gospel. The fictitious rendition of the Iconium encounter in *The Acts of Paul and Thecla* is entertaining, to be sure. Of particular interest is the description of Paul: He was "a man little of stature, thin-haired upon the head, crooked in the legs, of good state of body, with eyebrows joining, and nose somewhat hooked, full of grace: for sometimes he appeared like a man, and sometimes he had the face of an angel." However, this work is a forgery of the second century and the presbyter responsible for it was deposed from office. For a fuller account see Rackham (226-227). Nonetheless, the physical description of Paul performs a literary function of highlighting his noble character. This physiognomy is well defined by János Bollók, "The Description of Paul in the Acta Pauli," in *The Apocryphal Acts of Paul and Thecla* (ed. J.N. Bremmer; SAAA 2; Kampen: Kok Pharos, 1996), 1-15.

[3] The transition between vv. 2 & 3 is so unexpected, in fact, that some scholars accuse Luke of bungling his sources (e.g., Haenchen, 367-368). It is true that transposing vv. 2–3 would make for a smoother reading. However, there is no reason to suppose that such resistance could not make Paul stiffen his neck, redouble his resolve, and dig in his heels. At Philippi, Paul takes a beating (purposefully?) enabling the church to withstand secular authorities (16:35-40). In Thessalonica, Jason apparently made a pledge for Paul to leave the city *against his will* (17:1-9; cf. 1 Thess 2:18). In Ephesus, Paul nearly had to be hog-tied to keep him from preaching in the theater (19:30-31). And though he was warned not to go to Jerusalem, he willingly took the consequences for the opportunity to preach (Acts 21:4, 10-14). Paul was hardly the kind of guy to shy away from a good fight.

[4] The word "spent considerable time" (διατρίβω) is a favorite of Luke's. It is kind of like a chronological ellipsis which Luke uses to prolong the narrative without elongating text (John 3:22; Acts 12:19; 14:3, 28; 15:35; 16:12; 20:6; 25:6, 14).

Fortunately, the plot was discovered. Paul and Barnabas escaped before their enemies could latch onto them. They didn't just flee, they went into hiding. Rather than the major cities they had targeted, the two disappeared into the hinterlands of Lycaonia. Both Lystra and Derbe were minor blips on the radar, though Lystra was a kind of military outpost (since A.D. 6) and connected directly with Antioch.[5] Even in these out-of-the-way places Paul and Barnabas preached the good news . . . how could they not? News travels fast, and it wouldn't take long for the posse from Antioch and Iconium to align with each other in their fanatical hunt for Paul.

EXCURSUS
LUKE'S USE OF THE TITLE 'APOSTLE' IN ACTS

In verse 4, Paul and Barnabas were both labeled *apostles*. Surprisingly, the only place in the entire book where Paul is called an apostle is 14:4 & 14 and both times Barnabas is included. Clearly, Paul would agree with Luke's assessment that Barnabas was an apostle (cf. 1 Cor 9:5-6; Gal 2:9-10). And clearly, Luke knows that Paul was "sent with a commission" for twice he records Jesus' call of Paul with that very verb (*apostellō*, 22:21; 26:17). The problem is that Luke seems to reserve the title "Apostle" for the Twelve, as one might colloquially say, "with a capital A." As per the previous discussion on Apostles (see 1:2), a handful of others in the New Testament were also given the title[6] though the Twelve have a special place of authority. So does Luke consider Paul on par with the Twelve as a 13th Apostle to the Gentiles (cf. Rom 11:13; Gal 2:8)? Or does Luke see Paul, like Barnabas, merely a 'messenger' of the church of Antioch (e.g., 2 Cor 8:23)? Volumes of erudite speculation have yet to settle the issue.[7] Suffice to say for Luke, Barnabas and Paul are an anomaly. They are the only ones labeled apostles other than the Twelve. Hence, it appears that Luke regards Paul as partner with Barnabas though in some ways he is uniquely commissioned as were the Twelve. To attempt to say more would abuse the good reader's attention as well as an otherwise innocent sheet of paper.

[8]In Lystra there sat a man crippled in his feet, who was lame from birth and had never walked.[8] [9]He listened to Paul as he was speaking. Paul looked directly at him, saw that he had faith to be healed [10]and called out, "Stand up on your feet!" At that, the man jumped up and began to walk. [11]When the crowd saw what Paul had done, they shouted in the Lycaonian language, "The gods have come down to us in human form!" [12]Barnabas they called Zeus, and Paul they called Hermes

---

[5] There was a statue found in Antioch which was a gift of the Lystrans. Moreover, there was a direct Roman road between the two cities due to the military tie between them. This likely explains how Paul and Barnabas were located so quickly. Cf. Ramsay, *Cities*, 371-373.

[6] Apostles other than the Twelve include Paul and Barnabas (Acts 14:4, 14), Andronicus and Junias (Rom 16:7), unnamed brothers (2 Cor 8:23), James, the Lord's brother (Gal. 1:19), Epaphroditus, (Phil 2:25), and Jesus (Heb 3:1).

[7] Cf. Klaus Haacker, "Verwendung und Vermeidung des Apostelbegriffs im lukanischen Werk," *NovT* 30 (1988): 9-38; *Beginnings* 5:37-59; and Andrew C. Clark, "The Role of the Apostles," in *Witness to the Gospel: The Theology of Acts* (eds. I. Howard Marshall and David Peterson; Grand Rapids: Eerdmans, 1998), 182-185.

[8] Verse 8 showcases Luke's artistry as an author. The first half of the verse is a chiasm: Καί τις ἀνὴρ ἀδύνατος ἐν Λύστροις τοῖς ποσὶν ἐκάθητο. The second half has an alliterative play on words with "lame" (χωλός) and "womb" (κοιλίας).

because he was the chief speaker. ¹³The priest of Zeus, whose temple was just out-side the city, brought bulls and wreaths to the city gates because he and the crowd wanted to offer sacrifices to them. ¹⁴But when the apostles Barnabas and Paul heard of this, they tore their clothes and rushed out into the crowd, shouting:

14:8-10. Luke wastes no time getting to this miraculous healing. It is only a guess, but perhaps that is due to the fact that it took place in the city gate as Paul arrived. That would make sense. The city gate was a place of public gathering and discussion.[9] A traveler coming from a metropolis like Iconium would be a valuable source of public information (not to mention interesting gossip). If the crowd's curiosity stopped Paul short of entering the city, his discussion in the gates could have led to the healing of this lame man.

As Paul described the purpose of his visit, this lame man listened with par-ticular interest. Paul stared into his very soul, seeing that the man had faith.[10] Just how Paul did this is a mystery, but the very word (*atenizō*) reminds us of Peter's intense gaze at the beautiful gate (3:4). Both healings involve a man lame from birth. Both provided a platform for preaching Jesus. And both ultimately re-sulted in a pretty nasty beating for the miracle worker. These deliberate echoes take us back ever further—Jesus healed a lame man as well (Luke 5:18-26; cf. John 5:1-9).[11] It provided an opportunity for him to proclaim forgiveness of sins. Thus, the specific healing of a lame man becomes a metaphor for conversion in general. His physical transformation portrays our spiritual metamorphosis.

With a shout of authority, Paul orders the man to his feet. This lifelong crip-ple jumps up and begins to walk.[12] This story is thicker than it looks. The word for "**jump**" (*hallomai*) echoes that great Messianic promise of Isaiah 35:5-6, "Then will the eyes of the blind be opened and the ears of the deaf unstopped. Then will the lame **leap** like a deer, and the mute tongue shout for joy. Water will gush forth in the wilderness and streams in the desert."[13] Luke was, in fact, familiar with this Septuagint passage for he quotes part of it in Luke 7:22 (/Matt 11:5). His triple

---

[9] E.g., Gen 34:20; Deut 17:5; 22:15; 25:7; Josh 20:4; Ruth 4:11; 1 Kgs 22:10; 2 Kgs 7:1; Job 29:7; Psa 69:12; 127:5; Prov 24:7; 31:23, 31. Interestingly, the gate was also the place where people were stoned (Deut 21:19; 22:24; cf. Acts 14:19).

[10] Luke uses ἀτενίζω twelve of its fourteen times in the NT. Strelan argues that it indicates a kind of Spirit-possession, especially when combined with a "loud voice" (v. 10). This would account for why this is the only NT healing done without invoking the name of Jesus; cf. Rick Strelan, "Recognizing the Gods (Acts 14.8-10)," *NTS* 46 (2000): 488-503. While that is possible, Strelan does not account for the fact that half of the people who "stare" are not spirit-filled but staring at those who are (Luke 4:20; 22:56; Acts 1:10; 3:12; 6:15; 2 Cor 3:7, 13). In Acts, those whose gaze could be considered visionary or numinous are Peter (Acts 3:4; 11:6), Stephen (7:55), Cornelius (10:4), and Paul (13:9; 14:9; 23:1).

[11] This hermeneutical device is adequately described by Robert C. Tannehill, "The Composition of Acts 3–5: Narrative Development and Echo Effect," *SBLSP* 23 (1984): 217-240. Luke, of course, is particularly interested in physical healing as it relates to salvation. He uses the word σῴζω in v. 9. Cf. Ben Witherington, "Salvation and Health in Christian Antiquity: The Soteriology of Luke-Acts in Its First Century Setting," in *Witness to the Gospel: The Theology of Acts* (ed. I. Howard Marshall and David Peterson; Grand Rapids: Eerdmans, 1998), 145-166.

[12] It is difficult to miss the direct line Luke is drawing between the lame men healed by Paul and Peter. Acts 3:8 reads: καὶ ἐξαλλόμενος ἔστη καὶ περιεπάτει. Acts 14:10 reads: καὶ ἥλατο καὶ περιεπάτει. These two phrases are virtually identical save the inclusion of the word "stand" (ἵστημι) in 3:8, the prefix ἐξ on ἅλλομαι, and the change of "jump" in 14:10 from a present participle to an aorist middle indicative.

[13] The only other NT passage that uses ἅλλομαι (John 4:14) also alludes to Isaiah 35:6. Only instead of referencing the dear "leaping" he speaks of wells "gushing."

use of this paradigmatic healing of a lame man seems to be a deliberate reflection of the Messianic age where both physical and spiritual cripples are raised.[14]

14:11-14. Paul's healing made quite the impression. In fact, the locals were ready to treat them as gods (cf. Acts 28:1-6).[15] Most probably they have Ovid's tale in the back of their minds (*Metamorphoses* 8.631-720).[16] It is a quaint story set in the hills of Phrygia (from where Paul and Barnabas just came). So the legend goes: Zeus and Hermes[17] disguise themselves to test the hospitality of the region in order to determine if they would destroy the land. Going from door to door in the guise of vagrants, they were consistently rebuffed. Finally they came to the humble home of an elderly coupled named Philemon and Baucis. This kindly couple invited them in and stoked the fire with some twigs from their thatch roof. They served their guests all they could afford—a simple meal of peasant's fare. When they saw that their pitcher of wine never emptied no matter how much they refilled their guest's glasses, they suspected their guests were gods. At that they decided to kill and cook their pet goose. The bird proved nimbler than its elderly owners and evaded their grasp, even taking refuge with the divine guests. At this, Zeus and Hermes revealed their true identity. They offered a wish to the noble couple who forthwith requested that they become temple priests and die together. Their request was, of course, granted. The two gods transformed their humble home into a temple of Zeus and made Philemon and Baucis the priest and priestess of the local cult (the rest of the village was destroyed). Years later, the couple died simultaneously and were transformed into two intertwining trees. What a story!

It is not likely, even in rural Lystra, that such myths were taken seriously,[18] at least not until someone like Paul comes along and rocks their world with a prodigious miracle. What was taken seriously in Phrygia and Lycaonia, and with rapidly increasing frequency, was the emperor cult which deified the Roman ruler. This region was one of the primary areas for the Emperor Cult. Hence, these locals, given to human deification and faced with a notable healing, would reflect on an ancient myth and give it credence.

---

[14] It may also be significant that Luke chooses the word ἀνίστημι for "raised"—the very same word used throughout the NT for "resurrection." In light of this word as well as the general structure and vocabulary of the narrative, Dionne suggests that Luke expects the reader to understand the content of Paul's unreported sermon from the previous episodes in Antioch and Iconium; cf. Christian Dionne, "L'Épisode de Lystre (Ac 14,7-20a): une analyse narrative," *ScEs* 57 (2005): 5-33.

[15] There were precedents for treating healers as divine emissaries (Philostratus, *Apollonius* 1.1; 8.5; Diogenes Laertes, 8.62); cf. Strelan, "Recognizing the Gods," 488-489.

[16] There were, of course, a number to stories about gods (or angels) visiting incognito in both Jewish (e.g., Gen 18–19) and Greco-Roman literature; cf. Adelbert Denaux, "The Theme of Divine Visits and Human (In)Hospitality in Luke-Acts: Its Old Testament and Graeco-Roman Antecedents," in *The Unity of Luke-Acts* (ed. J. Verheyden; Leuven: Leuven University Press, 1999), 255-279.

[17] The original tale used their Latin names, of course, Jupiter (Zeus) and Mercury (Hermes). The importance of these two gods for the Lystrans was illustrated in a dramatic way when three inscriptions dedicated to this divine duo were discovered in the 1920s; cf. "Acts 14, 12," *ExpT* 37 (1925–26): 528.

[18] Depicting rustics as gullible was a common Greek *topos*. Normally such stories conclude by revealing how the charlatan had taken advantage of the unsuspecting illiterates. Luke's rendition, however, shows that Paul was not a charlatan that took advantage of others but was, in fact, the victim. Such an apologetic twist on the story could serve as an important social defense in the early church. Cf. Dean P. Béchard, "Paul among the Rustics: The Lystran Episode (Acts 14:8-20)," *CBQ* 63 (2001): 84-101.

Paul and Barnabas realized there was a stir but couldn't understand the hub-bub because the Lystrans reverted to their native language. The *lingua franca* of area was Greek, likely with a smattering of Latin.[19] But in times of particular excitement, people instinctively revert to their mother tongue.[20] So how was Paul to know he was being honored as Hermes (the chief speaker of the gods) and Barnabas as Zeus. Of course, when the priest of the local Zeus cult came around the corner with a bull dressed for sacrifice, this visual aid was all they needed to interpret what was going on. These pagans were acting like pagans; Barnabas and Paul respond like Hebrews. With a particularly Jewish gesture, they express their consternation by tearing their robes (cf. Gen 37:29, 34; Num 14:6; 2 Sam 13:19, 31, etc.). They even charged the 'mosh pit' and protested vociferously. What comes out of this chaos is the first of two sermons in Acts directed solely to pagans. Though all too brief, it is a gem of contextualized apologetics.

[15]**"Men, why are you doing this? We too are only men, human like you. We are bringing you good news, telling you to turn from these worthless things to the living God, who made heaven and earth and sea and everything in them.** [16]**In the past, he let all nations go their own way.** [17]**Yet he has not left himself without testimony: He has shown kindness by giving you rain from heaven and crops in their seasons; he provides you with plenty of food and fills your hearts with joy."** [18]**Even with these words, they had difficulty keeping the crowd from sacrificing to them.** [19]**Then some Jews came from Antioch and Iconium and won the crowd over. They stoned Paul and dragged him outside the city, thinking he was dead.** [20]**But after the disciples had gathered around him, he got up and went back into the city. The next day he and Barnabas left for Derbe.**

Paul's sermon to the pagans of Lystra is strikingly similar to his Areopagus address in Athens.[21] These are the only two places Luke recorded an evangelistic encounter with pure pagans. In both instances, rather than quoting Scripture, Paul referenced creation as the 'proof-text' for God's interaction with men.[22] Lystra represented illiterate rustics[23] while Athens was the epicenter of philosophic sophisticates. Thus, this message can play from the top of the educational ladder right down to the simplest folk.

---

[19] Cf. H. J. Cadbury, *Book of Acts in History* (London: Black, 1955), 21-22.

[20] Most local dialects of Anatolia have been lost except for rare inscriptional evidence. Unfortunately, that is the case for Lystra. The most educated guess is that it was a form of Luwian, a sub-species of the Indo-European family of languages; cf. Stanley Porter, "The Languages That Paul Did Not Speak," in *Paul's World* (ed. Stanley E. Porter; Leiden: Brill, 2008), 131-149.

[21] Nathalie Siffer-Wiederhold offers an indepth analysis of the linguistic and theological overlap of these two sermons; cf. "L'annonce du vrai Dieu dans les discours missionnaires aux païens: Ac 14,15-17 et 17,22-31," *RSR* 81 (2007): 523-544.

[22] Romans 1:18-32 also uses creation as an apologetic device but to a very different effect; cf. Philipp Vielhauer, "Zum 'Paulinismus' der Apostelgeschichte,"*PSTJ* 17 (1963): 5-17. In Acts, creation is the evidence for the goodness and patience of God in delaying his judgment. In Romans, because humankind rejected the truth of God embedded in creation, Yahweh gave them over to depraved passions which contradicted the created order. Both points are true, but truly very different.

[23] Béchard, "Paul among the Rustics," 89, provides convincing primary documentation.

LYSTRA, ACTS 14:15-17	ATHENS, ACTS 17:22-30
15a, "**Men** why are you doing this? "We too are only men, human like you."	22a, "**Men** of Athens"
15b, "We are bringing you good news," [An introduction to capture their interest.]	22b, "I see that in every way you are very religious." [An introduction to capture their interest.]
15c, "telling you to turn from these worthless things to the **living God**,"	23, Paul found in Athens an Altar to an **unknown god** who he will now **reveal as Yahweh.**
15d, "who **made heaven and earth** and sea and **everything in them**."	24, "The God who **made** the world and **everything** in it is the Lord of **heaven and earth** and does not live in temples built by hands."
	25-26, He is not dependent on us rather we are on him. Even our nations and boundaries are in his hand.
16, "In the **past**, he let all nations go their own way"	30, "In the **past** God overlooked such ignorance, but now he commands all people everywhere to repent"
17, God is a generous provider for humanity.	27-29, Creation calls us to seek a creator for in him we live and breathe. We are his children, made in his image.

14:15-18. Paul's reaction to their 'deification' of him and Barnabas could not have been more vigorous. Unquestionably, Paul is a monotheist who refused divine honors (as did Peter with Cornelius, see on 10:25). There was no question for Paul, God was one and all that exists was created by him. The triple term he used—heaven, earth, and sea—echoes Exodus 20:11, "For in six days the LORD made the heavens and the earth, the sea, and all that is in them . . ." What is most interesting is that this passage comes in the midst of the Ten Commandments. This is the core of the Jewish Law. Hence, part of the Mosaic Law was predicated on the creation account. This is not only the foundation for Jewish legislation, it was the foundation for natural theology.[24] This argument is the center of Paul's message both in Lystra and in Athens (14:15; 17:24).[25] In short, creation itself shouts of the goodness of God. Though the wayward nations know not the living god (v. 16) creation does (v. 17). The goodness of rain,

---

[24] Cf. Thomas B. Slater, "The Possible Influence of LXX Exodus 20:11 on Acts 14:15," *AUSS* 30 (1992): 151-152. This same tri-part division of creation is found elsewhere (Psa 146:6; Acts 4:24; Rev 5:13; 10:6-7).

[25] Interestingly, this argument was also used by Johanan ben Zakkai in *Deut. Rab.* 7.7: "Once it happened that a Gentile asked Rabban Johanan ben Zakkai saying to him: 'We have feasts and you have feasts. We have Kalendae, Saturnalia and Kratesis, and you have Passover, Pentecost and the Feast of Tabernacles. What is the day when both you and we rejoice?' Rabban Johanan ben Zakkai said to him: 'It is the day of rainfall, as it is written: "The meadows clothe themselves with flocks, the valleys deck themselves with grain, they shout and sing together with joy"'" (Psa 65:13[14]). What is written after these words? "To the choirmaster. A song. A Psalm. Make a joyful noise to God, all the earth" (Psa 66:1). It is not written "priests, Levites, and Israelites," but "all the earth."'" Cf. Colin Barnes, "Paul and Johanan ben Zakkai," *ExpT* 108 (1997): 366-367. For further parallels from Josephus see F. G. Downing, "Common Ground with Paganism in Luke and in Josephus," *NTS* 28 (1982): 546-559. Though the 'natural theology' of vv. 15-17 speaks to pagans, much of the language is indebted to the Septuagint; cf. Ernst Lerle, "Die Predigt in Lystra," *NTS* 7 (1960): 53-55.

seasonal crops, and the joy of life are gifts of God. This last point would carry a punch since Zeus was worshiped in this area as the god of rain and crops.[26]

One would expect at this point that Paul would preach the resurrected Jesus as he did in all his other sermons (even Athens!). Most likely, he has already done that *prior* to the healing of the lame man. After all, he never wasted much time getting to Jesus. Furthermore, the faith Paul saw in the lame man was most likely faith in the Name of the one who heals. What we have here is not really a sermon so much as a frenetic attempt to dissuade the locals from a blasphemous sacrifice. His words were barely effective.

14:19-20. Meanwhile, those who plotted Paul's assassination in Iconium have followed the trail to Lystra.[27] They burst on the scene with venomous accusations against the apostles which persuaded the Lystrans to lynch him. What could Paul's enemies have said that so quickly turned their adoration of a 'god' into a lethal attack on a 'demon'? The crowd may seem fickle. However, their operating logic makes sense: Paul has power; however, his power is disruptive and dangerous, not salutary. Obviously, they cannot deny Paul's miracles. They, could, however, relegate them to a dark force. The same logic is applied to the Man of Lawlessness: "The coming of the lawless one will be in accordance with the work of Satan displayed in all kinds of counterfeit miracles, signs and wonders" (2 Thess 2:9). The more impressive Paul's power the more potentially dangerous he was. Their admission of Paul's power did not change, but their assessment of it did. His power was malignant and thus must be brought to an abrupt end. Stoning will do.

Fortunately, they were one stone shy of the death blow. After they dragged Paul outside the city, perhaps even through the gate where the lame man leapt, the new believers gathered round. Their mourning was arrested when Paul groaned (or whatever made them realize he was alive). The brothers helped him to his feet and led him (surreptitiously?) into the city. This, of course, begs the question, "Was Paul really dead?" Perhaps he did actually die and his spirit went briefly to heaven. In c. A.D. 57 Paul will record a similar experience, though in the third person (2 Cor 12:1-5; cf. 2 Tim 3:11).[28] Still, a more naturalistic hypothesis may be simpler—Paul was knocked unconscious and Lois and Eunice nursed him back to health, making an indelible imprint on their child, Timothy (2 Tim 1:5). Paul took all of about twelve hours to recover from the most brutal beating of his life (cf. 2 Cor 11:25; 2 Tim 3:11) before hiking another sixty miles to Derbe.[29]

---

[26] For a survey of the primary data, cf. Cilliers Breytenbach, "Zeus und der lebendige Gott: Anmerkungen zu Apostelgeshichte 14.11-17," *NTS* 39 (1993): 396-413.

[27] There is no real time marker between vv. 18 & 19. The reader, however, senses that there must be some interval since Paul made a number of disciples (v. 20). The Western text fills the gap by adding at the end of v. 19, "spent some time [in Lystra] and taught."

[28] Since Paul places this visionary experience "fourteen years" earlier, that would put it at A.D. 43, a little early for this missionary tour, but not terribly far off.

[29] This is assuming that Kerti Hüyük is the site of Derbe. Cf. Bastiaan van Elderen, "Some Archaeological Observations on Paul's First Missionary Journey," in *Apostolic History and the Gospel* (W. Ward Gasque and Ralph P. Martin, eds.; Great Britain: Paternoster Press, 1970), 156-161, and *Beginnings* 5:227-230.

5. Paul and Barnabas Return to Antioch through the Fledgling Churches (14:21-28)

[21]They preached the good news in that city and won a large number of disciples. Then they returned to Lystra, Iconium and Antioch, [22]strengthening the disciples and encouraging them to remain true to the faith. "We must go through many hardships to enter the kingdom of God," they said. [23]Paul and Barnabas appointed elders[a] for them in each church and, with prayer and fasting, committed them to the Lord, in whom they had put their trust. [24]After going through Pisidia, they came into Pamphylia, [25]and when they had preached the word in Perga, they went down to Attalia. [26]From Attalia they sailed back to Antioch, where they had been committed to the grace of God for the work they had now completed. [27]On arriving there, they gathered the church together and reported all that God had done through them and how he had opened the door of faith to the Gentiles. [28]And they stayed there a long time with the disciples.

[a]23 Or *Barnabas ordained elders*; or *Barnabas had elders elected*

14:21-22. Luke shows little interest in Derbe except as the final stop on the tour. He simply reports an effective campaign before the missionaries retrace their steps to the very churches that persecuted them. If one were to look at a map at this point, one would see how close Paul was to his own home of Tarsus. From there Antioch is a short distance by land. This overland route was, by far, the easiest way to return to Antioch. But Paul's concern for the health of the churches drove him back the way he came even though it was longer and more dangerous. This penchant for succoring fledgling congregations would become a consistent pattern for Paul's ministry (cf. Acts 15:30-35, 41; 16:40; 18:23; 20:1-2). Perhaps the fracas had settled down in those cities since Paul's stoning. Or perhaps he threw caution to the wind in order to build up the body. More likely, his presence as a churchman was not as inflammatory as his presence as a missionary. Nevertheless, his exhortation recalls the persecution he experienced and which believers can expect: "We must go through many hardships to enter the kingdom of God" (v. 22; cf. 1 Thess 3:4).

Paul had a rather robust theology of suffering. He was convinced that it lead to greater good. In Romans 5:3-4 he claims, "We also rejoice in our sufferings, because we know that suffering produces perseverance; perseverance, character; and character, hope" (cf. 2 Cor 8:2; Eph 3:13; Col 1:24; 1 Thess 3:7). Therefore, to the great Apostle these were but "light and momentary troubles" (2 Cor 4:17). One might suggest that it was psychologically (if not sociologically) imperative for Paul to view suffering as advantageous since it was a perpetual part of his ministry (cf. Acts 20:23; 2 Cor 1:8; 6:4; Eph 3:13; Phil 1:17; 1 Thess 3:3) as well as a frequent experience of the churches he founded (Rom 8:35; 12:12; 2 Cor 1:4; 8:2; Phil 4:14; 1 Thess 1:6; 2 Thess 1:4). This reinterpretation of persecution as positive stands on the bedrock of God's eschatological justice (2 Thess 1:6). Because Paul believed God would soon intervene and set things right, he could live joyfully through trials (2 Cor 7:4; 8:2). The concept of the

"Kingdom of God" has eschatological overtones. Thus, Paul seems to be saying more than simply: "You will suffer as a member of the church." Rather, this passage implies: "Our suffering is an eschatological precursor to the full advent of the coming Kingdom."[30]

In the contemporary church, global persecution exponentially outweighs that of the first century. Because of this sad fact, Paul's theology of persecution as a means of accomplishing God's ultimate advent of the kingdom, is a tenet the church dare not obfuscate, particularly those living large in the west for whom persecution is but a disengaged sermon illustration.

14:23. Paul didn't just encourage them to remain faithful. He and Barnabas appointed local elders in each congregation to ensure the spiritual stability of the body.[31] Elders are crucial for New Testament churches (Acts 15:2-6; 20:17; 21:18; 1 Tim 4:14; 5:17; Tit 1:5; James 5:15; 1 Peter 5:1). Paul and Barnabas fasted and prayed, as they had done when they were initially set apart for this work (13:3). But where is the laying on of hands we saw earlier (13:3; 6:6; cf. 1 Tim 4:14; 5:22; 2 Tim 1:6)? It is likely implied in the word "appointed" (*cheirotoneō*) which etymologically means "to stretch out the hand."[32] To those avowedly committed to doing "Bible things in Bible ways," it would be right to ask why these three biblical practices are so rare among contemporary church leaders.

Detwiler makes an important observation.[33] In verse 21, Paul and Barnabas "made disciples" (*mathēteuō*). That's 'Great Commission' talk. An essential part of making disciples was establishing elders. We don't merely introduce individuals to Jesus; we incorporate them into his body. Disciples tend to grow in Jesus in direct proportion to their involvement in a healthy church. And churches tend to grow in faith, purpose, and outreach in direct proportion to the quality of local elders who tend to their needs.

14:24-28. The team now descends quickly across their one hundred and ten mile trek back to Perga. In a provocatively brief note, Luke mentions their preaching in Perga. They then hop a freighter in Attalia heading toward Syria. (For further travel details see notes on 13:14-15). Once they returned to their 'sending church' they submitted a full report, much to the delight of all. Of particular interest to the church of Antioch, not to mention Luke, God opened the door to the Gentiles. With this, their mission was accomplished. Without further detail, Luke leaves them in Antioch until the next major episode . . . and it will be *major!* It too has to do with God opening the door to the Gentiles.

---

[30] Cf. A. J. Mattill, "The Way of Tribulation," *JBL* 98 (1979): 531-546.

[31] Against Haenchen (379-381) etc., who casts aspersions on the historicity of Luke's report, Nellessen argues cogently that the establishment of Elders would not only be natural among Jewish Christians coming out of the synagogue but was strongly supported by Paul's own writings (e.g., Phil 1:1; 1 Cor 12:28-30, etc.). Ernst Nellessen, "Die Presbyter der Gemeinden in Lykaonien und Pisidien (Apg 14, 23)," in *Les Actes des Apôtres: Traditions, redaction, théologie* (ed. J. Kremer; Leuven: Leuven University Press, 1979), 493-498.

[32] It is theoretically possible, though hardly likely that those who "stretched out their hands" were the congregation rather than the apostles. However, the clear reading of the text points to Paul and Barnabas as the ones who laid hands on the newly appointed Elders; cf. John Ross, "The Appointment of Presbyters in Acts 14:23," *ExpT* 63 (1951): 288-289. It is true that the church of the late first and early second century already showed signs of electing church leaders (*Didache* 15.1; Ignatius, *Philadelphia* 10.1 and *Smyrna* 11.2). Nonetheless, there is no secure exegetical evidence that this text should be so read.

[33] David F. Detwiler, "Paul's Approach to the Great Commission in Acts 14:21-23," *BibSac* 152 (1995): 33-41.

ACTS 15

B. THE JERUSALEM COUNCIL (15:1-35)

There is no chapter in the book of Acts more central to Luke's theology, not to mention Paul's! Here we arrive at the theological epicenter of the book. It is also, however, the storm-center. This debate was charged with explosive emotions on both sides (e.g., Gal. 2:11-14). It is the epicenter and storm-center due to a single question: How are we saved? Is it "by grace through faith"? Or are there other requirements for Gentiles to enter the covenant salvation of Yahweh? On the one hand, some Jewish teachers pointed out that circumcision as the entrance into the covenant was an inviolable principle of fidelity to God (v. 1). Paul and Barnabas argued to the contrary that Jesus supersedes and supervenes all previous covenants. This is not a replacement of the older covenant but a fulfillment of it. The result is that Gentiles can enter the Kingdom of God without becoming Jewish. Such is the gist of the argument in Acts 15. Yet there are further questions begging for clarification.

What is the relationship between circumcision and table fellowship? Though it might appear that these are two separate issues, they are inextricably intertwined. Uncircumcised Gentiles were considered morally unclean even if they were exempt from rules of ritual purity.[1] Consequently, though table fellowship with Gentiles was not proscribed in the Old Testament, in Jewish practice it was uncomfortably strained (see comments on 10:13-16; cf. Jub 22:16; Tob 1:10-11; *Letter of Aristeas* 139-143). It was not merely that Gentile hosts might put nonkosher food on the table; their very presence was unholy, hence, defiling. The Gentile was unclean not because of what he ate or what he did but because of who he was. This was a huge problem in the early church which habitually practiced the Lord's Supper over a shared meal. At the most sacred moment of the church's *koinōnia* Jews and Gentiles were at their most bitter divide. It was bound to explode sooner or later. The 'Jewish' solution (v. 1) was to sanctify the Gentiles through circumcision. For Paul and Barnabas, however, such a compromise was tantamount to denying the sanctifying power of Jesus' substitutionary death.

Was James's decree a universal law for salvation or a cultural accommodation for unity? This is a complicated question, as we shall see below. Here's the skinny. In verses 19-21 James the Elder mandates four prohibitions for Gentiles: Food polluted by idols, fornication, meat of strangled animals, and blood. These look kind of like the rules for resident aliens among Israel (Leviticus 18–19) and kind of like the laws set down for Noah's family after the flood (Gen 9:4-6). If these are guidelines for Gentiles living among Jews, then they were given for the sake

---

[1] This complicated issue is helpfully explored by Jonathan Klawans, "Notions of Gentile Impurity in Ancient Judaism," *AJSR* 20 (1995): 285-312.

of the unity of the church. If, however, they are 'Noahic Laws', they are mandatory for Christians. Perhaps one might ask, "Would Paul not have a fit if James added to salvation by grace through faith?"[2] Probably not . . . at least not the way James framed it. These four guidelines, taken as a whole, prohibit idolatry and its concomitant practices. Paul would never argue that Gentiles could be idol worshiping Christians.[3] It appears, therefore, that Paul and James were of the same mind even if they expressed it differently. James is saying, "You Gentiles can't be doing that stuff in the church." If one has to ask whether idolatry is prohibited as a law or a practice of unity, they just don't get it.

Is Acts 15 the same meeting as Galatians 2?[4] Arguments both pro and con were already offered at 11:30 (see "Excursus on Paul's Visit to Jerusalem"). It is our tentative conclusion that Galatians 2 describes a private meeting that took place during Paul's second trip to Jerusalem when he arrived with famine relief (Acts 11:28-30).[5] Given this scenario, what can be said about the events leading up to the great council of Acts 15? (1) A group of pioneering missionaries breached the boundaries of Judaism by presenting the saving message of Jesus the Messiah to Gentiles (11:19-21). (2) The officials in Jerusalem sent Barnabas to validate the orthodoxy of this bold new move (11:22-24). He, in turn, hunted down Saul in Tarsus, who had already received a commission to preach to Gentiles (11:25-26; 26:16b-18). (3) These newly labeled "Christians" (11:26) were accosted by some representatives from Jerusalem concerning the need for circumcision (Gal 2:4).[6] It was now some fourteen years after Paul's conversion (Gal 2:1, c. A.D. 44). He goes to Jerusalem with Barnabas and Titus (as a test-case Gentile convert) so that the Apostles could confirm the orthodoxy of his preaching (Gal 2:2). They gladly did (Gal 2:9). They even affirmed the offering Paul and Barnabas brought from Antioch to alleviate the famine predicted by Agabus (11:27; Gal 2:10). (4) Very soon after this private Jerusalem meeting, Peter was nearly assassinated by Herod (Acts 12:3-17). He escaped with the help of an angel and then went 'underground'. One of the places to which he apparently traveled was Antioch. This makes sense. When Paul was a fugitive in Jerusalem, Barnabas brought him to Peter who harbored him for two weeks (Acts 9:27; Gal 1:18). Paul would gladly return the favor. It was during this stay, that some legalistic del-

---

[2] This is not an uncommon assertion; e.g., David Catchpole, "Paul, James and the Apostolic Decree," *NTS* 23 (1977): 428-444.

[3] In this sense, it is simplistic to suggest that James's solution is a 'compromise' between Paul and the Judaizers. Even so, Denis Fricker is correct to show that the method used in Acts 15 for dealing with division in the church is still an exemplary model of dialogue, accommodation, and decree; cf. "La crise d'Antioche et la gestion des conflits en église: exégèse et théologie pastorale," *RSR* 80 (2006): 349-370.

[4] Walter Radl, "Das Gesetz in Apg 15," in *Gesetz im Neuen Testament* (Freiburg: Herder, 1986), 169-174, wisely cautions that Acts 15 needs to be interpreted on its own terms without the imposition of Galatians 2.

[5] Some might object to two distinct meetings over the same issue. Would the Jerusalem leaders have to meet more than once to settle this issue? Yes, they did. There was a Jerusalem meeting after Cornelius' conversion by Peter (11:1-4) and another after Paul's mission to the Gentiles (15:1-4). The first answered the question, "Can Gentiles be seated at our table?" and the second, "Can Gentiles be saved without circumcision?" To propose a third at 11:28-30 is simply to recognize the very real difficulty this problem posed to the early church. Julius Scott, "The Church's Progress to the Council of Jerusalem According to the Book of Acts," *BBR* 7 (1997): 205-24, traces the long, arduous road in the book of Acts to arrive at this point in Gentile inclusion.

[6] These Jewish legalists may have arrived in Antioch as part of Barnabas's entourage (11:22), but more likely they came with the group of prophets along with Agabus (11:27).

egates came from Jerusalem, causing Peter and Barnabas to withdraw from table fellowship with Gentiles (Gal 2:12-13). Paul erupted with a vituperative public rebuke of Cephas (Gal 2:11, 14). Gauging from Peter's report (Acts 15:7-11), which sounds Pauline, he responded well to this correction. (5) Shortly after this event, the Holy Spirit called Barnabas and Saul on their first missionary journey, which lasted approximately three years. After their return to Antioch, the controversy over Gentile Christians had not yet subsided. Jerusalem legalists, perhaps in response to the missionary report of Gentile inclusion (14:27), surfaced in Antioch to restrain the doctrine of Free-Grace Salvation (Acts 15:1). Jewish tensions were nearly as high as Gentile jubilation. This brings us up to date.

1. Judaizers and a Question of Circumcision and Salvation (15:1-5)

¹Some men came down from Judea to Antioch and were teaching the brothers: "Unless you are circumcised, according to the custom taught by Moses, you cannot be saved." ²This brought Paul and Barnabas into sharp dispute and debate with them. So Paul and Barnabas were appointed, along with some other believers, to go up to Jerusalem to see the apostles and elders about this question. ³The church sent them on their way, and as they traveled through Phoenicia and Samaria, they told how the Gentiles had been converted. This news made all the brothers very glad. ⁴When they came to Jerusalem, they were welcomed by the church and the apostles and elders, to whom they reported everything God had done through them. ⁵Then some of the believers who belonged to the party of the Pharisees stood up and said, "The Gentiles must be circumcised and required to obey the law of Moses."

15:1. There are two questions introduced in verse one. First, who were these guys who advocated circumcision? All we know for sure about these shadowy figures is that they are from Judea (v. 1) and that they belonged to the party of the Pharisees (v. 5). Those two clues tell us a lot. That they were Pharisees tells us of their conservative zeal for Israel and her Scriptures.[7] To put it simply, they were Messianic Jews who still prioritized the Law of Moses. That they were from Judea probably means they leveraged the clout of the mother church in Jerusalem to substantiate their doctrine. In fact, when Paul reports the same argument in Galatians 2:4, he accuses the legalists of being spies. He says they came from James (Gal 2:12), although James (Acts 15:24) disavows their doctrine (if, indeed, the legalists of Galatians 2 and Acts 15 represent the same party).[8] The easiest solution seems to be to harmonize Paul and Luke: They *claimed* to be from James, but they did not actually have his approval. Or perhaps, as Bruce speculates (303),

[7] Alfons Weiser, "Das 'Apostelkonzil' (Apg 15, 1-35): Ereignis, Uberlieferung, lukanische Deutung," *BZ* 28 (1984): 145-167, considers the identification of Pharisees as one of the many Lucan redactions of this passage. He avers that Luke has deliberately included Septuaginalisms, archaisms, and ecclesiastical unity as he fused his various sources in order to give this passage an authentic tone. Weiser has not, however, explained how this passage would/should have looked differently had Luke simply recorded what actually happened.

[8] The Western text has an interesting variation at this point which says Paul and Barnabas were ordered to return to Jerusalem to testify before the Church authorities there: οἱ δὲ ἐληλυθότες ἀπό Ἱερουσαλήμ παρήγγειλαν αὐτοῖς τῷ Παύλῳ καὶ Βαρναβᾷ καί τισιν ἄλλοις ἀναβαίνειν (D—it^gig, syr^hmg, cop^G67).

James was capitulating to the weaker conscience of the Jewish legalists by allowing them to abstain from common meals with Gentile brothers. In all fairness, we must admit that this goes a bit beyond what the text actually says. Some, therefore, have argued that James approved of such a legalistic Christianity (with the approbation of Peter and Barnabas) in opposition to Paul who disavowed the Mosaic Law as a requirement for salvation.[9] There is no doubt that the issue of Gentile inclusion was not an issue easily settled. Nor did the key teachers of the church articulate their positions in the same language or at the same time—there was neither unanimity nor uniformity. Nonetheless, the least problematic view is still that Luke rightly recorded the general accord on this occasion between the most prominent teachers of the early church—Peter, Paul, James, and Barnabas.

The second question raised in verse one is this: Why were the Christian Pharisees mandating circumcision for Gentile believers? The question is more complicated than it would appear at first. Consider this: In all three pivotal texts for Gentile inclusion—Acts 10–11, 15 and Galatians 2—the 'Judaizers' objected to Messianic believers sharing meals with Gentile Christians. Thus, we must understand the mandate for circumcision as a twin issue of table fellowship.[10] With that in mind, why was circumcision a necessary prerequisite to table fellowship for the Judaizers? Circumcision and kosher food, along with Sabbath observance, were the three primary public distinctives of Jews. In an increasingly pluralistic world, these distinctives were imperative for Jews to survive as a recognizable ethnic identity.[11] The inclusion of Gentiles into the fold of Israel threatened the very fabric of Judaism. Gentiles practiced different "customs" (*ethos*).[12] If, however, Jewish Christians could not freely fellowship across a table with Gentiles, then even the Lord's Supper would be prohibited. Now what kind of fellowship is it when Christians can't even partake in the body and blood of Jesus over a common meal?

Furthermore, Gentiles were considered sinners *ipso facto*.[13] The normative religious and social practices of Gentiles rendered them unclean (see comments on 10:13-16). Such defilement would, necessarily, infect Messianic Jews

---

[9] Paul Achtemeier represented this position in his Presidential address of the Catholic Biblical Association in 1985; "An Elusive Unity: Paul, Acts, and the Early Church," *CBQ* 48 (1986): 1-26. In what could only be classified as radical historical revisionism (e.g., he claims Paul and Barnabas were not actually even involved in the conference of Acts 15!) he argues that Luke covered up the real division in the church where Paul preached salvation by grace through faith, and the other leaders advocated a messianic Judaism which included adherence to the Mosaic Law. Though Achtemeier adequately solved the problematic schism in Gal 2:11-14, he did so by the perilous introduction of even more perplexing historical and theological problems.

[10] Popkes explains the necessary sociological and theological connection between circumcision and table fellowship; cf. Enno Popkes, "'Bevor *einer* von Jakobus kam': Anmerkungen zur textkritischen und theolo-giegeschichtlichen Problematik von Gal 2,12," *NovT* 46 (2004): 259-260.

[11] Even Philo (*Migration of Abraham* 89-94) refused to reduce circumcision to an allegory. Its literal practice was imperative even, or especially, in the pluralistic social setting of Alexandria, Egypt.

[12] "Customs" were an especially big deal for Luke. He uses this word 10 of the 12 times it is found in the NT. In Acts, it has legal ramifications whether it is a Jewish custom being threatened (6:14; 15:1; 21:21; 26:3; 28:17) or a Roman custom (16:21; 25:16). Each time there was a potential riot or social disturbance as a result of the breached custom. Clearly we are well beyond the realm of personal preference here.

[13] Richard Bauckham, "James, Peter, and the Gentiles," in *The Mission of James, Peter, and Paul: Tensions in Early Christianity* (ed. Bruce Chilton and Craig Evans; Leiden: Brill, 2005), 91-142, helps matriculate the maze of contemporary Jewish literature concerning the Gentiles. His well-argued conclusion is that the danger in Acts 11, 15, and Gal 2 is not ritual contagion from food but moral contagion from Gentile's idolatrous practices.

who dared to ignore these social boundaries. The solution, of course, was circumcision. This *entre* into the Jewish system would render Gentiles clean, thus eliminating the danger of defilement.

15:2-3. For Paul and Barnabas, the solution of circumcision came at too high a price. It weakened the message of salvation by grace through faith. Moreover, it rendered Yahweh a parochial deity of one particular nationality. This issue is not merely how we are saved; it is about the very nature and domain of God. This is an issue for which Paul will go to the mat . . . or in this case, to Jerusalem. He sets off with a delegation appointed by the church. Who the others were is lost in the mist of history but it hardly matters.[14] The key figures are Barnabas and Paul from Antioch and Peter and James from Jerusalem. These latter two represent the "Apostles" and "Elders". It is a subtle reminder of the increasing role Elders play in the maturing church of Jesus Christ.[15] Luke leaves no room for misunderstanding. There is no question in the narrative which side will win the debate. Throughout their trek of more than three hundred miles, the delegation announces[16] in Phoenicia and Samaria the widening boundaries of the Kingdom of God. The churches receive the news with great joy. Question: Where did these churches come from? There were no evangelistic forays into these territories, save Philip's brief stint in Samaria. The salient point is that's all it takes. The gospel by its very nature expands. Jesus was right, it is like mustard seed and leaven. Once it is planted in an area, the surrounding region will soon be permeated with the message of Grace. Throughout the book of Acts we will notice this consistent pattern of the perpetually generative church.

15:4-5. Their arrival in Jerusalem looks a lot like their arrival in Antioch (14:27–15:1).[17] Paul and Barnabas report the progress of the gospel, the church rejoices, and the Judaizers attempt to mandate circumcision for the new Gentile believers. Of course, in Jerusalem, the big boys are there to arbitrate the dispute.[18]

2. Speech by Peter (15:6-11)

[6]The apostles and elders met to consider this question. [7]After much discussion, Peter got up and addressed them: "Brothers, you know that some time ago

---

[14] If one believes Acts 15 and Galatians 2 speak of the same event, then Titus was in the entourage as a kind of 'test case' for Gentiles (Gal 2:1). If Paul lost the debate, Titus would have undergone outpatient surgery. His zeal is commendable in this unenviable situation.

[15] Luke mentions the convention of "Apostles and Elders" only in this context, but he makes sure his readers don't miss it by repeating the refrain six times (15:2, 4, 6, 22, 23; 16:4).

[16] Luke uses a peculiar word to describe the "announcement" (ἐκδιηγέομαι) Paul and Barnabas delivered throughout Phoenicia and Samaria. The only other place it is found in the NT is Acts 13:41, that stern warning from Habakkuk with which Paul concludes his sermon. Robert Wall, "The Function of LXX Habakkuk 1:5 in the Book of Acts," *BBR* 10 (2000): 247-258, avers, perhaps making too much from the slightest clue, that Luke imports the warning against rejecting God's message (13:41) into the context of the Jerusalem council.

[17] The reader should bear in mind the unfortunate and arbitrary placement of the chapter division in Acts 15. The beginning boundary of the Jerusalem council narrative is 14:27 not 15:1. Cf. Alex Cheung, "A Narrative Analysis of Acts 14:27–15:35: Literary Shaping in Luke's Account of the Jerusalem Council," *WTJ* 55 (1993): 137-154.

[18] There is great wisdom in how the Jerusalem council handled this sensitive issue. It provides a continuing model for managing church disputes today; cf. Hyung Dae Park, "Drawing Ethical Principles from the Process of the Jerusalem Council: A New Approach to Acts 15:4-29," *TB* 61 (2010): 271-291.

God made a choice among you that the Gentiles might hear from my lips the message of the gospel and believe. ⁸God, who knows the heart, showed that he accepted them by giving the Holy Spirit to them, just as he did to us. ⁹He made no distinction between us and them, for he purified their hearts by faith. ¹⁰Now then, why do you try to test God by putting on the necks of the disciples a yoke that neither we nor our fathers have been able to bear? ¹¹No! We believe it is through the grace of our Lord Jesus that we are saved, just as they are."

15:6. It appears that the meeting of verse 6 is different from the gathering in verses 4-5. When the delegation arrives, *koinonia* naturally breaks out. In the midst of this robust fellowship it won't take long for someone to ask, "So, Barnabas, what have you and Saul been up to?" By now their report is undoubtedly a standard eulogy of God's grace among the Gentiles, which had been repeated dozens of times in Antioch, Phoenicia, and Samaria. As they excitedly rehearsed the tales of Acts 13–14, the Judaizers interpose their strenuous objection to a lawless covenant. This was not the first time Jewish factions came to theological loggerheads nor would it be the last. The Christian Church, like her Jewish ancestors, has always had to struggle with diversity of doctrinal opinions. It is true that some of our chapters have been written in vituperative slander and even blood. Nevertheless, the reader must bear in mind that this great debate (Acts 15) was generated, not by mutual hatred, but by Christ's love which successfully extended to outsiders. This painful chapter is the bi-product of two preceding chapters of successful evangelism. Now that the parties are convened and the cards are on the table, the council can ensue.[19]

15:7. After much banter it was time for some authoritative decisions. Is it really any surprise that impetuous Peter is the first to render his opinion? He did, actually, have first rights. Jesus had given him the keys to the Kingdom (Matt 16:19) which he successfully used to open the gospel to both Jews (ch. 2) and Gentiles (ch. 10). Now he leveraged his Apostolic authority and ecclesiastical experience to affirm the fact that Gentiles were *bona fide* members of the covenant community—the Christian *Qahal*. In fact, Peter connects the conversion of the Gentiles to God's 'ancient decision'. The NIV rendering "some time ago God made a choice" could be literally translated "from ancient [*archaios*] days God elected the Gentiles to hear the gospel through my mouth." This admittedly rough translation highlights two important points. First, this is not Peter's decision or Paul's or James's; it is God's will for the Gentiles to be saved by grace. Second, this is not a recent development or a novel innovation by men.[20] This carries the weight of ancient and ordained doctrine. Here we must don a yarmulke to appreciate Peter's subtlety. In the modern West the new is improved; not so in Peter's day. Ancient always trumped novel. Hence, the Judaizers raised a fuss about

---

[19] The phrase "consider this question" (NIV) is literally "look into the *matter*" (λόγος). This particular phrase is rare in Greek but fairly common in Latin, particularly in contexts of legal investigations. Cf. J. L. North, "Is IΔEIN ΠEPI (Acts 15.6 CF. 18.15) a Latinism?" *NTS* 29 (1983): 264-266. It appears that Luke may have adopted a Latinism from legal contexts that would add gravitas to the situation at hand.

[20] This theme of "God's ancient plan" is repeated in verse 14, "God at first (πρῶτον) showed his concern by taking from the Gentiles a people for himself;" verse 18, "that have been known for ages (γνωστὰ ἀπ' αἰῶνος);" and verse 21, "Moses has been preached in every city from the earliest times (ἐκ γενεῶν ἀρχαίων)."

Paul's innovative new doctrine of salvation: "We have to circumcise as we have always done." Peter counteracted that assertion by claiming this message to Gentiles was 'ancient' and 'ordained'. This was God's plan all along! We're not just talking about what happened with Cornelius, we're talking about God's ancient agenda for all the nations to be included in the covenant blessings of Israel.[21]

15:8-9. Peter's message hearkens back to the Cornelius episode with several verbal links.[22] (1) The **Holy Spirit** was given to the Gentiles as he had been to the Jews (10:44-47; 11:12). The possession of the Spirit trumps all other measures of covenant loyalty. Since the Holy Spirit is given by God, to question the inclusion of a Spirit-possessed person is to question the decision of Yahweh himself. This leads logically to the second connection: (2) Salvation is a **gift** of God (cf. 11:17-18) not an achievement of man. To append circumcision to the cross is to deny the absolute and sufficient power of the blood of Jesus to atone for sin. This leads inevitably to a third observation: (3) God **cleansed** the Gentiles through faith (cf. 10:15, 28). (4) Thus their **hearts** are right before God. *Heart* is found at the beginning of verse 8 and the end of verse 9. Hence, the heart is the heart of the matter. Salvation comes through faith, not ritual affiliation or ethnic identity. (5) Finally, God **judges** impartially a person's heart (cf. 10:34) not his ethnic appearance or ritualistic affiliation. Because he sees our interior, indeed he fashions our interior through the gift of his Spirit, he can rightly assess our standing with him and authenticate our inclusion through the manifestation of his Spirit in our lives. There could hardly be a clearer recapitulation of the Cornelius episode in such a brief synopsis.

15:10-11. The previous two verses are clearly Petrine. If you close your eyes in verses 10 and 11, however, you would swear it was the voice of Paul who famously said, "Stand firm, then, and do not let yourselves be burdened again by a yoke of slavery" (Gal 5:1).[23] Of course, Paul was not the only Rabbi to metaphorically call the law a yoke (Str-B 1:608-610).[24] Though a yoke is heavy, it is not

---

[21] See Huub van de Sandt, "An Explanation of Acts 15.6-21 in the Light of Deuteronomy 4.29-35 (LXX)," *JSNT* 46 (1992): 73-76.

[22] It also looks forward to Paul's epistles where he beats the drum of 'Salvation by grace through faith'. In fact, Peter sounds so much like Paul, that some have accused Luke of putting Paul's writings on the lips of Peter; e.g., Fracois Refoulé, "Le discours de Pierre à l'assemblée de Jérusalem," *RB* 100 (1993): 239-251. Aside from the obvious problem of assuming Luke knew of Paul's Epistles but never overtly used them, as well as the historiographical problem of accusing Luke of crediting the wrong Apostle with this brilliant discourse, there is the problematic assumption that Peter must be dependent on Paul for a gospel of grace. There is no real difficulty with Peter and Paul coming to the same general conclusion independently, or better yet, both dependent on the life and example of Jesus under the guidance of the Spirit.

[23] This Pauline theology on the lips of Peter might be chalked up to Lucan redaction (cf. Cheung, "Narrative Analysis," 150). But that is hardly necessary. If the Twelve were given the weight that Luke's narrative suggests (which is most certainly factual given the role leaders played in ancient Israel) and if Peter is chief among them, why could the direction of influence not have flowed from the 'Pillar', Peter, to the convert, Paul? Perhaps one would argue that Paul claims to have been taught the gospel by Jesus directly and not by the Apostles of Jerusalem (Gal 1:12-18). So be it, then Peter and Paul had the same teacher. Is it any wonder, therefore, that they would articulate the gospel in strikingly similar ways?

[24] Some of the New Perspectives on Paul have helped correct the caricature of the law as an oppressive burden demanded for salvation (cf. *y. Qidd* 1.8 [61d]; *b. Ros. Has.* 16b, 17a); cf. E. P. Sanders, "Judaism and the Grand 'Christian' Abstractions: Love, Mercy, and Grace," *Int* 39 (1985): 357-372. Although the prescient warning of Bruce (307, fn 28) is still valid: The rabbinic love for the law post A.D. 70 and the loosening of its absolute demands may not fully capture the oppressive legalistic requirements of a Pharisaic system of the Second Temple period, particularly the more stringent school of Shammai. Paul said, "All who rely on observing the law are under a curse, for it is written: 'Cursed is everyone who does not continue to do every-

necessarily odious (cf. Matt 11:29-30).[25] For the Jews, the law was a tremendous blessing not a baneful duty. It was the gift of God that not only identified them as the chosen people but also ordered their society with justice and compassion. Paul clearly had the highest regard for the law: "So then, the law is holy, and the commandment is holy, righteous and good" (Rom 7:12). The problem is that the law is incapable of making one righteous before God; only Jesus can do that. Paul put it this way: "Through him everyone who believes is justified from everything you could not be justified from by the Law of Moses" (Acts 13:39). Or again in Romans 8:3: "For what the law was powerless to do in that it was weakened by the sinful nature, God did by sending his own Son in the likeness of sinful man to be a sin offering."

Peter's conclusion, and his final words in the book, could hardly be more theologically astute: "It is through the grace of our Lord Jesus that we are saved, just as they are." To this Paul would surely add his hearty "amen!": "It is by grace you have been saved" (Eph 2:5); "For it is by grace you have been saved, through faith—and this not from yourselves, it is the gift of God" (Eph 2:8); "[Christ Jesus] has saved us and called us to a holy life—not because of anything we have done but because of his own purpose and grace" (2 Tim 1:9). According to Luke's report, Peter and Paul could not have had a closer accord on this core issue of salvation.

3. Barnabas and Paul Report; James Renders a Decision (15:12-21)

[12]The whole assembly became silent as they listened to Barnabas and Paul telling about the miraculous signs and wonders God had done among the Gentiles through them. [13]When they finished, James spoke up: "Brothers, listen to me. [14]Simon[a] has described to us how God at first showed his concern by taking from the Gentiles a people for himself. [15]The words of the prophets are in agreement with this, as it is written: [16]'After this I will return and rebuild David's fallen tent. Its ruins I will rebuild, and I will restore it, [17]that the remnant of men may seek the Lord, and all the Gentiles who bear my name, says the Lord, who does these things'[b] [18]that have been known for ages.'"

[a]14 Greek *Simeon*, a variant of *Simon*, that is, Peter   [b]17 Amos 9:11, 12   [c]17,18 Some manuscripts *things – / [18]known to the Lord for ages is his work*

15:12. The whole church sat in silence after Peter's testimony.[26] Though Luke now gives the floor to Barnabas and Paul, he doesn't give them a voice. Their virtual silence is noticeable. It was so troubling to Achtemeier in fact, that

---

thing written in the Book of the Law.' . . . Christ redeemed us from the curse of the law by becoming a curse for us" (Gal 3:10, 13). James reiterates the same point, "For whoever keeps the whole law and yet stumbles at just one point is guilty of breaking all of it" (Jas 2:10).

[25] Royce Dickinson, "The Theology of the Jerusalem Conference, Acts 15:1-35," *RQ* 32 (1990): 69-71; and John Nolland, "A Fresh Look at Acts 15.10," *Crux* 27 (1980): 105-115.

[26] The Western text adds "The Elders assented to Peter's words . . ." That is the obvious implication here. There was unanimous accord between the Jerusalem Elders, the Apostles, and the missionary team—Barnabas and Paul. Tissot interprets the variations of the Western text, particularly at Acts 15, as an early editing of Acts by an anti-Jewish element in the early church; cf. Yves Tissot, "Les prescriptions des presbytres," *RB* 77 (1970): 321-346.

he (among others) concluded that these heavyweights from Antioch weren't really even there![27] Seriously folks, Luke is not wont to simply invent material.[28] The report of the missionary team is specifically about the signs and wonders God did among the Gentiles which validated their inclusion in the Kingdom. Luke already narrated that with ample detail in the previous two chapters. Regurgitating it in the present context is hardly necessary.

One might ask, "What of Paul's theology of grace?" What could he add to what Peter already expounded? The answer to that lies in Paul's letters. Galatians and Romans are Paul's pulpit for preaching grace. Here in Jerusalem, he took a back-seat to those more qualified. It might come as a surprise, but in Jerusalem, Paul's clout is bested by Peter and James (even Barnabas for that matter). It is their responsibility, not Paul's, to make definitive doctrinal declarations in the mother church.

15:13-15. James now arbitrates the council, functioning as would the president of a synagogue or the *mebaqqer* at Qumran ◼ (i.e., "big chief").[29] He links Peter's detailed report[30] with prophecies concerning the fate of the Gentiles in the Kingdom of God. Notice that James refers to the prophets in plural (v. 15). The primary text is Amos 9:11-12 (LXX), but snippets from Jeremiah 12:15 and Isaiah 45:21 bracket the quotation.[31] Though Amos 9 would have been sufficient to support his decree, James aims at showing the breadth of prophetic expectation concerning the Gentiles.[32]

One peculiarity is that James calls Peter, "Simon." That, in itself, is natural enough—that was his name (cf. John 1:42). What is strange is how it is spelled. Forty Six times Peter is identified as Simon with the Greek spelling *Simōn*. Only twice is the more authentic Aramaic spelling used: *Sumeōn* (cf. 2 Pet 1:1). James, who himself had a brother named Simeon (Mark 6:3/Matt 13:55), shows his Aramaic heritage. This peculiarity led to some confusion since there are two others in the New Testament called *Sumeōn*. "Simeon the Black" was a leader of the church in Antioch (13:1), and Simeon the prophet met Jesus in the temple (Luke 2:25, 34). Chrysostom, (*Hom. Acts* 33.1) in fact, entertained the notion that the Simeon of Acts 15 was none other than the Simeon of Luke 2.[33] As

---

[27] Achtemeier, "An Elusive Unity," 6.

[28] The Greek historiographical rules under which Luke appears to operate (see in the introduction "(10) Was Luke an accurage historian?") expected writers to flesh out speeches from their sources. Even so, there was an obvious aversion to making stuff up. In other words, no one would be bothered if Luke crafted Peter's speech so the words artistically paralleled his earlier encounter with Cornelius. He would be censured, however, if he placed Barnabas and Paul in Jerusalem if they were not actually there at the time. Cf. A. W. Mosley, "Historical Reporting in the Ancient World," *NTS* 12 (1965): 10-26.

[29] Cf. Bruce Chilton, "James, Peter, Paul, and the Formation of the Gospel," in *The Mission of James, Peter, and Paul: Tensions in Early Christianity* (ed. by Bruce Chilton and Craig Evans; Leiden: Brill, 2005), 3-28.

[30] The word "described" (ἐξηγέομαι) is used for detailed reports, explanations, or interpretations, sometimes of divine mysteries (cf. Luke 24:35; John 1:18; Acts 10:8; 15:12, 14; 21:19).

[31] The introduction, "After this I will return," looks like Jeremiah 12:15 and the conclusion, "that have been known for ages," appears to come from Isaiah 45:21.

[32] Though not all Jewish traditions would be amicable to Gentile inclusion, there were some favorably disposed to outsiders and they certainly had sufficient scriptural support: Abraham's seed would bless the nations (Gen 12:3; Isa 42:6; 60:3); Yahweh would reign over all the earth (Psa 18:49; 67:2; 117:1; Isa 2:2; 49:6; Amos 9:11-12; Mal 1:11); his Messiah would gain international fame (Isa 11:10) and bring about global justice and salvation (Isa 49:22; 51:4; 52:10; Joel 2:28).

[33] Edgar R. Smothers, "Chrysostom and Symeon, (Acts xv, 14)," *HTR* 46 (1953): 203-216.

Riesner pointed out Symeon the Apostle and Symeon the Prophet both spoke with Aramaisms and both affirmed the inclusion of Gentiles (Luke 2:32).[34] It is not likely that Luke confused the two as did Chrysostom, but it is entirely possible that he used this idiosyncratic spelling to remind the reader of one of his earliest vignettes from volume one: "For my eyes have seen your salvation, which you have prepared in the sight of all people, a light for revelation to the Gentiles and for glory to your people Israel" (Luke 2:30-32).[35]

This is precisely the point Simon was getting at: God took from the Gentiles "a people for himself." Luke's words are deliberate, recognizable, and kosher: "You are a people holy to the LORD your God. Out of all the peoples on the face of the earth, the LORD has chosen you to be his treasured possession" (Deut 14:2).[36] The word "people" (*laos*) is used exclusively for the *Jewish* people, not the Gentiles (*ethnē*) except here and in Acts 18:10. This is the very eschatological expansion predicted by Zechariah (2:10-13):

> "Shout and be glad, O Daughter of Zion. For I am coming, and I will live among you," declares the LORD. "Many nations will be joined with the LORD in that day and will become my people. I will live among you and you will know that the LORD Almighty has sent me to you. The LORD will inherit Judah as his portion in the holy land and will again choose Jerusalem. Be still before the LORD, all mankind, because he has roused himself from his holy dwelling."

Moreover, James's brief allusion to Jeremiah 12:15 in the introduction would recall for his hearers, conversant with the Old Testament, this stern exhortation to national repentance for the Gentiles:

> But after I uproot them, I will again have compassion and will bring each of them back to his own inheritance and his own country. And if they learn well the ways of my people and swear by my name, saying, "As surely as the LORD lives"—even as they once taught my people to swear by Baal—*then they will be established among my people.*

Any of these passages would have been sufficient for James to make his point, but he bore down on Amos 9 as his proof-text. He used a *pesher* type interpretation to argue that what was unfolding in their midst was predicted long ago.[37]

15:16-18. James's meaning is straightforward enough: The Davidic Kingdom was restored and the Gentiles were now included in it. The "tent" of David now encompasses Gentiles formerly beyond the pale (cf. *b. Sanh.* 96b-97a; *Midr. Psa* 76 §3 (171b); *Gen. Rab.* 88.5.2f-3a; cited in Str-B 2:728-729). Just what this

---

[34] Cf. Rainer Riesner, "James's Speech (Acts 15:13-21), Simeon's Hymn (Luke 2:29-32), and Luke's Sources," in *Jesus of Nazareth: Lord and Christ* (ed. Joel B. Green and Max Turner; Grand Rapids: Eerdmans, 1994), 263-278.

[35] *Simon* and *Symeon* are used interchangeably by Josephus (*J.W.* 4.3.9 §159). Luke also uses two spellings for Saul: Σαῦλος and Σαούλ.

[36] The specific term "people for his name" is not found in the LXX but is in a number of Targumim; cf. Nils A. Dahl, "'A People for His Name' (Acts 15:14)," *NTS* 4 (1958): 320-321.

[37] Cf. Loveday Alexander, "'This Is That': The Authority of Scripture in the Acts of the Apostles," *PSB* 25 ns (2004): 189-204.

restored tent is has been a subject of debate.[38] It could either be the restoration of David's Kingdom (as in 4Q174 1.10-13) or, more likely, the eschatological temple built without hands (cf. 11QT 29.9-10; *1 En.* 90.29; *Jub.* 1.15-17)[39] perhaps hearkening back to Jesus' own words (Mark 14:58; cf. Heb 8:2).

The implications of James's interpretation can hardly be overstated. For Jews, whatever else the messianic age means, it must bring an end of exile by gathering the dispersed people of Yahweh in Israel. For James, the Diaspora *had* been reversed, not by an emigration of Israelites back to the ancestral borders but by an extension of the borders of Israel to encompass all God's people. Isaiah 54:1-3 carries this same idea:

> "Sing, O barren woman, you who never bore a child; burst into song, shout for joy, you who were never in labor; because more are the children of the desolate woman than of her who has a husband," says the LORD. "*Enlarge the place of your tent*, stretch your tent curtains wide, do not hold back; lengthen your cords, strengthen your stakes. For you will spread out to the right and to the left; *your descendants will dispossess nations and settle in their desolate cities.*"

If Yahweh now rules the world through Jesus Christ, the ancient boundaries are eradicated, the ethnic distinctions extinct. What demarks us now as "a people for his name" is the name of Jesus—the only "name under heaven given to men by which we must be saved" (Acts 4:12). This is a world-altering revelation and the most significant historical event of the first century.

Of course, the quotation (vv. 16-18) is problematic because the Septuagint version (LXX) of Amos 9:12 differs substantially from the Hebrew version (MT).[40] The MT implies that when God restores Israel, the Jews will overtake the nations by whom they were punished in exile, specifically Edom (as in *Tg. Jonathan* on Amos 9:11; cf. Num 24:18). The LXX, on the other hand, suggests that when Israel is restored, the nations among whom they were dispersed would seek Yahweh along with Israel. Though these two interpretations move in very different directions, they derive from nearly identical words. With the slightest modification of

---

[38] The *Damascus Document* from Qumran (7:15-17) understood it as the Law of Moses, though that hardly works for James's interpretation: "The books of the Law are the tabernacle of the king; as God said, 'I will raise up the tabernacle of David which is fallen.'"

[39] Cf. Bauckham, "James, Peter, and the Gentiles," 158, and Jostein Ådna, *Jesu Stellung zum Tempel: Die Tempelaktion und das Tempelwort als Ausdruck seiner messianischen Sendung* (WUNT 2.119; Tübingen: Mohr Siebeck, 2000), 35-49, 91-110. Some have argued this is the literal temple which is to be rebuilt during the millennial kingdom on earth after Jesus' return; see Allan A. MacRae, "The Scientific Approach to the Old Testament—A Study of Amos 9 in Relation to Acts 15," in *Truth for Today* (Chicago: Moody, 1963), 111-122. However, given the paucity of contextual clues in support, this argument has largely been abandoned even by premillennialists (e.g., Bock, 503-505).

[40] E. Haenchen accuses Luke of misinterpreting Amos and putting these Greek words into James's Aramaic mouth; "Quellenanalyse und Kompositionsanalyse in Act 15," in *Judentum, Urchristentun, Kirche: Festschrift für Joachim Jeremias* (ed. Walther Eltester; Berlin: Töplemann, 1960), 153-164. However, it remains to be proved that James would not have used the LXX in the presence of Greek-speaking brethren from Antioch or that the LXX does not represent an accurate Hebrew *Vorlage*. In fact, James used a complicated Jewish hermeneutic which depended upon the Hebrew text; Richard Bauckham, "James and the Gentiles (Acts 15.13-21)," in *History, Literature and Society* (ed. Ben Witherington; Cambridge: Cambridge, 1999), 154-184. Furthermore, James *did* use the LXX in his letter (James 4:6)! Even if his letter is deemed a forgery, it represents and authentic imitation of a Hebrew writer and thinker utilizing Greek Scriptures for Diaspora Jews. These facts leave little reason to acquiesce to Haenchen's critical assessment.

three Hebrew letters, the meaning of the sentence is substantially altered.[41]

But which is the original sense, the LXX or the MT? On the one hand, you have the MT, supported by the reading in *Targum of Jonathan*. On the other hand, you have the LXX supported by the reading in Acts 15. One might say, "Well, the Hebrew text is older, so James (or at least Luke) muddled it up." Not so fast. Both the MT and the LXX are witnesses to a pre-Christian Hebrew text tradition. Though the MT is generally to be preferred, there are some instances where the LXX may, in fact, retain an older reading.

It would help if the Qumran scribes 🖥 had cited Amos 9:12 and sided with either the MT or the LXX. Unfortunately they did not. However, two different scrolls cited Amos 9:11 (4Q174 1:12 and CD 7:16) with striking similarities to James's version in Acts 15:16.[42] In short, it looks like the Qumran community may have had access to a tradition similar to Luke's. This opens the possibility that there was an ancient Hebrew text that differed from the MT from which James quoted. The fact is, the LXX differs enough from Acts 15:16-17 that James may not have been using the LXX at all but a Hebrew original similar to that of the LXX and Qumran. If such a text did exist, that would explain the divergences of James from the LXX, as well as the LXX and Qumran from the MT.[43]

Regardless of the history of this textual transmission, whether in Hebrew or in Greek, the core message is unmistakable: Yahweh will restore Israel and the Gentiles will also be called by his name.[44] This idea is found not only in Amos 9:11-12 but in two passages appended to the beginning and end of this quote. This connection was noted above with Jeremiah 12:15-17, with which James begins his citation. It reappears now in connection with Isaiah 45:21-22 with which James concludes his quote: "Declare what is to be, present it—let them take counsel together. *Who foretold this long ago* [= Acts 15:18], who declared it from the distant past? Was it not I, the LORD? And there is no God apart from me, a righteous God and a Savior; there is none but me. *'Turn to me and be saved, all you ends of the earth;* for I am God, and there is no other.'"

---

[41] (1) If the Hebrew word "possess," יִירַשׁ, was read יִדְרֹשׁ, it would be translated in the LXX as "seek." (2) את means "the" while אתי means "me." By adding a *yod* (י) at the beginning of the word, the sentence would read "That the remnant of mankind might seek me" rather than "That they might possess the remnant Edom." (3) If one were to remove the *waw* (ו), "Edom" (אֱדוֹם) becomes "remnant of mankind" (אָדָם). Braun argues that the Masoretic pointing was deliberately designed to counter Christian claims on this verse; cf. Michael Braun, "James' Use of Amos at the Jerusalem Council: Steps toward a Possible Solution of the Textual and Theological Problems (Acts 15)," *JETS* 20 (1977): 116-117. That, however, is unlikely given the probable antiquity of the MT *Vorlage* as well as the meticulous care they took *not* to alter texts; cf. Larry Pechawer, "Reliability of the Manuscripts: Old Testament," in *Humble Defense: Evidence for the Christian Faith* (ed. Mark E. Moore; Joplin, MO: College Press, 2004), 57-73.

[42] Martin Stowasser, "Am 5,25-27; 9,11 f. in der Qumranüberlieferung und in der Apostelgeschichte," *ZNW* 92 (2001): 47-63, points out that the idiosyncratic introduction to the quotations is shared by Acts 7:42; 15:16; 4Q174 1.12. Moreover, all four passages (Acts 7:42-43; 15:16-18; 4Q174 3.12; and CD 7.16) are composite quotations which allude to or directly cite Nathan's promise to David that his throne would always have an heir (2 Sam 7:13-16/1 Chr 17:12-14). Furthermore, the editorial alterations in Luke's two Amos citations show no signs of Lucan redaction, thus pointing to a pre-Lucan tradition.

[43] This very argument is sustained by Jostein Ådna, "James' Position at the Summit Meeting of the Apostles and the Elders in Jerusalem (Acts 15)," in *Mission of the Early Church to Jews and Gentiles* (Tübingen: Mohr Siebeck, 2000), 125-161.

[44] Even if there were no textual variations between the LXX and MT, the message of Gentile inclusion is inherent in the phrase, "all the nations that bear my name"; see David M. King, "The Use of Amos 9:11-12 in Acts 15:16-18," *ATJ* 21 (1989): 8-13.

¹⁹"It is my judgment, therefore, that we should not make it difficult for the Gentiles who are turning to God. ²⁰Instead we should write to them, telling them to abstain from food polluted by idols, from sexual immorality, from the meat of strangled animals and from blood. ²¹For Moses has been preached in every city from the earliest times and is read in the synagogues on every Sabbath."

15:19-21. Though this passage has been fodder for much debate, there are three simple truths that are not to be missed. First, *this decree was intended to simplify Gentile conversion* in response to those who were trying to make it more difficult (cf. v. 10). The imposition of circumcision was merely the first step into a full-throttle Jewish lifestyle requiring dietary laws, fasts, feast, Torah regulations, Sabbath keeping, etc. James leveraged his ecclesiastical weight to settle the issue.[45] He decreed that none of these complexities would be demanded of Gentile converts. Indeed, *Jesus is the portal to the God, not Abraham or Moses.* This leads to a second principle.

These prohibitions are not imperatives for salvation but essentials for Christian unity. Since Moses was preached in all the synagogues of every city, Jewish sensibilities were acute (v. 21). There were certain behaviors that Jews simply could not countenance, nor should Christians for that matter. Taken as a collective whole, the prohibitions James lists were blasphemous disregard for Yahweh. These idolatrous practices, normative in pagan culture, were odious to people of faith in the one true God. Even so, no one is suggesting that Gentiles earn their salvation by keeping a new law. But neither are we suggesting these prohibitions are mere suggestions. What is at issue is not Gentile salvation but fellowship with Messianic believers. This does not mean that these prohibitions are somehow less important. In fact, biblically and theologically the unity of the body probably trumps the salvation of an individual, for the salvation of many depend on the unity of the body.

Bridging two cultures in one fellowship is most difficult. However, that bridge had already been crossed long ago—Gentiles living among Jews was an age-old issue. One can find similar regulations in the Old Testament, Apocrypha, and rabbinic literature. This leads to a third principle.

James's four prohibitions sound a lot like other lists of Gentile regulations. There is nothing new here; such lists were common. There are a number of ways of categorizing these sorts of rules but two deserve special mention. (1) The so called **Noahic commands** were universal laws extrapolated from Genesis 9:4-6 that prohibit eating blood (v. 4) and shedding blood (v. 6). Various rabbis offered

---

[45] Some have attempted to minimize James's authority in reaction to Catholic (ab)use of hierarchical systems of the church; see Telford Work, "Speaking for the Spirit in the Time of Division," in *Ecumenical Future* (Grand Rapids: Eerdmans, 2004), 198-217. However, Luke's language *is* authoritarian. In verse 19 James says, "I judge" (ἐγὼ κρίνω), and in verse 28, he justifies the decision by enlisting the support of the Holy Spirit. Consider the position of James in Acts: Upon Peter's escape from prison he enjoined the brothers to make sure James heard the report (12:17), and upon Paul's arrival in Jerusalem it was James who led the Elders in directing Paul to pay for the vow of four other worshipers in order to allay the accusations that he neglected Mosaic regulations (21:18-26). Furthermore, Paul recognized James as a pillar among the Jerusalem leaders (Gal 1:19; 2:12) and Jude augments his own authority by claiming kinship with his brother (Jude 1:1). James was incredibly influential. What we have here is an authoritative declaration not merely a personal opinion.

lists of Noahic commands ranging from four to seven, or even thirty items.[46] One might think of the Noahic commands as the 'Ten Commandments' for all humanity.[47] (2) The regulations for *resident aliens* (*gēr*), similarly, are bare-minimum rules for Gentiles living amidst Jews in Israel. These are most clearly stated in Leviticus 17–18 but are found throughout the Old Testament (cf. Exod 12:48-49; Lev 24:16, 22; Num 9:14; Deut 29:10-11; 31:12, etc.).[48]

The unalterable foundation of both kinds of lists is a prohibition against idolatry and blood (both shedding it and eating it). Other items migrate in and out of various lists in both Christian and Jewish literature. A few examples will show the similarities.

Jubilees 7:20-21 (c. 200 B.C.) says: "Observe righteousness, to cover the shame of their flesh, to bless their Creator, honor father and mother, love their neighbor and guard their souls from fornication, uncleanness and all iniquity." It continues with three prohibitions credited to none other than Noah: fornication, murder, and eating blood (vv. 22-39). Tosephta, *Abodah Zarah* 8.4-6, lists seven Nohaic admonitions: Establish courts of justice, abstain from idolatry, blasphemy, fornication, bloodshed, thievery, and eating flesh cut from a limb from a living animal.[49] The Talmud (*b. Sanh.* 74a) cites three laws which inevitably carry the death penalty: Idolatry, incest (including adultery), and murder [shedding of blood]. These three examples show the similarities in such lists as well as the variations surrounding the two dominant themes of idolatry and blood.

In James's list we find *similar kinds* of prohibitions, each of which *roughly* par-

---

[46] The popularity of four rules may be modeled on the refrain in Amos, "For three sins of [the places vary], even for four, I will not turn my back . . ." (1:3, 6, 9, 11, 13; 2:1, 4, 6). The popularity of seven is due to the numerological import of this 'complete' number. Cf. David Instone-Brewer, "Infanticide and the Apostolic Decree of Acts 15," *JETS* 52 (2009): 301-312, lists no less than eight! For longer moral lists cf. *Gen. Rab.* 34.13.1; *t. Abod. Zar.* 8.4; *b. Sanh.* 74a; *m. Gen. Rab.* 34.8.4, and Str-B 2:729-740.

[47] Savelle critiques the Noahic view as inadequate since that would impose additional laws on the Gospel of Free-Grace. Rather, he suggests, the resident alien (*gēr*) regulations are what James really has in mind. Although the form of James's prohibitions does not match the *gēr* regulations of Lev 17–18, they certainly fit the *Zeit Geist* of contemporary Judaism in setting ethical parameters for resident aliens; cf. Charles H. Savelle, "A Reexamination of the Prohibitions in Acts 15," *BibSac* 161 (2004): 449-465. As Judaism abutted Hellenistic culture, it was necessary to lay down some 'rules of engagement'.

[48] Hans Waitz argued that Lev 17–18 was the background of James's decree; see "Das Problem des sogenannten Aposteldekrets und die damit zusammenhängenden literarischen und geschichtlichen Probleme des apostolischen Zeitalters," *ZKG* 55 (1936): 228-231. The problem, as pointed out by Wilson, is that the prohibitions of James are substantially different from those of Lev 17–18; see S. G. Wilson, *Luke and the Law* (SNTSMS 50; Cambridge: Cambridge University, 1983), 84-102. In his mediating position, Callan has salvaged Waitz hypothesis from Wilson's criticism; see Terrance Callan, "The Background of the Apostolic Decree (Acts 15:20, 29; 21:25)" *CBQ* 55 (1993): 284-297; see also Charles Perrot, "Les decisions de l'Assemblée de Jérusalem," *RSR* 69 (1981): 195-208. His argument, adopted here, is that the general *topos* of *rules for Gentile residents* is the background for James's decree and that the list of rules as a whole is more important than the specific items on the list, which vary from list to list.

[49] *B. Sanh.* 56a-b cites this passage from the Tosephta, illustrating two important factors. First, it alters the original list slightly (transposing blasphemy and idolatry as well as replacing adultery with fornication). Second, it traces the rabbinic additions to the original list. We see these same two trends in the early church fathers (see below). "Our Rabbis taught: Seven precepts were the sons of Noah commanded: Social laws; refrain from blasphemy; idolatry; adultery; bloodshed; robbery; and eating flesh cut from a living animal. R. Hanania b. Gamaliel said: Also not to partake of the blood drawn from a living animal. R. Hidka added emasculation. R. Simeon added sorcery. R. Jose said: The heathens were prohibited everything that is mentioned in the section on sorcery. . . . Now, [the Almighty] does not punish without first prohibiting. R. Eleazar added the forbidden mixture [in plants and animals]: now, they are permitted to wear garments of mixed fabrics [of wool and linen] and sow diverse seeds together; they are forbidden only to hybridize heterogeneous animals and graft trees of different kinds."

allels one of the regulations for resident aliens in Israel (Lev 17–18). **(1) "Food polluted by idols" (cf. Lev 17:8-9)** would more accurately be translated "defilement of idols." The word "food" is not in the Greek text. However, it is probably implied. Though "defilement" (*alisgēma*) isn't found elsewhere in the NT, LXX, or Apocrypha, its verbal form appears several times and always with reference to food (Dan 1:8; Mal 1:7, 12; Sir 40:29).[50] Moreover, the word "idol offerings" (*eidōlothutōn*), replaces "defilement" the other two times this list is mentioned (15:29; 21:25), and this word also implies food in its other seven New Testament uses (1 Cor 8:1, 4, 7, 10; 10:19; Rev 2:14, 20). Hence, "Don't participate in feasts honoring pagan deities."

(2) Fornication (cf. Lev 18:6-29). Though "fornication" has obvious moral overtones, it relates to idolatry since sexual immorality was often part of cultic practices. Consequently, *fornication* became a virtual metaphor for *idolatry* (e.g., Hos 4:11-13; Isa 57:7; Jer 2:20-25; Ezek 16:26-41; Micah 1:7; James 4:4).[51] Obviously fornication is universally proscribed on moral grounds. Here, however, amidst these other three items, its implication is not an amorous couple in the backseat of a Chevy, but the revelry of a pagan cultic ceremony. Hence, sex as part of pagan worship is prohibited.

(3) Things strangled (Lev 17:13-14). This is a mysterious term (*pniktos*). The word itself means "to smother" or "to choke."[52] It is not typically used for sacrifices. Though Philo uses two related terms in just such a context: "They devise novel kinds of pleasure and prepare meat unfit for the altar by strangling (*agchō*) and throttling (*apopnigō*) the animals, and entomb in the carcass the blood which is the essence of the soul and should be allowed to run freely away" (Philo, *Special Laws* 4.122). It appears that both James and Philo consider strangled animals unkosher because they still have blood in them. Hence, don't drink blood or eat raw meat as the pagans do in ritual ceremonies of "extracting life" from a man or beast.[53]

(4) Blood (Lev 17:10-12) has a dual emphasis: Don't eat it (animals) and don't shed it (humans), (cf. Gen 9:4-6; *Jub* 7:22-39; Tertullian, *Apology* 9). Both are based on the axiom that life is in the blood (Lev 17:11, 14; Deut 12:23).[54] This helps clarify the previous prohibition of things strangled.

Witherington (461-463) rightly points out that all four items on the list could be related to idolatry. It might even be fair to punctuate the decree like

---

[50] This would continue to be one of the primary issues Christians wrestled with in the late first and early second century according to the Didache 6.3, "And concerning food, bear what thou art able; but against that which is sacrificed to idols be exceedingly on thy guard; for it is the service of dead gods." Cf. Clayton Jefford, "Tradition and Witness in Antioch: Acts 15 and Didache 6," *PRS* 19 (1992): 409-419.

[51] Cf. Albertus F. Klijn, "The Pseudo-Clementines and the Apostolic Decree," *NovT* 10 (1968): 306-312.

[52] Instone-Brewer makes an interesting and tenable argument that this may refer to (or include) infanticide rather than unkosher foods ("Infanticide," 301-312).

[53] Such dietary regulations sound strange to western ears. Blood is not typically on our menus. However, the following excerpt from Tertullian, exaggerated as it may be, shows what a pressing problem this was for the early church: "Those, too, who at the gladiator shows, for the cure of epilepsy, quaff with greedy thirst the blood of criminals slain in the arena, as it flows fresh from the wound, and then rush off—to whom do they belong? Those, also, who make meals on the flesh of wild beasts at the place of combat—who have keen appetites for bear and stag? . . . The entrails of the very bears, loaded with as yet undigested human viscera, are in great request" (*Apology* 9).

[54] Cf. Savelle, "Reexamination," 454-456.

this: "Avoid every corrupting influence of idolatry: fornication, cultic meals, and murder." James is clearly independent of both Leviticus 17–18 and Genesis 9:4-6. Nevertheless, the purpose of these lists is pretty much the same. They are regulations for Gentiles to live amidst Jews without causing a riot! Thus, it appears that James is prohibiting practices that are endemic in pagan culture that would irrevocably sever Christian fellowship with Messianic Jews for whom monotheism was the *sine qua non* of faith.

This list of Gentile regulations is a *topos* that is common in both Jewish and Christian literature, in biblical and extrabiblical literature. The individual items differ from list to list, but the differences are inconsequential.[55] The point is not the list of items but the overall thrust to avoid idolatry and blood. In fact, as the early church copied these prohibitions, it appears that they deliberately altered the list so that it was applicable to the changing needs of their own contemporary communities.[56] This is an important observation given that Paul seems to contradict one of James's prohibitions. He *approves* of eating meat sacrificed to idols when it is not a cause of offense. Of course, there is a substantial difference in eating meat purchased from a public market and sharing in a pagan feast in honor of a foreign god. This seems to be the difference in Paul's permission and James's prohibition.

Regardless, Paul offers the same warning as James not to offend brothers in exercising Christian liberty (cf. Rom 14:6, 21; 1 Cor 8:13; 10:25). The principle of restricting Christian freedom for the sake of unity is unalterable; the specific practices that cause a breach in unity morphed from place to place and from era to era.[57] Thus, *to be true to the principle of this text, sometimes churches reconfigured the items on the list.*[58]

---

[55] Variations in lists are normative such as lists of spiritual gifts (Eph 4:11; 1 Cor 12:28; Rom 12:5-8) or requirements for elders (1 Tim 3:1-7; Titus 1:6-8). The point is more about painting a portrait than creating a checklist. The following chart shows that even Luke didn't record the decree with exact precision, and it was modified by various manuscripts and church fathers; cf. Christian-Bernard Amphoux, "Les variants et l'histoire du 'décret apostolique' Actes 15,20.29; 21,25," in *New Testament Textual Criticism and Exegesis* (Leuven: Peeters, 2002), 209-216:

Acts 15:20	ἀλισγημάτων τῶν εἰδώλων	πορνείας	πνικτοῦ	αἵματος
Acts 15:29	εἰδωλοθύτων	αἵματος	πνικτῶν	πορνείας
Acts 21:25	εἰδωλόθυτον	αἷμα	πνικτόν	πορνείαν
P45	εἰδωλόθυτον		πνικτόν	
Codex D	εἰδωλόθυτον	αἵματος		πορνείαν
Irenaeus, Ad. Haer. 3.12.14	vanities of idols	fornication	"Don't do to others..." blood	"Don't do to others..."
Origin, Ad. Celsus 8.29	things offered to idols	strangled	blood	
Tertullian, Modesty 12	sacrifices	fornications	blood	
Ps.-Clement, Homilies 7.8	food offered to idols	dead carcasses	suffocated	blood

[56] See the chart in the previous footnote. These modifications show that the cultic regulations were sometimes recast as moral injunctions. This argument is advanced by J. Julius Scott, "Textual Variants of the 'Apostolic Decree' and Their Setting in the Early Church," in *The Living and Active Word of God* (ed. Morris Inch and Ronald Youngblood; Winona Lake: Eisenbrauns, 1983). Although C. K. Barrett rightly warns that there is nothing like a neat division in the Church Fathers between East/West or Cultic/Moral; cf. "The Apostolic Decree of Acts 15.29," *ABR* 35 (1987): 50-59, there is a mixture of both elements across the spectrum where these prohibitions are reproduced.

[57] This is hardly to suggest that the gospel is malleable or that it evolves through the history of religion, *pace* Joseph Pathrapankal, "The Polarity of Law and Freedom in Pauline Religion," *JD* 5 (1980): 343-351. The very nature of the council was to affirm the plan of God for Gentiles that was predicted in the prophets and consistent with the OT covenant of Abraham.

[58] The principles of this passage continue to be used to good effect in crosscultural missions. Cf. Kevin

4. The Dictate of the Council Sent Out
through James's Letter (15:22-35)

[22]Then the apostles and elders, with the whole church, decided to choose some of their own men and send them to Antioch with Paul and Barnabas. They chose Judas (called Barsabbas) and Silas, two men who were leaders among the brothers. [23]With them they sent the following letter: The apostles and elders, your brothers, To the Gentile believers in Antioch, Syria and Cilicia: Greetings.

15:22-23. An irrefutable conclusion had been reached: Gentiles are saved without circumcision. This conclusion has the consent of the Apostles, the Elders, and the "whole congregation" (although there is an admitted silence of the Judaizers who potentially were less than enthusiastic about the decision). This decision now needs to be communicated to the churches in Antioch and the surrounding regions. Two measures will ensure that the appropriate parties are adequately informed: eyewitnesses and written authorization. The eyewitnesses, aside from Barnabas and Paul, were Judas Barsabbas[59] and Silas. These two would act as authoritative leaders from the church of Jerusalem. Any accusations that Barnabas and Paul were fudging the facts would be swiftly refuted.

The eyewitnesses were augmented by a letter written in very fine Greek (vv. 24-26 are a single sentence). This is the first epistle of the New Testament, and though shorter than the other letters, it takes the exact same form: (1) senders—Apostles and Elders; (2) recipients—Gentile Christians in Antioch, Syria, and Cilicia; (3) greetings; (4) body (vv. 24-29); and (5) salutation. Structurally, this is standard fare.

[24]We have heard that some went out from us without our authorization and disturbed you, troubling your minds by what they said. [25]So we all agreed to choose some men and send them to you with our dear friends Barnabas and Paul—[26]men who have risked their lives for the name of our Lord Jesus Christ. [27]Therefore we are sending Judas and Silas to confirm by word of mouth what we are writing. [28]It seemed good to the Holy Spirit and to us not to burden you with anything beyond the following requirements: [29]You are to abstain from food sacrificed to idols, from blood, from the meat of strangled animals and from sexual immorality. You will do well to avoid these things. Farewell.

15:24-27. James's letter delivers three swift and decisive blows to Paul's opposition. First, he disassociates himself from those who claimed to be affiliated with the leaders of the Jerusalem church. He accuses them in the most stringent terms of being rabble-rousers[60] without the support of the Elders or Apostles.

Higgins, "Acts 15 and Insider Movements among Muslims: Questions, Process, and Conclusions," *IJFM* 24 (2007): 29-40; Hinne Wagenaar, "'Stop Harassing the Gentiles': The Importance of Acts 15 for African Theology," *JACT* 6 (2003): 44-54; John Proctor, "Proselytes and Pressure Cookers: The Meaning and Application of Acts 15:20," *IRM* 85 (1996): 469-483; Rodney Webb, "Missions in Multi-Cultural America: A Study of Acts 15:1-35," *JASCG* 8 (1997): 53-67.

[59] He shares the same surname as Joseph Barsabbas (1:23). Since both were prominent members of the Jerusalem church, it is possible that they may have been brothers, sons of (bar) Sabbas.

[60] There are two separate Greek verbs describing how the Judaizers stirred up trouble: "disturbed (ταράσσω) you, troubling (ἀνασκευάζω) your minds." Both verbs can carry the connotation of plundering or looting a town.

Second, he affirms Barnabas and Paul as men who had risked their lives for Jesus and who were dear friends (*agapētos*, cf. Gal. 2:9). This is a social mechanism of shaming. Paul and Barnabas put their lives on the line; anyone who stands against them should be publicly censured. Third, there was a unanimous decision (*homothumadon*) to elect/choose (*eklegomai*) Judas and Silas to confirm the council's decision by "word of mouth."[61] Both these men were eyewitnesses from Jerusalem and prophets personally selected by the Apostles and Elders (v. 32). This should effectively silence any opposition.

15:28-29. The authority of the Jerusalem Elders and Apostles, in alignment with the great missionaries (Barnabas and Paul) as well as the prophetic delegates (Judas and Silas) should be enough to silence any vestiges of legalistic opposition. Even so, James sequesters one final witness for his rhetorical *coup de grâce*. It is none other than the Holy Spirit of God! "It seemed good to the Holy Spirit . . ." sounds disconcertingly similar to "the Holy Spirit told me," which is often a theologically irresponsible and sociologically manipulative appeal to an unassailable authority. Is James really claiming a burning in his bosom or some similar existential revelation? While that is possible, the context points in a different direction. The two great witnesses of the council were Peter, followed by Paul and Barnabas. Peter's proof centered on the Holy Spirit's baptism of the house of Cornelius—a tangible, visible, and corporate miraculous manifestation. Barnabas and Paul, though their words are not recorded, recounted the "the miraculous signs and wonders God did among the Gentiles through them" (v. 12). It appears, therefore, that the Spirit validated the council's decision through the miracles worked among the Gentiles by the great Apostolic missionaries, not by an individual impression placed on James the Elder during the council.[62] Thus, the Holy Spirit's validation was historic, corporate, and tangible rather than mystical, individual, and existential.

Once again we read these four guidelines for maintaining the unity of a single church. They will come up again in 21:25. Two of these injunctions will surface yet again in the book of Revelation (2:14, 20): Food sacrificed to idols and sexual immorality. Some will argue that Paul really disagreed with James since these regulations never show up in his letters, particularly Galatians where he asserts that the Jerusalem leaders "added nothing to my message" (Gal 2:6). If we are correct that Galatians 2 is chronologically parallel with Acts 11 (as opposed to Acts 15) then Paul could not have included this decree because it had not yet been decreed! Even if, however, one assumes a later date for Galatians (post Acts 15), could it really be said that this decree *adds* to Paul's Gospel of Free Grace? Paul himself deals with two of the problematic social issues in

---

[61] It might come as a surprise to modern readers that eyewitnesses were more highly prized as valid testimony than written documents. Papias said, "If, then, anyone came, who had been a follower of the elders, I questioned him in regard to the words of the elders,—what Andrew or what Peter said, or what was said by Philip, or by Thomas, or by James, or by John, or by Matthew, or by any other of the disciples of the Lord. . . . For I did not think that what was to be gotten from the books would profit me as much as what came from the living and abiding voice," (Cited in Eusebius, *Eccl. Hist.* 3.39.4, cf. Quintilian, *Inst.* 2.2.8; Pliny the Younger, *Epistle* 2.3).

[62] This insight was gleaned from Josh McIntosh, "'For it Seemed Good to the Holy Spirit', Acts 15:28. How Did the Members of the Jerusalem Council *Know* This?" *RTR* 61 (2002): 131-147.

COLLEGE PRESS NIV COMMENTARY

1 Corinthians: sexual immorality (5–7) and food sacrificed to idols (8–10)—the very issues raised in Revelation (2:14, 20). His conclusions are no different from James's—don't sacrifice the unity of the body for the practice of individual freedom! He claimed to be a "slave to everyone" that he might win some to the gospel (1 Cor 9:19). He placed his own ban on eating meat so as not to offend a brother (Rom 14:1-23; 1 Cor 10:23-31), circumcised Timothy even on the heels of this conference (Acts 16:3), and paid for a ritual vow in the temple to conciliate offended legalists (Acts 21:20-24).[63] That James and Paul stress different aspects of the same issue(s) when writing to two different groups of people at two places and at two different times hardly counts as a contradiction. Finally, one might note that the question for the church was not what Peter, James, Paul, or Barnabas believed but what the Holy Spirit confirmed.

[30]The men were sent off and went down to Antioch, where they gathered the church together and delivered the letter. [31]The people read it and were glad for its encouraging message. [32]Judas and Silas, who themselves were prophets, said much to encourage and strengthen the brothers. [33]After spending some time there, they were sent off by the brothers with the blessing of peace to return to those who had sent them.ᵃ [35]But Paul and Barnabas remained in Antioch, where they and many others taught and preached the word of the Lord.

ᵃ*33 Some manuscripts them, [34]But Silas decided to remain there*

15:30-35. The delegation arrived with the letter in hand. When the whole congregation heard its contents, they celebrated the encouraging news. The theme of encouragement (*paraklēsis*) continues (v. 32), particularly through the prophetic ministry of Judas and Silas. We don't know how long they stayed in Antioch, but it was long enough to leave their imprint on the congregation. As they returned to Jerusalem the church sent them away with their blessing (v. 33). This "blessing of peace" (lit., "They sent them away with peace") likely reflects the Hebrew concept of *shalom*, a prayerful benediction for complete wholeness in body, soul, family, etc. (cf. Matt 10:12/Luke 10:5; 1 Sam 25:6; Psa 122:7 or "Go in peace" Mark 5:34; Luke 7:50; 8:48; Acts 16:36). Paul and Barnabas remained in Antioch. Verse 35 has another of Luke's infamous indeterminate chronological markers (*diatribō*) that gives space to the narrative somewhat like the margins of a book or the matting on a piece of art. Luke uses this word eight times, sometimes meaning days (Acts 16:12; 20:6; 25:6, 14), and other times it seems to mean weeks or even months (Acts 12:19; 14:3, 28; 15:35). It was long enough for a substantial ministry in the city where others joined Paul and Barnabas in teaching and preaching (lit. "evangelizing," *euangelizō*).

In the meantime, Silas and Judas returned to Jerusalem. The problem is that Silas suddenly reappears in verse 40 to join Paul for the second missionary journey. The ancient scribes noticed this obvious discrepancy and solved it by

---

[63] Edvin Larsson is right to point out that Luke's etic view of Paul may, in some respects, give us a *more* accurate view of his theology and praxis than Paul's epistles; cf. "Paul: Law and Salvation," *NTS* 31 (1985): 425-436. Hence, it is misguided to simplistically assert that Luke's view of Paul is different than Paul's own self-disclosure in his letters.

keeping Silas in Antioch. The addition of verse 34 in some of the manuscripts reads, "Notwithstanding, it pleased Silas to remain there." The textual support of this insertion is weak, and it should be rejected. Of course, this has led some critics to charge Luke with an obvious error—how can Silas accompany Paul when he was last seen in Jerusalem? The obvious answer is that *he came back!* Is it really difficult to believe that the Elders in Jerusalem would send Silas back to Antioch for a progress report? The Apostles sent Peter and John to Samaria to check out Philip's work (8:14); they sent Barnabas to Antioch to investigate the work there (11:22); Agabus later made a trip up to Antioch (11:27-28) as did the Judaizers (15:1). This says nothing of the frequent emissaries Paul sent out to encourage churches, deliver letters, and collect offerings. The loose chronological markers provide a flexible calendar that could easily absorb Silas's return from Jerusalem. And if one wonders why Luke didn't record it, then the same question needs to be asked of Paul's mysterious whereabouts after 9:30, Peter's disappearance in 12:17, and John Mark's defection in 13:13. This is no mere argument from silence. Silas had already visited Antioch as a delegate, Antioch already had a substantial connection with Jerusalem, and the precedent had already been established for sending authorized men to encourage new works in other cities.

Without a doubt, if such a delegate was sent to encourage the work in Antioch, Silas was the right fellow. Paul brought him on board as a full partner on the second missionary journey (15:40). Together they were arrested in Philippi (16:19, 22) and thrown into prison (16:25, 29). Both were able to exploit their Roman citizenship to good advantage for the church (16:37). Together they labored in Thessalonica and Berea (17:4, 10). The only time Paul let Silas out of his sight was when he went alone to Athens (Acts 17:14-15), but Silas soon caught up with him at Corinth (Acts 18:5). So it is little wonder (and beyond reasonable doubt) that Paul includes Silas in the Epistles to Corinth and Thessalonica, using his full Latin name, *Sylvanus* (2 Cor 1:19; 1 Thess 1:1; 2 Thess 1:1). Though it would be hard to prove, he is very likely the same *Sylvanus* who labored alongside Peter (1 Pet 5:12) and served as his amanuensis. They did, after all, run in the same circles in Jerusalem.

C. THE SECOND MISSIONARY JOURNEY: FROM GALATIA TO EUROPE (15:36–18:17)

This second missionary journey is a frenetic tour of adventure, danger, and cunning. Here Paul comes into his own as a missionary (not to mention Luke as a writer—this is just good stuff!). There are demons to be cast out, beatings to endure, courts to navigate, leaders to raise, and sermons to preach. From the military outpost of Philippi to the bustling port of Thessalonica, from the educational center of Athens to the commercial center of Corinth, Paul targets the major cities of Greece with shrewd political and rhetorical sophistication. Though there is constant opposition and trials, the success of the mission is undeniable. The gospel was preached, disciples were trained, and churches were planted.

1. The Establishment of a New Team and
a New Direction (15:36–16:10)

[36]Some time later Paul said to Barnabas, "Let us go back and visit the brothers in all the towns where we preached the word of the Lord and see how they are doing." [37]Barnabas wanted to take John, also called Mark, with them, [38]but Paul did not think it wise to take him, because he had deserted them in Pamphylia and had not continued with them in the work. [39]They had such a sharp disagreement that they parted company. Barnabas took Mark and sailed for Cyprus, [40]but Paul chose Silas and left, commended by the brothers to the grace of the Lord. [41]He went through Syria and Cilicia, strengthening the churches.

15:36-39. After awhile in Antioch, Paul got itchy feet. He proposed a pastoral visit[64] to the churches he and Barnabas planted a few years back. Like a doting mother, Paul wants to see the progress of these fledgling churches. Barnabas, of course, is on board. He's always eager for a road trip designed to encourage Christians. In fact, he had in mind to take John Mark. The word *wanted* (*boulomai*, v. 37) is more than a mere desire, it is a design. Paul refused. In fact, he accused John Mark of desertion. Then the gloves came off! Paul and Barnabas went at it. Undoubtedly Barnabas balked at Paul's accusation that John Mark was an unreliable deserter.[65] Paul must have retorted that the work was too important to take risks with questionable characters. In reply Barnabas surely reminded Paul of the risk he took to introduce the former persecutor to the Apostles (Acts 9:27). Perhaps Paul even revisited Barnabas's failure in Antioch with his misguided allegiance with Peter (Gal 2:11-14). It got ugly. In fact, the two great apostles parted ways.

It is always sad when Christians bicker. This is an unfortunate event. But let's be honest, sometimes good people just can't see eye to eye. There are even times when two stellar leaders might come to loggerheads and have to part ways. That is the inevitable and sad reality of human beings, Christians or not. So the issue is not how to *avoid* disputes in the church but how to *manage* them. This text offers three helpful principles.

15:40. First, *you can disagree with a brother without judging him.* Luke mentions the approval the church gave to Paul and Silas (v. 40), but there is not a word of condemnation of Barnabas. Luke just notes the fact of the dispute without any apparent need to side with one or the other. When will the church learn that two people can disagree without vilifying the other as Satan's spawn?

15:41. Second, *Paul and Barnabas divided strategically.* Barnabas went to Cyprus with John Mark. Not only was this his native land, it was the portion of the tour in which he took the lead. Paul, on the other hand, went though Syria and Cilicia, his home turf. He replaced Barnabas with Silas, a qualified leader from Jerusalem. Though the divorce of Barnabas and Paul is unfortunate, it is not without its

---

[64]In all of its 11 NT uses, ἐπισκέπτομαι implies caring for physical needs or providing protection for a beleaguered people group (Matt 25:36, 43; Luke 1:68, 78; 7:16; Acts 6:3; 7:23; 15:14, 36; Heb 2:6; James 1:27).

[65]The Western Text is even rougher on the lad by adding that he abandoned "the work to which they had been sent." Thus, he didn't complete his commission.

strategic advantage. Both teams effectively targeted the right territory.

Third, *though Paul rejected John Mark, at some point, he gave him a second chance.* After another tour with Barnabas, the young John Mark assisted Peter, who would refer to him as "my son Mark" (1 Pet 5:13). Years down the road, when Paul was abandoned during his house arrest, John came to him (Col 4:10; Phlm 1:24). Again at the end of Paul's life Paul begs Timothy (who replaced John Mark as Paul's junior assistant) to bring John Mark to his dungeon to be with him "because he is helpful to me in my ministry" (2 Tim 4:11).

One wonders what kind of psychological impression this dispute had on John. Whether it was a turning point or an albatross, this noble young disciple eventually eradicated all doubts as to his value in the Kingdom and his friendship with Paul.

ACTS 16

1. The Establishment of a New Team and
a New Direction (15:36–16:10 continued)

[1]He came to Derbe and then to Lystra, where a disciple named Timothy lived, whose mother was a Jewess and a believer, but whose father was a Greek. [2]The brothers at Lystra and Iconium spoke well of him. [3]Paul wanted to take him along on the journey, so he circumcised him because of the Jews who lived in that area, for they all knew that his father was a Greek. [4]As they traveled from town to town, they delivered the decisions reached by the apostles and elders in Jerusalem for the people to obey. [5]So the churches were strengthened in the faith and grew daily in numbers.

16:1-3. Heading northwest from Antioch, Paul and Silas undoubtedly passed through Tarsus, on through the mountain pass called the 'Cilician Gates', through Cappadoica , arriving in Derbe and Lystra. Thus, they begin the so-called 'Second Missionary Journey' from where Paul's previous tour ended. It was here in Lystra that Paul was stoned. Some anonymous benefactors had nursed him back from the precipice of death and sent him on his way to Derbe. If our suspicion is correct, we are reading the follow-up account of that terrible ordeal. It is likely that young Timothy, perhaps now only twenty years old, witnessed the assassination attempt on Paul's life. It is also plausible that Timothy's own mother, Eunice, and grandmother, Lois (2 Tim 1:5), had been Paul's nurses, saving his life through that dark night. If Timothy was privy to their rescue operation, it must have had a deep impact on his psyche. Now, some five years later, he had not only adopted the Messianic faith of his Jewish mother and grandmother, but had earned a reputation with the local believers as far away as Iconium (eighteen miles). He was the perfect replacement for John Mark as the junior assistant on the missionary team. Timothy eventually became Paul's most prominent and most loved disciple. While Titus and Philemon each received one small letter from Paul, Timothy received two, both longer and more impassioned. Moreover, six of Paul's other epistles were penned in partnership with Timothy (2 Cor 1:1; Phil 1:1; Col 1:1; 1 Thess 1:1; 2 Thess 1:1; Phlm 1:1). He was not merely Paul's coworker (Rom 16:21; 1 Cor 16:10; 1 Cor 1:19; Phil 2:19; 1 Thess 3:2, 6), he was his spiritual son (1 Cor 4:17; Phil 2:22; 1 Tim 1:2, 18; 2 Tim 1:2).[1]

The problem is that Timothy, according to his Jewish neighbors, was a "Mamzer"—the child of an illicit marriage. Though intermarriage was common

---

[1] It may be significant in this regard that Timothy's father was likely dead, at least such could be inferred from the imperfect verb in v. 3, "His father was (ὑπῆρχεν) a Greek" (*Beginnings*, 4:184).

in the Diaspora, some of the more rigid Hebrews would agree with the sentiment expressed in Jubilees 30:7-8, "And if there is any man who wishes in Israel
to give his daughter or his sister to any man who is of the seed of the Gentiles he
shall surely die, and they shall stone him with stones; for he hath wrought shame
in Israel; and they shall burn the woman with fire."

Though children belonged to their father, their ethnicity was determined
by their mother.[2] Consequently, Timothy, preaching the Jewish Messiah with
Paul, was not living in fidelity to his Jewish roots. But didn't we just come out
of the Jerusalem Council? Didn't Paul just fight for freedom from the Mosaic
Law? Didn't he argue against circumcision as a prerequisite for salvation (cf.
Gal 5:1-6; 6:12-15)?[3] Absolutely! Salvation by grace through faith is an inviolable
principle for Paul. So we can assert with complete confidence that Paul would
never circumcise Timothy for salvation. So why did he pull out his scalpel? It
was for evangelism, not salvation. Paul felt compelled to remove any barrier to
proclaiming Christ to his countrymen. Timothy's heritage was potentially offensive to more legalistic Jews. This simple out-patient procedure would effectively
silence contentious opposition. Timothy was a well-known figure in the area;
he could hardly hide his heritage. His willingness to submit to circumcision was
momentous. Since Greeks disdained circumcision, Timothy made a permanent
decision to identify himself with Judaism, knowing that he was thus aligned with
a maligned subculture of his world.[4] His model is still stellar for those called by
God to leadership ministry. Often that which is permissible is not advisable. We
deliberately refuse our 'rights' so that the gospel can go forth with the fewest
obstacles possible. The inalienable liberty in Christian salvation gives way to submission and deference for Christian ministers. In Paul's own words:

> To the Jews I became like a Jew, to win the Jews. To those under the
> law I became like one under the law (though I myself am not under
> the law), so as to win those under the law. To those not having the law I
> became like one not having the law (though I am not free from God's
> law but am under Christ's law), so as to win those not having the law. To

---

[2] This is an oversimplification challenged by Shane Cohen, "Was Timothy Jewish (Acts 16:1-3)? Patristic
Exegesis, Rabbinic Law, and Matrilineal Descent," *JBL* 105 (1986): 251-268, since both Roman and Rabbinic law on the subject postdates our text, and many of the Patristic Fathers called Timothy a Gentile.
However, the weight of the evidence still favors matrilineal descent; cf. Christopher Bryan, "A Further Look
at Acts 16:1-3," *JBL* 107 (1988): 292-294; e.g., *m. Qidd.* 3:12, "Wherever there is a potential for a valid marriage and the marriage would not be sinful, the offspring follows the male. . . . Wherever there is potential
for a valid marriage but the marriage would be sinful, the offspring follows the parent of lower status. And
what is this? This is a widow with a high priest, a divorcee or a 'released woman' [Deut 25:5-10] with a
regular priest, a *mamzeret* or a *nětînâ* [Ezra 2:43-58] with an Israelite, an Israelite woman with a *mamzēr* or
a *nātîn*. And any woman who does not have the potential for a valid marriage with this man but has the
potential for a valid marriage with other men, the offspring is a *mamzēr*. And what is this? This is he who
has intercourse with any of the relations prohibited by the Torah. And any woman who does not have the
potential for a valid marriage either with this man or with any other men, the offspring is like her. And what
is this? This is the offspring of a slave woman or a Gentile woman."

[3] Haenchen's (480-482) accusation that Luke misrepresents Paul who would never have circumcised
Timothy misses the point. Paul's argument in Galatians is about salvation; his action in Acts was about leadership in ministry. Even in Galatians Paul is not anticircumcision; he calls it irrelevant, not 'evil.'

[4] This complicated cultural setting of the diaspora is explicated by Irina Levinskaya, "Diaspora Jews in the
Book of Acts," in *The Book of Acts in its Diaspora Setting* (ed. Richard Bauckham, vol. 5 in *The Book of Acts in Its
First Century Setting*, Grand Rapids: Eerdmans, 1996), 1-17.

the weak I became weak, to win the weak. I have become all things to all men so that by all possible means I might save some. (1 Cor 9:20-22)

16:4-5. The effectiveness of Paul's strategy was undeniable. They plowed through Asia Minor, delivering the Jerusalem decree in town after town. The churches grew both deep and wide, in faith and in numbers. Mission accomplished.

⁶Paul and his companions traveled throughout the region of Phrygia and Galatia, having been kept by the Holy Spirit from preaching the word in the province of Asia. ⁷When they came to the border of Mysia, they tried to enter Bithynia, but the Spirit of Jesus would not allow them to. ⁸So they passed by Mysia and went down to Troas. ⁹During the night Paul had a vision of a man of Macedonia standing and begging him, "Come over to Macedonia and help us." ¹⁰After Paul had seen the vision, we got ready at once to leave for Macedonia, concluding that God had called us to preach the gospel to them.

16:6-8. Paul & Co. caravan[5] across Turkey passing through the territories of Phrygia and Galatia.[6] They likely had their sights set on Ephesus, the capital city of Asia and a major religious, political, and economic center in the Empire. When the Holy Spirit put the kibosh on their plans, they tried to turn north into Bithynia,[7] perhaps targeting important urban areas like Nicea, Nicomedia, and Byzantium. Again, the Spirit of Jesus wouldn't allow them to pass. So they found themselves passing through Mysia only to bump up against the Aegean Sea at Troas ■. This was a crucially important port on the Dardanelles, founded in 334 B.C. after the death of Alexander the Great by one of his generals, Antigonus (Strabo, *Geo.* 13.1.26).[8] Paul apparently stayed there long enough to establish a church (cf. Acts 20:5-6; 2 Cor 2:12; cf. 2 Tim 4:13).

Troas sat on momentous geography since it was in the vicinity of Troy. None can miss the importance of Troy for the Greeks due to the substantial influence of the Iliad as formative cultural document. But even for the Romans this fertile plain on the western coast of Asia Minor was a font of inspiration. A number of Roman rulers came here for career altering inspiration (e.g., Germanicus, Had-

---

[5] Robert Jewett offers a fascinating possibility that Paul travelled with a caravan across Asia Minor, repairing their tents in return for the protection such an entourage would afford in a region riddled with highway robbers; "Paul and the Caravanners: A Proposal on the Mode of 'Passing through Mysia'," *Text and Artifact in the Religions of Mediterranean Antiquity* (Waterloo, Ont.: Wilfrid Laurier University Press, 2000), 74-90.

[6] The geography here is a bit fuzzy; cf. Robert Jewett, "Mapping the Route of Paul's 'Second Missionary Journey' from Dorylaeum to Troas," *TB* 48 (1997): 1-22. We know we're talking about central Anatolia, but beyond that it is impossible to draw clear geographical boundaries. Ramsay proposes that the two territories are conflated—Phrygio-Galatia; cf. *Traveller*, 210-212; also Colin Hemer, "Adjective 'Phrygia'," *JTS* 27 (1976): 122-126. Conversely, J. Polhill argues that Luke intends the older Galatian kingdom in the north rather than the Roman province of Galatia in the south; cf. "Galatia Revisited: The Life-Setting of the Epistle," *RevExp* 69 (1972): 437-443.

[7] Bithynia had a substantial population of Jews (Philo, *Embassy to Gaius*, 281). It is thus hardly surprising that Christianity later flourished in the region (cf. 1 Peter 1:1; Pliny the Younger, *Epistle* 10.96).

[8] Colin Hemer, "Alexandria Troas," *TB* 26 (1975): 79-112, offers a robust description of this port and its significance. It was especially important because both land and sea routes between East and West (Asia and Europe) converged here. Suetonius (*Caes.* 79.3) reported a rumor that Julius thought of moving his political seat to Troas from Rome. This port city was equally important to Christians. The *Epistle of Ignatius* was addressed to the believers at Troas.

rian, Caracalla, Constantine, and Julian). That certainly captures Paul's career at the pivot point. It was God's sovereign destiny for him to preach in Europe.

A couple of questions come immediately to mind. First, is the Spirit of Jesus the same as the Holy Spirit? The answer is not so simple. The "Spirit of Jesus" echoes the Old Testament title for Yahweh, "Spirit of the Lord" or "Spirit of God."[9] Hence, it may carry a similar connotation: The force of God felt in earthly affairs. It was a way of putting Jesus in God's place of authority in the midst of Paul's mission. In this light, it is interesting to note that in verse ten God called Paul to preach in Macedonia. Thus we encounter the Holy Spirit (v. 6), the Spirit of Jesus (v. 7), and God (v. 10) in a single breath. This is the first time since Jesus' baptism that all three members of the Trinity have shown up in the same place and time.

A second question arises from this text: How was Paul hindered? It may have been through physical barriers such as floods, bandits, or rock slides. It may have been a prophetic word through Silas. However, the revelation that ultimately moved Paul to Macedonia was a dream (vv. 9-10). This may also have been the means that the Trinity used to get him to Troas. Dreams, particularly those with an audible voice attached to the apparition, were taken as a prophetic word from God (or the gods).

16:9-10. A Macedonian stood before Paul in a dream and pleaded for him to come and help.[10] Western readers, for whom dreams have been consigned to their Freudian subconscious, this text is rather eccentric. For those in the third world, this ancient appreciation of dreams is normative.[11] This is not to suggest that all dreams were gullibly accepted as divine communiqués. Both Aristotle and Cicero differentiated between natural and supernatural dreams (Aristotle, *On Sleep and Wakefulness*; Cicero, *On Divination*). Such a dream as this, however, with both vision and audition, in such a place as Troas, and substantiated with such marvelous confirmation as in Philippi, would clearly be understood as a message from God.[12] Moreover, such a dream would be read by Luke's audience in light of other political figures whose careers were altered by dreams at pivotal places and times. If we can listen with ancient ears, we hear Luke saying, "Paul's missionary career took a dramatic turn here in Troas." Furthermore, if

---

[9] Variations are found in Phil 1:19, "Spirit of Jesus Christ"; Rom 8:9; 1 Pet 1:11, "Spirit of Christ"; and Gal 4:6 "Spirit of his Son." This divine title, conflating Jesus with Yahweh, is explored by Gustav Stählin, "Tò πνεῦμα Ἰησοῦ (Apostelgeschichte 16:7)," in *Christ and the Spirit in the New Testament* (Cambridge: Cambridge University Press, 1973), 229-252.

[10] This text has been a major impetus for 'missions'; cf. Jean-Francois Zorn, "L'appel du Macédonien: un mythe biblique fondateur de la mission?" *ETR* 83 (2008), 249-269. On a different note, the fruitless speculation that Paul could recognize his nationality through his dress or accent or that the Macedonian was none other than Luke (Ramsay, *Traveller*, 200-202) or Alexander the Great (Barclay, 122) is neither exegetically sustainable nor theologically significant.

[11] Acts 16:9 is the only vision in Luke/Acts that is not a divine figure. Cf. John B. F. Miller, "Paul's Dream at Troas: Reconsidering the Interpretations of Characters and Commentators," in *Contemporary Studies in Acts* (ed. Thomas E. Phillips; USA: Mercer, 2009), 138-153, discerns from this fact that the dream was, in fact, open to interpretation and that Paul & Co. got it wrong! Unfortunately for Miller's thesis, however, is the fact that there is not the slightest indication by Luke that this trip into Macedonia was misguided.

[12] For a helpful synthesis on dreams in the ancient world, cf. Bart Koet, "Im Schatten des Aeneas, Paulus in Troas," in *Luke and His Readers* (Leuven: Leuven University Press, 2005), 415-439 and Derek Dodson, "Philo's *De somniis* in the Context of Ancient Dream Theories and Classifications," *PRS* 30 (2003): 299-312.

one caught the little word "we" in verse 10, one heard him say, "I was there to witness God's launching this critical new adventure."[13]

2. Philippi: Women, Slaves, and Gentiles (16:11-40)

One of the common daily prayers for Jewish men goes something like this, "God, I thank you that you did not make me a Gentile, a woman, or a slave" (cf. *b. Men.* 43b). One wonders whether Luke ever heard that prayer. Perhaps this chapter is his response as he describes how Paul's preaching impacted a woman, a slave, and a Gentile. The gospel in Philippi turned the city upside down, touching virtually every strata with the liberating message of Jesus.[14]

[11]From Troas we put out to sea and sailed straight for Samothrace, and the next day on to Neapolis. [12]From there we traveled to Philippi, a Roman colony and the leading city of that district of Macedonia. And we stayed there several days. [13]On the Sabbath we went outside the city gate to the river, where we expected to find a place of prayer. We sat down and began to speak to the women who had gathered there. [14]One of those listening was a woman named Lydia, a dealer in purple cloth from the city of Thyatira, who was a worshiper of God. The Lord opened her heart to respond to Paul's message. [15]When she and the members of her household were baptized, she invited us to her home. "If you consider me a believer in the Lord," she said, "come and stay at my house." And she persuaded us.

16:11-12. Leaving Troas in the rearview mirror, Paul & Co. made a beeline for Philippi with brief overnight stops on the island of Samothrace 🖻 and the quaint little port of Neapolis (modern Kavala) 🖻. Just eight miles to the northwest, Philippi sits in a marshy valley. It was not only a Roman colony with national pride and retired soldiers, but it was also famous for its medical training, a fact not likely lost on Luke. He euphemistically calls it *the* leading city of Macedonia (which, strictly speaking, was Thessalonica).[15]

16:13-15. After several days the Sabbath rolled around and Paul wanted to practice his traditional Jewish piety. Apparently there was no synagogue in town, because that required the presence of ten Jewish heads of household. So he went to the local river, Gangites, where the flowing waters would attract the few faithful Jews of the city for ritual washings. All he found were a few women who shared his

---

[13]This is the first of the "we" passages in the book (16:10-17; 20:5-21:18; 27:1-28:16). As was argued in the introduction (under "(2) Who is the author?"), these likely indicate Luke's presence during the travels of Paul.

[14]David Suazo argues that Luke presents us with a paradigm for preaching the gospel in such a way that it addresses the social needs of a community. In other words, there is no valid preaching of the gospel which only impacts one's soul without transforming one's society; cf. "El poder de la verdad para transformer culturas: El evangelio transforma a individuos, estructuras y sociedades (Hechos 16:11–40)," *Kairos* 37 (2005): 97-110. Similarly from a French perspective, cf. Yann Redalié, "Conversion or Liberation? Notes on Acts 16:11-40," *RR* 2 (1975): 102-108.

[15]Amphipolis was the leading city of the first district (μερίδος) of Macedonia and Thessalonica was the leading city of the entire province. It may be that "first—preeminent" (πρώτη) should be read as "first—in order," (πρώτης). It was the first major city one encountered when entering into Macedonia from Troas. Cf. Allen Wikgren, "The Problem in Acts 16:12," in *New Testament Textual Criticism: Its Significance for Exegesis* (Oxford: Clarendon Press, 1981), 171-178. For a fuller sociological description of Philippi, cf. Michael White, "Visualizing the 'Real World' of Acts 16," in *The Social World of the First Christians* (Minneapolis: Fortress, 1995), 234-261.

penchant for prayer. He started to preach. They listened attentively. One woman in particular was taken with his message. Her name was Lydia, though that might be her nickname since she was from the city of Thyatira ⬛ in the district of Lydda (i.e., "Lidian Lady"). She appears to be a single woman with a thriving business. She traded in purple dye, an occupation that could be both profitable and scandalous.[16] The merchants of this guild were notorious for substituting the hard-wrought dye of the murex shell (one drop per mollusk) with the less-permanent pigment of a native madder root. By the first few washings the coveted purple fabric of the fake dye would fade as quickly as the merchant that pawned it off on unwary customers (*caveat emptor*). There is no reason to accuse Lydia of such unscrupulous business practice, but her colleagues certainly did.

When she heard Paul's preaching, her heart was moved. More specifically, God "opened her heart to respond to Paul's message" (cf. 2 Macc 1:4). This does not mean she had no choice in the matter or that God's sovereignty paralyzed her personal volition (see comments on 13:48). However, this is a robust reminder that our conversion is initiated by God. Jesus put it this way, "No one can come to me unless the Father who sent me draws him" (John 6:44). Salvation was designed by God before the creation of the world, and was accomplished through his power and will in Jesus Christ. It is not as if God then removed himself from the equation. It is he who woos us, orchestrates our experiences, and prompts us through his Spirit to respond to the message of Christ when it is preached. Simply put, if you are a Christian, it is because God made you, bought you, sought you, accepted you, protected you, and sustained you. Though human volition is clearly part of individual conversion, it is far from a 50/50 proposition. God's calling precedes and dominates our response.

As a result of God's call through Paul's preaching, Lydia and her household were baptized. This does not necessarily imply that every single member was baptized, including infants (if there were any). It simply means that when the leader of the house follows Christ, the members of the house generally follow suit. Such is the nature of a patron-client culture. However, it should be apparent from the other two households baptized in Acts and that those baptized were volitional converts. Cornelius's household spoke in tongues (10:44-48) and the Jailer's household believed in Jesus (16:30-33). In addition, Stephanas' household (1 Cor 1:16; 16:15) devoted themselves to ministry. These activities, in conjunction with baptism, would more naturally be read as cognizant responses to the gospel than infants receiving baptism simply because they were in the household.[17] Thus, we read these household baptisms not as absolute statements of every member of the household but as those who responded to the gospel.

---

[16] Thyatira was apparently a center for this guild according to a monument excavated at Thessalonica in honor of one master dyer named Menippus (Haenchen, 438); cf. Rev 2:18-29; and Homer, *Iliad* 4.141-142.

[17] Contra J. Jeremias, *Infant Baptism in the First Four Centuries* (London: SCM, 1960). For the classic argument against infant baptism, see G. R. Beasley-Murray, *Baptism in the New Testament* (Grand Rapids: Eerdmans, 1972, c. 1962), 306-386. Ayson Clifford, "A Paedobaptist Proof-Text," *RevExp* 54 (1957): 426-431, adds this interesting argument from a Calvinistic perspective: Infant baptism fails to account for the fact that not all the infants in a given household could be known to be elect and should thus be debarred from the sacrament until they can confirm their own faith in Jesus.

Another important point raised in this story is the dominant role women played in the church of Philippi. Lydia established the church in her home, even persuading Paul to stay at her home (she must have been among the elite few who persuaded Paul of anything!). Such hospitality by wealthy patrons was the primary mechanism for church gatherings in the first three centuries of the Christian era.[18] Lydia was not alone. Through Paul's later letter, we meet Euodia and Syntyche who, despite their bickering, were identified as Paul's colleagues and fellow laborers (Phil 4:3).[19] It was because of these stellar women and their consistent financial support that the church flourished not only in Philippi but also in Thessalonica (Phil 4:15-18). These kinds of contributions by women were common in the early church[20] but especially in Greece where women appear to have enjoyed more social freedoms (e.g., signing contracts, holding certain honorific titles, and initiating divorce).

[16]Once when we were going to the place of prayer, we were met by a slave girl who had a spirit by which she predicted the future. She earned a great deal of money for her owners by fortune-telling. [17]This girl followed Paul and the rest of us, shouting, "These men are servants of the Most High God, who are telling you the way to be saved." [18]She kept this up for many days. Finally Paul became so troubled that he turned around and said to the spirit, "In the name of Jesus Christ I command you to come out of her!" At that moment the spirit left her.

16:16. Here the story takes a most interesting twist. On one of their frequent

[18] One of the more spectacular archaeological finds of such a house church was in Dura-Europas where a Christian home was found in proximity to a synagogue in the midst of a Roman military outpost. For a description of the house and its floor-plans cf. Armin von Gerkan, "Zur Hauskirche von Dura-Europos," in *Mullus: Festschrift Theodor Klauser* (Münster: Aschendorfe, 1964), 143-149. For more information on house churches, see Greg Lockwood, "The House Church: From Acts to Constantine," *LTJ* 43 (2009): 97-100.

[19] Cf. Francis Malinowski, "The Brave Women of Philippi," *BTB* 15 (1985): 60-64; and Derek Thomas, "The Place of Women in the Church of Philippi," *ExpTim* 83 (1972): 117-120. Because churches met in homes, a realm where women were free to exercise more authority, women may have been allowed greater involvement in the church than they might otherwise have experienced in the synagogue or society at large; cf. Rosalie Beck, "The Women of Acts: Foremothers of the Christian Church," in *With Steadfast Purpose: Essays on Acts in Honor of Henry Jackson Flanders* (ed. Naymond Keathley; Waco: Baylor University, 1990), 296. In fact, Joel B. Green argues that Luke deliberately showed how God moved the locus of power for both Jews and Gentiles into the home. The Jewish temple and the Roman government were less authoritative for Christians than the church which met in homes. Cf. "'She and Her Household Were Baptized' (Acts 16.15): Household Baptism in the Acts of the Apostles," in *Dimensions of Baptism* (New York: Sheffield, 2002), 72-90. The Jewish temple and the Roman government were less authoritative for Christians than the church which met in homes.

[20] Women were the first to announce the coming of Jesus (Luke 1:39-55) as well as his resurrection (Matt 28:1-8; Mark 16:1-8; Luke 24:1-9; John 20:1, 2). Mary held a prayer meeting in her house (Acts 12:12 16) and Lydia used her home for a church (Acts 16:11-15) as did Nympha (Col 4:15; cf. Rom 16:1-15). Priscilla and her husband worked with Paul both at Corinth and at Ephesus; together they taught Apollos correctly about baptism (Acts 18:18-28) and hosted a church in their home (1 Cor 16:19). Philip's four daughters were prophetesses (Acts 21:8-10; cf. 1 Cor 11:5-16), Phoebe was a "deaconess" (Romans 16:1-2), and Mary was recognized as a hard-working kingdom associate (Romans 16:16). Euodia and Syntyche were Paul's associates (Phil 4:2, 3). Women were included in the instructions to church leaders (1 Tim 3:11; cf. 5:14; Prov 31:10-31), and some were eligible for a stipend from the church (1 Tim 5:9-10); of particular value were those who taught younger women how to live as Christians (Titus 2:3-5).

The contribution of women continued well beyond the NT. Given the number of women martyrs, we can ascertain that they held considerable positions of influence. After all, it was most often the church leaders who were targeted for persecution, not the laity. Moreover, there is considerable inscriptional evidence for women as deacons, teachers, and "overseers" (πρεσβῦτις or a variant thereof). Cf. G. R. Horsley (ed.), *New Documents Illustrating Early Christianity* (North Ryde: Macquaire University, 1984) 1:121.

treks to the place of prayer down by the river they ran across a fortune-teller. She was a slave, probably a teen,[21] exploited for her uncanny ability to predict the future. She was possessed by a 'Python' spirit (*pneuma pythōna*). She was akin to the famous cult of soothsayers from Delphi ⬤ in southern Greece (described by Plutarch, *Moralia*, "Obs. Orac." 414). These fortune-tellers were placed on a stool over a gaseous vapor which emanated from the ground. Thus intoxicated, they would begin to babble under the guidance of the spirit, and the priests of the cult would interpret their words for customers who paid for such divine counsel.[22]

We mustn't reduce this woman to a quack with a crystal ball at a carnival.[23] These 'prophetesses' were taken seriously.[24] Even emperors and generals consulted them before major decisions. Their male counterparts, likewise, were often political advisors (e.g., Bar Jesus) or, alternatively, enemies of the state whose prophecies were so influential that they were not infrequently expelled from Rome (e.g., Tacitus, *Ann.* 12.52).[25] There were many people who sought her council, much to the economic delight of her owners.

16:17-18. She tagged along with the small entourage of believers, bellowing all the way about Paul and Barnabas. Notice that Luke includes himself in this vivid eyewitness account. She acclaimed them as servants of the "Most High God" announcing salvation in their fair city. At first blush that sounds great—free press for the gospel. However, "most high god" was found not infrequently in Greco-Roman inscriptions for both men and gods and Philippi was no exception.[26] Furthermore, this was the very kind of claim made by demons about Jesus

---

[21] The word (παιδίσκη) is used for the young gate-keepers in Caiaphas's courtyard who intimidated Peter (Mark 14:66-69/Matt 26:69/Luke 22:56/John 18:17) and of Rhoda (Acts 12:13). When Paul uses the term for Hagar, she is obviously an older servant (Gal 4:22, 23, 30, 31).

[22] Frederick Brenk, "The Exorcism at Phillippoi in Acts 16.11-40: Divine Possession or Diabolic Inspiration," *FilNoet* 13 (2000): 3-21, argues that there is no evidence that the Python prophetesses uttered garbled speech, contra L. Maurizio, "Anthropology and Spirit Possession: A Reconsideration of the Pythia's Role at Delphi," *JHS* 115 (1995): 69-86.

[23] Though there were charlatans running amok in the Roman world, according to Philo, they could be distinguished from *bona fide* fortune-tellers (*Spec. Leg.* 3.100-101). Surprisingly, the Jewish populace was as fascinated with the divine arts as any other group in the Middle East (Pliny, *Nat. Hist.* 30.11; Josephus, *Ant.* 20.7.21 §142; Luke 11:19; *PGM* IV 3007-3027).

[24] *Selected Papyri*, LOEB, 1:436-439, illustrates the kind of questions one might ask an oracle: 193: "O Lord Sarapis Helios, beneficent one. (Say) whether it is fitting that Phanias my son and his wife should not agree now with his father, but oppose him and not make a contract. Tell me this truly. Goodbye." 195:73, "Shall I remain where I am going?" 74, "Am I to be sold?" 76, "Has it been granted to me to make a contract with another person?" 77, "Am I to be reconciled (?) with my offspring(?)?" 79, "Shall I get the money?" 80, "Is he who left home alive?" 81, "Am I to profit by the transaction?" 82, "Is my property to be put up to auction?" 85, "Am I to become a beggar?" 86, "Shall I be a fugitive?" 88, "Am I to become a senator?" 90, "Am I to be divorced from my wife?" 91, "Have I been poisoned?"

[25] For an excellent summary of the *Zeit Geist* of magical practices in Paul's world, cf. Bernhard Heininger, "Im Dunstkreis der Magie: Paulus als Wundertäter nach der Apostelgeschichte," in *Biographie und Persönlichkeit des Paulus* (ed. Oda Wischmeyer, Eve-Marie Becker, and Peter Pilhofer; Tubingen: Mohr Siebeck, 2005), 271-291.

[26] Even so, as pointed out by Irina Levinskaya, "God-fearers: Epigraphic Evidence," in *The Book of Acts in Its Diaspora Setting* (ed. Richard Bauckham, vol. 5 in *The Book of Acts in Its First Century Setting*, Grand Rapids: Eerdmans, 1996), 83-104, "Most-High" was predominantly a Jewish term for Yahweh even if it was sometimes used for pagan deities (Pindar, *Nemean Odes* 1.90; 11:2; Aeschylus, *Eumenides* 28), e.g., Pindar, *Nemean Odes* 1.90; 11:2; Aeschylus, *Eumenides* 28). Although Paul R. Trebilco, "Paul and Silas—'Servants of the Most High God' (Acts 16.16-18)," *JSNT* 36 (1989): 51-73, traces this term through Luke, showing that when Jews use the term they just use "most high" (ὕψιστος) without the superlative addition "god" in order to avoid implications of polytheism. Hence, the girl's declaration in Philippi, like the demons', comes from a Greek polytheistic context open to misunderstanding.

that was silenced for good reason (Luke 4:34; 8:28/Mark 1:24; 5:7). In addition, though the NIV says she proclaimed "*the* way of salvation," there is no definite article in Greek so she may be saying little more than that they introduced *a* way of salvation. All told, her declaration is open to substantial misinterpretation. This is hardly the kind of PR Paul wants for the gospel.

This went on for days. Finally, Paul had had enough. Just as Jesus silenced the demons, so also Paul puts the kibosh on this girl's incessant clamoring. Paul does not perform a standard exorcism which would include elaborate rituals, charms, and incantations.[27] He simply orders the demon out. Luke adds a touch of humor by using the same word (*exerchomai*) for the demon "exiting" (v. 18) and the owners' revenue "evaporating" (v. 19). Their greed will cause serious problems for Paul (cf. Acts 19:24-28). This stands in oppositions to Lydia's generosity which so blessed the progress of the gospel.

[19]When the owners of the slave girl realized that their hope of making money was gone, they seized Paul and Silas and dragged them into the marketplace to face the authorities. [20]They brought them before the magistrates and said, "These men are Jews, and are throwing our city into an uproar [21]by advocating customs unlawful for us Romans to accept or practice." [22]The crowd joined in the attack against Paul and Silas, and the magistrates ordered them to be stripped and beaten. [23]After they had been severely flogged, they were thrown into prison, and the jailer was commanded to guard them carefully. [24]Upon receiving such orders, he put them in the inner cell and fastened their feet in the stocks.

16:19-21. When the owners realized their golden goose just got cooked, all Gehenna broke loose. They accosted Paul and Silas and dragged them into the agora (marketplace) ⬛. This is the central gathering place of the city where business, law, education, and social life converged. There they stood before the civic leaders,[28] and the accusations began to fly. Interestingly, the offended parties never mentioned their own personal agenda. Rather, they scandalize the two preachers in the most dangerous possible way with three accusations.[29] (1) "They are Jews." This hardly seems like a valid criminal charge, particularly with post-Holocaust sensitivities to anti-Semitism. It was, in fact, a meaningful accusation in Paul's social world. According to the Rhetoricians, one of the ways a person can sway a judge is by identifying (or vilifying) your opponent's national character (Cicero, *Inv.* 1.15.20; Quintilian, *Inst.* 4.1.1-4). Since Jews typically rejected Roman religion and social customs and since they were a small minority

[27]One such incantation invoked, "the god of the Hebrews, Jesu, Jaba, Jae, Abraoth, Aia, Thoth, Ele, Elo," cf. Adolf Deissman, *Light from the Ancient East* (Grand Rapids: Eerdmans, 1965), 260.

[28]This Greek term στρατηγοί was essentially equivalent to the Latin *duumviri* or *praetor* but can also indicate consuls, proconsuls, or a combination thereof. It is a pretty generic term for a civic authority.

[29]Craig de Vos argues that Paul did exorcise the girl and this caused him to be labeled a magician; "Finding a Charge That Fits: The Accusation against Paul and Silas at Philippi (Acts 16:19-21)," *JSNT* 74 (1999): 51-63. Such a label would be effective libel. His conclusion, however, that these three accusations are Luke's redaction, obfuscating the real issue of magic, misses the point that magicians and soothsayers in the first century *were* politically dangerous. This was particularly true during the latter half of Nero's reign when Luke was presumably writing. For an excellent analysis of the typical social/legal charges made against Christians see Gregory Sterling, "Customs Which Are Not Lawful: The Social Apology of Luke/Acts," *Leaven* (1997): 19-23.

in Philippi, they were easy targets. More than this, if their exorcism was viewed as part and parcel with general magic practices, this could have caused substantial disturbance.[30] (2) "They are throwing our city into an uproar." It may seem like 'disturbing the peace' would be a misdemeanor. Not so. Because the Roman Empire had grown so large, it took considerable effort to sustain the *Pax Romana.* Thus, Rome took seriously any threat to social equilibrium. A city that rioted would be dealt with most severely, even brutally. This would have been particularly true of Philippi as a Roman colony. They had Roman rights that others did not. If they could not keep order within their walls, they would be stripped of these rights and reduced to rubble. Their special privileges required a stringent example for others to follow. (3) "They advocate unlawful customs." This is the least serious of the three criminal charges. Essentially they are saying Christianity was an illicit religion. However, Christianity was not a new religion but an extension of Judaism. Furthermore, the law prohibiting proselytizing Romans was inscribed under Hadrian in the second century.[31] Perhaps this accusation reflects an earlier law, or perhaps it is merely a local prejudice. For example, Tacitus said, "To establish his influence over this people for all time, Moses introduced new religious practices, quite opposed to those of all other religions. The Jews regard as profane all that we hold sacred; on the other hand, they permit all that we abhor" (*Hist.* 5.4).[32] Nonetheless, proselytizing was seldom banned in the first century and it could hardly be proved illegal.

16:22-24. Paul and Silas had no chance for a fair trial. When the crowds turned against the preachers, popular outrage outweighed legal procedures. The crowds were nearly as angry as the owners, for they too lost something precious—the ability to foresee their fate. The magistrates ordered the missionaries stripped and beaten by the 'sergeant at arms' (Greek *rhabdouchoi* for the Latin *lictors*).[33] The rods they used were as thick as billy clubs but as long a broom sticks.[34] They gave a wicked blow. Two more times Paul suffered this brutal form of torture (1 Cor 11:25) though Luke only records this one.

After this thrashing the pummeled pair were handed over to the chief jailer and thrown into maximum security ◻.[35] Ancient prisons were harsh with a complete disregard for human rights. The interior dungeon was particularly odious. In all likelihood there were no windows, no toilets, no food or water.

[30] E.g., Pliny, *Nat. Hist.* 30.11; Juvenal, *Sat.* 6.542-545; Josephus, *Ant.* 8.45-48; Lucian, *Lover of Lies* 16; *Gout* 171-173; *Val. Max.* 1.3.3.

[31] A. N. Sherwin-White, *Roman Society and Roman Law in the New Testament* (Oxford: Clarendon, 1963), 81-82.

[32] Unnik concludes that sentiments such as Tacitus's suggest that the accusation in Philippi would have social significance even if it would not be granted legal weight until the second century; cf. W. C. van Unnik, "Die Anklage gegen die Apostel in Philippi," in *Mullus* (Aschendorff: Münster Westfalen, 1964), 366-373.

[33] Though literally Luke says the magistrates stripped Paul and Silas and ordered them beaten, it is unlikely that they stripped them with their own hands. There were police standing at the ready for just such duties.

[34] ◻ The *lictors* came equipped with a bundle of rods surrounding an axe in the middle, tied together with a red band called the *fasces*.

[35] Of the six imprisonments mentioned in the book of Acts, this is the only true public jail. In Acts 4–5 the Apostles were held in the Hall of Gazith in Jerusalem, part of the High Priestly complex. Peter and James were locked up in Herod's Praetorium (12). In chapters 22–23 Paul was in the Roman fortress of Antonia in Jerusalem and transferred to the Governors palatial holding cell in Caesarea (24–26). Finally, in Rome (28) Paul was in house arrest, not the local dungeon. This is not to say these other facilities were cozy, but they were likely a good bit more accommodating than the rat-hole in Philippi.

In fact, the only amenity was a pair of wooden beams that locked around their ankles to prohibit an escape. Paul and Silas had their legs stretched after their beating and fastened in the stocks ◨. They might be thrown on their faces into the urine-soaked soil of the dungeon floor or thrown on their bruised backs and cracked ribs. Though Paul's stoning was worse than this, Silas had not likely experienced such physical pain in his life.

[25]About midnight Paul and Silas were praying and singing hymns to God, and the other prisoners were listening to them. [26]Suddenly there was such a violent earthquake that the foundations of the prison were shaken. At once all the prison doors flew open, and everybody's chains came loose. [27]The jailer woke up, and when he saw the prison doors open, he drew his sword and was about to kill himself because he thought the prisoners had escaped. [28]But Paul shouted, "Don't harm yourself! We are all here!" [29]The jailer called for lights, rushed in and fell trembling before Paul and Silas.

16:25-26. Against all odds, Paul and Silas worshiped God.[36] Specifically they were singing prayers to God.[37] Granted, their songs might be the Blues (otherwise known as Lament Psalms). Nonetheless, in this dark and violent place, their prayers permeated the prison, and the inmates eavesdropped incredulously (*epakroaomai*). Their recital was interrupted by God's stomping; at least that would have been how the Philippians interpreted the earthquake (cf. Psa 114:7; Isa 29:6; Ezek 38:19; Matt 27:54; 28:2; Acts 16:26; Rev 6:12; 8:5; 11:13, 19; 16:18).[38] It rocked the Richter Scale enough to damage the very foundation of the prison. Obviously, if the foundation twists the doors will pop open. But chains falling off the prisoners cannot be explained through naturalistic means. The force required to rattle chains from your wrists would beat you to death before it freed you. Clearly, Luke is portraying this as a miraculous release from prison—what was good enough for Peter (Acts 5:19-21; 12:5-11) is now replicated for Paul.

16:27-29. The jailer, probably dozing on the outside of a secured door, is jarred to full attention by the earthquake. In the dead of night and a bit dazed, he saw the prison doors ajar. Both the door leading out of the prison, and the door into the maximum security cell, were open.[39] The jailer, assuming the prisoners had escaped (or were about to rush him), drew his sword. It was more honorable in his culture to end his own life voluntarily than to be subjected to the punishments due the prisoners. Though he was obviously not culpable for the prisoner's escape, he would, nonetheless, be held responsible (cf. Acts 12:19; 27:42). Divine Justice must be served.

---

[36] This motif of singing in prison is also found in Pagan literature (Lucian, *Icarom.* 1; Philostratus, *Apollonius* 4.36; *T. Joseph* 8.5; Epictetus, *Disc.* 2.6.26-27) and Jewish literature (*T. Jos.* 8.5; cf. Parsons, 233).

[37] The single Greek verb (ὑμνέω) is rendered by two English words "sing hymns." But the Greek construction suggests that what they were "hymning" were their prayers, represented by a participle connected to the main verb "sing."

[38] Pieter W. van der Horst, "Hellenistic Parallels to Acts (Chapters 3 and 4)," *JSNT* 35 (1989): 44-45.

[39] A number of the thematic details of Paul's miraculous escape can be found in other 'prison break' stories (cf. Bruce, 337, ftn 51 & 52). For example, Joseph supposedly sang praise to God before his release (*T. Jos.* 8.5; cf. Tertullian, *To the Martyrs*, 2), and Euripides recounts how doors flew open and fetters fell in *Bacchae* 443-448. These are recognizable themes in Mediterranean literature.

Paul screamed at him, "Don't hurt yourself." Paul had no personal agenda in saving this guy's life except, perhaps, his adoption of Jesus' principle to love one's enemies. This impulse was instinctive—there was no time for a premeditated response. There was no need for the jailer to off himself since all the inmates were still in their cells. That was too much to believe, but his assistants rushed in with lamps (or torches) and sure enough, the head-count proved that every prisoner was accounted for.[40]

The jailer was still terrified but not because of who might have escaped from prison but because of who was still in prison. If the earthquake was a sign of god(s)'s perturbation, then Paul and Silas were the source of his angry outburst. They had divine approbation, and the jailer was on the wrong side of heavenly justice. That's why he burst into their cell and fell at their feet.

[30]He then brought them out and asked, "Sirs, what must I do to be saved?" [31]They replied, "Believe in the Lord Jesus, and you will be saved—you and your household." [32]Then they spoke the word of the Lord to him and to all the others in his house. [33]At that hour of the night the jailer took them and washed their wounds; then immediately he and all his family were baptized. [34]The jailer brought them into his house and set a meal before them; he was filled with joy because he had come to believe in God—he and his whole family.

16:30-32. The jailer's question about 'salvation' was not about 'rescue'. Paul already rescued his physical life. His question was about getting on the right side of divine justice. At this point, he was pretty open to whatever demands they might place on him. Is he ever in for a surprise! Salvation is not about righting your wrongs or appeasing God's wrath. That was all accomplished in Christ. What he must do is put his faith in the Lord Jesus. It is interesting that the jailer called Paul and Silas "Lords" (NIV = "Sirs"), but they deflected this honorific title to Jesus, the one true Lord. This message was not only for him but also for his household over which *he* is 'lord'. The jailer, of course, was delighted with this précis of the gospel. He escorted the evangelists to his home where he gathered his family (no doubt also awakened by the tremor) for a full rendition of the gospel message of salvation in Jesus the Messiah.

16:33-34. Verses 30-31 introduce an interesting paradox: the jailer called Paul and Silas "Lords," but they introduce him to the one true Lord. Here we find two more paradoxes. (1) Right then, right there in the middle of the night, the jailer washed the wounds of the evangelists, and they reciprocated immediately by washing his household in baptism. (2) With classic Middle Eastern hospitality he offered them a meal as an enacted metaphor for the joy with which they had filled him. What a celebration that must have been. Can there be any doubt that this jailer celebrated his first communion at his own dinner table? In the early church, the natural setting of the Eucharist was the home, not a separate and artificial edifice constructed to detach the affair of God from daily life. With these two

[40] The Western text makes a reasonable addition that the jailer secured all the other prisoners before leading Paul and Silas to his home.

sacraments (baptism and Lord 's Supper) the jailer launched his journey of faith. His home was consecrated as a place where fidelity to God would be lived out in community. This is now the second house church Paul planted in Philippi.

[35]When it was daylight, the magistrates sent their officers to the jailer with the order: "Release those men." [36]The jailer told Paul, "The magistrates have ordered that you and Silas be released. Now you can leave. Go in peace." [37]But Paul said to the officers: "They beat us publicly without a trial, even though we are Roman citizens, and threw us into prison. And now do they want to get rid of us quietly? No! Let them come themselves and escort us out." [38]The officers reported this to the magistrates, and when they heard that Paul and Silas were Roman citizens, they were alarmed. [39]They came to appease them and escorted them from the prison, requesting them to leave the city. [40]After Paul and Silas came out of the prison, they went to Lydia's house, where they met with the brothers and encouraged them. Then they left.

16:35-36. How awkward it must have been for the jailer to return his preachers to prison. He was barely dry from the baptistery when he had to refasten the stocks on the feet of those who brought him good news. His soul had been released from bondage by the very evangelists he had to incarcerate in a dirty dungeon. Meanwhile, the magistrates were shaken up by the earthquake.[41] This natural phenomenon convinced them that their bludgeoned visitors were divine envoys. So at first light they sent a delegation to release the Jewish exorcists.

16:37-38. The jailer's joy at their release was immediately doused by their resolute refusal to leave the prison. Paul was wronged! As a Roman citizen he had certain rights that had been violated. Specifically, *Lex Porcia* and *Lex Valeria* forbade the binding and beating (respectively) of Roman citizens without a proper trial.[42] For noncitizens binding and beating were standard interrogation techniques from which Paul should have been exempt. We see him invoke this right to good effect in Acts 22:24-29. He was strung up under Claudius Lysias, but as soon as he announced his citizenship, he was released and not without a good deal of trepidation by the governor. The question here, then, is why Paul did not invoke the right the day before. Perhaps the clamoring crowd drowned out their protests so they could not be heard. However, this seems unlikely. Even if one of the soldiers heard the word "citizen" he would have backed off. The penalty for violating this law was a severe beating commensurate with what you dished out. It is likely, therefore, that Paul and Silas deliberately withheld this information,[43] took the beating, and are now leveraging this judicial error for the security of the fledgling church.[44]

---

[41] This is a natural implication which the Western text turns into an overt statement.

[42] Cicero (*Against Verres* 2.5.161-162; cf. Cicero, *Pro Rabirio* 12) records how disgraceful it was to beat a Roman citizen. When this very thing happened in the marketplace of Messina, Sicily, the citizen cried out "I am a Roman citizen!" (*"Civis Romanus sum"*).

[43] Though this theory cannot be proved, it should be noted that part of the political apology Luke offers in Acts is how the church can capitalize on Roman law and practice. His realistic assessment of both the positive and negative behaviors of Roman rulers provides helpful principles for carrying out Acts 1:8 under Roman rule; cf. Steve Walton, "The State They Were In: Luke's View of the Roman Empire," in *Rome in the Bible and the Early Church* (ed. Peter Oaks; Grand Rapids: Baker, 2002), 1-41.

[44] It is unclear how Paul and Silas would have proved their citizenship. Records were kept, often on wooden diptychs small enough to be carried. However, there is no evidence that the average citizens, most

Paul demanded that they not be expelled (*ekballō*) secretly (*lathra*). He will not walk out of that prison unless it is with an escort by the very magistrates that unjustly beat him. Such a demand shamed the civic leaders; it was an admission of their error. When the citizens of Philippi saw their leaders parading Paul from the prison, they would recognize that Paul was being vindicated. That was a tough pill for the magistrates to swallow, but if they don't take it on the chin, Paul could cause some serious damage to their careers, even having them expelled from office (Cicero, *In Verrem*, 5.66), and Philippi could lose its status as a Roman colony (e.g., Suetonius, *Claudius*, 25). So they had to humble themselves and capitulate to his demand. Paul's primary purpose was not self-justification. His interest is not his own vindication or personal retaliation. His interest was in the health of a fledgling church. Due to this one night of humiliation and physical torture (and undoubtedly a few weeks of rehabilitation), Paul and Silas provided the church with a good bit of immunity from the social pressure that other congregations had to face. After this incident, there was little chance that the church would undergo persecution from the power brokers of Philippi.

16:39-40. The leaders capitulated and escorted Paul and Silas out of the prison but pleaded with them to leave the area. Fair enough. That was a compromise Paul was willing to accept, but not before meeting with the church in Lydia's house. What a prayer meeting that must have been. Paul undoubtedly had much to say about living as the community of God in the midst of a pagan society. Surely he instructed them about the jailer and incorporating him into the body so that the believers would include both Jews and Gentiles. Finally, he must have had something to say about Luke's leadership for he would not join them on the next stage of the journey. It would be another five years or so before Luke rejoined the entourage en route back to Jerusalem. This church had political peace, ethnic integration, and a stellar disciple as a new pastor. They were poised to become one of the great churches of the New Testament . . . and they do not disappoint.

---

of whom would scarcely travel, would have carried these with them. Cf. H. J. Cadbury, *Book of Acts in History* (London: Black, 1955), 68-78; and Sherwin-White, *Roman Law*, 151-152.

ACTS 17

3. Thessalonica: Hooligans in the Square (17:1-9)

Paul's brief stint in Thessalonica appears as a blip on the radar and is then gone. One is tempted to wonder why Luke bothered to recount the details of this city rather than listing it along with Amphipolis and Apollonia (v. 1) and moving on to more fertile ground. It is, however, important for several reasons. First, Paul wrote two letters to this city which exponentially expand our knowledge of the church that met there. Aside from Galatians, these are probably the earliest extant correspondence from the Apostle to the Gentiles. Second, Thessalonica is a narrative bridge between Philippi and the churches of Achaia. This story shows how the persecution continued unabated from the synagogue. Third, and perhaps most importantly for Luke's audience, this story illustrates the kind of political trouble the church can encounter and the shrewd maneuvering sometimes necessary to avoid such unfortunate glitches.

¹When they had passed through Amphipolis and Apollonia, they came to Thessalonica, where there was a Jewish synagogue. ²As his custom was, Paul went into the synagogue, and on three Sabbath days he reasoned with them from the Scriptures, ³explaining and proving that the Christ[a] had to suffer and rise from the dead. "This Jesus I am proclaiming to you is the Christ,'" he said. ⁴Some of the Jews were persuaded and joined Paul and Silas, as did a large number of God-fearing Greeks and not a few prominent women.
ª3 Or Messiah

17:1. Though Amphipolis and Apollonia are only mentioned in passing, one should not mistake them as insignificant cities. Amphipolis was the major city of the region. Its entrance boasted a majestic lion which dates back to the time of Alexander the Great (4th cen B.C.). Paul surely saw this same monument as he passed through the city. It is likely these two cities were where Paul spent the night on his way to Thessalonica. It was thirty-three miles to Amphipolis, thirty more to Apollonia, and another thirty-seven to Thessalonica. That is an impressive day's trek to each of these cities, especially for a couple of guys still recovering from such a brutal beating even if they were on horseback rather than on foot (which is most probable). Luke likely breezed by these cities because there was no church planted there. It is as if he counts the significance of a city not by the number of citizens but by the number of Christians.

17:2-3. After several days, Paul, Silas, and Timothy arrived at Thessalonica. It was the capital city of Macedonia and one of the major ports of the Mediterranean Sea (and still is today) . It, of course, had a synagogue. Paul, of course, made a beeline to worship with the Jews of the city and announce the wonderful news that their Messiah had come. That was a world-altering message and it took some time to unpack. For three weeks running[1] Paul plowed through the ancient scrolls.[2] The most difficult 'sell' was that their Messiah was not a victorious warrior but a suffering servant. This was, by far, the minority view of the Messiah, supported by two primary texts: Isaiah 53 and Zechariah 12:10. So why did it take three Sabbaths to explain? Though there are only two proof-texts, there are lots of precursors to the suffering Messiah. All those forefathers who foreshadowed the Christ had biographies that told of suffering. From Abraham to Moses, from David to Jeremiah, from Elijah to Joshua, all suffered in their vocational service to Israel. Thus, while the proof-texts are thin, the metanarratives are vast. In fact, the entire story of Israel is one of death and resurrection. If Jesus is the embodiment of Israel and all her heroes, then how could he escape suffering? Normally the cross would be shameful, but the fact of the resurrection reversed this curse. It is now a symbol of victory and hope. The Messiah's suffering, vindicated by exaltation, was the message of Jesus (Luke 24:26, 46), Peter (1 Peter 1:11), and Paul (Acts 26:23; 1 Cor 15:3-4)—it is the core of Christian *kerugma*. Bottom line: Jesus absorbed the suffering of Israel into his body on the cross and through the resurrection defeated death. As one should expect, God's greatest servant, Jesus, suffered supremely and rose victoriously. The shame of the cross is thus turned on its head; it is now a signal victory of vicarious redemption.

17:4. As the reader has come to expect, Paul's preaching split the synagogue.[3] To some this message made sense. A few of the Jews and many of the God-fearing Greeks gave allegiance to Jesus the Messiah in affiliation with Paul and Silas. To most of the Jews, however, this bizarre teaching smacked of heresy. To make matters more chaotic, some of the new believers were prominent women of Thessalonica who undoubtedly shared with their husbands their newfound faith.[4] Thus the local synagogue debate would soon become a public debacle.

[5]But the Jews were jealous; so they rounded up some bad characters from the marketplace, formed a mob and started a riot in the city. They rushed to Jason's house in search of Paul and Silas in order to bring them out to the crowd.[a] [6]But when they did not find them, they dragged Jason and some other brothers before the city officials, shouting: "These men who have caused trouble all over the world have now come here, [7]and Jason has welcomed them into his house.

---

[1] Paul was likely in Thessalonica longer that the three Sabbaths he spent in the Synagogue. After all, he received multiple gifts from the new church in Philippi (Phil 4:16), and he earned a reputation for working hard, apparently in his own trade (1 Thess 2:9). Paul had a ministry well beyond the synagogue in which idolaters turned to God (1 Thess 1:9), implying a much longer time than Luke's compressed 'three Sabbaths'.

[2] The words "explaining" (διανοίγω) and "proving" (παρατίθημι) are less authoritative than they sound in English. Literally they could be rendered "opening" and "laying out." Paul was doing cognitively what he had just done literally with the scroll—he opened it and laid it before his interlocutors. He provided the materials; the Holy Spirit provided the conviction.

[3] By now the reader has come to expect Luke's standard presentation of Paul's preaching: Synagogue, Scriptures, division, persecution, civic intervention, and narrow escape. For careful examination of this pattern see Néstor Míguez, "Lectura socio-politica de Hechos 17:1-10," *RevB* 50 (1988): 183-206.

[4] As a matter of historical record, women of high standing were often attracted to Christianity. It is even rumored that Nero's wife had sympathies for believers (Josephus, *Ant.* 20.8.11 §195).

They are all defying Caesar's decrees, saying that there is another king, one called Jesus." [8]When they heard this, the crowd and the city officials were thrown into turmoil. [9]Then they made Jason and the others post bond and let them go.

a5 Or the assembly of the people

17:5-7. Enraged with jealousy, some of the Jews took to the streets. The market was the center of town and often a magnet for scalawags—the lazy, shiftless rabble who were ever eager for a row (e.g., Aristophanes, *Frogs* 1015; Plato, *Protagoras*, 347c; Plutarch, *Aemilius Paulus*, 38.3). They were easily fanned into a frenzied mob who marched to Jason's house . They were looking to lynch these divisive preachers.[5] Fortunately, they were not at home. Unfortunately, Jason[6] and several other brothers bore the brunt of harboring these 'outlaws'. Though we don't know their names, it is possible that Aristarchus and Secundus were among them (Acts 20:4; 27:2). They were dragged before the city officials, more specifically, the *politarchs.*

17:8-9. Jason & Co. were accused of harboring these criminals and eventually forced to post bond. The charges laid against Paul and Silas were twofold. First, they stirred up trouble "all over the world" (meaning, of course, the Roman Empire). Where did they come up with such a charge? Probably from Paul himself. After three weeks in the synagogue, he likely gave them all the ammunition they needed as he recounted his persecutions in Damascus, Jerusalem, Antioch, Iconium, Lystra, etc. Thus Paul's preaching caused riots, starting in the East and creeping across the Mediterranean, finally reaching their noble city. This was a serious charge. The second charge was even more serious: They defied Caesar's decrees by claiming another king, namely, Jesus.[7] Pilate had heard the same thing and would have dismissed it had it not been for the incessant demands of the Jewish leaders. This is much the same. Paul's accusers are Jews who forced a negative verdict against their own countrymen from Roman rulers who would otherwise have been relatively unconcerned about such an intramural debate. (One suspects that Luke intends his readers to see the comparison and discern Paul's innocence.) Nevertheless, the way they couched the charges cannot be ignored.

Just what were these charges? At first blush it appears they are being charged with treason (*maiestas*)—claiming another king. However, such a charge would surely have been taken to the proconsul of Macedonia (conveniently located in Thessalonica) rather than the local *politarchs* who arbitrated lesser affairs. Furthermore, if Paul and Silas were accused of treason, it is difficult to imagine that Jason would have been allowed to post bond and let the preachers escape to another unsuspecting city to propagate their rebellion against Caesar. Two other theories have been put forward that carry more weight.

---

[5] Verse 5 says they wanted to bring Paul and Silas "out to the crowd." The Greek word for "crowd" (δῆμος) is more specific than the general rabble. It signifies the 'citizenry' of a city with rights and privileges. In other words, it is not merely a lynching but a public verdict against these evangelists that would lead to public defamation and appropriate punishment.

[6] Jason was a name equivalent to "Jesus/Joshua" often used by Diaspora Jews.

[7] It is probably best to understand the word "king" (βασιλεύς) as "Emperor" since the Caesars never used the title "king" for themselves (*Beginnings* 4:206).

E. Judge argues that Paul and Silas were treated as Jewish soothsayers who predicted the overthrow of Caesar at the return of Jesus.[8] Both Augustus (Cassius Dio, *Hist.* 56, 25.5-6) and Tiberius (Cassius Dio, 57.15.8) forbade predictions about the death of the Emperor. By such prognostication, soothsayers could foment self-fulfilling prophecies of the Emperor's demise. By predicting a regime change, a prophet/magician could embolden assassins to carry out the inevitable and imminent fate of the gods. It could very well be that Paul's teaching on the return of Jesus and the inbreaking Empire of God made the synagogue rulers nervous. Concerning the Man of Lawlessness, Paul said:

> He will oppose and will exalt himself over everything that is called God or is worshiped, so that he sets himself up in God's temple, proclaiming himself to be God. Don't you remember that when I was with you I used to tell you these things? . . . Then the lawless one will be revealed, whom the Lord Jesus will overthrow with the breath of his mouth and destroy by the splendor of his coming. (1 Thess 2:4-5, 8)

In short, during the time when the Emperors prohibited inflammatory soothsaying, Paul's predictions of Jesus' return were presented as political propaganda against Caesar. There was enough truth in what they said to make their argument compelling. Although, asserting Jesus as a rival to Claudius vastly underestimates Paul's actual presentation of the Kingdom of God. It would have seemed scandalous at the time, but from our vantage point, we can see that the Emperors were not even close to the clout of the Exalted One.

A second theory is presented by Justin Hardin, who argues that the charge was an illegal assembly of a voluntary association that was prohibited by Julius (Suetonius, *Jul.* 42.3) and Augustus after him (Suetonius, *Aug.* 32.1; cf. Philo, *Flacc.* 4; Tacitus, *Ann.* 14.17).[9] This would explain not only the public outcry against Paul and Silas, but the fine levied against Jason and the other brothers who likewise participated in the meetings. Furthermore, it explains why Paul and Silas would have been released after the fine was paid and allowed to leave the city.[10] Finally, it would explain why the Christians of the city continued to experience persecution from their fellow countrymen (1 Thess 2:14) and why Paul could not return to Thessalonica without significant repercussions to Jason and the brothers (cf. 1 Thess 2:18).

4. Berea: Nobles in the Synagogue (17:10-15)

[10]As soon as it was night, the brothers sent Paul and Silas away to Berea. On arriving there, they went to the Jewish synagogue. [11]Now the Bereans were of more noble character than the Thessalonians, for they received the message with great eagerness and examined the Scriptures every day to see if what Paul

---

[8] E. Judge, "Decrees at Thessalonica," *RTR* 30 (1971): 1-7.

[9] Justin Hardin, "Decrees and Drachmas at Thessalonica: An Illegal Assembly in Jason's House (Acts 17.1-10a)," *NTS* 52 (2006): 29-49.

[10] One document shows that a fine was sometimes levied against illegal gatherings; cf. J. González, "The *Lex Irnitana*: A New Flavian Municipal Law," *JRS* (1986): 147-243.

said was true. [12]Many of the Jews believed, as did also a number of prominent Greek women and many Greek men. [13]When the Jews in Thessalonica learned that Paul was preaching the word of God at Berea, they went there too, agitating the crowds and stirring them up. [14]The brothers immediately sent Paul to the coast, but Silas and Timothy stayed at Berea. [15]The men who escorted Paul brought him to Athens and then left with instructions for Silas and Timothy to join him as soon as possible.

17:10-11. Paul and Silas were evacuated in the dead of night to Berea.[11] It was a substantial town of the area, fifty miles west of Thessalonica on the *via Egnatia* 🔲. In a discussion about another fugitive from Thessalonica, Cicero described Berea as "out of the way" for anyone traveling to Rome (*Against Pison*, 36.89). It was not likely the first place Paul's opponents would come looking for him.

Paul and Silas were hardly whipped pups with their tails between their legs. Even though they were attempting to fly under the Thessalonian radar, they were neither silent nor passive. They headed to the synagogue straight away and this time with some notable results. The Bereans were more noble than the Thessalonians. The word Luke used literally means "well-born" (*eugenēs*), and it speaks of the high caste of Roman society. In this context, of course, it is a metaphor for the children of God who have demonstrate their nobility by their receptivity to the Scriptures. What made them noble was their eagerness for truth and their effort to judge the message against Scripture. There is hardly a more important personal characteristic than this for spiritual growth.

17:12-15. Typically after Paul preached, the audience was divided. A few Jews and a bunch of Greeks believed the gospel, but a crowd of Jews and a few prominent Greeks stirred up trouble (cf. Acts 13:50; 14:2, 5). Here in Berea, however, there was a preponderance of Jews who believed along with the prominent Greek God-fearers. Sadly, the only name we have from this circle of new believers is Sopater, son of Pyrrus (Acts 20:4).

Persecution was inevitable but not because of the Bereans. Somehow the Thessalonians discovered Paul's whereabouts and hunted him down. Perhaps the most likely explanation was that Timothy was followed on one of his itinerant trips to/from Philippi. The Philippians generously supported Paul's ministry, and Timothy was the messenger (Phil 4:15-16; cf. Phil 2:19; Acts 17:1). Obviously he would pass through Thessalonica, even delivering the letters Paul wrote to the fledgling congregation (1 Thess 1:1; 3:2, 6; 2 Thess 1:1). Likely, on one of his return trips to Berea, he was spotted by an enemy and followed back to Berea. It would not take long for a report to get back to the capital and a posse dispatched to round up this rebel who had evaded their grasp.

[11] It is an interesting fact that Silas receives more prominence in Acts than does Timothy though the reverse appears to be the case in the Epistles; cf. Bruce N. Kay, "Acts' Portrait of Silas," *NovT* 21 (1979): 13-26. This may be due to the fact that Silas worked alongside Paul in preaching/teaching and as an authoritative preacher whereas Timothy spent more time delivering the letters and collecting offerings (e.g., 1 Cor 4:17; 16:10; 2 Cor 1:1; Phil 1:1; 2:19; Col 1:1; 1 Thess 1:1; 3:2, 6). This would explain Silas's prominence in Acts where Paul's ministry is described and Timothy's prominence in the Epistles where he is an envoy to the churches.

Once the mob arrived, the brothers ushered Paul furtively to the coast, ostensibly to board a ship headed south (perhaps the paucity of details reflects the actual secrecy of Paul's escape route). Silas and Timothy stayed behind. Silas, no doubt, continued to teach and train the elders of the new church while Timothy traveled back to Thessalonica and Philippi to update the church on Paul's status. As for Paul, he was in the good hands of a Berean delegation, assigned to escort him safely to Athens. This majestic city had to be an overwhelming experience for an intellectual like Paul. It was the center of learning, even in Paul's day, three hundred years after its zenith. The weather, architecture, intellectual climate, and social history are all eminently wonderful. But Paul was troubled, not least by the fact that he was now alone. He sent orders for Silas and Timothy to join him *posthaste*. By the time they arrived, however, they would find Paul had already stirred quite a controversy.

5. Athens: Intellects on the Hill (17:16-34)

Paul's famous sermon in Athens has generated volumes of discussion, far more than one would expect from ten brief verses.[12] Perhaps that's appropriate since the city of Athens itself carried far more weight culturally than its five thousand residents would seem to merit. This message, like its location, has density as well as all the marks of authenticity. The details of the *agora*, Areopagus, Stoics, and Epicureans are all true to the local color of the city.[13] Furthermore, the figures of speech[14] and the quotations from pagan poets[15] tell of a speech particularly suited for its audience and setting.

Paul's Areopagus address is a model of preaching to pagans.[16] It is similar to

---

[12] Two of the most classic and comprehensive treatments of this speech come from Martin Dibelius, "Paul on the Areopagus," in *Studies in the Acts of the Apostles* (ed. Heinrich Greeven; London: SCM Press, 1939, 1956), 26-77, representing classic German liberalism, and from a more conservative perspective, Bertil Gärtner, *The Areopagus Speech and Natural Revelation* (Uppsala, Sweden: C W K Gleerup, 1955).

[13] Colin Hemer, "The Speeches of Acts II: The Areopagus Address," *TynBul* 40 (1989): 239-259, makes a strong case that these authentic details more likely derive from Paul's personal experience than Luke's literary flair. Several points of the sermon have specific cultural connections that Luke does not highlight but could hardly have been accidental by Paul. Moreover, if Paul had not mastered this kind of contextualization, one wonders how he earned the reputation as the quintessential apostle to the Gentiles. This is not to deny Lucan redaction. The intricate chiasm suggested by Robert O'Toole demonstrates that when Luke reduced Paul's address to eighty seconds of text he shaped it into an articulate nugget of Greek rhetoric; cf. "Paul at Athens and Luke's Notion of Worship," *RB* 89 (1982): 187.

[14] E.g., assonance, ζωήν καὶ πνοὴν (v. 25); alliteration, ἐπὶ παντὸς προσώπου (v. 26); paronomasia, πάντας πανταχοῦ (v. 30).

[15] Aside from the recognized quotes of Aratus and Epimenides (v. 28 below), Witulski points out a host of other allusions: Verse 24a and Epictetus, *Disc.* 4.7.6; v. 24c and Lucian, *Sacrifices* 11; v. 25 and Euripides, *Heracles* 1345-1355; v. 26 and Plato, *Tim.* 34; v. 27 and Dio Chrysostom, *Or.* 12.28; v. 28 and Plato, *Tim.* 37; v. 29 and Plutarch, *Stoic Contradictions* 1034b-c, and Clement of Alexandria, *Strom.* 5.11.76. Cf. Thomas Witulski, "Apologetische Erzählstrategien in der Apostelgeschichte—Ein neuer Blick auf Acts 15:36–19:40," *NovT* 48 (2006): 338-339.

[16] Missiologists have latched onto this text as a model for contextualization. E.g., Dean Flemming, "Contextualizing the Gospel in Athens: Paul's Areopagus Address as a Paradigm for Missionary Communication," *MIR* 30 (2002): 199-214; Tomás Halík, "The Soul of Europe: An Altar to the Unknown God," *IRM* 95 (2006): 265-270; Johnson Samuel, "Paul on the Areopagus: A Mission Perspective," *BTF* 28 (1986): 17-32 (from an Indian perspective): or from an apologetic perspective: Daryl Charles, "Engaging the (Neo)Pagan Mind: Paul's Encounter with Athenian Culture as a Model for Cultural Apologetics (Acts 17:16-34)," *TJ* 16ns (1995): 47-62; John J. Kilgallen, "Acts 17, 22-31: An Example of Interreligious Dialogue," *StudMiss* 43 (1994): 43-60; Javier Sánchez Cañizares, "Filosofía griega y revelación cristiana: las recepción del discurso del Areópago," *ScrTh* 39 (2007): 185-201 (from a Catholic perspective), Kurt Koch, "Glaubensüberzeu-

his briefer discourse to the pagans at Lystra (Acts 14:15-17) as well as to his own summaries of pagan preaching in Romans 1:19-32[17] and 1 Thessalonians 1:9-10.[18] In days gone by, scholars liked to question Paul's methodology in Athens, criticizing his philosophical capitulation to pagans based on his own self-critique in Corinth: "When I came to you, brothers, I did not come with eloquence or superior wisdom as I proclaimed to you the testimony about God" (1 Cor 2:1). Today, however, it is the near unanimous opinion that Luke intended for Acts 17 to be a model sermon to pagans just as chapter 13 was a model to Jews and chapter 20 a model to Christians. He hardly would have included it in such detail had he not intended it as a praiseworthy paradigm.

One debate continues, however. What kind of speech is this? There were three primary kinds of speeches in Paul's day: epideictic (praise or lament of a hero), forensic (legal defense), and deliberative (considering a question). Clearly this is not epideictic but it could be either forensic or deliberative. If Paul is defending himself before a legal body, then this would be a forensic speech. However, since there are no charges leveled and no verdict given, one suspects this as a deliberative speech in which Paul will answer the question about the one true God. Following this line of thought, Sandnes offers a most interesting proposal.[19] According to the rhetorical rules of the day, if your audience was antagonistic, the deliberative speech should proceed allusively (*insinuatio*), drawing the readers along in a Socratic fashion.[20] The purpose of such a speech

gung und Toleranz: interreligiöser Dialog in christlicher Sicht," *ZMR* 92 (2008): 196-210; Lars Dahle, "Acts 17:16-34: An Apologetic Model Then and Now?" *TynBul* 53 (2002): 313-316; and Marilyn McCord Adams, "Philosophy and the Bible: The Areopagus Speech," *FPh* 9 (1992): 135-150.

[17] There are some substantive differences between the 'natural revelation' of Romans 1 and Acts 17. Primarily, in Romans 1, the pagans were blinded by a wrathful God when they rejected his natural revelation. Conversely, in Acts 17, God turned a 'blind eye' to their ignorance and through natural revelation called them to recognize God as a loving father. Even so, at the macro level, the idea of knowing God through his physical creation has the same tone in both passages. Both have a polemic against idolatry and a warning of coming judgment; cf. Huw P. Owen, "The Scope of Natural Revelation in Rom. I and Acts XII," *NTS* 5 (1959): 133-143. The difference between Romans 1 and Acts 17 is more likely due to the different audience than the different author. In other words, both texts derive from the mind of Paul as opposed to the independent pens of Paul and Luke. Furthermore, Romans 2:14-16, *does* express the sentiments of Acts 17. Namely, pagans who seek God through natural revelation will be able to repent at the preaching of Jesus the Christ; cf. Heinrich Schlier, "Über die Erkenntnis Gottes be den Heiden," *EvT* 2 (1935): 9-26; and James Barr, "La foi biblique et la théologie naturelle," *ETR* 64 (1989): 355-368.

[18] The verbal similarities between these texts is striking; cf. Lucien Legrand, "The Unknown God of Athens: Acts 17 and the Religion of the Gentiles," *IJT* 30 (1981): 160-161:

	1 Thess 1:9-10	Acts 14:15	Acts 17:24, 31
Theological *kerygma*	You **turned to God** from idols to serve the living and true God	**Turn** from these worthless things to the living **God**, who made heaven and **earth** and sea and everything in them.	The **God** who **made** the world and everything in it is the Lord of **heaven and earth** and does not live in temples built by hands
christological *kerygma*	and to wait for his Son from heaven, whom he **raised from the dead**—Jesus, who rescues us from the **coming wrath**.		He has set a day when he will **judge the world** with justice by the man he has appointed. He has given proof of this to all men by **raising him from the dead**

In fact, the substance of Paul's message in Acts 17 can be found throughout the book of Acts; this is hardly an isolated and idiosyncratic speech; cf. Sjef van Tilborg, "Acts 17:27—'that they might feel after him and find . . .'" *HvTsT* 57 (2001): 86-104; and Simon Légasse, "Le discours de Paul à Lystres," in *Penser la Foi* (Joseph Doré, Christoph Theobald, and Joseph Moingt, eds.; Paris: Cerf, 1993), 127-136.

[19] Karl Olav Sandnes, "Paul and Socrates: The Aim of Paul's Areopagus Speech," *JSNT* 50 (1993): 13-26; cf. Witulski, "Apologetische Erzählstrategien," 335.

[20] Sandness, "Paul and Socrates," 21, notes several similarities between these two great teachers. Both met

is not to persuade but to generate interest. It is, so to speak, priming the pump for further discussions in which a more deliberate decision would be possible. Seen in this light, Paul's speech is hardly a failure as some discern from a mere two converts.[21] Rather, he successfully established a conversation that continued productively in the epicenter of philosophy.[22]

[16]While Paul was waiting for them in Athens, he was greatly distressed to see that the city was full of idols. [17]So he reasoned in the synagogue with the Jews and the God-fearing Greeks, as well as in the marketplace day by day with those who happened to be there. [18]A group of Epicurean and Stoic philosophers began to dispute with him. Some of them asked, "What is this babbler trying to say?" Others remarked, "He seems to be advocating foreign gods." They said this because Paul was preaching the good news about Jesus and the resurrection. [19]Then they took him and brought him to a meeting of the Areopagus, where they said to him, "May we know what this new teaching is that you are presenting? [20]You are bringing some strange ideas to our ears, and we want to know what they mean." [21](All the Athenians and the foreigners who lived there spent their time doing nothing but talking about and listening to the latest ideas.)

17:16-17. Paul was waiting in Athens for Timothy and Silas to arrive. They eventually did (cf. 1 Thess 1:1; 3:1-2). In the meantime, however, Paul was hardly sedentary. He toured the city, the home of Socrates and Plato, and the place where Aristotle, Zeno, Epicurus and scores of others carried out their careers. Here he encountered a veritable forest of idols ⬛.[23] Petronius jested, "Indeed the gods walk abroad so commonly in our streets that it is easier to meet a god than a man" (*Satyricon*, 17, cf. Livy 45.27; Strabo, *Geo.* 9.1.16). This sent Paul into a conniption.[24] So he preached in three separate places that represented virtually every part of the city: The synagogue, the *agora*, and the Areopagus. The synagogue was a semiprivate religious association. The *agora* was the public gathering place for business, law, and education. The Areopagus was a meeting of the elite philosophical minds.

Naturally, Paul heads first to the synagogue. These were his people and worship was his practice. Following his *modus operandi*, he opened the scrolls

their disputants in the marketplace of Athens (Xenophon, *Mem.* 1.1.7); both dialogued (διαλεγομαι); and both were charged with introducing foreign gods (Plato, *Euthyphro* 3; Xenophon, *Mem.* 1.1.1; Philostratus, *Apollonius* 7.11). Also helpful on this subject is Mark D. Given, "The Unknown Paul: Philosophers and Sophists in Acts 17," *SBLsp* 35 (1996): 343-351.
[21] Paul's success among the Areopagites, which likely maintained a mere thirty members, may be no less, statistically, than in many of his synagogue sermons. Moreover, by any standard, the conversion of a single Areopagite is a huge gain for the influence of the church in Athens. Cf. Bruce W. Winter, "Introducing the Athenians to God: Paul's Failed Apologetic in Acts 17?" *Them* 31 (2005): 38-59.
[22] It is also interesting that the form of the speech follows other missionary documents intended to present the monotheistic God to pagans: (1) creation of humans in God's image, (2) times and/or boundaries ordained by God, and (3) salvation. Cf., e.g., *Apostolic Constitutions* (7 §34; 8 §12); Clement, *Strom.* 1.2; Eusebius, *Prep. Gospel* (8.9-10; 13.12); *1 Clement* 19.2-20.12; 33.2-8.
[23] A "forest of idols" is a rather literal rendering of κατείδωλος. The word was used for forests, luxurious vegetation, and even "a good head of hair." Cf. R. E. Wycherley, "St. Paul at Athens," *JTS* 19 (1968): 619-621.
[24] The word for "greatly distressed" (παραξύνω) is a cognate of παραξυσμός which Luke used to describe the quarrel between Paul and Barnabas (15:39). The English word "paroxysm" (which means "convulsion") is based on the Greek word which means "angered, irritated, or upset."

and reasoned through the messianic claims of Jesus. Each Friday evening and Saturday he could be found there debating and teaching. During the rest of the week, he stood on the speakers' platform facing the famed portico of the Greek *agora*. It was kind of like a Hyde Park of London where street preachers and performers could always find curious spectators. As his audiences grew, some of the educational elite took notice. That's when things got really interesting.

17:18. Stoics and Epicureans came to check out the 'competition'. Who were they? Well, defining these groups is kind of like describing Democrats and Republicans over a two-hundred-year period. Not only do they evolve over time but at any given time, any given individual may or may not share all the classic tenets of the party. So also the Stoics and Epicureans were two of the dominant philosophical schools of the day (among many) with no real membership or checklist for what one had to believe. We often find writers espousing tenets of Stoicism who never claimed to be Stoic. That being said, there are a few things that can and should be said about these two philosophies.

The **Stoics** inherited their philosophy from Zeno of Cyprus (335–263 B.C.) who regularly held his classes in the "Painted Porch" (*stoa poikile*) from which they derived their nickname "Stoics."[25] They were a rather monastic lot, holding that happiness comes from detachment. If you love something, they said, you would be sad if you lost it. Thus, the highest pleasure could be attained by craving nothing.

Some of their beliefs are quite compatible with Christianity: (1) The world was created and god was in it—a kind of pantheism, (2) the gods determined the destiny of the world, (3) self-denial led to the happiest life since one was not enslaved to earthly passions, and (4) *logos* became a synonym for "god" as it maintained order in the world. On the other hand, the Stoics denied some key Christian tenets such as the immortality of the soul and the existence of an immaterial world. Thus, Paul's preaching would receive a mixed review from the Stoics. There was both common ground as well as considerable, even incompatible, differences.

The **Epicureans** followed the teachings of Epicurus (341–270 B.C.). He had more devoted followers and bitter enemies than any of the early philosophers. Unlike the Stoics, no other figure of importance arose from his school. Their spiel was essentially, "Eat, drink, and be merry, for tomorrow you will die."[26] They were not, however, raw hedonists. For example, one would abstain from drunkenness to avoid a nasty hangover or from adultery if the woman's husband was insanely jealous. They believed that pleasure was the greatest good but that certain pleasure should be avoided if it would lead to a painful consequence. Aside from this primary belief in pleasure, they also held that matter was eternal, death was final and *not* to be feared, acquiring friends is vital, humans operate under freewill—a kind of deism, and that one gained knowledge through logical reasoning and the five senses. Because of this 'scientific' and rationalistic epistemology, they disdained religion as irrational. Diogenes (c. A.D. 200) aptly

---

[25] Some of the more famous Stoics include Aratus of Soli (c. 315–240 B.C., quoted by Paul in v. 28), Brutus, one of Julius Caesar's key assassins (85–42 B.C.), Seneca (c. A.D. 1–65, a key advisor to Nero), Epictetus (c. 55–135 A.D.), and Emperor Marcus Aurelius (A.D. 121–180).

[26] Among the best sources for Epicureans is Lucretius, *On the Nature of Things*.

summed up Epicureanism: "Nothing to fear in God; Nothing to feel in Death; Good [pleasure] can be attained; Evil [pain] can be endured." Obviously, they will have problems with much of Paul's preaching. Paul, however, is up to the challenge. His formative years in Tarsus, the third greatest university town of the Empire, prepared him well for such a time as this.

The Stoics and Epicureans asked, "What is this babbler trying to say?" The Greek word for "babbler" (*spermalogos*) originally referred to the birds that went about pecking at seeds. They could be seen all over the *agora* picking up scraps from various stalls. It was an insulting term for loafers and chatterers of low status. This, in sociological terms, is a label used for libel and a cheap attempt to win over the crowd by disparaging Paul's character. As we shall see soon enough, Paul, the able orator, will turn this label around and show that it is not he who peddles inferior philosophy, but these resident ideologues of Athens.

Part of what upset the Stoics and Epicureans was that Paul appeared to be introducing new gods into the Greek Pantheon.[27] Paul touted Jesus as the divinely raised son of God. The "Resurrection" (*anastasis*, a feminine noun in Greek) they might have mistaken as some divine counterpart to Jesus though this is not likely.[28] Clearly Paul had a great deal of explaining to do. His answer was that the God he was introducing was not, in fact, new, but they had known him all along! Interestingly, that is essentially the same response he offered when the Jews accused him of altering ancient customs of Judaism.[29] He argues, "This is what you've been looking for all along!"

17:19. The philosophical powerhouses took Paul off to the side to discuss his theology. That actually was part of the official role of the Areopagus as a ruling body in Athens.[30] The real question is where they took him. Just south of the *agora* is a bald limestone hill that sits in the shadow of the Acropolis ◙. It would be a three minute walk from where they stood but it would afford a quieter space for an intellectual deliberation. This rock is called the Areopagus (or Mars Hill) and was, in fact, the original meeting place of the legal body. However, the legal body also went by the designation "Areopagus." Thus it represented not only the *place* but also the *people* who met there, kind of like "Wall Street." However, the Areopagus also met in the main *Stoa Basileios* of the *agora*, not just atop that notable rock. That too would have provided the privacy necessary for the oratorical foray we are about to relish. It hardly matters where they met historically, although any visitor to Athens can attest that Paul preaching atop the majestic rock towering over the city is far more picturesque than a stuffy old counsel chamber of the marketplace.[31]

---

[27] The word "advocate" (καταγγελεύς, v. 18) was also used for the herald of the Imperial Cult.

[28] Cf. K. L. McKay, "Foreign Gods Identified in Acts 17:18?" *TynBul* 45 (1994): 411-412.

[29] Cf. Witulski, "Apologetische Erzählstrategien," 341-346. Luke's polemical strategy here in Acts 17 is similar to his description of Philippi (16:19-22), Thessalonica (17:5-8), and Corinth (18:12-13). Namely, those who accuse Paul of innovation and public disturbance are actually the ones guilty of those charges.

[30] There were major changes in the theological landscape of Athens during Paul's time, particularly the explosion of the Imperial Cult. The Areopagus was the official body that would have arbitrated any theological or philosophical innovations of the city; cf. Bruce Winter, "On Introducing Gods to Athens: An Alternative Reading of Acts 17:18-20," *TynBul* 47 (1996): 71-90.

[31] William Morrice, "Where Did Paul Speak in Athens—on Mars' Hill or before the Court of the Areopagus? (Acts 17:19)," *ExpT* 83 (1972): 377-378, comes down on the side of this hill.

Paul now has the undivided attention of the undisputed gurus of ancient philosophy.[32] Luke, however, never takes the spotlight off of Paul. He is not enamored in the least with these great intellects or their philosophical prowess. In fact, he kind of paints them in a negative light. This is true in at least two ways. *First, he portrays them as ignorant.* That's worse than it appears initially, for the Athenians prided themselves on being well-informed, cutting edge, and in-the-know.[33] To call an Athenian intellectual ignorant is 'fightin' words'. *Second, he emphasizes their curiosity.* While that may seem good for an academic, in the ancient world, idle curiosity was portrayed as spurious and infantile.[34] And the Athenians were particularly noted for their insatiable curiosity. Demosthenes, four hundred years earlier, admitted of his fellow Athenians, "Now all the Athenians and the foreigners who lived there spent their time in nothing except telling or hearing something new" (*Philippic*, 1.10). Hence, to say that they spent their time on idle gossip over the latest cognitive fads (v. 21) is a functional retort for calling Paul an intellectual scavenger (18).

Paul's Sermon to the Areopagus

The following speech has three definite movements.[35] (1) Paul used a local idol dedicated to an unknown god to introduce the one true God (vv. 22-23). (2) He then described how God created (vv. 24-25), ordained (vv. 26-27), and lovingly sustained (vv. 28-29) the world. None of these are new topics either in the *agora* or the Areopagus—pagans had already been debating whether and how god/s created the world and whether he/they should be honored with idols and/or temples. (3) There is a coming eschatological judgment where we will stand before the one true God.

22Paul then stood up in the meeting of the Areopagus and said: "Men of Athens! I see that in every way you are very religious. 23 For as I walked around and looked carefully at your objects of worship, I even found an altar with this inscription: TO AN UNKNOWN GOD. Now what you worship as something unknown I am going to proclaim to you. 24The God who made the world and everything in it is the Lord of heaven and earth and does not live in temples built by hands. 25And he is not served by human hands, as if he needed anything, because he himself gives all men life and breath and everything else. 26From one man he made every nation of men, that they should inhabit the whole earth; and he determined the times set for them and the exact places where they should live.

---

[32] When they asked Paul, "May we know what this new teaching is," the word they used was δύναμαι. At its root is the word "power". Hence, the way they phrase the question may imply their authority to arbitrate the new doctrine Paul was espousing.

[33] It was not merely an insult from a Greek standpoint; it was also an insult from a Jewish standpoint. In the OT, ignorance led to sin (e.g., Deut 27:18; 1 Sam 26:21; Isa 28:7); cf. Heinz Külling, "Zur Bedeutung des Agnostos Theos: eine Exegese zu Apostelgeschichte 17,22.23," *TZ* 36 (1980): 65-83.

[34] E.g., Seneca, *Ep.* 88.36-38; Demosthenes, *Or.* 4.10. Luke's characterization of the Athenians as busybodies through unwise curiosity fits the known topos and reflects a necessarily negative connotation of the word δεισιδαιμονέστερους (v. 22); cf. Patrick Gray, "Athenian Curiosity (Acts 17:21)," *NovT* 47 (2005): 109-116.

[35] This speech conforms to the rhetorical form of Paul's day: *Exordium* (vv. 22-23), *Probatio* (vv. 24-29), and *Peroratio* (vv. 30-31); cf. Dean Zweck, "The *Exordium* of the Areopagus Speech, Acts 17.22, 23," *NTS* 35 (1989): 94-103.

[27]God did this so that men would seek him and perhaps reach out for him and find him, though he is not far from each one of us. [28]'For in him we live and move and have our being.' As some of your own poets have said, 'We are his offspring.' [29]Therefore since we are God's offspring, we should not think that the divine being is like gold or silver or stone—an image made by man's design and skill. [30]In the past God overlooked such ignorance, but now he commands all people everywhere to repent. [31]For he has set a day when he will judge the world with justice by the man he has appointed. He has given proof of this to all men by raising him from the dead."

17:22-23. The Unknown God: The fact that the highest council of Athens took Paul off to a private meeting certainly indicates something serious is taking place. Like the Sanhedrin of Israel, or the *Politarchs* of Thessalonica, the Areopagus was an administrative body. Though their judicial functions were limited under the Roman government, they could flex their political clout in a number of areas including education, religion, civic affairs, and even legal matters (Cicero, *Nat. of the gods* 2.29). Yet there are no official charges brought up nor any punishment meted out. Perhaps we could see this as an official inquiry to determine the nature or legality of Paul's preaching—whether he would be accepted, ignored, or run out of town.

Paul opens his speech with a most titillating statement:[36] "I see that in every way you are very religious." The last word, "religious" (*deisidaimōn*), could be rendered either as "pious" (if it is a compliment [cf. Cicero, *Nat. of the gods*, 2.3]) or "superstitious" (if it is an insult).[37] Though Paul surely intended it as a compliment as part of his *capitatio benevolentiae*,[38] to be sure they would have to listen attentively to what comes next. It was a rather clever way to engage his audience from the opening line of his address.

What came next could hardly be construed as a compliment. Paul points out their plethora of idols which were congested in the *agora*. It was a veritable rock garden of gods and emperors, immortals engraved in silent stone. To the tourist it was an outdoor museum, honoring both the Greek Pantheon and the Roman Forum. To the apostle it was rampant paganism that nearly sent him into convulsions.

Paul even found one idol dedicated "to an unknown god." While archaeologists have not found such a statue in Athens, Pausanias (c. A.D. 150) attested to multiple such idols en route to Athens from Phalerum (1.1.4; 5.14.8).[39] This

---

[36] Though Paul's speech is peppered with reference to and from pagan philosophy, it is also thoroughly enmeshed with OT allusions and ideology, a point most ably demonstrated by Gärtner, *The Areopagus Speech*; A. M. Dubarle, "Le Discours à L'Aréopage [Acts 17:22-31] et son Arrière-plan Biblique," *RSPT* 57 (1973): 576-610; and Kenneth Litwak, "Israel's Prophets Meet Athen's Philosophers: Scriptural Echoes in Acts 17,22-31," *Bib* 85 (2004): 199-216. Paul never abandons his Jewish roots no matter how far from home he travels philosophically. The two systems of thought are not completely antithetical. It is Paul's intention to show the overlap.

[37] H. Armin Moellering, "Deisidaimonia, a Footnote to Acts 17:22," *CTM* 34 (1963): 466-471, shows that the most common meaning of this word was "uncommonly scrupulous."

[38] Lucian (*Anacharsis*, 19) says it was forbidden to use compliments to court the favor of the Areopagus in one's *exordia*. Whether that was rigidly followed by Paul (or anyone else) is doubtful.

[39] Philostratus, (*Apollonius* 6.3.5), similarly testifies to altars "to unknown gods" in the third century A.D. For a thorough survey of altars to unknown gods, cf. *Beginnings* 5:240-246, and Witherington, 521-523.

shows the reality of the pagan penchant to cover all the bases. The basic idea is that if a god showed up in Athens and felt jilted for lack of a monument, the citizens could point to this altar as the overlooked memorial. This, in theory, would assuage the wrath of a capricious and potentially lethal god.[40] It is not so dissimilar from a soldier who wears a cross, a Star of David, and a rabbit's foot into battle with a Koran in his backpack.

This may well answer the question as to whether Paul was calling them "pious" or "superstitious." If he did intend this as a compliment, it was backhanded for sure. The Athenians prided themselves on being in-the-know. To call an Athenian ignorant is akin to calling a New Yorker a hick or a Texan a sissy. This can't sit well with the Areopagites who, of all people, held pride of place in their educational and philosophical world.

17:24-29. The God to Be Known—Summary: In this second movement of the sermon, Paul offered three attributes of the one true God. First, he is the creator of the whole world and thus humanity is beholden to him, not he to them (vv. 24-25). Second, since God is one, so too is humanity. Our ethnic, political, and geographic differences are ordained by that one true God so that we will be in a position to find him (vv. 26-27). Third, God is near and he is our father (vv. 28-29). He is neither out of touch nor out of reach. If we seek him, we will find him, for he wants desperately to be found by his children.

17:24-25. In these two verses, Paul affirms two things with which most Stoics would agree.[41] First, **God created the world.** Epictetus said the same thing: "God has made all things in the cosmos" (*Disc.* 4.7.6). Consequently, **God cannot be confined to a human edifice.** On this point even the Epicureans would agree. Perhaps it sounds strange coming from a Jew that a temple cannot contain the Almighty, but even at the dedication of the temple, Solomon gave lip service to this idea: "But will God really dwell on earth? The heavens, even the highest heaven, cannot contain you. How much less this temple I have built!" (1 Kgs 8:27; cf. Isa 66:1; Philo, *Moses* 2.88). Euripides said much the same thing (*Frag.* 968; Bruce, 336): "What house built by craftsmen could enclose the form divine within enfolding walls?" Plutarch accuses Zeno, the founder of Stoicism at just this point:

The fact that Paul identifies the statue as dedicated to a single god, whereas all other references are to plural "gods" may suggest that Luke was summarizing the broader concept into a singular and localized instance.

[40] Though this idea is never articulated as such, there is an illuminating story told by Diogenes Laertius (*Lives of Philosophers* 1.110): "They sent a ship and Nicias the son of Niceratus to Crete, to invite Epimenides to Athens; and he, coming there in the forty-sixth Olympiad, purified the city and eradicated the plague for that time; he took some black sheep and some white ones and led them up to the Areopagus, and from thence he let them go wherever they chose, having ordered the attendants to follow them, and wherever any one of them lay down they were to sacrifice him to the God who was the patron of the spot, and so the evil was stayed; and owing to this one may even now find in the different boroughs of the Athenians altars without names, which are a sort of memorial of the propitiation of the Gods that then took place."

[41] This passage is one of the few in Acts that manifests 'intertextuality' with the Greek classics. Though Paul (and Luke) was clearly familiar with the major Greco-Roman philosophic traditions, he lacked the subtlety of a classically trained student in *paideia* (as one would expect from a rabbi). Cf. Osvaldo Padilla, "Hellenistic παιδεία and Luke's Education: A Critique of Recent Approaches," *NTS* 55 (2009), 416-437.

Moreover, it is a doctrine of Zeno's not to build temples of the gods [ἱερὰ θεῶν μὴ οἰκοδομεῖν]. . . . Yet they think that the Epicureans are confuted by the fact that they sacrifice to the gods, whereas they are themselves worse confuted by sacrificing at altars and temples which they hold do not exist and should not be built. (*Stoic Self-contradictions*, 1034b)

There was a disconnect. As Balch ("Posindonius," 68) points out, "Stoics reverence statues of the gods and goddesses in temples, neither of which, they think, should ever have been made, whereas Epicureans offer sacrifice before the human shapes of divinities who do nothing." Plutarch satirizes the situation:

What then? Does it not seem to you that the feeling of the atheists [ἀθέων] compared with the superstitious [δεισιδαίμονας] presents just such a difference? The former do not see the gods at all, the latter think that they do exist and are evil. The former disregard them, the latter conceive their kindliness to be frightful, their fatherly solicitude to be despotic, their loving care to be injurious, their slowness to anger to be savage and brutal. Then again, such persons give credence to workers in metal, stone or wax, who make their images of gods in the likeness of human beings [ἀνθρωπόμορφα τῶν θεῶν τὰ εἴδη ποιοῦσι]. . . . Atheism is an indifferent feeling towards the Deity, which has no notion of the good, and superstition is a multitude of differing feelings with an underlying notion that the good is evil. (Plutarch, *Superst.* 167de)

What these quotes clearly demonstrate is that Paul was arguing as a monotheistic Jew but jumped into the middle of a discussion that had been raging already for some time. Many of the Stoics and Epicureans would share his critique of temples and idols.

Paul's second presupposition is that **God is self-sufficient**. Psalms 50:9, 12 says, "I have no need of a bull from your stall or of goats from your pens. . . . If I were hungry I would not tell you, for the world is mine, and all that is in it" (e.g., Isa 42:5; 2 Macc 14:35; 3 Macc 2:9).[42] This biblical truth was recognized by a number of pagan philosophers.[43] For example, Euripides said, "God, if he be truly God, has need of nothing" (*Heracles*, 1345). It is God who provides for human needs, not *vice versa*. Our very life and breath come from God.

17:26-27. For the average Greek philosopher, there are two striking statements in these verses. In verse 26, Paul avers that *there is really only one race of people.* In a world that assumed in-group ethnic superiority, such a claim could

---

[42] Not only does this thought reflect Paul's Jewish background, an allusion to Isaiah 42:1-9 might be particularly relevant to Paul since it goes back to his own commission by Jesus to be the Apostle to the Gentiles (Acts 13:47 citing Isa 49:6). Cf. Edward Fudge, "Paul's Apostolic Self-Consciousness at Athens," *JETS* 14 (1971): 193-198.

[43] For other parallels showing Paul's points of connection with the Greek philosophy, cf. David L. Balch, "The Areopagus Speech: An Appeal to the Stoic Historian Posidonius against Later Stoics and the Epicureans," in *Greeks, Romans, and Christians* (Minneapolis: Augsburg Fortress, 1990), 52-79; Eduard des Places, "Des temples faits de main d'homme (Actes des Apôtres 17, 24)," *Bib* 42 (1961): 217-223; Dean Zweck, "The Areopagus Speech of Acts 17," *LTJ* 21 (1987): 111-122; and Kilgallen, "Interreligious Dialogue," 52-55.

be dismissed with a supercilious air (Bruce, 357-358). The Jews claimed to be God's elect with a stubborn resilience that befuddled their neighbors who disregarded their eccentric ways. The Egyptians cherished their ancient mysteries in architecture, navigation, agriculture, mummification, astrology, and the gods. The Romans, of course, could boast of political and military dominance. But perhaps the Greeks, of all the Mediterranean peoples, held pride of place. In medicine, language, culture, art, literature, architecture, etc., they had bragging rights of which they were not shy. For Paul to come in and level their cultures to one theocratic humanity, stemming from Adam, would have tested the patience of this august council. Nonetheless, his claim is straightforward and simple: The geopolitical divisions are not a result of one's superiority but rather of God's sovereignty (cf. Deut. 32:8).[44]

Somehow these divisions logically led to a search for the one true God (lit., "grope after" him as if in the dark). How so? There are two viable options. First, these geopolitical boundaries and seasons indicate that Yahweh is moving Caesars and generals like pawns on a chessboard (e.g., Dan 2:36-45; Luke 21:24). He establishes societies so as to posture people to receive his loving-kindness (Marshall, 288). Second, God's boundaries and seasons are not about nations but about nature.[45] The ordered universe declares the goodness and immanence of God. Greek philosophy praised the well-designed world, its natural boundaries and ordered seasons. This is similar to the appeal Paul made in Lystra, "Yet he has not left himself without testimony: He has shown kindness by giving you rain from heaven and crops in their seasons" (Acts 14:17; cf. Matt 5:45).[46] Everything has a time, place, and purpose; such order indicates a celestial 'orderer' who is calling his creation to himself.

The second big surprise is that *God is not far from us.* Christian readers, attuned to the concept of incarnation, easily miss the magnitude of this revelation. Most of the world has held God at arm's length. He is believed to be distant, even unconcerned. After all, isn't that what you'd expect from an all-powerful, sovereign God? How could he deign to meddle in the petty affairs of humans? That is precisely the beauty of the Jewish concept of God that was magnified exponentially in the revelation of Jesus. For deists like the Epicureans this is a hard sell; for pantheists like

[44] This important idea, shared among Jews and pagans alike, that God(s) determined times and places of habitation, is explicated by Édouard des Places, "Tempora vel Momenta (Act 1,7; cf. 17,26 et 30)," in *Mélanges Eugène Tisserant* (Città del Vaticano: Biblioteca apostolic, 1964), 105-117.

[45] Though καιρός generally refers to the four seasons, one could argue that in this context it implies the evolutionary seasons of the human races and governments; cf. Roger Lapointe, "Que sont les *kairoi* d'Act 17:26: Étude semantique et stylistique," *EgT* 3 (1972): 323-338.

[46] Paul's argument is quite like Dio Chrysostom, *Or.* 12.27-29: "Now concerning the nature of the gods in general, and especially that of the ruler of the universe, first and foremost an idea regarding him and a conception of him common to the whole human race, to the Greeks and to the barbarians alike, a conception that is inevitable and innate in every creature endowed with reason, . . . for inasmuch as these earlier men were not living dispersed far away from the divine being or beyond his borders apart by themselves, but had grown up in his company and had remained close to him in every way, they could not for any length of time continue to be unintelligent beings, especially since they had received from him intelligence and the capacity for reason, illumined as they were on every side by the divine and magnificent glories of heaven and the stars of sun and moon, by night and day. . . . How, then, could they have remained ignorant and conceived no inkling of him who had sowed and planted and was now preserving and nourishing them, when on every side they were filled with the divine nature through both sight and hearing, and in fact through every sense?" Cf. Wis. 7:17-22; 13:6-9; *1 Clem.* 20.1-12.

the Stoics, it requires serious clarification. Perhaps that's why Paul emphasized the point most ardently (v. 27). Though it doesn't show up in English, Paul punctuates both halves of this sentence with an emphatic particle (*ge*) and emphasizes not merely that God *is* near us, but that he *exists* in that state of proximity.

17:28-29. Paul proof-texted his claims, not with Jewish Scripture, but with pagan poets. This first sentence, "In him we live and move and have our being," is preserved in Epimenides,[47] though he is hardly the only philosopher to express such a sentiment.[48] The second line, "We are his offspring" (Aratus, *Phaen.* 5),[49] likewise is a not uncommon idea in Greek literature and lore.[50] Dio Chrysostom, for example, described God as the "Giver of our material and physical life . . . , Father and Savior and Guardian of humankind" (*Or.* 12.74). Paul, using familiar words and ideas, leads his audience to the God of the Bible.

If we are created in the image of God, then the idea of idolatry is ridiculous. We are sentient beings, like our father in heaven. How can a mute stump or a deaf stone replicate or represent a living God?! Clever human design, even if it is embossed with gold, can never approximate the glory of the one true God. Thus, Paul comes full circle to his opening line—"an altar to an unknown god." It is time to drive to a decision.

17:30-31. The God before Whom We Will Stand: God had been patient with humanity's ignorance.[51] Prior to the revelation of Jesus, we were not in a position to know God—not sufficiently. That has all changed now that the Christ has been revealed. This is not to say that God did not hold humanity accountable for sin or take seriously its moral consequences. In other words, God was not winking at sin but nodding toward Jesus (Acts 14:16; Rom 3:25; Wis 11:23).

God has set a day of eschatological judgment—a foreign thought to these philosophers but thoroughly at home in Jewish thinking. The whole world will stand before him and give an account for the deeds done in the body. Even more shocking than the idea of eschatological judgment was the fact that it would be adjudicated by Jesus (cf. Acts 10:42). Though Paul preached Jesus both in the marketplace and in the Areopagus, he never mentioned him by name. And though the center of this sermon is about God the creator, the resurrected Jesus receives pride of place at both the beginning and end of the narrative.

To the Christian, Jesus as Judge is familiar talk (Matt 7:22 [cf. Luke 11:24-

---

[47] The documentation, however, is quite late, being quoted in a 9th cen. Syriac commentary by Ischoʻdad (cf. *Beginnings* 5:246-251). Another line from this same poem is quoted by Paul in Titus 1:12, "The Cretans, always liars, evil beasts, idle bellies." There is a tenable argument that the original source is not actually Epimenides, but Euripides, *Bacchae*, 506; cf. Peter Colaclides, "Acts 17,28a and Bacchae 506," *VC* 27 (1973): 161-164).

[48] E.g., Epictetus, *Disc.* 1.14.6, "But if our souls are so bound up with God and joined together with him as being parts and portions of his being, does not God perceive their every motion as being a motion of that which is his own and of one body with himself?"

[49] Τοῦ γὰρ καὶ γένος ἐσμέν; cf. M. J. Edwards, "Quoting Aratus: Acts 17,28," *ZNW* 83 (1992): 266-269.

[50] Paul affirms that multiple poets had said these things: "as some of your own poets have said" (v. 28). He is not claiming to quote verbatim a specific line from a particular poet.

[51] This is a difficult phrase to render into English. First, what God overlooked is the time of ignorance, not the ignorance itself. A subtle difference, perhaps, but the point is that in former times, mankind was incapable of responding to God until the revelation of Jesus introduced a new age which had now dawned. Second, it is a participial phrase which would more literally be rendered, "Therefore, God, having looked past the epoch of ignorance, now orders all people everywhere to repent."

30]; 12:39-42 [/11:29-32]; 16:27; 25:31-46; Luke 10:13-16; John 5:22-30; 12:47-48; 2 Cor 5:10; 2 Tim 4:1; Rev 19:11). To a pagan, however, a crucified Jew hardly had the gravitas of a universal judge. What evidence is there that Jesus stood on par with the monotheistic God (cf. John 5:27; Dan 7:13)? For Paul Jesus' validation is the resurrection. This was not a belief held among the Greeks (or Romans). On the contrary, they scoffed at the idea.[52] Rather, they agreed with what the god Apollo purportedly said at the founding of the Areopagus: "But when the dust has drawn up the blood of a man, once he is dead, there is no resurrection [*anastasis*]" (Aeschylus, *Eumenides*, 647). The Greeks hoped to escape the body, the prison house of the soul. The Jews were the ones who cherished the hopes of eschatological resurrection. As a point of historical fact, however, it matters little (at least to Paul), what people expected. What mattered was what actually happened. Jesus of Nazareth was crucified under Pontius Pilate and three days later was reported by the Twelve Apostles, the authorized witnesses, to have been raised. One would like to know the apologetic tack Paul took in addition to this brief statement recorded by Luke. At the end of the day, however, it was not enough to turn the tide of skepticism in the Areopagus.

[32]When they heard about the resurrection of the dead, some of them sneered, but others said, "We want to hear you again on this subject." [33]At that, Paul left the Council. [34]A few men became followers of Paul and believed. Among them was Dionysius, a member of the Areopagus, also a woman named Damaris, and a number of others.

17:32-34. The response to Paul's address was *underwhelming*.[53] The audience, as usual, was split.[54] On the one hand, some just scoffed at the objectionable notion of resurrection. On the other hand, there were a goodly number for whom this speech pricked their curiosity. Though there was no revival that day, it would be grossly unfair to label it a failure.[55] Not only did Paul posture the gospel to get

---

[52] Cf. N. T. Wright, *Jesus and the Resurrection of God* (Minneapolis: Fortress), 32-84.

[53] Patrick Gray believes this may be Luke's way of reminding his readers that the Gentile mission was not so stunning that it overshadowed Jewish evangelism; "Implied Audiences in the Areopagus Narrative," *TynBul* 55 (2004): 205-218.

[54] Some have speculated that the split was not between those who believed and those who rejected but between the Stoics (who were more favorable) and the Epicureans (who mockingly rejected Paul); e.g., Clayton Croy, "Hellenistic Philosophies and the Preaching of the Resurrection (Acts 17:18, 32)," *NovT* 39 (1977): 21-39.

[55] Many have followed Tertullian's distaste for philosophy when he queried: "What has Athens to do with Jerusalem?" (*Heretics*, 7.9). This antiphilosophical bias has led many to criticize Acts 17 as inappropriate intellectualism. Paul is even cited against Luke's rendition: "When I came to you, brothers, I did not come with eloquence or superior wisdom as I proclaimed to you the testimony about God. For I resolved to know nothing while I was with you except Jesus Christ and him crucified. I came to you in weakness and fear, and with much trembling" (1 Cor 2:1-3). From this, some misconstrued Paul as repenting from his philosophical apologetic in Athens when he went to Corinth. It is, however, a separate context and a separate argument. Luke, most certainly, presented Paul's speech with approbation. This once popular view that Paul's Areopagus speech was a failure has largely been abandoned. From time to time, however, it resurrects. For example, Joseph Pathrapankal, "From Areopagus to Corinth (Acts 17:22-31; 1 Cor 2:1-5): A Study on the Transition from the Power of Knowledge to the Power of the Spirit," *MissSt* 23 (2006): 61-80, with more sophisticated exegetical nuance, asserts that the history of Christian mission has moved from a power-based evangelism to a more irenic spirit–based presentation of the gospel. While that is true, Pathrapankal equating Paul's Areopagus speech with Constantinian Imperialism is befuddling. In Athens, Paul was christocentric, courteous, and open-minded.

a further hearing—a major gain for a *deliberative* address (see above)—he convinced a number of people to follow Jesus.[56] A small band of disciples was birthed that day; one of them was a prominent member of the Areopagus, named Dionysius[57] and another was a notable woman named Damaris.[58] Dionysius most certainly would have used his position and clout to fast-track the church, especially among the educated elite.[59] Damaris, likewise, would leverage her own notoriety in order to make Jesus famous.[60] Though one could hope for greater numbers, they could hardly ask for more influential leaders for this new church.

---

[56] Several, in fact, have found Paul's sermon a model for homiletics in a postmodern world; cf. Michael Rogness, "Proclaiming the Gospel on Mars Hill," *WW* 27 (2007): 274-294; G. A. Lotter and G. G. Thompson, "Acts 17:16-34 as Paradigm in Responding to Postmodernity," *IDS* 39 (2005): 695-714; and Raymond Bailey, "Acts 17:16-34," *RevExp* 87 (1990): 481-485.

[57] Dionysius was the most common name in Athens (and Greece) of Paul's day. This fact led David Gill to conclude that Luke merely made up these names to give the story an authentic flare; cf. "Dionysios and Damaris: A Note on Acts 17:34," *CBQ* 61 (1999): 483-490. However, it is highly unlikely that Luke would attempt to pass off fiction as history during the lifetime of eyewitnesses. Even more mystifying is how Gill can assert that Luke invented Dionysius *because* it was the most common name while "Damaris" has yet to be verified in any inscription or document of the period. If both the commonality and anonymity of names disproves Luke's veracity, then our poor author is condemned no matter what he writes.

[58] "Damaris" is likely a variant of "Damalis" which means "heifer". One interesting hypothesis is that Damaris is a Greek corruption of the Egyptian name *T'-mr* and that she had emigrated to Athens from her homeland where she was a cult leader; cf. Gwyn Griffiths, "Was Damaris an Egyptian?" *BZ* 8 (1964).

[59] Eusebius (*Ch. Hist.* 3.4.11 & 4.23.3) twice mentioned Dionysius of Corinth (c. A.D. 180) in a letter to the Athenians claiming that Dionysius the Areopagite was ordained by Paul as the first bishop of Athens. Though interesting, it is impossible to establish this tradition with any credibility.

[60] Though some have suspected she was Dionysius' 'escort', there is no real evidence to support that supposition. Nor can one confirm Chrysostom's speculation that she was Dionysius' wife. We simply do not know who she was. Regardless whether she was famous or infamous, her notoriety could still be used to promote the fledgling church.

ACTS 18

6. Corinth: Jews in the Court (18:1-17)

Part of what makes this episode so fascinating is its comparison with Paul's correspondence to the Corinthians. Paul's letters add to our reading of Acts and vice versa. Another interesting facet of this episode is that it lasted so long. Paul stayed in Corinth for a year and a half, far longer than any other church to date and only to be surpassed by his three years in Ephesus (Acts 19). This may mark a transition in Paul's mission strategy in that he stays for much longer in his last two church plants and reaches out more deliberately to Gentiles.[1]

[1]After this, Paul left Athens and went to Corinth. [2]There he met a Jew named Aquila, a native of Pontus, who had recently come from Italy with his wife Priscilla, because Claudius had ordered all the Jews to leave Rome. Paul went to see them, [3]and because he was a tentmaker as they were, he stayed and worked with them. [4]Every Sabbath he reasoned in the synagogue, trying to persuade Jews and Greeks.

18:1. Paul moved from Athens, the educational capital of the Roman world, to Corinth, its commercial center. This renowned city was located seven miles west of the Saronic Gulf and two miles south of the Gulf of Corinth that fed into the Ionian Sea and probably had about fifty to eighty thousand inhabitants. It was a perfect intersection for Mediterranean shipping, what Strabo called a "master of two harbors" (*Geo.* 8.6.20a), as well as a bridge between the mainland of Greece and the Peloponnese.[2] Consequently, Corinth had a perpetual flow of people, goods, and wealth. The city had been leveled by the Romans in 146 B.C. after it revolted but was reestablished by Julius Caesar in 44 B.C. as a Roman colony. It became the capital of Achaia in 27 B.C. and remained a magnificent city up through Paul's day. Even after two millennia the dust cannot obscure the grandeur of this ancient San Francisco.[3] Due to the diligent work of archaeologists, one can walk the marble Lechaion through the major shopping district , sit beside the pool of Peirene , admire the monolithic columns of the Temple of Apollo , stand before the Bema where Gallio dismissed the charg-

---

[1] This argued by Philip H. Towner, "Mission Practice and Theology under Construction (Acts 18–20)," in *Witness to the Gospel: The Theology of Acts* (ed. I. H. Marshall and David Peterson; Grand Rapids: Eerdmans, 1998), 417-436.

[2] The isthmus connecting mainland Greece to the Pelopennesus narrows at one point to a mere 3½ miles. Nero began a canal at that strategic crossing for ships to pass. It was not finished until late in the nineteenth century with the help of modern engineering .

[3] Victor P. Furnish, "Corinth in Paul's Time: What Can Archaeology Tell Us?" *BAR* (May/June 1988): 14-27; and Jerome Murphy-O'Connor, "The Corinth That Saint Paul Saw," *BA* 47 (1984): 147-159, offer clear and accessible descriptions of Corinth.

es against Paul ◗, and gaze up to the temple of the licentious Aphrodite atop Acro-Corinth, nineteen hundred feet above ◗.

Where there are sailors and money one suspects there would be prostitution. That certainly fits Corinth whose very name became a euphemism for fornication. It was a crossroad for the Empire and, in many ways, a cesspool of humanity. In this sin-city that could make Las Vegas blush, Paul finds himself preaching the simple and shameful message of the cross:

> When I came to you, brothers, I did not come with eloquence or superior wisdom as I proclaimed to you the testimony about God. For I resolved to know nothing while I was with you except Jesus Christ and him crucified. I came to you in weakness and fear, and with much trembling. My message and my preaching were not with wise and persuasive words, but with a demonstration of the Spirit's power, so that your faith might not rest on men's wisdom, but on God's power. (1 Cor 2:1-5)

18:2-4. In order to survive in an ancient city, one needed a network—a group of people with whom one could live, work, and find protection. That is part of the reason Paul went first to the synagogue. There he was sure to find some like-minded Jews who would host him until he could get himself established. In this case, Paul's hosts were Aquila and Priscilla, fugitives from Rome.

They apparently got caught in the crossfire when Emperor Claudius expelled the Jews from Rome because of some sort of hullabaloo over "Chrestus" (c. A.D. 49–50,[4] cf. Suetonius, *Claudius*, 25.4).[5] The details are a bit sketchy because of this strange name "Chrestus." Though it was a common Roman name, it has never been found as a name for a Jew in Rome in the hundreds of catacomb inscriptions or other sources. Thus, it is not likely speaking of a contemporary Jew in Rome. Most likely, it is a misspelling of *Christ*, exchanging the "i" for an "e", a common error (which is understandable since Hellenistic Greek pronounced *iota* and *eta* virtually identically).[6] In this case, it is not merely a group of Jews that were fighting, but non-Messianic Jews were fomenting an uproar over the Christian message of Jesus. This has become standard fare by now in Acts and comes as no surprise. The practical result for Paul, Aquila, and Priscilla, however, is that any riot here in Corinth could run a short track back to Rome, leading to an Empire-wide ban on Christianity. Paul had better tread lightly.

Since Paul did not baptize Priscilla and Aquila (cf. 1 Cor 1:14) it's likely that they were already believers when Paul met them. That may be why he is wel-

---

[4]This is the date assigned by the later church historian Orosius. For a discussion on the validity of this date, cf. *Beginnings* 5:459-460, and for a full discussion of the incident cf. F. F. Bruce, "Christianity under Claudius," *BJRL* 44 (1962): 309-326.

[5]It is unlikely that all 50,000 Jews in Rome at the time were expelled. This probably refers to those directly or indirectly involved in the disturbance. Dio Cassius (*Hist.* 60.6) mentions an earlier incident (c. A.D. 41) in which the Jews were forbidden to meet, which was tantamount to expulsion; cf. Dixon Slingerland, "Acts 18:1-17 and Luedemann's Pauline Chronology," *JBL* 109 (1990): 686-690; and Robert Hoerber, "Decree of Claudius in Acts 18:2," *CTM* 31 (1960): 690-694. Hence, a precedent had likely already been set for misbehavior among some of the synagogues in Rome.

[6]A point noted by Tertullian (*Apologeticum* 3.5) and manifested in codex ℵ which reads Χρηστιανός in Acts 11:26; 26:28; and 1 Pet 4:16.

comed so quickly into their tent-making guild.[7] Etymologically, Paul's occupational title means "tent-maker." In actual practice, he probably worked with all sorts of leather and woven goods, producing whatever products deemed necessary by those with the ability to pay (*Beginnings*, 4:223).[8] Just what Priscilla's role was in the family business is hard to say. We do know that when they took Apollos aside to instruct him about baptism, her name is first, receiving pride of place. This may be due to her dominant personality, her unusual ability, or her family history.[9] Nonetheless, she is almost always mentioned first, indicating that she is a key player in the narrative (Acts 18:18, 26; Rom 16:3; 2 Tim 4:19). Together these three plied their trade and preached their gospel in the synagogue among both Jews and Greeks.[10] In other words, "Here we go again!"

[5]**When Silas and Timothy came from Macedonia, Paul devoted himself exclusively to preaching, testifying to the Jews that Jesus was the Christ.[a] [6]But when the Jews opposed Paul and became abusive, he shook out his clothes in protest and said to them, "Your blood be on your own heads! I am clear of my responsibility. From now on I will go to the Gentiles." [7]Then Paul left the synagogue and went next door to the house of Titius Justus, a worshiper of God. [8]Crispus, the synagogue ruler, and his entire household believed in the Lord; and many of the Corinthians who heard him believed and were baptized. [9]One night the Lord spoke to Paul in a vision: "Do not be afraid; keep on speaking, do not be silent. [10]For I am with you, and no one is going to attack and harm you, because I have many people in this city." [11]So Paul stayed for a year and a half, teaching them the word of God.**

[a]*5 Or Messiah; also in verse 28*

18:5. When Silas and Timothy arrived from Macedonia (cf. 2 Cor 1:19), Paul quit working with Aquila and spent all his time preaching. Perhaps Timothy and Silas were put to work paying the bills or, more likely, Timothy arrived from Philippi with yet another generous offering (Phil 4:16). Paul mentioned to the Corinthians that other churches supported his work there (2 Cor 11:8-

---

[7] Unlike democratic capitalism, the patron-client economy favored corporate guilds rather than competitive entrepreneurs. It wasn't exactly "the more the merrier" but since only a handful of families were actually paying for the goods, cooperation within the guild had a better chance of producing the quantity and quality of goods demanded by these elite families. We know that Paul practiced his trade in at least three cities: Thessalonica (1 Thess 2:9), Corinth (Acts 18:3; 1 Cor 9:12), and Ephesus (Acts 20:33-34).

[8] Paul would have learned this trade as a boy growing up in Tarsus. There, their tents would likely have been made from Cilician goat hair. Rabbis would later teach the importance of learning a trade, "All study of the Torah which is not combined with work will ultimately be futile and lead to sin" (*m. Abot* 2.2; cf. 4.7). Ronald Hock, disagrees, arguing that Paul actually demeaned manual labor as did other aristocrats but was forced by poverty to learn a trade after he began his itinerant preaching ministry. He gleans this from Paul's own (supposedly) disparaging comments about his labors (1 Cor 4:9; 9:19; 2 Cor 6:5; 11:7, 23, 27; 2 Thess 2:9; 3:7-9); cf. "The Problem of Paul's Social Class: Further Reflections," in *Paul's World* (ed. Stanley E. Porter; Leiden: Brill, 2008), 7-18. It is likely, however, that he makes too much of too little in the Epistles and too little of too much from Acts; cf. Todd Still, "Did Paul Loathe Manual Labor? Revisiting the Work of Ronald F. Hock on the Apostle's Tentmaking and Social Class," *JBL* 125 (2006): 781-795.

[9] "Priscilla" is a diminutive of "*Prisca*," one of the leading families in Rome. Perhaps she came from a higher class than her husband. Luke seems to prefer more personal names (whereas Paul often uses more formal names in his epistles): Priscilla vs. Prisca; Silas vs. Silvanus; Sopater vs. Sosipater; and Lucius vs. Luke.

[10] A fragmentary door inscription (c. A.D. 100-200) has been found that originally probably read "Synagogue of the Hebrews" ([συνα]γωγη εβρ[αιων]) ◻; cf. W. A. McDonald, "Archaeology and St. Paul's Journeys in Greek Lands: Part III—Corinth," *BA* 5 (1942): 36-48.

9). The travel log at this point is somewhat complex: It appears that Silas and Timothy caught up with Paul in Athens, but Timothy was immediately sent back to Thessalonica with the Epistle (1 Thess 1:1 & 3:1-2), and Silas may have made a return trip to Berea. If Timothy went clear to Thessalonica, he almost certainly paid another visit to Philippi. The lad had been busy!

This verse introduces several important financial principles of Pauline Missions. (1) He never took money from a church he was planting. He boasted about this to the Thessalonians (1 Thess 2:9-10), the Corinthians (1 Cor 9:15-19; 2 Cor 11:7-13), and the Ephesians (Acts 20:35). (2) He was not opposed to "tent-making ministry," but always preached full-time when he had the resources. A Christian worker is certainly worthy of wages (1 Cor 9:14; Gal 6:6; 1 Tim 5:17). (3) He expected the churches he planted to participate in funding other church plants (Rom 15:27; Phil 4:10-19).

18:6-8. The consequence of Paul's preaching to his Jewish compatriots was predictable: abuse (*blasphēmē*) and division. This is the European version of Paul's Turkish troubles in Pisidian Antioch. We recall the conclusion of Paul's first recorded sermon:

> When the Jews saw the crowds, they were filled with jealousy and talked abusively against what Paul was saying. Then Paul and Barnabas answered them boldly: "We had to speak the word of God to you first. Since you reject it and do not consider yourselves worthy of eternal life, we now turn to the Gentiles." (Acts 13:45-46)

Because of Jewish rejection, Paul concentrated his efforts in Corinth on Gentiles. This is not a permanent rejection of Jewish evangelism but a local shift in emphasis—a pattern now well established in Acts.[11] Paul's reaction in Corinth is the same as in Antioch: He shook the dust from his garment as a bit of Jewish theatrics saying, "I curse you for your stubbornness" (cf. Luke 9:5/Mark 6:11/Matt 10:14; Luke 10:11; Acts 18:6; 22:22-23; Str-B 1:571). His words matched his actions: "Your blood be on your own heads." This was Jewish imprecation releasing the speaker from any culpability in the punishment that would surely follow a grievous disobedience (Josh 2:19; 2 Sam 1:16; 3:29; 1 Kgs 2:33, 37; Ezek 18:13; 33:4-5). The most telling parallel is from Ezekiel's prophecy concerning the watchman on the wall (33:4-5). If the watchman sounded the trumpet, warning the city, and they ignored it, the watchman was not guilty of the destruction of the city. Similarly, Paul is saying, "I warned you. Because you ignored the warning, I am free from guilt when you meet your judgment."

With this ominous warning, Paul turns to the Gentiles, fulfilling his apostolic call (Acts 9:15; 22:15; 26:16-18). He left the synagogue with Crispus, its former ruler (or at least one of its key leaders; cf. *Beginnings* 4:225) and went right next door to the home of Titius Justus (his Roman names might suggest he was a

---

[11] See Acts 13:46-47 for comments concerning Paul going to the Jew first and then turning to the Gentiles; cf. Robert C. Tannenhill, "Rejection by Jews and Turning to Gentiles: The Pattern of Paul's Mission in Acts," *SBLsp* 25 (1986): 130-141.

citizen). Thus, these three—Paul, Crispus, and Titius—founded the first house church in Corinth.[12] Because of the two long letters Paul sent to this church, we know quite a lot about the composition of this community:

(1) Paul only baptized two initial converts, Crispus and Gaius (1 Cor 1:14), and the household of Stephanas (1 Cor 1:16). Since Crispus's whole family was baptized, either Paul allowed Crispus the honor of baptizing the rest of his family or he delegated that work to Silas or Timothy.[13] This turned out to be a wise decision since those baptized were soon boasting about who baptized them (1 Cor 1:12). We know about Crispus, but who is this Gaius? There is a clue in Romans 16:23 where Paul boasts about the hospitality of one Gaius. If this is the same man as is mentioned in 1 Corinthians 1:14, then it is possible (though still conjectural) that Gaius (*praenomen*) is Titius (*nomen*) Justus (*cognomen*). Whereas Luke calls him by his *nomen* and *cognomen*, Paul identifies him by his *praenomen* or perhaps a new name, given to him at baptism.[14]

(2) The members came from just about every racial, religious, and economic strata of the city, though most were lower class (1 Cor 1:26). While this diversity is wonderful, it caused a variety of problems. For example, there was boasting over who baptized whom (1 Cor 1:12), who was whose mentor (1 Cor 3:4-9; 4:14-15), and who spoke in tongues the most (1 Cor 14:12, 18). A couple of brothers bore a lawsuit against each other (1 Cor 6:1-11). One man didn't have enough sense to abstain from sex with his father's wife (1 Cor 5:1) while others were frequenting the brothels (1 Cor 6:16). There were wealthy people who could afford enough wine at the Lord's Supper to get drunk while the poor were ostracized and went away from the meal hungry (1 Cor 11:17-22). This, of course, seems trivial in light of the fact that some were still sacrificing to idols before coming to the communion table (1 Cor 10:14-22). It was a mess . . . but what a beautiful mess! The message of the cross, in all its weakness (1 Cor 1:18-31), had penetrated the bowels of Rome's economic center. The power of the resurrection (1 Cor 15:1-58) was transforming the elect in the midst of the world's worst vices.

Some will criticize Corinth as a corrupt church. I cannot share that sentiment, for all her problems stemmed from the one thing she was doing well: Calling all sorts and sundry to the cross with the promise that a resurrection changes everything. There was no other social group in all the ancient world that successfully bridged the social divides of economics, race, gender, and politics. The church of Jesus Christ was the only truly inclusive group. Though that caused some of her deepest problems, it is yet her greatest boast.

18:9-11. Just as the tensions were heating up, the Lord Jesus stepped in. Normally at this point in the narrative we read about Paul being beat up, thrown

---

[12] Another would soon be established in the home of Chloe (1 Cor 1:11) as well as that of Priscilla and Aquila (1 Cor 16:19). In addition, Erastus, the director of public works in the city, joined the church (cf. Rom 16:23). This may be the same Erastus whose name was inscribed on a dedication stone found in the plaza next to the theater in Corinth 🖾.

[13] Or perhaps Paul did baptize his whole house, as he did Stephanas's (1 Cor 1:16), and speaks only of Crispus as a synecdoche.

[14] The giving of a Christian name at baptism was not an uncommon occurrence; cf. G. H. R. Horsley, "Name Change as an Indication of Religious Conversion in Antiquity," *Numen* 34 (1987): 1-17.

into jail, and/or run out of town. Not this time. Jesus appeared in a vision and promised Paul a pass from persecution.[15] Such an 'appearance' would have been familiar to those steeped in the Old Testament traditions. Mighty men of God often received important confirmations at pivotal points (Exod 3:12; Deut 31:6; Josh 1:5, 9; Jer 1:8). One can only imagine the relief this brought to Paul as well as the extra zeal this might add to his already feverish preaching.

Jesus promised Paul that he would not be persecuted. Why? The Lord said, "because I have many people in this city." The specific Greek word used for "people" (*laos*) was used in Jewish literature to designate the Jews—God's chosen people (see on Acts 15:14; Titus 2:14; 1 Pet 2:9-10). That is both mysterious and beautiful. It can be read in at least three different ways. (1) Jesus protected Paul from persecution *in order that* he could reach those who Jesus foreknew would respond to the gospel (cf. 1 Pet 1:2).[16] The Gentile believers are thus invited into the 'people of Yahweh'.[17] In this case, Jesus exercised sovereignty over Paul's persecution but allowed freewill with the Corinthians' conversions. (2) Jesus protected Paul from persecution so that he could irresistibly call those Corinthians whom God had ordained for salvation. In this case, Jesus exercises sovereignty over both Paul and the Corinthian converts. (3) Paul avoided persecution because, as Jesus foreknew, "God's servants" in the city (such as Gallio) would protect God's assets through their righteous behavior. The "many people" Jesus had in the city were not necessarily prospects for salvation but civil servants rightly carrying out their social responsibilities. In this case, Jesus foreknew what "God's servants" would do and did not need to intervene sovereignly. The way one reads this text probably has less to do with words Luke wrote than the theological presuppositions one brings to the text.

The end result was a year-and-a-half ministry for Paul in this famous city. Though Paul would not be beaten during that time, he would face the second most important trial of his life. Aside from his defense before Nero, Paul's encounter with Gallio would have the greatest potential impact on the church of Jesus Christ. This verdict could echo all across the Mediterranean.

[12]While Gallio was proconsul of Achaia, the Jews made a united attack on Paul and brought him into court. [13]"This man," they charged, "is persuading the people to worship God in ways contrary to the law." [14]Just as Paul was about to speak, Gallio said to the Jews, "If you Jews were making a complaint about some misdemeanor or serious crime, it would be reasonable for me to listen to you. [15]But since it involves questions about words and names and your own law—settle the matter yourselves. I will not be a judge of such things." [16]So he had them

---

[15] Other visions of Paul (in chronological order) include the prediction of Ananias coming to heal him (9:12), Jesus' warning for him to get out of Jerusalem (22:17-21); the appeal to come to Macedonia (16:6-10); the promise that he would stand before the Emperor (23:11); and the assurance of rescue from the shipwreck (27:23-24).

[16] Although Jesus has not protected Paul from suffering in the past, and the gospel seems to have fared fairly well in the midst of, or even because of, persecution.

[17] This is the argument made well by Jacques Dupont, "Un people d'entre les nations (Actes 15.14)," *NTS* 31 (1985): 321-335.

ejected from the court. [17]Then they all turned on Sosthenes the synagogue ruler and beat him in front of the court. But Gallio showed no concern whatever.

18:12-13. Thanks to the discovery of an inscription at Delphi , we can be fairly certain that Gallio was Proconsul of Achaia from May, A.D. 51, to April, A.D. 52.[18] If Gallio served a second year as Proconsul, Paul's stay in Corinth could be as late as A.D. 54. Thus, Paul's year-and-a-half stint in Corinth fell between A.D. 49–54 depending on whether Gallio was Proconsul for one or two years and whether Paul's trial was at the beginning of Gallio's term or at the end of it.[19]

Gallio was a major player in Roman politics. His real name was Marcus Annaeus Novatus, the son of Seneca, the famous rhetorician (c. 50 B.C.–c. A.D. 40) though he took the name of his adopted father Lucius Junius Gallio upon coming to Rome. Though he rose to considerable influence, Gallio was noted for his mild disposition (Seneca, *Nat. Quest.* 4; *Ep. Mor.*, 104) and wit (Dio Cassius, *Hist.* 61.35). That will be particularly important during this trial. His younger brother, Seneca, grew even more powerful. He was a Stoic philosopher employed as a tutor for the child Nero. He rode Nero's coattails all the way into the imperial palace.[20] Therefore, the outcome of Paul's trial could quickly reach the ears of the emperor. A verdict against the Way could spread across the Mediterranean world with frightening severity. That makes this Paul's most important trial to date.

The Jews of the city banded together to present a united attack against Paul at the *bema* (Judgment Seat) in the center of the *agora* . The accusation against Paul is similar to what was leveled against him at Philippi: Paul advocates unlawful customs (see notes on 16:21). Of course there the charge was made by Romans, and here in Corinth it was his own Jewish compatriots accusing him of changing ancestral customs. This will come up again several times. Paul's defense before Governor Felix (24:14-15) and Herod (26:22) concentrates on the continuity between Christianity and Judaism—he is merely fulfilling his ancestors hopes and aspirations. Governor Festus will articulate this same conclusion (25:19). This is what Paul would have had to prove at this trial.

18:14-15. Fortunately, Gallio already came to the conclusion that this was an intramural debate between two rival Jewish sects. Paul's offense was not even a misdemeanor, let alone a felony. Therefore, Gallio simply threw the case out of court. This had two important legal implications. First, this trial could be used as precedent for further cases against the Way. Since the Proconsul of Achaia rejected the charge as bogus, it would be much more difficult for a lawyer in any

---

[18] Cf. A. Plassart, "L'inscription de Delphes mentionnant le proconsul Gallion," *REG* 80 (1967): 372-378.

[19] Cf. Dixon Slingerland, "Acts 18:1-18, The Gallio Inscription, and Absolute Pauline Chronology," *JBL* 110 (1991): 439-449. Since this is the most secure date of all the events in Acts, it becomes foundational for constructing a Pauline chronology which shows substantial correspondence with Paul's letters; cf. Albrecht Scriba, "Von Korinth nach Rom: Die Chronologie der letzten Jahre des Paulus," in *Das Ende des Paulus: Historische, theologische und literaturgeschichtliche Aspekte* (Berlin: Walter de Gruyter, 2001) 157-173.

[20] Unfortunately, Nero would later assassinate Seneca to gain his considerable wealth, and the mild-mannered Gallio would be carried away in his brother's wake, also dying at the hand of Nero. Some have slandered Gallio (even in ancient times, his inscription at Delphi was defaced) particularly because of his illness which caused him to leave his post as Proconsul in Achaia. A close scrutiny of his career and the ancient sources, however, tell of a noble Roman politician; cf. Bruce Winter, "Rehabilitating Gallio and His Judgement in Acts 18:14-15," *TynBul* 57 (2006): 291-308, for an excellent biographical summary.

other part of the Empire to successfully level that same charge again. Second, since Gallio declared the legitimate connection between the church and the synagogue, Christians could be exempt from making sacrifices to the Emperor in the burgeoning idolatrous cult of Emperor Worship.[21]

18:16-17. Gallio ejected them from court, Sosthenes got pummeled, and Gallio didn't care. This raises three interrelated questions: Who was Sosthenes? Who beat him? And why didn't Gallio care? The Western text claims "all the Greeks" beat Sosthenes while other texts state conversely that it was the Jews. Clearly there is a difference of opinion. Hubbard, tracing the common occurrence of urban uprisings, argues that "all" means "all," both Jews and Greeks. In short, there was an outburst of violence during which the flash-mob exploded on Sosthenes.[22] His theory is helpful for understanding the social dynamic but fails to account for Gallio's unconcern. More likely, therefore, those that did the beating were the Jews themselves (likely accompanied by the unruly rabble in the *agora*, as Hubbard argued). If that is the case, it would appear that they turned on their own synagogue ruler who botched the case. This becomes even more interesting in light of the fact that Sosthenes is a partner with Paul in the first letter to the Corinthians (1:1).[23] One possibility is that Sosthenes replaced Crispus as the synagogue ruler after his mentor's conversion and was privately vacillating about the claims of Christ.[24] His own questions may have been exposed as he presented the case against Paul. If his fellow Jews picked up on his sympathies, they could have accused him of throwing the case on purpose. He would be punished with blows. This very beating may have been the thing that threw him over edge and into the church. His own conversion would have put him in a precarious position in the city, especially if Gallio didn't protect him even while standing before the *bema*. That would explain why he left town with Paul.[25]

[21] Cf. Bruce W. Winter, "Gallio's Ruling on the Legal Status of Early Christianity (Acts 18:14-15)," *TynBul* 50 (1999): 213-224.

[22] Moyer V. Hubbard, "Urban Uprisings in the Roman World: The Social Setting of the Mobbing of Sosthenes," *NTS* 51 (2005): 416-428.

[23] Sosthenes is an extremely rare name, comprising a mere .028% of Greek names. Hence, the Sosthenes of Acts 18 and 1 Cor 1:1 are likely the same person; cf. Christos Karakolis, "Alle schlugen Sosthenes, Gallio aber kümmerte sich nichts darum," *ZNW* 99 (2008): 239-243.

[24] Though the synagogue may have had a council of elders that led services and handled its internal affairs, there probably was one man (perhaps on a rotating basis) who would represent the group to Roman authorities in such cases. For a description of the clout and responsibilities the *archisynagōgos* would bear, cf. Winter, "Gallio's Ruling," 221. Most probably they were more patrons than managers; cf. Tessa Rajak and David Noy, "*Archisynagogoi*: Office, Title, and Social Status in the Greco-Jewish Synagogue," *JRS* 83 (1993): 75-93.

[25] There is yet another (speculative) possibility, first argued by Chrysostom (*Hom. Acts* 39.1-2) and defended by Richard Fellows, "Renaming in Paul's Churches: A Case of Crispus-Sosthenes Revisited," *TynBul* 56 (2005): 111-130; and Augustine Myrou, "Sosthenes: The Former Crisupus (?)," *GOTR* 44 (1999): 207-212. Namely, Paul changed Crispus's name to Sosthenes (meaning "saving strength") after his baptism, a common practice signifying religious conversion; cf. Horsley, "Name Change," 1-17. Thus, *Crispus and Sosthenes are the same person*. He was beaten, not as a negligent Jewish lawyer, but as a faithful friend of the defendant (cf. Jason, Acts 17:6-9). Gallio ignored it, not because he was unjust, but because he threw the case back into the Jewish court who handled the case according to their own jurisprudence. While they got away with a single beating, they could not get away with a widespread persecution because that would be seen as riotous behavior in a city already sensitive to the Roman expulsion under Claudius. The fly in the ointment, however, is why Paul would speak of Sosthenes in 1 Cor 1:1 and then change his name to Crispus (1 Cor 1:14) without warning or explanation.

D. THE THIRD MISSIONARY JOURNEY: FROM EUROPE TO ASIA (18:18–20:38)

It is, frankly, a bit generous to call this a missionary journey. The only city highlighted was Ephesus, and Paul had already preached there at the tail end of the second tour. It is, however, a critically important place, the most notable religious center of the Roman world, and the place where Paul held his longest ministry. Luke has arranged the narrative in such a way that we read Paul's biography from Ephesus in chapter 19 and his diary (of sorts) in chapter 20 when he exposes his heart to the Ephesian Elders, exhorting them in their leadership ministry.

1. Interlude: Apollos the Eloquent Alexandrian (18:18-28)

This interlude is rather complex. There is a lot of movement. Paul goes from Corinth to Ephesus then on to Antioch via Jerusalem. Priscilla and Aquila travel with Paul as far as Ephesus where they stay long enough to meet Apollos. Apollos preaches powerfully in Ephesus and then more accurately in Corinth after a session with Paul's protégés, Priscilla and Aquila. The bottom line is that Paul moves from Corinth to Ephesus while the powerful Apollos moves from Ephesus to Corinth. This brief interlude functions like a set change at a play.

[18]Paul stayed on in Corinth for some time. Then he left the brothers and sailed for Syria, accompanied by Priscilla and Aquila. Before he sailed, he had his hair cut off at Cenchrea because of a vow he had taken. [19]They arrived at Ephesus, where Paul left Priscilla and Aquila. He himself went into the synagogue and reasoned with the Jews. [20]When they asked him to spend more time with them, he declined. [21]But as he left, he promised, "I will come back if it is God's will." Then he set sail from Ephesus. [22]When he landed at Caesarea, he went up and greeted the church and then went down to Antioch.)

18:18. After Paul's most considerable ministry in Corinth, it was time to set sail for Syria. As was his custom, he took a couple of disciples with him from the city. They would prove to be a strategic addition to the new church work in Ephesus. They head west seven miles to Cenchrea 📷, the nearest port on the Aegean. There Paul shaved his head, and frankly, we don't know why.[26] Obviously it was some sort of vow. However, the only vow that requires a haircut is the Nazirite vow, and that is supposed to be carried out in Israel where the head is shaved to complete the vow (cf. Num 6:1-21; *m. Mid.* 2.5; *m. Naz.* 7.3).[27] Admittedly, the information we have on the Nazirite vow for Jews in the Diaspora is rather sketchy (cf. 1 Macc 3:49; Josephus, *Ant.* 19.6.1 §293; *m. Naz.* 2.5-6; 3.6).[28] Our best guess is that Paul was keeping a vow of his own creation to the best of his ability while away from the temple in thankfulness for Jesus' keeping him safe in Corinth.

---

[26] It is grammatically possible that it was Aquila (not Paul) who shaved his head, but that is unlikely given that Paul is the center of Luke's attention, and it is he, not Aquila, who was heading to Jerusalem.

[27] Cf. Roger Tomes, "Why Did Paul Get His Hair Cut? (Acts 18.18; 21.23-24)," in *Luke's Literary Achievement*, JSNTsupp 116 (ed. C. M. Tuckett; Sheffield: Sheffield Academic Press, 1995), 188-197.

[28] Cf. Friedrich Horn, "Paulus, Das Nasiräat und die Nasiräer," *NovT* 39 (1997): 117-137.

18:19-22. Paul had a wonderful reception in the synagogue at Ephesus. They wanted him to stay longer but he had his heart set on Antioch. It was time to report back home about the extraordinary things God was doing across the Mediterranean. Paul did promise his fellow Jews in Ephesus that he would return if God allowed it. Of course, that's no sure thing. The last time Paul tried to target Ephesus, the Holy Spirit hindered him (16:6). His passion for his people drove him home, yet it would not be long before his passion to proclaim Christ drove him back to this important city. The Western text of verse 21 has a most likely addition that Paul wanted to reach Jerusalem in time for the "Festival." In A.D. 52 Passover fell in early April. If that is what Paul wants to attend, there's no time to waste since the shipping lanes of the Mediterranean were generally closed up through March 10.

Paul landed at Caesarea, the major port on the eastern seaboard, and "went up" to greet the church. That most surely refers to the mother church at Jerusalem particularly since Caesarea is two hundred and fifty miles south of the main port for Antioch. From there he descends to Antioch to report to his 'sending church'.

Priscilla and Aquila parted company with Paul at Ephesus. They stayed on, enjoying a fruitful ministry themselves, particularly with Apollos (more on him in a moment). By the time Paul returned to Ephesus, his friends were gone (at least from the narrative). It is likely that when Claudius died in A.D. 54, they felt safe to return to Rome. When Paul writes his letter to the Romans (c. A.D. 57), he sends Priscilla and Aquila warm greetings (Rom 16:3).

[23]After spending some time in Antioch, Paul set out from there and traveled from place to place throughout the region of Galatia and Phrygia, strengthening all the disciples. [24]Meanwhile a Jew named Apollos, a native of Alexandria, came to Ephesus. He was a learned man, with a thorough knowledge of the Scriptures. [25]He had been instructed in the way of the Lord, and he spoke with great fervor[a] and taught about Jesus accurately, though he knew only the baptism of John. [26]He began to speak boldly in the synagogue. When Priscilla and Aquila heard him, they invited him to their home and explained to him the way of God more adequately. [27]When Apollos wanted to go to Achaia, the brothers encouraged him and wrote to the disciples there to welcome him. On arriving, he was a great help to those who by grace had believed. [28]For he vigorously refuted the Jews in public debate, proving from the Scriptures that Jesus was the Christ.)
[a]*25 Or with fervor in the Spirit*

18:23. From Antioch, Paul heads across northern Turkey through the regions of Phrygia and Galatia. Luke, in the most summary fashion, covers some fifteen hundred miles in verses 22-23; Paul's blistered feet undoubtedly testified to the true length of this difficult journey. As was Paul's custom, he revisited the churches he had established, strengthening the disciples. This particular word "strengthened" is used four times, always in Acts and always in reference to an itinerant tour through churches (14:22; 15:32, 41; 18:23). In other words, Paul didn't just plant churches, he grew them.

18:24-25. Flashback to Ephesus: Apollos, the eloquent Alexandrian. Luke describes this preacher with unusual detail. He was from Alexandria, a city second only to Athens as an intellectual center. It had a substantial Jewish population where Apollos would be at home with his own Hebrew heritage. Apollos was a follower of Yahweh, thoroughly trained in the Old Testament. He was also a fan of John the Baptist and hence, got turned on to Jesus. His preaching was powerful, fervent, and accurate, except that he didn't know of Christian baptism. Thus his teaching needs to be tweaked.

18:26. Apollos, like Paul, used the synagogue as a platform for preaching Jesus. That's natural. It was there he met Paul's former companions. Undoubtedly Priscilla and Aquila were delighted to meet a brother so like Paul. Both were Hellenistic Jews from a major university town; both preached Jesus from the Old Testament with zeal[29] and accuracy;[30] both were itinerant evangelists with powerful personalities. Though there is no apparent animosity between Paul and Apollos ("I planted the seed, Apollos watered it, but God made it grow," 1 Cor 3:6), the people of Corinth had taken sides (cf. 1 Cor 1:12). Not only in Corinth but in Ephesus the two great teachers apparently worked together. In fact, Paul was unsuccessful in urging Apollos to return to Corinth (1 Cor 16:12). In short, there is a lot of similarity between Paul and Apollos.

Apollos, however, did not know about Christian baptism. For many, this seems like a minor doctrine. We will see in the following chapter the substantial ramifications of a doctrinal deficit in baptism—it matters! For now, suffice to say that Priscilla and Aquila thought it important enough to have him to their home to teach him more accurately so that his preaching could fully represent Jesus. Before moving on, two ecclesiastical comments should be made. First, they did not confront Apollos publicly. They took him aside so that he could deal with doctrine without the added pressure of pride from public rebuke. Simply put, they were courteous. We all have doctrinal shortcomings and we should welcome correction. Practically, however, pride and public shame often deter open inquiry. Second, Priscilla is mentioned first in the teaching of Apollos. The *least* we can say, therefore, is that she was Apollos's co-teacher. Any theory of women's roles in the church must certainly account for Priscilla as an instructor of this prominent preacher.[31]

---

[29] Literally, "zeal in spirit" (ζέων τῷ πνεύματι). The "spirit" spoken of here is likely Apollos's spirit (cf. Rom 12:11) rather than the Holy Spirit, contra J. D. G. Dunn, *Baptism in the Spirit* (Philadelphia: Westminster, 1970), 88-90. This is especially so since the disciples of Apollos in the following pericope have not even heard of the Holy Spirit. If Apollos is preaching by the Holy Spirit, how could his disciples be ignorant of him? The NIV leaves out this important word "spirit," likely to avoid this very confusion. Nonetheless, the language is (deliberately?) polyvalent, and the reader should be given the option to wrestle with the possibility as the Greek readers would have. To that end the KJV offers "fervent in the spirit" which the NKJV improves with "fervent in spirit" (also ESV, NASB, RSV, ASV).

[30] One might wonder how he could preach Jesus accurately and not know about baptism or how his disciples in Ephesus (19:1-2), if that is a fair ascription, could not have known about the Holy Spirit. Several comments are apropos: (1) He accurately taught about Jesus, particularly that he was the Messiah (cf. 18:28). This may not have included post-Pentecost Christianity. (2) Evangelicals often measure doctrinal accuracy with far more rigorous demands than are exegetically warranted or ecclesiastically gracious. Luke may be giving Apollos the benefit of the doubt, particularly given his teachable spirit. (3) Coming from Alexandria, where both allegory and Gnosticism thrived, the surprise is not that he needed correction but that he had not been seduced by rampant heresy.

[31] Of the plethora of works on women's roles, two stand out as particularly instructive for the role of women in early Christianity: Ben Witherington, *Women in the Earliest Churches* (New York: Cambridge University Press, 1988), and Carroll Osburn, *Essays on Women in Earliest Christianity* (Joplin, MO: College Press, 1993).

18:27-28. Apollos set his sights on Achaia and probably Corinth in particular. His influence there could easily be exported across the empire. The brothers at Ephesus agreed. In fact, they did a bit of name-dropping in a letter of affirmation (cf. Rom 16:1; 2 Cor 3:1-3). This was just the kind of connection needed in the ancient world to move from one social network to another. This was a well-conceived plan. Apollos was particularly adept at debate. He virtually shut down the opposition, using the Old Testament as a foundation for proving that Jesus was the promised Messiah. One is struck not only with the similarity in spirit and style between Apollos and Paul but also with Apollos's greater success than the famed Apostle. Perhaps Luke simply doesn't share with his readers the opposition Apollos received whereas Paul is open about his own detractors (e.g., 1 Cor 4:1-21). Or perhaps Apollos really did have better success. In any event, Luke's portrait of Apollos puts him on par with his own mentor and hero.

ACTS 19

2. Ephesus: Jesus Is Better (19:1-35)

This is one of the most compelling series of stories in all of Acts. The narrative is fast-paced and riveting, moving consecutively through the stories of Paul's (re)baptizing Apollos's disciples (vv. 1-10), the failed exorcism attempt of Sceva's sons (vv. 11-22), and the uproar in the theater over Artemis (vv. 23-41). What binds these diverse stories is the single theme: *Jesus is better*. His Spirit baptism trumps the mere immersion of John. His miraculous power overshadows any other exorcism or magical incantation. He makes irrelevant the revered gods of the Greeks and Romans. He is simply better than anything on offer in the megalopolis of Ephesus.

It would be difficult to overestimate the importance of Ephesus to the New Testament. No other place has so much biblical literature directed its way. Acts 19–20 are about this city as is the Epistle which bears its name. To that, one can add the Pastoral tractates of 1 & 2 Timothy and the excerpt from Revelation 2, chiding this city for her lost first love. A stroll through the city, even today, reveals its grandeur, violence, wealth, sexual profligacy, and sophistication.

Ephesus was the fourth largest city of the Empire behind Rome, Alexandria, and Antioch but had the most famous of some thirty-three temples devoted to Artemis. It boasted one hundred and twenty-seven 60′ columns ■ surrounding a temple measuring 425′ × 225′ (Pliny, *Nat. Hist.* 36.21), four times larger than the Parthenon of Athens! ■[1] The theater of the city was just as majestic, with seating sufficient for some twenty-five thousand people ■. The marble streets ■ tell of the economic prowess of the city, but even this is trumped by the mosaic street facing the homes of the wealthy elite ■. There was every kind of diversion one could want: baths ■, gladiatorial games ■, prostitutes ■, gambling ■, markets ■, and a magnificent library (though it postdates Paul) ■. Ephesus was the most important religious center of the Roman world, and Jesus trumped everything it had to offer.

Jesus Is Better Than John the Baptist (19:1-10)

[1]**While Apollos was at Corinth, Paul took the road through the interior and arrived at Ephesus. There he found some disciples** [2]**and asked them, "Did you receive the Holy Spirit when**[a] **you believed?" They answered, "No, we have not even heard that there is a Holy Spirit." **[3]**So Paul asked, "Then what baptism did you receive?" "John's baptism," they replied.**

[a]2 Or *after*

---

[1] Today only a single column stands on the site in Ephesus ■. However, one can see several surviving columns in Istanbul which Constantine took (rescued?) from Ephesus for the construction of his church, the Agia Sophia ■.

19:1. Paul finally arrived in Ephesus for his long-awaited ministry. Luke specifies that he passed through the interior of the country. This would most likely take him through the Lycus valley were Colossae, Hieropolis, and Laodicea were located. While there is no mention of any ministry there, this itinerary might explain Paul's interest in the area.[2]

The mention of Apollos and Corinth takes us back to 18:24-28. *Literarily,* these two texts are intended to be read as concentric circles.[3] *Geographically,* we see the crisscross on the map: Paul from Corinth to Ephesus and Apollos from Ephesus to Corinth. *Historically,* Paul and Apollos would eventually meet (1 Cor 16:12), though Luke keeps them apart in his treatise.[4] *Theologically,* Apollos needed correction in his doctrine of baptism. All this seems clear.

19:2-4. What is less clear is whether Luke understands these "disciples" to be Christians. On the one hand, the twenty-seven other uses of "disciple" in the book refer to Christians.[5] Thus, one naturally suspects this one does as well.[6] Furthermore, if Paul did not consider them Christians, why did he inquire about their initial belief? Their response may have changed Paul's mind, but at first he took them to be believers.

On the other hand, one rightly wonders how a person without the Holy Spirit can be considered a Christian (John 3:5; Rom 8:9; 1 Cor 12:3; Gal 3:2-3; 1 Thess 1:5; Titus 3:5; Heb 6:4; 1 Pet 1:2; 1 John 3:24; 4:13; cf. Marshall, 305). What Apollos preached about Jesus was accurate (18:25) but incomplete. Perhaps he was ignorant of John's prediction that Jesus would follow him with a baptism of the Holy Spirit or perhaps his own lack of experience prohibited him from prioritizing this sacrament. Either way, his disciples were deficient. Bottom line: Luke has not given us enough information to determine whether he and Paul considered these twelve men to be Christians. Perhaps that is the lesson. They needed correction, just as Apollos before them; what they didn't need was judgment. There is a graciousness in Luke's lack of definition that we would do well to imitate.

Paul noticed an absence of the Spirit in their lives and began to inquire about their baptism. He clearly believed there was a connection between water baptism and the Spirit.[7] *Is immersion, therefore, somehow related to receiving the Holy*

---

[2] The Western text at 19:1 differs considerably. It says that Paul wanted to return to Jerusalem but the Holy Spirit commanded him to go into Asia; cf. W. A. Strange, "The Text of Acts 19.1," *NTS* 38 (1992): 145-148.

[3] Though some would argue that the disciples of chapter 19 were not necessarily Apollos's, the literary exchange between these texts argues otherwise not to mention the unlikelihood of finding John's disciples in Ephesus apart from a charismatic evangelist like Apollos. While Apollos is not directly charged with a theological error, nonetheless his disciples were clearly deficient in Luke's view. Michael Wolter, "Apollos und die ephesianischen Johannesjünger," *ZNW* 78 (1987): 49-73, offers an interesting suggestion that Luke felt a need to correct Apollos's error but did not want to personally attack such a noted and revered evangelist.

[4] Paul seems to have had great respect for Apollos (1 Cor 3:5-6, 22; 4:6; Titus 3:13) even though others pitted them against each other (1 Cor 1:12; 3:4).

[5] Although grammatically this is the only plural use of "disciples" in Acts that is anarthrous. That *may* be Luke's way of subtly suggesting to his reader that something odd is going on here.

[6] A number of scholars have argued cogently that these are to be seen as Christians; cf. F. W. Norris, "Christians Only, but Not the Only Christians (Acts 19:1-7)," *RQ* 28 (1985–1986): 97-105 [from a Campbellite perspective]; Mark Lee, "An Evangelical Dialogue on Luke, Salvation, and Spirit Baptism," *Pneuma* 26 (2004): 81-98 [from a Pentecostal perspective]; also Wilson Paroschi, "Acts 19:1-7 Reconsidered in Light of Paul's Theology of Baptism," *AUSS* 47 (2009): 73-100; and Bruce, *Acts*, 384-387.

[7] What Paul saw lacking was likely the outward expression of spiritual gifts as opposed to the indwelling of

Spirit? Scriptures teach this very thing. This is not only true of the baptism of the Holy Spirit (Matt 3:11; Acts 1:5; 2:1-4; 10:44-46; 11:16). The same is said about water immersion. Several "New Birth" texts mention both the water and Spirit as effective forces in conversion (John 3:3-7; 1 Cor 6:11; Titus 3:3-7). Though "water" *may* be a mere metaphor in these texts,[8] it is most certainly literal immersion in Acts 2:38-39; 19:1-6, and probably 1 Corinthians 12:13. The bottom line is that the Holy Spirit is clearly connected with water baptism in the process of conversion. This doesn't mean the Spirit is shackled to the water and can only "seal" a person at immersion. It does mean, however, that our vocabulary in the baptistery is biblical if we talk about receiving the Holy Spirit through faith expressed in the sacrament of baptism (cf. Acts 2:38-39). Baptism is not a work by which we earn the presence of the Holy Spirit. Rather it is an expression of our faith which causes us to open our lives to the Spirit's control.

⁴Paul said, "John's baptism was a baptism of repentance. He told the people to believe in the one coming after him, that is, in Jesus." ⁵On hearing this, they were baptized into[a] the name of the Lord Jesus. ⁶When Paul placed his hands on them, the Holy Spirit came on them, and they spoke in tongues[b] and prophesied. ⁷There were about twelve men in all.

ᵃ5 Or *in*   ᵇ6 Or *other languages*

19:4-7. Two things happen in this text: baptism and the laying on of hands. Which of these granted the disciples the gifts of tongues and prophecy? Since Luke doesn't say, it may be mere speculation. However, in no other text does baptism grant spiritual gifts of any kind. However, when the Apostles (Acts 6:6, 8; 8:18; 19:6; 2 Tim 1:6) or Elders (1 Tim 4:14) laid their hands on people, spiritual gifts were imparted. Hence, one might assume that immersion marked the transition of the twelve into full faith in Jesus (and hence their new relationship with the Spirit), but it was Paul's touch that bestowed the miraculous gifts of the Spirit.[9] As a result of the visible sign, no one could question the spiritual transformation that took place due to their faith, expressing itself in the obedience of baptism.

⁸Paul entered the synagogue and spoke boldly there for three months, arguing persuasively about the kingdom of God. ⁹But some of them became obstinate; they refused to believe and publicly maligned the Way. So Paul left them. He took the disciples with him and had discussions daily in the lecture hall of Tyrannus. ¹⁰This went on for two years, so that all the Jews and Greeks who lived in the province of Asia heard the word of the Lord.

19:8-9a. This is one of Paul's longer runs in a synagogue, but eventually a

---

the Spirit for salvation and sanctification (cf. v. 6). When Luke speaks of the Spirit, he generally has in mind the power of the Spirit working *through* a person in contradistinction to Paul's pneumatological emphasis of the Spirit working *in* a person for salvation; cf. Mark E. Moore, "The Comforter Has Come with Power," in *Fanning the Flame: Probing the Issues in Acts* (ed. Mark E. Moore; Joplin, MO: College Press, 2003), 192-209.

[8] Which is hardly surprising given the metaphoric comparisons of the Spirit to water in the OT (Psa 46:4-5; Isa 32:15; 44:3; 55:1; 58:11; Ezek 39:29; Joel 2:28).

[9] Paul bestowing the Spirit through the laying on of hands is reminiscent of Peter and the Samaritan believers (8:17). Here is yet another comparison between the two great Apostles in Acts.

blowout was inevitable. In typical fashion, he *boldly* argued about the Kingdom of God. This particular word is a favorite of Luke. Seven of its nine New Testament uses are in Acts, and all of them refer to Paul's intrepid preaching, save 18:26 which describes Apollos in this same city (cf. Acts 9:27, 28; 13:46; 14:3; 19:8; 26:26; Eph 6:20; 1 Thess 2:2). So this synagogue had been subjected to two particularly aggressive and persuasive preachers. Some had apparently had enough and retaliated with public libel. It is probable that Paul's opponents here in Ephesus became his persecutors at Jerusalem, responsible for his ill-fated arrest (cf. 21:27-29).

19:9b. Paul had to withdraw from the synagogue and relocate in the lecture hall of Tyrannus (likely a nickname for a particularly demanding teacher with whom Paul had some affinity). According to the Western text, he was given free use of the building from 11 a.m. to 4 p.m. during the traditional hours of 'siesta'. "At 1 P.M. there were probably more people sound asleep than at 1 A.M." (*Beginnings* 4:239).

19:10. His pupils were hard-core disciples who chose the study of Scriptures rather than an afternoon nap, a sacrifice of no small significance to a Mediterranean. Because of Tyrannus's generosity, during the next two years, churches grew all over Asia Minor. This, undoubtedly, included the other six churches to which John would address the Revelation.

Jesus Is Better Than Magic (19:11-22)

¹¹God did extraordinary miracles through Paul, ¹²so that even handkerchiefs and aprons that had touched him were taken to the sick, and their illnesses were cured and the evil spirits left them. ¹³Some Jews who went around driving out evil spirits tried to invoke the name of the Lord Jesus over those who were demon-possessed. They would say, "In the name of Jesus, whom Paul preaches, I command you to come out." ¹⁴Seven sons of Sceva, a Jewish chief priest, were doing this. ¹⁵One day the evil spirit answered them, "Jesus I know, and I know about Paul, but who are you?" ¹⁶Then the man who had the evil spirit jumped on them and overpowered them all. He gave them such a beating that they ran out of the house naked and bleeding.

19:11-12. Can you have a regular old run-of-the-mill miracle? Aren't they all amazing? Well, apparently, some are more extraordinary than others. When Paul's handkerchiefs and workshop aprons[10] worked wonders, the whole city began to buzz. The Ephesians had never seen anything like that, though Luke's readers are familiar with the "extraordinary miracles" done by Peter's shadow

---

[10] The words "handkerchief" (σουδάριον, cf. Luke 19:20; John 11:44; 20:7) and "apron" (σιμικίνθιον) were actually Latin words (not found at all in the LXX). We are guessing when we translate them with the specific terms "handkerchief" and "apron", but they are both cloths used in the workshop, so these speculative translations certainly give the right impression even if they are not the exact technical terms. The few Latin uses of "apron" (σιμικίνθιον) more likely indicate a "belt"; cf. T. J. Leary, "The 'aprons' of St Paul—Acts 19:12," *JTS* 41 (1990): 527-529. And the σουδάριον may indicate the appropriate apparel of an orator rather than a tent-maker; cf. Rick Strelan, "Acts 19:12: Paul's 'Aprons' Again," *JTS* 54 (2003): 154-157. For a comprehensive overview of Paul's clothes and their relation to the Greco-Roman world—cost, style, social value, etc—see Ceslas Spicq "Pèlerine et vetements (A propose de II Tim IV,13 et Act XX,33)," in *Mélanges Eugène Tisserant* (ed. Eugène Tisserant, Vaticano: Biblioteca apostolic vaticana, 1964), 389-417.

(Acts 5:15) and the fringes of Jesus' prayer shawl (Luke 8:43-44/Mark 5:25-29/ Matt 9:20-21; cf. Mark 6:56/Matt 14:36). Luke's language is picturesque at verse 12. With a clever chiasm he portrays the departure of illnesses and demons— both were sent packing.

19:13. Exorcism in the ancient world was generally an elaborate ritual. It could include incantations, bloodletting, amulets, and dances, in short, a whole bunch of folderol. There are a number of surviving texts and amulets that offer a sampling of the kinds of rituals popular in Paul's day.[11] One of the most popular techniques was name binding. If the exorcist had access to the authority inherent in the name of a powerful spiritual figure, either by genealogical bloodline or religious devotion, he could invoke that name against another spiritual entity. If a demon was of a lesser rank than the invoked figure, it would be obligated to obey the binding oath of exorcism. That's the theory anyway. In actual practice, both then and now, exorcism was likely more of a trial and error art than a precise science. This, however, should be clear: neither Jesus nor his disciples were classic exorcists. They performed none of the elaborate rituals of their Jewish or Greek counterparts. They simply said the word and the name of Jesus effectively exorcised the demon.

19:14-16. Ephesus was as well known for practicing magic as Athens was for dabbling in philosophy (cf. Clement, *Strom.* 5.8.45; Plutarch, *Symp.* 7.5.4). Western rationalists may question the whole exorcistic enterprise or explain it as a psychological expression. The Seven Sons of Sceva, however, had no doubt of the reality of demons nor the power of Jesus' name to overwhelm these evil entities. The problem was, they did not have the right relationship with Jesus to pull it off. Just because they were Jewish and their father was an important priest[12] did not give them access to the power of the Messiah.[13] That kind of power comes through a relationship of faith rather than mere lineage.

One occasion went very badly for the boys. The seven of them were ganging up on a particularly potent demon. They attempted to invoke the name of Jesus to force the demon out. Its retort is particularly interesting. This unclean spirit knew Jesus (cf. James 2:19) and had heard about Paul, but had no respect for these seven sons of Sceva. For their misappropriation of power they were thor-

---

[11] For example, Paris Magical Papyrus reads, "The god of the Hebrews, Jesu, Jaba, Jae, Abraoth, Aia, Thoth, Ele, Elo," cf. Adolf Deissman, *Light from the Ancient East* (New York: Harper, 1927), 260. Another reads (PGM IV. 3019-3020), "I adjure thee by Jesus the God of the Hebrews." It was common enough for Jewish exorcists and healers to invoke the name of Jesus that there was later a prohibition for doing so: "And Jacob of Kefar Sama came to heal him in the name of Jesus son of Pantera. And R. Ishmael did not allow him [to accept the healing]" (*t. Hullin* 2.22-23; cf. *b. Abod. Zar.* 27b; *y. Shab.* 14.4 [14d]; *y. Abod. Zar.* 2.2.40d-41a).

[12] In this instance "chief priest" surely means "important" or "influential" rather than an actual "Chief Priest" as one would encounter in Jerusalem. The fact that he is an otherwise unknown figure living in Ephesus makes it unlikely that he is a High Priest of the temple hierarchy. Cf. E. Delebecque, "La mésaventure des fils de Scévas selon ses deux Versions (Actes 19, 13-20)," *RSPT* 66 (1982): 225-232, points out how the Western text "downgrades" Sceva to simply a "priest."

[13] Jews were widely noted exorcists, and Solomon particularly was a name invoked for casting out demons. Beginning with the LXX of 1 Kgs 5:9-14, Solomon's exorcistic powers are exaggerated, see Josephus, *Ant.* 8.2.5. §46-48; *Testament of Solomon; The Apocalypse of Adam* 7.13; cf. D. C. Duling, "Solomon, Exorcism, and the Son of David," *HTR* 68 (1975): 235-252, and "Matthew's Plurisignificant 'Son of David' in Social Science Perspective: Kinship, Kingship, Magic, and Miracle," *BTB* 22 (1992): 99-116.

oughly thrashed and sent running from the house bloodied and bludgeoned.[14] They ran naked down the marble streets of Ephesus,[15] chased furiously by the rumors of their failed attempt. News spread of the power of the name of Jesus and the respect of Paul in the world of spirits. The great Apostle's name was recorded not only in the Lamb's book of life but in the hit list of the Devil, men of God not to be trifled with.

[17]When this became known to the Jews and Greeks living in Ephesus, they were all seized with fear, and the name of the Lord Jesus was held in high honor. [18]Many of those who believed now came and openly confessed their evil deeds. [19]A number who had practiced sorcery brought their scrolls together and burned them publicly. When they calculated the value of the scrolls, the total came to fifty thousand drachmas.[a] [20]In this way the word of the Lord spread widely and grew in power.

[a]19 A drachma was a silver coin worth about a day's wages.

19:17. It was impossible to keep this bit of gossip contained. Both Jews and Greeks heard Paul's name but more importantly revered Jesus' fame. It was not so much that Paul was a superhero but that he was the servant of a super power. The power of Jesus rendered all others frivolous, even idolatrous by comparison. Who needs an amulet when you are clothed with Christ? Why recite an incantation when one can petition the one enthroned on high? The blood of Jesus subverts all other powers. To put one's faith in anything other than Jesus is a striking act of disbelief.

19:18-19a. This realization struck fear in the Ephesian believers who had clung to the dark arts. The incident of the exorcists convinced them that their dual dependence on Jesus and magic was offensive to his majesty. It is spiritual polygamy and practical idolatry. This reality terrified them, and they repented forthwith, revealing their stash of magical scrolls. These scrolls were one-of-a-kind copies of carefully kept secrets. The power of these incantations was (supposedly) in their secrecy. If the incantation became known, it ceased to be effective. Therefore, once the books were burned, the magic was lost forever.

19:19b-20. Some Christian accountant apparently tallied the scrolls and estimated the cost. The collection came to fifty thousand drachmas (day's wages)! If we figure an average of three hundred work days per year and an average working life-span of thirty years (generous for the first-century world), we are watching the net worth of more than five lifetimes of labor go up in smoke. Why not sell the books and give the money to the poor? There is a spiritual principle at play. One does not advance the church by profiting from paganism. These books were evil contraband, testimonies to illicit powers in opposition to the

---

[14]Though the term ἀμφοτέρων (v. 16) generally means "both," it can be used for "all of them." Hence, this term does not necessarily mean that only two of the seven sons attempted the exorcism. Though one demon thrashing seven sons seems difficult to manage, that appears to be the meaning in context (v. 16). Charles Torrey, "Two Sons in Acts 19:14," *ATR* 26 (1944): 253-255, suggests that the "seven" of v. 14 is a textual variant for "two" which mistakenly was adopted by the dominant MSS. This is an unlikely hypothesis.

[15]Nakedness, especially for Jews, was a sign of abject humiliation. The word likely refers not to complete nakedness but to being stripped of one's robe even if the loincloth was still intact.

Kingdom of God. They were treated as incendiaries in imitation of God casting the powers of darkness into the flames of hell (Rev 20:14-15).

²¹After all this had happened, Paul decided to go to Jerusalem, passing through Macedonia and Achaia. "After I have been there," he said, "I must visit Rome also." ²²He sent two of his helpers, Timothy and Erastus, to Macedonia, while he stayed in the province of Asia a little longer.

19:21-22. Once again Paul sets his sights on Jerusalem and thereafter Rome. Literally, "He resolved in the spirit." The question is whether the word "spirit" should be capitalized. Is this Paul's spirit or the Holy Spirit? The reader is left to guess. Perhaps this ambiguity is deliberate. Sometimes differentiating one's own desires from the prompting of the Spirit is difficult indeed.

Verse 21 records the same itinerary Paul described in his letter to the Romans (15:23-33). In a real sense, 19:21 marks a transition in the narrative when Paul heads hard to Rome in the same way that Luke 9:51 marks Jesus' journey toward Jerusalem. Paul loved his own people and their festivals. The one he hopes to attend on this trip is probably Pentecost. He couldn't board a ship on the Mediterranean until the winter storms subsided around March 10. That would be too late to get to Israel for Passover. As Paul had done before, he wanted to greet his people with a substantial gift from the Gentiles (cf. 11:29-30). Luke doesn't make much of this offering. In fact, he only alludes to it when Paul stands before Felix (cf. 24:17). However, it was a big deal to the Apostle who mentions it several times in his correspondence (1 Cor 16:1-4; 2 Cor 8:1-15; Rom 15:25-27). To that end he sends two of his most trusted companions around the horn of Macedonia to take up a collection from Philippi, Thessalonica, and Berea, as well as any daughter churches these have now spawned. Timothy is the obvious choice to lead in the collection. He has been with Paul since the beginning of the second missionary tour and is well known by these churches as Paul's envoy. Erastus was a famous CFO from Corinth whose name is still embedded in stone there as a Patron of the marketplace (discovered in 1929, it reads, "Erastus, procurator of public buildings, laid this pavement at his own expense"). We cannot, of course, prove the Erastus of the Bible (cf. Rom 16:23; 1 Tim 4:20) is the same Erastus of this inscription.[16] Nonetheless, both were directors of public works, both were associated with Corinth, and both come from this same time period. Paul obviously had some friends in high places along with his converts of humble origins.

Jesus Is Better Than Diana (19:23-41)

²³About that time there arose a great disturbance about the Way. ²⁴A silversmith named Demetrius, who made silver shrines of Artemis, brought in no

---

[16] For a helpful description of the inscription and its potential relevance to the biblical Erastus, cf. David Gill, "Erastus the Aedile," *TynBul* 40 (1989): 293-301; John K. Goodrich, "Erastus, Quaestor of Corinth: the Administrative Rank of *oikonomos tēs poleōs* (Rom 16.23) in an Achaean Colony," *NTS* 56 (2010): 90-115; and H. J. Cadbury, "Erastus of Corinth," *JBL* 50 (1931): 42-58. For a second "Erastus" inscription in Corinth, found in 1960, cf. Andrew D. Clarke, "Another Corinthian Erastus Inscription," *TynBul* 42 (1991): 146-151. In contradistinction, Meggitt questions the high rank of Erastus; cf. Justin J. Meggitt, "The Social Status of Erastus (Rom 16:23)," *NovT* 38 (1996): 218-223.

little business for the craftsmen. [25]He called them together, along with the workmen in related trades, and said: "Men, you know we receive a good income from this business. [26]And you see and hear how this fellow Paul has convinced and led astray large numbers of people here in Ephesus and in practically the whole province of Asia. He says that man-made gods are no gods at all. [27]There is danger not only that our trade will lose its good name, but also that the temple of the great goddess Artemis will be discredited, and the goddess herself, who is worshiped throughout the province of Asia and the world, will be robbed of her divine majesty."

19:23-24. Toward the end of Paul's three years in the city there was one particularly close call that Luke records. This is not likely the first fracas Paul encountered in Ephesus. He had probably already written 1 Corinthians 15:32, "If I fought wild beasts in Ephesus for merely human reasons, what have I gained?" (cf. 2 Cor 1:8-10). In fact, Paul may have been imprisoned during his Ephesian ministry and suffered other beatings as well (cf. 2 Cor 11:23).[17] It was a perilous time that came to a head due to Demetrius, a vociferous organizer of the profitable silversmith guild.[18] These men were cashing in on a monopoly of miniature idols they produced for the pious pilgrims devoted to the goddess Artemis (or Diana in the Roman pantheon). Their goddess was popular across the empire and appeared in various forms (cf. Pausanias, *Descr.* 4.31.8).[19] Sometimes she was a virgin huntress, but most often she was this grotesque figure with a bunch of nodules protruding from her chest ◘. These nodules have been interpreted as breasts but they appear more like bull testicles or eggs, each of which are obvious symbols of fertility.

19:25-27. Demetrius called a meeting of the silversmith union workers as well as other associated trades. His speech was compelling at two levels. First, Paul was converting great numbers of people in Asia. Part of the core message of Christianity was the monotheistic impulse of Judaism. If there was but one God, every idol was either an empty farce or a deceptive demon. Either way, they are to be abandoned as readily as magic scrolls are to be burned. Demetrius appealed to their piety, warning that the honor and worship of their great goddess was in jeopardy if the preaching of Paul spread. Oddly, here was one pagan who really did perceive the reality of the situation. It would take longer than Demetrius expected, but Christianity did eventually dominate the area and Diana fell into disrepute. Her worship waned and her temples were ultimately aban-

---

[17] Cf. *Beginnings* 4:245, and G. S. Duncan, "Paul's Ministry in Asia—The Last Phase," *NTS* 3 (1957): 211-218.

[18] Reinhard Selinger, "Die Demetriosunruhen (Apg 19:23-40): Eine Fallstudie aus rechthistorischer Perspektive," *ZNW* 88 (1997): 244-248; *Beginnings* 4:245-246. Though there are inscriptions which speak of silver shrines of Artemis, so far archaeologists have only found pieces in terracotta. This is hardly surprising, however, given the value of silver and the disdain of idols in a Christianized Empire. Those made of silver would inevitably be melted down and recast as saints.

[19] For a fuller description of Artemis and a historical reconstruction of this event in particular, cf. C. L. Brinks, "'Great Is Artemis of the Ephesians': Acts 19:23-41 in Light of Goddess Worship in Ephesus," *CBQ* 71 (2009): 777-794. Epigraphic evidence amply illustrates the kind of honor granted to Artemis in Ephesus; cf. Richard Horsley, "The Inscriptions of Ephesos and the New Testament," *NovT* 34 (1992): 105-168; and Richard Oster, "Acts 19:23-41 and an Ephesian Inscription," *HTR* 77 (1984): 233-237.

doned.[20] Pliny (c. 110) as the governor of Bithynia, wrote to the Emperor Trajan, bemoaning the "deserted temples," "neglected worship," "hardly a single purchase" because "Christians converted the whole region" (Pliny, *Letters* 10.96-97). The temple was finally destroyed in A.D. 262 by Goths. Today, the single entity in all the world that still has any practical appreciation for Artemis is a lonely stork which has made her home atop the single remaining pillar of the once majestic temple of Artemis, one of the seven wonders of the ancient world .

Demetrius's speech was compelling for a second reason that ought not to be underestimated. He appealed not only to their piety but to their pocketbooks. Paul's preaching was costing them. Granted, Demetrius's harangue may have included a bit of hyperbole. His prognostication of the demise of the cult, however, was spot on. Paul was accosting not only the Temple of Artemis but the central bank of Asia. Consequently they accosted him.[21] Missionaries and apologists must not underestimate the deep connection between piety and economics. Popular piety often produces economic security for those who construct and control the sacred shrines. Just as the owners of the slave girl in Philippi turned against Paul when he turned out their fortunetelling demon, so here, Paul threatened to reduce the income of the idolaters; for this they want him to pay dearly.

[28]When they heard this, they were furious and began shouting: "Great is Artemis of the Ephesians!" [29]Soon the whole city was in an uproar. The people seized Gaius and Aristarchus, Paul's traveling companions from Macedonia, and rushed as one man into the theater. [30]Paul wanted to appear before the crowd, but the disciples would not let him. [31]Even some of the officials of the province, friends of Paul, sent him a message begging him not to venture into the theater. [32]The assembly was in confusion: Some were shouting one thing, some another. Most of the people did not even know why they were there. [33]The Jews pushed Alexander to the front, and some of the crowd shouted instructions to him. He motioned for silence in order to make a defense before the people. [34]But when they realized he was a Jew, they all shouted in unison for about two hours: "Great is Artemis of the Ephesians!"

19:28-29. The fury of the craftsmen spilled out onto the streets. Their "uproar" was dangerously close to a riot. This same word (*synchysis*) was used in the LXX for the confusion at Babel (Gen 11:9), the tumult of war (1 Sam 14:20), and a spreading plague (1 Sam 5:6, 11). This kind of public outcry commonly got out of hand as the rabble fomented disorderly conduct.[22] The *hoi polloi* marched through the marble streets of Ephesus, chanting for their favored deity. They gathered momentum as they converged onto the open-aired theater .[23] The

---

[20] *Beginnings* 5:255-256, records a decree by the Ephesian Senate (A.D. 160) to attempt to restore the worship of Diana to its former glory. Again, Christians were probably the cause of its decline.

[21] An inscription found in Ephesus dating back several hundred years B.C. confirms the very real threat Paul was facing. It records the death sentence pronounced against forty-five inhabitants of Sardis who mistreated a sacred Artemisian delegation; cf. Franciszek Sokolowski, "A New Testimony on the Cult of Artemis of Ephesus," *HTR* 58 (1965): 427-431.

[22] This is amply documented by Moyer V. Hubbard, "Urban Uprisings in the Roman World: The Social Setting of the Mobbing of Sosthenes," *NTS* 51 (2005): 416-428.

[23] Josephus has his own descriptions of such public protests in theaters (cf. *B.J.* 2.18.7 §487; 7.5.2 §110-

mood was electric and volatile. Their voices swelled and their numbers grew to some twenty-five thousand. They were frenzied and confused, even ignorant of the purpose for their assembly.

19:30-31. Paul saw this sea of people and decided to preach.[24] The great Apostle appears to have had an exaggerated view of his ability to calm crowds. Had he gone into the theater, there would have been a bloodbath. It was dangerous enough for Gaius and Aristarchus (Paul's companions) who got dragged into the theater when the mob couldn't get their hands on Paul. These two were among Paul's inner circle. Though Gaius is only mentioned by Luke here and in 20:4, he was obviously more important to Paul who baptized him at Corinth (1 Cor 1:14) and continued to rely on his hospitality and patronage (Rom 16:23). The Apostle John, who also held a considerable ministry in Ephesus, devoted his final letter to this dear brother (3 John 1:1, assuming this is the same famed leader of Ephesus). Aristarchus not only followed Paul to Jerusalem (Acts 20:4) but even on to Rome (Acts 27:2) as Paul's comrade in chains (Col 4:10; cf. Phlm 1:24).

Fortunately, the Disciples persuaded Paul to stay put. They had a bit of help from an unlikely source. Luke calls them "officials of the province," literally "Asiarchs." These men were officials from the various major cities of the province who were responsible for the Emperor Cult (*Beginnings* 5:256-262). This put them in direct contact with the cult of Artemis that had been co-opted by the Emperor Claudius for political propaganda. This is seen in two separate coins minted in Ephesus (c. A.D. 49–54) depicting Artemis on one side of the coin and Claudius and his wife Agrippina respectively on the reverse.[25] The gathering of Asiarchs in Ephesus might best be explained by the annual month-long celebration of the goddess (Artemisian) complete with athletic competitions, musical performances, dancing, and ample sacrifices to Artemis. If this is a fair assumption, then Paul's "friends" were heavily involved in the very festival that gave rise to the religious fervor that endangered Paul's life. At the very least it meant that Paul made friends with powerful men of high status.[26] They cared enough about him to seek his safety even before they had adopted his faith. This holds a lesson not to be lost on modern evangelists.

19:32-34. Meanwhile, the crowd[27] is seething but they don't know why. Various camps seized the opportunity to shout their grievances (some of which may have had little to do with Paul's preaching). The majority was swept up in the excitement which transported them to the theater, but they had yet to identify the

115). Luke adopts the same apologetic strategy to show that it was not the Jews who started riots but pagans; cf. Robert F. Stoops, "Riots and Assembly: The Social Context of Acts 19:23-41," *JBL* 108 (1989): 73-91.

[24] The NIV translation "wanted to appear before the crowd" does not capture the full connotation of the word βούλομαι. It speaks of Paul's will or decision. Paul's had a determined plan not just a vague desire. This is made obvious by the need for both his Christian brothers and non-Christian friends to dissuade him.

[25] Cf. Larry J. Kreitzer, "A Numismatic Clue to Acts 19.23-41: The Ephesian Cistophori of Claudius and Agrippina," *JSNT* 30 (1987): 59-70.

[26] Craig Keener, "Paul's 'Friends' the Asiarchs (Acts 19.31)," *JGRChJ* 3 (2006): 134-141, makes a strong argument that they were not merely Paul's friends but potentially his patrons in the city of Ephesus, sponsoring his development of the Christian community. If this is true, it explains all the more why Paul would have avoided offending the cult of Artemis.

[27] Lit. ἐκκλησία, "assembly." "The inscriptions of Ephesus constantly refer to the ἐκκλησία and they indicate that it was held in the theatre" (*Beginnings* 4:248).

point of the assembly. The Jewish contingent, likely wanting to distance themselves from the Pauline party, pushed Alexander to the stage. Thus, the crowd began shouting at Alexander.[28] His fellow Jews, undoubtedly, shouted instructions
about what to say to quell the crowd. The crowd, on the other hand, used him as
a target for their mounting aggression. He was going to attempt to identify Paul
as a rogue Jew who did not represent the community of law-abiding Hebrews
in their midst. Alexander did not want the synagogue, where Paul spent three
months teaching, to be associated with the Christian movement now maligned
as having an anti-Artemis agenda. The paradox is twofold. First, Paul never maligned the goddess (as we will soon hear from the city clerk), and Alexander
surely shared the same disdain for idolatry as that of which Paul is now accused.

Alexander raises his hand like a good Roman rhetorician, calling for the
attention of his audience. The crowd recognizes him as a prominent Jew, and
that's all it took for their anti-Semitism to erupt into a unified chant for two
hours! This is an unbelievably long, sustained, and unified objection to Alexander's Jewish presence. This certainly would explain why Paul's friends had
sufficient time to learn of his predicament and send a message to him to stay
clear of the theater.

**[35]The city clerk quieted the crowd and said: "Men of Ephesus, doesn't all
the world know that the city of Ephesus is the guardian of the temple of the
great Artemis and of her image, which fell from heaven? [36]Therefore, since
these facts are undeniable, you ought to be quiet and not do anything rash. [37]You
have brought these men here, though they have neither robbed temples nor
blasphemed our goddess. [38]If, then, Demetrius and his fellow craftsmen have a
grievance against anybody, the courts are open and there are proconsuls. They
can press charges. [39]If there is anything further you want to bring up, it must
be settled in a legal assembly. [40]As it is, we are in danger of being charged with
rioting because of today's events. In that case we would not be able to account
for this commotion, since there is no reason for it." [41]After he had said this, he
dismissed the assembly.**

19:35-36. Alexander was unable to quiet the crowd; the city clerk had more
success. He was the liaison between the political rulers of Ephesus and those in
Rome. It was a position of substantial power, particularly in situations like this
since he was responsible for reporting to Roman rulers the significant events of
the city. Were he to send a message that a riot broke out in the theater, the entire
city's privileged position could be jeopardized. He had their undivided attention.

With somewhat exaggerated claims, he calms their anxiety concerning the
honor of Artemis. The Clerk asserts that **all the world** recognizes **Ephesus** as the
guardian of Artemis's image which fell from **heaven** (perhaps a meteor whose
'human' appearance gave it divine status; cf. *Beginnings* 4:250-251; cf. Cicero,

---

[28] The word συμβιβάζω in v. 33 implies either *unity* or *instruction*. Hence the various translations, "The
crowd *concluded* it was Alexander" (NASB) or "The crowd *shouted instructions to* him" (NIV). Luke's Greek,
intentional or not, appropriately reflects the confusion of the occasion. The crowd, as a whole, did not
know why they were there, who Alexander was, or what was being said by him or to him.

Verr. 2.5.187, who records a similar phenomenon). In short, the Clerk's claims
are universal and, according to him in verse 36, undeniable. Hence, there is
no need to get all bent out of shape because some itinerant Jewish preacher
claims the god of resurrection is greater than the goddess of reproduction. The
inflated claims concerning Artemis are matched by the Clerk's intense demand
(v. 36) that they settle down.

19:37-39. Gaius and Aristarchus (and Paul by extension), have done nothing criminal. This, of course, is a pet theme for Luke. He has already shown
several times the legal innocence of Christianity. Though this is not a formal
trial, the church does stand before the *demos* (city population) as its jury and
the Clerk serves as a judge, effectively throwing the case out of court as Gallio
had done. As a point of practical ministry, Paul and his associates did not find
it necessary to attack pagan systems of religion in order to promote Jesus. Just
presenting the truth, without demolishing error, is sufficient not only for salvation but for public opposition.

The Clerk challenged Demetrius and his guild to challenge Paul legally if
they could (v. 38). The courts were open and the proconsuls available. There
are two delightful observations in this verse, one literary and the other historical.
First, Luke's rendition of the Clerk's remarks borders on poetic. "The courts are
open" is, in Greek, a lovely assonance: *agoraioi agontai.* In this public address, the
Clerk is demonstrating oratorical skill commensurate with the occasion. Second,
Luke asserts there are *politarchs.* Normally, that would be an historical error since
only *one* Politarch ruled at any given time, unless, of course, Luke was speaking
generically: "There are such things as Politarchs" (cf. Bruce, 401; Haenchen,
552). However, in October of A.D. 54, Silanus was murdered (likely by orders of
the Emperor), and two Proconsuls replaced him—Helius and Celer—until order could be reestablished in the region.[29] There is nothing inconsistent in this
timing with the chronology of Acts. Moreover, it would explain the sensitivity of
the Clerk to a potential riot in Ephesus. In any event, the Clerk warns them to
redress their grievances through the proper legal challenges. The courts, open
three times a month (cf. Chrysostom, *Homily* 42.2), were functioning properly.

19:40-41. The Clerk says they were in danger of being accused of a riot. The
real danger, therefore, was not Paul, but this unlawful assembly. This can only
be read as a veiled threat since he was the one responsible for making such a
report. In other words, "Either you people dismiss, disassemble, and go home,
or I will be forced to send a report to Rome in which I will name names." Not
surprisingly, with that warning, the assembly was dismissed legally and orderly.
Paul's danger, as well as his ministry in Ephesus, was over.

---

[29] Maurice Carrez, "Note sur les événements d'Éphése et l'appel de Paul á sa citoyenneté romaine," in
Á cause de l'Evangile (Paris: Cerf, 1985), 769-777, speculates that (a) Paul was imprisoned in Ephesus on
capital charges and that (b) it was Silanus's murder that offered a window for Paul's escape (cf. 1 Cor 15:32;
2 Cor 1:8; 4:8-11). This explains why Paul would not reenter Ephesus in Acts 20:17.

ACTS 20

3. Interlude: Paul's Preparations for His Return to Jerusalem (20:1-12)

¹When the uproar had ended, Paul sent for the disciples and, after encouraging them, said good-by and set out for Macedonia. ²He traveled through that area, speaking many words of encouragement to the people, and finally arrived in Greece, ³where he stayed three months. Because the Jews made a plot against him just as he was about to sail for Syria, he decided to go back through Macedonia. ⁴He was accompanied by Sopater son of Pyrrhus from Berea, Aristarchus and Secundus from Thessalonica, Gaius from Derbe, Timothy also, and Tychicus and Trophimus from the province of Asia. ⁵These men went on ahead and waited for us at Troas. ⁶But we sailed from Philippi after the Feast of Unleavened Bread, and five days later joined the others at Troas, where we stayed seven days.

20:1-3. After things settled down in Ephesus, it was time for Paul to bring his longest local ministry to a close. Sometime in the fall of A.D. 56 he convened the congregations of Ephesus and bade them farewell. Paul set out on a tour of Macedonia and Greece. Luke emphasized the encouragement Paul provided the congregations; Paul emphasized the offerings these churches were to provide for the poor in Jerusalem (1 Cor 16:1-4; 2 Cor 8:1-15; Rom 15:25-27; cf. Acts 24:17 and Gal 2:10). Afterward,[1] he wintered in Greece, from whence he likely composed the book of Romans, his theological *magnum opus*.[2] Hey, if you're going to get stuck waiting for the winter storms to subside on the Mediterranean, Athens, Corinth, or some other coastal village in Greece is not a bad stint. Just as he was about to set sail, the local Jews hatched an assassination plot. They likely boarded the vessel upon which Paul was to sail. If it was heading to Syria, it must have been a sizeable ship. Luke doesn't give any details as to how Paul eluded their grasp. Perhaps our imaginations are more interesting than historical details. Nonetheless, one can picture Paul slipping off the boat just before she sailed, leaving his assailants searching the crowded vessel on the high seas. This is hardly the first time his life had been threatened. He was one cagey evangelist who knew how to handle himself.

20:4-5. Rather than a rough sea voyage, Paul opted for an overland journey. This allowed him the benefit of visiting a few old friends along the way, not to mention the extended conversations with his disciples. Here we have the longest list of Paul's traveling companions. At first it looks like a random list of

---

[1] Luke doesn't say how long this tour of Macedonia took. Bruce speculates that it was a rather extended period that included his famed visit to Illyricum (Rom 15:19) which doesn't fit any other period of the book of Acts.

[2] Luke narrates this season of Paul's ministry with disappointing brevity. There is so much more we would like to know. As a consolation one can turn to 2 Cor 1–7 which offers tantalizing details such as a 'painful visit' to Corinth (2 Cor 2:3-4) and an unsuccessful attempt to intercept Titus at Troas (2 Cor 2:12-13).

people associated with Paul. However, because Luke tags them geographically, it is more likely a list of those individuals sent by the local congregations to escort Paul to Jerusalem with their offerings. The mundane purpose for this group is obvious—the larger the entourage, the less likely they are to be robbed. There is a deeper purpose that pertains to ministry. One of the great dangers of the early church was the inevitable distance between churches geographically, ethnically, and culturally. This offering was a massive project that unified the churches from a vast disparity of places and cultures. It was both benevolent and brilliant on Paul's part.

REGION	CITY	INDIVIDUAL	OTHER TEXTS MENTIONING THIS PERSON
Macedonia	Berea	Sopater son of Pyrrhus	Acts 20:4
	Thessalonica	Aristarchus	Acts 19:29; 20:4; 27:2; Col 4:10; Phlm 1:24
		Secundus	Acts 20:4
	Philippi	Luke	Acts 20:6
Galatia	Derbe	Gaius	Acts 19:29; 20:4; Rom 16:23; 1 Cor 1:14; 3 John 1
	Lystra	Timothy	Acts 16:1, 3; 17:14-15; 18:4; 19:22; 20:4; Rom 16:21; 1 Cor 4:17; 16:10; 2 Cor 1:1, 19; Phil 1:1; 2:19, 22; Col 1:1; 1 Thess 1:1; 3:2, 6; 2 Thess 1:1; 1 Tim 1:2, 18; 6:20-21; 2 Tim 1:2; Phlm 1; Heb 13:23
Asia		Tychicus	Acts 20:4; Eph 6:21, 24; Col 4:7, 18; 2 Tim 4:12; Titus 3:12
		Trophimus	Acts 20:4; 21:29; 2 Tim 4:20
Achaia	Corinth	Titus	*Not in Acts;* see 2 Cor 8:16-24; also 2:13; 7:6, 13-14; 8:6; 12:18; 13:14; Gal 2:1, 3; 2 Tim 4:10; Tit 1:4; 3:15

20:6. Most of the men boarded the ship in Greece that was headed for Troas. This may have been a tactical diversion for Paul's assassins. Paul and Luke, however, trekked north through Macedonia and celebrated one last Passover with the Messianic believers of Philippi. There is a deep tenderness in this verse. Philippi was Paul's first church plant in Europe as well as Luke's preaching post for some five years. For the first time in half a decade, Paul and Luke are reunited and headed for Troas, where they apparently met. These are vivid memories for Luke; he literally counts the days: five en route from Philippi[3] and another seven in his old hometown of Troas.

[3] This is considerably longer than the two-day trip earlier from Troas to Neapolis (16:11); wind and waves were less amiable heading east.

[7]On the first day of the week we came together to break bread. Paul spoke to the people and, because he intended to leave the next day, kept on talking until midnight. [8]There were many lamps in the upstairs room where we were meeting. [9]Seated in a window was a young man named Eutychus, who was sinking into a deep sleep as Paul talked on and on. When he was sound asleep, he fell to the ground from the third story and was picked up dead. [10]Paul went down, threw himself on the young man and put his arms around him. "Don't be alarmed," he said. "He's alive!" [11]Then he went upstairs again and broke bread and ate. After talking until daylight, he left. [12]The people took the young man home alive and were greatly comforted.

20:7-9. The weeklong reunion came to a close on a Sunday. Naturally, the believers gathered for a celebration service that included the Lord's Supper and one *very* long sermon.[4] Since Sunday was a workday, the Christians convened in the evening, somewhat bedraggled from the labor of the day. For most of them, work meant hard manual labor. The fact that they were meeting on the third story suggests they were a congregation of poor people living in the least enviable accommodations. Upper stories were inconvenient because of the stairs one had to climb and unsafe when fires broke out, which happened not infrequently due to the lack of central heating or reliable chimneys. They were tired yet eager to hear Paul's farewell address. One young man was particularly tired. He sat in the window; probably an attempt for fresh air after the oil lamps sucked the oxygen out of the room. Because these lamps were small, they lit a bunch of them to provide enough light but that also meant a bunch of smoke. As Paul droned on, Eutychus nodded off.[5] Have you ever had one of those dreams where you were falling but you never land? Eutychus landed. It didn't just knock the breath out of him, it knocked the life out of him.[6]

20:10-12. The sermon took an abrupt intermission as the concerned congregation raced down the stairs. Luke, undoubtedly, took his turn examining

---

[4]The early practice of Sunday meetings is best explained by the resurrection of Jesus. The Jewish impulse was Sabbath celebrations and Romans had nothing akin to what we would call a weekend. Hence, the reverence of Sunday as "The Lord's Day" (Acts 20:7; 1 Cor 16:2; Rev 1:10) is a striking sociological phenomenon that demands an explanation most fittingly found on the third day after Jesus death. On the early acceptance of Sunday as "The Lord's Day" cf. S. R. Llewelyn, "The Use of Sunday for Meetings of Believers in the New Testament," *NovT* 43 (2001): 205-223.

[5]Like Venerable Bede (A.D. 709-716), Andrew Arterbury takes Eutychus's sleep to be a metaphor for negligence, which was one of the common figurative uses of sleep in the ancient world. Though "sleep" is the chiastic center of this text, there is nothing else contextually, nor any statistical dominance in the use of "sleep" figuratively, that would compel such an interpretation; contra "The Downfall of Eutychus: How Ancient Understandings of Sleep Illuminate Acts 20:7-12," *Contemporary Studies in Acts* (ed. Thomas E. Phillips; USA: Mercer, 2009), 201-221. More profitable is a semiotic approach to the text that pays attention to the oppositions of light/dark, up/down, in/out; cf. Bernard Trémel, "A propos d'Actes 20,7-12: Puissance du Thaumaturge ou du témoin," *RTP* 112 (1980): 359-369; and Alan Bulley, "Hanging in the Balance: A Semiotic Study of Acts 20:7-12," *EgT* 25 (1994): 171-188, who believe that these textual clues point to the ultimate wholeness and encouragement of the community through Paul's presence.

[6]Some suggest that Eutychus was not dead. Rather, when Paul declares, "He's alive," it is his *discovery* not his *miracle.* This is not what Luke intends. (1) The story of Eutychus is another deliberate parallel between Paul and Peter, who raised a dead woman in an upper room (ὑπερῷον, is found four times and only in Acts 1:13, 9:37, 39; 20:8). (2) Just as Peter's miraculous resuscitation imitated Jesus' methodology, so Paul's imitates Elijah's. Thus, it has all the trappings of a raising from the dead. (3) It is not likely that Luke would include this story, which breaks up the narrative flow toward Jerusalem, were it not for this substantive miracle.

the young man. He may have even known the family from five years earlier when he practiced medicine in this very city. The stunned and grieving parents stood breathless as Paul stretched his body across the lad's limp corpse. He was imitating one of his own historic heroes who had a 'raising' under his prophetic belt. Elijah laid on top of the widow's son at Zarephath three times, pleading with Yahweh for the life of the child (1 Kgs 17:21) as did Elisha after him (2 Kgs 4:34-35). In both instances, God heard their prayers to the delight of the family.

The jubilant church, undoubtedly waking the neighbors, returned upstairs for the Eucharist and a love-feast that followed.[7] One can only imagine the significance that sacred meal held on the heels of this youth returning to life. Unbelievably, Paul *kept on preaching*! It was the sunrise and the impending sailing of his ship that finally quieted the Apostle's unflagging sermon.

4. Miletus: Paul's Farewell Address to the Ephesian Elders (20:13-38)

This is the last of Paul's three main sermons in Acts and the only one directed to believers. It should come as no surprise, therefore, that this narrative sounds most like the Paul of the Epistles.[8] It is a masterpiece of ministry advice in the form of a 'farewell speech'.[9] Paul stresses four major themes that summarize his entire missionary career: preaching the Gospel of Grace (vv. 21, 25-27, 31-32), suffering (vv. 19, 22-23), giving/working (vv. 18, 33-35), and leadership (vv. 28-31).[10] Obviously, this exhortation has relevance far beyond the geographic and chronological boundaries of Ephesus.[11] It is a message to the Church, not merely a congregation. Finally, this sermon has two unique and interesting features. (1) Paul never cites Scripture. Rather, his 'text' is the testimony of his own life of service and suffering for the believers. (2) Paul does quote Jesus, but it is a saying never recorded in the Gospels. This free-floating proverb is appended to Paul's sermon as its finale. How fitting that Jesus gets the last word in Paul's final sermon.

---

[7] The breaking of bread undoubtedly indicates a communion service. The word "ate" (γεύομαι), however, describes a full meal. Eating is often used as a narrative clue that a sickness or trial has come to an end (e.g., Mark 5:43; Acts 9:19).

[8] Armin D. Baum, "Paulinismen in den Missionsreden des lukanischen Paulus: Zur inhaltlichen Authentizität der *oratio recta* in der Apostelgeschichte," *ETL* 82 (2006): 405-436, demonstrates this through a meticulous evaluation of the overlapping vocabulary and ideology between this sermon and the undisputed Pauline Epistles.

[9] For other farewell speeches, cf. Gen 49:1-33; Josh 23:1–24:28; 1 Sam 12:1-25; 1 Macc 2:49-70; Tobit 14:3-11; John 13–17. Lawrence Wills argues that this "word of exhortation" presented by Paul represents well a common sermonic form of the early church, differentiated from both Jewish sermons and Greco-Roman rhetoric; cf. "The Form of the Sermon in Hellenistic Judaism and Early Christianity," *HTR* 77 (1984): 277-299.

[10] This sermon has been criticized for its apparently loose, even 'chaotic' structure (cf. Dibelius, 157). Cheryl Exum, however, offers a compelling case that Luke has here a balanced chiasm: A—Paul testifies to his witness (vv. 18-21); B—Foreboding: Paul in Jerusalem (vv. 22-24); C—Paul's final farewell (v. 25); B'—Foreboding: False teachers (vv. 26-30); A'—Paul testifies to his witness (vv. 31-35). The center of the chiasm, hence, the central thought of the sermon, is Paul's prediction that he is departing for the last time. Cf. "The Structure of Paul's Speech to the Ephesian Elders (Acts 20,18-35)," *CBQ* 29 (1967): 233-236.

[11] Beverly Roberts Gaventa, "Theology and Ecclesiology in Miletus Speech: Reflections on Content and Context," *NTS* 50 (2004): 36-52, presents a convincing argument that this speech is meant to be read as a paradigm for all missionary congregations not merely Ephesus. Its major themes of suffering and false teaching certainly run heavy through the NT Epistles; cf. Ramon Tragan, "Les 'Destinataires' du Discours de Milet," in *À Cause de l'Évangile: Études sur les Synoptiques et les Actes* (Cerf: Sainte-André, 1985), 779-798.

¹³**We went on ahead to the ship and sailed for Assos, where we were going to
take Paul aboard. He had made this arrangement because he was going there on
foot. ¹⁴When he met us at Assos, we took him aboard and went on to Mitylene.
¹⁵The next day we set sail from there and arrived off Kios. The day after that we
crossed over to Samos, and on the following day arrived at Miletus. ¹⁶Paul had
decided to sail past Ephesus to avoid spending time in the province of Asia, for
he was in a hurry to reach Jerusalem, if possible, by the day of Pentecost.**

20:13. After preaching all night (punctuated with raising Eutychus from the
dead), Paul chose to walk more than twenty miles to Assos rather than sail all
the way around the Cape of Lectum. It may be that he was so wound up from
the emotional meeting that he had energy to burn. On the other hand, he may
have just not liked ships. Perhaps he suffered from seasickness or perhaps he
just got tired of ships sinking when he was aboard, which had already happened
three times (2 Cor 11:25). Either way, Paul, now somewhere in his late fifties,
shows impressive physical stamina.

20:14-15. It took one day to get from Assos to Mitylene, the chief city on the
eastern coast of the island of Lesbos (30 miles). The following day they sailed
south to the island of Chios (55 miles), the next day to Samos (60 miles) and
one more day to Miletus (35 miles). One can hardly be criticized for asking,
"Who cares?" The most likely answer is: The guy onboard! These vivid details
surely come from Luke's personal recollection.[12]

20:16. As desperately as Paul wanted to see the congregation(s) of Ephesus,
he dare not make a personal visit to the city or he would never escape their
loving embrace prior to Pentecost. If he is going to reach Jerusalem for the sacred festival, he would unfortunately have to limit his conversation to the Elders
alone. There is, perhaps, another reason Paul wanted to avoid the city. Paul had
encountered potentially lethal opposition in Ephesus (1 Cor 15:32; 2 Cor 1:8;
4:8-11). Carrez provocatively speculates that his narrow escape from his enemies
made him wary of showing his face again.[13] It wasn't just the church that would
love to get their hands on the Apostle.

a. Paul Testifies to His Witness (20:17-21)

¹⁷**From Miletus, Paul sent to Ephesus for the elders of the church. ¹⁸When
they arrived, he said to them: "You know how I lived the whole time I was with
you, from the first day I came into the province of Asia. ¹⁹I served the Lord
with great humility and with tears, although I was severely tested by the plots of
the Jews. ²⁰You know that I have not hesitated to preach anything that would be
helpful to you but have taught you publicly and from house to house. ²¹I have
declared to both Jews and Greeks that they must turn to God in repentance and
have faith in our Lord Jesus."**

---

[12] The "we" passages of Acts are still a conundrum for Acts scholars—what do they tell us about Lucan
redaction, sources, and potential participation in the events? We are still far from a consensus; cf. Susan
Praeder, "The Problem of First Person Narration in Acts," *NovT* 29 (1987): 193-218. Nonetheless, the
simplest and most satisfying explanation of these sections, to this author, is that Luke was a traveling companion of Paul on several of his journeys.
[13] Carrez, "Les événements d'Éphésse," 769-777.

20:17-19. It took the better part of a week for the envoys to get to Ephesus, round up the Elders, and escort them back to Miletus, more than thirty miles to the south. When they arrived, Paul reminded them of his ministry. What he said is most interesting from a sociological perspective. Verse nineteen uses several terms that would normally be interpreted as objects of shame rather than badges of honor. He was the Lord's "*slave*," serving with *humility*, in spite of Jewish *plots* against him.[14] These terms describe a person living in the shadow of shame. For Paul, honor and shame had been reversed in the Kingdom. That which the world prized he considered shameful and vice versa. Even his own noble pedigree he considered excrement (*skubalon,* Phil 3:1-11). His ministry, like Jesus', was at its best when he was absorbing in himself the worst this world had to spew.

20:20-21. In the face of threats from pagans like Demetrius and plots from his own countrymen, Paul persisted in preaching the full gospel both "publicly and from house to house."[15] Luke's summary of Paul's preaching is what he had been saying all along—Paul was a "servant" and a "witness" (cf. Acts 26:16-18).[16] This dual characterization has a particularly authentic ring against echoes of the Epistles. This is precisely how Paul portrayed his own ministry.[17]

b. Foreboding: Paul in Jerusalem (20:22-24)

[22]**"And now, compelled by the Spirit, I am going to Jerusalem, not knowing what will happen to me there. [23]I only know that in every city the Holy Spirit warns me that prison and hardships are facing me. [24]However, I consider my life worth nothing to me, if only I may finish the race and complete the task the Lord Jesus has given me—the task of testifying to the gospel of God's grace."**

20:22. Paul is both headstrong and Spirit-filled. This makes it difficult to know whether to capitalize the word "Spirit" in verse twenty-two. Was it *his* spirit that drove him back to Jerusalem or *God's* Spirit? This is the same question we asked back in 19:21 and it will come up again in 21:4, 11, when the Spirit warns the believers that Paul will be arrested in Jerusalem. There it will be given full consid-

---

[14]Though "plots" (ἐπιβουλή) against Paul were common (Acts 9:23-24; 20:3, 19; 23:30; cf. 9:29; 13:50; 14:5, 19; 16:19-20; 17:5; 21:27-32; 22:22; 23:12; 25:2), the only recorded incident in Ephesus was the near riot fomented by Demetrius. That there were others is beyond dispute based upon Paul's own reflections in 1 Corinthians concerning his ministry in Ephesus (1 Cor 15:32; 2 Cor 1:8; 4:8-11).

[15]These terms describe the various forums in which one could speak in the ancient world. As Neyrey demonstrates, Paul is consistently portrayed as successful in public spaces such as the agora and the governor's residence as well as in the private spaces of homes and schools, but not in the private–nonkinship space of the synagogue; cf. Jerome Neyrey, "'Teaching You in Public and from House to House' (Acts 20.20): Unpacking a Cultural Stereotype," *JSNT* 26 (2003): 69-102.

[16]This is particularly interesting in light of the same twofold characterization of the "Servant of the Lord" (Isa 43:10, 12). For a careful study of these two characteristics in the life of Paul, cf. P. Boyd Mather, "Paul in Acts as 'Servant' and 'Witness'," *BR* 30 (1985): 23-44.

[17]There are multiple echoes in Acts 20 of Paul's Epistles: (1) He reminded them of how he lived among them (20:18; cf. 1 Thess 2:1-2; 4:11). (2) He considered himself vocationally a "servant of the Lord" (20:19; cf. Rom 1:1, 9; 1 Cor 3:5; 4:1; 9:6-7; 2 Cor 6:4; Gal 1:10; Eph 3:7; Phil 1:1; Col 1:7; 1 Tim 1:12; Titus 1:1). (3) He pointed out his humility (20:19; cf. 2 Cor 10:1; 11:7). (4) He showed sorrow (20:19; cf. Rom 9:2; 2 Cor 2:4; Phil 3:18). (5) He was persecuted by his fellow Jews (20:19; cf. 2 Cor 11:24, 26; 1 Thess 2:14-16). (6) He targeted both Jews and Gentiles (20:21; Rom 1:13-16; 11:11-24; 15:7-13; 1 Cor 1:23; 9:20; Gal 3:14). (7) He was willing to risk his life (20:22; 2 Cor 4:7–5:10; 6:4-10; Phil 1:19-26; 2:17; 3:8).

COLLEGE PRESS NIV COMMENTARY

eration. Suffice to say here that it is often difficult to discern the inner promptings of the Spirit and tease them apart from our own impulses and desires.

20:23-24. Nonetheless, Paul set his sights on Jerusalem in spite of the inevitable persecutions that await. As he points out, he is bound to be beaten in every city in which he preaches. He might as well take a shot for his own people in hope that they too will accept Jesus as God's Messiah. To him, this is part of the race he's been given to run (cf. 2 Tim 4:7). His life was not his own. He had been bought with a price and destined to the duty of proclaiming this marvelous message of God's grace. If he died in that task he was confident of a waiting reward.

c. Paul's Final Farewell (20:25)

[25]"Now I know that none of you among whom I have gone about preaching the kingdom will ever see me again."

20:25. This sentence stands at the center of this chiastic sermon. Thus, it punctuates the message with particular emphasis. Though it appears that Paul did, in fact, revisit Ephesus after his Roman imprisonment,[18] the Apostle was convinced at that time that this was his final farewell before traveling to preach in Spain where he would likely end his career on the western frontiers of Europe.

b'. Foreboding, Part 2: False Teachers (20:26-30)

[26]"Therefore, I declare to you today that I am innocent of the blood of all men. [27]For I have not hesitated to proclaim to you the whole will of God. [28]Keep watch over yourselves and all the flock of which the Holy Spirit has made you overseers.[a] Be shepherds of the church of God,[b] which he bought with his own blood. [29]I know that after I leave, savage wolves will come in among you and will not spare the flock. [30]Even from your own number men will arise and distort the truth in order to draw away disciples after them."

[a]28 Traditionally *bishops*   [b]28 Many manuscripts *of the Lord*

20:26-27. Because Paul never neglected his duty to preach, he was innocent of any punishment due to the unrepentant. This is a well-worn principle from Ezekiel 3:17-19 (cf. Ezek 33:1-9). God ordains the prophet to function like a watchman on the wall, warning the nation of a coming invasion. If the watchman says exactly what God tells him, regardless of how painful the message, he escapes the punishment inflicted on an unrepentant city. If, however, he neglects his duties, their blood will be on his head.

20:28-30. As Paul leaves, he charges *the Elders* with this responsibility; they are the watchmen over the church. Hence, it behooves them to guard themselves,[19]

---

[18] If we are correct that 1 & 2 Timothy were written after Paul's first Roman imprisonment, then it seems clear that Paul was in Ephesus (cf. 1 Tim 1:3; 3:14; 4:13; 2 Tim 4:13, 20). This should hardly come as a surprise given how often Paul's plans changed (cf. Acts 16:620; 20:3; Rom 1:13; 2 Cor 1:15; 1 Thess 2:18).

[19] The word "keep watch" (προσέχω) is used 24 times in the NT and 12 of those are exhortations to guard against false doctrine (Matt 7:15; 16:6, 11-12[/Luke 12:1]; Luke 20:46; Acts 20:28; 1 Tim 1:4; 4:1; Titus 1:14; Heb 2:1; 2 Pet 1:19).

as watchmen, and the 'city' over which God had given them care.[20] Whether they are labeled Elders,[21] Overseers,[22] or Shepherds,[23] their role is essentially threefold. (1) They **feed** the flock.[24] This necessitates teaching. It is the job of the Elders to ensure a proper indoctrination of the congregation. They may themselves teach or they may supervise the implementation of teaching programs by other Spirit-endowed teachers. Nonetheless, the education and edification of the flock is one of the primary tasks of Elders. (2) They **visit** the flock. This is inherent in the word "overseer" which implies not only the presence of the Pastor/Shepherd, but also providing for their needs. It certainly includes godly counsel for the confused, advocacy for the disenfranchised, and benevolence for the needy. If anything involves the emotional, spiritual, or physical health of the sheep, it is the role and responsibility of the Elders. (3) They **protect** the flock. Paul spends most time here. There were then, as there are today, a plethora of wolves in sheep's clothing (e.g., Matt 7:15; 4 Ezra 5:18; *1 En* 89.13-15). They introduce false doctrine and lead away the lambs to the slaughter to slake their own appetites and stroke their own egos. A godly Eldership is vigilant against heresies, particularly those that arise from within the fold.

In the New Testament there was a fairly extensive list of heresies constantly infiltrating the church. The Epistles give voice to the kind of confrontation needed from Elders in order to protect the flock from false doctrine. There were Judaizers (Gal), Gnostics (1 John); Nicolaitans (Rev 2:6) and other miscellaneous bothersome deviants (cf. Matt 7:15; Eph 5:6-14; Col 2:8; Rev 2:2) particularly prevalent in Ephesus (cf. 1 Tim 1:4, 7, 19-20; 4:1-3; 2 Tim 2:17-18; 3:1-9; 4:4).[25]

---

[20] The entire Trinity shows up in verse 28. The presence of Jesus (vv. 21, 24, 28, 35), the Spirit (vv. 22, 23, 28), and the Father (vv. 19, 21, 24, 27, 28, 32) mark this discourse as a Trinitarian text; cf. Abdón Moreno García, "Constituidos Pastores por el Espíritu Santo: El Discurso de Mileto (Hch 20,17-38)," *EB* 62 (2004): 27-48.

[21] Elders (*presbuteros*) and Overseers are used synonymously in this text and probably throughout the NT. These men were to be respected both inside and outside the church (cf. 1 Tim 3:1-7; Titus 1:5-9) with sufficient age to carry the gravitas of this sacred stewardship. Some have claimed that we can discern specific leadership structures based on this and other texts in Acts and the Pastoral Epistles; e.g., David Miller, "The Uniqueness of New Testament Church Eldership," *GTR* 6 (1985): 315-327. The biblical texts, however, are open to polyvalent readings, evidenced by multiple leadership structures in a plethora of global denominations. What can be definitively stated and defended is that there were multiple Elders in each local congregation. Anything beyond this is speculation that would be better relinquished to the guidance of the Spirit who ultimately establishes both the individual leaders and the corporate structures appropriate to culturally embedded bodies of believers (v. 28!; cf. 13:2-4).

[22] The word ἐπίσκοπος, translated in the KJV as "bishop," is composed of two compound words, *epi* "over" and *skopos* "seeing." It implies looking into a situation analytically (often with a physical visit) with the intent of responding appropriately to the needs of the situation (TDNT 2:600-605). In the NT, the overseer and elder seem to be synonymous as opposed to the later development where the "bishop" supervised the work of several churches.

[23] Shepherds and Pastors, of course, are the same thing. Both words play off a metaphor with deep roots in the OT: Ezek 34:12-16; Jer 23:2; Zech 10:3; 11:4-17; cf. John 10:1-18; 21:15-17; 1 Pet 2:25; 5:2. It is common for the terms "shepherd" and "overseer" to be used together (cf. 1 Pet 2:25; 5:2; LXX Jer 23:2; Ezek 34; Zech 10:3; 11:16). A similar combination is found in CD 13.7-12 where the word *mˀbaqqēr* "supervisor" is combined with a shepherding motif; cf. Evald Lövestam, "Paul's Address at Miletus," *ST* 41 (1987): 6-7.

[24] Feeding is implied in the word ποιμαίνω "shepherd." The KJV of v. 28, in fact, translates it "to feed the church of God."

[25] G. W. H. Lampe, "'Grievous Wolves' (Acts 20:29)," in *Christ and the Spirit in the New Testament* (Cambridge: Cambridge Univ. Press, 1973), 253-268; and Tragan, "Les 'Destinataires' du Discours de Milet," 784-787, offer a helpful survey of false teachers in the NT and in the early church—what they promoted and how they were handled.

Obviously, there's no litmus test for false doctrine, and wolves don't wear badges that identify themselves. Practically speaking, most of them don't even believe they are damaging the flock. That being said, there are several signs that should raise red flags for Elders. First, an individual who gathers people around himself for his or her self-aggrandizement is dangerous. Verse 30 warns: "they draw away disciples after them." When people give allegiance to a human personality above the Lord Jesus Christ, take heed! Second, individuals who fleece the flock financially are heading toward heresy. Paul makes a point in this passage that he gave rather than received. He worked for the benefit of others rather than allowing the church to support him. Obviously, there is nothing wrong with a Pastor receiving a salary (1 Tim 5:18). However, there is a fine line that wolves dance across when the flock is a means to ungodly gain; take heed. Third, though this passage doesn't address sexual immorality, church history and contemporary experience are rife with examples of wolves who abuse sheep for their own sexual pleasure. Flirting Pastors are not innocent; they are pernicious. It is perhaps an oversimplification, but a helpful rule nonetheless to suggest that with these three strikes an Elder is out.

The Blood of God. Verse 28 introduces a theologically striking statement. It claims that the church was purchased (*peripoieō*, or "obtained") with "his own blood." This is remarkable for two reasons, best addressed through two questions. (1) *Can God bleed?* If Jesus is fully endowed with deity, this turn of phrase presents no problem (cf. Heb 9:12).[26] However, to many it has been a problem, even to those who preserved and translated the Bible. Multiple manuscripts replace "God" with "Lord," thus softening the strong language of verse 28.[27] In other words, it is Jesus (alone) bleeding, not God the Father. Others have argued that "blood" doesn't refer to the liquid flowing from veins but the "offspring." Thus understood, God rescued the church through the life of his son, Jesus, not by his death.[28] This not only removes the difficult reading, it softens the emphasis on blood atonement which is admittedly muted in Luke's writings. This introduces our second question: (2) *Would Luke talk about the bloody sacrifice of Jesus as a payment for human sin?* There are limited references in Luke/Acts to substitutionary atonement (cf. Luke 22:19-20).[29] However, that Luke does not emphasize a particular theme is not to say he objects to it. The sources Luke <u>faithfully followed</u> (Mark/Matthew) and the mentors he valorized (Peter/Paul)

381-408.

[27] The manuscript evidence (barely) favors the reading "church of God" (א, B, 614, 1175, 1505, al vg, sy, bo^{ms}, Cyr.). However, there is also strong manuscript evidence for "church of the Lord" (P⁷⁴, A, C*, D, E, ψ, 33, 36, 453, 945, 1739, 1891, al gig, p, syh^{mg}, co). To this manuscript evidence should be added the observation that "church of the Lord" is never used in the NT while "church(es) of God" is common parlance (cf. 1 Cor 1:2; 10:32; 11:16, 22; 15:9; 2 Cor 1:1; Gal 1:13; 1 Tim 3:5, 15; 1 Thess 2:14; 2 Thess 1:4); cf. Kevin Giles, "Luke's Use of the Term 'ΕΚΚΛΗΣΙΑ' with Special Reference to Acts 20:28 and 9:31," *NTS* 31 (1985): 135-142.

[28] For a typical linguistic argument to this effect see Karl Gustav Dolfe, "The Greek Word of 'Blood' and the Interpretation of Acts 20:28," *SvEA* 55 (1990): 64-70, also *Beginnings* 4:262.

[29] Though there are far more than is often granted. For a full list of suggestive texts, see David Moessner, "The 'script' of the Scriptures in Acts: Suffering as God's 'plan' (βουλή) for the World for the 'release of sins'," in *History, Literature and Society* (ed. Ben Witherington; Cambridge: Cambridge, 1999), 218-250.

unquestionably taught substitutionary atonement through the blood of Jesus.[30] It would be difficult for him to tell their stories without some allusion to this theme. In summary: this passage, though stated strongly, means what it says: *God, in Christ, redeemed the church through his blood.*

a'. Paul Testifies to His Witness, Part 2 (20:31-35)

[31]**"So be on your guard! Remember that for three years I never stopped warning each of you night and day with tears. [32]Now I commit you to God and to the word of his grace, which can build you up and give you an inheritance among all those who are sanctified. [33]I have not coveted anyone's silver or gold or clothing. [34]You yourselves know that these hands of mine have supplied my own needs and the needs of my companions. [35]In everything I did, I showed you that by this kind of hard work we must help the weak, remembering the words the Lord Jesus himself said: 'It is more blessed to give than to receive.'"**

20:31-35. Paul ends where he began by testifying to his own unrelenting witness. With a final foray, he warns the elders to be vigilant. "Be on your guard" (*grēgoreō*) is a single Greek word that implies staying alert or awake.[31] With that, he takes two parting shots. In the first, he symbolically places these Elders into the hands of God, whose message of grace can keep them unto the day of salvation (v. 32). In the second, he reminds them of his self-supporting, tent-making ministry (vv. 33-35). None of this is particularly new, except, of course, the quotation of Jesus: "It is more blessed to give than to receive." This particular logion is fascinating, not because it is in any way inconsistent with Jesus' preaching (e.g., Luke 6:30, 38; 12:33; 18:22) but because no one bothered to record it until here. There may have been dozens, if not hundreds of quips and quotes of Jesus which didn't make it into the canon.[32] This one barely made it and only because it resonated so well with one of Paul's core ministry values—economic compassion.[33] It is fitting that the last word in Paul's public missionary sermon

---

[30] Though Luke generally offers his own etic view of Paul, there are two important glimpses of Paul's own (emic) soteriological emphasis on Jesus' substitutionary death (Acts 13:38 and 20:28); cf. Edvin Larsson, "Paul: Law and Salvation," *NTS* 31 (1985): 425-436. Both the etic view of Paul in Acts and Paul's own emic view in the Epistles have valid claims to authenticity. The supposed contradiction between the Paul of Acts and the Paul of the Epistles is to a large degree artificial, overblown, and sociologically naïve; cf. Witherington, 430-438, for a fair and balanced treatment of the major issues.

[31] Peter uses this word once (1 Pet 5:8), Paul five times (Acts 20:31; 1 Cor 16:13; Col 4:2; 1 Thess 5:6, 10). The other sixteen uses of this word in the NT are all on the lips of Jesus (Matt 24:42, 43; 25:13; 26:38, 40, 41; Mark 13:34, 37, 38; Luke 12:37; Rev 3:2, 3; 16:15). Moreover, 10/22 uses are imperatives—commands to stay alert.

[32] However, there are no extrabiblical sayings of Jesus that can be securely traced back to him; cf. Ofried Hofius, "Unbekannte Jesusworte," in *Das Evangelium und die Evangelien* (Tübingen: J. D. B. Mohr, 1983), 355-381. All attempts to find alternative sayings of Jesus not recorded in the Gospels have proven speculative at best.

[33] Thucydides has a quote that is the antithesis of this one (2.97.4). He records the habit of the Odrysian kingdom to "receive rather than to give." Some, therefore, assert that Luke is really quoting Thucydides and giving Jesus credit, via his hero Paul; cf. Eckhard Plümacher, "Eine Thukydidesreminiszenze in der Apostelgeschichte (Apg. 20,33-35—Thuk. II 97,3f.)," *ZNW* 83-4 (1992): 270-275; and Haenchen, 526. However, John Kilgallen has rightly questioned how close the unwritten antithesis would have been to this logion; cf. "Acts 20:35 and Thucydides 2.97.4," *JBL* 112 (1993): 312-314. One might also question whether Luke would have felt comfortable attributing a logion to Jesus that he did not find attached to the Lord in his sources. Moreover, one certainly could wonder why Thucydides has to be the singular source behind

is given to the Lord Jesus Christ.[34] It might not be so bad if he got the final say in all our sermons.

[36]When he had said this, he knelt down with all of them and prayed. [37]They all wept as they embraced him and kissed him. [38]What grieved them most was his statement that they would never see his face again. Then they accompanied him to the ship.

20:36-38. Paul had a particularly rich investment into these people who would eventually influence all of Asia for the gospel. His tears are understandable. They too weep for him, especially since they also believed it was their final farewell with their founder and friend. They sent him off with tears, prayers, hugs, and kisses. The ship's departure forces an end to their reunion.

---

this common sentiment (cf. Plutarch, *Moralia* 2.173d and Sir 4.31; for other examples cf. *Beginnings* 4:264) when Jesus is indubitably a creative moral genius.

[34] Functionally, this 'proof-text' adds gravitas to Paul's sermon and emphasizes the theme of benevolence that is so critically important to Luke (cf. Acts 2:42-45; 4:32-35; 11:28-30; 12:25; 24:17); cf. Robert O'Toole, "What Role Does Jesus' Saying in Acts 20,35 Play in Paul's Address to the Ephesian Elders?" *Bib* 75 (1994): 329-349, "One might well say that Luke, by placing this saying of Jesus at the end of Paul's speech to the Ephesian elders, has anticipated the recent theological and spiritual concern of 'faith and justice'" (349).

ACTS 21

IV. WITNESS SHIFTS FROM JERUSALEM TO ROME (21:1–28:31)

This rather long section is a series of legal briefs that fulfill the promise Jesus made to Paul at his conversion. He said, "This man is my chosen instrument to carry my name before the *Gentiles* and their *kings* and before the people of *Israel*" (9:15). The three primary speeches of this section are to the people of *Israel* (22:1-22), to the *Gentile governors* Felix (24:10-21) and Festus (25:8-11), and finally to *King* Agrippa II (26:2-29).

Taken together, these legal briefs paint a portrait with three broad brush strokes. *First, the passion narrative of Paul mirrors that of Jesus.* Luke lays out five trials of Jesus—Caiphas, the Sanhedrin, Pilate, Herod, than back to Pilate. Paul's five trials are almost identical—the Jewish populace (ch. 22) replaces Jesus' trial before the high priest, and there are two separate governors rather than two trials before the same governor. The striking historical similarity is a deliberate device to show that "so goes Jesus, so goes Paul." Hence, Paul's trials are not an appendix to the action of Acts. Rather, they function, as do Jesus' trials in Luke, as a climactic summary at the end of the book. *Second, Christianity is the legal heir of Judaism* (cf. Polhill, 441). Though maligned, misrepresented, and abused, the church was never found wanting in the halls of justice. No Roman court ever rendered a "guilty" verdict against the people of God. *Third, the resurrection reigns supreme.* Paul's trials serve as a platform for preaching the reality and reasonableness of the resurrection of Jesus. What is on trial is really not the person of the Apostle, but the core of Christianity—the resurrection of Jesus.

A. PAUL'S JOURNEY TO JERUSALEM (21:1-36)

Paul's journey to Jerusalem is a climactic moment in Acts. It is a hinge upon which the book swings into its final movement toward the trials of Paul. Yet this ascent to the city is more than a climactic literary motif. For Paul it is a homecoming of sorts though with ominous clouds looming about. There is tension for the reader, who senses Paul's career as an evangelist is nearing an end when he jeopardizes his freedom for the chance to preach to his own people. There is also an excitement building in this text through Luke's repetition of the word "we." He was there, on sacred soil, meeting for the first time the early believers who could serve as eyewitnesses for his historical project.

1. Travel Itinerary and the Church's Reception (21:1-16)

[1]After we had torn ourselves away from them, we put out to sea and sailed straight to Cos. The next day we went to Rhodes and from there to Patara. [2]We found a ship crossing over to Phoenicia, went on board and set sail. [3]After sighting Cyprus and passing to the south of it, we sailed on to Syria. We landed at Tyre, where our ship was to unload its cargo. [4]Finding the disciples there, we stayed with them seven days. Through the Spirit they urged Paul not to go on to Jerusalem. [5]But when our time was up, we left and continued on our way. All the disciples and their wives and children accompanied us out of the city, and there on the beach we knelt to pray. [6]After saying good-by to each other, we went aboard the ship, and they returned home.

21:1-3. It was a difficult and tearful farewell in Miletus. However, the clock was ticking toward Pentecost; it was time to move and the wind was blowing in the right direction.[1] Once again Luke carefully traces their itinerary. The first three days took them from Miletus to Cos[2] (50 miles), on to Rhodes (roughly 75 miles), and then to Patara (another 75 miles). This was the normal shipping route along the coast of Asia Minor (Cf. Lucan, *Pharsalia* 8.243-244; Livy 37.16). Likely they paid for passage on a local coasting vessel that skipped from port to port. From Patara, however, they changed ships, probably a larger cargo vessel setting sail for Phoenicia, a straight 475 miles across the depths of the Mediterranean. This is the cultural equivalent of a direct flight but hardly first class. Paul & Co. would have slept on the deck or in the cargo hold with no meals provided. They sailed to the south of Cyprus, close enough to spot the island off the left side of the boat. This was a welcomed sign that they were nearing Syria, or more specifically, the coast of Phoenicia and its major port of Tyre.

21:4-6. The cargo destined for Syria was off-loaded and undoubtedly replaced with wares headed south. All this took a week, offering Paul the opportunity to hunt down the disciples of the area. The first word of verse 4 (*aneuriskō*) implies a deliberate search. The only other time Luke uses it is to describe Joseph and Mary frantically looking for their son in Jerusalem (Luke 2:16). What is most interesting about this tidbit is that Luke has not previously informed Theophilus of any evangelistic campaign in Syria. He does mention that some of those scattered by Stephen's persecution preached in Tyre but only to the Jews (11:19). Nothing more is said. These disciples were the product of the natural and inevitable spread of the kingdom.

During the week, some of the Spirit-inspired brothers told Paul not to go to Jerusalem. Obviously, he went anyway. Does this mean that Paul was disobedient to the Spirit? That's a real possibility; he was a fallible human being like the rest of us. However, Luke gives no clue that Paul should be rebuked for his belligerence.

---

[1] The winds are normally from the northeast during the summer in western Turkey, alternating between several days of strong winds punctuated with a couple of calm days (cf. *Beginnings* 4:264). The speed of their southward journey indicates they have favorable winds.

[2] Cos was not merely the island as a whole, but also the capital city of that island. It was the famed home of the physician Hippocrates (5th cen. B.C.). Rhodes, their next stop, was also the island as well as its capital city.

In fact, there is a clue in verse 11 that points in a different direction. There the believers at Caesarea likewise begged him not to go to Jerusalem. Even Agabus the prophet weighed in on the issue, warning him to steer clear of the capital. However, the specific message the Spirit gave Agabus was not a prohibition against going to Jerusalem. Rather, it was a prediction that if he did, Paul would be arrested by his countrymen and handed over to the Romans. Even without this prophetic input, Paul could probably have predicted what was coming. It's not like he had no track record of riling up his fellow Jews. Putting these pieces together renders the following portrait: The Spirit warned that if Paul went to Jerusalem, he would be arrested and turned over to the Romans. Those that heard this message tried to talk Paul out of going. When Paul heard it he said, "So? Been there; done that." Paul's desire to evangelize his own people despite personal peril is impressive.

This is a not an uncommon literary theme: a hero marches resolutely into the face of death despite the protest of family and friends.[3] It was used with Hector and Socrates prior to Paul and Perpetua and Polycarp after him. The point is not really that the hero and his friends have a dispute but that the hero has unflagging resolve. Read against this motif of Greco-Roman literature, the apparent paradox effectively dissolves.

The ship was ready to sail again, for Paul had a date with destiny. The brothers escorted him to the shore. This is the same scene we saw at Miletus where the church saw Paul to the ship, knelt in prayer, and sent him on his way. The only real difference is that here the wives and children were able to participate, but no one burst into tears like at Miletus.

[7]We continued our voyage from Tyre and landed at Ptolemais, where we greeted the brothers and stayed with them for a day. [8]Leaving the next day, we reached Caesarea and stayed at the house of Philip the evangelist, one of the Seven. [9]He had four unmarried daughters who prophesied. [10]After we had been there a number of days, a prophet named Agabus came down from Judea. [11]Coming over to us, he took Paul's belt, tied his own hands and feet with it and said, "The Holy Spirit says, 'In this way the Jews of Jerusalem will bind the owner of this belt and will hand him over to the Gentiles.'"

21:7. The ship sailed less than thirty miles down the coast to Ptolemais (modern Acre, ancient Acco, cf. Jdg 1:31). Once again, the entourage was greeted by the believers of the area who detained them for a single day. The next day they headed south again; another forty miles and they were at Caesarea, a coastal city that had been home to Herod, Pilate, Cornelius, and for the last twenty years, Philip the Evangelist (cf. 8:40).

21:8-9. This must have been immensely exciting to Luke who was, at this time, in the throes of his historical research. He was able to meet Philip, the Evangelist.[4] This title "Evangelist" would later become an official role in the

---

[3] Gratitude goes to Francois Bavon for recognizing and explicating this literary motif; cf. "Le Saint-Esprit, l'Église et les relations humaines selon Actes 20, 36–21, 16," in *Les Actes des Apôtres: Traditions, redaction, théologie* (ed. J. Kremer; Leuven: Leuven University Press, 1979), 339-358.

[4] Philip the Evangelist was sometimes confused with or conflated with Philip the Apostles. For example,

church (Eph 4:11; 2 Tim 4:5). Though the role is never clearly defined, "Evangelist" comes from the verb meaning "to announce good news." It may be that pastors spent more time teaching and edifying the saints while evangelists concentrated on telling unbelievers the message of Jesus. That certainly fits Philip's *M.O.* (Acts 8:4, 12, 35, 40). He was one of the original seven chosen by the Apostles to administrate the benevolence for widows (Acts 6:1-6). He had been in close proximity to the Apostles, as well as the front-runner in Samaria where the first non-Jews turned to Christ. Luke had *so* much to ask him. He would have his chance, but not on this visit; they were racing to Jerusalem. Philip wasn't the only one who caught Luke's attention. Though he doesn't record anything they said or did, Luke remembers fondly Philip's four single daughters. Literally, the text says they were *virgins*. The point is not that they were marriageable nor that they were sexually pure. The point is that they were singly devoted to God.[5] Equally impressive is the fact that they were all prophetesses, practicing one of the most important charismatic leadership gifts of the early church (cf. 1 Cor 11:5; 12:28; 14:1-6; cf. Joel 2:28-29/Acts 2:17-18).[6]

21:10-11. Apparently they made good time getting to Israel and could afford a few days in Caesarea with the believers. During that time, Judea got word that Paul was back in the country. Paul's old friend Agabus (cf. 11:28) made a beeline for Caesarea, seventy-five miles NNW of Jerusalem. Like the Asiarchs in Ephesus (19:31), he is going to attempt to dissuade the apostle from a dangerous (nearly suicidal) mission. Agabus was less effective than his pagan counterparts in spite of his theatrics.[7] He took Paul's belt and bound his own hands and feet as a vivid visual to augment his "word from the Lord." For most, this might have been effective. For Paul, mere chains would be a welcome reprieve from the brutal beatings he experienced elsewhere. He's still going!

Had Luke made up the story of Agabus, he certainly could have aligned more closely Agabus's words with the later narrative. For, in fact, the Jews did *not* bind Paul; it was the Romans who put him in chains. Furthermore, the Jews did not "hand him over" to the Gentiles. Rather, the Roman authorities forcibly extracted Paul from the murderous mob. These superficial differences would hardly have given the ancients pause. Modern scholars have been much less generous in their critique of Luke and Agabus. Besides, Luke's wording may

---

Polycrates, bishop of Ephesus (c. A.D. 190) described Philip as one of the Twelve who had three virgin daughters and claimed he was buried at Hieropolis near Laodicea (Eusebius, *Eccl. Hist.*, 3.31).

[5] Singleness in the early church was honored as an office to which one could aspire. It was not quite like the celibacy practiced by modern Catholic clergy, but it was closer to that than the singles ministry in most evangelical churches. Foreign to this text is the subtle assumption that singles are somehow broken and need to be 'fixed up'. The church is poorer for her attitude toward those blessed with celibacy. There is no other group in the church that people so desperately try to get out of than the singles ministry. Cf. W. A. Heth, "Unmarried 'For the Sake of the Kingdom' (Mt 19:12) in the Early Church," *GTJ* 8 (1987): 55-88.

[6] Though male prophets far outnumber female prophets in the Scriptures, there have always been women through whom God spoke by his Spirit: Miriam (Exod 15:20-21); Deborah (Jdg 4:4-5); Huldah (2 Kgs 22:12-20); Isaiah's wife (Isa 8:1-3); Anna (Luke 2:36).

[7] Theatrics were common among the prophets. For example, Ahijah tore a cloak into twelve pieces to illustrate the rending of Israel (1 Kgs 11:29-31); Isaiah went around for three years stripped and barefoot (Isa 20:1-4); Jeremiah had to carry a yoke into the temple (Jer 27:1-22); Ezekiel built a model of the temple (Ezek 4:1-17), and Hosea was ordered to marry a prostitute (Hos 1:2). These are pretty radical visual aids for a sermon.

have been partially influence by his desire to match Paul's fate in Jerusalem with Jesus' (cf. Matt 20:18-19; Luke 18:32). In short, Agabus's prophecy fits Jesus' experience in Jerusalem much more closely than it does Paul's.

[12]When we heard this, we and the people there pleaded with Paul not to go up to Jerusalem. [13]Then Paul answered, "Why are you weeping and breaking my heart? I am ready not only to be bound, but also to die in Jerusalem for the name of the Lord Jesus." [14]When he would not be dissuaded, we gave up and said, "The Lord's will be done." [15]After this, we got ready and went up to Jerusalem. [16]Some of the disciples from Caesarea accompanied us and brought us to the home of Mnason, where we were to stay. He was a man from Cyprus and one of the early disciples.

21:12-14. A sympathetic chorus echoed Agabus's petition for Paul to alter his itinerary. He uses a picturesque word "breaking my heart" (*synthryptō*) which implies the pounding of clothes in the wash. Their petitions were giving him a beating. Yet they underestimated his resilience and his determination to evangelize his own countrymen. Agabus's threat of "binding" is but a minor inconvenience to one willing to die for his people, nay, for his Lord. If Paul was willing to die for the Jews (Rom 9:3), how much more would he die in solidarity with Jesus in the very city where he suffered? His friends were left speechless. All they could say was "The Lord's will be done."

21:15-16. From this point on, they prepared[8] for their final ascent to Jerusalem. The Christians of Caesarea figured, "If you can't beat 'em, join 'em." They accompanied Paul's entourage. The enthusiasm was contagious; the anticipation was palpable. Off they go to make history. Somewhere along the seventy-five mile hike, they would need to stop for the night at least once. A certain Cypriot named Mnason was gracious enough to provide hospitality for a group of at least ten men, not to mention the friends who followed from Caesarea. There had to have been dozens of these overnight stays through the years that Luke had never deemed worthy to mention. This one stuck out to Luke particularly. One suspects that it was due to the fact that Mnason was "one of the early disciples." This may have been the first time that Luke personally met someone who had encountered Jesus incarnate. This journey was Paul's homecoming and Luke's pilgrimage—both are beside themselves with excitement.

2. Paul's Arrival and Consultation with James (21:17-26)

[17]When we arrived at Jerusalem, the brothers received us warmly. [18]The next day Paul and the rest of us went to see James, and all the elders were present. [19]Paul greeted them and reported in detail what God had done among the Gentiles through his ministry.

---

[8] Ramsay, *Traveller*, 302, points out that the word "prepare" (ἐπισκευάζομαι) was often used in classical Greek to describe travel preparations that included saddling pack animals. Paul may have been afforded the luxury of a rented mule for his final ascent to Jerusalem.

COLLEGE PRESS NIV COMMENTARY

21:17-19. At last, they arrived at Jerusalem.[9] Once again, James is center stage with the Elders around him. Together they arbitrated the actions of Christians in Jerusalem, even of one as prominent as Paul. It is not, however, a time of antagonism. Quite the contrary, these verses are filled with greetings and warm reports. The church welcomes Paul with open arms. His missionary efforts and benevolent collections must have been the boast of the Jerusalem believers. Paul, for his part, brings a thrilling report of God's ever-expanding kingdom and limitless grace among the Gentiles. The glory of Israel is becoming the light to the nations.

²⁰**When they heard this, they praised God. Then they said to Paul: "You see, brother, how many thousands of Jews have believed, and all of them are zealous for the law. ²¹They have been informed that you teach all the Jews who live among the Gentiles to turn away from Moses, telling them not to circumcise their children or live according to our customs. ²²What shall we do? They will certainly hear that you have come, ²³so do what we tell you. There are four men with us who have made a vow. ²⁴Take these men, join in their purification rites and pay their expenses, so that they can have their heads shaved. Then everybody will know there is no truth in these reports about you, but that you yourself are living in obedience to the law. ²⁵As for the Gentile believers, we have written to them our decision that they should abstain from food sacrificed to idols, from blood, from the meat of strangled animals and from sexual immorality." ²⁶The next day Paul took the men and purified himself along with them. Then he went to the temple to give notice of the date when the days of purification would end and the offering would be made for each of them.**

21:20-21. James and the Elders were as happy about Paul's success as anyone else. However, as leaders, they dared not ignore this real and pressing problem. Paul's reputation preceded him. To some it was a message of liberation, grace, and God's ever-expanding glory. To others, however, it was a sign of heresy. Paul's preaching was threatening the purity of their native Judaism. If they let him continue, God's revealed religion would be diluted to an unrecognizable syncretism. There were thousands upon thousands of these legalistic Jewish Christians who were ready to take up arms against Luke's hero. And because of their penchant for defending the Law of Moses, they readily believed the anti-Pauline propaganda. There was just enough truth in the slander to make it dangerous.

It was actually reported that Paul told Jews to abandon (*apostasia*) circumcision and the other accoutrements of Jewish religion and practice. That's not far from the truth. Paul put it in black and white years earlier, "Mark my words! I, Paul, tell you that if you let yourselves be circumcised, Christ will be of no value to you at all" (Gal 5:2). He continued in Galatians 5:6, "For in Christ Jesus neither circumcision nor uncircumcision has any value. The only thing that counts

---

[9] Luke includes himself in the entourage with the word "we." He has done so six times in chapter 20 and fourteen times in chapter 21. But here in 21:17 the "we" passage ceases until 27:1 when Luke leaves with Paul for Rome.

is faith expressing itself through love." Or again, "Was a man uncircumcised when he was called? He should not be circumcised. Circumcision is nothing and uncircumcision is nothing" (1 Cor 7:18b-19, cf. Gal 6:13-15; Rom 2:25-29; 3:30; 4:9-12; Phil 3:2-3; Col 2:11; 3:11). Several things should be readily apparent. *First, these sound bites are part of a larger argument* that can hardly be viewed as abandonment of Judaism in general or the Mosaic Law in particular. Paul's heart is revealed in Romans 3:1-2a, "What advantage, then, is there in being a Jew, or what value is there in circumcision? Much in every way!" Taken out of context, however, they can make Paul look like a Jewish apostate. *Second, Paul's own actions have to shape how these isolated statements are interpreted.* He lived as a kosher Jew, attending feasts in Jerusalem (Acts 18:21 [KJV]; 19:21; 20:16, 22), taking vows (e.g., Acts 18:18), teaching from the Old Testament, and bringing much needed financial relief to the poor of his own people (e.g., Acts 11:29-30; 12:25; Rom 15:25-26; 1 Cor 16:3; cf. Gal 2:10). Furthermore, Luke recorded the story of Paul's circumcising Timothy (16:3); this is an effective apologetic against this unwarranted accusation.[10] *Third, this was hardly a new accusation.* This was precisely what was leveled against Steven (Acts 6:13-14). Paradoxically, Paul was complicit in Stephen's trial, accusing him of *changing customs.* He is now on the other side of the charge.

The accusation that Paul was changing ancestral customs was a dangerous one.[11] This is difficult for modern Westerners to appreciate. We tend to see customs as old-fashioned and limiting. That was not the perception of Jews or even Romans in the first century. As the Roman military machine marched across the Mediterranean, it took control of the political and economic affairs of the locals, but pacified them with broad self-governance over religious affairs. Consequently, the Jews held tenaciously to their ancestral customs and punished with impunity those who threatened their way of life. Though this is an oversimplification of an immensely complicated sociopolitical situation, it captures adequately the essence of the pressure James felt from the vast numbers of Messianic Jews who felt their ancestral ways were being threatened.

21:22-24. James offered a straightforward solution. Paul was directed to pay for the vow of four Pentecost pilgrims. That was a noble act of Jewish piety that would bode well for Paul.[12] This is, in all probability, a Nazirite vow.[13] If so, they had to purchase a dove, a yearling lamb, and a haircut (full shave). Of course,

[10] Cf. Richard Thompson, "'Say It Ain't So, Paul!': The Accusation against Paul in Acts 21 in Light of His Ministry in Acts 16–20," *BR* 45 (2000) 34-50, reflects on the ambiguity of this passage. Since the accusations of chapter 21 do not match the actual ministry Paul performed in chapters 16–20, the reader is drawn into the story through this narrative tension.

[11] The danger of this charge has been well documented by a survey through Josephus; cf. David L. Balch, "'. . . you teach all the Jews . . . to forsake Moses, telling them not to . . . observe the customs' (Acts 21:21; cf. 6:14," *SBLsp* 32 (1993): 369-383. The Jews were radically protective of their heritage, especially under the mounting pressure of Hellenization. And the Romans gave them generous liberties to punish violators.

[12] Agrippa I likewise paid the expenses of many Nazirites to court favor with the Jewish populace (Josephus, *Ant.* 19.6.1 §294).

[13] See comments on 18:18; Num 6:1-21; *m. Naz.* 6.6ff; as well as Friedrich Horn, "Paulus, Das Nasiräat und die Nasiräer," *NovT* 39 (1997): 117-137; and Jacob Neusner, "Vow-Taking, the Nazirites, and the Law: Does James' Advice to Paul Accord with Halakhah?" in *James the Just and Christian Origins* (Leiden: E. J. Brill, 1999), 59-82.

Paul was not participating in their vow, which would be thirty days; he was mere-ly joining them in the seven-day ritual of purification.[14] Essentially, Paul was join-ing these other four men in the standard pre-Pentecost purification rites. As pilgrims made their way to Jerusalem, they would inevitably become ritually un-clean by inadvertent contact with a grave, an idol, a ritually impure person, or a thousand other items that could render them unclean. Bottom line: Paul's pub-lic solidarity with one of the most revered Jewish institutions would go a long way to squelching the rumors that he was abandoning his heritage. This is hardly too much to expect of one who began this journey with his own vow and haircut (Acts 18:18). Some scholars have objected that the 'real' Paul would never have submitted to such a demand lest he contradict his message of salvation by grace. This objection is nonsensical. It ignores the simple fact that Paul never objected to Jews being Jews. For one to participate in his or her native culture is hardly a subversion of salvation by grace. Paul's objection was never to Judaism, per se, but to its inappropriate imposition on Gentiles as a condition of salvation.

21:25. James was *well* aware that Gentiles were not obligated to practice Ju-daism in order to be saved. He rehearsed again the decision of the Jerusalem Council (Acts 15:20, 29), liberating Gentiles from oppressive and excessive de-mands that they look and act like their Jewish brothers and sisters. This was obvi-ously a massively important decree, repeated in Acts for the third time.[15] Luke apparently does not want us to miss it!

21:26. Paul gladly capitulates. If he said, "circumcision is nothing," how much less of an imposition would he consider a mere vow? This is no problem for Paul. As he said himself, "I have become all things to all men so that by all pos-sible means I might save some" (1 Cor 9:22). He lived as a Gentile to win them. Now he has the special delight of practicing his own beloved traditions for the benefit of his own people. The details of verse 26 are as kosher as a dill pickle.

3. Paul's Arrest (21:27-36)

[27]When the seven days were nearly over, some Jews from the province of Asia saw Paul at the temple. They stirred up the whole crowd and seized him, [28]shouting, "Men of Israel, help us! This is the man who teaches all men ev-erywhere against our people and our law and this place. And besides, he has brought Greeks into the temple area and defiled this holy place." [29](They had previously seen Trophimus the Ephesian in the city with Paul and assumed that Paul had brought him into the temple area.) [30]The whole city was aroused, and the people came running from all directions. Seizing Paul, they dragged him from the temple, and immediately the gates were shut. [31]While they were trying

---

[14] Archaeologists have uncovered forty-eight ritual baths adjacent to the temple for just such purifi-cation rituals; cf. Eyal Regev, "The Ritual Baths near the Temple Mount and Extra-Purification before Entering the Temple Courts," *IEJ* 55 (2005): 194-204; and Ronny Reich, "The Great Mikveh Debate," *BAR* 19 (1993): 52-53.

[15] The Jew/Gentile controversy was a major issue in Paul's Epistles as it was in Acts. Though Paul articu-lates the issue in his own idiosyncratic terms, his epistles are consistent with the historical material in Acts; cf. Frank Stagg, "Paul's Final Mission to Jerusalem," in *With Steadfast Purpose: Essays on Acts in Honor of Henry Jackson Flanders* (ed. Naymond Keathley; Waco: Baylor University, 1990), 259-278.

to kill him, news reached the commander of the Roman troops that the whole city of Jerusalem was in an uproar. [32]He at once took some officers and soldiers and ran down to the crowd. When the rioters saw the commander and his soldiers, they stopped beating Paul. [33]The commander came up and arrested him and ordered him to be bound with two chains. Then he asked who he was and what he had done. [34]Some in the crowd shouted one thing and some another, and since the commander could not get at the truth because of the uproar, he ordered that Paul be taken into the barracks. [35] When Paul reached the steps, the violence of the mob was so great he had to be carried by the soldiers. [36]The crowd that followed kept shouting, "Away with him!"

21:27-29. Ritual purification took a week to complete. Toward the tail end of the ritual some Jews from Asia stirred up a hullabaloo. These may well be the very Jews bested by Paul in Ephesus. Alexander (cf. Acts 19:33-34) and his ilk must have had a serious grudge they would like to settle. They knew all too well Paul's penchant for Gentile inclusion *without* any imposition of Jewish ritual. He preached in one of their synagogues for three months and propagated his ideas throughout the entire region for nearly three years. They saw their opportunity in the temple and seized it.

Paul's enemies clamored for their comrades to help. The word "help" (*boētheō*) usually means "to rescue" (from danger, 2 Cor 6:2; Heb 2:18; Rev 12:16; or demons, Matt 15:25; Mark 9:22, 24). Thus, they spoke as if they were in trouble when, in fact, they were the aggressors causing trouble for Paul. They apprehended Paul (literally, "laid their hands on him") with two accusations: anti-Semitic propaganda and temple violation. The first accusations sounds a lot like what some of the Christian-Jewish legalists were saying (v. 21). Both Christian and non-Christian Jews picked up on the same themes in Paul's preaching. Paul really did say some things that his countrymen considered dangerous to the stability and perpetuation of their traditional way of life. This is hardly surprising given the oppressive weight of Hellenization in Israel from 200 B.C. up through the second century A.D. This first accusation also is of a piece with what Paul and his cohorts leveled against Stephen:

ACCUSATION AGAINST STEPHEN, 6:12-14	ACCUSATION AGAINST PAUL, 21:27b-28
So **they stirred up the people** and the elders and the teachers of the law.	**They stirred up the whole crowd**
They **seized Stephen** and brought him before the Sanhedrin.	and **seized him**
They produced false witnesses, who testified, "**This fellow never stops speaking against this holy place** and against **the law.**	shouting, "Men of Israel, help us! **This is the the man who teaches all men everywhere against** our people and our law and **this place.**
For we have heard him say that this Jesus of Nazareth will **destroy this place** and change the customs Moses handed down to us.	And besides, he has brought Greeks into the temple area and **defiled this holy place.**

Luke could hardly be more overt in comparing the persecution of Stephen, promulgated by Paul, with the predicament in which Paul now finds himself. Moreover, since Stephen's martyrdom was deliberately patterned after Jesus', the reader gets this sense: So goes Jesus, so goes Stephen, so goes Paul. The pattern of Jesus' passion in Paul's procession to Rome will continue through the end of the book.

The second accusation is that Paul brought a Gentile into the temple. That is hardly likely. Luke's explanation makes sense. Trophimus the Ephesian was recognized by the Asiatic Jews. When they saw Paul hobnobbing with a dirty ol' Gentile in the city streets during the sacred festival, they concluded from that *faux pas* that Paul actually took Trophimus into the temple. This would have been a 'felony' for Trophimus. There was a proscription inscribed in stone, warning Gentiles not to trespass the sacred precincts. Two such inscriptions have actually been found, one in 1871 (Museum of Ancient Orient in Istanbul) and another in 1935 (Palestine Archaeological Museum in Jerusalem). The first reads as follows ■:[16] "No foreigner may enter within the barricade which surrounds the temple and enclosure. Anyone who is caught doing so will have himself to blame for his ensuing death." This barricade was well-known and well-attested in antiquity (e.g., Josephus, *J.W.* 5.5.2 §193-194; *Ant.* 15.11.5 §417; Philo, *Embassy to Gaius*, 212; *m. Mid.* 2.3; *m. Kel.* 1.8; Eph 2:14). The Romans had actually permitted the Jews hegemony in their sacred space.[17] They could have brutally executed punishment on any Gentile who ignored the warning sign and set foot in the Jewish courts. The crime, of course, would not have been Paul's but Trophimus's who was nowhere to be found. If the accusation were true, where was the offending party?

This second accusation, defiling the temple, is also a deliberate parallel to Stephen's trial. It has every earmark of historical veracity; Jesus also was arrested on this very charge.[18] It is not surprising that his followers were also perceived as proponents of a prophetic critique of the temple. This caused problems since the temple was the central symbol of Israel. Any offense against its sanctity would certainly rouse the patriotic ire of the more conservative citizens (see comments on 6:12-15).

21:30-32. Suddenly a flash-mob burst into a frenzy. With pardonable hyperbole, Luke portrays the whole of Jerusalem drawn into the disturbance. The scene is violent and frenetic. Paul was dragged from the temple and the gates

[16] Cf. F. F. Bruce, *The New Testament Documents: Are they Reliable?* (Downers Grove, IL: InterVarsity, 1934, 2003), 94-101.

[17] Titus, during the siege of Jerusalem, rebuked the Jewish rebels for desecrating their own temple over which the Romans had given them control. He mentions the barrier they erected as well as the death penalty attached to trespassing beyond it (Josephus, *J.W.* 6.2.4 §124-128).

[18] Jesus predicted the temple's demise three times: before the temple cleansing (Luke 13:34-35; 19:42-44; John 2:19-20) and twice afterwards (Matt 23:37-39 and Mark 13:1-37/Matt 24:1-51/Luke 21:5-36). Jesus' critique echoes the prophets of old (e.g., Isa 1:11; 28:7; Jer 6:13; 19:1-15; 26:6; Lam 4:13; Ezek 4:1-17; 22:23-31; Hos 6:6; Micah 3:9-12; Zeph 3:1-8; Zech 14:20-21; Mal 3:1; cf. *T. Levi* 10:3; *Liv. Pro.* 10:10-11; 12:11; *T. Judah* 23:3; Josephus, *J.W.* 6.4.5 §250; *Sib. Or.* 3:337-340; *1 Enoch* 90:28-29a) as well as later rabbis and rabble rousers (cf. *Tg. Isa.* 5:5; *t. Menah* 13.22; *b. Yoma* 39b; *Lam. Rab.* 31.2). Cf. Craig A. Evans, "Predictions of the Destruction of the Herodian temple in the Pseudepigrapha, Qumran Scrolls, and Related Texts," *JSP* 10 (1992): 89-147.

were immediately shut behind him as if to protect its sacred precincts from defilement. By closing the gates behind Paul, they were saying he was a bane, banned from the temple. This action would dissuade any potential converts from following Paul.

A brutal beating commenced. It is impressive how quickly the Commander (*chiliarchos*[19]) reacted. He certainly saved Paul's life. Whatever criticisms might fairly be leveled against the Romans, dilatory military duty is *not* one of them. The troops stood at the ready in the fortress of Antonia on the northwest corner of the temple . It had towers a hundred feet high, affording a clear view of the entire temple mount, and two stairs which fed directly into the courts (*J.W.* 5.5.8 §238-247). This fortress was built by Herod the Great for the strategic protection of the temple. When the security forces heard the uproar, they raced to the scene and rescued Paul from his would-be assassins. The mob gave way at the sight of a lethal military force racing in formation to squelch the riot. The officers (lit., centurions), with their trusted troops, were a well-oiled machine, fiercely determined to keep peace in the name of Rome. The plural "centurions" suggest the presence of at least two hundred men. This is a realistic number of troops for putting down mob violence.

21:33-36. The Commander, Claudius Lysias (cf. Acts 23:26), wisely bound Paul with chains, likely to a soldier on each wrist. This effectively said to the crowd, "Paul will be dealt with legally." Though the crowd was not allowed to lynch him, neither was he going to escape the long arm of the law. In fact, the Commander began the investigation immediately: "Who is this guy and what has he done?" Various boisterous zealots immediately belch their opinion. It was chaos. They were shouting in unison but without consensus. Such is the nature of the mob. They don't have a clear purpose, a singular leader, or a reasoned reaction. The Commander was getting nowhere, so he took Paul elsewhere. Perhaps a change of venue would produce a clearer picture of what Paul did to cause this riot.

Paul was escorted back to barracks. The troops, badly outnumbered, whisked Paul away, even carrying him up the stairs. By the time they started up the stairs the crowd congealed with a single demand: "Away with him." This is nearly identical to the words of a similar crowd in this very city some twenty-five years earlier when they clamored for Jesus' execution (cf. Luke 23:18; John 19:15).

B. PAUL'S APOLOGIA (21:37–26:32)

Back in chapter nine, Jesus appeared to Ananias, commissioning him to baptize the repentant Paul. Understandably, Ananias was reticent. This guy was bad news. Jesus, looking toward Paul's future rather than to his past, revealed to Ananias how this persecutor would turn preacher: "Go! This man is my chosen instrument to carry my name before the Gentiles and their kings and before

---

[19] This word literally means "ruler of a thousand," which represents (theoretically) the actual number of troops under his control: 760 foot soldiers and 240 cavalry. The Roman term for the Commander was *tribunes militum.*

the people of Israel" (9:15). From 21:37–26:32 Luke revisits that vision showing how Jesus' prophecy was fulfilled point for point. Chapters 22–23 record Paul's testimony before "the people of Israel," chapters 24–25 tell of his trials before Gentile governors, and chapter 26 finds him before Agrippa II, the last king of Israel. These trial transcripts stress Paul's penchant for preaching the resurrection. This is the irreducible center of Christianity for him. In addition, they underscore the theme of the legal innocence of Christianity. Virtually everyone Paul stood before declared him innocent. That is most true of his trials before the Gentile governors and King Agrippa. Yet even when Paul stood before his own countrymen, he is portrayed as innocent. The angry mob of chapters 21–22 had no valid charge and the Sanhedrin (ch. 23) was divided over him.

1. To the Jews (21:37–23:35)

To the Jewish People in Jerusalem and an Escape from Flogging (21:37–22:29)

[37] As the soldiers were about to take Paul into the barracks, he asked the commander, "May I say something to you?" "Do you speak Greek?" he replied. [38] "Aren't you the Egyptian who started a revolt and led four thousand terrorists out into the desert some time ago?" [39] Paul answered, "I am a Jew, from Tarsus in Cilicia, a citizen of no ordinary city. Please let me speak to the people." [40] Having received the commander's permission, Paul stood on the steps and motioned to the crowd. When they were all silent, he said to them in Aramaic[a]:
[a] *40 Or possibly Hebrew; also in 22:2*

21:37-38. Paul saw a crowd of his own countrymen standing before him and he was eager to turn the stairstep into a pulpit. He didn't want to let this opportunity slip by even if his audience was less than sympathetic. He requested the Commander's permission to address the crowd. Claudius Lysias was somewhat surprised to learn that Paul spoke Greek. He had assumed that Paul was the Egyptian[20] rebel who, three years earlier, had lead four thousand rebels against Roman troops in Jerusalem.[21] Josephus described this Egyptian as a false prophet who led thirty thousand freedom fighters to the Mount of Olives with the promise that the walls of Jerusalem would fall at his command (*J.W.* 2.13.5 §261-263; *Ant.* 20.8.6 §167-172).[22] That didn't happen. Instead, the Roman troops

---

[20] It may seem odd than an Egyptian would fight for the liberation of Israel. However, Egypt was a haven for Jews who fled from the political and social upheaval of their homeland. Undoubtedly, the Egyptian was, in fact, a Jew in 'exile'.

[21] This brief encounter shows that *Paul is no rebel* threat to the Roman government. The word "terrorists" (v. 38) is σικάριος, a term used to describe a particularly lethal group of assassins who surreptitiously killed with a dagger those Jewish leaders complicit with Roman rule in Israel (Josephus, *J.W.* 2.13.3 §254-257; *Ant.* 20.8.5, 10 §160-166, 185-188). These *sicarii* arose during the reign of Felix, which was replete with rebel movements. They were part of the larger Zealot movement; cf. Martin Hengel, "Zeloten und Sikarier," *Die Zeloten,* zweiten Auflage (Leiden: Brill, 1976), 387-412. This passage also shows how badly *Claudius miscalculated who Paul was.* These two themes capture, in a nutshell, all the trials Paul faces through the rest of the book. Cf. Dean Béchard, "The Disputed Case against Paul: A Redaction-Critical Analysis of Acts 21:27–22:29," *CBQ* 65 (2003): 232-250.

[22] If so, it may demonstrate Luke's greater reserve compared to Josephus's exaggerated numbers: 4,000 (Luke) vs. 30,000 (Josephus). Another common proposal is that the 30k represents a scribal error, misreading Λ (= 30k) for Δ (= 4k).

attacked with a vengeance, killing four hundred Jewish patriots and capturing another two hundred. The Egyptian fled into the desert and was henceforth considered a seducer and deceiver. Claudius assumed Paul was the Egyptian who came back and got a well-deserved beating by his own countrymen.

21:29-40. Far from being an Egyptian rebel, Paul was a Jew from Tarsus. He was well-traveled, sophisticated, and noble. We don't tend to consider a person's birthplace part of his resume in the modern world. In the ancient world, however, they did. Consider how often genealogies included a person's geographic origin along with their family history. It was assumed that people inherited the dignity inherent to certain regions. Cilicia in general, and Tarsus in particular, had a reputation as a noble region that produced men of valor and intelligence.[23] This qualified Paul to speak to the crowd. Claudius capitulated. Paul raised his hand in a standard gesture of Roman oratory. The crowd fell silent. He addressed them in their native language. The NIV assumes this was Aramaic, the *lingua franca* of Ancient Israel (cf. Bruce, 437 and *Beginnings* 4:278). However, the word (*Hebrais*) would naturally be rendered "Hebrew." The NIV translators assume that Paul would have spoken to the crowd in the common tongue rather than the lesser known sacred language of Hebrew (contra RSV, NASB, ESV, KJV).[24] Obviously Paul would have been fluent in Hebrew (as well as Aramaic and Greek). The question is whether the crowd would have been able to understand what he said. Paul would have reason to speak in Hebrew rather than Aramaic—it would show that he was a kosher Jew. This would also explain why the crowd fell silent (cf. 22:2). They would have to listen carefully and concentrate heavily when Paul spoke in their second (or third) tongue.

---

[23] If Ramsay is correct, Tarsus afforded Paul Roman citizenship by birth; cf. Ramsay, *Cities*, 174-180. This detail was apparently lost on Claudius Lysias who had to be informed of Paul's citizenship.

[24] Though Aramaic was the common language of Israel at the time, Hebrew was not unknown. While Grintz probably overstates his case, he certainly has shown that Hebrew would have been understood by many; cf. J. M. Grintz, "Hebrew as the Spoken and Written Language of the Last Days of the Second Temple," *JBL* 79 (1960): 32-47.

ACTS 22

1. To the Jews (21:37–23:35 continued)

To the Jewish People in Jerusalem and an Escape
from Flogging (21:37–22:29 continued)

[1]"Brothers and fathers, listen now to my defense." [2]When they heard him speak to them in Aramaic, they became very quiet. Then Paul said: [3]"I am a Jew, born in Tarsus of Cilicia, but brought up in this city. Under Gamaliel I was thoroughly trained in the law of our fathers and was just as zealous for God as any of you are today. [4]I persecuted the followers of this Way to their death, arresting both men and women and throwing them into prison, [5]as also the high priest and all the Council can testify. I even obtained letters from them to their brothers in Damascus, and went there to bring these people as prisoners to Jerusalem to be punished."

22:1-3. Paul went out of his way to prove he was a 'True-Blue Jew'. There are four elements to his shrewd rhetorical strategy. (1) He opened with a standard respectful Jewish address: "Men—brothers and fathers, listen now to my defense" (cf. 2:29, 37; 7:2; 13:15, 26, 38; 15:7, 13; 23:1, 6; 28:17). The word "defense" is *apologia*. This is Luke's way of framing what follows as a formal trial. Though legally this was hardly a formal trial, it does, in fact, function as such in the literary structure of chapters 22–26.[1] (2) Paul chose to address the crowd in the sacred Hebrew language [see comments on 21:40]. This kosher move captured their attention. Intuitively a hush came over the crowd so they could clearly hear the language of the sages and prophets. (3) Paul began in Tarsus, a city which afforded him a noble birth. Then he moved to Jerusalem, most probably in his early teens.[2] In all likelihood, Paul's father moved the family to the sacred center so his precocious son could train under the famed rabbi Gamaliel.[3] Moreover, Paul stresses that his legal studies were in line with the Jewish Fathers. He is, therefore, not a theological deviant. His teaching extrapolates from and fulfills the ancient traditions so cherished by their nation.

---

[1] Allison Trites, "The Importance of Legal Scenes and Language in the Book of Acts," *NovT* 16 (1974): 278-284, offers a helpful and brief survey of the judicial scenes and language of Acts.

[2] The word ἀνατρέφω "grow up" usually meant early childhood development. It can, however, include rabbinic training during puberty; cf. Andrie du Toit, "A Tale of Two Cities: 'Tarsus or Jerusalem' Revisited," *NTS* 46 (2000): 375-402.

[3] Literally "at his feet." Gamaliel was a grandson of the great Hillel. Of Gamaliel the Mishnah says, "Since Rabban Gamaliel died, the glory of the Law has ceased" (*m. Sotah* 9.15). He is one of the most quoted rabbis in the Mishnah and Talmud, though much of the material attributed to him should be taken with a grain of salt. Even so, there is a strong degree of congruence between Paul's thought processes in the Epistles and the body of literature attributed to Gamaliel even if there is a paucity of verbal or even topical overlap; cf. Bruce Chilton and Jacob Neusner, "Paul and Gamaliel," in *In Quest of the Historical Pharisees* (ed. Jacob Neusner and Bruce Chilton; Waco: Baylor University Press, 2007), 175-223; and Everett Harrison, "Acts 22:3—A Test Case for Luke's Reliability," in *New Dimensions in New Testament Study* (Grand Rapids: Zondervan, 1974), 251-260.

(4) Paul's final strategy was to affirm his own religious zeal. He doesn't merely say he was zealous (NIV). The Greek word is a noun, not an adjective: "I am (exist as) a zealot for God."[4] Though the formal Zealot party cannot be identified securely prior to A.D. 66, the violent impetus behind it certainly predates Paul. Even Jesus had a man in his inner circle who could be identified as a zealot (Mark 3:18/Matt 10:4/Luke 6:15; Acts 1:13). It described a person who was willing to put teeth to their zeal in the form of violence. That was Paul (Acts 8:8; Gal 1:13-14; 1 Tim 1:13). As Paul notes, this is an apt description of the present crowd (v. 3b). In short, Paul was saying, "I can relate to you people."

22:4-5. Not only could Paul relate to his persecutors, he could 'out-zeal' them (cf. Rom 10:2). He had killed Christians in Jerusalem and then chased them down to Damascus—both men and women! He obtained letters of extraditions some twenty years earlier to which the High Priest and Council could presently testify [see comments on 9:1-3]. Some of those who were now elders had been Paul's contemporaries, fellow rabbinic students outstripped by his zeal. They may disagree with Paul's conversion but they cannot deny that he used to be one of them.

[6]"About noon as I came near Damascus, suddenly a bright light from heaven flashed around me. [7]I fell to the ground and heard a voice say to me, 'Saul! Saul! Why do you persecute me?' [8]'Who are you, Lord?' I asked. 'I am Jesus of Nazareth, whom you are persecuting,' he replied. [9]My companions saw the light, but they did not understand the voice of him who was speaking to me. [10]'What shall I do, Lord?' I asked. 'Get up,' the Lord said, 'and go into Damascus. There you will be told all that you have been assigned to do.' [11]My companions led me by the hand into Damascus, because the brilliance of the light had blinded me."

22:6-11. [See comments on 9:1-9.] This is the second of three accounts of Paul's conversion.[5] There are differences in emphasis and wording between the three accounts as well as with Paul's own autobiographical descriptions (Gal 1:13-15; 1 Cor 9:1; 15:8; 2 Cor 11:32-33; Phil 3:4-6; 1 Tim 1:12-16). This is to be expected. Even so, there is nothing inconsistent between Luke's renditions of Paul's conversions and Paul's own autobiographical descriptions.[6] Furthermore, these three accounts should be read in conjunction with one another rather than in opposition to each other. Thus read, the *differences* between Acts 9, 22, and 26, are not problems to be solved but keys to identifying Luke's development of the story throughout his work. In the first account, Paul was portrayed

---

[4] This is quite a strong and specific statement in Greek: ζηλωτὴς ὑπάρχων τοῦ θεοῦ. This is Paul's own self-designation in Gal 1:14 (cf. Num 25:13; Rom 10:2; Epictetus, *Disc.* 2.14.13); cf. Mark Fairchild, "Paul's Pre-Christian Zealot Associations: A Re-Examination of Gal 1.14 and Acts 22.3," *NTS* 45 (1999): 514-532.

[5] Literarily this repetition has at least two important effects according to Marie-Eloise Rosenblatt, "Recurrent Narration as a Lukan Literary Convention in Acts: Paul's Jerusalem Speech in Acts 22:1-22," in *New Views on Luke and Acts* (ed. Earl Richard; Collegeville, MN: The Liturgical Press, 1990), 94-105. First, it forces the reader to flash back in the narrative which effectively slows the forward progress creating a sort of "narrative hologram" (104) of Paul's conversion. Second, it extends this story through the whole of Acts emphasizing Gentile mission as a unifying theme of the whole book.

[6] Cf. Manfred Diefenbach, "Das 'Sehen des Herrn' vor Damaskus: Semantischer Zugang zu Apg 9, 22 und 26," *NTS* 52 (2006): 409-418.

as a converted persecutor (9:1-19), in the second (22:3-16) Luke stresses Paul's genuine Jewish heritage, and in the third (26:12-18) Paul will defend the legality of the Christian mission.[7]

The only important difference between the first two accounts is whether Paul's companions heard the heavenly voice (9:7 vs. 22:9). As was concluded in 9:7 [see comments there], Luke says they didn't hear the voice in the first account whereas they *did* hear the voice in this second account. Though *grammatically* that is a contradiction, *thematically* it is a subtle maneuver to pull the *witnesses* from the shadows closer to the center of the stage in the second account. In other words, Paul the persecutor needs no witnesses in chapter 9 and thus had no audience. In chapter 22, however, Paul the preacher has witnesses who can authenticate his conversion. In short, the point of the "voice" is not whether or not they heard it, but to what extent they participated in the action. Chapter 9 sidelines them for ideological effect whereas chapter 22 brings them forward to help paint a progressing portrait of Paul's conversion.[8]

There are two other bits of data only found in this account:[9] Nazareth (v. 8) and "What shall I do?" (v. 10a). Both fit the portrait of a native Jew who knew the local geography and one who was sufficiently pious to ask the voice from heaven to direct his consequent response. All in all, the texts tell of a zealous Jew who piously responded to a theophany.

[12]"A man named Ananias came to see me. He was a devout observer of the law and highly respected by all the Jews living there. [13]He stood beside me and said, 'Brother Saul, receive your sight!' And at that very moment I was able to see him. [14]Then he said: 'The God of our fathers has chosen you to know his will and to see the Righteous One and to hear words from his mouth. [15]You will be his witness to all men of what you have seen and heard. [16]And now what are you waiting for? Get up, be baptized and wash your sins away, calling on his name.'"

22:12-13. [See comments on 9:10-19]. Luke's earlier rendition of Ananias is quite a bit longer than this one.[10] That makes sense since this current account is from Paul's perspective. He tells of his own experience rather than Ananias's vision (9:10-16). What Paul added here is a description of Ananias: "He was a devout observer of the law and highly respected by all the Jews living there"

---

[7] Cf. Ronald D. Witherupp, "Functional Redundancy in the Acts of the Apostles: A Case Study," *JSNT* 48 (1992): 67-86.

[8] The later detail about "hearing/not hearing" is not a blunder but a rhetorical variation deliberately used to push the Narrative forward. Cf. Daniel Marguerat, "Saul's Conversion (Acts 9, 22, 26): and the Multiplication of Narrative in Acts," in *Luke's Literary Achievement*, JSNTss 116 (ed. C. M. Tuckett; Sheffield: Sheffield Academic Press, 1995), 127-155. More specifically, "hearing" and "seeing" are common elements in theophanies which indicate an individual was part of the action. To say these traveling companions of Paul did not hear the voice simply means they were not involved substantively in the theophany; cf. Marvin W. Meyer, "The Light and Voice on the Damascus Road," *Forum* 2 (1986): 27-35.

[9] The new datum that it was noon (περὶ μεσημβρίαν, v. 6) is repeated in 26:13 in a slightly different form (ἡμέρας μέσης). It adds little to the narrative, except to highlight how bright the heavenly light must have been to overshadow the noonday sun, a point stressed by Luke in v. 6 "a bright light (φῶς ἱκανὸν) from heaven flashed (περιαστράπτω) around me" and v. 11 "the brilliance (δόξα) of the light had blinded me."

[10] According to Kathy R. Maxwell, "The Role of the Audience in Ancient Narrative: Acts as a Case Study," *RQ* 48 (2006): 171-180, the reader is expected to fill in the missing details from their previous knowledge.

(v. 12). This was important to Paul existentially. It was also important to Luke thematically. Remember, this second conversion account is designed to stress Paul's genuine Jewish heritage. That Ananias was a devout law-abiding Jew, respected in Antioch, bodes well for the validity of Paul's 'conversion'. In other words, he was not seduced by a heretic to denounce Judaism. Rather he was led by an orthodox adherent to fulfill his faith by pledging allegiance to the nation's Messiah.

22:14-15. These verses also offer something entirely new to the account though they will be expanded further in 26:17-18. Once again, they highlight the orthodox validity of Paul's conversion. Their ancestral God selected Paul to be his witness. Notice the emphasis on Jesus ("the Righteous One") and the Gentiles ("witness to all men") is muted. Paul is articulating his testimony in the most palatable terms possible.

22:16. The detail of Paul's baptism is also expanded from 9:18b that simply says, "He got up and was baptized." Here the verb tense suggests that Paul was actively involved in the action (aorist, middle, *active*, imperative). Normally, one thinks of a convert "being baptized" (*passive*). But in this text Ananias orders Paul to baptize himself. This does not mean that he dunked himself as Ananias watched. Rather, it implies that Paul caused himself to be baptized by submitting to Ananias's instructions.[11] (Since Ananias had just restored his sight, Paul would be prone to be agreeable!). One might render it: "Get yourself baptized" (Bruce, 442). Three other observations stick out in this little verse. First, there is urgency in the command: "What are you waiting for?" Second, baptism is connected to forgiveness of sins "wash your sins away." Third, it is an enacted prayer of repentance, "calling on his name." Ananias, Paul, and Luke seem to share the opinion that baptism is an integral and immediate element of conversion.

[17]"When I returned to Jerusalem and was praying at the temple, I fell into a trance [18]and saw the Lord speaking. 'Quick!' he said to me. 'Leave Jerusalem immediately, because they will not accept your testimony about me.' [19]'Lord,' I replied, 'these men know that I went from one synagogue to another to imprison and beat those who believe in you. [20]And when the blood of your martyr[a] Stephen was shed, I stood there giving my approval and guarding the clothes of those who were killing him.' [21]Then the Lord said to me, 'Go; I will send you far away to the Gentiles.'"

[a]*20 Or witness*

22:17-21. In Galatians 1:18, Paul says, "Then after three years, I went up to Jerusalem to get acquainted with Peter and stayed with him fifteen days." Thus he identified a three-year hiatus between his conversion and his return to his boyhood home. Clearly he wanted to stay in Jerusalem longer but was forced out in just two weeks. It didn't take long for Paul to cause a ruckus. We read earlier that, "He talked and debated with the Grecian Jews but they tried to kill him. When the brothers learned of this, they took him down to Caesarea and

---

[11] For the most detailed examination of the grammatical and exegetical issues involved with this sentence, see Stanley Porter, "Did Paul Baptize Himself? A Problem of the Greek Voice System," in *Dimensions of Baptism: Biblical and Theological Studies* (London: Sheffield, 2002), 91-109.

sent him off to Tarsus" (9:29-30). In spite of fierce antagonism, Paul was still absolutely confident in his ability to sway his fellow Grecian Jews. It was totally unrealistic, and Jesus told him so during a trance (*ekstasis*, cf. 10:10; 11:5). Paul, in one of the bolder self-assessments in Scripture, argued with Jesus that his past as a persecutor, particularly Stephen's murderer, would persuade those of the same zealot spirit to transfer their allegiance to Jesus. The Lord refused to argue with him. He simply reiterated the command to leave Jerusalem, and he redirected Paul's focus from his fellow Jews to those Gentiles for whom Paul formerly had so much disdain.

There is an interesting fact presented in verse 20: Paul held the cloaks at Stephen's stoning.[12] Unfortunately, there is no other historical data which allows us to interpret the sociological implications of holding cloaks at a stoning. It could mean that he was supervising the execution, or it could simply mean that he was cheering from the sidelines. It may be that he was not one of the witnesses at the trial, hence did not have the legal authority to participate in the execution. It at least means that Paul approved to such an extent that this action could be referenced later with the Jews as a sign of his zeal against Christians.

[22]The crowd listened to Paul until he said this. Then they raised their voices and shouted, "Rid the earth of him! He's not fit to live!" [23]As they were shouting and throwing off their cloaks and flinging dust into the air, [24]the commander ordered Paul to be taken into the barracks. He directed that he be flogged and questioned in order to find out why the people were shouting at him like this. [25]As they stretched him out to flog him, Paul said to the centurion standing there, "Is it legal for you to flog a Roman citizen who hasn't even been found guilty?" [26]When the centurion heard this, he went to the commander and reported it. "What are you going to do?" he asked. "This man is a Roman citizen." [27]The commander went to Paul and asked, "Tell me, are you a Roman citizen?" "Yes, I am," he answered. [28]Then the commander said, "I had to pay a big price for my citizenship." "But I was born a citizen," Paul replied. [29]Those who were about to question him withdrew immediately. The commander himself was alarmed when he realized that he had put Paul, a Roman citizen, in chains.

22:22-26. The mention of Gentiles sent the crowd into a frenzy . . . yet again. It was a spectacle. They shouted to the heavens, disrobed, and threw dust into the air. Most probably they were shaking the dust out of their garments as a sign of protest, like Paul did with his sandals in 13:51 (cf. Luke 9:5/Mark 6:11/Matt 10:14; Luke 10:11; Acts 18:6; 22:22-23; Str-B 1:571). It was a visual symbolic act to say, "Even your dust defiles us." It may not appear to make much sense, but it clearly communicated their anger in the moment. They are seething, and could they, they would tear Paul limb from limb. The Commander was no fool; it is time to get Paul out of sight. It rested on his shoulders to keep the tenuous peace in Jerusalem, and he finds himself on the razor's edge of a revolt. Yet he

---

[12] Stephen is identified as a *martyr*. This is the first instance where this word implies one who died for their testimony rather than just giving it. This definition of *martyr* would soon become common parlance (e.g., Rev 1:5; 2:13; 3:14).

still has no clue what Paul has done to earn their ire. He was determined to find out, this time with a corporeal inquiry.

Flogging was one of the more vicious inventions of humanity. It involved a series of leather thongs attached to a sturdy handle. Sometimes the thongs were merely knotted to create welts; at other times there were sharp objects embedded into the strands such as bone, glass, or metal shards. These were raked across the victim's naked body as he was tied taut to a pillar or hung by a ring from a wall. Often men were blinded as the jagged shards wrapped around their heads and gouged out their eyes. It was common for vertebrae and intestines to be exposed. In more brutal beatings, survival was less than fifty percent. The pain of this punishment would exceed anything Paul had heretofore experienced save the stoning at Lystra.

Now it may seem a horrid thing to us to beat a criminal *in order to discover his crime.* However, in many parts of the modern world, corporeal interrogation is still used under the assumption that one is more likely to tell the truth under torture.

As his hands were being bound and his body stretched for beating, Paul asked the centurion if it was legal to flog a Roman citizen prior to trial.[13] The answer was obviously and emphatically, "NO!" There were specific laws prohibiting the binding (*Lex Porcia*) and beating (*Lex Valeria*) of a Roman citizen without due process of trial. Cicero said, "To bind a Roman citizen is a crime, to flog him is an abomination, to slay him is almost an act of murder," (*Against Verres* 2.5.66). The Commander had made a serious miscalculation of Paul (again!). He never considered the possibility that this man might be a Roman citizen. The centurion was shaken, rightly so, for military personnel could receive the punishment they inappropriately inflicted on others. He made a mad dash for Claudius to inform him of the hazard they were running.

22:27-29. The Commander came to question Paul personally: "Are you a Roman citizen?" (v. 27). Paul affirmed emphatically that he was. Just how that would be proved is a bit of a mystery.[14] However, that it could be confirmed is beyond dispute, and that a false claim would incur brutal retaliation is indubitable.

---

[13] Throughout chapters 22–28 Paul proves resourceful in leveraging legal rights and privileges for the proclamation of the gospel. He claims his Roman citizenship here and appeals to Caesar in 25:8-12. He shrewdly divides the Sanhedrin who otherwise would likely have condemned him (23:6-10) and craftily discloses the assassination plot to Claudius (23:12-19). He builds a relationship with Felix (24) and the Centurion (27-28). And he manages his trials so that each of the Roman rulers (23-25), as well as Herod (26), proclaims his innocence. Cf. Robert Linthicum, "The Apostle Paul's Acts of Power," in *Mission in Acts: Ancient Narratives in Contemporary Context* (ed. Robert Gallagher and Paul Hertig; Maryknoll: Orbis, 2004), 297-312.

[14] For a discussion on the process see A. N. Sherwin-White, *Roman Society and Roman Law* (Oxford: Clarendon, 1963), 144-171; and Witherington, 679-684. There is evidence of wooden placards recording citizenship, normally protected by the family, but these could potentially be carried by a traveler. There were few Jews who had obtained citizenship. This explains why neither the magistrates at Philippi nor Claudius stopped to consider whether Paul was a Roman citizen. Wolfgang Stegemann, "War der Apostel Paulus ein römischer Bürger?" *ZNW* 78 (1987): 200-229, doubts that Paul was a Roman citizen because of the "infinitesimally" small percentage of Jews who acquired citizenship compounded with the fact that Paul's letters show virtually no evidence of his citizenship. However, to posit that Luke gratuitously created the citizenship of Paul (not to mention that of Silas) at three places (16:37-38; 22:25-29; 23:27; cf. 25:10-12; 26:32; 28:17-19) is unwarranted skepticism, particularly in light of the real historic possibility of citizenship acquisition. Furthermore, if Paul was not a Roman citizen, then the entire narrative of his appeal to Caesar is a ruse which would be difficult to promulgate amidst a church that knew well the contours of Paul's personally history.

Claudius took him at his word. However, he wanted to know what *quality* of citizenship Paul had. Claudius himself had paid a pretty penny for his citizenship (v. 28). Under the reign of Emperor Claudius, citizenship was being sold for less and less, not only by the Emperor, but by his wife, Messalina (Dio Cassius, 60.17.5-6). Some suspect the proceeds of her sales funded her rampant liaisons. Though it can't be proved, one suspects that this Claudius Lysias bribed Messalina for citizenship and was granted a new Roman name.[15] Paradoxically, he was named Claudius, after the Emperor against whom Messalina was cheating! Ah, the twisted irony of Roman nobility. At first, the price of citizenship was very high, but later in the reign of Claudius it got cheaper and cheaper. This may be what Lysias referred to when he charged Paul: "You must have just recently gotten your citizenship with little expense."

In contrast to Claudius, however, Paul was actually *born* a citizen. It could be that all the citizens of Tarsus received citizenship in 171 B.C. when the city received its constitution as a Greek city (Ramsay, *Cities*, 185). Or it could be that Paul's father or grandfather was granted citizenship due to a particularly valuable contribution to Antony or Pompey in their conquest of the region (c. 42–40 B.C.). However, these are mere guesses. Regardless of how Paul obtained citizenship, he was fully and irrefutably Roman. Claudius dared not touch him. The 'inquisitors' withdrew immediately, Claudius was disconcerted, and Paul had a newfound clout in the barracks. He'll not be mishandled again under the Commander. This left Claudius with two problems. First, he had strung up a Roman without trial, for which he could be punished. Second, he still had no clue what Paul had done. His interrogation amidst the crowd created chaos; Paul's speech drew dust rather than shedding light; and his attempted corporeal interrogation was a fiasco. Perhaps a civil inquiry among the Sanhedrin would provide a more dispassionate setting for a formal inquiry . . . or perhaps not.[16]

---

[15] *Lysias* was a Greek name, likely given to him at birth. *Claudius*, of course, is Latin, the likely cognomen assigned to him upon receiving citizenship.

[16] Throughout this section, the Roman authorities never are able to come up with a valid charge against Paul (cf. 22:30; 23:28-29; 24:22; 25:20, 26-27).

ACTS 23

1. To the Jews (21:37–23:35 continued)

To the Jewish Leaders and an Escape from an Assassination Plot (22:30–23:35)

²²:³⁰The next day, since the commander wanted to find out exactly why Paul was being accused by the Jews, he released him and ordered the chief priests and all the Sanhedrin to assemble. Then he brought Paul and had him stand before them. ²³:¹Paul looked straight at the Sanhedrin and said, "My brothers, I have fulfilled my duty to God in all good conscience to this day." ²At this the high priest Ananias ordered those standing near Paul to strike him on the mouth. ³Then Paul said to him, "God will strike you, you whitewashed wall! You sit there to judge me according to the law, yet you yourself violate the law by commanding that I be struck!" ⁴Those who were standing near Paul said, "You dare to insult God's high priest?" ⁵Paul replied, "Brothers, I did not realize that he was the high priest; for it is written: 'Do not speak evil about the ruler of your people.'ᵃ"

ᵃ5 Exodus 22:28

22:30. After three attempts, the Commander had yet to discover Paul's crime. So he convened the Sanhedrin. There is some doubt as to just how much authority Claudius held over the Sanhedrin. Even so, the Sanhedrin would likely welcome the opportunity to investigate Paul in the Commander's presence so as to persuade him to punish their nemesis. This meeting was probably held at the Tower of Antonia rather than the Hall of Gazith where the Sanhedrin normally met. In other words, it's on Claudius's turf and terms.

23:1. The seventy members of the Sanhedrin typically sat in three concentric semicircles (the most powerful in the center) with the defendant standing before them (*m. Sanh.* 4.3).[1] Paul had every right to be intimidated. However, like Peter and John before him, he preached with power (cf. 4:8-13). He stared hard at his accusers[2] and boldly claimed to have lived his life in all good conscience (cf. 24:16; Phil 3:6). Now there's a theological thunderbolt! The Sanhedrin would hardly view this claim as conciliatory. If Paul was on trial before them, they had good reason to believe he was culpable. With this audacious denial Paul established a confrontational tone for the trial. Not only that, one wonders how he could claim a clean conscience given his own confession of being the worst of sinners (1 Tim 1:13, 15b; cf. Acts 22:4; 26:10; 1 Cor 15:9; Gal

---

[1] Every major Jewish city had its own Sanhedrin with at least twenty-three judges (*m. Sanh.* 1.1). The Sanhedrin of Jerusalem had seventy judges plus the high priest (*m. Sanh.* 1.6). This high court morphed into its second-temple configuration in the second century B.C., but its roots went back to Moses' seventy elders (Num 11:16, 24-25).

[2] This word ἀτενίζω means to stare or gaze intently. Paul uses it twice (2 Cor 3:7, 13) and the remainder of its 14 NT uses are Lucan (Luke 4:20; 22:56; Acts 1:10; 3:4, 12; 6:15; 7:55; 10:4; 11:6; 13:9; 14:9).

1:13, 22-23). Two things should be observed. First, the word translated "fulfilled my duty" (*politeuomai*) has particular reference to one's public duties.[3] Paul was not claiming he never sinned. Rather, he claimed to have admirably carried out his public affairs consistently with what he thought was most honoring to God. Even his persecutions of the church were his attempt to serve the greater good of Yahweh's rule in this world. A second thing to bear in mind is that one's conscience can be terribly misguided (e.g., Rom 2:14-16). Paul now knows how wrong were his murderous designs, but it took an appearance of Jesus to correct his thinking.

23:3-5. Paul's bold claim to innocence was a slap in the face to the Sanhedrin. The high priest Ananias retaliated.[4] At his order Paul got popped by the Sergeant at Arms. Once again, we hear echoes of Jesus' trial when he was subjected to the same indignity (John 18:22) though the Lord bore it in silence (1 Pet 2:23). It's not a knockout punch but a disciplinary slap to put him in his place. Even so, it was rather inhospitable. More importantly it was illegal! The spittin' match is well underway. It's Paul's volley and he lobs an impertinent retort right in the lap of the high priest, "God will strike you, you whitewashed wall!" To us that may sound silly—"you cracked wall covered with plaster" (cf. Ezek 13:10-15; 22:28; cf. Job 13:4; Matt 23:27). In Paul's day, however, *them's fightin' words.* Paul was correct (though not politically correct); the high priest did *not* have the right to slap a defendant. Of course, that was a minor peccadillo compared to Ananias's more vicious crimes during his eleven or twelve years in office (A.D. 47–c. 59).[5] Then again, Paul does not have the right to revile the high priest . . . at least that was the opinion of his fellow Sanhedrinites.

23:5. Paul backed off, even quoting Exodus 22:28 against himself.[6] Did Paul just apologize? That seems to be the most straightforward reading. Even a corrupt ruler deserves honor in God's economy. It is not ours to retaliate; only God is capable and just to punish those who mismanage the stewardship he invests

---

[3] The verbal form of this word is only found elsewhere at Phil 1:27, ". . . *conduct yourselves* in a manner worthy of the gospel of Christ." This was directed to citizens of a Roman colony; they certainly understood the implication of public behavior as a mechanism of representing and glorifying a kingdom. The word itself has at its roots in "politics" (πολιτεύομαι; cf. 2 Macc 11:25). The noun form of the word is found only at Phil. 3:20 and is translated "citizenship." Cf. Raymond Brewer, "The Meaning of *Politeuesthe* in Philippians 1:27," *JBL* 73 (1954): 76-83.

[4] Divine justice will follow closely on his heels. In A.D. 66 Ananias was assassinated by the Zealot party who paradoxically represented the antithesis to Paul's doctrine (Josephus, *J.W.* 2.17.9 §441). Little did he know that Paul was not his worst threat.

[5] What makes his longevity so impressive is that there were twenty-eight high priests between A.D. 37–70 He survived by rapacity, greed, power, and violence. Josephus describes how his servants beat other priests and stole their portion of the tithes (*Ant.* 20.9.2 §204-207). The Talmud (*b. Pesachim* 57a) lampooned him with a variation on Psalm 24: "The temple court cried out, 'Lift up your heads, O ye gates'; and let Yochanan [Hebrew for Hananiah or Ananias] the son of Narbai, the disciple of Pinqai [="meat dish"—a word play off Phinehas indicating his avarice in stealing meat tithes of other priests] enter and fill his stomach with the divine sacrifices." As an interesting aside, his name may have been etched on an ostracon found at Masada (Mas no. 461): "A[nani]as the high priest, 'Aqaia his son"; cf. Y. Yadin, J. Naveh, and Y. Meshorer, *Masada I: The Yigael Yadin Excavations 1963–1965 Final Reports. The Aramaic and Hebrew Ostraca and Jar Inscriptions/The Coins of Masada* (Jerusalem: Israel Exploration Society, 1989), 37 & pl. 30.

[6] Paul's citation is straight from the LXX (with a minor transposition of the words ἐρεῖς and κακῶς). Both Paul and the LXX make "ruler" singular while the MT intends a more broad application of the principle to all rulers. Cf. Gert J. Steyn, *Septuagint Quotations in the Context of the Petrine and Pauline Speeches of the Acta Apostolorum* (Netherlands: Kok Pharos Publishing House, 1995), 203-212.

in them. Some have defended Paul, suggesting that he would not have known Ananias was the high priest. A rushed assembly, an altered seating arrangement, and Paul's poor eyesight could combine to blind him to Ananias's identity. Paul had been away from Jerusalem for the entirety of Ananias's tenure in office, and there were frequent changes in high priests. Even so, Ananias clearly acts as the high priest in ordering the guard to slap Paul. Hence, it is unlikely that Paul is unaware of his position. Another possibility is that Paul is using irony: "Oh, I didn't know the high priest acted like that!" He may have even been subtly accusing Ananias of usurping the role. None of these theories, however, are as likely as a straightforward reading wherein Paul apologizes for his impetuous (though ultimately correct) slander of the high priest.

⁶**Then Paul, knowing that some of them were Sadducees and the others Pharisees, called out in the Sanhedrin, "My brothers, I am a Pharisee, the son of a Pharisee. I stand on trial because of my hope in the resurrection of the dead." ⁷When he said this, a dispute broke out between the Pharisees and the Sadducees, and the assembly was divided. ⁸(The Sadducees say that there is no resurrection, and that there are neither angels nor spirits, but the Pharisees acknowledge them all.) ⁹There was a great uproar, and some of the teachers of the law who were Pharisees stood up and argued vigorously. "We find nothing wrong with this man," they said. "What if a spirit or an angel has spoken to him?" ¹⁰The dispute became so violent that the commander was afraid Paul would be torn to pieces by them. He ordered the troops to go down and take him away from them by force and bring him into the barracks. ¹¹The following night the Lord stood near Paul and said, "Take courage! As you have testified about me in Jerusalem, so you must also testify in Rome."**

23:6-7. Civility degenerated to a dangerous degree. It was obvious that Paul was not going to get a fair trial. So, he shrewdly adopted a divide-and-conquer strategy.[7] If he could get them to fight amongst themselves they would be unable to articulate a unified accusation for Lysias. He lobs a theological grenade right in the middle of the Sanhedrin. Knowing what a hot button the resurrection was, Paul made a beeline for it. Some have accused him of blatant subversion. That's not quite fair. Though he is on trial for temple violation (an unfounded, bogus charge), the real issue really is the resurrection. This, according to Paul, was Israel's hope (cf. 24:15; 26:6-7; 28:20), not merely life after death, but a national resurrection. The *apology* Paul gave on the stairs of Antonia the day before, was testimony to the resurrection of Jesus, the proleptic promise of the nation's destiny.[8] Paul was *not* 'skirting the issue'. He was boring down on the

---

[7] The last word of v. 7 "divided" (σχίσμα) testifies to the effectiveness of Paul's strategy. This word most often describes the rending of a cloth (Mark 15:38/Matt 27:51/Luke 23:45; Luke 5:36; John 19:24) or a net (John 21:11), and figuratively of the sky as if it were a curtain (Mark 1:10). It's a word one can almost hear. Luke uses it twice in Acts, both times to describe the dissection of an audience due to Paul's divisive preaching (Acts 14:4; 23:7)

[8] This theory was happily introduced to me by Klaus Haacker, "Das Bekenntnis des Paulus zur Hoffnung Israels nach der Apostelgeschichte des Lukas," *NTS* 31 (1985): 437-451; cf. Anton Deutschmann, "Die Hoffnung Israels (Apg 28,20)," *BN* 105 (2000): 54-60.

deeper issue and the core of Christianity. That it conveniently divided his accusers is a bonus.

Paul courts the favor of the more conservative side of the Sanhedrin claiming affinity with them: "I am a Pharisee, the son of a Pharisee." He similarly boasted to the Philippians (3:4b-5), "If anyone else thinks he has reasons to put confidence in the flesh, I have more: circumcised on the eighth day, of the people of Israel, of the tribe of Benjamin, a Hebrew of Hebrews; in regard to the law, a Pharisee. . . ." The Pharisees were staunch advocates of the bodily resurrection at the end of the age. The Sadducees denied it (cf. Josephus, *J.W.* 2.8.14 §164-165; *Ant.* 18.1.4 §16). The architects of the Mishnah (*Sanh.* 10.1) subtly alluded to their extinct adversaries when they said, "And these are the ones who have no portion in the world to come: He who says, the resurrection of the dead is a teaching which does not derive from the Torah. . . ." Even Jesus was drawn into this debate (Mark 12:18-27/Matt 22:23-33/Luke 20:27-40).

23:8. There is no question that the Sadducees denied the resurrection. However, there is no evidence that they ever denied angels or spirits. How could they if they believed in the Pentateuch that is populated with both? The English translation misleads the reader and frankly makes Luke blunder. The Sadducees did not deny the existence of angels or spirits. What they denied was that a human being could attain a postmortem existence as either one. Perhaps it could be understood this way: "The Sadducees say that there is neither resurrection (in a body) nor a postmortem existence either as an angel or as a spirit." This suggestion is confirmed by the last word of the sentence (*amphotera*). Nearly every major translation renders this word "all" in this passage, though its primary meaning is "both." The Sadducees denied both eschatological bodily resurrection *and* an interim postmortem existence as either a spirit or angel.[9] That's why Paul's claim that Jesus appeared to him was rejected out of hand by the Sadducees.

23:9-11. Paul's strategy worked. The Pharisees suddenly come out of the woodwork to defend one of their own. Verse 9 likely refers back to Paul's testimony on the stairs the day before. He claimed that Jesus appeared to him on the road to Damascus. Though the Pharisees were hardly prepared to admit Jesus was Lord or that he rose in bodily form, they wonder if perhaps his departed spirit appeared to Paul in some form.

That's when the meeting degenerated into fisticuffs. The two parties were playing tug-o'-war with the Apostle, and the Commander feared for Paul's life. Once again Claudius dispatched his soldiers to rescue Paul from a savage death. The Commander wasn't the only one to intervene. Just when things looked hopeless, Jesus appeared to Paul that night (likely in a dream). He promised

---

[9] David Daube, "On Acts 23: Sadducees and Angels," *JBL* 109 (1990): 493-497, points out the goodly number of texts from the second temple milieu that speak of departed humans as spirits or angelic figures in the interim before the final bodily resurrection (1 Sam 28:7-19; Mark 12:25/Matt 22:30/Luke 20:36; Acts 12:15; Luke 24:36-43; *1 En.* 45:4-5; *2 Bar.* 51.5, 10-12; *b. Sabb.* 152b; cf. Str-B 2.707). Though the matter is hardly this simple. As Floyd Parker points out, resurrection for the Jews meant both an eschatological and corporeal experience, neither fit the context of present angelic/spiritual apparitions to Paul; cf. "The Terms 'Angel' and 'Spirit' in Acts 23,8," *Bib* 84 (2003): 344-365. Hence, it is not merely that they reject resurrection *as* angel or spirit, but that they reject both resurrection *and* interim existence of human souls.

the Apostle that he would reach his dream destination of Rome.[10] Undoubt-edly Paul would replay that message a thousand times over the next two years. His imprisonment looked like an impossible situation; Jesus' pledge surely sustained our beleaguered hero.

[12]The next morning the Jews formed a conspiracy and bound themselves with an oath not to eat or drink until they had killed Paul. [13]More than forty men were involved in this plot. [14]They went to the chief priests and elders and said, "We have taken a solemn oath not to eat anything until we have killed Paul. [15]Now then, you and the Sanhedrin petition the commander to bring him before you on the pretext of wanting more accurate information about his case. We are ready to kill him before he gets here." [16]But when the son of Paul's sister heard of this plot, he went into the barracks and told Paul. [17]Then Paul called one of the centurions and said, "Take this young man to the commander; he has something to tell him." [18]So he took him to the commander. The centurion said, "Paul, the prisoner, sent for me and asked me to bring this young man to you because he has something to tell you." [19]The commander took the young man by the hand, drew him aside and asked, "What is it you want to tell me?" [20]He said: "The Jews have agreed to ask you to bring Paul before the Sanhedrin tomorrow on the pretext of wanting more accurate information about him. [21]Don't give in to them, because more than forty of them are waiting in ambush for him. They have taken an oath not to eat or drink until they have killed him. They are ready now, waiting for your consent to their request." [22]The commander dismissed the young man and cautioned him, "Don't tell anyone that you have reported this to me."

23:12-15. Forty Jews pledged on oath to assassinate Paul. This was more than a simple oath. They called a curse on themselves or literally *anathematized themselves* should they fail to kill Paul. Plots against Paul were nothing new (Acts 9:23-24, 29; 13:50; 14:5, 19; 16:19-20; 17:5; 20:3, 19; 21:27-32; 22:22; 23:12, 30; 25:2). However, this was a particularly nefarious scheme in that it was a *bona fide* suicide mission.[11] They were ready to fast from all food and drink until they had accomplished their mission.

They asked the Chief Priest for assistance, and offered him plausible deniability. All he had to do was request a meeting on behalf of the Sanhedrin, this time on their turf. It may be that the previous meeting was held at a place designated by Lysias, after all, he called the meeting. If that was the case, then Ananias could claim that a meeting *he* called would have very different results since it would take place under Jewish jurisdiction. That would be a hard sell for Claudius given Ananias's track record. Nonetheless, it was worth a try. If Claudius capitulates, the assassins could station themselves on a crowded narrow street ◖ where the entourage had to pass en route to the Hall of Gazith where the Sanhedrin normally met. At a given signal, assassins would pour forth

---

[10] The first word on Jesus' lips, "Take courage" (θαρσέω) is almost exclusively from his lips in the NT (Matt 9:2, 22; 14:27 [/Mark 6:50]; John 16:33). The only exception is Mark 10:49 when the crowd told the blind man to take courage *because Jesus called for him.* θαρσέω, therefore, sounds like the verbiage of Jesus.

[11] The Western text makes this overt by adding to the end of v. 15, "even if we ourselves should die for it."

from the houses and shops, even diving out two-story windows, breaking apart the center of the Roman protection detail and hacking Paul to death with daggers or swords. Undoubtedly most of the assassins would die in the foray, but there's no way the troops could stop all of them in such a surprise attack. They were willing to make widows of their wives and orphans of their children for the satisfaction of ridding Israel of this baneful apostate. Though the names have changed, the Middle East has not.

Since the assassins never had the chance to attack Paul, did they die of starvation in keeping their oath? The answer is simple: No. According to Jewish law, life trumps all other laws, especially impetuous vows that could not be accomplished (cf. *m. Ned.* 3.1-3). As soon as Lysias whisked Paul away to Caesarea the assassins would be released from their vow of fasting. They would not, however, lose their thirst for Paul's blood.

23:16-18. Paul's nephew foiled the plot. This raises several questions. Obviously Paul had a sister, but did he have any other siblings? Were they still living in Jerusalem? How old was this kid? How did he discover the plot? Was he risking his own life by coming to Paul? What happened to him afterwards? Why did he want to save Paul? Speculation is all we really have, but here we go. Given that the Commander took the young man by the hand (v. 19) and given that he is called a "young man" (v. 18), it is possible that he was still a teenager and still living with his mother and/or extended family in Jerusalem. Although, according to Philo, the word (*neaniskos*) referred to a man between twenty-two and twenty-eight (*On Creation* 105). Since Paul divided his audiences everywhere he went, there's good reason to believe his own family was sharply divided over this black sheep who shamed them. Since they are not mentioned by Luke until now, one has to wonder why Paul didn't avail himself of the family's hospitality. The most likely supposition is that Paul's family despised him (cf. Phil 3:8). It is entirely possible, in fact, that the plot was spawned in their home when several relatives attempted to recover the family's honor by sacrificing one of their own. Perhaps the nephew overheard the hatching scheme and surreptitiously stole away to uncle Saul.

Notice the kid gloves worn by both Paul and Claudius in handling this situation. Paul sends his nephew to the Commander without telling the centurion why (and the centurion is in no position to argue with Paul after the near flogging two days earlier). The Commander sends the young man home under a veil of secrecy (v. 22). That alone could have protected him, though there is no assurance that it did. No one is safe—not the assassins, Paul, Lysias, the soldiers, or this noble young informant.

23:18-22. All of this is cloak and dagger sort of stuff. Lives hung in the balance. Paul's nephew was escorted straight away to Claudius who drew him off to the side so even the centurion was kept in the dark. As far as we can tell, only Paul, his nephew, and now Claudius know of the plot. The lad shared the secret scheme with the Commander to which the reader is already privy (vv. 13-15). This makes for great literary tension. The Commander wisely sends the boy away without telling him how he plans to respond. This is going to require a bit of sophisticated political maneuvering. The easiest solution would be to go ahead and send Paul to the Sanhedrin, without telling the troops of the danger. He would have gotten away with it at the cost of a handful of foot soldiers. The thorny problem of Paul would conveniently go away. The Jews would have been proud of themselves, and Rome would have been pleased with Lysias for putting down a rebellion, particularly after he massaged his version of the story in the official report. We will soon see just how capable Claudius is of rewriting history to his own advantage (vv. 26-30). Fortunately, Claudius has too much of a conscience to simply throw Paul to the wolves. His second solution would be to keep Paul in lockdown and refuse the High Priest's request. That, of course, could cause a riot unless the Commander offered a valid reason for his refusal to release Paul to the Sanhedrin. If he revealed his knowledge of the plot, he would jeopardize his informant and the Chief Priests would vociferously deny any plot was afoot. Such a head-on collision with political terrorists is seldom one's best option. Claudius chose a third alternative—send the prisoner to Caesarea. This would subvert the plot *and* place Paul in the procurator's court. That, for Claudius, was a win-win. Now all he had to do was whisk Paul out of Jerusalem under the cover of darkness and draft a letter to Felix explaining why he was forfeiting jurisdiction of this predicament called "Paul." Getting Paul out was the easy part (vv. 23-24); writing the letter required more delicacy (vv. 25-30).

[23]Then he called two of his centurions and ordered them, "Get ready a detachment of two hundred soldiers, seventy horsemen and two hundred spearmen[a] to go to Caesarea at nine tonight. [24]Provide mounts for Paul so that he may be taken safely to Governor Felix." [25]He wrote a letter as follows: [26]Claudius Lysias, To His Excellency, Governor Felix: Greetings. [27]This man was seized by the Jews and they were about to kill him, but I came with my troops and rescued him, for I had learned that he is a Roman citizen. [28]I wanted to know why they were accusing him, so I brought him to their Sanhedrin. [29]I found that the accusation had to do with questions about their law, but there was no charge against him that deserved death or imprisonment. [30]When I was informed of a plot to be carried out against the man, I sent him to you at once. I also ordered his accusers to present to you their case against him.

[a]*23* The meaning of the Greek for this word is uncertain.

23:23-24. Claudius prepared a military escort of four hundred and seventy men: Seventy cavalry were augmented by two hundred foot soldiers and two hundred "throwers." The NIV translates this esoteric term as "spearmen" which is as good a guess as we have. However, the term itself literally means "to hold with the right hand." We just don't know what they were holding—javelins, slings, clubs, or spears. By any account, that is an impressive entourage, particularly since it represents nearly half of the Chiliarch's one thousand troops.[12] To

---

[12] The Western text adds an explanation for Claudius's action: "For he was afraid that the Jews would seize him (Paul) and kill him, and afterwards he would incur the accusation of having taken money" [i.e., bribed to throw Paul under the bus], cf. *Beginnings*, 4:294. G. D. Kilpatrick speculates the 200 'throwers'

some this might seem excessive. However, to those familiar with terrorist threats in the Middle East, this appears both reasonable and historically tenable. Outnumbering the assassins ten to one is sensible, particularly given the fact that the guerrillas all have family in the area who might easily be called to arms in the event of an open attack. This says nothing about *Paul's* supporters who the commander might imagine could hear of the plot and weigh in on the fray.

They plop Paul on a horse (or mule, *ktēnē*) and set him off in the center of the troops. They strategically made their exodus around nine-thirty p.m.,[13] unnoticed by most of the population who would be nestled in their homes. Paul was being transferred to the jurisdiction of the procurator Felix who held the same office that Pilate had earlier. Frankly, Felix was pretty poor at it (cf. Josephus, *J.W.*, 2.12.8-18.7 §247-493; *Ant.*, 20.7.1–8.9 §137-184).

Felix was born a slave and raised in Caesar's household until freed by Antonia, Claudius's mother. His brother, Pallas, was a favorite advisor to Claudius, offering Felix considerable political advancement, well beyond his ability or nobility. In A.D. 48 he was granted rule over Samaria. Judea was added four years later (A.D. 52). During this period there was a disturbing rise of insurrection and anarchy to which Felix responded with heartless cruelty. Even the Roman historian Tacitus (no friend of Jews) described him as, "A master of cruelty and lust who exercised the powers of a king with the spirit of a slave" (*Annals*, 12.54; *History*, 5.9). In A.D 59 Nero recalled him, but that was two years after Paul suffered from his political corruption.

23:25-30. Claudius can't send a political prisoner without a letter of explanation. Technically, he needs to provide Felix with the charges for which Paul was arrested as well as an explanation of why he couldn't handle it at the local level. His letter is a commendable example of political casuistry, shrewdly crafted to save his own skin. The letter itself is a standard first century communiqué.[14] It opens, like all letters, by greeting the recipient: "To His Excellency (*kratistos*), Governor[15] Felix: Greetings." Curiously, Luke offers this same appellation, "Excellency," to Theophilus (Luke 1:3), the patron of his two-volume work.

The body of the letter is devoted to the details of Paul's situation. It is a pretty decent summary of the events that transpired. However, there were two points upon which Claudius fudged the facts. First, he claimed that he rescued Paul *because* he *had* learned he was a Roman. *Actually*, he didn't learn Paul was

---

were part of the local police force and not part of the imperial forces under Lysias since that would leave their troops too thin; cf. "Acts 23:23 *dexiolbous*," *JTS* 142 (1963): 393-394.

[13] This would be the approximate time of the "third hour" at Passover (*Beginnings*, 4.293).

[14] This is the second embedded letter in the book (cf. Acts 15:23-29). Such letters, folded into the narrative, were common in historical documents as well as in novels. They served two functions. First, they reiterated the main points of the story. Second, they provided a sense of reality to the narrative (Parsons 217). Justin Howell, "Embedded Letters and Rhetorical αἴξησις in Sallust, Chariton and Luke," in *Contemporary Studies in Acts* (ed. Thomas Phillips; Atlanta: Mercer University Press, 2009), 154-180, proposes that this letter is a Lucan creation rather than an actual document he copied. While it is certainly possible for a novelist to create a letter to bolster the believability of a story, one wonders how it would look any different from an actual historical document. In other words, if novelists cleverly replicated reality, how could one differentiate a Lucan fiction from a genuine historical document? This makes Howell's confidence in Luke's fictional creativity both indemonstrable and inexplicable.

[15] The Greek term ἡγεμών is a generic term for "ruler" or "governor." In point of fact, Felix's specific title was *procurator*.

a Roman until after he strung him up and nearly flogged him. One can sympathize with his desire to cover this up. However, had Paul called him on it, he would have had some real explaining to do. The second disingenuous point is the very last sentence. He had not actually ordered the accusers to present their case to Felix when he wrote the letter. That would take place the following morning. Of course, by the time Felix reads the letter it would be accurate as written, hence, no foul.

When one reads this letter, two things stand out with striking clarity. First, Paul is innocent in the eyes of this Roman Chiliarch. This theme will run thick through the remainder of the book. Second, Claudius is kind of stuck on himself. He uses nine verbs or participles in just four verses to refer to what *he* did. He is certainly the hero of his own story. He would likely be scandalized by the paucity of attention he received by later historians in lieu of this wandering Jew.

[31]So the soldiers, carrying out their orders, took Paul with them during the night and brought him as far as Antipatris. [32]The next day they let the cavalry go on with him, while they returned to the barracks. [33]When the cavalry arrived in Caesarea, they delivered the letter to the governor and handed Paul over to him. [34]The governor read the letter and asked what province he was from. Learning that he was from Cilicia, [35]he said, "I will hear your case when your accusers get here." Then he ordered that Paul be kept under guard in Herod's palace.

23:31-33. Paul had to be exhausted. Day 1: thorough thrashing in the temple followed by a disappointing *apology*; spent the night in custody as a political prisoner. Day 2: Paul creates a rift in the Sanhedrin over the resurrection; they return the favor, nearly tearing him in two. Day 3: Plot discovered and Paul whisked away in the dead of night. He traveled thirty-five miles to a military station at Antipatris on a donkey (or horse).[16] That's gotta rattle the bones of a man in his late fifties. Day 4: No rest for the weary. They power their way through another twenty-seven miles, arriving at Caesarea the following afternoon. [For a brief description of Caesarea, see comments on 10:1.]

The four hundred foot soldiers returned to Jerusalem posthaste. They have to get back to the barracks in case their comrades need their support when the assassins discover that their target had been extricated. One can only imagine the debate before Claudius. They asked for Paul to be transferred to the Sanhedrin for trial. He refused, informing them the prisoner had been taken to the Governor in Caesarea. Both parties knew why but would feign ignorance of the whole nasty business. Eventually Claudius would have had to send Paul to the procurator, Felix. He had jurisdiction over capital cases.[17]

Meanwhile, back in Caesarea, the cavalry surely caught the attention of the locals. Some villain had been captured, perhaps a rebellion squelched. One wonders if Philip's four virgin daughters were among the crooked necks as the parade passed by. As speculation began to spread, they saw a familiar face, now

---

[16] Thirty-six miles in one night is really an incredible distance. The upper limit of a military march in a single day was traditionally set at 24 miles (*Beginnings*, 4:293).

[17] Cf. A. N. Sherwin-White, "The Early Persecutions and Roman Law Again," *JTS* 3 (1952): 199-213.

in chains, less than two weeks after Agabus's prophecy was first uttered. They knew it was coming . . . but so soon?!

23:34-35. Felix read the letter. In an initial inquiry he learned Paul was from Cilicia and therefore fell within his jurisdiction. He agreed to hear the case, but, of course, had to wait for the prosecution to arrive. Meanwhile, Paul was kept in the political prison in Herod's palace . No Caesar's Palace, to be sure, but not a dungeon either. Paul's friends were able to provide for his needs. Philip undoubtedly came with food, supplies, and perhaps an "I told you so."

ACTS 24

1. To the Gentiles (24:1–26:32)

To the Gentile Governor Felix and Two-Year Imprisonment (24:1-27)

This trial before Felix is the most fully developed legal narrative in Luke's two-volume work in spite of the fact that nothing was decided and Paul remained in custody! Given that the trial itself was inconclusive, one wonders why Luke gave it so much space. One possibility is that Luke was granted access to the legal briefs recorded during the trial itself. The defendant and his 'staff' would be allowed access to the abbreviated transcripts of the trial. This could account for the length of chapter 24—we may be reading something like a court stenographer's transcript which Luke utilized for this narrative.

In spite of the fact that the (mis)trial was a 'draw', it is still significant at several levels. (1) It continues the well-worn path of comparing Paul to Jesus and thus portraying the apostle as a model to follow. (2) It shows historical verisimilitude. In other words, both the content and form of both Tertullus and Paul are exactly what one would expect from a legal trial at that time. (3) An analysis of Paul's legal strategy, particularly in light of the rhetorical schools and Roman legal precedents, shows him to be as astute in the court as he was in the synagogue. Paul was a person of extraordinary rhetorical and intellectual prowess.

An analysis of Tertullus (Acts 24) and Paul (Acts 24 & 26) shows just how closely they followed the rhetorical guidelines established by Quintilian.[1] The rhetorical handbooks suggest a legal address should consist of the following five components:

QUINTILIAN'S GUIDE, *INSTITUTIO ORATORIA*	TERT.	PAUL 24	PAUL 26
Exordium, **4.1** (introduction) predisposes the judge to your case[2]	2-4	10B	2-3
Narratio, **4.2** (facts) a persuasive exposition of what should or did take place	5-7	11	4-21
Probatio, **5.1-4, 7-12** (proof) provides evidence of the veracity of the details[3]			22-23
Refutatio, **5.5, 13** (refutation) denies, rebuts, defends, or makes light of accusations		12-20	25-26
Peroratia, **6.1** (conclusion) An emotional recapitulation of the important points	8	21	27-29

---

[1] The following chart was developed based on the work of Derek Hogan, "Paul's Defense: A Comparison of the Forensic Speeches in Acts, *Callirhoe*, and *Leucipe and Clitophon*," *PRS* 29 (2002): 73-87. Others offer similar analyses: Bruce Winter, "Official Proceedings and the Forensic Speeches in Acts 24–26," in *The Book of Acts in Its Ancient Literary Setting* (ed. Richard Bauckham, vol. 1 in *The Book of Acts in Its First Century Setting*; Grand Rapids: Eerdmans, 1993), 322-327; Ben Witherington, *The Acts of the Apostles: A Socio-rhetorical Commentary* (Grand Rapids: Eerdmans, 1998), 709-710; and Jerome Neyrey, "The Forensic Defense Speech and Paul's Trial Speeches in Acts 22–26: Form and Function," in *Luke-Acts: New Perspectives from the Society of Biblical Literature Seminar* (ed. C. H. Talbert; New York: Crossroad, 1984), 221.

[2] An exordium can contain information on the character of the defendant, prosecution, judge, hearers or certain facts of the case; cf. *Ad Herennium* 1.4.8. He may even threaten the judge, especially with a public riot if the case is not in his favor (Quintilian, *Inst.* 4.1.21).

[3] Probatio might contain: witnesses, documents, oracles, court findings, or logical syllogisms.

¹**Five days later the high priest Ananias went down to Caesarea with some of the elders and a lawyer named Tertullus, and they brought their charges against Paul before the governor. ²When Paul was called in, Tertullus presented his case before Felix: "We have enjoyed a long period of peace under you, and your foresight has brought about reforms in this nation. ³Everywhere and in every way, most excellent Felix, we acknowledge this with profound gratitude. ⁴But in order not to weary you further, I would request that you be kind enough to hear us briefly. ⁵We have found this man to be a troublemaker, stirring up riots among the Jews all over the world. He is a ringleader of the Nazarene sect ⁶and even tried to desecrate the temple; so we seized him. ⁸By^a examining him yourself you will be able to learn the truth about all these charges we are bringing against him." ⁹The Jews joined in the accusation, asserting that these things were true.**

^a *6-8 Some manuscripts* him and wanted to judge him according to our law ⁷But the commander, Lysias, came and with the use of much force snatched him from our hands ⁸and ordered his accusers to come before you. By

24:1. It took about a week for Ananias to prepare his prosecution and get down to Caesarea. Their hired gun was a lawyer named Tertullus. He was likely a professional, whose Latin name suggests he was fluent in the language of the court. It was as common then as it is today to secure the services of a professional lawyer in such disputes (e.g., Philostratus, *Apollonius* 4.44). His speech gives every indication that he not only knew the case and the culture but was also a trained rhetorician. He makes all the classic moves appropriate to the legal profession of his day. His services were purchased by the High Priest to represent the grievances of the Jewish community in which he lives but of which he may or may not be a part. It is not possible to tell whether he is a Latin-speaking Roman living in Jerusalem or whether he is a Diaspora Jew retiring to the homeland. On the one hand, he aligns himself with the Jews using the word "we" (vv. 3, 4, 6), but that may merely indicate affinity with his clients. In verse 7 he spoke of "our law" though this textual variant may not be part of the original transcript (see below). On the other hand, verse 2 "this nation" and verse 5 "the Jews" may suggest he is an outsider. This mixed evidence does not allow us to make any firm decision as to Tertullus's identity.

24:2-4. Tertullus opens with a standard *captatio benevolentiae*. In ancient schools, lawyers were taught how to court favor with the judge prior to presenting their case. To modern Westerners this may seem like a bit of 'brownnosing', but it was normal jurisprudence in Paul's day. The purpose was not merely to court favor with the judges but to recognize the judge's particular experience or expertise that qualified him to capably adjudicate the current case.⁴ Tertullus says two things, neither of which is true to any considerable degree. First, he tells Felix how profoundly grateful the Jewish people were for his stellar leadership and social reforms. While it is true that Felix responded promptly to the rising tide of banditry under his administration, it is also true that he did so with ruthless brutality. Moreover, the rise of banditry was probably prompted by his oppres-

---

⁴ Tertullus' *captatio benevolentiae* compares favorably with other extant judicial introductions; cf. Bruce Winter, "The Importance of the *captatio benevolentiae* in the Speeches of Tertullus and Paul in Acts 24:1-24," *JTS* 42 (1991): 505-531.

sive policies, and the people hated him for it. Even his fellow Roman, Tacitus accused him of being a scoundrel: "[He] had for some time been governor of Judaea, and thought that he could do any evil act with impunity, backed up as he was by such power. . . . Felix meanwhile, by ill-timed remedies, stimulated disloyal acts" (*Annals* 12.54). Second, Tertullus promised to be brief. This is almost always a disingenuous promise from both lawyers and preachers. Though Luke's summary of his prosecution is abbreviated, compared to Paul's response, Tertullus's speech is longer . . . and that's saying something next to Paul!

24:5-9. The original charge leveled against Paul was desecrating the temple by bringing a Gentile into its precincts. Granted, it was a mob action (a 'citizen's arrest' at best). Here, however, the charges have changed. The primary accusation is now that Paul caused riots all over the Roman world (*oikoumenē*).[5] This is a dangerous indictment and provable to a considerable degree, although Paul could easily have turned that around on the whole Jewish community. In places like Damascus, Jerusalem, Pisidian Antioch, Thessalonica, and Corinth, it was his Jewish adversaries, not Paul, who fomented a public disturbance. The second charge is that Paul was a "ringleader of the Nazarene sect."[6] The term "sect" was used of any idiosyncratic group such as the Sadducees (Acts 5:17) or the Pharisees (Acts 15:5; 26:5) without necessarily implying the group was heretical (though it can mean that, cf. 2 Pet 2:1). Implied in this charge in this context is that Christianity is a novel religious offshoot that is problematic. As discussed earlier, there is no evidence that Rome kept a list of 'authorized' religions, at least not at this early date (cf. Witherington, 539-544). However, new religious innovations would have been viewed with suspicion and disdain. The third charge, desecrating the temple, was the original one. Tertullus challenges Felix to investigate the charges that will surely render Paul guilty. When he finished his harangue, the Jews accompanying him heartily affirmed what he said against Paul.

One will notice that verse seven is missing from modern translations, and without it, verse 8a is somewhat confusing. Would Tertullus really suggest Felix investigate *Paul* to get at the truth? Most criminals don't readily incriminate themselves. Hence, it appears that some of the later scribes added this bit for clarification at verse 6b: "So we seized him *and wanted to judge him according to our law.* [7]*But the commander, Lysias, came and with the use of much force snatched him from our hands* [8]*and ordered his accusers to come before you.* By examining him . . ." This addition, though it may not be in the original text Luke wrote, makes Tertullus's statement more understandable. Rather than investigating Paul directly, the addition suggests that Felix would investigate Claudius Lysias, as confirmed by verse 22. It would be natural to summon him for details on the case.

[10]**When the governor motioned for him to speak, Paul replied: "I know that for a number of years you have been a judge over this nation; so I gladly make**

[5] The initial charge (v. 5) that Paul was a "troublemaker" (λοιμός) could literally be rendered "plague" (cf. Luke 21:11). It is to be read in conjunction with the second charge of stirring up riots.
[6] The term "Nazarene" was first applied to Jesus because of his hometown (Matt 2:23; Mark 14:67; 16:6; John 1:46). It became a designation for Christians, especially among the Jews who as early as A.D. 100 condemned the *nosrîm* in a synagogue prayer known as *Shemoneh 'Esreh* 12 (cf. Jerome, *On Illustrious Men* 3, *Epist.* 120.3; Epiphanius, *Heresies* 29.7, 9).

my defense. [11]You can easily verify that no more than twelve days ago I went up to Jerusalem to worship. [12]My accusers did not find me arguing with anyone at the temple, or stirring up a crowd in the synagogues or anywhere else in the city. [13]And they cannot prove to you the charges they are now making against me. [14]However, I admit that I worship the God of our fathers as a follower of the Way, which they call a sect. I believe everything that agrees with the Law and that is written in the Prophets, [15]and I have the same hope in God as these men, that there will be a resurrection of both the righteous and the wicked. [16]So I strive always to keep my conscience clear before God and man."

24:10. It is now Paul's turn. What he does is masterful.[7] First, his *captatio benevolentiae*, though briefer than Tertullus's, is no less astute. In order to correctly adjudicate Paul's case, Felix will need a sophisticated knowledge of idiosyncratic Jewish concerns. His nine years in the province (five or six as governor) afforded him intimate knowledge of Jewish affairs. Hence, without disingenuous flattery, Paul recognizes Felix's experience and understanding (v. 10).

24:11-13. Second, Paul has been charged with disorderly conduct and fomenting a riot. Verses 11-13 give evidence to the contrary. Paul has only been in the province for twelve days.[8] It would be difficult to organize a revolt in less than two weeks. There is no evidence that Paul was carrying on publicly in the temple, in synagogues, or in any other public space. He was not preaching to crowds or debating with opponents. There is simply no proof of the allegations. Quite the contrary, Paul had come to worship. The word for "worship" (*proskuneō*) was commonly used for pilgrimage and was a term of piety (*Beginnings* 4:301). He's no radical rebel; he's a pious pilgrim.

24:14-16. Third, the single concession Paul makes is that he is a follower of the Way. Here Paul makes two brilliant rhetorical moves, one sociological and the other political. First, he claims "the Way" was ancient. In sociological terms, this gives it authenticity. It is the 'kosher' faith of the Fathers, the well-worn path of the prophets. As Paul had done a number of times before, he presented Christianity not as a novel deviation due to eschatological events but as the fulfillment of ancient hopes and promises to the people of Israel. Pure

---

[7] "The author of Acts intends his readers to see Paul handling his defense with great dexterity, refuting serious charges. His prescribing of the limits of evidence based on Roman law, his proscribing the charges of absent accusers, his use of forensic terminology, his construction of 'lawyerlike' phrases, and, not least of all, his presentation of a well-argued defense, even if preserved in a summary form, is meant to point to the fact that Paul conducted his own defense in an able manner against a professional forensic orator," Winter, "*Captatio Benevolentiae*," 526. For another excellent analysis of Paul's rhetorical and legal strategy before Felix, see Craig Keener, "Some Rhetorical Techniques in Acts 24:2-21," in *Paul's World* (ed. Stanley E. Porter; Leiden: Brill, 2008), 221-251.

[8] Though there is no question that Paul had been in Jerusalem a short time, it is a mystery how he came up with the specific number of twelve days. There are approximately 18 days between his arrival in Jerusalem and his trial before Felix: day 1, Paul arrived (21:17); day 2, he met with James (21:18); day 3, he paid for purification vow in the temple (21:26); days 4-9, he waited nearly seven days for purification vow to be complete (21:27); day 10, he was arrested (21:27); day 11, trial before the Sanhedrin (22:30); day 12, assassination plot and escape (23:12); day 13, arrival in Caesarea (23:33); days 14-17, he awaited the arrival of Tertullus (24:1); day 18, trial (24:1). The simplest solution is that Paul only counted the twelve days he was in Jerusalem. Another possible solution is to add the days enumerated in the text—seven (21:7) and five (24:1)—without counting the days in the middle. Though we don't know how Paul (or Luke) counted the twelve days, his point is indisputable—this is too short a period to be responsible for a national rebellion.

and simple: Christianity is Judaism—Abrahamic, Mosaic, Davidic, and Messianic. Paul's second shrewd strategy, political in force, was to remove the allegation from Roman provenance to Jewish. The issue is *not* that Paul is a militaristic threat to Roman security but that he is preaching the resurrection of Jesus. As was discussed at 23:6, the key issue of the resurrection is not merely a diversionary distraction. By "resurrection" Paul means not merely the raising of Jesus, nor simply of the Elect of Israel, but of all humanity, both the righteous and the unrighteous (cf. John 5:28-29; Matt 25:31-46; Rev 20:11-15). The reality of the resurrection, proleptically promised in Jesus, is the source of Paul's conversion, the cause of Gentile inclusion, and the hope of ancient Israel.[9] As such, this is not a point of litigation for a Roman procurator; it is a discussion for the leaders of Israel. [See comments on 23:1 for Paul living with a clear conscience.]

[17]**"After an absence of several years, I came to Jerusalem to bring my people gifts for the poor and to present offerings. [18]I was ceremonially clean when they found me in the temple courts doing this. There was no crowd with me, nor was I involved in any disturbance. [19]But there are some Jews from the province of Asia, who ought to be here before you and bring charges if they have anything against me. [20]Or these who are here should state what crime they found in me when I stood before the Sanhedrin— [21]unless it was this one thing I shouted as I stood in their presence: 'It is concerning the resurrection of the dead that I am on trial before you today.'"**

24:17-18. Paul now addresses the final charge—temple violation. This was the foundation of Tertullus's most serious charge that Paul caused riots. Paul offered three evidences against this accusation. (1) He provided benevolence for his fellow Jews as well as pious offerings to God in the temple. This hardly sounds like the rabble-rouser Tertullus is attempting to convict. As an aside, the offering that Paul makes so much about in his letters, gets a brief mention here. Though Luke does not stress the yearlong collection preceding Paul's arrival in Jerusalem, it is pretty clear from verse 17 (not to mention Paul's accompanying entourage) that part of Paul's purpose in the city was to bless the poor.[10] (2) Paul was ceremonially clean in the temple. In other words, he was playing by the rules with all due diligence and respect for his ancestral traditions. (3) He was all alone. He had no band of brigands or chorus of rebels as a bodyguard to carry off some subversive attack. He was the only one attacked that day, and those responsible were now nowhere in sight. This leads to a major legal point that should have ended the proceedings on the spot.

24:19-21. As the reader is aware, the problem started when some Asiatic Jews got out of sorts. They were the ones to cry out in the temple that Paul had to be apprehended. They were the ones who commenced with a beating. On what charge? That Paul brought a Gentile into the temple. However, Trophimus

---

[9] Especially important here is Klaus Haacker, "Das Bekenntnis des Paulus, 437-451.

[10] Contra David Downs, "Paul's Collection and the Book of Acts Revisited," *NTS* 52 (2006): 50-70, who contends that if Acts is read on its own terms there is no mention of the offering. Acts 24:17, according to Downs, describes Paul's personal piety rather than a corporate collection from the Gentiles.

was never produced and now these original accusers can't be produced either. That is a serious legal problem.[11] Either they need to come to court to present an eyewitness case, or those currently in attendance need to offer a substantial and sustainable charge from the Jewish high court of the Sanhedrin.

The only potential crime Paul committed is in disrupting the Sanhedrin meeting with his outburst about the resurrection. That did, indeed, cause an uproar. However, Paul knows that this confession is not going to get him imprisoned. After all, the meeting had already degenerated to a slapping match before he brought up the resurrection. Furthermore, there are enough members of the Sanhedrin who approved of what he said that he can hardly be accused of a heretical outburst that caused a riot. The very fact that the Sanhedrin rioted over the resurrection proves that Paul has enough recognized leaders on his side of the argument to sustain it as an intra-Jewish debate as opposed to a culpable outsider's imposition. What he concedes should actually support his defense.

22Then Felix, who was well acquainted with the Way, adjourned the proceedings. "When Lysias the commander comes," he said, "I will decide your case." 23He ordered the centurion to keep Paul under guard but to give him some freedom and permit his friends to take care of his needs. 24Several days later Felix came with his wife Drusilla, who was a Jewess. He sent for Paul and listened to him as he spoke about faith in Christ Jesus. 25As Paul discoursed on righteousness, self-control and the judgment to come, Felix was afraid and said, "That's enough for now! You may leave. When I find it convenient, I will send for you." 26At the same time he was hoping that Paul would offer him a bribe, so he sent for him frequently and talked with him. 27When two years had passed, Felix was succeeded by Porcius Festus, but because Felix wanted to grant a favor to the Jews, he left Paul in prison.

24:22. Felix was well acquainted with Judaism and its major sects, even "The Way," those messianic Jews who included Gentile God-fearers. It's no great wonder that he would keep his finger on the political pulse of his subjects. He had a number of sources informing him about this growing Christian movement. Certainly his wife Drusilla could tell him about her own father who had executed James and nearly executed Peter before his dramatic escape (Acts 12). His escape was presumably due to the secret help of several soldiers who lost their lives for their traitorous conspiracy. Felix might also have heard a more sympathetic account from Cornelius, a centurion famed for being the first Gentile convert to The Way some fifteen years earlier. If he retired in the area, he might still be an informant at Felix's disposal. Philip also had been in Caesarea for twenty years with broad connections that might include politicians and military leaders. This says nothing about the general gossip and secret police employed by Roman rulers of the region. Felix had plenty to go on. He is 'in the know'. He shrewdly adjourned the court without coming to a decision. He has an ex-

[11] *Destitutio* was the abandonment of a charge brought against another person, and it was considered a serious offense in Roman litigation (e.g., Appian, *Rom. Hist.: Civ. Wars* 3.54); cf. A. N. Sherwin-White, *Roman Society and Roman Law* (Oxford: Clarendon, 1963), 52-53.

cuse—Claudius Lysias needs to return to Caesarea and fill in the details. This postponement bought him some time, potentially enough time for tempers to cool. Felix had to handle the situation carefully. His favor in Rome was tenuous, particularly after Nero took the throne and deposed his brother Pallas (Tacitus, *Ann* 13.14). He no longer has a privileged advocate in the royal court of Rome and his reputation as a brute was filtering back to the capital.

24:23-25. In the meantime, Paul was kept in protective custody with considerable freedom for his friends to come and go. During this time, Luke could have had full access to Paul, not to mention the court records. This special courtesy is commensurate with a political prisoner who has yet to be convicted and who has shown considerable education, intelligence, and legal sophistication.

This period of time also afforded Drusilla (still a teenager)[12] the opportunity to hear the famed rabbi whose sect was at odds with her now deceased father. We have no way of knowing if she connected the worms that consumed her father with the wrath of God as did Luke. Notwithstanding, her interest in the Christian movement is understandable in that it intersected with her father who assassinated the first Apostolic martyr, her uncle who tried Jesus prior to his crucifixion, and her grandfather who attempted to murder the Christ-child. Her own Jewish roots undoubtedly pricked her curiosity in the Messiah of whom Paul preached.

His preaching, however, got prickly. He prodded uncomfortable issues for a Herodian queen who divorced her first husband to align with a Roman ruler. Righteousness (probably implying social justice), self-control (often in reference to sexuality), and judgment to come (undoubtedly in connection to the imminent return of Jesus)[13] were uncomfortable topics, somewhat inconsiderate of Paul to probe in the presence of these particular dignitaries. Felix was disconcerted enough to cut him short and lock him up. Apparently Felix feared more becoming a slave (again) to Jesus than falling under his impending judgment. There is a lesson here for those with ears to hear. This was the closest Felix ever came to giving his life to Jesus. It is not that his opportunities were cut off or his life cut short. It was that the preaching of the word hardened his heart so that the good seed was incapable of penetrating trampled soil.

24:26-27. Felix promised to call on Paul again. He did. Again and again he heard Paul preach, partly through fascination, but partly due to a desire to extort a bribe. Paul confessed he had made a considerable offering to his people in Jerusalem. Perhaps these same people would grease the wheels of justice with a voluntary offering to the Roman Governor. Bribes were illegal (*Lex Iulia de*

---

[12] She was born in A.D. 38, the youngest daughter of Agrippa I (we will meet her two siblings in chapter 26). Josephus (*Ant.* 20.7.2 §141-144) catalogues the scandalous affairs of her marriages. At fourteen she married Azizus, the king of Emesa. Through the help of a magician named Atomos from Cyprus, Felix convinced her to divorce Azizus in favor of him. This stunningly beautiful sixteen-year-old decided to trade up to a husband of greater clout and power, perhaps to trump her older sister who had not been particularly kind to her. She was 19 when she met Paul, two years before her brother and sister would have the privilege.

[13] Many scholars believe that Luke sees the return of Jesus at a distance, not as imminent. However, this text, as well as 10:42; 17:31; 24:15 suggests it is near. According to Luke, both Peter and Paul warn of the soon return of Jesus. Cf. A. J. Mattill, "*Naherwartung, Fernerwartung,* and the Purpose of Luke-Acts: Weymouth Reconsidered," *CBQ* 34 (1992): 276-293.

repetundis, in *Digest* 48.11; cf. Cicero, Pro Rabirio 12) but still all too common. Paul refused to capitulate. For two years he was kept in prison. He and Luke likely wrote a lot. Eventually Felix was recalled for his brutal intervention of a civil strife in Caesarea between local Jews and Syrians (Josephus, *J.W.* 2.13.7 §266-270; *Ant.* 20.8.7-9, §173-178).[14] Felix's forces ransacked the Jewish fighters and many of the nobles lost their lives. Their delegation in Rome complained to Nero who ruled in their favor, ending the career of Felix. He was replaced by Porcius Festus in A.D. 60, a virtual unknown.[15] What little we do know of him suggests he was of more noble character but no more successful in carrying out justice for Paul.

---

[14] The historical records of Felix's dismissal are difficult. Josephus claims that Felix got off lightly through the intervention of Pallas. However, Pallas had been deposed in A.D. 55, several years earlier, making it doubtful that he had much influence in the court. Eusebius gives A.D. 55 as the date of Felix's dismissal, which would potentially solve the problem of Pallas but is certainly too early for the chronology of Acts as well as the Roman records. This is one of the many details of ancient history for which horseshoes and hand grenades will have to suffice. (For a detailed discussion on this difficulty, see *Beginnings* 5:464-467.)

[15] Aside from Acts 25, he is only mentioned in Josephus, *J.W.* 2.14.1 §271 and *Ant.* 20.8.9-10 §182-188, both of which recount the great number of robbers and *sicarii* with whom he had to deal.

ACTS 25

1. To the Gentiles (24:1–26:32 continued)

To the Gentile Governor Festus and Paul's Appeal to Caesar (25:1-12)

This is now the second procurator before whom Paul stood. Josephus describes Festus as a noble ruler who worked hard to rid Israel of its many brigands who arose under the wicked rule of Felix. Festus would eventually deal with those guerilla rebels, but right now he has a more pressing problem with a certain Jewish rabble-rouser incarcerated two years earlier. Some of the Jewish leaders are still seething over Paul. He's not only still on their radar, he is in their sights. They are dead set on execution. Try as he might, Festus will not be able to navigate this particular political landmine. Festus would have a short reign, lasting from A.D. 58 or 59 until A.D. 62 when he died suddenly from some undetermined illness.[1] The pressure of Paul at the beginning of his term certainly did nothing helpful for Festus's fragile constitution.

¹Three days after arriving in the province, Festus went up from Caesarea to Jerusalem, ²where the chief priests and Jewish leaders appeared before him and presented the charges against Paul. ³They urgently requested Festus, as a favor to them, to have Paul transferred to Jerusalem, for they were preparing an ambush to kill him along the way. ⁴Festus answered, "Paul is being held at Caesarea, and I myself am going there soon. ⁵Let some of your leaders come with me and press charges against the man there, if he has done anything wrong."

25:1. Festus had no sooner set foot in the province but that he paid a courtesy visit to the capital city of the Jews. It would take the better part of three days to get there, and he's only been in country three days. In other words, he is making a major investment of time in this trip, indicating how important it was to him to curry the favor of the Jewish population under his jurisdiction. He is trying to get off on the right foot.

25:2-3. The most important representatives of Israel pleaded with Festus to bring Paul down to Jerusalem. On the surface, it appears to be a reasonable request. The previous trial before Felix proved this was an intramural theological discussion concerning the resurrection. That is certainly beyond the pale of a Roman governor to arbitrate adequately. Nonetheless, just below the surface of the request was a plot afoot. They were planning on ambushing Paul along the lonely route from Caesarea to Jerusalem. It was Jewish territory and they could certainly count on the support of a village or two to sacrifice their social security

---

[1] Josephus, *Ant.* 20.9.1 §200; *J.W.* 2.14.1 §271-276. He was succeeded by a wicked ruler, Albinus. Before Albinus was able to take control of Israel, Ananias, the High Priest, convinced the council to execute James, Jesus' brother. In other words, what the Jewish leaders attempted to do with Paul under Festus, they succeeded in doing to James at the beginning of Albinus's reign. These political dangers were all too real.

for the glory of their country. Contemporary events in the Middle East provide ample illustrations of how this might work.

They know their request is beyond the normal bounds of jurisprudence. Verse 3, "they urgently requested" is literally, "they asked for a favor (*charis*)." Both the "request" and the "ambush" are reminiscent of the language found in 23:15-16, "Now then, you and the Sanhedrin *petition* the commander to bring him before you. . . . But when the son of Paul's sister heard of this *plot* . . ." Luke is reminding his readers that this is the same song, second verse.[2] After two years the venom of Paul's enemies has not subsided nor has their strategy changed. They would request certain privileges under the guise of justice in order to assassinate Paul in a suicide mission.

25:4-5. Festus wisely declined their offer to take Paul off his hands. Though Festus is a newbie, he's not naïve. He may or may not know of the previous assassination plot attempted under Claudius Lysias (all that was pretty hush, hush). Nonetheless, he had a sense that justice would better be served in Caesarea than Jerusalem. Festus offers the excuse that he is soon returning to Caesarea, suggesting the transfer of the prisoner could not take place in time. As it turns out, he spent eight to ten days in Jerusalem (v. 6), which would have been sufficient for the transfer and trial of Paul. Festus challenged Paul's accusers to present their charges in a court of law over which he would preside. His little jab at the end, "*if* he has done anything wrong," may suggest Festus suspected foul play. At the very least, it suggested he would put up with none.

[6]**After spending eight or ten days with them, he went down to Caesarea, and the next day he convened the court and ordered that Paul be brought before him. [7]When Paul appeared, the Jews who had come down from Jerusalem stood around him, bringing many serious charges against him, which they could not prove. [8]Then Paul made his defense: "I have done nothing wrong against the law of the Jews or against the temple or against Caesar." [9]Festus, wishing to do the Jews a favor, said to Paul, "Are you willing to go up to Jerusalem and stand trial before me there on these charges?" [10]Paul answered: "I am now standing before Caesar's court, where I ought to be tried. I have not done any wrong to the Jews, as you yourself know very well. [11]If, however, I am guilty of doing anything deserving death, I do not refuse to die. But if the charges brought against me by these Jews are not true, no one has the right to hand me over to them. I appeal to Caesar!" [12]After Festus had conferred with his council, he declared: "You have appealed to Caesar. To Caesar you will go!"**

25:6-8. Festus wasted no time attending to the thorny problem of Paul. The first full day he was back in Caesarea he convened court. There Paul stood, surrounded by his fellow Jews repeating their serious, though ultimately unprovable, accusations. So as not to weary his reader, Luke doesn't repeat the Jewish charges though we have a pretty good idea what they were based on Paul's cur-

---

[2] A speculative marginal note in one ancient manuscript (Harclean) says it was not merely the same plot but the same forty men (23:12-15).

sory response: He had not violated Jewish law by introducing a new sect, he had not violated the temple by bringing into it a Gentile, and he had not violated Caesar's rule by proclaiming Jesus as King of the Jews. Paul's reply can be adequately paraphrased: "I didn't do it, and you can't prove I did."

25:9-11. Festus invited Paul to voluntarily move the legal proceedings from Caesarea to Jerusalem. This is a surprising misstep on his part. He attempted to grant the Jews the very favor they asked for ten days earlier. This capitulation was at least a sign of weakness on his part (a fatal political flaw in the Middle East) and perhaps a calculated and nefarious attempt to rid himself of a difficult dilemma he unfairly inherited from Felix. On the surface, it looks like Festus merely offered a change of venue. After all, he told Paul he would stand before *him* (not the Jews) down in Jerusalem. Paul saw through the ruse. His immediate and strident response unmasked Festus's motive to transfer jurisdiction from the Roman to the Jewish court. That would be suicide for Paul. Now, it may look like Paul is just trying to save his own skin. He vociferously denies any cowardice (or in ancient terms any lack of honor). If he deserved to die he would die with the dignity due him. But if not, then no one, including the procurator, could force his head into a noose. One picks up on Paul's subtle rebuke of Festus— the governor was acting ignobly. He was forfeiting justice for a man he *knew* was innocent. The adverb in the phrase "you *well* know" is particularly emphatic. In other words, Paul is verbally pointing his finger at Festus, calling him out on his attempt to subvert justice.

So, just as Paul disrupted the Sanhedrin meeting with a reference to the resurrection, he brought a swift and serious halt to these legal proceedings by appealing to Caesar (*Ad Caesarem prouoco*). The specifics of an Imperial Appeal have been lost with time. In other words, we can't know with certainty who could appeal and under what circumstances.[3] There are several things, however, one can assume: (1) Under certain circumstances, Roman citizens had the right to appeal to Caesar as protection against just such a mistrial. This was particularly true where there was not yet a legal precedent established as in Paul's case. (2) The judge was then obligated to immediately halt the proceedings and send the prisoner on to the Emperor with a record of the case up to that point (v. 11). (3) An appeal to the Emperor was risky business. Emperors could be capricious, and their political power was virtually unchecked. Paul was throwing himself into the hands of Nero.

Nero Claudius Caesar Germanicus was born in A.D. 37 to Agrippina. She had married Emperor Claudius when she was merely thirty-four years old (in A.D. 49). He was fifteen years older than she and a lifelong victim of cerebral palsy. He suffered a limp, drooling, and a stutter that led most of his contemporaries to treat him as a half-wit in spite of his superior intelligence. One suspects her motives in marriage were less noble than love. When Claudius died in A.D. 54, rumor had it that he had been poisoned by Agrippina so that her seventeen-

[3] For the little we do know cf. *Beginnings* 5:312-319; Sherwin-White, *Roman Law*, 57-70; and Boyd Reese, "The Apostle Paul's Exercise of His Rights as a Roman Citizen as Recorded in the Book of Acts," *EvQ* 47 (1975): 138-145.

year-old son could inherit the crown. She apparently had the help of Claudius's primary advisors Pallas, Seneca, and Burrus, each of whom were later repaid by Nero with assassination and confiscation of their estates. Agrippina herself, apparently an incestuous collaborator of Nero, was murdered when he could no longer stand her scheming manipulations. This was a minor offense for a man who killed his second wife, Poppaea, by kicking her in the stomach while she was pregnant (A.D. 66; P.S. the baby died as well). It would take too much space to catalogue his vices and crimes. Suffice to say, Paul was taking his life in his hands by appealing to Nero even though the first five years of his rule were a "golden age" in Rome. After that the monster emerged from under the watchful eye of Seneca and Burrus (c. A.D. 62). It was a couple of years after Paul's trial when the Emperor was suspected of setting fire to a large area of Rome, killing thousands of poor people who lived in the area and clearing it for Nero's "Golden Palace" in the center of the city. As a scapegoat for the allegations, Nero enacted the first official Roman persecution against Christians who subsequently acquired the sympathy of even Tacitus, certainly no friend of the church (cf. *Ann.* 15.44).

25:12. Festus was taken aback by Paul's surprising maneuver. He was new at all this and fumbled his first big case. That must have been embarrassing, having to explain to the Emperor why he abdicated a case in his first two weeks in office. He conferred with his legal advisors who simply shrugged their shoulders— there was nothing to do but send him on to Caesar. The die had been cast.

To King Agrippa and Paul's Proclamation of Innocence (25:13–26:32)

This story about Paul before Herod Agrippa II is not merely tangential window dressing. Though we learn virtually nothing new about Paul's political situation or his conversion account, the story plays an important theological function. Luke alone tells about Jesus' trial before Herod Antipas. Now he shows how Paul's trials recapitulate Jesus' as he too stands before a Herod who finds no guilt in him. The point is not merely, "Hey, look at Paul, he looks like Jesus." Rather, Luke is offering a living example for his readers to follow as well. We are to imitate Paul as he imitates Christ (1 Cor 11:1; cf. Acts 26:29).[4]

¹³A few days later King Agrippa and Bernice arrived at Caesarea to pay their respects to Festus. ¹⁴Since they were spending many days there, Festus discussed Paul's case with the king. He said: "There is a man here whom Felix left as a prisoner. ¹⁵When I went to Jerusalem, the chief priests and elders of the Jews brought charges against him and asked that he be condemned. ¹⁶I told them that it is not the Roman custom to hand over any man before he has faced his accusers and has had an opportunity to defend himself against their charges. ¹⁷When they came here with me, I did not delay the case, but convened the court the next day and ordered the man to be brought in. ¹⁸When his accusers got up to speak, they did not charge him with any of the crimes I had expected. ¹⁹Instead, they had some points of dispute with him about their own religion and about

---

[4] Robert O'Toole, "Luke's Notion of 'Be Imitators of Me as I Am of Christ' in Acts 25–26," *BTB* 8 (1978): 155-161, develops this idea to good effect.

a dead man named Jesus who Paul claimed was alive. [20]I was at a loss how to investigate such matters; so I asked if he would be willing to go to Jerusalem and stand trial there on these charges. [21]When Paul made his appeal to be held over for the Emperor's decision, I ordered him held until I could send him to Caesar." [22]Then Agrippa said to Festus, "I would like to hear this man myself." He replied, "Tomorrow you will hear him."

25:13. King Agrippa was the last king of Israel though he never ruled over Galilee, Samaria, or Judea. He was king in the sense that he controlled the High Priestly appointment as well as their vestments. Born in A.D. 27, he spent the first twenty-one years of his life in Rome and was a court favorite. When his uncle died in A.D. 48, Agrippa II inherited his kingdom of Chalcis as well as his wife Bernice (or so the rumors said). This is a bit messy. Bernice, Agrippa's sister, had married her own uncle, Herod of Chalcis. When Agrippa II inherited their uncle's kingdom upon his death, she moved in with her brother. This raised suspicions of an incestuous liaison. Frankly, the rumors were probably true. Bernice, rightly called the "Jewish Cleopatra," would later become the mistress of Titus, the son of Emperor Vespasian and the conqueror of Jerusalem. That created as much scandal in Rome as her relationship with Agrippa did in Israel because a noble Roman courting a Jew was disreputable (cf. Juvenal, *Sat.* 6.155-160; Tacitus, *Hist.* 2.2; Suetonius, *Titus* 7; and Dio Cassius, 65.15; 66:18).

The visit of Herod and Bernice presented a golden opportunity to Festus. He could utilize Herod's expertise in Jewish affairs to figure out what in the world he would write to Nero. He had to explain to the Emperor why he was sending this prisoner. If he's lucky, Herod would offer him insight and perhaps even some clout. His name might offer Festus some leverage in the Roman court, justifying why he was unable to manage the case he had inherited from his predecessor.

25:14-19. Festus rehearsed the basic history of the case, offering the reader a few pregnant details. We learn that the leaders in Jerusalem asked that Paul be condemned (v. 15). This comes as no surprise, but it is thicker detail than was given earlier. Verse 16 is also a richer detail than was offered earlier. Festus defended his actions as consistent with the noble Roman penchant for justice. Of course he conveniently left out the detail that he invited Paul to waive his Roman rights and be tried in Jerusalem before a seething court that had already determined he must die! There was nothing new in the charges from the previous trial. Yet Festus was surprised by the nature of the case—it centered on the resurrection of Jesus. So, Festus either had not yet read the docket or he had not understood from what he read just how theological the charges were. It really was about the Jewish religious[5] belief in resurrection—a concept that befuddled this Roman governor. What is interesting is that the text of chapter 25 mentioned nothing about the resurrection either from Paul or from his accusers. Obviously Paul said more than Luke recorded in his brief categorical denial.

---

[5] The word for "religion" (δεισιδαιμονία) is the same root word found in Acts 17:22 when Paul describes the Athenians as "religious/superstitious/pious." It may be a polite way of referring to another's religious beliefs which one does not share.

25:20-22. For Festus, Paul was a real conundrum. He didn't understand the nature of the charges, he was caught short by Paul's appeal to Caesar, and he had nothing definitive to write to the Emperor explaining why the prisoner was being sent to Rome. As he described the situation to Herod, he understandably portrayed himself as competent and in control: "I ordered him held until I could send him to Caesar." The truth is, however, that he really had no choice. The only good news for Festus was that Herod was as curious about Paul as were Felix and Drusilla. He would be delighted to hear him personally. This might give Festus some desperately needed insight. Arrangements were set for the following day.

²³**The next day Agrippa and Bernice came with great pomp and entered the audience room with the high ranking officers and the leading men of the city. At the command of Festus, Paul was brought in.** ²⁴**Festus said: "King Agrippa, and all who are present with us, you see this man! The whole Jewish community has petitioned me about him in Jerusalem and here in Caesarea, shouting that he ought not to live any longer.** ²⁵**I found he had done nothing deserving of death, but because he made his appeal to the Emperor I decided to send him to Rome.** ²⁶**But I have nothing definite to write to His Majesty about him. Therefore I have brought him before all of you, and especially before you, King Agrippa, so that as a result of this investigation I may have something to write.** ²⁷**For I think it is unreasonable to send on a prisoner without specifying the charges against him."**

25:23. The pompous[6] parade of dignitaries was a veritable "who's who" of the region. Herod, Bernice, and the royal guests were surrounded by the highest military officers (*chiliarchs*) of Caesarea as well as the wealthy and powerful who were likely as eager to meet the Herods as the Herods were to meet Paul. Anachronistically speaking, this is a grand photo-op. There are glamorous garments, sparkling jewelry, puffed up chests weighted with medals, red carpets, regalia, and in the center of it all, a solitary Jew in chains. Boy, was he out of place. One can only imagine how scandalized this crowd would be to learn that Paul was the only one in the room who is still well-known. In fact, far more know his name than even the Emperor to whom he appealed.

25:24-27. Before Festus gave Paul the floor, he explained the nature of the proceedings. This is not merely a 'meet-and-greet'. It is an official meeting whereby Herod and the other potentates can help Festus compose a letter to the Emperor whom he identifies with the titles "Sebastos"[7] (v. 21, 25) and "Lord" (*kurios*, v. 26). This must have made Paul's skin crawl!

Festus makes several things clear in this brief introduction. First, he's not

---

[6] The Greek word for "pomp" is φαντασία. This word would become the root of our English word "fantasy." Obviously it would be anachronistic to retroject the definition of the modern word "fantasy" into the Greek text of Acts 25:23. Paradoxically, however, their perception of their own importance was a figment that would dissolve in time. The unlikely figure in the center of the room was, in reality, the most influential and socially significant personage. This is significant in light of how Epictetus uses this term (more than all other ancient writers, 116×) in the sense of "appearance" or even "imagination." He would argue that the true philosopher must use god-given rationality to see the reality of a situation.

[7] This Greek word translates into Latin as "Augustus" and is the standard inscriptional title for the Emperor. It carries religious connotations of "piety" since the Emperors were seen as the High Priest of the nation. Hence it could be translated "Reverend" or "Venerable."

so keen on the Jews at this point. They clamored for Paul's death (v. 24) even though Festus found nothing so deserving in Paul's life. According to Festus, what the Jews lacked in evidence, they made up for with volume (v. 24).[8] Festus suggested he would have released Paul had the prisoner not appealed to Caesar (v. 25). This, however, is a rather generous self-assessment since he had asked Paul to forfeit his Roman privileges to stand trial in Jerusalem. It was Festus's misstep, not the Jewish antagonists, which forced Paul's hand. Second, Paul was innocent in terms of the Roman law. He may be offensive to his own country-men, but that is a different matter for a different court. This was now the second Roman declaration of Paul's innocence (cf. 22:29). Finally, it was clear that Festus had nothing to write to the Emperor (vv. 26-27). This could be a costly mistake, perhaps even political suicide. One cannot court imperial favor if his first case in office is botched. If Festus couldn't handle local affairs, the Emperor would likely find someone who could.

---

[8] Βοάω is, in Acts, a rather unflattering term, reserved for the demonized and riotous rabble (cf. 8:7; 17:6; 25:24). Elsewhere it simply indicates the excessive volume of a shout or cry.

ACTS 26

1. To the Gentiles (24:1–26:32 continued)

*To King Agrippa and Paul's Proclamation
of Innocence (25:13–26:32 continued)*

¹Then Agrippa said to Paul, "You have permission to speak for yourself." So Paul motioned with his hand and began his defense: ²"King Agrippa, I consider myself fortunate to stand before you today as I make my defense against all the accusations of the Jews, ³and especially so because you are well acquainted with all the Jewish customs and controversies. Therefore, I beg you to listen to me patiently.

26:1-3. In 25:24-27, Festus stated the purpose of the day's investigation—to determine what to write to the Emperor concerning Paul—and handed the proceedings over to King Agrippa. The King, without further ado, gave the floor to Paul (26:1). In the previous trials, the orators made a point to be brief (e.g., 24:4; 25:8). Brevity was an important rhetorical strategy; the lawyer who wearied the judge could thereby lose the case. This, however, is not a court case. It is an investigation into the unique Jewish concerns over the resurrection which found Paul crosswise with his countrymen. In order to understand the intricacies of this argument, it will take some familiarity with Jewish sects and not a little bit of theological sophistication. Fortunately, Herod Agrippa II has both due to his family heritage as well as his many years of public office in the region. Paul's *captatio benevolentiae* recognizes that he finally has a judge competent to comprehend the intricacies of his case. *Therefore*, Paul pleaded for Herod's patience; this could take a while. (That's saying something for a guy who preached past midnight in Troas!) Undoubtedly it did take a while. This narrative is more than twice as long as the Areopagus address and no less sophisticated in its Greek and rhetorical strategy. Paul raised his hand like a classic Roman rhetorician and offered his defense (*apologeomai*). Here will culminate every major argument in the last five chapters—Paul's legal innocence, the total transformation of Paul's life, and the centrality of the resurrection of Jesus.[1]

⁴"The Jews all know the way I have lived ever since I was a child, from the beginning of my life in my own country, and also in Jerusalem. ⁵They have known me for a long time and can testify, if they are willing, that according to the strictest sect of our religion, I lived as a Pharisee. ⁶And now it is because of my hope in what God has promised our fathers that I am on trial today. ⁷This is

---

[1] Robert O'Toole rightly calls this *The Christological Climax of Paul's Defense* (Rome: Biblical Institute Press, 1973). The length of this discourse, particularly given the fact that it changed nothing of Paul's course, shows how important the content was to Luke's summation of Paul's preaching of Jesus.

the promise our twelve tribes are hoping to see fulfilled as they earnestly serve God day and night. O king, it is because of this hope that the Jews are accusing me. [8]Why should any of you consider it incredible that God raises the dead?"

26:4-5. Paul opened with a biographical description of his kosher heritage. This was precisely his argument in 22:3-5 (cf. Gal 1:13-14; Phil 3:4b-6). In essence, he was showing what a great guy he was according to all the standards of Judaism. To modern ears this sounds somewhat egotistical and would be quite unconvincing in a court of law. (For example, what difference does it make, legally speaking, where a person is born?)[2] That's why we must listen with ancient ears.[3] According to the standards of Paul's day, the defendant's character was inherited through father, land, occupation, and education. Though Paul does not mention his occupation here, all the other primary barometers of character are called to bear witness to Paul's honor: trained as a Pharisee, raised in Jerusalem, and an observant Jew.

26:6-8. What caused the rift was the belief in the resurrection. This theological tenet divided the Pharisees from the Sadducees. What divided Paul further was the specific belief in Jesus' resurrection which was the proleptic promise of the eschatological resurrection that all Pharisees hoped for. According to Paul, this *was* the hope God promised to the "twelve tribes" of Israel.[4] He is not suggesting that there is a proof-text that points to the resurrection of Jesus as the one historical moment when God fulfills his covenant with Israel. Rather, Paul is pointing toward the metanarrative of the Jewish people. The whole story, from the Exodus through the Exile, is about how God elected, sustained, and raised his people from the jaws of death. Jesus, God's beloved son, his envoy and representative to the nation, embodied the entire history of his people. Thus, his personal experience of resurrection is irrefutable proof for Paul that God will ultimately raise his Messianic heirs.

Problem: Dead men don't rise. That was conventional wisdom of both Greeks and Romans. Paul was swimming upstream, and he knew it. Trying to convince the nominally religious of God's eminent work in the world is difficult indeed. However, Paul's argument is sound (v. 8). If there is a God who created and sustained this world (the dominant view of Jews, Greeks, and Romans), what would keep him from raising the dead? What kind of neutered theology portrays a god lacking either the power or the love to give life to his own creation with whom he desires a relationship?

---

[2] Verse 4 is translated in the NIV so as to differentiate Paul's "own country" (ostensibly Tarsus) from Jerusalem. Grammatically speaking, it could also be read, "my own country, *even* Jerusalem." The NIV is likely correct, however, since Paul, in his previous biographical defense mentioned his early life in Tarsus (22:3). For an argument that Paul did not move to Jerusalem until his teen years, cf. du Toit, "A Tale of Two Cities," 375-402.

[3] Frank Crouch, "The Persuasive Moment: Rhetorical Resolutions in Paul's Defense before Agrippa," in *Society of Biblical Literature 1996 Seminar Papers* (Evanston, IL: American Theological Library Association, 1996), 333-342, is particularly helpful in allowing modern readers to hear this passage in the context of ancient rhetorical standards.

[4] This is the only time in the NT the word δωδεκάφυλον is used and surprisingly it does not occur at all in the LXX, Josephus, or Philo, though James 1:1 has a similar expression: ταῖς δώδεκα φυλαῖς.

⁹"I too was convinced that I ought to do all that was possible to oppose the name of Jesus of Nazareth. ¹⁰And that is just what I did in Jerusalem. On the authority of the chief priests I put many of the saints in prison, and when they were put to death, I cast my vote against them. ¹¹Many a time I went from one synagogue to another to have them punished, and I tried to force them to blaspheme. In my obsession against them, I even went to foreign cities to persecute them."

26:9-11. Paul is ready for his second argument—God would raise the dead (vv. 12-18). His evidence was simple: "I saw it!" This is the kind of thing you expect a committed Christian to say. Paul's point in verses 9-11 is that he was not *always* a Christian. In fact, formerly, he was the nastiest persecutor the church had ever seen. His biography is well-known enough by now there's no need to repeat it. Suffice to say, all his brutality against believers bolstered the credibility of his conversion. It is true that some dramatic conversions can be explained through psychological phenomenon. However, Paul showed none of the necessary emotional or psychosocial signs—deep angst, erratic or bipolar tendencies, pounding guilt, close connections to or broken relationships with Christians, etc. There is no psychological explanation of Paul's conversion more compelling than his own testimony: "I saw the risen Christ and that changed the course of my life." Though the resurrection is difficult to believe, it is the only explanation that adequately accounts for Paul's dramatic transformation. Paul understands that the resurrection is a lot to swallow. That's why he so carefully supports it with the testimony of his own life.

Most of what Paul says in verses 9-11 is old news. There are, however, four tidbits of local color we've not seen before. (1) Paul called the Lord "Jesus of Nazareth", the very appellation Jesus himself used (22:8, not to mention Peter, 2:22; 3:6; 4:10; 10:38; see comments on 24:5, fn. 63). (2) Saul was not alone in his rampage against the church. Executions were done under the authority of the High Priest through a vote. The phrase "I cast my vote" is literally "I cast my pebble" (v. 10).[5] The council of judges, of which Saul was a part, would throw in a stone, probably either white or black, to indicate their verdict. (3) As one suspected as early as 8:3, Saul was not just terrorizing the church by going from house to house. He was infiltrating the social networks of the synagogues in Jerusalem, forcing informants to notify the authorities of any Narazenes amidst their congregation (v. 11). (4) Paul attempted to compel Christians to blaspheme by renouncing their faith in Jesus. A century later, Pliny (*Letters* 10.96.5), writing to the governor of Bithynia, said about Christians, "Those who denied they were, or ever had been, Christians, who repeated after me an invocation to the gods . . . and who finally cursed Christ—none of which acts, it is said, those who are really Christians can be forced into performing—these I thought it proper to discharge."

---

[5] Rev 2:17b is the only other passage to use this Greek word for stone (ψῆφος), "I will also give him a white stone with a new name written on it, known only to him who receives it." The word is also used for jewels, particularly in rings (Philostratus, *VA* 3.27), stones in an abacus (Herodotus, 2.36.4), magical incantation pebbles (*PMag. Par.* 1.1048), pieces on a board game, etc. So one should not assume that Rev 2:17b is speaking of a legal verdict though that is a strong possibility.

¹²"On one of these journeys I was going to Damascus with the authority and commission of the chief priests. ¹³About noon, O king, as I was on the road, I saw a light from heaven, brighter than the sun, blazing around me and my companions. ¹⁴We all fell to the ground, and I heard a voice saying to me in Aramaic,ᵃ 'Saul, Saul, why do you persecute me? It is hard for you to kick against the goads.' ¹⁵Then I asked, 'Who are you, Lord?' 'I am Jesus, whom you are persecuting,' the Lord replied. ¹⁶Now get up and stand on your feet. I have appeared to you to appoint you as a servant and as a witness of what you have seen of me and what I will show you. ¹⁷I will rescue you from your own people and from the Gentiles. I am sending you to them ¹⁸to open their eyes and turn them from darkness to light, and from the power of Satan to God, so that they may receive forgiveness of sins and a place among those who are sanctified by faith in me.'"

ᵃ14 Or Hebrew

This is the third time Luke's readers have been privy to Paul's conversion (cf. 9:1-9; 22:4-11). As was mentioned earlier, this triple account is not just about Paul's past. It shows the development of his ministry from a passive persecutor to an active preacher. Here, standing before the King of the Jews, Paul boldly fulfills the call of Christ.

26:12-16a. All the details are essentially familiar though Paul's companions feature more heavily. They too are surrounded by this exceptionally bright light (v. 13), and they too fell to the ground (v. 14). The voice of Jesus also has added color. We learn here that Jesus spoke in Aramaic (or Hebrew, see comments on 21:40),[6] and the following words are new to the reader: "It is hard for you to kick against the goads." This was a popular proverb[7] and simple enough to understand: The farmer plowing with an ox keeps a long stick on the plow with a sharp spike on the end. Should the ox object to his manual labor, the farmer can prod him with a strategically placed jab with the goad. The ox may express his objections to such abuse by kicking against the goad. This is not a particularly bright idea, but what can you expect from a bovine? Paul was called/forced into service of the master and his kicking backfired. The question is "Against what did Saul kick?" Most likely, particularly read against the other ancient uses of this type of proverb, was that Paul was resisting God's sovereign will.[8] The point is that Paul got the point and thereby fell in line with God's call on his life. That is what landed him in the lap of Agrippa on this particular occasion.

26:16b-18. This was Saul's call to become the Apostle to the Gentiles (cf. Eph 2:19; 3:1-6). Glimpses of this commission were given to Ananias (9:15-16): Saul would preach to both Jews and Gentiles, even to their highest authorities, and he would suffer significantly in his new vocation (cf. vv. 16b-17). Verse 18, however, is new and fresh. It is Jewish at its core, echoing two prominent passages from Isaiah.

---

[6] Although Jesus' vernacular might be discerned from vocative spelling of Σαούλ, a Hebrew form of Σαῦλε (9:4; 22:7).

[7] Pss. Sol. 16:4; Philo, Decalogue 87; Euripides, Baccae, 794-795; Aeschylus, Agamemnon 1624; Pindar, Pythian Ode 2.94-95.

[8] The psychological interpretations that Saul was fighting his own conscience are surely an anachronistic imposition of Freudian psychology; cf. Krister Stendahl, "The Apostle Paul and the Introspective Conscience of the West," HTR 56 (1963): 199-215.

The closest verbal parallel is Isaiah 42:1, 6b-7a, "Here is my *servant*, whom I uphold, my *chosen*, in whom my soul delights; I have put my spirit upon him; he will bring forth justice to the *nations*. . . . I have given you as a covenant to the people, a *light* to the *nations*, to *open the eyes* that are blind." Isaiah 42:1-7 was also Jesus' commission (Matt 11:5/Luke 7:22). A second passage reflected in this text also comes from Isaiah 9:2, "The people walking in darkness have seen a great light; on those living in the land of the shadow of death a light has dawned." This too was taken as a description of Jesus in Matthew 4:16 as well as the ministry of John the Baptist (Luke 1:79).[9] Furthermore, the wording of verses 16-23 is strikingly similar to that of Luke 24:46-48,[10] Jesus' final commission to his Apostles: "He told them, 'This is what is written: The Christ will suffer and rise from the dead on the third day, and repentance and forgiveness of sins will be preached in his name to all nations, beginning at Jerusalem. You are witnesses of these things.'"

Paul stood in pretty stout company since his commission at several levels connected with that of Jesus and John. Paul put this commission into practice, bringing people out of darkness into the light: "For you were once darkness, but now you are light in the Lord. Live as children of light" (Eph 5:8). Paradoxically, Paul does not mention his own blindness in this account; rather he is the one who heals the spiritual blindness of those who hear his preaching. The soteriological language of verse 18, prefaced with Hebrew prophecy, is an authentic touch, likely reflecting the actual words of Paul. For example, Acts 26:17-18 sounds quite like Colossians 1:12-14 "[God] has qualified you to share in the inheritance of the saints in the kingdom of light. For he has rescued us from the dominion of darkness and brought us into the kingdom of the Son he loves, in whom we have redemption, the forgiveness of sins."

[19]"So then, King Agrippa, I was not disobedient to the vision from heaven. [20]First to those in Damascus, then to those in Jerusalem and in all Judea, and to the Gentiles also, I preached that they should repent and turn to God and prove their repentance by their deeds. [21]That is why the Jews seized me in the temple courts and tried to kill me. [22]But I have had God's help to this very day, and so I stand here and testify to small and great alike. I am saying nothing beyond what the prophets and Moses said would happen— [23]that the Christ[a] would suffer and, as the first to rise from the dead, would proclaim light to his own people and to the Gentiles."

[a]23 Or *Messiah*

26:19-20. Paul began to drive to a point of decision. One senses that we are getting a rare glimpse of the kind of conclusion Paul came to in synagogue after synagogue. He pushed for a practical repentance that proved authentic through appropriate deeds (v. 20) which sounds a lot like John the Baptist (Luke 3:8; cf.

---

[9] Isaiah 9:6 is not the only description of John the Baptist that was also applied to Paul. Isaiah 49:6, "I will also make you a light for the Gentiles, that you may bring my salvation to the ends of the earth," is also applied to both John the Baptist (Luke 2:32) and to Paul (Acts 13:46).

[10] Jacques Dupont traces the dominant connections of these two texts; cf. "La mission de Paul d'après Actes 26:16-23 et la mission des Apôtres d'après Luc 24:44-49 et Actes 1:8," in *Paul and Paulinism* (London: SPCK, 1982), 290-301.

Luke 3:3; Acts 13:24; 19:4). This call, in no way, reduces salvation by grace to an act of repentance. However, authentic repentance necessarily responds to grace. Particularly in a Jewish context, repentance has always been practical. It includes things like restitution, breaking addictions, altering habits, and reconciliation. One does not repent merely by feeling sorry. Repentance is a changed lifestyle as Paul asserts elsewhere (e.g., Eph 2:10; Titus 2:14; 3:8).

26:21-23. It's a pretty gutsy move to call the king to such transformative repentance. Paul justifies his bold call in several ways. First, he references his vision of the risen Christ. Paul had to be obedient to God's call after such a radical revelation and Herod should follow suit. Second, this call was not for Paul or Herod alone. It had been proclaimed from Damascus to Jerusalem, to Jews and Gentiles (v. 20), before both small and great (v. 22).[11] In fact, his invitation for Gentiles to repent is what brought on the present imprisonment (v. 21). Had he only made the offer to his own people, the Asians would never have hounded him in the temple of Jerusalem. Third, Paul is doing the will of God with the help of God (v. 22). He is accomplishing what the prophets and Moses predicted. This is no new innovation; it is the long-awaited Messianic age. How can we know? This is Paul's fourth and final point: Jesus suffered and rose again. This grand message is too colossal to be contained by just one people-group. The God of Israel must now become the God of the nations.

Though many Gentiles heard this good news and rejoiced, Festus was flustered. What kind of nonsense is this that from the Jews would come the salvation of mankind? Festus considered them small, petty, and mean. They mutilated their bodies in circumcision, they abstained from good food, they were lazy in their rigid Sabbath adherence, they were arrogant in their ethnocentrism, and they were constantly fighting with everyone including themselves. *They* were the source of salvation?! Furthermore, the idea that a man would raise from the dead is simply nonsense. Not only did Festus 'know' that didn't happen, Romans and Greeks wouldn't *want* it to happen. Death was that sweet release from the prison of a mortal body. This was too much to stomach in silence.

[24]**At this point Festus interrupted Paul's defense. "You are out of your mind, Paul!" he shouted. "Your great learning is driving you insane."** [25]**"I am not insane, most excellent Festus," Paul replied. "What I am saying is true and reasonable.** [26]**The king is familiar with these things, and I can speak freely to him. I am convinced that none of this has escaped his notice, because it was not done in a corner.** [27]**King Agrippa, do you believe the prophets? I know you do."** [28]**Then Agrippa said to Paul, "Do you think that in such a short time you can persuade me to be a Christian?"** [29]**Paul replied, "Short time or long—I pray God that not only you but all who are listening to me today may become what I am, except for these chains."**

---

[11] The phrase "then to those in Jerusalem and in all Judea," is grammatically awkward since it is in the accusative case while the other phrases are in the dative case. It is also historically awkward since it is out of chronological sequence. Bruce (492, fn 24) suggests the simplest solution is to take the phrase to mean: "in every land to both Jews and Gentiles." Regardless, it communicates the unquestionably historical sense that Paul preached to Jews (first) and to Gentiles the saving message of faith in the Messiah, Jesus.

26:24. Festus couldn't contain himself. His belligerent outburst bordered on rude. It could be rendered literally, "Your studies have driven you insane." From the word "insane" (*mania*) we have derived "maniac." The implication is one who is raving, frenzied, and/or enraged (*TDNT* 4:360-361). Such a person is highly emotional and volatile. In the current context, however, that looks more like Festus than Paul. One must admit, the resurrection is a wild idea. It is not impossible to believe, but it does demand the kind of stellar evidence Paul has provided if Festus only had ears to hear. Festus was right about one thing: Paul was one of those 'scary-smart' people who could run intellectual circles around his peers. Such unique minds have a tendency to be misunderstood and vilified as unstable, perhaps even crazy (e.g., *Tg. Num.* 22.5, Str-B 2:770).

26:25-26. Paul's measured retort[12] goes a long way to disarming Festus's libel.[13] We must bear in mind that all such public verbal forays were contexts for honor. Normally the crowd arbitrated the contest by granting approval or disapproval to one of the parties. In this scenario, however, Herod holds the key to victory in this contest of honor. Hence, Paul deflects Festus's insult and zeros in on Herod. By reminding Festus that Herod was familiar with the intricacies of this Jewish debate, he was also subtly rebuking Festus for speaking out of ignorance. Paul, with appropriate decorum, suggested Festus keep his mouth shut when he said, "I can speak freely *to him.*"

Indeed Herod must have been familiar with the debate over resurrection in general and over Jesus' resurrection in particular. After all, it was not something done in a corner (v. 26). This argument, it should be pointed out, was pretty standard fare for philosophers.[14] Since they were often accused of esoteric, secret discussions, they replied by pointing out the public nature of their discourse. Jesus offered a similar retort to Annas who questioned him about his teaching, "I have spoken openly to the world. I always taught in synagogues or at the temple, where all the Jews come together. I said nothing in secret" (John 18:20). Likewise, those who testified to the resurrection did so in public discourse. Herod had to have heard of all this.

26:27-29. It was time to press for a decision from the king. Beyond familiarity with contemporary witnesses, Herod should concur with the ancient prophets. Paul presses the point (v. 27). Of course, the "King of the Jews" can't very well publicly deny familiarity with or fidelity to the Old Testament! Agrippa surely felt the glaring eyes of his colleagues. On the one hand, he likely had a sense that what Paul was saying was true and had enough of a conscience not to deny it but had not the wits to decry it. On the other hand, he could hardly afford to convert under the pressure of a prisoner. He had to save face without denying faith. His smokescreen was incredibly clever: "Do you think that in such a short time you can persuade me to be a Christian?" (v. 28). It is, perhaps, the

---

[12] The word "reasonable" (σωφροσύνη, v. 25) is the antithesis of "mania" (e.g., Xenophon, *Mem.* 1.1.16; Luke 8:38; 2 Cor 5:13).

[13] For a similar accusation and measured response, see Justin, *Dialogue* 39.4.

[14] E.g., Origen, *C. Celsus* 6.78; cf. Abraham Malherbe, "'Not in a Corner': Early Christian Apologetic," *SC* 5 (1985/1986): 193-210 (esp. 202-203).

most nebulous statement recorded in all Scripture. The problem is fourfold. First, we don't know exactly what the "little/much" is. The NIV supplies the word "time" (v. 28, 29) which would be the normal accusative for "little" (*oligō*) in such a Greek construction. However, the nebulous nature of the sentence opens the possibility for other meanings such as "paucity of evidence," "few words," or "minimal effort." Second, we can't tell whether it is a statement or a question. Third, we don't know if the king is serious or sarcastic.[15] Fourth, we can't tell if "Christian" is pejorative or merely descriptive [for comments on the term "Christian" see 11:26]. This leaves a dizzying array of possibilities such as: "You seriously think you can convert me with this brief argument?" "Surely you don't think I'll covert so soon (or so easily)." "Paul, you almost had me . . . with a little more discussion I might concur." "I'm pretty close to becoming a Christian." "Paul, I'm almost ready [wink]." All this ambiguity should not distress the reader. Narrative ambiguity, at least in this instance, is not a hindrance to grasping the meaning of the text, it *is* the meaning of the text! Herod throws out this nebulous smokescreen to keep Paul at bay.[16]

Paul doesn't linger long over the invitation. It was offered, rejected, and there's no use pushing Herod further into a corner, particularly amidst his peers with whom he must save face. He simply takes one parting shot: "I pray you all would become Christians like me . . . well, without the chains." Notice the subtle jibe against Festus—these chains are unjust and should have been removed long ago by civic rulers with the courage to do what is right. Paradoxically, the Roman ruler won't do what is right for fear of the Jews, and the Jewish ruler won't do what is right for fear of the Romans.

[30]The king rose, and with him the governor and Bernice and those sitting with them. [31]They left the room, and while talking with one another, they said, "This man is not doing anything that deserves death or imprisonment." [32]Agrippa said to Festus, "This man could have been set free if he had not appealed to Caesar."

26:30-31. Herod was pretty uncomfortable with where all this was headed and brought the investigation to a swift and definitive end. He stood, all the court stood with him, and the session was thus adjourned. This inquiry, though interesting, offered nothing of substance for Festus to write. Herod only offered this, "Paul is guilty of no capital offence." This, of course, was nothing new. Festus (25:18-19) and Claudius (23:29) had already come to that same conclusion. The Roman consensus is clear: Paul was innocent of any major crime but somehow inextricably embroiled in litigation that kept him in chains.

26:32. Agrippa claims that Paul could have been released had he not appealed to Caesar. Technically, that is probably true. Practically, however, that is doubtful on several counts. First, Paul had been kept in prison for two years un-

---

[15] Sarcasm is, by far, the greater likelihood; cf. Pat Harrell, "Almost Persuaded' Now to Believe? Acts 26:28," *RQ* 4 (1960): 252-254.
[16] Paul Harlé, "Un 'Private-Joke' de Paul dans le Livre des Actes (XXVI. 28-29)," *NTS* 24 (1978): 527-533, suggests that Paul got the joke and responded accordingly, changing the metaphor from time (ὀλίγος) to the high social status of King Herod (μεγάς).

der Felix, an unjust procurator who courted the favor of Jewish politicians who practiced violence and plotted assassinations. It was not likely that Festus would soon have resisted their pressure. Second, Festus asked Paul to go to Jerusalem and stand trial there. That was a lethal political compromise that Paul would not likely have survived. Festus may have convinced *himself* he was just. The historian, however, rightly questions his self-assessment as either self-deception or sheer bravado in the face of a fellow politician he would like to impress. Third, had Festus thought Paul was in any way connected with an anti-imperial movement, there is little chance he would have released him in case the emperor should find out. Rumors spread quickly and usually run downhill, and Rome was filled with influential Jewish patrons who had the Emperor's attention. Festus's fledgling career could hardly survive such a misstep.

ACTS 27

C. JOURNEY TO ROME (27:1–28:31)

This is the climactic movement in Acts—the journey to Rome. The narrative is gripping at a couple of important levels. *Historically*, we are witnessing an extraordinary true-to-life adventure, what Bruce (498) calls "a classic in its own right, as graphic a piece of descriptive writing as anything in the Bible." These kinds of maritime voyages are recorded a plenty.[1] Homer's *Odyssey* set a standard for sea voyages that was difficult to avoid in practically every novel that followed. Though Acts 27 conforms to the standard story form, [2] it also shows signs of historical veracity.[3] Luke identifies the right places (in disproportionate detail), the right nautical practices (though he lacks the technical vocabulary of a sailor[4]), the right timing, and the right persons in leadership onboard.[5] Furthermore,

[1] Charles Talbert and J. H. Hayes, "A Theology of Sea Storms in Luke-Acts," in *Society of Biblical Literature Seminar Papers* no. 34 (January 1, 1995): 268-269, offers a striking array of primary sources: (1) Greek—Homer, *Odyssey* 4.499-511; 5.291-453; 12.403-428; Aeschylus, *Agamemnon* 647-666; Herodotus, *Histories* 7.188-192; 8.12-14; Euripides, *Daughters of Troy* 77-86; *Iphigeneia in Taurica* 1391-1498; *Helen* 400-413; Apollonius Rhodius, *Argonautica* 2.1093-1121; Polybius, *Histories* 1.37; Chariton, *Chaereas and Callirhoe* 3.3; Chion of Heraclea, 4; Dio Chrysostom, *Oration* 7.2-7; Xenophon of Ephesus, *Ephesian Tale* 2.11; 3.2; 3.12; Lucian, *Toxaris* 19-21; *The Ship* 7-9; Aelius Aristides, *Sacred Tales* 2.12-14; 2.64-68; Achilles Tatius, *Leucippe and Clitophon* 3.1-5; *Apollonius King of Tyre* §265-267; Heliodorus, *Ethiopian Story* 1.22; 5.27; Quintus of Smyrna, *The Fall of Troy* 14.359-527. (2) Roman—Plautus, *The Rope* 62-78; Virgil, *Aeneid* 1.122-252; 3.253-275; 5.14-43; Ovid, *Metamorphoses* 11.477-574 and *Tristia* 1.2.1-110; Curtius, *History of Alexander* 4.3.16-18; Phaedrus, *Fables* 4.23; Petronius, *Satyricon* 7.11.89; Seneca, *Agamemnon* 456-578; Lucan, *Civil War* 4.48-120; 5.560-577; 9.319-347; 9.445-492; Statius, *Thebaid* 5.361-430; Valerius Flaccus, *Argonautica* 1.614-658; Silius Italicus, *Punica* 17.244-290; Tacitus, *Annals* 2.23-24. (3) Jewish—Jonah 1:3-17; the *Testament of Naphtali* 6:1-10; Josephus, *War* 1.279-280; *Life* 13-16. (4) Christian—*Acts of Philip* 3.33-36; Pseudo-Clementine *Homilies* 1.8.

[2] Acts 27 shares many of the major themes of these fictive stories. Talbert and Hayes, "Theology," 269-270, identify more than a dozen: warning not to sail, dangerous season for sailing, chaotic winds, darkness during the storm, sailors scurrying about, cargo and tackle jettisoned, ship driven at sea and finally being broken up, abandoning all hope, wreckage on rocks or shallows, survivors drifting on planks and others swimming to shore, and simple local folk helping the victims. In other words, Luke was clearly writing within a standard story form.

[3] Susan Praeder, "Acts 27:1–28:16; Sea Voyages in Ancient Literature and the Theology of Luke-Acts," *CBQ* 46 (1984): 683-706, points out that though Acts 27 taps into the topos of sea voyages, there is not a demonstrable dependence on them. "It cannot be said that it simply follows a literary model for storm scenes" (693); so also Ernst Haenchen, "Acta 27," in *Zeit und Geschichte; Dankesgabe an Rudolf Bultmann zum 80 Geburtstag* (Tübingen: Mohr, 1964), 235-254. There are, in fact, a number of classic narrative descriptions that are lacking in Acts 27 that one would expect from a literary fiction (694). Marius Reiser, "Von Caesarea nach Malta: Literarischer Charakter und historische Glaubwürdigkeit von Act 27," in *Das Ende des Paulus: Historische, theologische und literaturgeschichtliche Aspekte* (Berlin: Walter de Gruyter, 2001): 51-61, goes further, stating that there are no true parallels to Acts 27 in other ancient *Seenotrettungswunder* (dangerous sea voyage accounts).

[4] Luke uses more than two dozen words or phrases found only here in the NT (though familiar to the LXX, Josephus, Philo, and other pagan literature). Most of these terms pertain to the ship or the sailing conventions, but they are not the technical terms used in conventional nautical literature; cf. Adrian Hummel, "Factum et fictum: Literarische und theologische Erwägungen zur Romreise des Paulus in der Apostelgeschichte (Apg 27,1–28,16)" *BN* 105 (2000): 48-49. He rightly concludes that though Luke's presentation is both literary and theological, it is, nonetheless, no less historical.

[5] J. M. Gilchrist, "The Historicity of Paul's Shipwreck," *JSNT* 61 (1996): 29-51, is so confident of the historicity of this account that he offers it as a credible guide for archaeologists to locate the wreckage in St. Paul's Bay. Another classic piece, still of great value, that confirms the factual nature of the account is James Smith, *The Voyage and Shipwreck of St. Paul* (Grand Rapids: Baker, 1978, 1848).

the use of the first person in the narrative is a likely sign of historicity.[6] In short, it looks like Luke was on board recording his experiences in vocabulary and style familiar to him from his own literary milieu.

The journey to Rome is gripping at a second level—*theologically.* Just as the book of Luke pointed toward and culminated in Jerusalem (Luke 9:51; 19:28), so Acts begins in Jerusalem and drives toward Rome (Acts 19:21; 28:14-16). This is more than geography; it is theology. The point is not *where* they were but that they had arrived at the capital city under the sovereign protection of God with the Lord's promise that Paul would preach to the Emperor himself. Thus the gospel had reached the ends of the earth, fulfilling the commission Jesus laid out in 1:8, "But you will receive power when the Holy Spirit comes on you; and you will be my witnesses in Jerusalem, and in all Judea and Samaria, and to the ends of the earth."

The journey has introductory and concluding itineraries (27:1-8; 28:11-16) that bracket three dynamic scenes: The storm (27:9-20), the shipwreck (27:21-44), and salvation on shore (28:1-10). The first two sections open with a prediction (27:9-10, 21-22) that describes for the reader precisely what will take place. This subtly, yet irrevocably, places Paul center stage. His life determines the destiny of all 276 people on board. The ancient reader was more adept at catching the parody in the situation. They were familiar with stories like Jonah where one wayward sinner could cause a catastrophe at sea. The gods were keen to punish criminals through the waves.[7] Our story, however, contains a twist. It is not the villain who caused the catastrophe but it was God's vessel who averted it. Against all odds they landed safely at shore because God's hand of protection was on Paul.

1. The Storm (27:1-20)

[1]When it was decided that we would sail for Italy, Paul and some other prisoners were handed over to a centurion named Julius, who belonged to the Imperial Regiment. [2]We boarded a ship from Adramyttium about to sail for ports along the coast of the province of Asia, and we put out to sea. Aristarchus, a Macedonian from Thessalonica, was with us. [3]The next day we landed at Sidon; and Julius, in kindness to Paul, allowed him to go to his friends so they might provide for his needs. [4]From there we put out to sea again and passed to the lee of Cyprus because the winds were against us. [5]When we had sailed across the open sea off the coast of Cilicia and Pamphylia, we landed at Myra in Lycia. [6]There the centurion found an Alexandrian ship sailing for Italy and put us on board. [7]We made slow headway for many days and had difficulty arriving off Cnidus. When the wind did not allow us to hold our course, we sailed to the lee of Crete, opposite Salmone. [8]We moved along the coast with difficulty and came to a place called Fair Havens, near the town of Lasea.

---

[6] Colin Hemer, "First Person Narrative in Acts 27–28," *TynBul* 36 (1985): 79-109, and C. K. Barrett, "Paul Shipwrecked," in *Scripture: Meaning and Method* (Hull, England: Hull University Press, 1987), 51-64, contra Vernon Robbins, "The We-Passages in Acts and Ancient Sea-Voyages," *BR* 20 (1975): 5-18.

[7] Especially helpful with this *topos* are Gary Miles and Garry Trompf, "Luke and Antiphon: The Theology of Acts 27–28 in the Light of Pagan Beliefs about Divine Retribution, Pollution, and Shipwreck," *HTR* 69 (1976): 259-267, and the more carefully argued article by David Ladouceur, "Hellenistic Preconceptions of Shipwreck and Pollution as a Context for Acts 27–28," *HTR* 73 (1980): 435-449.

27:1-3. A number of prisoners were in the same boat as Paul, including his friend Aristarchus of Thessalonica.[8] There's no way to know whether the others had appealed to Caesar like Paul, but they were headed to Rome just the same. They too were in the custody of Julius, a Centurion who treated Paul with considerable philanthropic respect. The fact that Julius gave Paul such latitude and the fact that he was accompanied by at least two helpers (whom Julius might have seen as servants), indicates the significant social status Paul was able to claim.[9] He is the last Centurion in the New Testament, and like all the others was portrayed in a positive light. Julius was from the Imperial (*Sebastēs*) Regiment.[10] This might merely be a title of special honor (Bruce, 500, fn. 9). However, Ramsay (*Traveller*, 315) offers the likely suggestion that this regiment was composed of officer-couriers (*frumentarii*) who supplied a communicative link between the Emperor and his troops in the far-flung provinces. If that is so, it would be natural for Julius and his troops to return to Rome with news of the province and escort these prisoners to the imperial court.

Luke includes himself in the travel log by picking up the "we" narrative left off in 21:18. Moreover, just as he carefully catalogued his overnight stops in 16:11-12; 20:13-16; and 21:1-8, so here he gives a detailed itinerary of every port of call for this Adramyttium ship heading back home to Mysia in Asia Minor. The first day they went about seventy miles from Caesarea to Sidon, a major import/export center in Phoenicia (modern Lebanon). There Julius allowed Paul to visit local Christian 'friends'.[11] These brothers and sisters supplied Paul's needs for the trip, primarily food. There were no food stores on board for passengers. They ate what they carried with them. Julius was strategically kind to Paul—a well-fed prisoner was less of a risk for flight or fight.

27:4-6. After off-loading cargo in Sidon and loading goods for transport to Asia, the crew was off again. Due to inclement weather, they chose to sail along the east shore of Cyprus ("to the lee"), using the island as a buffer against the blustery west winds.[12] Luke likely recalls the same strategy from chapter 21:1-3

---

[8] The text does not say Aristarchus was a prisoner, he might just be returning home to Thessalonica. However, he does show up in Rome with Paul and is called a "fellow-prisoner" (Col 4:10; cf. Phm 1:24). So if he is not a prisoner now, he must have been arrested somewhere along the way, perhaps in Rome itself, unless the term "fellow-prisoner" is a figure of speech for "faithful companion" of the imprisoned Paul. The Western text also adds Secundus as a traveling companion of Paul but this is most certainly because of his literary connection to Aristarchus in Acts 20:4. In addition the Western text adds that the governor [Festus] decided to send Paul to Rome and the very next day called Julius to escort him. For other differences in the Western text of vv. 1-13, some of which are substantial, see Marie Boismard and Arnaud Lamouille, "Le texte Occidental des Actes des Apôtres: à propos de Actes 27:1-13," *ETL* 63 (1987): 48-58.

[9] This status of Paul under Julius's jurisdiction is part and parcel with a very complicated and intricate social system of honor, the details of which are explicated by Michael Labahn, "Paulus—ein *homo honestus et iustus*: Das lukanische Paulusportrait von Act 27–28 im Lichte ausgewählter antiker Parallelen," in *Das Ende des Paulus* (Berlin: Walter de Gruyter, 2001): 75-106. Chapters 27 and 28 consistently portray Paul as a man of honorable social status with clout and influence in whatever company or circumstance he finds himself.

[10] A number of inscriptions attest to this title for auxiliary troops in various provinces (*ILS* 1, 2683; *OGIS* 421; *CIL* 6, 3508); cf. Labahn, "Paulus—ein *homo honestus et iustus*," 79 fn 13. Josephus (*J.W.* 2.3.4 §52; 2.4.2 §58, 2.4.3 §63, 2.5.2 §74, 2.12.5 §236) uses the term for the royal troops of Jewish kings.

[11] "Friends" may have been one of the early titles for the church (cf. Luke 12:4; 16:9; John 15:13-15; Acts 24:23; 3 John 15) that fell into disuse due to its adoption by Gnostics.

[12] Jean Rougé disagrees, arguing that they sailed to the south of Crete and then north on the western side of the island; cf. "Actes 27:1-10," *VC* 14 (1960): 195-196. He also makes an interesting observation that Festus probably intended Julius to take Paul to Rome by land, following the basic trek of the second

when they sighted Cyprus on the left side of the ship as they sailed to the south of it en route to Syria. After crossing the open sea between Cyprus and Cilicia, they were blown to the east and had to creep along the coast against a heavy west wind, finally arriving at Myra in the region of Lycia. They would have had to tack back and forth, taking advantage of the wind (particularly at night) which came off the coastal mountains. Their progress would have been aided slightly by the westward current along the coast of Cilicia and Pamphylia which typically runs about two miles per hour. According to the Western text, this jaunt from Cyprus to Myra took fifteen days.

From here the Adramyttium ship would soon head north. Since they wanted to head west, they found an Egyptian cargo vessel carrying grain from Alexandria. This was not hard to do; Myra was one of the major ports between Alexandria and Rome for the grain trade. It would be difficult to overestimate the importance of Alexandria's grain to Rome. In fact, grain commerce was its own 'state department' in Rome. Due to the relationship between Rome and the grain trade, Julius would have had little trouble booking passage for his chained gang and the soldiers who guarded them. This particular ship was built for cargo, not for speed. From bow to stern it might reach two hundred and forty feet (and sixty feet wide), carrying up to 2,000 tons of grain (though most were, in all probability, considerably smaller)! But fully loaded she could probably not exceed nine miles per hour (seven knots).[13]

27:7-9. At this point the poor weather took a turn for the worse. What should have been a single day's journey to Cnidus was remembered by a seasick physician as "many days" full of "difficulty." Rather than stopping for the winter in Asia Minor (southern Turkey), these foolhardy seamen risked a precarious journey that would gain them a couple hundred miles. They allowed the vessel to be driven south to Crete, where they (again) used the southern side of the island as a shield from the relentless northwest gale. They crept along the coast to a little inlet called "Fair Havens," which is likely to be identified with *Lime[o] nas Kalous*, about twelve miles east of Cape Matala. The nearest town, Lasea, was some five miles to the east and hardly suitable for their needs.[14] Two hundred and seventy-six men had certain physical and social needs that could scarcely be met by the local farmers and barmaids.

⁹Much time had been lost, and sailing had already become dangerous because by now it was after the Fast.ᵃ So Paul warned them, ¹⁰"Men, I can see that our voyage is going to be disastrous and bring great loss to ship and cargo, and to our own lives also." ¹¹But the centurion, instead of listening to what Paul said,

missionary journey and then on to Italy via the Egnatian way (197). Julius, however, decided that the ship would be easier and faster.

[13] For more detail on these types of ships, see Nicolle Hirschfield and Michael Fitzgerald, "The Ship of St. Paul," *BA* 53 (1990): 25-39; cf. Seneca, *Epistles* 77.1-2; Lucian, *The Ship or the Wishes* 4: "What a huge ship! A hundred and twenty cubits long, the ship-wright said, and well over a quarter as wide, and from deck to bottom where it is deepest, in the bilge, twenty-nine. Then what a tall mast, what a yard to carry! . . . She was said to carry corn enough to feed all Attica for a year. And all this a little old man, a wee fellow, has kept from harm by turning the huge rudders with a tiny tiller."

[14] There are some ruins in this vicinity that have been postulated to be Lasea though this is far from certain.

followed the advice of the pilot and of the owner of the ship. [12]**Since the harbor was unsuitable to winter in, the majority decided that we should sail on, hoping to reach Phoenix and winter there. This was a harbor in Crete, facing both southwest and northwest.**

[a]9 That is, the Day of Atonement (Yom Kippur)

27:9-10. Their trip so far had been slow and tedious, delaying them past the reasonable season for sailing. It was already past Yom Kippur ("The Fast") which fell on October 5 in A.D. 59. Sailing on the Mediterranean was dangerous between September 15 and November 11, after which sailing ceased altogether until February at the earliest (cf. Vegetius, *On Military Affairs* 4.39). There is a thin line between courage and foolhardiness that even seasoned sailors should not cross. Paul predicts trouble. Though Luke may intend to portray Paul's prediction as a prophecy, it hardly takes a seer to prognosticate disaster on the high seas of the Mediterranean after November 1. Since Paul has already been shipwrecked three times (2 Cor 11:25), he can sense the danger and he isn't eager for round four. This warning is standard fare in sea-voyage stories. In effect, it allows the reader to know what is coming. Paul's prediction, however, is not a mirror image of what will happen. He said there would be loss to the ships and cargo (which is exactly right) but also that there would be loss of life. Jesus' later revelation would correct Paul's misperception (v. 22).[15] The ship would sink, but against all odds, every life would be spared from the sea.

27:11. Predictably, the Centurion heeds the advice of the ship's captain and owner (over against Paul). The captain of the ship was a professional sailor whose expertise guided the precious cargo to Rome; the owner of the ship was probably on contract with the Roman government and had much to gain from this shipment. This was especially true for grain arriving in Rome during the dangerous season for sailing. While they had to brave the dangers at sea in the fall, they could also charge exorbitantly for the precious cargo they carried. These two had far more experience than Paul and more vested interests in the cargo and crew, the majority of whom sided with the captain. (The fact that Paul was even given voice in the ship's council says a lot about his influence and travel experience). If this ship was, in fact, under contract with the Roman government, then Julius was the highest ranking official on board, hence, responsible for the final decision whether to stay or sail. You can't blame Julius for following the advice of the captain and owner rather than heeding Paul's warning. Any reasonable military man would have done the same.

27:12. Since Fair Havens was inadequate for the needs of soldiers and sailors, they decided to sail on to Phoenix and winter there *if they could*. The Greek construction reflects the real danger of the situation: "if they might, perhaps, be able to reach Phoenix." Had they reached Phoenix, they would have been rewarded with a much larger city to host the crew and a particularly safe harbor for their ship. Luke describes this harbor as facing both southwest and north-

---

[15] This may be a pretty good indication that Paul's prediction is based on human experience while the later revelation is exactly correct that there would not be a single life lost (v. 22).

west. "*Phineka*" fits that description perfectly. *Phineka* is not quite as impressive a *Lutro* on the eastern side of the promontory that protects ships in all directions but about 25° of the compass, but it was also known as a suitable harbor for wintering.[16] Even so, Luke doesn't think it's worth the risk. Of course, this friend of Paul writes with the advantage of 20/20 hindsight. The sailors, on the other hand, are willing to risk the short little jaunt of fifty miles while hugging the coast. This should not have been a terribly difficult trip . . . but it was.

[13]When a gentle south wind began to blow, they thought they had obtained what they wanted; so they weighed anchor and sailed along the shore of Crete. [14]Before very long, a wind of hurricane force, called the "northeaster," swept down from the island. [15]The ship was caught by the storm and could not head into the wind; so we gave way to it and were driven along. [16]As we passed to the lee of a small island called Cauda, we were hardly able to make the lifeboat secure. [17]When the men had hoisted it aboard, they passed ropes under the ship itself to hold it together. Fearing that they would run aground on the sandbars of Syrtis, they lowered the sea anchor and let the ship be driven along. [18]We took such a violent battering from the storm that the next day they began to throw the cargo overboard. [19]On the third day, they threw the ship's tackle overboard with their own hands. [20]When neither sun nor stars appeared for many days and the storm continued raging, we finally gave up all hope of being saved.

27:13. It was the dangerous season for sailing, but it was not so late that shipping ceased. One could, therefore, expect a reprieve between storms when one could cautiously sail a short distance. That's the plan. When the northwesterly storms gave way to a gentle south breeze from the coast of Africa, the warmer weather and milder conditions lulled the sailors into an ill-fated optimism. All they had to do was round the cape of Matala and gently guide the ship along the coast. It should have taken less than eight hours.

27:14. Problem: As they rounded the cape and headed north, the wind dramatically changed course. The gentle breeze from the south was pummeled by a blast from the northeast. This furious gale had its own name: Euroquilo or in English "northeaster."[17] It built up force as it swept across the island and gained a full head of steam as it descended eight thousand feet down the slopes of Mt. Ida. By the time it funneled into the valley, it gained the strength of a hurricane (*typhōnikos*).[18]

27:15-18. There was just no way they could hold their course; literally, they

---

[16] One inscription tells of an Alexandrian ship wintering there in the time of Trajan; cf. Hemer, "First Person Narrative," 97-98. Some scholars believe that Luke actually intended *Lutro*. It does not, in fact, face southwest and northwest but faces southeast and northeast. It is possible, though not likely, that Luke described the port not from land but from the perspective of the ship. This, however, would make his description confusing. Another option is that Luke, who never actually saw the harbor, had the compass points heading in the wrong direction (cf. Ramsay, "Traveler," 326).

[17] Euroquilo is a hybrid *hapax legomenon* combining the Greek word Εὖρος "east wind" and the Latin *Aquilo* "northwind." There was a large compass found in North Africa that confirmed the use of this term. Inscribed in stone were the names of all the winds from the various directions. The northeast compass point had the name "Euroaquilo," cf. Reiser, "Von Caesarea nach Malta," 64-66.

[18] For a helpful description of the physics involved in the Euroquilo coming off Mt. Ida, cf. R. W. White, "A Meteorological Appraisal of Acts 27:5-26," *ExpT* 113 (2002): 403-407.

could not "look the wind in the eye" (*antophthalmein*).[19] They were blasted out to sea with no other option but to allow the wind to drive them westward. Fortunately, there is a little island about twenty-five miles west of the coast of Crete called Cauda. Under the protection of its southern shore, the sailors frantically made preparations for a wild ride on the chaotic waves at the mercy of the nautical gods. Since Cauda is a mere six-and-a-half miles long, their window was slim. They did three things to improve their chances of survival. First, they secured the lifeboat. That would mean pulling it on deck and strapping it down. Should the ship sink, this little lifeboat might be the only source of salvation. Since most ancients could not swim, there was an urgency to preserve this dinghy. Luke apparently helped hoist a waterlogged dinghy, remembering the difficulty, and perhaps a few blisters.

A second precautionary action was to 'frap' the ship (v. 17). They literally tied the ship together with ropes (cf. Philo, *Joseph*, 33). This likely meant passing ropes under the hull and securing them on deck, but it might also include securing beams below deck with ropes or somehow securing the ropes across the deck (cf. Polhill, 521, fn. 3). The pressure of the waves could literally separate the beams in the hull of the ship, allowing water to careen into the lower deck. The ropes helped minimize the amount of water that could seep in. Finally, fearing that they would be driven aground off the coast of Africa on the treacherous sandbars of Syrtis (Polybius 1.39; Strabo, *Geo.* 2.5.20), they lowered the sea anchor, literally, "the equipment." This probably refers to the stone anchors dragged behind the drifting vessel, slowing its inevitable course.[20] With these three preparations, they were at the mercy of the waves.

27:18-20. Before the ship ever sank, the sailors' spirits did. Their hopes were battered by the storm. In three successive movements, Luke takes his readers down the rabbit hole of despair. First, the ship was battered so badly they decided to throw the precious cargo overboard (cf. Jonah 1:5). The weight of the grain sank the ship deeper into the waves, all the more if the ship took on water and the grain absorbed it. When they jettisoned the cargo, the ship rode higher on the waves rather than taking on the full brunt of the waves battering the side of the ship. One shudders to think that part of what was pitched overboard were the sacred scrolls of Paul or perhaps letters he had written that were yet unsent. The lighter load helped, but it was still not enough. Three days later, they cast the ship's tackle into the sea. Luke's description is heart-wrenching. The sailors, *with their own hands*, "ripped" off the rigging and threw it overboard. The ropes, sails, pulleys, yardarm, etc. were heavy and could substantially lighten the ship's load. But when a sailor loses his tackle, he loses control. When he loses control, he loses hope. Added to that, the storm concealed the sun and stars. This is not a comment on how dreary the weather was. Luke is saying they were sailing

---

[19] Cf. Polybius, *Hist* 1.17.3. Witherington suggests: "This last expression likely comes from the practice of painting eyes on each side of the bow of a ship" (765).

[20] A less likely interpretation of "lowering the sea anchor" was that they cut off the heavy mast (or yardarm) whose weight would not only lower the ship in the waves but could torque the sides of the ship, allowing water to pour into the hull; cf. James Smith, *The Voyage and Shipwreck of St. Paul* (4th edition; Grand Rapids: Baker, 1978, 1880), 111-116.

blind. Before the invention of the compass, the sun and stars were the navigation system for a sailor. The captain lost his cargo, the crew was riding blind and lame without their tackle and navigation, so everyone lost all hope of surviving. They were soaked to the bone, chilled to the core, desperately fatigued, and limp from more than a week of perpetual seasickness and vomiting. A thick cloud of despair shrouded this skeleton of a ship that the raging ocean flicked across her currents. They lost hope of being saved.[21]

2. The Shipwreck (27:21-44)

[21]After the men had gone a long time without food, Paul stood up before them and said: "Men, you should have taken my advice not to sail from Crete; then you would have spared yourselves this damage and loss. [22]But now I urge you to keep up your courage, because not one of you will be lost; only the ship will be destroyed. [23]Last night an angel of the God whose I am and whom I serve stood beside me [24]and said, 'Do not be afraid, Paul. You must stand trial before Caesar; and God has graciously given you the lives of all who sail with you.' [25]So keep up your courage, men, for I have faith in God that it will happen just as he told me. [26]Nevertheless, we must run aground on some island."

27:21-22. Paul apparently never read the book *How to Win Friends and Influence People.* He attempted to encourage a shipload of terrified, hungry, and seasick, sailors, soldiers, and prisoners. How did he get their attention? With a good old fashioned "I told you so." The fact that he was right may have done little to win their approval. His purpose, of course, was to convince them that he did, in fact, know what he was talking about. Even if they agreed that Paul was competent, what he said next was still a difficult sell: The ship would be destroyed but not a single person would drown. The first half was all too tenable. It's the second part that made no sense. If the ship sank, the nonswimmers (the majority) would likely drown in the storm-tossed surf. Weak as they were, chances were slim that every individual would safely float to shore on a piece of willing wreckage.

27:23-26. Paul's evidence was an angel who appeared to him the previous night. Now they had no anti-supernatural bias as most modern westerners today. But that did not mean they would buy Paul's story. The Greco-Roman gods were capricious, often unmerciful, and not uncommonly deceptive. Hence, the sailors might ask, "If your God wanted to save us, why did he send the wind and waves to beat us down?" They had no trouble believing there was divine intervention in the storm. They would, however, have had difficulty believing that the end of the chronicle would be better than the beginning.

Verse 24, coming from anyone else, would sound incredibly arrogant. Paul

---

[21] Luke's salvation vocabulary in this chapters is likely a double entendre of both physical and spiritual rescue: σώζω (27:20, 31), διασώζω (27:43, 44; 28:1, 4), σωτηρία (27:34); cf. Karl Löning, "Das Gottesbild der Apostelgeschichte im Spannungsfeld von Frühjudentum und Fremdreligionen," in *Monotheismus und Christologie: zur Gottesfrage im hellenistischen Judentum und im Urchristentum* (ed. Joachim Gnilka and Hans-Josef Klauck; Freiburg: Herder, 1992), 88-117.

not only claims to be the servant of God but the savior of the ship and destined to stand before their Caesar. There is a truth here that should not be missed. In the words of F. F. Bruce (512), "The world has no idea how much it owes, in the mercy of God, to the presence in it of righteous men." This was intended to encourage them, and Paul's own faith in God was to bolster theirs. Whether it worked or not is irrelevant. In a few days they would look back on Paul's prediction and see just how true were his words. At that point their faith could grow. Paul adds one P.S.: "Oh, by the way, we will run aground on some island." As a point of encouragement, this last statement is probably better left off. As a point of predictive prophecy, it would add yet another bullet point to the accuracy of God's revelation to Paul.

27On the fourteenth night we were still being driven across the Adriatica Sea,22 when about midnight the sailors sensed they were approaching land. 28They took soundings and found that the water was a hundred and twenty feetb deep. A short time later they took soundings again and found it was ninety feetc deep. 29Fearing that we would be dashed against the rocks, they dropped four anchors from the stern and prayed for daylight. 30In an attempt to escape from the ship, the sailors let the lifeboat down into the sea, pretending they were going to lower some anchors from the bow. 31Then Paul said to the centurion and the soldiers, "Unless these men stay with the ship, you cannot be saved." 32So the soldiers cut the ropes that held the lifeboat and let it fall away.

a27 In ancient times the name referred to an area extending well south of Italy.
b28 Greek *twenty orguias* (about 37 meters)   c28 Greek *fifteen orguias* (about 27 meters)

27:27-29. After two weeks of helpless, hopeless drifting, the adrenaline kicked in at the sound of land. They apparently heard some breakers in the middle of the night. On the one hand, that was very good news. Paul's prophecy might just come true; they might get out of this alive. On the other hand, it was the middle of the night and they had no idea where they were. If they plowed into some cliff face while it was dark, they would most surely drown. Hence, as a means of assessing their situation, they took a sounding. This consisted of a heavy weight at the end of a rope. The rope was knotted about every six feet, that is, the span of a man's arms from fingertip to fingertip. They dropped the weight until it hit the ocean floor and then counted the knots as they pulled it back up. The first sounding they counted twenty knots or "fathoms" (*orguia*). That comes to one hundred and twenty feet. Just a short way further, their sounding showed only fifteen fathoms (ninety feet). They were approaching land *fast*. It was time for precautionary measures. Some of the sailors dropped four anchors from the stern (the back of the ship). This would hold the ship in place until they could see the land in the daylight. All they could do now was pray.

There is some debate about where the ship landed. Most concur that the island was Malta, a rather paltry piece of real estate less than eight miles wide and twenty-five miles in length if you include the two nearly contiguous islands

22 This is not to be confused with the modern designation "Adriatic" between the Balkan and Italian peninsulas. The ancients identified the Adriatic as the north-central Mediterranean ocean extending south of Greece and Italy.

to the north.[23] It was a Roman colony but not of great account. The specific inlet where the ship 'landed' is probably "St. Paul's Bay" on the northeast side of the island. It fits the biblical description quite accurately. Coming into the bay from the west, the ship would have passed the promontory—point of Koura—which juts out more than a mile and a half from the center of the bay. Waves crashing against this rocky outcrop would be heard well before the ship entered the bay. Furthermore, the soundings in the bay would have quickly gone from twenty to fifteen fathoms. Finally, according to the careful calculations of Smith, a ship adrift from Crete to Malta would take fourteen days to arrive.[24] Obviously, without video cameras there will never be proof positive, but the physical features of the island fit the biblical description with striking accuracy.

27:30-32. With all due respect, certain sailors were not willing to wait to see if Paul's prophecy would come true. They took matters into their own hands. In an act that could only be described as selfish cowardice, they planned on escaping in the lifeboat under the ruse of setting anchors in the bow (front) of the ship. There *may* be a valid reason for doing this; namely, to secure the front of the ship as well as the back. However, if the anchors at the stern were not holding, putting anchors at the front may endanger the vessel worse by allowing the ship to turn broadside to the pounding waves. Rather than the ship being thrust against a cliff it would have been broken up in the bay. Paul saw what they were doing. His experience with both sailing and with people raised a red flag which he called to the attention of the Centurion. The soldiers forthwith drew their swords and cut the boat loose. The dinghy blasted away in the angry surf and the sailors most certainly exploded (if the reader would allow a bit of imaginative reconstruction): "That's our lifeboat you fools! You know nothing about sailing!" The soldiers' retort would have been equally animated, "You cowards! You know nothing about honor and discipline." Both sailors and soldiers were culpable. The sailors, obviously, were abandoning the ship prematurely. The soldiers cut loose a lifeline that would have been incredibly helpful the following morning. It was good for all involved that God's sovereignty rather than men's impetuousness was orchestrating the events in St. Paul's Bay.

[33]Just before dawn Paul urged them all to eat. "For the last fourteen days," he said, **"you have been in constant suspense and have gone without food—you haven't eaten anything. [34]Now I urge you to take some food. You need it to survive. Not one of you will lose a single hair from his head." [35]After he said this,**

---

[23] One of the abler defenses of the traditional location is offered by Colin Hemer, "Euraquilo and Melita," *JTS* 26 (1975): 100-111. Agnes Seppelfricke, "Paulus war nie auf Malta," *Zeite* 52 (1988): 33-34, created quite a stir when this self-taught historian claimed with a bit of bravado that he had overturned the scholarly consensus by 'proving' that the island was actually Kephallenia just off the western coast of Greece! See also H. Warnecke, *Die Tatsachliche Romfahrt des Apostels Paulus* (Stuttgart: Katholisches Bibelwerk, 1987). This claim has been debunked convincingly (and not so gently) by Jürgen Wehnert, "Gestrandet: Zu einer Neuen These über den Schiffbruch des Apostels Paulus auf dem Wege nach Rom (Apg 27–28)," *ZTK* 87 (1990): 67-99, and Basel Reinhardt, "Zum Seeweg Alexandrien-Rom," *TZ* 47 (1991): 208-213.

[24] Smith calculated a ship adrift would go 36 miles in 24 hours. From Cauda to the point of Koura is 476.6 miles. Hence, following Smith's calculations, the ship would arrive 13 days, 1 hour, and 21 minutes. If it did not drift in an exactly straight line, which is most certain, it would take slightly longer . . . like 14 days (Smith, 126-128).

he took some bread and gave thanks to God in front of them all. Then he broke it and began to eat. [36]They were all encouraged and ate some food themselves. [37]Altogether there were 276 of us on board. [38]When they had eaten as much as they wanted, they lightened the ship by throwing the grain into the sea.

27:33-34. It had been the longest two weeks of their lives. The conditions had been miserable both physically and psychologically. Now the sailors and soldiers were at each other's throats and the tension was palpable. They were hungry, sick, angry, and afraid. In short, they were in the wrong state of mind for the ordeal they were about to face. Paul already predicted the ship would sink. Without the lifeboat, he knew that everyone would have to swim to shore. Hence, it was imperative that they eat something for strength. If they followed his advice, which they were finally prepared to do, no one would die (the obvious implication of Paul's hyperbole: "not one of you will lose a single hair from his head" cf. Luke 21:18).

27:35-38. Paul successfully persuaded all 276 passengers to eat.[25] Obviously, they had not jettisoned all their food supplies. Of course, for the past fourteen days they had not tapped into their reserves since they were too sick to eat. So they prepared a *last supper* and threw the rest overboard in one last effort to lighten the load. The language "last supper" is deliberately suggestive; so is Luke's. He uses several phrases in verse 15 reminiscent of the language of Luke 22:19.[26] Paul "took some bread," "gave thanks" to God, "broke it," and they "began to eat" (Luke 22:15-16; cf. Acts 20:11 and 1 Cor 11:23-24). This is not to say that Paul saw this as a Eucharistic meal. That would be reserved for believers. It is to say, however, that Luke provocatively compared Jesus' passion event to Paul's final course in Acts.[27] Already we have seen the deliberate overlap of Jesus' five trials with Paul. Now we get a glimpse of the death and resurrection motif as Paul administrates a final meal before passing through a watery grave. The allusion is subtle enough that some have difficulty seeing it.[28]

[39]When daylight came, they did not recognize the land, but they saw a bay with a sandy beach, where they decided to run the ship aground if they could. [40]Cutting loose the anchors, they left them in the sea and at the same time untied the ropes that held the rudders. Then they hoisted the foresail to the wind and made for the beach. [41]But the ship struck a sandbar and ran aground. The bow stuck fast and would not move, and the stern was broken to pieces by the

[25] Though it has been noted that 276 is the sum of the numbers 1-23, there is no apparent symbolic meaning to this number; contra F. H. Colson, "Triangular Numbers in the New Testament," *JTS* 16 (1915): 72 (who mistakenly ascribes the 276 as the sum of 1-24 rather than 1-23). This was simply a headcount, perhaps for the necessary meal preparations. This may seem like an exaggerated number of people on board a vessel likely measuring 180' by 50' but Josephus (*Life* 1.1.3 §15) tells of 600 on board his ship that also sank in this same Adriatic Sea. This is even more striking since the 'slop' buckets, full of diarrhea and vomit, would likely have spilled more than they held and most were too sick to care.
[26] The comparison is even more overt in Greek; cf. Barrett, "Paul Shipwrecked," 59-63, and Praeder, "Sea Voyages," 699.
[27] This position is ably argued by Bo Reicke, "Die Mahlzeit mit Paulus auf den Wellen des Mittelmeers Act. 27, 33-38," *TZ* 4 (1948): 401-410, and equally ably controverted by Witherington (772-773).
[28] Bernard Robinson, "The Place of the Emmaus Story in Luke-Acts," *NTS* 30 (1984): 481-497, is able to see this and (too?) much more.

pounding of the surf. **⁴²The soldiers planned to kill the prisoners to prevent any of them from swimming away and escaping. ⁴³But the centurion wanted to spare Paul's life and kept them from carrying out their plan. He ordered those who could swim to jump overboard first and get to land. ⁴⁴The rest were to get there on planks or on pieces of the ship. In this way everyone reached land in safety.**

27:39-40. Once it was light enough to see where they were going they were ready to drive to shore. None of the sailors were familiar with this bay nor should they have been. The main port of Malta is Valetta, seven miles southeast of St. Paul's Bay. They set their sights on a sandy beach where they could safely run the ship aground. Most of the bay is surrounded by rocky outcrops so this was their best bet. They cut loose the four anchors and lunged forward. They lowered two large oars from the back of the ship that served as rudders. These had been secured against the deck during the fortnight of drifting. Then they raised the foresail, one of the few pieces of rigging they retained for just such an emergency landing. The sail caught the wind, the ship surged forward and drove hard toward the beach.

27:41. Unfortunately, there was a sandbar that lay between the ship and the shore. Had they been familiar with the bay, they would have known that the sandy beach that lured them was a treacherous trap. Just to the north of the beach was a small island. It looked like part of the shoreline from their vantage point in the bay. However, as they pressed toward land, they could see that it was not, in fact, attached to the mainland. It was, as Luke says, "where the two seas met" (v. 41, *dithallassos*).[29] This caused currents to jut through the narrow passage between the islands, bringing with it sandy debris that settled in an unseen mound in the middle of the bay. By the time they realized what was there, it was too late. They were stuck. A ship stuck in a sandbar only causes accumulation of sand. The relentless surf pounded the stern. Already badly battered, she soon gave way, scattering her skeleton across the bay.

27:42-44. Julius's troops were ready to dispatch the prisoners. It would be easier to justify to Rome why they executed accused criminals than to explain why they let them escape. This is truly an extraordinary and foreign judicial system, but they knew they would bear the punishment of convicted felons who were allowed to escape. Fortunately, Julius halted their plans because of his affinity for Paul. Once again, the life of the apostle spared those with him (cf. Gen 8:1-14). He allowed those who could swim to make for shore first. Afterward, soldiers, sailors, and prisoners alike clung to the wreckage that the sea tossed ashore. Those soldiers who preceded them were standing at the ready to round up their prisoners. Undoubtedly it was terrifying and chaotic, but when the adrenaline rush subsided, all were accounted for. Unbelievably, two hundred and seventy six shivering, wet, and exhausted survivors stood in solidarity on the shore, thankful to the gods, and perhaps even to Paul's God, who rescued them from the bowels of the angry sea in precise fulfillment of Paul's most unlikely prophecy.

---

[29] Although, *dithallassos* may, in fact, merely be a description of the sandbar and not the channel between the two islands; cf. Gilchrist, "Historicity," 42-46.

ACTS 28

3. Salvation on Shore (28:1-10)

[1]Once safely on shore, we found out that the island was called Malta. [2]The islanders showed us unusual kindness. They built a fire and welcomed us all because it was raining and cold. [3]Paul gathered a pile of brushwood and, as he put it on the fire, a viper, driven out by the heat, fastened itself on his hand. [4]When the islanders saw the snake hanging from his hand, they said to each other, "This man must be a murderer; for though he escaped from the sea, Justice has not allowed him to live." [5]But Paul shook the snake off into the fire and suffered no ill effects. [6]The people expected him to swell up or suddenly fall dead, but after waiting a long time and seeing nothing unusual happen to him, they changed their minds and said he was a god. [7]There was an estate nearby that belonged to Publius, the chief official of the island. He welcomed us to his home and for three days entertained us hospitably. [8]His father was sick in bed, suffering from fever and dysentery. Paul went in to see him and, after prayer, placed his hands on him and healed him. [9]When this had happened, the rest of the sick on the island came and were cured. [10]They honored us in many ways and when we were ready to sail, they furnished us with the supplies we needed.

28:1-6. The rescue operation caused quite a stir among the natives. As they rose for their morning rounds, the fishermen and farmers saw the listing ship in the bay and a few bedraggled survivors on shore. Scores of others were still clinging to wreckage in the angry waves. This must have been one of the most exciting events to take place on their sleepy little island in a long time. Neighbors called for reinforcements until all 276 were accounted for. Only after they took a head count and caught their breath did the passengers learn they had landed on Malta.

The locals (*barbaroi*)[1] showed unusual kindness (*philanthrōpia*). Luke mentions the fire they built to warm the shivering survivors. Surely they also provided shelter, food, and perhaps some dry clothes. In addition, it is hard to believe they would not have used their own little fishing boats to round up a few of the survivors struggling to make it ashore. The average overnight temperature on Malta during November is not terribly cold by most standards (around 40–45°F). Even so, if one were submerged in the frigid ocean waves and then stood on the shore in blustery winter rain he would be extremely grateful for a fire stoked by the locals.

Paul participated in rounding up firewood. It would take a lot of brush to

---

[1]Luke calls them βάρβαροι, the word from which we get "barbarians." The term arose among Greeks who looked down on those who were unable to speak their native tongue, hence, could only babble syllables that sounded like "bar bar bar" or in English vernacular "ga ga goo goo" (cf. 1 Cor 14:11). It was a term for foreigners that was not particularly malicious but neither was it complementary. It fit the locals who were of Phoenician descent and spoke in a Punic dialect.

build a blaze sufficient for 276 shivering survivors, particularly since the kindling was soaked. As Paul positioned one load on the fire, a viper was awakened by the heat and latched on to his hand. The locals concluded that Paul had escaped his fate at sea so that Justice (i.e., the punishment of the gods) could reserve for him some greater retribution.[2] They saw he was a prisoner and concluded he must be a hardened criminal such as a murderer. Hence, the gods would smite him. They were looking for the telltale signs of venom—red streaks on his arm and severe swelling. However, nothing happened. Paul simply shook the snake into the fire and went about his business.[3] As time passed, their minds changed. Rather than concluding he was a criminal, they thought he was a god, immune to the suffering of humanity. Amazingly, Luke provides no other commentary. There is none of the standard Jewish objection to human deification—no rent clothes or loud lamentations. Perhaps he expected his comments from Lystra (14:14-18) to be appropriately supplied by the reader. Nevertheless, this miracle provided Paul considerable clout on the island for the remainder of their three-month stay. This is the only documented fulfillment of Mark 16:18, a promise of divine intervention in the midst of evangelistic activity. Thus, this is precisely the kind of 'sign' one would expect from God's pledge to protect those who "Go into all the world and preach the good news to all creation" (Mark 16:15).

Some have suggested that the snake was harmless and the natives were simply superstitious.[4] After all, there are no venomous snakes on the island today. That, however, is hardly credible. Those who have lived near rural communities have heard the colloquial wisdom for discerning between venomous and non-venomous snakes. Moreover, Luke, as a physician, would have been well versed in caring for victims of snakebite. Poisonous snakes tend to be hacked with hoes by farmers. Benign snakes tend to be appreciated for their voracious appetites for rodents. Hence, it is difficult to believe that the locals, on such a small island, could not tell the difference between the two. Furthermore, it is *not* difficult to believe that the increased human population on the island eventually eradicated the venomous snakes from their little plot of ground.

28:7-10. Paul's breathtaking encounter with the viper made him somewhat

---

[2] Cf. Miles and Trompf, "Beliefs about Divine Retribution," 259-267; and Ladoceur, "Hellenistic Preconceptions," 435-449. There is a parallel to this account recorded in *The Greek Anthology* 7.290: "The shipwrecked mariner had escaped the whirlwind and the fury of the deadly sea, and as he was lying on the Libyan sand not far from the beach . . . naked and exhausted by the unhappy wreck, a baneful viper slew him. Why did he struggle with the waves in vain, escaping then the fate that was his lot on the land?" (LCL), cf. Talbert and Hays, "Sea Storms," 273.

[3] If one could survive a viper, he proved he was approved by God. Thus, rabbi Haninah ben Dosa was said to have rid his village of a tormenting viper by allowing it to bite him. Rather than Haninah dying as his fellow villagers had, the snake died. Thus the saying, "Woe to the man whom the snake meets, and woe to the snake whom Haninah ben Dosa meets," (*b. Ber.* 33a; cf. *t. Sanh.* 8.3).

[4] William Ramsay, *Luke the Physician* (Grand Rapids: Baker, 1979 [1908]), 63-64, brings up an interesting point that venomous snakes generally strike rather than bite. They pierce the flesh with their fangs only long enough to deliver their venom. Since the snake that bit Paul "latched onto" (καθάπτω) Paul's hand and the villagers saw it "hanging there," Ramsay concluded that it must be a nonvenomous snake. There are, however, venomous snakes that bite and latch on, for example, the North American Cottonmouth. Hence, one should probably accord Luke the physician the benefit of the doubt in one of his areas of expertise.

of a local celebrity. Publius, the head honcho (literally "the preeminent one") of the island, entertained Paul for three days.[5] The language Luke used is not so much about throwing a party as showing honor.[6] It would be like a visit from a neighboring statesman. The receptions and banquets were not for entertainment so much as respectful dialogue between persons of power. Notice that Luke (and probably Aristarchus and Julius) was invited along with Paul (v. 7). They were, after all, part of his entourage.

During these three days (perhaps a subtle allusion to the "period of resurrection") Paul "raised" Publius's father.[7] Two observations add color to this healing. First, if Publius is the chief of the island, he is most probably past forty years old. That would likely put his father somewhere in the vicinity of seventy years old. For an ancient, that's ancient. His age only exacerbated the illness. Second, though the NIV translates "fever" as singular, the word is actually plural. This likely suggests recurring fevers that were accompanied by dysentery (i.e., extreme diarrhea). One likely cause is the infamous "Maltese Fever" caused by infected goat's milk. Picture here a feeble, bedridden old man making a dozen or more trips a day to the outhouse. This noteworthy miracle not only endeared him to Publius, the chief of the island, but also to the locals. They flooded Publius's estate with their own loved ones on pallets, crutches, and cots. Remember, the island is only 8 × 25 miles. Word spread, people rejoiced, and Publius's villa became an outpatient clinic. Paul was overrun. Fortunately, he had a physician on staff who could help. Verse 10 says, "They honored us . . ." The word (*timaō*) indicates financial remuneration and Luke includes himself.[8] Perhaps this is his subtle way of saying he too was involved. In fact, the word "healed" (*iaomai*, v. 8) seems to suggest miraculous healings while the word "cure" (*therapeuō*, v. 10) would suggest more medical treatment. The miracles of Paul and the cures of Luke were working in tandem to bless the citizens of Malta who had been so kind to them. On their departure, the people of Malta felt compelled to supply the apostolic entourage with the necessary supplies to continue their journey to Rome.

---

[5] This title, πρῶτος, has been confirmed by both Greek and Latin inscriptions on Malta (*Beginnings* 4:342). Elsewhere it was used to identify the priest of the Emperor Cult (*flamen Augustalis*; cf. Alfred Suhl, "Zum Titel πρῶτος τῆς νήσου (Erster der Insel) Apg 28:7" *BZ* 36 (1992): 220-226. If Publius was, in fact, a priest of the Emperor Cult, his response to Paul's preaching would be most interesting indeed.

[6] Literally, Publius "hospitably welcomed [Paul] as a guest," (φιλοφρόνως ἐξένισεν). The first of these two words is the adverb for "friendly"; the second term, "to receive/welcome/host," is a favorite of Luke's. He uses it seven times (Acts 10:6, 18, 23, 32; 17:20; 21:16; 28:7) always in the context of hospitality (except the figurative use in Acts 17:20). Outside of Luke, the term is only found in 1 Peter 4:4, 12, and Heb 13:7, again, in the sociological context of hospitality (cf. Plutarch, *Lysander* 4.1-3; *Pericles* 7.1; Pindar, *Olympian* 6.98; Josephus, *J.W.* 1.6.1 §122).

[7] This is the only time in Acts where laying on of hands, combined with prayer, brought about a healing, though this seems to have been a normative practice in Judaism (cf. Jas 5:14; 1Q20 20.29); cf. W. Kirschslager, "Fieberheilung in Apg. 28 und Lk. 4," *Les Actes des Apôtres* (ed. J. Kremer; Gembloux: Duculot, 1979), 514-515. As an aside, this healing parallels the healing of Peter's mother-in-law on several points (Luke 4:38-41): (1) a parent is healed of fever through physical touch (2) causing a stir in the neighborhood so that (3) many other sick people are brought to be healed. (4) The healed person then provides service to the healer.

[8] Sirach 38:1-2, "Honor physicians for their services, for the Lord created them; for their gift of healing comes from the Most High, and they are rewarded by the king" (NRSV), cf. Cicero, *Ad Fam.* 16.9; 1 Tim 5:17.

4. Arrival in Rome—the Unhindered Gospel (28:11-31)

If Acts were a symphony, this is where the tympani drums would thunder, the strings would crescendo, and the brass would blast the signal of a rousing ovation. Stand to your feet, for this is the finale. This is not merely Paul's arrival in Rome; it is the symbolic fulfillment of Acts 1:8. The gospel had penetrated the epicenter of the Empire's power. As promised, Paul would stand before Nero and present to the Lord of Rome, the galactic King of kings. Interestingly, the dramatic encounter is not even narrated. *Historically*, that may be because Luke went to press before Paul was released. *Literarily*, the ambiguity of a 'balked' nonending fortuitously forces the reader to complete the story him or herself. Such conjecture draws the reader into participating in writing the end of the story. One's own imagination inflates the flat narrative into a 3D experience. *Missiologically*, the abortive ending of Acts sucks the reader into the narrative. One intuitively asks, "How does the story then end?" The answer comes as easily as the question, when the Spirit retorts, "You tell me!" We have the divine privilege of making history with the God who transcends human affairs. Rome, as the symbolic end of the world, is still experiencing the arrival of the gospel. We, like Paul, still dripping from our own shipwreck, march relentlessly toward the imposing city armed with the power of the word and the promise of God that we will stand fearless before rulers because this gospel message is not our own. We are but the conduit of the Holy Spirit.

[11]**After three months we put out to sea in a ship that had wintered in the island. It was an Alexandrian ship with the figurehead of the twin gods Castor and Pollux.** [12]**We put in at Syracuse and stayed there three days.** [13]**From there we set sail and arrived at Rhegium. The next day the south wind came up, and on the following day we reached Puteoli.** [14]**There we found some brothers who invited us to spend a week with them. And so we came to Rome.** [15]**The brothers there had heard that we were coming, and they traveled as far as the Forum of Appius and the Three Taverns to meet us. At the sight of these men Paul thanked God and was encouraged.** [16]**When we got to Rome, Paul was allowed to live by himself, with a soldier to guard him.**

28:11-13. They were stranded on Malta for about three months—November, December, and January. They then set sail as soon as it was safe, around February 8 (Pliny, *Nat. Hist.* 2.122).[9] The ship that transported them was another Alexandrian vessel whose figurehead was a pair of twins, Castor and Pollux, the sons of Zeus. These guys form the Zodiac sign "Gemini," called in Greek *Dioscuri*. Since they were the guardians of the sea, their presence on the ship gave comfort to the crew. Little did they know (and perhaps this is the point of Luke's reference) it was not Zeus's sons but God's servant, Paul, who secured the fate of this vessel.[10]

---

[9] This was likely the date for 'safe' travel near the shore. Ships crossing the Mediterranean wouldn't dare venture out before March 10 (cf. Vegetius, *On Military Affairs* 4.39).

[10] The *Dioscuri* were common fare in ancient literature, mentioned 90× by Pausanius alone (e.g., Euripides, *Electra* 1238ff.; Pausanias 1.18.1; Herodotus, *Hist.* 2.43.2-3; Thucydides, *Peloponnesian War* 3.75.3). They were not only protectors at sea but also punishers of perjurers and guardians of truth. This too could

Once again, Luke recounts their itinerary in detail. They likely left Malta from the port of Valletta, sailing north to Syracuse just shy of one hundred miles. With good winds they could make it in a single day. They were in port at Syracuse for three days, either transferring cargo or just waiting for the southerly breeze to pick back up. From Sicily they sailed for Rhegium, a port just south of the Straight of Messina, where Sicily and Italy nearly kiss. This seventy-five mile jaunt along the eastern coast of the island was apparently a bit more taxing. Luke used a word that means "sailed around" (*periaireō*) probably suggesting how the ship tacked back and forth against the wind. The next stop was Puteoli (modern Naples), two hundred and ten miles north. With the help of a fine southern breeze they made it in two days. It was (and is) the most protected port of southern Italy and the grain ships arriving here were celebrated. Seneca (*Epistle* 77) describes how every other ship had to lower their foresail but the grain ships were allowed immediate access and were easily identified by the *suppara* flying proud, boasting another arrival of the lifeblood of Rome. Alas on land, the passengers were still over a hundred miles from Rome but the rest of the trip would be covered by land, a fact for which Paul was undoubtedly grateful.

28:14-16. In Puteoli, Paul once again located Christians who invited him to spend a full week.[11] Until now, their itinerary had been determined by the ship's captain. Here, however, it seems as if Paul set his own agenda, obviously with the permission of Julius. That's extraordinary. This centurion has been so taken with Paul that he seems to have relinquished the itinerary to his discretion. Of course, it helps that Paul & Co. were in possession of the supplies provided by the grateful citizens of Malta and that the hospitality of the Christians in Puteoli ensured the soldiers were well fed and housed. It was in Puteoli where Luke recorded that colossal moment: "And so we came to Rome." However, they were still over a hundred miles away. This is not a geographical error; it is a theological truth. It is the Christians in Rome who comprise the true city. Paul was now in the orbit of the Roman church, hence, he had arrived at his destination.

In light of this, Paul did not just "come to Rome;" Rome came to Paul. The Christians of the capital learned of Paul's arrival and ran to greet him at Three Taverns about thirty-three miles south on the Appian Way (Cicero, *Ad Atticum*, 2.10). Others went another ten miles to the Forum of Appius.[12] Paul's weeklong stint in Puteoli allowed word to reach Rome. Most likely Christian businessmen or envoys en route to Rome informed the brothers that Paul was in country. They rushed out to meet him. Some got all the way to the Forum of Appius, others left later and only made it to Three Taverns. The picture Luke paints is of an increasing entourage as Paul parades into the capital. For those familiar with political literature of the first century, this has shades of a triumphal entry. Paul, like a victorious general, marched into the capital with an entourage of admiring followers.[13] The

---

be a purpose of Luke's reference—a veiled jab at the Roman rulers who could not see what even the deaf-mute gods of the Greeks seemed to affirm; cf. Ladouceur, "Hellenistic Preconceptions," 445.

[11] Josephus twice mentions the large Jewish settlement in Puteoli (*J.W.* 2.7.1 §104; *Ant.* 17.12.1 §328).

[12] Or the "Market at Appi" (Cicero, *ad Att.* 2.10; Suetonius, *Tib.* 2: Horace, *Satire* 1.5; Pliny, *Nat. Hist.* 3.9).

[13] The word ἀπάντησις is often used in the context of going out to meet foreign dignitaries (e.g., Judg 11:31 LXX; Matt 25:6; 1 Thess 4:17; Josephus, *Ant.* 7.11.5 §276).

point is not primarily the aggrandizement of Paul but the glory of the gospel. The ever-increasing victorious kingdom of God was being celebrated by her citizens.

Paul was escorted into the city, giving thanks to God for these hospitable brothers who had read his letter three years earlier and knew how badly he wanted to see them (Rom 1:9-13; 15:23-29). Many in the entourage were likely the very ones named at the tail end of the letter (Rom 16:1-16). Once he arrived, he was given considerable freedom, even his own rented apartment. The Western text adds that Paul was handed over to the *stratopedarch* to guard him. Technically, he was under house arrest but with considerable latitude for hosting visitors. Really, his only limitation was the soldiers who took turns 'babysitting' him while he entertained guests and discussed the gospel. Paradoxically, the soldiers, chained to Paul's wrist, were the captive audience. Many of them consequently converted, a fact noted twice in Philippians (1:12-14):

> Now I want you to know, brothers, that what has happened to me has really served to advance the gospel. As a result, it has become clear throughout the whole *palace guard* and to everyone else that I am in chains for Christ. Because of my chains, most of the brothers in the Lord have been encouraged to speak the word of God more courageously and fearlessly.

Again, at the tail end of the letter (4:22), Paul wrote, "All the saints send you greetings, especially those who belong to *Caesar's household.*" Paul's shipwreck and imprisonment turned out to be one of his most effective ministries! Most of us are ill equipped to evaluate the ultimate outcomes of the opportunities God provides which we consider inconvenient tragedies.

[17]Three days later he called together the leaders of the Jews. When they had assembled, Paul said to them: "My brothers, although I have done nothing against our people or against the customs of our ancestors, I was arrested in Jerusalem and handed over to the Romans. [18]They examined me and wanted to release me, because I was not guilty of any crime deserving death. [19]But when the Jews objected, I was compelled to appeal to Caesar—not that I had any charge to bring against my own people. [20]For this reason I have asked to see you and talk with you. It is because of the hope of Israel that I am bound with this chain." [21]They replied, "We have not received any letters from Judea concerning you, and none of the brothers who have come from there has reported or said anything bad about you. [22]But we want to hear what your views are, for we know that people everywhere are talking against this sect."

28:17-19. It didn't take long for Paul to get down to business. In just three days he had gathered the Jewish leaders in Rome. It was a gutsy move. The Jews had been expelled from the capital by Claudius a decade earlier due to a hullabaloo over "*Chrestus*" (see comments on 18:1-4). If our assumption is correct that this was a disturbance over Christ whom some Jewish believers had adopted as Messiah, then Paul is opening a can of worms that could bite him. It is impossible to tell how long these Jews had been back in the city, but caution would be called for on both sides. The incident of Philippi (16:20-21), the beating of Sosthenes in Corinth (18:17), and the rejection of Alexander in Ephesus (19:33) show how tenuous was the Jewish footing in Roman environments. In the capital city, their status would have been precarious. Hence, they can no more afford to cause a disturbance than Paul.[14] If a riot results from Paul's rendezvous with the Jewish leaders, this political prisoner's fate would be sealed and the Jewish patriots expelled again. Given Paul's track record in previous synagogues, this is, at minimum, a foreboding moment.

Paul appears to be treading lightly. His opening (vv. 17-20) could not be more congenial, and the Jewish response was equally amiable (vv. 21-22). He *briefly* summarizes his situation (and Luke has likely pared it down to bare bones, which the reader is supposed to flesh out from the previous narratives). Though he looks like a criminal in house arrest, he categorically denies any culpability. Notice, he never implicates his fellow Jews. The reader knows he was brutalized by Jews in Jerusalem and that they plotted his assassination more than once. They hired a lawyer to convict him on charges they could not substantiate without the eyewitnesses who had long since returned to Asia. No one would really blame Paul if he was a bit bitter against his countrymen.[15] None of this, however, is recalled. Paul puts the entire onus on the Romans. Obviously there was tension between Paul and the Jerusalem Jews since they blocked his release. Paul immediately affirms that he had no charge against his own people. Paul is stating, in the clearest possible terms, that he is no threat to the Jewish community of Rome. Be that as it may, no one winds up in shackles without *some* enemies. Even so, the tension between Paul and his people is muted by him as well as by his interlocutors. Neither have any plans of doing the other dirty.

28:20. On the contrary, Paul's goal is to share with them the "hope of Israel," for which he stood in chains. This concept of the "hope of Israel" has already emerged three other times in Acts [See comments on 26:6-7; cf. 23:6; 24:15].[16] In short, it was the hope for the reemergence of the nation under the resurrection power of the Messiah. It was the hope that God would truly reign through his eschatological intervention. And it was the hope that Israel would be the gravitational center for all the Gentiles to attach themselves to the seed of Abraham and enjoy together the rule of God. This was the prophetic announcement of John the Baptist, the core of Jesus' preaching (esp. Luke 4:16-30),[17]

---

[14] Cf. Conrad Gempf, "Luke's Story of Paul's Reception in Rome," in *Rome in the Bible and the Early Church* (ed. Peter Oakes; Grand Rapids: Baker Academic, 2002), 42-65.

[15] There is a rather brisk debate about whether Luke was anti-Semitic, particularly in this text. Most notably, J. T. Sanders, *The Jews in Luke-Acts* (Philadelphia: Fortress, 1987), confidently claims that he was. J. Jervell, *Luke and the People of God* (Minneapolis: Augsburg, 1972) is more cautious, even turning the discussion on its head: "One usually understands the situation to imply that only when the Jews have rejected the gospel is the way opened to Gentiles. It is more correct to say that only when Israel has accepted the gospel can the way to Gentiles be opened" (55).

[16] On the "hope of Israel" see Haacker, "Das Bekenntnis des Paulus, 437-451; and Anton Deutschmann, "Die Hoffnung Israels (Apg 28,20)," *BN* 105 (2000): 54-60.

[17] Paul's sermon in Acts 28 parallels Jesus' inaugural sermon in Nazareth. Both quote from Isaiah, both

as well as the primary message of the Apostles. The "hope of Israel" was none
other than "the Kingdom of God." Paul summarized this hope for Herod in
26:23, "that the Christ would suffer and, as the first to rise from the dead, would
proclaim light to his own people and to the Gentiles."

28:21-22. The Roman Jews assured Paul that they had no gripe against
him (an important message for the person with an appointment to see Nero).
There's no local agenda or plot against the apostle. That does not mean they
had never heard about Paul. It certainly doesn't mean that they were ignorant
of Christianity. They knew well the sect which Paul advocated, and frankly, they
had not heard favorable reports about it. Christianity was maligned from every
direction in the first century. Jews considered it an aberrant sect which threatened to alter the customs of Moses in a place and time when Judaism was under
immense pressure to conform to Hellenism. Romans grew to hate Christians
who gave their ultimate loyalty to another king, refused cultural entertainments
(gladiatorial games, brothels, and bawdy theater), eschewed military service,[18]
etc. Naturally, therefore, the local Jewry would be most interested in Paul's opinion on this maligned sect. Arrangements were set for a full hearing. Paul would
have an eager audience of Roman Jews, willing to hear him out.

[23] **They arranged to meet Paul on a certain day, and came in even larger numbers to the place where he was staying. From morning till evening he explained
and declared to them the kingdom of God and tried to convince them about
Jesus from the Law of Moses and from the Prophets. [24]Some were convinced by
what he said, but others would not believe. [25]They disagreed among themselves
and began to leave after Paul had made this final statement: "The Holy Spirit
spoke the truth to your forefathers when he said through Isaiah the prophet:
[26]"'Go to this people and say, "You will be ever hearing but never understanding; you will be ever seeing but never perceiving." [27]For this people's heart has
become calloused; they hardly hear with their ears, and they have closed their
eyes. Otherwise they might see with their eyes, hear with their ears, understand
with their hearts and turn, and I would heal them.'[a] [28]"Therefore I want you to
know that God's salvation has been sent to the Gentiles, and they will listen!"[b]**

[a]27 Isaiah 6:9,10   [b]28 Some manuscripts *listen!" [29]After he said this, the Jews left, arguing vigorously
among themselves*

28:23-24. The Jews came to Paul's apartment in droves (lit., "larger numbers"). Paul got started early in the morning and went until suppertime (*hes-
pera*). He plowed his way through the sacred Scriptures ("Law and Prophets"),
scouring passages that proved Jesus was the long-awaited Messiah. He taught, argued, warned, and perhaps even cajoled, attempting to convince his compatri-

---

mention eyes and ears, both commission a preacher, both encounter unbelief, and both point toward Gentile inclusion; cf. Donald Miesner, "The Circumferential Speeches in Luke-Acts: Patterns and Purpose,"
SBLsp 14 (Missoula: Scholar's Press, 1978): 223-237.
   [18]Cf. Ignatius, *Eph.* 12; Irenaeus, *Ad. Haer.* 4.34.4; Tertullian, *Of the Soldier's Crown*, 11; Origen, *Ad. Celsum*
5:33; cf. Alan Kreider, "Military Service in the Church Orders," *JRE* 31 (2003): 415-422; and John Yoder,
"War as a Moral Problem in the Early Church: The Historian's Hermeneutical Assumptions," in *The Pacifist
Impulse in Historical Perspective* (ed. Harvey L. Dyck; Toronto: University of Toronto Press, 1996), 90-110.

ots to accept Jesus as Lord. Some did; others refused. This division (*asymphōnos*, v. 25) was par for Paul's course.[19]

28:25-27. As the dissidents headed for the door, Paul got in this one final shot.[20] It is a nearly exact quotation from the LXX version of Isaiah 6:9-10 that is peppered throughout the New Testament.[21] Matthew puts it on the lips of Jesus as an explanation of why he spoke in parables (Mark 4:12/Matt 13:14/Luke 8:10). John cites this passage as explanation for the recalcitrance of the Jews even after all Jesus' miracles (John 12:40). And Romans 11:8 has an allusion in the context of Gentile inclusion (though the wording is closer to Isaiah 29:10). The original text concerns the call of Isaiah. In the midst of a smoking vision of God's throne room, the terrified Isaiah responds to the call of God, "Who will go for us?" Not that he had a lot of choice, but he volunteers to preach for Yahweh. Yet what shall he preach? This is his message he was ordered to preach: "You will be ever hearing but never understanding; you will be ever seeing but never perceiving." This mournful message is due to the perpetual rejection of God. Consequently, God would respond to their rejection by hardening their hearts, closing their eyes, and deafening their ears so they could never again hear the message and repent.[22] What mechanism would God use to accomplish this baneful rejection? Preaching! That's right, preaching was the tool God used to ensure that those who rejected him would never again have the opportunity to hear and repent. It was the preaching of parables that allowed Jesus to open the hearts of the repentant and close the minds of the arrogant (Mark 4:12/Matt 13:14). It was the miracles of Jesus that God used to enliven faith in the faithful and blind the eyes of the unbelieving (John 12:40). And it was the preaching of Paul that allowed the open mind to understand and the closed mind to sit comfortably and consign themselves to darkness.

This is not so much God determining the destiny of the damned. It is God confirming the damned destiny of the determined. In other words, God wants all to respond to his son Jesus in faith (2 Pet 3:9). That is his will. If, however, his call is rejected, if his invitation is flouted, God responds with a rejection of his own. We often preach and teach as if death is the only end to God's gracious invitation. It is not. According to this passage, there is a line men cross when their rejection leads to God's renunciation and their fate is sealed. Though God's

---

[19] This all-too-brief summary of Paul's full day of teaching has striking similarities to the arguments Paul elaborates in Romans 11. Kenneth Litwak used this overlap to argue that Luke's Paul, at least (or especially) in Acts 28, is the historical Paul; cf. "One or Two Views of Judaism: Paul in Acts 28 and Romans 11 on Jewish Unbelief," *TynBul* 57 (2006): 229-249.

[20] "It is a typical and doubtless lifelike touch in Acts that Paul always gets the last word—generally with devastating effect," *Beginnings* 4:347.

[21] The textual details are explicated carefully by Gert Jacobus Steyn, *Septuagint Quotations in the Context of the Petrine and Pauline Speeches of the Acta Apostolorum* (Netherlands: Kok Pharos, 1995), 213-229. The theme of obduracy of the Jews also has substantial parallels in Ezek 3:4-7; cf. Hubertus Sandt, "Acts 28,28: No Salvation for the People of Israel? An Answer in the Perspective of the LXX," *ETL* 70 (1994): 341-358.

[22] Martin Karrer attempts to translate "and I would heal them" not as a subjunctive but as an indicative. Thus, God promised to heal Israel *regardless* of her stubborn rejection; cf. "'Und ich werde sie heilen': Das Verstockungsmotiv aus Jes 6,9f in Apg 28,26f," in *Kirche und Volk Gottes* (Neukirchen: Neukirchener Verlag, 2000), 255-271. Unfortunately his theory runs afoul of linguistic evidence. The translation of the LXX is a fair representation of the MT. Both Isaiah and Paul intend this not as a promise of healing but as a threat against rejection.

patience is immense, it is not eternal. There comes a time when his call is closed (cf. Matt 22:1-14). If we reject his offer of grace beyond his limits, he withdraws his 'drawing' Spirit which is the sole means by which one can come to him (John 6:44). Human nature alone, especially in its present depravity, will never suffice to draw a person to salvation. We need the Spirit. If God gets fed up with us and withdraws his Spirit, game over.

28:28. Of course, this passage, particularly in this present context, is not primarily about individual election. It is about national calling. Even back in Isaiah's day, God warned of a national rejection that would result in a spiritual decimation—only the remnant would survive. That was the warning God commissioned Isaiah to announce. Does this mean that for Paul the mission to the Jews was over? Is this the final rejection of Israel so she could be replaced by the church? Absolutely not!

First of all, Paul never saw a dichotomy between the church and Israel. The Elect of Israel, that is Messianic Jews, were to invite the nations to Yahweh's rule. Those who accepted the invitation were adopted as children of Abraham (Gal 3:26-29). Conversely, Jews who rejected God's ordained Messiah forfeited their spiritual heritage and were excised from the will (Rom 11:17-24). However, Israel is still Israel, still the elect, and still the people of God. Secondly, on two previous occasions Paul rejected the Jews in order to reach out to Gentiles. When Paul abandoned his Jewish mission in Antioch (13:46), he fled to Iconium and made a beeline for the Synagogue. Likewise, after excoriating the Jews of Corinth (18:6) he preached in Ephesus, you guessed it, *in the synagogue*. Hence, on neither of the previous two instances where Paul "turned to the Gentiles" did he cease to preach "to Jews first" in other localities. Though some might argue for 'three strikes you're out', particularly since Paul had reached the literary "end of the earth," nonetheless, there is no necessary reason to assume the Roman rejection means anything different than that of Antioch or Corinth.[23] All Luke likely intends to convey is that Paul had sought out these Roman Jews for the last time. Thirdly, the subtle anti-Semitism that undergirds this 'final rejection' theory is nowhere to be found in the Apostle Paul. His Epistles, from start to finish, are a Jew inviting Gentiles to join with the people of God (i.e., the remnant of Israel) never to replace them. This is not to say that Israel has higher status with Yahweh. God's blessing is *through* the Jews, not merely *to* the Jews. Hence, the universal love of God is extended through this chosen people to the ends of the earth. That did not change after Acts 28:28.

[30]For two whole years Paul stayed there in his own rented house and welcomed all who came to see him. [31]Boldly and without hindrance he preached the kingdom of God and taught about the Lord Jesus Christ.[24]

---

[23] Cf. Darryl Palmer, "Mission to Jews and Gentiles in the Last Episode of Acts," *RTR* 52 (1993): 62-73, contra Karl Löning, "Das Gottesbild der Apostelgeschichte im Spannungsfeld von Früjudentum und Fremdreligionen," in *Monotheismus und Chistologie* (Freiburg: Herder, 1992): 88-117.

[24] Verse 29 is not included in modern versions because the overwhelming manuscript evidence indicates it is a later addition. It reads "After saying these things the Jews left and had a big debate over these things," Καὶ ταῦτα αὐτοῦ εἰπόντος, ἀπῆλθον οἱ Ἰουδαῖοι, πολλὴν ἔχοντες ἐν ἑαυτοῖς συζήτησιν.

28:30. And so we come to the 'end'. Yet the reader is left wanting! What, pray tell, happened when Paul stood before Nero? What did he say? How did the Emperor respond? Would Paul have been released after a couple of years when some statute of limitations would kick in?[25] Where did he go?[26] How large was the church when he left? Were Trophimus and Luke still with him? Did Timothy show up? Was John Mark reconciled to Paul during this imprisonment? Luke offers not a word. Pardon my blatant honesty but I find this to be the most unsatisfactory ending of any book I've ever read![27]

Perhaps Luke was planning a trilogy. This cliff-hanger is the perfect stage for a sequel. There is, however, another possibility. Perhaps Luke intends an Acts 29. Perhaps he deliberately left the ending open so the reader could add his or her own verse.[28] Part of the beauty of this book is the number of anonymous contributors. There are a lot of little people whose lives extended the gospel:

[25] This theory was first argued by O. Eger, *Rechtsgeschichtliches zum Neuen Testament* (Basel: Reinhardt, 1919), 20-23, but on tenuous evidence. There is no definitive proof for a two-year statute of limitations on holding a prisoner. Nonetheless, there is no better explanation for the meaning of the two years; cf. *Beginnings* 5:332-336, and A. N. Sherwin-White, *Roman Society and Roman Law* (Oxford: Clarendon, 1963), 112-119. D. Mealand's hypothesis that it may be related to a two-year rental contract on Paul's apartment is interesting but less likely; cf. "The Close of Acts and Its Hellenistic Greek Vocabulary," *NTS* 36 (1990): 583-597. In fact, Ernst Hansack, "Er lebte . . . von seinem eigenen Einkommen (Apg 28, 30)," *BZ* 19 (1975): 249-253, makes a fairly strong case that the Greek phrase should not be rendered "His own rented quarters," but rather, "He lived at his own expense."

[26] *1 Clement* 5.6 (C. A.D. 100) says Paul reached the "farthest bounds of the west," a likely allusion to Rom 15:24, "I plan to do so when I go to Spain," though some would have him travel all the way to Britain. Eusebius (*Eccl. Hist.* 2.22, c. A.D. 400) intimates this happened after Paul's release from his "first Roman imprisonment" (cf. 2 Tim 4:16). Thus arose the theory of Paul's "fourth missionary journey." It is speculative but nonetheless probable that Paul was released and eventually traveled to Spain; cf. Bernd Wander, "Warum wollte Paulus nach Spanien? Ein forshungs-und motivgeschichtlicher Überblick," in *Das Ende des Paulus* (ed. Friedrich Horn, Berlin: Gruyter, 2001), 175-195, on the plausibility of Paul's Spanish mission. The strongest evidence is the fact that none of the Pastoral Epistles can be fit into the chronological framework of Acts. Our best reconstruction would look something like this: Paul anticipated being released A.D. 62 (cf. Phil. 1:26; 2:24; Phm 22: Acts 28:30). At some point he planned on visiting the church at Philippi and then the churches of the Lycus Valley (Colossae, Laodicea, and Hieropolis). Before that, however, he likely set sail for Spain directly after his release. Returning from Spain, it would make sense to stop off and see Titus in Crete (Tit 1:5) perhaps spending the winter there in A.D. 64–65. As he sailed north to Asia, he left Trophimus sick at Miletus (2 Tim 4:20), and he went to visit the church of Colossae in the Lycus Valley (Phm 1:22). Moving west again, he, of course, paid Timothy a visit in Ephesus where he also took care of Onesiphorus (cf. 1 Tim 1:3; 3:14-15; 2 Tim 1:18). On his way to Macedonia he stopped over in Troas, enjoying the hospitality of Carpus (cf. 2 Tim 4:13). He paid one last visit to his cherished friends in Philippi (Phil 2:23-24; 1 Tim 1:3) and possibly spent the following winter in Nicopolis, A.D. 66–67 (Titus 3:12). Thus he came to Rome again in A.D. 67 and was eventually arrested a second time and thrown in the Mamertine Prison ◘. According to tradition Paul was beheaded on the Ostian Way by Nero in the last year of his depraved reign (A.D. 68) ◘. This story was embedded in the Ethiopian ending of Acts: "For it happened that he [Paul] appeared before Nero the first time and won his case and went free. And he remained there for about two years before heading out. Afterward he returned and baptized the relative of Nero. And he died by the sword as an unwavering martyr . . ." Cf. Siegbert Uhlig, "Ein pseudepigraphischer Actaschluss in der äthiopischen Version," *OC* 73 (1989): 129-136.

[27] In all fairness to Luke, his is not the only book with an open ending. Witherington offers 2 Kings 25:28-30 as an example Luke might have followed (a not unlikely suggestion given Luke's affinity for the LXX). Here King Jehoiachin remains in prison in exile and is granted considerable freedom. Though the parallels are clear, Acts clearly has substantively more unfinished business than 2 Kings.

[28] Open endings were not an uncommon rhetorical device in ancient novels. They are found in both Homer and Herodotus and commended by Quintilian (2.13.12-13). Cf. Daniel Marguerat, "The End of Acts (28:16-31) and the Rhetoric of Silence," in *Rhetoric and the New Testament* (Sheffield: JSOT Press, 1993), 74-89, E.T. of his "'Et quand nous sommes entrés dans Rome': L'énigme de la fin du livre des Actes (28:16-31)," 73 (1993): 1-21. This rhetorical explanation for the open ending of Acts is far more likely than Jerome Quinn's hypothesis that the Pastoral Epistles are actually the disconnected "appendix" to the book; cf. "The Last Volume of Luke: The Relation of Luke-Acts to the Pastoral Epistles," in *Perspectives on Luke-Acts* (Edinburgh: T & T Clark, 1978), 62-75.

the unnamed evangelists who planted the first multiethnic church in Antioch, those brave believers who fled Saul's rampage, the Christians in Mary's house who prayed for Peter, the brothers who ran from Rome to escort Paul on his final leg to the capital. *We are they!* Acts 29 has millions of verses that will only be read in eternity. They tell of brutal beatings and mundane faithfulness. They recount mothers praying for the salvation of their children and prophets mocked on street corners. They memorialize extraordinary sacrifices sometimes tallied in meager coins as well as a million acts of kindness carried out in the shadow.

"Boldly and without hindrance" Paul preached the kingdom of God.[29] As Peter stood in the shadow of Jesus in the first half of this book, and as Paul stood on his shoulders in the second, so too, Christian, you carry out a legacy that traces back to the Master himself. The Kingdom of God, with which this book began (1:3) now drips from the final ink of Luke's quill. This is the core message of the book: The Kingdom of God irresistibly, powerfully, perpetually, miraculously, inevitably expands. This Kingdom now rests in your hands. What's your verse?

[29] The last word in the book in Greek is "unhindered" (ἀκωλύτως), giving the finale to the book a victorious ring. This is a rather unusual adverb that often is used in civil contracts for free uses of rented houses or unrestricted access to property, which might relate to Paul's rental contract on his apartment. However, given Jesus' initial promise in that book that the Apostles would be his witnesses to the ends of the earth, this nebulous term of unrestricted freedom was a clever way for Luke to thrust the narrative beyond the boundaries of his own quill; cf. Gerhard Delling, "Das letzte Wort der Apostelgeschichte," *NovT* 15 (1973): 193-204.

Authors Cited in Footnotes Index

Topical Index

437

People of Acts Index

Places of Acts Index